Arizona Territory
1863-1912

A Political History

PROCLAMATION.

TO THE PEOPLE OF ARIZONA:

I, JOHN N. GOODWIN, having been appointed by the President of the United States, and duly qualified, as Governor of the TERRITORY OF ARIZONA, do hereby announce that by virtue of the powers with which I am invested by an Act of the Congress of the United States, providing a temporary government for the Territory, I shall this day proceed to organize said government. The provisions of the Act, and all laws and enactments established thereby, will be enforced by the proper Territorial officers from and after this date.

A preliminary census will forthwith be taken, and thereafter the Judicial Districts will be formed, and an election of members of the Legislative Assembly, and the other officers, provided by the Act, be ordered.

I invoke the aid and co-operation of all citizens of the Territory in my efforts to establish a government whereby the security of life and property will be maintained throughout its limits, and its varied resources be rapidly and successfully developed.

The seat of government will for the present be at or near Fort Whipple

JOHN N. GOODWIN.

By the Governor:

RICHARD C. M'CORMICK,

Secretary of the Territory.

Navajo Spring

FORT WHIPPLE, ARIZONA

December 29th 1863-

TERRITORY
1863-1912
A Political History

Jay J. Wagoner

 The University of Arizona Press
Tucson, Arizona

About the Author . . .

JAY J. WAGONER is particularly interested in the political and ranching aspects of Arizona history. He is the author of *The History of the Cattle Industry in Southern Arizona, 1540–1940,* and of articles in journals such as the *New Mexico Historical Review* and *The Journal of Arizona History.* He holds an M.A. in history from the University of Arizona, and has done further graduate work at UCLA, Stanford, Columbia, and American University. His keen interest in history stems from his acquaintance with many of the first settlers of the Oklahoma Panhandle, where he grew up during the "Dust Bowl" days. A Fulbright scholar to Brazil in 1960, he has also traveled extensively to historical sites in both the United States and Europe. Since 1949 he has taught in the Phoenix Union High School system where for some years he has been head of the Social Studies department at East Phoenix High School.

THE UNIVERSITY OF ARIZONA PRESS

S.B.N. 8165-0176-9
L.C. No. 69-16331

Foreword

One of the most interesting phenomena of modern history has been the growth of the United States from a small republic of thirteen Atlantic seaboard states to a vast nation of fifty commonwealths. Curiously, however, the story of the westward expansion has been told almost exclusively in terms of social and economic developments. Though settlement of most of the Trans-Appalachian region took place within the framework of the territorial system that provided government and laws, scant attention has been given to the political development in the Western territories that emerged as states between 1803 and 1958. The neglect of this phase of frontier history is partly explained by the fact that the similarity of experiences with the territorial form of government has made it relatively easy to dismiss the subject with a few descriptive generalizations.

The purpose of this study is to provide a documented political history of one of the territories, namely Arizona. The scope of the work encompasses more than an analysis of the activities of local political parties and the operation of the machinery of government. The pattern of administration used in Arizona, and in all the other territories, was a unique combination of federal supervision with a measure of local autonomy. Because of this characteristic of the territorial political system, I have searched for basic primary source materials in both national and local depositories.

The National Archives and the Library of Congress in Washington, D.C., yielded many of the territorial records and official correspondence that were once scattered over the capital city in sundry bureaus and agencies of the Departments of Interior, State, War, Justice, Post Office, and Treasury. Though many records have been lost or destroyed, there is still an abundance of previously unused materials available to piece together the story of federal tutelage over the Territory of Arizona between 1863 and 1912.

v

In addition to the federal documents, many valuable personal papers of territorial politicians, local official records, old newspaper files, and miscellaneous materials were located in the Arizona Pioneers' Historical Society in Tucson, the State Library and Archives in Phoenix, the Sharlot Hall Museum in Prescott, the Phoenix Public Library, the Maricopa County Law Library, and the special collections in the libraries of the state universities of Arizona. Additional materials were found at the Columbia University Library and the New York City Public Library, both of which have large collections of national periodicals and old pamphlets, and at the Bancroft Library in Berkeley, California, which has a good Arizona collection. Some useful sources were also found at the Huntington Library in San Marino, California, the Southwest Museum, Los Angeles, and the California State Library in Sacramento. I am indebted to librarians and research personnel in all of these institutions for assistance in locating materials used in the preparation of this book.

One of the most famous documents on parchment in the National Archives, as far as Arizona is concerned, is the Organic Act upon which President Lincoln scrawled his signature on February 24, 1863. By this law, the Territory of Arizona was carved out of the western portion of New Mexico, a vast territory which had been created by the Compromise of 1850 from the spoils of the Mexican War and then enlarged further in 1854 by the Gadsden Purchase Treaty. The new desert lands acquired by this treaty attracted several hundred settlers and prospectors from the States. And by the time the U. S. soldiers arrived in Tucson to take formal possession with a flag-raising ceremony, on March 10, 1856, the people were already agitating for separate civil government.

Feeling their remoteness from distant Santa Fe and resentful of a condition appropriately described by the phrase "no law west of the Pecos," the Tucson pioneers held a convention on August 29, 1856; they resolved not only to send a memorial to Congress urging the organization of the Territory of Arizona, but also elected Nathan Cook to represent them in Washington. Cook was denied a seat in the House but persuaded the delegate from New Mexico, Miguel A. Otero, to introduce the memorial. This petition, which was signed by more than 260 residents, including men such as Granville Oury and Peter R. Brady who were later to become prominent in Arizona politics, was referred to the House Committee on Territories but brought no immediate relief. During the next six years the people signed more petitions, held mass meetings, wrote constitutions, and sent delegates to lobby in the national capital. A full account of these early frustrations and the tireless efforts of enthusiastic boosters like Sylvester

Mowry, Charles Poston, and Samuel P. Heintzelman, can be found in Dr. Benjamin Sack's scholarly *Be It Enacted,* and hence is not repeated in this work.

Most of the early plans which were suggested for an "Arizona Territory," including one offered by Mowry, would have embraced only the southern parts of present-day Arizona and New Mexico, leaving out the unsettled reaches north of the Gila. Whatever the size and shape recommended in the various proposed plans for a new territory, however, all efforts were doomed to failure until 1863. The pre-Civil War struggle over slavery simply precluded the formation of any new political units in the West during the "fitful fifties." The separation of New Mexico into two territories came only when the nationalistic Republican Party gained control of Congress. This party wanted to assure its future political success by binding the agricultural and mining West to the industrial North. The creation of new territories and states likely to be loyal to the Union was a part of the overall strategy, especially after the outbreak of the War Between the States. The war indirectly aided Arizona's cause by bringing about a rivalry for control of the Southwest. The new Confederate government served as a catalyst for action in Washington by creating its own elongated version of an "Arizona Territory" comprising the southern segment of New Mexico between Texas and California. Faced with this threat to the Union, the House finally endorsed the Organic Act on May 8, 1862. Then, after the deletion of a clause which would have located the capital in Tucson, where Southern sympathies were known to prevail, the law cleared the Senate on February 20, 1863, and was sent to President Lincoln's desk.

The act, as signed four days later, provided that the territorial government would be continued "until such time as the people residing in said Territory shall, with the consent of Congress, form a State government . . . and apply for admission into the Union as a State, on an equal footing with the original States." This latter provision was placed in all organic acts, but it seems remarkable, considering that Arizona was then one of the least known and most thinly populated areas of the United States. The census of 1864 showed a total of 4,573, exclusive of Indians. The largest concentration of people was around Tucson where over two thousand were counted, most of whom were of Mexican origin. There were a few scattered settlements south of Tucson in the valleys of the Santa Cruz and Sonoita. Small settlements could be found also along the Colorado, such as Yuma and La Paz, and several parties of gold seekers were mining in the foothills of the Bradshaws in central Arizona. With the addition of a few widely spaced military posts, that was about it! When the first governor, John Good-win, arrived at Fort Whipple on January 22, 1864, he found no gov-ernment, no laws except those passed by the legislature in Santa Fe, no office buildings, no railroads, no mail service, and scarcely any civili-zation. There were hostile Indians who roamed the territory almost unchecked, miners and trappers who called no place home, Southern sympathizers who wanted the new territorial government to fail, and even some officials who were more interested in "striking it rich" than in the affairs of state. These were the conditions under which Governor Goodwin began his duties.

The government which he launched was to last for nearly forty-nine years, until February 14, 1912. Only two other territories — New Mexico for sixty-one years and Hawaii for fifty-nine — remained "state-less" for a longer time. During this period of preparation for statehood, Arizona was administered by sixteen appointed governors and twenty-five elected legislatures. The territory was represented in Washington by twelve different non-voting delegates to Congress, beginning with Charles Poston, who has been called the "father of Arizona" because of his part in helping to bring about the passage of the Organic Act.

The governors who came into the political limelight for a little while and played a leading role in territorial affairs were of widely varying heritage and talent. They represented all the types of public men, from a presidential aspirant and former United States senator from California to local politicians. They hailed from different walks of life, most of the governors having had experience in several vocations. Nine of the sixteen had practiced law; two were professional army men who also engaged in mining enterprises and other business activities; one was a civil engineer; and three were in business, mining, and real estate almost exclusively. Several served in the Union Army and one, Ben-jamin Franklin, was in the Confederate forces. Nearly all of them had some previous political training — three of them, for example, had served in the U. S. House of Representatives, and one, John C. Fré-mont, had been the first Republican candidate for President. Half of the governors were in their forties when appointed, though the ages ranged from McCormick's youthful thirty-three to Frémont's sixty-five.

Though most of the governors were not appointed from the states of their birth, all were born east of the Mississippi — five in Pennsyl-vania, three in Ohio, two in Maine, two in New York, and one in each of the following states: Kentucky, Georgia, Indiana, and Vermont. More than half of the governors — all except Irwin after 1889 — were classi-fied as residents of Arizona at the time of their appointments. Of the sixteen, however, only five had resided in the territory as long as ten years. Every president from Lincoln through Taft, with the exception of Garfield, made at least one appointment. Cleveland, who was the only Democrat elected during this era, chose the three governors of that party — Conrad Zulick during his first term, Louis C. Hughes and Franklin during the second. In contrast to the near-monopoly of the Republican Party on the governorship, most of the elective offices were usually in the hands of the Democrats.

After the political parties became active in the territory, the governor was in a difficult, and often untenable, position. In the first place, his appointment was the result of a certain amount of political activity, wire pulling, and loyalty to the President in office. To keep his post he had to hold the favor of the national government and, at the same time, to win the support of the territorial majority as well. Since the legislature was generally in control of the opposite party, or a different faction of the same party, the governor had to exercise much political acumen and tact to get along harmoniously. Local newspapers frequently took the side of the elected legislators and exhausted vials of frontier invective on the governor and on the other federal appointees who were unfortunate, at least in the eyes of the local residents, to be Republicans when they should have been Democrats, Stalwarts when they should have been Halfbreeds, or simply appointed Easterners of either party when they should have been elected Westerners.

Much of the political activity during territorial days had to do with the election of the delegate to Congress every two years. That Arizona should "blaze forth a new star in the galaxy of states" became the slogan of every congressional campaigner in the territory and the "Holy Grail" of each elected delegate sent to Washington. The United States House *Journals* are filled with statehood bills that died in committee. It was Marcus Aurelius Smith, the perennial delegate after 1886 and one of the first two United States senators from Arizona when statehood was achieved, who finally convinced the House to pass enabling legislation in 1892. But the Republican Senate, ever protective of its restrictive membership, refused to go along at that time. The Republican politicians in the East had no intention of admitting two radical, silver Democrats to the club; in President Harrison's words, they were "opposed to the free coinage of Western Senators." As statehood seemed more imminent at the turn of the century, the Eastern establishment resorted to the ruse of joint statehood with New Mexico in order to limit any increase in Western influence in the Senate.

But, after persistent knocking at the door, Arizona finally was admitted into the Union when President William Howard Taft signed the Proclamation of Statehood on February 14, 1912. The long tutelage of the federal government ended. In retrospect, granted that at times the territory suffered some of the worst effects of carpetbag rule, it seems that Arizona had much for which to be grateful to the nation during the years 1863 to 1912. The territory cost "Uncle Sam" millions of dollars during its growing years as a political minor. Practically all the expenses of operating the territorial government were appropriated by Congress, including the cost of the Constitutional Convention in 1910. And it is difficult to see how the hostile Apaches could have been subjugated without federal assistance. This does not diminish the brave accomplishments of the pioneers who overcame the problems of nature in a desert country and laid the firm foundations for community life on the frontier. For them, the territorial period seemed too long, as they impatiently sought home rule and freedom from "colonial peonage." But the era was a necessary and interesting period of growth in the political development of Arizona, a phase of the state's history that has been much neglected.

I hesitate, for fear of omission, to try acknowledging all of the people who have been of assistance to me in locating source materials and in readying this book for publication. In addition to the personnel in the libraries and the archives mentioned above, however, I would like to express my appreciation to Marshall Townsend, Mrs. Elizabeth Shaw, Doug Peck, Erv Acuntius, and Miss Kit Scheifele of the University of Arizona Press for their help and encouragement. The advice and experience of Miss Scheifele, who edited the manuscript, has been invaluable to me. I am also indebted to Don Bufkin for the cartography and to my colleague, Hal Luck, for photographing some of the pictures from the State Archives. And finally, I am grateful to members of my family and to friends for their helpfulness and patience while the book was being researched and written.

Jay J. Wagoner

Contents

List of Maps

Arizona Territory
1863-1912

A Political History

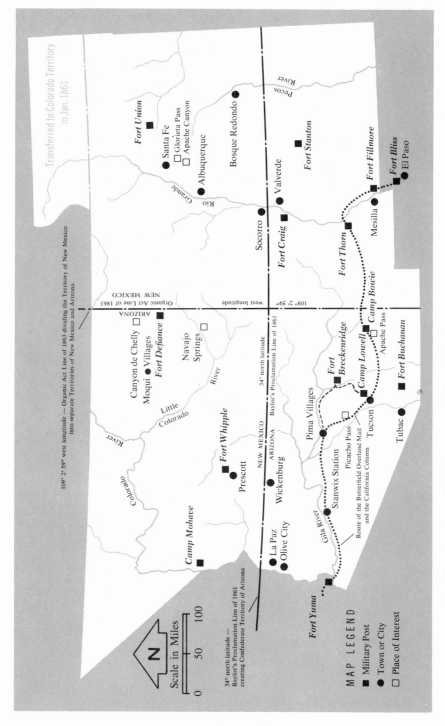

Territories of Arizona and New Mexico During the Civil War

Chapter I

War Baby:
Arizona and the Civil War

Probably no era in our country's history has held the enduring interest of Americans as has the Civil War. The impact of this great conflict did not even escape such a remote frontier section as the Southwest. Because of its geographic position, this region played a significant role in the power struggle between the North and the South. Jefferson Davis wished to annex California to the Confederacy and fully appreciated the importance of the New Mexico Territory (which until 1863 comprised the area that is now the states of Arizona and New Mexico) as the connecting link between seceded Texas and the Golden State. With an outlet to the Pacific Coast, the Confederate States would be open to the world and free from the shackles of an effective Union naval blockade. The precious minerals in California and in the present-day states of Arizona, Nevada, and Colorado would also bolster the South's inflated currency and strengthen its position in international trade. In addition, the conquest of such a vast domain would be impressive to the European nations from whom the South hoped to gain recognition as an independent country.[1]

Not only were the reasons for invasion of the western territories substantial but the chances for success were encouraging. The strategists in Richmond had cause to believe that many of the citizens of New Mexico were pro-Southern. In 1856, for example, the territorial legislature had passed an act restricting free Negroes and, three years later, enacted a slave code.[2] Several territorial newspapers, including Sylvester Mowry's Tucson *Arizonian,* were sympathetic to Southern principles.[3]

---

[1]Charles S. Walker, "Causes of the Confederate Invasion of New Mexico," *New Mexico Historical Review* [hereafter *NMHR*], Vol. 8, No. 2 (1933), pp. 76-97; see also, W. H. Watford, "Confederate Western Ambitions," *The Southwestern Historical Quarterly,* Vol. 44, No. 2 (1940), pp. 161-87.

[2]Speech of John A. Bingham of Ohio, *U. S. Congressional Globe,* 36th Cong., 2d Sess., January 22, 1861, Appendix, p. 83.

[3]*Weekly Arizonian* (Tucson), March 9, 1861.

On March 16, 1861, shortly after Lincoln was inaugurated as President, a secession convention met at Mesilla, a town on the Rio Grande in southern New Mexico. Claiming to represent the people of "Arizona," the name then often applied to the southwestern part of the New Mexico Territory, the convention repudiated the "Black Republican Administration" and attached "Arizona" to the Confederate States of America.[4] The South was pleased by this demonstration of support, even though Santa Fe ultimately decided to remain loyal to the Union, preferring to follow the hesitant "wait and see" policy of Missouri.[5] Northern New Mexico depended on trade with Missouri and was also held in check by the presence of federal troops, most of whom remained loyal.

The effectiveness of the United States Army in New Mexico was diminished, however, by the defection of many of its officers to the Confederacy.[6] Even the Departmental Commander, Colonel William W. Loring, "took the Texas route." Others who resigned their commissions in 1861 were Lieutenant Joseph Wheeler, Colonel George B. Crittenden (whose father had replaced Henry Clay in the Senate from Kentucky and unsuccessfully attempted to save the Union by compromise), Major James Longstreet, Captain Richard S. Ewell, and Captain Cadmus M. Willcox — all to become Southern generals.

The commander at Fort Union, Major Henry H. Sibley, was another officer who ended a long career in the U. S. Army by tendering his services to the South. He returned to New Mexico, however, as a brigadier-general in command of an army to be known as the Confederate States of America Army of New Mexico. Following his resignation, Sibley had traveled to Richmond where he convinced President Davis that New Mexico was the natural gateway for an expedition that could eventually conquer not only that region but also what is now Arizona, Colorado, and possibly California.[7] Arriving in San Antonio in August, Sibley organized three regiments of the Texas Volunteer Cavalry and made preparations for the New Mexico campaign.

The actual invasion had already begun, however. On July 1,

---

[4]Letter of James A. Lucas, President of the Convention, to Dr. Lorenzo Labado, from Mesilla, New Mexico, June 14, 1861, in U. S. War Department, *The War of the Rebellion: A Compilation of the Official Records of the Union and Confederate Armies,* Series I, Vol. 4, p. 39. [Hereafter *War of the Rebellion*].

[5]*Mesilla Times,* May 11, 1861.

[6]Ray C. Colton, *The Civil War in the Western Territories* (Norman: University of Oklahoma Press, 1959), p. 8.

[7]Letter of S. Cooper to General Henry H. Sibley, from Richmond, Virginia, July 8, 1861, in *War of the Rebellion,* Series I, Vol. 4, p. 93; see also, Hubert H. Bancroft, *History of Arizona and New Mexico, 1530–1888* (San Francisco: The History Company, 1889), pp. 510-11.

Lieutenant-Colonel John R. Baylor reached and occupied the deserted Fort Bliss (near El Paso, Texas) with a regiment of rough, tough, and determined Texas riflemen. These men were recruited ostensibly "to hunt buffalo on the plains" and furnished their own horses, saddles, guns, and ammunition. On July 25 the Texans took possession of the town of Mesilla where they were welcomed by Southern sympathizers. Major Isaac Lynde advanced with several companies of federal troops toward the town from nearby Fort Fillmore but retreated after a brief and indecisive skirmish. On July 27 the panicky Lynde abandoned the fort and started northeast toward Fort Stanton.

Many of Lynde's soldiers emptied their canteens and refilled them with high-quality hospital brandy and medicinal whiskey. By the time Baylor caught up with the thirsty stragglers they were quite willing to surrender in exchange for water. Pushing on in hot pursuit, the Confederates cut the main body off at San Augustine Pass in the Organ Mountains. There Major Lynde cowardly and disgracefully surrendered his entire command without firing a shot.[8] As a result of his capitulation Fort Stanton was also abandoned, and the South had won its first territory with little opposition.

Flushed with victory, Baylor, on August 1, 1861, proclaimed the Confederate Territory of Arizona with the capital at Mesilla and himself as the military governor.[9] The territory was to comprise all of the New Mexico Territory south of the 34th parallel, an east-west line that passes near present-day Socorro, New Mexico, and Wickenburg, Arizona. Thus, Confederate Arizona extended from Texas to California and lay generally south of the Gila River in the southern parts of what are now Arizona and New Mexico. The Confederate Congress passed an enabling act on January 18, 1862, and on February 14, President Jefferson Davis formally proclaimed the Arizona Territory to be a part of the South.[10]

Baylor had given Tucson some recognition — on paper, that is — by making it the seat of the second judicial district, the first being at Mesilla. About the same time as the issuance of his proclamation, some sixty-eight Americans assembled in Tucson and passed an ordinance of

---

[8]Letter of Major Isaac Lynde to Acting Assistant Adjutant-General, from Fort Craig, New Mexico, August 7, 1861, in *War of the Rebellion,* Series I, Vol. 4, pp. 5-7.

[9]"Proclamation to the People of the Territory of Arizona," signed by John R. Baylor, Governor and Lieut. Col., Commanding Mounted Rifles, Confederate States Army, Mesilla, August 2, 1861, in *Confederate Victories in the Southwest: Prelude to Defeat* (from the *Official Records*), (Albuquerque, N. Mex.: Horn and Wallace, 1961), pp. 37-39 [hereafter *Confederate Victories*]; see also, *War of the Rebellion,* Series I, Vol. 4, pp. 20-21.

[10]*War of the Rebellion,* Series I, Vol. 4, pp. 853, 859, and 930.

Colonel John R. Baylor, governor of the Confederate Territory of Arizona. This picture is from a painting hanging in the Alamo, San Antonio, Texas.

Granville H. Oury, Arizona delegate to the Confederate Congress. Like his brother William S., "Grant" was prominent in early Arizona politics, serving more than once as Speaker of the territorial Assembly, and as delegate to Congress.

secession. The Stars and Stripes were tossed away to the summer breezes as Granville Oury was selected territorial delegate to the Confederate Congress and Jefferson Davis was petitioned for troops.[11] This sympathy for disunion can be traced partly to the Southern origin of many of the residents. But the abrupt departure of Union troops in July was perhaps the strongest factor. Suddenly abandoned to the wild Apaches and lawless desperadoes, the people were willing to accept protection from any government.

The evacuation of troops from Forts Breckenridge and Buchanan, in the southern part of present-day Arizona, had been ordered by the military headquarters in New Mexico when Baylor invaded the territory. The Union officers had decided it best to destroy the Arizona posts rather than risk losing them to the South. Breckenridge was abandoned on July 10 after its supplies and buildings were burned. Joining with the force at Buchanan, the entire command of some four hundred departed for Fort Fillmore on July 21, Captain Isaiah N. Moore in command. Distant columns of smoke were still rising from deserted Buchanan when General Albert Sydney Johnston passed through Tucson the following day en route from California to join the Confederacy at Richmond.[12] By the time Johnston reached the Rio Grande a week later, Baylor had captured Fort Fillmore. The Arizona Unionists were warned in time, however, to bypass this post, and joined Colonel Edward R. S. Canby at Fort Craig, on the Rio Grande nearly halfway from El Paso to Santa Fe. Canby was then the Union commander in New Mexico and, interestingly enough, the brother-in-law of the Confederate officer, General Sibley, who arrived at El Paso in mid-December, 1861, to assume command of all Southern forces in the area.

Early in 1862 Sibley's force of hardy Texas Volunteers moved up the Rio Grande and on February 21 engaged the Union troops under Canby in the Battle of Valverde, the first major conflict of the Civil War in the Southwest. The fighting took place on the east side of the river, a few miles above Fort Craig. After a fierce struggle which included several hand-to-hand encounters, the Texas sharpshooters succeeded in routing the Federals. "Kit" Carson, however, distinguished himself in the battle as his New Mexico Volunteers stood firm in the Union center and repulsed a charge of yelling Rebels armed with double-barreled shotguns, squirrel rifles, revolvers, and lances. But another spirited Texan charge on the Union left overwhelmed the

[11]*Ibid.*, Vol. 4, pp. 1-45.

[12]William A. Keleher, *Turmoil in New Mexico* (Santa Fe: The Rydal Press, 1952), pp. 213-19.

defenders along the river.[13] Theophilus Noel of the Texas cavalry wrote that "in this charge we carried everything before us, routing the enemy, we drove them to the river, where they 'took water,' on short notice, more like a herd of frightened mustangs than like men."[14]

Canby retreated to Fort Craig and let the Confederates march up the valley to capture Albuquerque and Santa Fe without much opposition. The Texans largely subsisted "on the country" but soon ran low on supplies because of their own vandalism and the indifference of the majority of the New Mexicans. So, on March 25, Sibley ordered an advance on Fort Union with the dual objectives of capturing military stores and removing the last obstacle to the South's possession of nearly all of New Mexico. Three days before the departure of the Confederates, however, more than thirteen hundred men under Colonel J. P. Slough left Fort Union, following the Santa Fe Trail. This force consisted mainly of Colorado Volunteers. These "Pike's-Peakers," as they were called, had been resting at the fort after a cold mid-winter journey of over four hundred miles from Denver. They were a hardy breed of frontiersmen, a good match for the tough Texans.

The two armies clashed about twenty miles southeast of Santa Fe in the "Gettysburg of the West." Engagements at Apache Canyon on March 26 and at Glorieta Pass on March 28 proved to be the turning point in the war in saving this area for the Union. One Texan wrote that instead of meeting "Mexicans and regulars," they had encountered "regular demons, upon whom iron and lead had no effect." Major J. M Chivington, a Bible-pounding preacher who had turned soldier, is given credit for assuring a Union victory by maneuvering so as to flank and surprise the Texas rear guard.[15] His charging column swooped down upon the Confederate camp, burned the supply train, and bayoneted several hundred horses and mules which could not be driven over the rugged mountains to the Federal lines.[16]

The tired, hungry, and demoralized Texan army retreated and probably would have been quickly wiped out had Canby permitted Slough to follow up the advantages won at Glorieta. But Canby had

---

[13]Ovando J. Hollister, *Boldly They Rode: A History of the First Colorado Regiment of Volunteers* (Lakewood, Colorado: The Golden Press, 1949) p. 110.

[14]Theophilus Noel, *Autobiography and Reminiscences of Theophilus Noel* (Chicago: Theophilus Noel Company Print, 1904).

[15]Report of Major John M. Chivington, First Colorado Infantry to Brigadier General E. R. S. Canby, U. S. Army, Commanding Department of New Mexico, March 26, 1862, in *Union Army Operations in the Southwest: Final Victory* (from the *Official Records*), (Albuquerque, N. Mex.: Horn and Wallace, 1961), pp. 20-21. [Hereafter *Union Army Operations*].

[16]*War of the Rebellion*, Series I, Vol. 9, pp. 531-45; J. F. Santee, "The Battle of Glorietta Pass," *NMHR*, Vol. 6, No. 1 (1931), pp. 66-75.

no intention of risking his own army by attempting to annihilate the enemy and allowed Sibley to lead the remnant of his column back into Texas.[17] The desperate retreat route veered west of the Rio Grande through the San Mateo Mountains, where there was less chance of harassment by Union troops. Struggling through difficult country, the troopers suffered terribly. One Confederate soldier, the above-mentioned Theophilus Noel, said that they "walked and staggered along like the reeling hungry, thirsty wretches" they were. Everything that the men could not personally carry was abandoned, including the sick and lame. The bloodthirsty Dog Canyon Apaches scalped the unfortunate boys whose blistered feet and weariness caused them to falter. Finally, the ill-fated expedition reached Fort Bliss in early May, a third to one-half of the original force of 3,700 having been left behind — killed, wounded, or captured.

Heroes when they marched northward two months before, the men were now released to find their way back to Texas any way they could. The attitude of the soldiers concerning Sibley's leadership was expressed by a Private George M. Brown, who wrote to his wife on April 30, 1862, that he hoped General Sibley would soon be hanged.[18] Noel even expressed regret that the often-intoxicated general had escaped starvation during the retreat. There may be some doubt as to whether the general's addiction to alcohol and his personal cowardice had anything to do with the outcome of the New Mexican campaign. But certainly his failure to conquer the upper Rio Grande doomed Baylor's Confederate Territory of Arizona and the other strategic schemes which hinged upon the possession of New Mexico.

Meanwhile, the region that is now Arizona became more involved in the war. As Sibley was preparing to march up the Rio Grande during January, 1862, he detached a company of mounted rifles under Captain Sherod Hunter to take possession of friendly Tucson for the Confederacy. The purpose of the expedition was to protect the South's growing interest — chiefly mineral — in western Arizona and to open communications to southern California. Hunter's cavalrymen encountered no opposition as they rode into the chief town of Arizona on February 28 and ran up the Confederate Stars and Bars.[19] Union sympathizers who had not already departed were given the choice of swearing allegiance

---

[17]Record Group 59, Territorial Papers: New Mexico; see also, "Report of Brigadier General Henry H. Sibley, Confederate States Army, to General S. Cooper, Adjutant and Inspector General at Richmond, Va.," from Albuquerque, N. Mex., March 31, 1862, *Union Army Operations,* p. 30.

[18]Hollister, pp. 166-70.

[19]Letter of Captain Sherod Hunter to Col. John R. Baylor, from Tucson, Arizona, April 5, 1862, *Confederate Victories,* pp. 200-201.

to the Confederacy or leaving the territory. Solomon Warner, the store-keeper whose goods were confiscated by the troopers, was one of those who left for Sonora.

A party of Confederates also went south of the border, but for a different reason. Colonel James Reily, traveling from Chihuahua to Sonora on a diplomatic mission, happened to stop over in Tucson shortly after Hunter arrived.[20] After making a speech and participating in a formal flag-raising ceremony in the town plaza, Reily departed for Hermosillo with his escort of twenty men under Lieutenant James H. Tevis. Carrying a letter of introduction from Sibley, he was to negotiate with Governor Don Ignacio Pesqueira in behalf of the Confederacy.[21] Reily reported to the Southern leaders that he had made a favorable treaty; yet he actually accomplished very little except to obtain permission to purchase supplies in gold or silver, the Mexicans refusing to accept Confederate currency.

Unfortunately for the South, an enterprising reporter for the *San Francisco Bulletin* had managed to steal copies of Reily's letter of introduction and other notes, which he sent to General George Wright, the commander of the Army of the Pacific. Any inclination that Pesqueira might have had to cooperate with the Confederate States was soon forgotten with the arrival off Guaymas of a Union gunboat. In a letter containing veiled threats of invasion, Wright congratulated the governor for having refused Reily.[22] The show of force was effective, for Pesqueira promised, in a letter dispatched to Wright on August 29, that he would consider the presence of any Southern force on Mexican soil as "an invasion by force of arms."[23] By this time, of course, the Southwest had been saved for the Union. The struggle might have been prolonged, however, if Pesqueira had placed his weight behind the rebels.

Just as Reily's mission was barren of results, so was Captain Hunter's occupation of Tucson. The soldiers "lived off the country" as Sibley's force was doing in the Rio Grande Valley. Using Tucson as a base they confiscated food, animals, and other property, including some mines owned by Northerners. On March 3, the same day that Reily left for Sonora, Hunter led his command over the old emigrant trail to

---

[20]*War of the Rebellion*, Series I, Vol. 4, pp. 167-74 and Vol. 9, p. 708.

[21]Letter of James H. Carleton to Brigadier General George Wright, from Camp Drum, March 22, 1862, *War of the Rebellion*, Series I, Vol. 50, Part 1, pp. 944-45.

[22]Letter of General George Wright to Governor Ignacio Pesqueira, State of Sonora, May 3, 1862, *ibid.*, Part 1, pp. 1047-48.

[23]Letter of Pesqueira to Wright, from Ures, August 29, 1862, *ibid.*, Part 2, p. 93.

the Pima Indian villages on the Gila River. There he arrested Ammi M. White, a miller and federal purchasing agent who had been buying grain, forage, and other supplies for use by the Union troops on their eastward advance from California. Among the articles confiscated were 1,500 sacks of wheat. "This," Hunter reported to Baylor, "I distributed among the Indians, as I had no means of transportation, and deemed this a better policy of disposing of it than to destroy or leave it for the benefit (should it fall in their hands) of the enemy."[24]

While at the Pima villages Hunter learned that every station of the old Butterfield Overland Mail between that place and Fort Yuma had been provided with hay for use of the Union government. His raiding parties burned six of these stations, and the Rebel scouts came within a few miles of the Colorado River. Fort Yuma on this river was of great concern to Hunter because it was the planned base of operations for the California Volunteers, or California Column as they were generally called. In March and April, 1862, the infantry and cavalry were concentrating for an invasion of Arizona. Even before leaving Los Angeles, Colonel (later General) James H. Carleton, the energetic commander, had been informed of Hunter's activities and dispatched Captain William McCleave with a squad of cavalry to learn the strength and disposition of the Confederate forces.

McCleave's personal orders from Carleton were to stop at the Pima villages to construct a building in which to store the wheat and flour from Ammi White's mill. He was also to reconnoiter Tucson and to take the town by surprise, capturing "Mr. Hunter and his band of renegades and traitors." As it turned out, however, the Union soldiers were the victims of clever strategy. McCleave and his advance guard of nine picked men were sighted by Confederate scouts in time for a trap to be laid at the villages. Unaware that White had been arrested, McCleave knocked on his door and was greeted by Captain Hunter posing as the miller. In the meantime, the Confederates gathered around and easily made the Yankees prisoners. McCleave and White were eventually escorted to General Sibley's headquarters on the Rio Grande by Lieutenant Jack Swilling, a man who was to reappear often in Arizona history.

When news of McCleave's capture reached Fort Yuma, the officers and men were eager to find out what under the Arizona sun was going on. Captain William P. Calloway was sent into Arizona with a Union vanguard of 272 men, consisting of California infantry, cavalry, and

---

[24]Letter of Hunter to Baylor, *Confederate Victories,* pp. 200-201.

a battery of two twelve-pound howitzers. Plans called for the establishment of a base at the Pima villages and a hasty dash toward Tucson to recapture McCleave before he could be taken east to Mesilla. At Stanwix Station, one of the Butterfield Overland posts about eighty miles from Yuma, Calloway's men encountered some Texan troopers destroying hay stored there. Shots were exchanged and a Californian was wounded. The Confederates then succeeded in eluding Captain N. J. Pishan's cavalry detachment which was sent in pursuit. Though hardly a battle of the magnitude of a Gettysburg or Bull Run, this action was actually the westernmost skirmish of the Civil War.

Upon reaching the Pima villages, the Federals learned that some Confederate soldiers were in the vicinity. Calloway directed Lieutenant James Barrett to circle about in a flanking movement and to strike the Confederates from the east with a dozen cavalrymen. The main body under Lieutenant Baldwin would attack on the front. On April 15, 1862, however, Barrett unexpectedly caught up with the Southerners at Picacho Pass, about forty-five miles northwest of Tucson. Ordered to charge, the Yankees forced the Texans into the chaparral where a few minutes of fierce fighting ensued. Lieutenant Barrett was hit in the neck and died instantly. Two Union privates, George Johnston and William S. Leonard, were also killed and three others were wounded. All the Confederates escaped except for two wounded and three who were taken prisoner. Known as the "Battle of Picacho Peak," this engagement is traditionally described as the westernmost action of the Civil War, though, as we have seen, there was an earlier conflict nearly a hundred miles farther west at Stanwix Station.

Neither side actually won the battle and each withdrew from the area. The Confederates fell back to Tucson; Calloway ordered a retreat back to Stanwix to join with a larger advance unit of Federals under Colonel Joseph R. West. The united Union force continued on to the Pima villages which were reached near the end of April. Fort Barrett was constructed there and named in memory of the lost lieutenant. Little more than an "earthworks thrown around a trading post" near present-day Sacaton, the fort served as a resting place while the troops prepared for the advance on Tucson. Supplies that Colonel West expected to purchase from the Pimas were furnished only in limited quantities. He had nothing to offer the Indians for forage and wheat except "promises" to deliver "manta," a kind of white cloth. Thus only trifling day-by-day rations of hay, wheat, and *pinole* (ground corn) were produced by the Pimas. As a result, Colonel West did not have a large store of supplies when he left the villages for Tucson near the middle of May.

He traveled by way of the deserted Fort Breckenridge and reestablished that post on the eighteenth. The United States flag was hoisted as the soldiers cheered. When Carleton arrived at the Pima villages a few days later he ordered that Fort Breckenridge be renamed Fort Stanford in honor of the Governor of California and stationed Colonel Edward E. Eyre's First California Cavalry regiment there. Meanwhile, on May 20, West occupied Tucson without a shot being fired.[25] His advance cavalry detachment under Captain Emil Fritz charged into town from three directions only to find that it had been abandoned by the Confederates. Hunter had evacuated on May 4, leading his Texan troopers and several Southern sympathizers toward the Rio Grande. While en route the party was attacked near Dragoon Spring, some fifty miles east of Tucson, by Apaches who killed four men and drove away a number of horses and mules. Hunter can hardly be criticized for giving up the idea of holding Arizona. His small band was no match for the approaching California Column of eighteen hundred volunteers.

Colonel Carleton himself reached Tucson on June 7, 1862, having delayed his arrival so that Lieutenant John B. Shinn's artillery battery would get there first to fire a salute in his honor. Carleton wasted no time in asserting the authority of the Federal government. On June 8, he declared Arizona a territory of the United States, designated himself military governor, and proclaimed martial law until such time as the President of the United States would otherwise direct.[26] He contended that an assertion of military authority was necessary because Arizona was in a chaotic state with no civil officers to protect life and property.

The proclamation contained certain rules and regulations which were to be rigidly enforced. All citizens of legal age were compelled to take an oath of allegiance to the United States. No unpatriotic words or acts would be tolerated. Every man who remained in Arizona was required to have some legitimate means of livelihood. And, in the absence of civil courts, provision was made for the conduct of trials before a military commission in cases involving either minor or capital offenses.

Carleton let his axe fall on Confederate sympathizers as well as on the desperadoes. Among the political prisoners was Colonel Palatine

[25]Report of Brigadier General James H. Carleton, U. S. Army, commanding expedition from California, to Major Richard C. Drum, Ass't. Adjutant General, U. S. Army, San Francisco, from Fort Barrett, Pima Villages, Arizona, May 25, 1862, *Union Army Operations,* p. 39.

[26]Proclamation of James H. Carleton, Colonel First California Volunteers, Major Sixth U. S. Cavalry, at Tucson, Arizona, June 1, 1862, *Union Army Operations,* pp. 47-48.

Robinson who had recruited troops for the South.[27] But the most notable man arrested was Sylvester Mowry. A West Point graduate, Mowry was stationed at Fort Yuma in the mid-1850s. His travels in Arizona convinced him that this region had boundless mineral resources. Resigning his commission as a lieutenant in 1858, he worked relentlessly for the creation of a separate territory for Arizona.[28] In 1860 he purchased a silver mine in the Patagonia Mountains, some seven miles from the Mexican border, and immediately began developing the property. The Mowry Silver Mine was soon prosperous, supporting a camp of some four hundred inhabitants by 1862.

After Carleton arrived in Tucson, he received a letter, marked Mowry Silver Mine and signed by "T. Scheuner, Mettallurgist, M.S.M." In the letter Mowry was accused of having aided the Confederate cause by selling ammunition to the Rebel forces and of having boasted that with twenty Southerners he could whip a hundred Northerners. On the basis of this information, as well as a statement by William Pyburn, another Arizona citizen, that Mowry had furnished Captain Hunter with percussion caps, Carleton sent Colonel Eyre with a detachment to Patagonia. Mowry was charged with having written letters to Jefferson Davis, Brigadier General Henry H. Sibley, and Captain Sherod Hunter; he was arrested and his silver mine confiscated on June 13, 1862.[29] His arrival in Tucson was dramatic. When he made his appearance, his demeanor was lordly, his rage Olympian; his entourage included his private secretary, his personal servant, and his mistress.[30] A board of officers headed by Colonel West quickly convened in Tucson and found sufficient evidence of "collusion with well known secessionists" to restrain Mowry from his liberty.[31] On July 2, Carleton confirmed the findings of the board and directed that the prisoner be confined at Fort Yuma where he remained until November 4.[32]

---

[27]Frank C. Lockwood, *Life in Old Tucson, 1854–1864* (Los Angeles: The Ward Ritchie Press, 1943), pp. 128-37. Lockwood's account of Robinson's trial and imprisonment, by a military board appointed by Carleton, is based upon records of the War Department that Senator Carl Hayden had photostated for the author.

[28]Sylvester Mowry, *Memoir of the Proposed Territory of Arizona* (Washington, D.C.: Henry Polkinhorn, Publisher, 1857). [Reprinted by Territorial Press, Tucson, 1964.]

[29]Letter to Colonel James H. Carleton to Major R. C. Drum, Ass't. Adj.-General, San Francisco, from Tucson, Arizona Territory, June 10, 1862, in *War of the Rebellion,* Series I, Vol. 50, Part 1, pp. 1128-29.

[30]Benjamin Sacks, "Sylvester Mowry," *The American West,* Vol. 1, No. 3 (1964), p. 23.

[31]*War of the Rebellion,* Series I, Vol. 9, pp. 694-95.

[32]U. S. Senate, *Message of the President of the United States,* 38th Cong., 1st Sess., 1863-64, Sen. Exec. Doc. No. 49, pp. 1-3.

*General James H. Carleton (above), commander of the California Column
that occupied Tucson and restored it to the Union. He proclaimed martial law
and confiscated the property of those he thought were Confederate sympathizers, including Sylvester Mowry (below). A soldier and mining entrepreneur,
Mowry was an early advocate of separate territorial status for Arizona. His*
Memoir of the Proposed Territory of Arizona *was published in 1857.*

Mowry was held "for aiding and abetting the enemy." However, he consistently claimed absolute innocence of any treasonable actions. Well-liked by the officers at Fort Yuma, he was often taken for rides and furnished with choice bourbon that had been confiscated in Kentucky. After his case was investigated by General Wright, commander of the Department of the Pacific, Mowry was acquitted and given his unconditional release since the charges against him were not supported with sufficient evidence. But the matter did not end there. The bitter Carleton-Mowry feud continued until the latter's death in 1871. Convinced that Mowry was a secessionist, Carleton went beyond military arrest, court martial, and imprisonment. By a United States District Court order obtained in Albuquerque, he confiscated Mowry's property and had it sold at public auction on July 18, 1864, for a mere $2,000. The properties of W. S. and Granville H. Oury, Southern sympathizers beyond doubt, were sold on the same date.

Meanwhile, Mowry wrote letters to influential people, published newspaper articles, and sought vindication through legal channels. In December, 1862, he filed damage claims for more than a million dollars against Carleton and others in California's Fourth District Court.[33] Eventually, in 1868, he received approximately $40,000 from the federal government. But his reputation was never completely redeemed. A Senate Resolution, a formal gesture that was introduced in 1864 calling for a Congressional investigation, received scant attention. Mowry was consoled, however, by another resolution that was passed by Arizona's First Territorial Legislature.[34] In this resolution, the legislature censured General Carleton for expelling Mowry and for subsequently ordering his arrest the moment he arrived back in Arizona. The lawmakers were partially motivated by a desire to hasten the development of the mineral resources in this region. Along this line Mowry went to London to raise money for refinancing his Arizona properties. While there he became ill and died in October, 1871. Commenting upon his death the *Arizona Miner* said, "This is sad news for Arizona. In the death of Mr. Mowry this Territory has lost as faithful a friend as it ever had in the person of one man."[35]

In addition to Mowry and Robinson, about twenty other political prisoners were arrested by Carleton and sent to California during the

---

[33]Aurora Hunt, *The Army of the Pacific: Its Operations . . . 1860–1866* (Glendale, Calif.: Arthur H. Clark Co., 1951), pp. 113-14.

[34]"Concurrent Resolution Relative to Sylvester Mowry," *Acts, Resolutions, and Memorials,* First Legislative Assembly, Arizona, 1864, p. 70.

[35]*Arizona Miner,* October 19, 1871.

summer of 1862. At the same time, some of the Union sympathizers who had fled from the Confederates to Sonora, returned to Tucson and found that Carleton was reestablishing orderly government within the town itself. As the self-appointed military governor of Arizona, Carleton instructed Lieutenant Benjamin Clarke Butler, his secretary of state for the territory, to levy a tax on all business establishments in Arizona. Only concerns selling forage, subsistence stores, fruits, and vegetables were exempted. Merchants whose monthly sales amounted to $500 or less were taxed $5 per month. Another dollar was assessed for each additional $100 in sales. Gambling houses were obliged to pay $100 per month for each table in operation. Every keeper of a bar was charged $100 per month for the privilege of selling his liquors. Violation of the provisions of the license-tax order subjected the gambling and liquor dealers to a fine and the seizure of all equipment and stocks upon the second offense. All money collected was earmarked exclusively for the hospital fund established for the benefit of the sick and wounded soldiers of the California Column.

While bringing some semblance of order to the frontier community of Tucson, Carleton was mainly occupied with preparations for the next leg of his army's eastward advance. The column had to be provisioned for the journey to Mesilla and contact made with the Union forces in New Mexico under Canby. For the latter purpose, Carleton sent an express rider named John Jones, Sergeant William Wheeling, and a Mexican guide known as Chávez. Only Jones escaped the Apache's scalping knife and he was captured by the Confederates under the command of Colonel William Steele at Mesilla. Jones did manage, however, to smuggle word to Canby that Carleton was in Tucson.[36]

On June 21, six days after Jones's departure, a reconnaissance guard of 140 men under Lieutenant Colonel Edward Eyre started from Tucson for the Rio Grande. Following the route used by the Overland Mail stages before the war, the detachment had to travel about three hundred miles under a broiling sun and over a country destitute of water for distances ranging from thirty-five to sixty miles. While watering and grazing their horses at Apache Pass the troopers were approached by a mounted party of about a hundred well-armed Indians carrying a white flag of truce. The warriors asked for and were given food and tobacco, promising in return not to molest either the soldiers or the horses. Three men, however, who disobeyed orders and wandered off, were killed and stripped of their clothing and firearms. And that evening

---

[36]Report of Brigadier General James H. Carleton, U. S. Army, San Francisco, Calif., from Tucson, Arizona, July 22, 1862, *Union Army Operations,* pp. 40-41.

the Indians fired into the Union camp, wounding Acting Assistant Surgeon Kittridge. Proceeding on without further trouble with the Indians, Eyre reached the Rio Grande on the Fourth of July. Appropriate to the occasion and day, the Stars and Stripes were unfurled amid the wild cheers of the volunteers. This was the first time that Old Glory had floated over the Rio Grande south of Fort Craig since the occupation of New Mexico by the Confederates nearly one year before.[37]

On July 5, the detachment marched down the river and occupied the gutted ruins of old Fort Thorn, which had been abandoned by the Rebels. Eyre was eager to engage the Confederates under Colonel Steele. In defiance of orders from General Canby, Eyre crossed the flooding Rio Grande on July 17 in a small boat and pursued the retreating Southerners as far as Las Cruces. Meanwhile, however, Steele had evacuated Mesilla on July 8 and El Paso on July 12. In a letter written on the latter date to the Confederate government in Richmond, he explained that he could not hold the Territory of Arizona with four hundred men against the combined forces of some three thousand soldiers under Canby and Carleton.[38] Into Texas with Steele went the dream for a transcontinental Confederacy. Southern authority along the Rio Grande had evaporated and the Union had only to solidify its jurisdiction to be in complete control.

The second detachment of the California Column left Tucson on July 10. Under the command of Captain Thomas S. Roberts, the 126 men, twenty-two wagons and two howitzers proceeded via the Butterfield route toward Mesilla. About noon on July 15 the advance troops were ambushed near Apache Pass by Indians led by two of the most feared of all Apaches, Mangas Coloradas and Cochise. After a sharp skirmish the Indians were driven off. But when the main body of troops moved into the pass approaching a spring for water, the Apaches began firing from behind rocks along the rim of the canyon. The "Battle of Apache Pass" that followed was one of the largest-scale engagements ever fought between Federal troops and Apache Indians in Arizona history.

After a stubborn resistance, the Apaches were finally dislodged by bursting howitzer shells which were fired from the mysterious "wagons on wheels." By late afternoon Roberts gained control of the water and

---

[37]Report of Lieut. Col. Edward E. Eyre, First California Volunteer Cavalry, to Lieutenant Benjamin C. Cutler, A.A.A.G., Column from California, Tucson, Arizona, from Fort Thorn, Arizona [now in New Mexico], July 8, 1862, *ibid.*, pp. 72-76.

[38]Report of Colonel William Steele, Seventh Regiment of Texas Volunteers, to General S. Cooper, Adjutant and Inspector General, Richmond, Va., from El Paso, Texas, July 12, 1862, *Union Army Operations,* pp. 129-30.

sent Sergeant Titus B. Mitchell with five men back to warn Captain John C. Cremony, who was guarding the supply wagons with part of the cavalry. These couriers were attacked a few miles from the pass but managed to reach the supply train. Private John Teal had to walk the last eight miles, however. After his horse was shot from under him he crouched behind the carcass and shot a big chief of the circling Apaches with his breech loading rifle. Little did he know at the time that he had hit the great Mangas Coloradas. After the attackers departed with their wounded leader, Teal frugally picked up his saddle and walked to Cremony's camp.

The next day Roberts grouped his entire command and forced his way through the pass, again having to use his howitzers and sharpshooting riflemen. The Battle of Apache Pass was regarded as a victory for the troops since their casualties consisted of only two killed and three wounded, while estimates of Indian losses vary from ten to sixty-eight.[39] The battle was significant in that it focused the attention of Carleton on the importance of controlling the strategic Apache Pass. On July 27, 1862, he gave orders for the establishment of a military camp there. It was named Fort Bowie in honor of General George W. Bowie of the Fifth California Cavalry. For years to come, the garrison at this post was to give protection to travelers, wagon trains, and stagecoaches passing through the Apache danger zone.[40]

Meanwhile, the main body of the California Column started from Tucson on July 17, 1862. Because of the scarcity of water 1,400 men were separated into sections to march one or two days apart. Several garrisons were left in Arizona with Major David Fergusson at Tucson in charge. Brigadier General Carleton, who had been promoted from colonel in June, left on July 23, 1862, confident that he had brought law and order to Arizona during his two months' sojourn in Tucson. He reached the Rio Grande on August 7 and the last units arrived about a week later. On September 18, 1862, Carleton replaced Canby in command of the Department of New Mexico. It had taken him nine months to move the California Column across the hot, dry desert and to occupy Arizona, southern New Mexico, and western Texas. With the Confederate danger removed, his most pressing problem during the

---

[39]Letter of Brigadier General James H. Carleton to Lieut. Colonel Richard C. Drum, Ass't. Adj. General, U. S. Army, San Francisco, Calif., from Santa Fe, N. Mex., September 20, 1862, *ibid.,* p. 50; *War of the Rebellion,* Series I, Vol 9, p. 565; and John C. Cremony, *Life Among the Apaches* (San Francisco: Roman and Company Publishers, 1868), p. 164.

[40]Ray Brandes, *Frontier Military Posts of Arizona* (Globe, Arizona: Dale Stuart King, Publisher, 1960), pp. 14-21.

next four years was to subdue the Indians of New Mexico and Arizona.

The hostile Indians saw in the Civil War an opportunity to slaughter the white intruders or to expel them from the land of their fathers. So savage was the death and destruction that they carried to the mines, ranches, and settlements, that Southern and Union leaders alike considered the Indian menace a major obstacle to the occupation of the Southwest. Colonel Baylor, the Governor of Confederate Arizona, had very early decided upon a policy of extermination and on March 20, 1862, he wrote a most infamous order to Captain Helm in command of the Arizona Guards at Tucson. He urged Helm to use all available means of persuasion, including whiskey, to bring the Indians in for peace talks. Then all grown Indians were to be killed and the children sold to defray expenses of the operation.[41] There is no evidence that the order was obeyed, however, and Baylor was stripped of his command when President Davis learned of the incident.

Like the Confederate government, the Union at first supported a policy of extermination. On October 12, 1862, just a few weeks after Federal troops had been forced to fight a coalition of Apaches under Mangas Coloradas and Cochise at Apache Pass, General Carleton ordered that all Indian men were to be killed whenever and wherever they could be found. He was determined to keep the lines of communication open to the west coast at all costs. After first conducting a relentless campaign to subdue the Apaches in New Mexico, Carleton extended his military protection westward into Arizona, which officially became a territory separate from New Mexico on February 24, 1863.

Brigadier General Joseph R. West, who was placed in command of the military district that included Arizona, sent expeditions from Mesilla to fight the Apaches.[42] In January, a detachment under Captain Edmond D. Shirland induced the feared Mangas Coloradas to enter the camp of Joseph Walker, the leader of a party of gold seekers en route to Arizona.[43] At the camp, near present-day Silver City in New Mexico, the huge Apache chief was treacherously killed under circumstances that have been described as everything from attempted escape to cold-blooded murder. His successor, Cochise, enraged by what he believed was American perfidy, swore that a hundred whites would die for every Apache killed. Holding religiously to this Indian oath, Cochise

---

[41]*War of the Rebellion,* Series I, Vol. 50, Part 1, p. 942.

[42]Letter of Brigadier-General Joseph R. West to Governor Ignacio Pesqueira, from Mesilla, January 30, 1863, in *War of the Rebellion,* Series I, Vol. 50, Part 2, p. 300.

[43]Letter of Brigadier-General Joseph R. West to Captain Ben C. Cutler, Assistant Adjutant-General, Santa Fe, from Mesilla, January 28, 1863, *ibid.,* pp. 296-97.

murdered, tortured, and pillaged his chosen enemies almost to the end of his own life in 1874. The influx of American miners and ranchers after 1863 gave him plenty of opportunity to wreak vengeance.

One of the main objectives of General Carleton's extermination policy was to encourage prospecting parties to develop the gold deposits which had been discovered in 1863 in the mountains of central Arizona. Though the government's policy now called for peace agreements, neither the military nor the settlers seemed to have any scruples about ejecting the red man from his homeland. The rush of several hundred miners and ranchers to the new diggings led to the establishment of Fort Whipple, in the new military district known as Northern Arizona.[44] Originally located in Little Chino Valley about twenty-two miles north of Prescott, the fort was occupied in December, 1863, by two companies of California Volunteers. Major Edward B. Willis immediately negotiated a peace treaty with a local band of some three hundred Tonto Apaches who lived in the vicinity. Unfortunately, the soldiers who were escorting the officials of the recently organized Arizona Territory to Fort Whipple attacked and slew twenty of the bewildered Indians.

Following this engagement the Tontos went on the warpath and threatened to end the white occupation of the territory. Ranches were swept bare of stock and miners were killed at work as the Indians made raids through the Peeples, Hassayampa, and other valleys of north-central Arizona. The men who were erecting the buildings for the new capital of Prescott went armed, and feared to venture beyond the town limits. Not all the Indian fighting was done by the soldiers, however. Hardly a week passed during 1863–1864 without an encounter between the settlers and the Apaches. The frontiersmen mobilized under the leadership of King S. Woolsey, a prominent rancher who had accompanied the Walker party on its prospecting tour in the Prescott area.[45] Though a leader in territorial politics, ranching, and business, Woolsey is best remembered as an Indian fighter of the school that believed that the only good Indian was a dead one.

In January, 1864, Woolsey led an expedition of settlers and friendly Maricopas in pursuit of Apaches who had stolen livestock in the Peeples Valley. Coming upon a large concentration of Indians near the present site of Miami, Arizona, he arranged a peace council with about thirty chiefs. After the conferees were seated in a circle, Woolsey

---

[44]Assistant Adjutant-General Ben C. Cutler, *General Orders No. 27,* from Santa Fe, N. Mex., October 23, 1863, *ibid.,* pp. 653-55.

[45]Letter of Major Edward B. Willis to Captain Benjamin C. Cutler, from Fort Whipple, Arizona Territory, May 27, 1864, *ibid.,* pp. 868-69.

King S. Woolsey, commander of the territorial militia, rancher, miner, and legislator.

— Sharlot Hall Museum

touched his hat as the signal for his aides to draw pistols and start shooting the chiefs who sat next to them. The fight then became general as Woolsey's men fired upon the savages in the nearby hills. The actual number of Apaches killed in this treacherous episode is not a matter of record though there must have been at least twenty-four since the Maricopas brought back that many scalps.[46]

The punishment administered to the Apaches in the so-called "Massacre at Bloody Tanks" temporarily slowed up but did not end the Indian hostilities. The Indians and settlers continued to return bloody deed for bloody deed.[47] The first Arizona Legislative Assembly in 1864 commended Woolsey and bestowed the rank of colonel upon him. It also called for a war of extermination and authorized the raising of a regiment of voluntary infantry for this purpose.[48]

Conditions were equally bad in the southern and eastern parts of the territory. The military annals contain accounts of many expeditions sent out to punish the Apaches for their depredations. Two examples illustrate the type of activity in which the soldiers engaged. In May,

---

[46]Clara T. Woody, "The Woolsey Expeditions of 1864," *Arizona and the West,* Vol. 6, No. 2 (1962), pp. 159-64; see also, J. Ross Browne, *Adventures in the Apache Country* (New York: Harper and Brothers, 1869), pp. 99-102.

[47]*Arizona Miner,* May 11 and 25, 1864; September 7 and 21, 1864.

[48]*Acts, Resolutions and Memorials,* First Legislative Assembly, Arizona, 1864, pp. 69-70.

1863, Captain T. T. Tidball, in command of California Volunteers and some civilians from Fort Bowie, trailed a band of Aravaipa Apaches to Aravaipa Canyon in southeastern Arizona and killed fifty savages with the loss of only one soldier. The men had traveled steadily at night for five days over ground previously untrodden by whites in order to surprise the Indians. Almost a year later, on April 7, 1864, Captain James H. Whitlock led sixty-one California Volunteers in pursuit of Chiricahua Apaches. Some 250 redskins were routed from their camp near Grey's Peak in present-day Greenlee County. In his report on this episode, Whitlock wrote:

> . . . just as the savages were awakening from their slumbers, between daylight and sunup, I charged their camp. The fight lasted about one hour, at the end of which I had in my possession their entire "Campoody," with all its property, including forty-five head of horses and mules and the dead bodies of twenty-one Indians. I am satisfied that as many as thirty were killed in this fight. Some of my men fired as many as eighteen shots from their minie muskets. I could form no idea how many of those wretches went away with holes in their hides, but suffice it to say, a great many.[49]

These expeditions were typical of a considerable number of military and civilian forays in 1863, 1864, and 1865 to carry out General Carleton's extermination order. For the most part the campaign was ineffective and, at the end of the Civil War, the Apaches remained unsubdued in their mountain fastnesses. The desolation they caused was so complete in southern Arizona that no man's life was safe outside the walled pueblo of Tucson.

Of all the mines and ranches of the Santa Cruz and San Pedro valleys, only the ranch of Pete Kitchen remained occupied. His fortified home on Potrero Creek, about six miles north of the border in the upper Santa Cruz Valley, was the only safe place between Tucson and Magdalena, Sonora. It was Pete Kitchen who coined the phrase concerning the road to Sonora: "Tucson, Tubac, Tumacacori, and to Hell." The Apaches killed his employees, drove his stock away, and filled his famous pigs, which were so much in demand in Tucson, with arrows. Yet he stayed on as the one spark of civilization that could not be extinguished.

Quite in contrast with the unsuccessful and unsystematic attacks upon the Apaches was the Navajo campaign, which partly affected

---

[49]Letter of Captain James H. Whitlock to Captain C. A. Smith, Ass't. Adjutant-General, District of Arizona, from Camp Miembres, N. Mex., April 13, 1864, in *War of the Rebellion,* Series I, Vol. 50, Part 2, pp. 827-29.

Arizona. With the coming of the Civil War the Navajos became more aggressive because they interpreted the withdrawal of troops as evidence that the white man had been defeated. Raiding down the Rio Grande Valley they defied any attempt to pursue them into their strongholds centering around the magnificent Canyon de Chelly in northeastern Arizona. Their marauding days were numbered in 1863, however, when Colonel Kit Carson was appointed by General Carleton to organize an expedition against them. Determined to remove the Navajo threat to white civilization, Carleton notified the Indians that they had until July 20, 1863, to surrender and go to the Bosque Redondo Reservation in New Mexico. After that date every Navajo male capable of bearing arms was to be killed. The Indians, who had often heard "big talk" that meant nothing, were surprised when Carson arrived at Fort Defiance in Arizona Territory on July 20.

At the fort a band of Ute Indian scouts, anxious to fight their traditional enemies, the Navajos, joined the more than seven hundred troops in Carson's command. The armed Utes proved to be good marksmen and were very skilled in tracking and killing the Navajos, some of whom they scalped. So effective were Carson's encircling attacks that by the end of November all the Navajos outside the snow-choked entrances to Canyon de Chelly had either surrendered, been killed, or fled southward. All means of livelihood were destroyed as the soldiers tore up cornfields and slaughtered thousands of sheep, leaving them in piles to rot. All that remained to subdue the tribe completely was an invasion of the canyon itself. This stronghold had long been regarded as impregnable, even in summertime. But Carson chose to strike in mid-winter. With a force of 375 men and 14 officers, he moved to the west end of the canyon in January.[50]

A detachment of New Mexico Volunteers under Captain Albert Pfeiffer entered from the east and marched through ice and snow to unite with Carson's force. En route the Volunteers were rudely welcomed by Navajos who moved along the high ledges like mountain cats, yelling, cursing in Spanish, and throwing rocks on the soldiers. Next, Captain Asa B. Carey retraced Pfeiffer's route from west to east with another detachment. After these maneuvers, Colonel Carson returned to his field headquarters at Fort Canby, a supply depot that he had established at a place called Pueblo Colorado some twenty-one miles west of Fort Defiance. The immediate results were insignificant but by the end of February the fighting spirit of the Navajos seemed to be broken. By that time there were several thousand Indians at

---

[50]*War of the Rebellion*, Series I, Vol. 34, Part 1, p. 76.

Fort Canby awaiting a trip to Bosque Redondo. On January 14, 1865, Carleton reported that 8,354 Navajos had taken the "long walk" to the reservation.[51] Eastern New Mexico did not prove to be a good country for them, however.

In the first place, they were interned with several hundred Mescalero Apaches, their enemies of old. Tribal jealousies were aggravated when the reservation authorities forced the Mescaleros to give up cultivated lands to the more numerous Navajos. But even when the disappointed Apaches sneaked away from the reservation early in 1865, there was still insufficient land to sustain the Navajo population. The soil was unproductive, wood scarce, and the water unhealthy. Without the livestock and the grasslands that had supported them in their own country, the Indians made a half-hearted attempt to farm. Yet, because of several crop failures due to cutworms and bad irrigation practices, and because there were no subsistence berries and roots to be foraged for as in their homeland, the Navajos were forced to become expensive wards of the federal government. Though they submitted to the daily counting and accepted the rations, they refused to look upon the Bosque Redondo as a permanent residence and longed for the day when they could return to their own territory. Demoralized by a smallpox epidemic that took the lives of over two thousand of their people in 1865, and by the neglect of corrupt agents who were in charge of doling out rations and blankets, the Indians began quarreling with the soldiers.

Finally, after four years of dismal failure, the War Department realized that Carleton's plan for relocating the hostile Navajos needed to be reconsidered. In May, 1868, two Peace Commissioners, General William T. Sherman and Colonel Samuel F. Tappan, were sent to the Bosque Redondo to investigate. Satisfied that the Navajos would never be self-supporting on the New Mexico reservation, these men entered into a treaty agreement with the Indian leaders, one of whom, Barboncito, had previously made a trip to Washington, D. C., to report on conditions at Bosque Redondo. The Navajos were permitted to return to a defined portion of their former lands and were provided with liberal federal assistance to get them back on their feet again. During the 1870s, the Navajos began to change from a band of paupers to a nation of industrious, nearly self-sustaining people. At last, a policy had been developed that seemed to take the interests of the Indians into account.

Meanwhile, despite the Indian turmoil of the Civil War era, there were prospectors searching for precious metals in northern Arizona

---

[51]*Ibid.,* p. 523.

during the Civil War period. Early in 1862, Pauline Weaver and others struck pay dirt on the Colorado about ten miles north of Ehrenberg, where Michael Goldwater had established a trading post two years earlier. The discovery of gold placers brought people flocking to the spot. La Paz, as the new town was named, became Arizona's chief city with a population of probably 1,500 living in tents or houses made of brush and logs. The newly established territorial government, to be described shortly, had hardly begun to consider La Paz as a possible site for the capital, however, when the boom was over. The collapse that came in 1864 was due mainly to the difficulty of extracting the gold, and the high prices charged by merchants for dry goods and liquor. Within a few years most of the residents drifted away and La Paz became a mere shell of a place.

In the year 1863 there was great mining activity in north-central Arizona around present-day Prescott and Wickenburg. Famous pioneers like Pauline Weaver, Joseph Walker, Jack Swilling, and Henry Wickenburg located placers and veins of gold and silver along the Hassayampa, Big Bug, Lynx and Weaver creeks. The first organized group of white men to invade Arizona with the gold fever was the party of more than thirty hardy frontiersmen led by Captain Joseph R. Walker.[52] From a point on the north bank of the Hassayampa, about five miles south of the present city of Prescott, the men explored the surrounding country and experienced "booming times" in panning gold and killing Indians. A lot of gold was also picked up on the surface in the mountains. Jack Swilling, who had joined the Walker party following his sojourn in the Confederate Army, sent two specimens of pure gold to General Carleton. The general, envisioning "vast gold fields" in the area, forwarded the samples to Secretary of Treasury Salmon P. Chase in September, 1863, for presentation to President Lincoln.[53]

Another party was guided from California to the Prescott region in May, 1863, by Pauline Weaver. Organized by Abraham H. Peeples, this group followed the Colorado River to La Paz and crossed over to the creek which they named Weaver Gulch in honor of their guide. A nearby mountain, some eighty-five miles northwest of present-day Phoenix, was named Antelope Peak because the party killed several antelope on its slope. The miners struck it rich in both the creekbed and in the mountains. Just to the east of the creek, nugget gold was

---

[52]Daniel Ellis Conner, *Joseph Reddeford Walker and the Arizona Adventure* (Norman: University of Oklahoma Press, 1956), pp. 67-105.

[53]U. S. Bureau of Indian Affairs, *Report of the Commissioner of Indian Affairs, 1867*, p. 140.

found barely beneath the surface in a small saddleback of a mountain which was soon called Rich Mountain. Within a few months the prospectors were able to gather thousands of dollars worth of gold, using no more than knives to force out the metal. Needless to say, newcomers came from all directions to investigate reports of the discoveries made by the Walker and Peeples parties.

Perhaps the richest deposit was the Vulture mine, which was located in 1863 by Henry Wickenburg some ten miles south of the town which now bears his name. Wickenburg, who had arrived in Arizona the year before, seemed especially suited to prospecting by virtue of geological and mineralogical studies in his native Austria. Acting upon a tip from Colonel Woolsey that gold ore had been seen in the Harquahala Mountains, Wickenburg left his land in Peeples Valley and struck it rich. Supposedly he named his mine after the turkey buzzards which hovered above the region. Within a year after the discovery of the Vulture, probably two hundred people were living at the new town of Wickenburg where the ore was hauled to the Hassayampa's waters.[54] Along with some eighty miners who worked for Wickenburg, there were the usual saloonkeepers, gamblers, and gunmen who flocked into the mushrooming town.

Unfortunately, the "vast gold fields," about which Carleton wrote to officials in Washington, proved to be a mirage. In the years following the Civil War, copper, not gold, was the important mineral in Arizona's economy. Discovery of gold, however, was a factor that helped influence Congress to create Arizona as a territory separate from New Mexico. The Union government badly needed gold and was anxious that the potential mineral wealth of this region not fall into Confederate hands. The Arizona Organic Act was introduced on March 12, 1862, by Congressman James H. Ashley of Ohio. Already, a crosswise version of Arizona, approximating the southern parts of present-day Arizona and New Mexico, had been admitted to the Confederacy. Ashley's bill called for a vertical division of the New Mexico Territory along the meridian 109°2′59″. Lively debate followed the introduction of the measure. Proponents contended that Arizona's white population of 6,500 and the 4,000 civilized Indians were entitled to civil government.

The opposition argued that all but about 600 of the estimated 6,500 whites were Mexicans and that the loyal American population had probably been driven out by the Confederates. Opposing orators also claimed that the act was intended only to benefit office seekers and

---

[54]Conner, p. 85.

would serve only to divert monies from the war effort. The bill squeaked through the House, however, by a narrow vote on May 8, 1862. But it was not until February of the following year that Senator Benjamin F. Wade of Ohio was able to guide it through the Senate. Final action followed the deletion of a clause which designated Tucson as the capital. Arizona became a territory when President Lincoln signed the bill on February 24, 1863.[55]

Chief lobbyist for the bill was Charles D. Poston who is called the "Father of Arizona." The extent of his influence in bringing about passage of the measure is uncertain, though his account of what happened is interesting. In his *Reminiscences* he wrote:

> At the meeting of Congress in December, 1862, I returned to Washington, made friends with Lincoln, and proposed the organization of the Territory of Arizona. Oury was in Richmond cooling his heels in the ante-chambers of the Confederate Congress without gaining admission as a delegate from Arizona. Mowry was a prisoner in Yuma, cooling his head from the political fever that had afflicted it, and meditating on the decline and fall of a West Point graduate. There was no other person in Washington, save General Heintzelman, who took any interest in Arizona affairs. They had something else to occupy their attention, and did not even know where Arizona was. Old Ben Wade, Chairman of the Senate Committee on Territories, took a lively and bold interest in the organization of the Territory, and Ashley, Chairman of the Committee of the House, told me how to accomplish the object. He said there were a number of members of the expiring Congress who had been defeated in their own districts for the next term, who wanted to go west and offer their political services to the "galoots," and if they could be grouped and a satisfactory slate made, they would have influence enough to carry the bill through Congress. Consequently an "oyster supper" was organized, to which the "lame ducks" were invited, and then and there the slate was made, and the territory was virtually organized. So the slate was made and the bargain concluded, but toward the last it occurred to my obfuscated brain that my name did not appear on the slate, and in the language of Daniel Webster, I exclaimed, "Gentlemen, what is to become of me?" Gurley promptly replied, "O, we will make you Indian agent." So the bill passed and Lincoln signed all the commissions, and the oyster supper was paid for, and we were all happy, and Arizona was launched upon the political sea.[56]

This account of what happened is interesting, but Poston probably assumed too much glory for himself. Sam Heintzelman, who had served

---

[55]*U. S. Statutes at Large,* Vol. XII, 37th Cong., 3d Sess., 1863, Chap. LVI. pp. 664-65.

[56]Charles D. Poston, *Building A State in Apache Land,* John M. Myers, ed., (Tempe, Ariz.: Aztec Press, 1963), pp. 112-113 (originally in *Overland Monthly,* Vol. 24, October, 1894, p. 404).

Charles D. Poston, called the "Father of Arizona" because of his work in helping to bring about the creation of Arizona as a territory separate from New Mexico. The original of this photograph is in the Brady Collection of the National Archives.

John A. Gurley, the first appointee as governor of the Territory of Arizona. Although he died before he could assume his post, both a street in Prescott and Gurley Mountain in Yavapai County are named for him.

The silver inkstand presented to President Abraham Lincoln by Charles D. Poston in commemoration of the signing of the Organic Act creating Arizona as a separate territory. The inkstand today is in the Library of Congress.

as commander of Fort Yuma and founded a large mining company in Arizona, worked with certain Cincinnati mining investors to bring pressure on Ohio congressmen, who, with the able assistance of Delegate John S. Watts of New Mexico, were influential in pushing the Organic Act through Congress. Regardless of who deserves the greatest praise, however, it is certain that Poston played an active part.

To dramatize the event, Colonel Poston designed a massive inkstand which he intended to present to Lincoln with the request that it be used in affixing his signature to the Organic Act. Made by Tiffany's and purportedly costing $1,500, the gift was fashioned from the purest Arizona silver. In the center was the dome of the capitol building which covered the inkwell itself. On one end was the figure of an Indian woman which has since been described as Comanche-type and hence not typical of Arizona tribes. On the other end was the figure of a frontiersman with rifle in hand. "Abraham Lincoln" was inscribed on one side of the base. The inscription on the other side, "From Charles D. Poston, Arizona — 1865" would indicate that the gift was about two years too late for the signing ceremony. Lincoln was privileged to use it for only about a month before his assassination. A prized item today, the inkstand is in possession of the Library of Congress.

The officers of the new territory were mostly defeated "lame-duck" politicians.[57] Ohio Congressman John A. Gurley headed the slate as governor, but he became ill, delaying the departure of the appointees for Arizona. Gurley died on August 18, and John N. Goodwin of Maine was promoted from chief justice of the Arizona Supreme Court to governor. Richard C. McCormick of New York was appointed secretary of the territory. William F. Turner of Iowa became chief justice, with William T. Howell of Michigan and Joseph P. Allyn of Connecticut as his associate judges. The other officers were: District Attorney Almon Gage of New York, Surveyor-General Levi Bashford of Wisconsin, United States Marshal Milton B. Duffield of New York, and Superintendent of Indian Affairs Charles D. Poston of Kentucky and Arizona. Reverend Hiram W. Read, who had been a missionary in New Mexico in 1855, accepted the position of postmaster for the new territory, hoping that he might be useful in the evangelical field.

Poston did not travel with the main party of Arizona officials. He crossed the continent to Sacramento via stagecoach which he boarded in Kansas City. From Sacramento he took a river steamer to San Francisco. There he met an old friend, J. Ross Browne, agent for the Department of the Interior, who agreed to accompany him to Arizona. Browne described their boat trip to Los Angeles and the overland journey to Tucson, where they arrived on January 17, 1864, in his book, *A Tour Through Arizona in 1864.* Poston guided Browne through southern Arizona and distributed presents to various Indian tribes before joining the other officials at Prescott.

Except for Marshal Duffield and his deputy, Robert F. Greely, who accompanied Poston, the rest of the territorial government party traveled from Washington to Fort Leavenworth, located on the Missouri River, and then over the historic Santa Fe Trail to Santa Fe, where they were welcomed on November 26. Until that time the exact destination in Arizona was not certain, some members of the party even expecting that Tucson would be the new capital. General Carleton, however, argued against a location where Mexican and secessionist influences were strong. He favored Chino Valley, near the geographical center of the 126,141 square miles of territory and where a miniature gold rush had drawn several hundred miners. In October, the general had sent troops ahead under Major E. B. Willis to protect the miners and give security to property pending the arrival of the civil officers of Arizona. A military post, known as Fort Whipple, was established and became the first capital of the Arizona Territory.

---

[57]*New York Times,* March 10, 1863.

Some of the first officials of the Territory of Arizona. Seated *(left to right):*
Associate Justice Joseph P. Allyn, Governor John N. Goodwin, and Secretary
Richard C. McCormick; standing *(left to right): the Governor's private secre-*
tary, Henry W. Fleury, U. S. Marshal Milton B. Duffield, and U. S. District
Attorney Almon P. Gage.

The Goodwin party reached the fort after following the 35th-
parallel route which had been pioneered by Spanish conquistadors
and U.S. Army explorers. Sometime on December 27, 1863, the officials
crossed the eastern boundary of Arizona with their military escort. To
make certain that they *were* in Arizona territory, the wagon train traveled
for two more days before creaking to a halt beside a waterhole called
Navajo Springs, just south of the present town of Navajo on Highway 66. There, on the snowy afternoon of December 29, 1863, the
Territory of Arizona was formally established.[58] After Reverend Read
opened the ceremony with a prayer, Governor Goodwin and the other
officers took the oath of office.[59] Secretary McCormick delivered a brief

---

[58]Letter of Secretary Richard C. McCormick to President Abraham Lincoln,
from Prescott, Arizona Territory, December 1, 1864, Record Group 59, Territorial
Papers: Arizona, Vol. I.

[59]Letter of Governor John N. Goodwin to Secretary of State William H.
Seward, from Tucson, Arizona, April 4, 1864, *ibid.*

but stirring oration and hoisted the Stars and Stripes. He also read the Governor's Proclamation which announced that a census would be taken, judicial districts formed, and an election held for members of a legislature. In his own handwriting Goodwin specified that "the seat of government will be for the present at or near Fort Whipple." Nearly a month elapsed after this ceremony before the territorial officials reached the provisional capital on January 22, 1864.[60] But the Territory of Arizona had been established in the name of the Union. It was now a separate and distinct territory, divided from New Mexico approximately at the 109th meridian.

---

[60]*Arizona Miner,* March 9, 1864; see also, letter of Jonathan Richmond, a member of Governor Goodwin's party, to his parents, from Navajo Springs, Arizona, December 29, 1863. The original letters written by Richmond on this trip are in the Arizona Department of Library and Archives.

— Courtesy Bill Young

Marker at Navajo Springs where the first officials of the Territory of Arizona took the oath of office and formally established the territorial government.

Chapter 2

Man From Maine:

The Goodwin Administration

J. Ross Browne, who toured Arizona in 1864, summarized his impressions as follows:

> I believe it to be a Territory wonderfully rich in minerals, but subject to greater drawbacks than any of our territorial possessions. It will be many years before its mineral resources can be fully and fairly developed. Emigration must be encouraged by increased military protection; capital must be expended without the hope of immediate and extraordinary returns; civil law must be established on a firm basis, and facilities of communication fostered by legislation of Congress.[1]

Governor John Goodwin spoke similarly to the First Legislative Assembly of the Territory of Arizona which convened at Prescott in September, 1864. Identifying the Apache as the chief obstacle to the growth of civilization, he described how the murdering savages had desolated southern Arizona and northern Mexico following the withdrawal of troops at the commencement of the Civil War. "But for them," he said, "mines would be worked, innumerable sheep and cattle would cover these plains, and some of the bravest and most energetic men that were ever the pioneers of a new country, and who now fill bloody and unmarked graves, would be living to see their brightest anticipations realized." He suggested that there was only one policy that could be adopted in regard to the warlike Indians: "A war must be prosecuted until they are compelled to submit and go upon a reservation."[2]

Prior to delivering his message to the legislature, Goodwin had been working vigorously for several months to organize the government. After his arrival in Chino Valley the previous January, he had

---

[1]Browne, *Adventures in Apache Country,* p. 288.

[2]"Message of Governor John N. Goodwin," *Journals of the First Legislative Assembly,* 1864, p. 43.

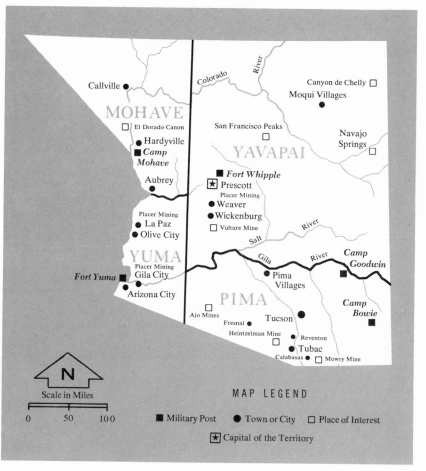

Arizona in 1865

The first change in the political map of Arizona came in December of this year when the legislature created the county of Pah Ute with Callville as the county seat. Prescott was the capital of the territory from 1864 to 1867.

set out with a military escort to become acquainted with the domain over which he was to preside and to select an appropriate site for the territorial capital.[3] He spent a month visiting the mining districts around Fort Whipple and then traveled eastward to the Verde and Salinas (Salt) rivers. During April and May he toured southern Arizona. While at Tucson on May 11, he proclaimed that town to be an incorporated municipality and appointed William S. Oury the first mayor. Tucson was the only community in the territory of any size and stability and probably would have been selected as the first capital except for the fact that it was tainted by Confederate sympathy.

One point should be made clear, however: Goodwin and his successors, down to the late 1870s, were inclined to mollify Southerners and other divergent groups in Arizona; by appearing to be nonpartisan they hoped to unify the territory and to tie it more closely to the federal kite. Accordingly, Goodwin established one of three district courts at Tucson. By his proclamation of April 9, the First Judicial District comprised all of Arizona south of the Gila and east of an artificial north-south boundary line approximating the 114th meridian. Judge William T. Howell held the first term of court in Tucson near the end of May. All of Arizona west of the 114th meridian constituted the Second Judicial District with Joseph P. Allyn presiding at La Paz. The northeast part of the territory was the Third Judicial District and was assigned to William F. Turner, who eventually held court in a log hut, later known as Old Fort Misery, in the town of Prescott.[4]

Goodwin carefully considered several possible locations for the territorial capital before deciding to start a brand-new town, nearly twenty miles south of the temporary seat of government at Fort Whipple. Situated in a picturesque spot on the west side of Granite Creek, the new "mile high" capital was surrounded by mountains covered with pines and abounding in game.[5] It was also near a small mining community and just south of the new military post of Fort Whipple. The fort was moved along with the seat of government and the original site in Little Chino Valley was renamed Camp Clark. A name for the new townsite and a method for the disposition of lots that had been surveyed by Robert W. Groom were decided upon at a public meeting of citizens on May 30, 1864. The town was named in honor of William H. Prescott,

---

[3]Letter from Secretary R. C. McCormick, Fort Whipple, to Mr. Hemphill Jones, Esq., 1st Comptroller's Office, Washington, D.C., April 20, 1864, Record Group 217, Territorial Letters Received, Vol. 8; see also, *Arizona Miner,* April 6 and May 25, 1864.

[4]*Journals of the First Legislative Assembly,* Appendix, pp. iv-v.

[5]*Arizona Miner,* June 22, 1864.

John N. Goodwin, governor of Arizona Territory from 1863 to 1866.

William S. Oury, brother of Granville, and first mayor of Tucson. An early Arizona cattleman and politician, he was also the leader of the famous Camp Grant Massacre.

Robert W. Groom, surveyor of the original townsite of Prescott, miner, and member of the first two territorial legislatures. Groom Creek near Prescott and Groom Peak in Mohave County carry his name.

the historian who was recognized as an authority on the Aztecs and Spanish-American history.[6] The name seems logical when one considers that one of William Prescott's theses was that the West should be Anglicized; Goodwin, McCormick, and the federal clique which they headed were of like mind. The capital planners showed no obvious Eastern prejudices, however, naming the streets after persons identified with the history of Arizona and Mexico, such as Montezuma, Cortéz, Marina, Alarcón, Coronado, Aubrey, Leroux, and Walker.

Three commissioners (Van C. Smith, Hezekiah Brooks, and Groom) were appointed to direct the appraisal and auctioning of lots in accordance with a law passed by Congress in March, 1863, to increase the revenue derived from the sale of public land for town sites.[7] At the first sale, on June 4, seventy-three lots were sold for $3,927.50, considerably more than their appraised value of $910. The first lot, which was sold for $175, was soon occupied by the corner store of "J. Goldwater & Bro." By July 4, 1864, 232 lots had been sold in Prescott. R. C. McCormick paid the highest price, $245, for a lot upon which was constructed a building made of hand-hewn boards for the office of the *Arizona Miner*. This newspaper began publication in Prescott on June 22 though it had been in operation on a semi-monthly basis at Fort Whipple since March 9. It was printed on a Ramage press that McCormick, the owner, had brought to Arizona. Published by Tisdale A. Hand, the paper kept its readers informed on the latest Indian atrocities, mineral discoveries, and official proclamations.

In a June issue of the *Miner,* the territorial government called for bids on the "Governor's Mansion," the first public building erected in Prescott. The mansion was constructed of logs that were cut and sawed entirely by hand from trees near the site. The carpenters who built the two-story, eleven-room house had to be armed against Indian attack. On one occasion a band of hostiles was killed within two hundred yards of the building, just as the Indians were preparing to descend upon the workers. Because of the high cost of materials — $1.75 per pound for tenpenny nails, for example — the contracting partners (Blair, Hotz, and Raible) went $1,500 into debt with only the "broad canopy" overhead for a roof. Since there was no watchdog of the treasury at the time, a new specification was inserted in the contract and the work continued, being finished at a cost of $6,000.

------

[6]"Letter of Secretary McCormick to Mr. Cepheus Brainerd (of New York) from Prescott, Arizona, July 11, 1864," [In files of the Arizona Pioneers' Historical Society] *Arizoniana,* Vol. 5, No. 3 (1964), pp. 61-62.

[7]*U. S. Statutes at Large,* Vol. XII, 37th Cong., 2d Sess., March 3, 1863, Chap. 80, pp. 754-55.

The Governor's Mansion in Prescott, constructed in 1864, and now a part of the Sharlot Hall Museum. The man seated under the tree is believed to be Henry W. Fleury, who lived there both while it was an official residence and for many years thereafter.

During the early period of its official life, the mansion was occupied in succession by Governor Goodwin, Secretary McCormick, Chief Justice Turner, and Henry W. Fleury.[8] As a member of Goodwin's private staff, Fleury had begun living in the house as early as 1864; when the capital was moved to Tucson in 1867, he continued to occupy the mansion as a private home until his death in 1896. At that time, the property was in the estate of the late Chief Justice C. G. W. French, who had acquired it from Fleury and generously permitted the former owner to reside there as long as he lived. The Congregational Church of Prescott then fell heir to the building and eventually sold it to Joseph Dougherty who attempted to modernize it by covering the pine logs with weatherboards. Finally, in 1917, the state legislature appropriated $7,000 to apply on the purchase of the historical structure. Thanks to restoration work begun by Sharlot Hall, historian and poet, one can still see the Governor's Mansion and a large collection of guns, furniture, and other articles used by the first white settlers in Prescott.

All that remains of the first capitol, on the other hand, is a marker on the north side of Gurley Street which reads:

> Arizona's First Territorial Legislature met in a log house at this site, September 26, 1864. The log structure served the pioneer government until the capital was removed to Tucson in 1867. The building later housed a store, post office, and brewery. It was destroyed by the great fire in 1900.

When the legislature convened in the two-room log cabin, there was only a dirt floor from which wild grass had been cleared but a short time before. The pine logs smelled of fresh balsam and still oozed pitch in tearlike drops. The building had been erected in such haste that the logs were only roughly faced with an axe. They had not yet been "chinked" and the cold autumn wind blew freely through the crevices. There were no glass windows, only holes with shutters of whip-sawed lumber. The seats and tables were also made of rough boards and the cuspidors that usually adorned legislative halls were missing. Tallow candles were provided for illumination at night. When the legislators assembled, their building was not quite completed and an unusually early winter storm drove them out. They adjourned temporarily to the Governor's Mansion where they conducted the territorial lawmaking.

The bicameral legislature consisted of councilmen and representatives who were apportioned to the judicial districts on the basis of

---

[8]*Arizona Graphic*, I, No. 5 (October, 1899), pp. 1-3.

population. An official census was taken by the United States Marshal, Milton B. Duffield, with the aid of a corps of assistants including soldiers and interpreters.[9] No settlement, mining district, or ranch in the territory was overlooked. The 4,573 people, exclusive of Indians, who were questioned, had come from nearly every state then in the Union and from many foreign countries, Mexico in particular. Mexicans who were residents of this region in 1848, and who had not declared their intentions of remaining citizens of Mexico within one year after the ratification of the Treaty of Guadalupe Hidalgo, were considered by the census takers to be citizens of the United States in accordance with Article 8 of that treaty.[10] The richest man in the territory was found to be Mark Aldrich, of Tucson, who listed his total fortune at $52,000 and his occupation as farming. The possessions of another prosperous Tucson pioneer, Charles Trumbull Hayden, father of Senator Carl Hayden, were valued at $20,000. Most of the laborers and persons engaged in mining, soldiering, farming, and cattle raising (the most common occupations listed) were less affluent than Aldrich and Hayden. The net worth of Thomas J. Goodman, for example, was recorded as only 25 cents. The census breakdown by districts is most interesting, both for the absence of such modern centers of population as Phoenix, and as an indication of the frontier status of Arizona in 1864.

The following figures were submitted by Marshal Duffield: First District (total of 2,377) — Tucson (1,568), Mowry Mine (145), women and children at the Mowry Mine (107), Apache Pass (74), Cerro Colorado Mine (45), Pima Villages (29), San Pedro (6), Raventon and Calabasas (183), San Xavier (112), and Fresnal (91).

Second District (total of 1,157) — La Paz (352), Arizona City (151), Fort Mojave (120), La Laguna (113), El Dorado Cañon (90), San Francisco District (62), New Water (61), Hughes Mines (54), Castle Dome and Potato (32), Hardy's Landing (32), Olive City (19), Mineral City (16), Los Pasos (14), Plomoso Placers (14), Apache Chief Mine (8), Picacho Mine (7), Salizar Mine (5), Scottie Mine (4), and Apache Wide West (3). The total of the more sparsely settled Third District was 1,039 persons.[11]

On the basis of the census tabulation, Governor Goodwin issued a proclamation on May 26, providing for the election of the First

[9]Letter of Secretary McCormick to Marshal Milton B. Duffield, Fort Whipple, February 25, 1864, Record Group 59, Territorial Papers: Arizona.

[10]*Ibid.*

[11]"The Special Territorial Census of 1864 Taken in Arizona," in U. S. Senate, *Federal Census: Territory of New Mexico and Territory of Arizona.* 89th Cong., 1st Sess., 1965, Sen. Doc. 13, pp. 49-124.

Charles Trumbull Hayden, an early Tucson merchant who later moved to Tempe where he ran a store, a blacksmith and wagon shop, and a grist mill. Because of the ferry that he operated across the Salt River whenever it was unfordable, Tempe was for many years also known as Hayden's Ferry. "Don Carlos," as he was often called, was the father of long-time U.S. Senator Carl Hayden.

— Arizona Pioneers' Historical Society

Michael Goldwater, another early Arizona merchant, with his brother Joe opened the first store in La Paz on the Colorado about 1860. The store was later moved to Ehrenberg and Prescott, and then to Phoenix. He was the father of Baron and Morris — who was vice president of the Arizona Constitutional Convention in 1910 — and the grandfather of U.S. Senator Barry Goldwater.

— Arizona Historical Foundation

Legislative Assembly and the delegate to Congress. Accordingly, on July 18, the voters cast their ballots for the first time in Arizona. Looking at the following list of successful candidates to the nine-member Council and the eighteen-member House of Representatives, one could surmise that the mining interests had a strong voice in Arizona's first election.[12]

MEMBERS OF THE FIRST LEGISLATIVE ASSEMBLY OF THE TERRITORY OF ARIZONA

COUNCIL

Name	Residence	Occupation	Age	Where Born
Coles Bashford	Tucson	Lawyer	47	New York
Francisco S. León	Tucson	Farmer	42	Arizona
Mark Aldrich	Tucson	Merchant	62	New York
Patrick H. Dunne	Tucson	Printer	40	Maine
George W. Leihy	La Paz	Miner	47	New York
José M. Redondo	Arizona City	Rancher	40	Mexico
King S. Woolsey	Agua Fria Ranch	Farmer	32	Alabama
Robert W. Groom	Groomdale	Miner	40	Kentucky
Henry A. Bigelow	Weaver	Miner	31	Massachusetts

HOUSE OF REPRESENTATIVES

W. Claude Jones	Tucson	Lawyer	46	Ohio
John G. Capron	Tucson	Merchant	35	Ohio
Daniel H. Stickney	Cababi	Miner	52	Massachusetts
Gregory P. Harte	Tucson	Surveyor	24	Ohio
Henry D. Jackson	Tucson	Wheelwright	40	New York
Jesús M. Elías	Tucson	Rancher	35	Arizona
Nathan B. Appel	Tubac	Merchant	36	Germany
Norman S. Higgins	Cerro Colorado	Mining Engineer	28	Ohio
Gilbert W. Hopkins	Maricopa Mine	Mining Engineer	35	New York
Luis G. Bouchet	La Paz	Carpenter	32	California
George M. Holaday	La Paz	Hotel Keeper	46	Indiana
Thomas J. Bidwell	Castle Dome	Miner	31	Missouri
Edward D. Tuttle	Mohave City	Miner	28	New York
William Walter	Mohave City	Miner	28	Pennsylvania
John M. Boggs	Prescott	Miner	32	Missouri
Jackson McCrackin	Lynx Creek	Miner	36	South Carolina
James Garvin	Prescott	Physician	33	Illinois
James S. Giles	Prescott	Miner	28	Delaware

Charles D. Poston, the newly appointed Superintendent of Indian Affairs, was elected delegate to Congress from a field of five candi-

---

[12]*Journals of the First Legislative Assembly,* p. 6.

dates.[13] Already known as the "Father of Arizona" and running on a platform favoring the Union, he easily defeated his opponents. He received 514 votes; Charles Lieb, another Union man, 226; William D. Bradshaw, an avowed Democrat, 66; William J. Berry, 48; and Sam Adams, 31. The runnerup, Lieb, was a newcomer with an interesting background. His friend, President Abraham Lincoln, had appointed him Quartermaster of the Army of the Potomac. Though honest himself, some corrupt Army contractors used him as a tool to fleece the government and ended his career in short order. About his only claim to fame was a German campaign song that he composed for German soldiers in the Union Army. William D. Bradshaw owned a Colorado River ferry with his brother, Isaac, at Olive City, a one-shanty town about six miles south of La Paz, but spent most of his time prospecting and exploring. Though personally likeable, he was an alcoholic and eventually slit his own throat in a fit of delirium tremens at La Paz. Berry and Adams were less well known pioneers.

After the campaigning was over, Poston departed for Washington D.C., by way of Panama, a trip that cost the taxpayers $7,000, and the legislature began convening in Prescott on September 26, 1864. The first meeting was called to order by Secretary McCormick. However, several members had not yet arrived and only one action was apparently taken before adjournment. By common consent they sent out for a generous supply of tobacco and liquid refreshments. It was not until September 29 that all the members had arrived. Most of them had traveled many miles through a country full of Indians and lacking in good trails and wagon roads. They came dressed in frontier clothes and were armed as men must be to safeguard their lives in a relatively unsettled wilderness.

In organizing for Arizona's first lawmaking session, the legislators elevated two Tucson lawyers to positions of leadership. Coles Bashford was chosen president of the Council, and W. Claude Jones, speaker of the House.[14] Bashford, who doubled as attorney general by appointment of Governor Goodwin, was especially well trained in law and government. A native New Yorker, he had served as a district attorney in that state before moving to Wisconsin where he was elected to the state senate as a member of the Whig Party. Ardently opposed to the extension of slavery into any state or territory, Bashford was active in

---

[13]U. S. House, *Journal of the House of Representatives of the U. S.,* 38th Cong., 2d Sess., 1864, p. 6; and Proclamation of Governor John N. Goodwin, August 20, 1864, *Journals of the First Legislative Assembly,* p. xviii.

[14]*Journals of the First Legislative Assembly,* pp. 20, 22.

the founding of the Republican Party, and in 1855 was elected governor of Wisconsin. After one term he returned to the more profitable practice of law. When Arizona was created as a territory in 1863, he was living in Washington, D.C., and, in true pioneer spirit, decided to accompany the territorial officials westward. Bashford had the distinction of being the first lawyer admitted to practice in the Arizona courts. He was elected in 1866 as the delegate to Congress. After one term he returned to accept an appointment from President Grant to be secretary of the territory, a position which he held until 1876. Perhaps his outstanding achievement was the compilation of all the session laws of the legislatures up to 1871 into one volume. The home he built in Prescott, a year before his death in 1878, is considered to be the oldest private residence still standing in that city.

After the two branches had organized, they met in joint session on September 30 to hear Goodwin's message. The Governor covered a wide range of subjects and demonstrated an understanding of the territory's history, problems, needs, and prospects. He reminded the Legislative Assembly that the laws of New Mexico (which included Arizona before 1863) had been extended to the Arizona Territory by the Organic Act and would remain in force until repealed or amended.[15] He recommended that the lawmakers provide for the appointment of a commission to carefully study and submit a new code of laws but urged the immediate repeal of the inherited New Mexican act which permitted peonage and imprisonment for debt. The Governor believed that involuntary labor and the detention of debtors in jail were barbarous and inconsistent with the Union's goals in the great civil conflict being waged in the East.

In responding to these recommendations, the first territorial legislature performed some of its best work. The basic research for a much-needed code had already been done for the lawmakers by Associate Justice William T. Howell. As the presiding judge at Tucson, Howell fully appreciated the impossibility of administering justice without a guide that was applicable to Arizona's legal problems. So, in March, 1864, he commenced preparation of a tentative code — more than six months before the "Founding First" convened. Howell, who had gained experience as an attorney and as a member of the Michigan legislature, was assisted in this endeavor by Coles Bashford. Together, the

---

[15]*U. S. Statutes at Large,* Vol. XII, 37th Cong., 3d Sess., 1862-63, Chap. 56, pp. 664-65; see also U. S. Senate, *Message from the President of the United States Transmitting a Copy of the Constitution adopted by . . . New Mexico . . . ,* 31st Cong., 1st Sess., 1850, Sen. Exec. Doc. No. 74, p. 1150.

Coles Bashford, president of the
Council of the First Legislative
Assembly, and at various times
delegate to Congress and territorial attorney general and secretary.

Judge William T. Howell, principal author of Arizona's first
code of laws.

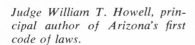

two lawyers sifted through the statute books of California, New York, and other states for laws suitable for the territory. Believing the New Mexico enactments to be "ill-adapted to our condition," they listened to the views of interested citizens and, in about ninety days, compiled a comprehensive code that ran more than four hundred pages in length when printed.[16]

In order to expedite action on the proposed laws, the legislature went through the motions of authorizing the Governor to select a commissioner to draft a code. Accordingly, Goodwin appointed Howell, who had by that time returned to Michigan, to the "new" position; and two days later, the Governor "miraculously" submitted the bulky code to the Assembly for study. The frontier solons naturally had many ideas of their own and did not accept the judge's suggested laws *in toto,* though they were strongly influenced by them. In fact, the compiled laws which they enacted during the historic first session were called the "Howell Code," in honor of the principal draftsman. Besides this recognition, Howell was well compensated financially for his work. The "three dollars a day" members of the "Founding First" appropriated $2,500 for his special services. In addition, he drew his judicial salary of $2,500 per year, beginning with his appointment in February, 1863 — eleven months before his arrival in the territory — and continuing until March, 1865, when he resigned. Altogether, then, he received $7,500 for about six months' time on the job. As we shall see, not all of the territorial employees were so well paid — certainly not the men who volunteered to take the field against the hostile Apache.

In 1864, more than laws was needed to bring order and civilization to Arizona. In his message, Governor Goodwin also dwelled at some length on the Indian situation that was stymieing progress. He suggested that the legislature provide for the organization of territorial ranger companies to cooperate with federal troops then in the field and praised the expeditions that Lieutenant-Colonel King S. Woolsey had led into Apache country. The Governor emphasized the need for confining the hostile Apaches to reservations. He also urged that Congress be memorialized for an appropriation to construct an irrigation canal on the Colorado River lands that had been selected by the Superintendent of Indian Affairs as a reservation for friendly tribes.[17]

The First Legislative Assembly of the Territory of Arizona, recog-

---

[16]*Acts, Resolutions and Memorials,* First Legislative Assembly, 1864, pp. 19, 62, 71; *Arizona Miner,* April 10, 1864; and Gilbert J. Pedersen, "The Founding First," *The Journal of Arizona History,* Vol. 7, No. 2 (1966), pp. 45-58.

[17]"Message of Governor John Goodwin," *Journals of the First Legislative Assembly,* pp. 43-44.

nizing the wisdom of Goodwin's suggestions, asked Congress to appropriate $250,000 for the organization of volunteer rangers to aid in the war against the Apaches. It requested $150,000 more for placing the amicable Yavapais, Yumas, Mohaves, and Hualapais on the Colorado River reservation. In spite of the untiring efforts of Delegate Poston, however, the Thirty-eighth Congress, convening in December, 1864, gave the requests little consideration. A reservation of 75,000 acres was set aside on the Colorado, but no money for settlement and irrigation was voted until 1867, and that was a meager $50,000. So the Indians were left to roam and to prey upon their white neighbors. For the time being, the responsibility for defense of homes and possessions was almost entirely in the hands of the settlers. In the absence of a sufficient number of United States troops, five companies of volunteers, totaling 350 men and 11 officers, were mustered into service.

The men of Companies A, E, and F were natives of Arizona, or Mexicans, and the officers were mainly Anglo-Americans. Company B was composed of Maricopa Indians raised by 1st Lieutenant Thomas Ewing, while C was a company of Pima Indians headed by 1st Lieutenant (later Captain) J. D. Walker. The Indian contingents were stationed at Fort McDowell and were responsible for killing and capturing a large number of Apaches. Company F, under Lieutenant Oscar Hutton, was located in Skull Valley and did efficient work in escorting and scouting for hostiles. Companies A and E, under Lieutenant William H. Ford and Captain Hiram S. Washburn respectively, were stationed at Camp Lincoln in the Verde Valley. These latter two units were credited by the Adjutant-General of the Territory of Arizona, William H. Garvin, with killing or capturing about one hundred Apaches between February and October, 1866.[18]

Considering that the Arizona Volunteers were poorly equipped, clothed, and fed, they rendered valuable service in hunting and destroying the wily and implacable Apache. The Third Legislative Assembly expressed the gratitude of the people after the troops had been mustered out in the fall of 1866. The resolution stated that the Volunteers "have inflicted greater punishment upon the Apache than all other troops in the Territory, besides ofttimes pursuing him barefoot and upon half-rations, to his fastnesses, cheerfully enduring the hardships encountered on mountain and desert."[19] The rangers undoubtedly appreciated

[18]"Report of the Adjutant General, William H. Garvin to Governor Richard C. McCormick, October 1, 1866," in *Journals of the Third Legislative Assembly,* pp. 250-54.

[19]*Acts, Resolutions and Memorials,* Third Legislative Assembly, 1866 (printed in 1867), p. 61.

this sentiment, especially since the financial condition of the territory did not permit the payment of the hundred-dollar bounty each recruit had been promised at the time of his enlistment.

Another important Arizona problem that the Governor mentioned to the legislature was the lack of mail facilities. He said, "Since the discontinuance of the overland mail in 1861, and until the action of the present Congress, no mail routes have been established in any part of this territory. We have been indebted to the courtesy of the military authorities for the means of communication between the principal points in the territory, and the mail routes in New Mexico and California." The semi-monthly military express, connecting Mesilla and Los Angeles by way of Tucson and Pima, was appreciated. But an increasing population required regular and more frequent mails. Advertisements in the *Arizona Miner* describing the comfortable and speedy coach transportation between El Paso and Kansas City tended to stimulate the pioneers' desire for a westward extension of this service. Goodwin recommended that the legislature memorialize the postmaster general for the establishment of an east-west route across the territory, a north-south route from Tubac or Tucson via Prescott to Fort Mohave and Utah, and branches to La Paz and other points.[20]

Following the Governor's lead, the lawmakers instructed Poston to request weekly postal service on each of about a dozen routes that connected the major towns of Arizona to each other and to the outside world.[21] This proved to be a large order for the delegate since the federal government had previously considered Arizona too sparsely settled for even one mail route. Poston's labors were successful, however, for the Thirty-eighth Congress voted to give Arizona several post roads: from Agua Caliente to La Paz; from La Paz, via Williamsport, Castle Dome City, Laguna, Arizona City, to Fort Yuma; from Mohave City to La Paz via Aubry; from Mohave City to Fillmore City in the Utah Territory; from Mohave City to Los Angeles via San Bernardino; from Prescott to Mohave City; from Prescott to Casa Blanca via Weaver, Walnut Grove, and Upper Hassayampa; from Tucson, via Tubac, to Patagonia Mines; from Tubac, via Cerro Colorado, Fresnal, and Cababi, to Tucson.[22]

By December, 1865, Acting Governor Richard C. McCormick was able to report that during the preceding year mail routes had been

---

[20]*Journals of the First Legislative Assembly,* p. 42.

[21]"Instructions to Charles D. Poston, concerning Arms and Mail Routes with Postal Service," *Acts, Resolutions and Memorials,* First Legislative Assembly, p. 64.

[22]*U. S. Statutes at Large,* Vol. XIII, 38th Cong., 2d Sess., 1865. p. 525.

established that connected Prescott with Los Angeles, Santa Fe, and Tubac. He was not pleased, however, with the mail facilities during the early years of the territory and urged the legislature to petition the federal government for other routes, including the old southern — or Butterfield — route and one to accommodate people along the Colorado River from Fort Yuma to Callville. McCormick also criticized the irregular service given by the first contractor whose contract had expired the previous June. "The hostile Indian," he said, "is scarcely more inimical to the progress and prosperity of a new country than the mail contractor who by his faithlessness interrupts the business and social intercourse of the people, and deprives them of their only means of communication with the outer world."[23] Fortunately, most of the later mail contractors during the territorial period performed their obligations in the highest tradition of the postal service. Among them can be found such well-known names as Charles T. Hayden (father of Senator Carl Hayden), William Zeckendorf, and Sanford Poston (brother of Charles Poston). But no territory suffered as much as Arizona did in the beginning for want of proper mail facilities.

Education was another topic that Governor Goodwin discussed in his message to the legislature. A firm believer in learning, he stressed the idea that universal education and self-government are inseparable, that one can be exercised only as the other is enjoyed. He recommended that the common school (public grade school), high school, and a university should all be established, and that a proportion of the tax monies, though small in the beginning, be appropriated for educational purposes. The Governor pointed out that sections 16 and 36 in each township had been set aside, by the Organic Act organizing the Territory of New Mexico, for the support of schools and would eventually be available for that purpose. He also informed the lawmakers that Arizona was entitled to a donation under the Morrill Act of 1862 for the establishment of an agricultural college. And finally, he recommended that assistance be given to the church school at San Xavier del Bac that he had visited.

It is understandable that few of the pioneer legislators who sat in the log capitol at Prescott could imagine the establishment of a public school system as extensive as that outlined by the Governor. On the frontier of a nation still engaged in the Civil War, they were naturally more preoccupied with developing the territory's resources and just keeping alive under the threat of Indian attack, than with

---

[23]"Message of Governor Richard C. McCormick," *Journals of the Third Legislative Assembly,* p. 37.

the educational needs of their children. However, the Assembly did give some consideration to Goodwin's pleas. Chapter XXXIII, section 11, of the Howell Code provided for a "system of common school education at the public expense." But the law was meaningless since neither a school system was proposed nor taxes levied for support of education. An act was passed, nevertheless, that gave $250 to the mission school at San Xavier where Father Mesaya was teaching some Mexican and Indian children. The money was to be used for the purpose of purchasing books of instruction, stationery, and furniture; it was a "fitting compliment for the first school opened in Arizona."

The county-seat towns of Prescott, La Paz, and Mohave were each granted $250 for public schools with the proviso that each town so aided would raise an equal amount. A further string was attached to an offer of $500 to Tucson, in that the English language would have to become part of the daily instruction for the predominantly Spanish-speaking students.[24] Only two schools actually benefited. San Xavier collected $250 outright and Prescott qualified for the grant when the school started by S. C. Rogers was assisted by matching funds from the community. Not one of the other towns raised its stipulated share. The first legislature also give lip service to higher education when it appointed a board of regents for a university in an undesignated location.

Goodwin's successor, McCormick, postponed the initiation of a school system. He told the Second Legislative Assembly, "I am inclined to think that the existing provisions for schools in various parts of the Territory are now sufficient."[25] It was not until after Anson P. K. Safford was appointed in 1869 by President Grant to be the third governor that the education picture began to change. Known as the "father of Arizona schools," Safford was mortified and humiliated by the results of the 1870 census. There were 1,923 children between the ages of six and twenty-one but not a single public school in the territory. Other things had obviously seemed more pressing to the early pioneers.

Governor Goodwin believed the development of mineral wealth and transportation were extremely important concerns of the territory. To encourage the mining industry, he advised the legislature to adopt a just and liberal mining code. He thought that the development of mines would serve as an inducement for the construction of a railroad into Arizona from the east. The legislature could expedite the latter by following New Mexico's lead in incorporating the Kansas, New

---

[24]*Acts, Resolutions and Memorials,* First Legislative Assembly, pp. 41-42.
[25]*Journals of the Second Legislative Assembly,* 1865, p. 47.

Early scenes in Prescott — the first school, built in 1865; a wagon train on the main street; and the territorial homes of Coles Bashford (on left) and of Levi Bashford, his brother (on right).

Mexico, and Arizona Railroad Company, giving it "ample powers and liberal provisions."

The legislators responded to the Governor's suggestions by including in the Howell Code some well-digested mining laws that would secure the rights of mine developers. One act allowed military personnel to locate claims on mineral lands. Territorial protection was assured, too, for all persons who had occupied and claimed a tract up to 160 acres under the preemption laws of the United States. Two railroad companies were incorporated, though not the one mentioned above.[26] Goodwin himself was involved in mine and railroad speculation and was the recipient of at least one legislative boon. He, along with Secretary McCormick and several others, was given territorial sanction to build a railroad that would connect Guaymas, Mexico, with La Paz on the Colorado River by way of Tubac, Tucson, and Picacho Peak. The organization, called the Arizona Railway Company, was incorporated by the legislature in an act that showed an awareness of the need for improved transportation. However, neither this line nor the railroad that Henry Sage, Richard Gird, and others were authorized to operate between Castle Dome City and the Castle Dome mines in Yuma County, was constructed.

The first legislature also granted liberal franchises to six toll-road companies.[27] These companies were permitted to charge exorbitant rates for the simple reason that the territorial government could not afford to build the needed roads and had to depend on private enterprise. One of the best roads in the territory was built by the Santa Maria Wagon Road Company. It ran westward from Prescott along the present route of the Santa Fe Railroad to the steamboat landings on the Colorado River. The toll rates established by the legislature ranged from one-eighth cent per mile for each sheep, goat, or pig, to four cents per mile for each wagon drawn by two horses, mules, or oxen. There was an extra charge of one and a half cents per mile for each additional span of animals. For each rider on horseback, two and one-half cents per mile was assessed. These rates would be considered quite excessive today, particularly where a road was over level ground which required little work to make it passable for a team. Yet the Santa Maria Road became one of the most used roads in the territory.

Another one of the chartered companies was the Tucson, Poso Verde and Libertad Road Company. The incorporators, who included a number of legislators, were authorized to build several roads — a

---

[26]*Acts, Resolutions and Memorials,* First Legislative Assembly, pp. 25 and 51.
[27]*Ibid.,* pp. 21, 27, 30, 32, 53, 57.

Edmund W. Wells, a Prescott lawyer who represented Yavapai County in the Council of the Legislative Assembly, and served both as attorney general and as a federal judge. He was a delegate to the Constitutional Convention in 1910.

— Special Collections, University of Arizona Library

main road from Tucson to Libertad on the border of Mexico, a branch from Tucson, Cababi, and Fresnal to some point to be selected on the main road; and another branch from the San Antonio, Mowry, and Esperanza mines, via Tubac, to Sopori on the main thoroughfare. The company was required to build bridges, to grade the road, and to maintain wells along the routes. No pedestrian was required to pay, but toll rates ran up to four cents per mile for each wagon with one span of draft animals plus one cent per mile for each additional span.

Four other companies were permitted to build roads into the temporary capital at Prescott. The Arizona-Central Road Company was authorized to build from La Paz to Weaver and on to Prescott. Another was the Mohave and Prescott Toll Road Company headed by Rufus E. Farrington. A third, the Prescott, Walnut Grove, and Pima Road Company, was authorized to build the first north-south highway. Among the incorporators of this latter road were some well-known pioneers, including Richard C. McCormick, King S. Woolsey, Jack Swilling, Bob Groom, and Dr. John T. Alsap (the first treasurer of the territory as well as a joint owner of the first saloon in Prescott). Woolsey was also involved in another enterprise, along with Edmund W. Wells (author of *Argonaut Tales*) and others. Their Prescott and Fort Wingate Road Company was granted the privilege of constructing and operating a toll-road across northern Arizona to Fort Wingate in New Mexico.

The first legislature also helped to promote transportation to California by granting exclusive ferry franchises on the Colorado River.[28] Samuel Todd received the privilege at Mohave, and William D. Bradshaw, one of the defeated candidates for delegate to Congress in 1864, was granted a franchise at La Paz. The ferry tolls authorized by the acts were high: four dollars for a one-team wagon plus one dollar for each additional pair of animals; one dollar for every horse with its rider; fifty cents for every person on foot and for each head of loose horses, mules, jacks, or cattle; and twenty-five cents for each hog, sheep, or goat. Obviously, travel by any mode was not cheap in Arizona.

The first legislature could not agree on the location of the permanent capital. In fact, the argument continued until Phoenix was finally selected, a quarter of a century after the inauguration of the territorial government. Governor Goodwin was almost asking the humanly impossible when he said in 1864,

> I can only urge that no considerations of local advantage, or sectional feeling and jealousy, should be suffered to control a question of so great public importance, but that a point should be selected which will become the centre of population, and aid in the development of the Territory. The claims and advantages of the different sites should be carefully weighed, and a location be made that will not require an immediate change. The advantages to the territory of a permanent settlement of this question are too obvious to require enumeration.[29]

Several bills were introduced in the first session to take the capital away from Prescott. The measures were in favor of La Paz, which was the short-lived county seat of Yuma County, another town called Walnut Grove on the lower Hassayampa that had a population of forty in the 1870 census, and a nonexistent town to be founded "at a point within ten miles of the junction of the Rio Verde with the Rio Salado" and to be called Aztlan. All of these suggested changes were voted down in the House by the narrow margin of nine to eight. So Prescott remained the temporary seat of government, by virtue of the Governor's proclamation, until the legislature moved the "capital on wheels" to Tucson in 1867. It was moved back to Prescott in 1877 and finally to Phoenix in 1889. This shifting of the capital's location emphasized the sectional rivalry between the older and newer portions of the territory.

The legislature had less difficulty dividing Arizona into four counties, which were named for Indian tribes inhabiting the areas. Pima

---

[28]*Ibid.*, pp. 24, 36.

[29]"Message of Governor John Goodwin," *Journals of the First Legislative Assembly*, pp. 38-39.

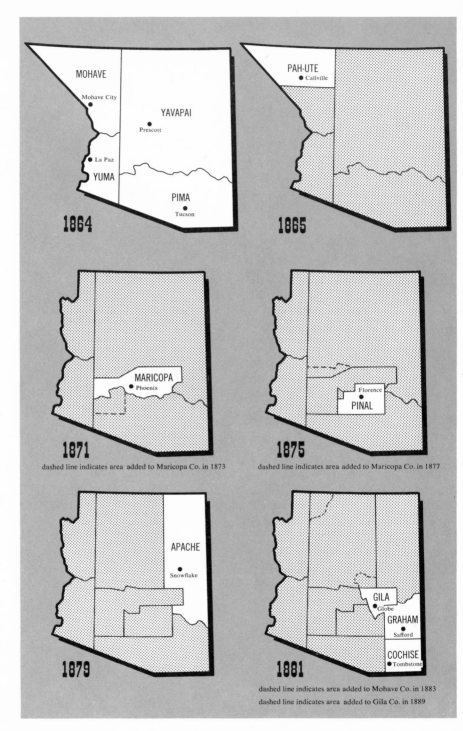

1864

MOHAVE
Mohave City
YAVAPAI
Prescott
La Paz
YUMA
PIMA
Tucson

1865

PAH-UTE
Callville

1871

MARICOPA
Phoenix

dashed line indicates area added to Maricopa Co. in 1873

1875

Florence
PINAL

dashed line indicates area added to Maricopa Co. in 1877

1879

APACHE
Snowflake

1881

GILA
Globe
GRAHAM
Safford
COCHISE
Tombstone

dashed line indicates area added to Mohave Co. in 1883
dashed line indicates area added to Gila Co. in 1889

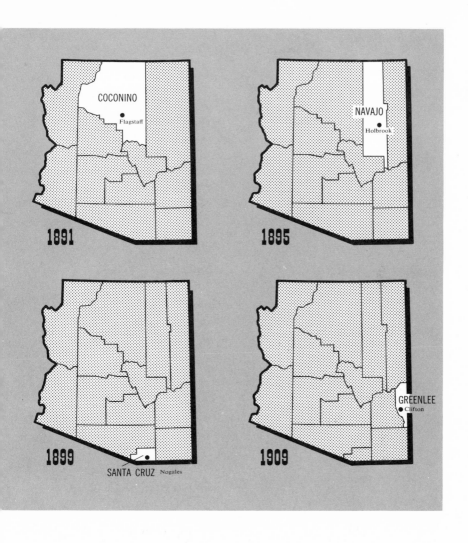

Counties of the Territory of Arizona

The present fourteen counties of Arizona were created, as shown here, by the territorial legislatures. County seats were also changed occasionally by statute.

County, with the county seat at Tucson, comprised the land south of the Gila and east of longitude 113° 20′; Yuma County was west of this line and extended from Mexico on the south to the Bill Williams River on the north with La Paz as its first county seat; Mohave County was north of Yuma and was administered from Mohave City; Yavapai made up the vast northeast part of the territory, that is, everything north of the Gila and east of 113° 20′. Prescott was selected as its county seat. Of the four original counties, only Yuma now has the same boundaries.

The first boundary change came in December, 1865, when the second legislature cut off the northern part of Mohave County to form Pah Ute County. Initially Callville, but later the little Mormon community of St. Thomas, served as the county seat. The new county had been recommended by Acting Governor McCormick because farmers were rapidly populating the area along the Colorado River. On May 5, 1866, however, Pah Ute became Arizona's "lost county" when Congress transferred the portion west of the river to the new state of Nevada. After vain protests against this action, the legislature in 1871 grudgingly repealed the act creating Pah Ute and restored what was left to Mohave County. Today the sites of Callville and St. Thomas are submerged under Lake Mead behind Hoover Dam and the "lost county" (now called Clark County) is better-known for another town, the gambling city of Las Vegas, Nevada. The latter town was founded in 1855 as a Mormon agricultural colony on the Old Spanish Trail that ran from Santa Fe to Los Angeles. The post office that was established there in the same year was the first of eleven such offices established in the Arizona part of the New Mexico Territory. The acquisition of Pah Ute by Nevada did not change the natural trade and mail connections between Las Vegas, and six other settlements, which had been located by 1866, within Arizona. The county was represented in the Arizona legislature until 1868 and the U.S. post offices at St. Thomas, St. Joseph, and Overton were listed in the federal records as located in the Arizona Territory until the early 1870s.[30]

Parts of Yavapai County, the so-called "mother of counties," were taken to form Maricopa in 1871, Apache in 1879, and Coconino in 1891. Pinal County was organized in 1875 from parts of Yavapai, Maricopa, and Pima but had other boundary adjustments later. Gila County was created in 1881 from portions of Pinal and Maricopa. Pima County not only lost some of its original land to Pinal but also gave

---

[30]Don Bufkin, "The Lost County of Pah Ute," *Arizoniana*, Vol. 5, No. 2 (1964), pp. 1-11.

Prescott as it looked in 1868

up other areas: one was annexed to Maricopa in 1873, and another was combined with part of Apache County to form Graham County in 1881; Cochise County was carved out of Pima in the same year and Santa Cruz in 1899. Greenlee was the fourteenth and last unit to be organized. Needless to say, the step-by-step changing of the original four counties into the present fourteen involved considerable complication and legislative manipulation.

Just as the territorial legislatures were never completely free of pressure resulting from sectional interests and political ambitions, so occasionally they were also called upon to solve personal problems that ordinarily would be settled in the courts. Divorces were an example. Not long after the first legislature convened, it passed a law annulling the marriage of John G. Capron, a member of the House of Representatives who had been a cross-country mail carrier in the late 1850s, and one Sarah Rosser Capron.[31] Since there was no law of divorce in the territory, the annulment was granted by the legislature on the vaguely worded grounds that Capron had been induced into marriage "by fraudulent concealment of criminal facts." Another act divorced Elliott Coues, the post surgeon at Fort Whipple and later the author of books

---

[31]*Acts, Resolutions and Memorials,* First Legislative Assembly, p. 19.

on Father Garcés and Zebulon Pike, from Sarah A. Richardson Coues.[32]

Later territorial legislatures were to continue this practice. Two bills in particular stand out. The seventh legislature in 1873 passed an act divorcing Governor A. P. K. Safford from his wife Jennie, though the circumstances of his family troubles were not quite clear. Then, in 1879, the tenth legislature passed the Omnibus Divorce Bill, which Governor Frémont approved. This measure released fifteen couples from the bonds of matrimony.[33] Among them was Secretary of the Territory — and one-time acting governor — John J. Gosper, who was freed from Waitie E. Gosper. It seems that Gosper had left a wife behind in Nebraska and he wanted to remarry in Arizona. Apparently all the divorces granted by the legislatures were considered legal because the U.S. Supreme Court had affirmed the validity of this type of divorce in an Oregon test case in 1852. The British Parliament and the American colonial assemblies had set the precedent. The Forty-ninth Congress stopped the practice, however, in the 1880s.

Altogether, the First Legislative Assembly was in session forty-three days. Out of seventy-seven bills introduced in the House and forty-five in the Council, forty laws were enacted. Governor Goodwin interposed no veto and withheld his signature in only one instance, a memorial to Congress asking that Arizona be transferred from the Military Department of New Mexico to that of the Pacific. All in all, the Governor and the legislature cooperated splendidly in organizing and launching the new government. In his farewell address to the legislature the Governor said,

> The task before you was indeed one of no ordinary difficulty. Since its acquisition by the United States, the Territory has been almost without law or government. The laws and customs of Spain and Mexico had been clashing with the statutes and the common law of the United States, and questions of public and private interest had arisen, which demanded careful but decided action. These questions have been met and satisfactorily settled.[34]

Actually, most of the topics considered appeared again and again in subsequent legislatures: location of the capital, Indian hostilities, schools, roads, codification of laws, mail routes, and boundaries. Nevertheless, great strides were made in the initial years despite the many handicaps presented by a raw frontier.

One member of the First Assembly, Edward D. Tuttle, captured the atmosphere of this legislative session in a letter to his sister, Cate Slade Auburn:

[32]*Ibid.,* p. 20.

[33]*Acts, Resolutions and Memorials,* Tenth Legislative Assembly, 1879, pp. 4-7.

[34]"Message from Governor John N. Goodwin," *Journals of the First Legislative Assembly,* pp. 241-42.

Legislature of Arizona
House of Representatives
October 31, 1864

My Dear Sister Cate,

I gave you a scolding in my last and would not pen this did I not believe that a letter from you was on the way to me now. No mail communication exists now between here and Mohave and I must compose myself until I return to Mohave about ten days hence. The weather is cool to excess now and reminds me much of an October in N.Y. but old residents inform me that it gets but little colder at any time in the winter and that we may look for fine weather after the cold snap. Last night snow enough fell to whiten the ground but the sun soon dissipated it. I have good health all the time, and have enjoyed myself largely all the time.

The members of both branches are with a few exceptions an intelligent set of fellows and I shall part with them with regret. No Indian difficulties have occured [*sic*] of late and only about a dozen [*sic*] Apaches have been killed since I came out. We have passed a good "Code" of laws and I trust have laid the corner stone of our jurisprudence well and deep and hope our young Territory may prosper under it.

Your aff. Brother
E. D. Tuttle[35]

One interesting thing about this letter is that it was written by a young man who had changed his mind about Arizona. Some fifteen months earlier, when he was a first lieutenant in the 4th Infantry of the California Volunteers stationed at Fort Yuma, he wrote a letter in which he said, "I don't believe any amount of gold would tempt me to remain in this country if I were out of the service."[36]

Unlike Tuttle, Governor Goodwin left Arizona at the first opportunity. Though he was governor from 1863 until April 10, 1866, he actually was serving in another capacity, too, during the last part of his term. At the first regular election held in September, 1864, he was elected delegate to Congress, his vote totaling 717 in comparison to 206 for the incumbent, Charles D. Poston, and 381 for Joseph P. Allyn. On March 4, 1865, Goodwin began a two-year term in Washington, D.C. Secretary McCormick assumed most of the real work of the gubernatorial office and, after more than a year as acting governor, he received the full title. During the interim Goodwin drew two salaries, but failed to reimburse the government for the overpayment, in spite of several requests from the Treasury Department to do so. For example,

---

[35]See Journal and Letters of E. D. Tuttle, University of Arizona Library, Special Collections.

[36]Letter of 1st Lieutenant E. D. Tuttle to the Slades, from Fort Yuma, July 17, 1863, *ibid*.

Acting Comptroller William Hemphill Jones wrote the following to him as late as July 25, 1872:

> I desire to call your attention to the amount $2692 with which you stand charged on the books of the Treasury Department, which was paid to you for salary of Governor, from March 4th, 1865 to March 31, 1866. You have been elected Delegate to Congress from said Territory and received pay as said Delegate for the above named period and request that you deposit said amount with some U. S. Depository, and transmit the proper certificate to this office.[37]

There is no record that the money was ever repaid, and the debt was still carried on the department's ledgers as late as 1884.[38]

As a delegate, Goodwin was not outstanding. The one speech credited to him in the *Congressional Globe*[39] was in opposition to the transfer of Pah Ute County to Nevada, but there is no evidence that he tried to stop the passage of this bill when it came up for final consideration. Poston wrote in an open letter to the people of Arizona that he believed Goodwin's election was fraudulently secured through a combination of military and federal authorities and that the new delegate never really identified himself with the interests of the territory.[40] Without confirming the charge, Major General Irvin McDowell nevertheless ordered all military personnel to take no part in Arizona elections, except to vote.[41] Much of Poston's criticism was unfair even though Goodwin never returned to Arizona. He resumed the practice of law in New York, and in 1870 obtained a position in the Internal Revenue Department. He died at Paraiso Springs, California, in 1887, at the age of sixty-three.[42]

---

[37]Letter from William H. Jones to Hon. John N. Goodwin, June 25, 1872, Record Group 217, Territorial Letters Sent, Vol. 8.

[38]Account of John N. Goodwin, Record Group 217, Accounting Office Records, Treasury Auxiliary Ledger #2, p. 35.

[39]U. S., *Congressional Globe,* Part 3, 39th Cong., 1st Sess., May 3, 1866, pp. 2369-70.

[40]U. S. House, *Biographical Directory of the American Congress, 1774–1961,* 85th Cong., 2d Sess., 1961, House Doc. No. 442, p. 958; see also, *Yuma Sentinel,* May 14, 1887.

[41]U. S. Army, Department of California, *General Orders No. 35,* July 14, 1866, signed by Assistant Adjutant General R. C. Drum by command of Major General McDowell.

[42]Lawrence Poston III, "Poston vs. Goodwin, A Document on the Congressional Election of 1865," *Arizona and the West,* Vol. 3, No. 4 (1963), pp. 351-54.

Chapter 3

Newspaperman at the Helm:

The McCormick Administration

"And the Governors of Arizona! . . . . Not one remains to air his rubicund visage in the Arizona breeze. They are not much to blame. Arizona has been a poor goose to pluck." Thus wrote Charles Poston in his *Reminiscences* in 1884. Arizona suffered the usual experiences of remote territories. Governors came from afar, having been appointed by the President for political reasons that were in no way related to the problems of Arizona Territory. They generally accepted the office as a steppingstone to more lucrative positions in the government, secured any extra remuneration that could be culled from local business enterprises, and then departed for the East as suddenly as they had come. The record of Governor Goodwin was illustrative of this pattern.

The second governor of the Territory, Richard C. McCormick, was one of the most popular and distinguished of the eastern appointees. Born in New York City in 1832, he entered business on Wall Street at the age of twenty and five years later became a journalist. Working as a reporter for the *New York Evening Post,* he visited the scenes of the Crimean War and then was a correspondent with the Army of the Potomac during the early years of the Civil War. For a time he served as chief clerk in the Department of Agriculture and in 1863 was chosen by President Lincoln to be secretary of the Arizona Territory. From 1866 to 1869 the handsome, red-haired New Yorker functioned officially as Governor and was then elected to three two-year terms as delegate to Congress. Among his extra-governmental activities during these years was the publication of two newspapers, the *Journal-Miner* of Prescott, started in 1864, and the *Arizona Citizen* that was begun in Tucson in 1870.

Following his Arizona service, McCormick returned to his native New York and received a number of political honors: U.S. commissioner to Philadelphia's Centennial Exposition in 1876, first assistant secretary of the Treasury Department in 1877, and commissioner general to the Paris Exposition in 1878. He declined ministerships to Brazil and Mexico but reentered politics as an unsuccessful Republican candi-, date for Congress in 1886. Defeated, but not deterred, he tried again in 1894 and was elected to represent the First District of New York for one term.[1]

When he passed away in 1901, Arizonans had good reason to remember both him and his two wives. He had met his first one, Margaret, on board the steamer carrying him on the last leg of a trip to New York City via the Isthmus of Panama in 1865. After a quiet wedding McCormick returned to Arizona where his bride became the first wife of a governor to live in the territory.[2] She died in Prescott during childbirth in the spring of 1867, after having traveled extensively in the territory with her husband during the previous winter.

McCormick was married again in 1873, this time to the daughter of Senator Allen Thurmond of Ohio in a grand nuptial ceremony attended by Secretary of State Hamilton Fish, General William T. Sherman, several senators, and other Washington dignitaries.[3] Rachel, or "Lizzie" as she was called, accompanied McCormick to Arizona in 1875. The *Arizona Citizen* (December 11, 1875) reported the visit in these words:

> Hon. R. C. McCormick and his wife arrived in Tucson on Thursday last, and are the guests of Mssrs. Tully, Ochoa & Co., at their house on Pennington Street. Mr. McCormick, having completed twelve years of honorable and active public life in and for Arizona, is with us for the first time as a private citizen. He will meet here, as he has elsewhere in the territory, a very cordial and sincere welcome. Having been with us in the dark and bloody days, no one can better appreciate the peace, order and prosperity we now as a people enjoy.[4]

As governor, McCormick was associated with four of the territory's twenty-five legislatures. At the time of the second in 1865, he was acting governor. In his message to the second group of lawmakers to convene in Prescott, McCormick emphasized the need for encouraging agricultural development of the territory's rich soil and grazing lands and for "the subjugation, even to extermination," of the hostile Apache. He recommended that Congress be petitioned for appropriations to provide a geological survey of unexplored portions of Arizona, to remove obstacles that impeded navigation on the Colorado River, and

[1]U. S. House, *Biographical Directory of the American Congress, 1774–1961,* 85th Cong., 2d Sess., 1961, House Doc. No. 442, p. 1289.

[2]*Arizona Citizen,* December 11, 1875.

[3]*Ibid.,* December 20, 1873.

[4]*Ibid.,* December 11, 1875.

to acquire the port of Libertad on the Gulf of California so that Arizona might have a seaport. The Governor gave the high cost of private transportation as the reason why many people had not entered the territory, and encouraged the establishment of both steamer and coach lines. These proposals guided the second legislature in their deliberations.

In a twenty-four-day session, the solons, who were led by Council President Henry A. Bigelow (a miner from Wickenburg) and House Speaker James S. Giles of Prescott, passed some notable acts. Two taxes were provided for future levying while current expenses were limited to the appropriation made by Congress. An *ad valorem* tax of twenty-five cents was levied upon each one hundred dollars of assessed property and a poll tax of three dollars was to be collected from all persons except Negroes, Indians, and Mongolians.

Two laws concerning matrimony were passed, the first of which is still part of the Arizona Code. This law enacted the old Spanish principle of community property whereby all property accumulated during the marriage was owned jointly by husband and wife. The other act prohibited the marriage of a white person to a Negro, Mulatto, Indian, or Mongolian. It is interesting to note that the latter law was enforced in Arizona for nearly a hundred years, until a Tucson schoolteacher of Japanese origin won a court decision recognizing his marriage to an airline employee of white ancestry.

Other acts of the second legislature created the county of Pah Ute described above; set December 4, 1865, as the date for the first meeting of the territorial Supreme Court; and provided for an elective board of supervisors with three members to control the affairs of each county. Several resolutions, including one that expressed the sorrow of Arizonans over the death of Abraham Lincoln, were passed. These were transmitted to President Andrew Johnson by the Acting Governor along with a copy of his message.[5]

Several changes occurred in the governmental personnel during the interim between the second and third legislatures. Coles Bashford defeated two opponents, Charles Poston and Samuel Adams, for the office of delegate to Congress. When the legislature convened at Prescott in October, 1866, two Tucsonans were elected to leadership positions. Mark Aldrich took over as president of the Council, and Granville Oury as speaker of the House. And at the top level, McCormick was officially appointed governor by President Andrew Johnson.

------

[5]Two letters of Secretary and Acting Governor Richard C. McCormick to President Andrew Johnson from Prescott, Arizona, December 23, 1865, Andrew Johnson Papers, Series 1, Vol. 64, Library of Congress.

*Richard C. McCormick, gover-
nor of Arizona Territory, 1866
to 1869.*

— Arizona Department of Library and Archives

A number of leading Arizona residents objected, though belatedly, to McCormick's elevation to the governorship. Among these were members of the strongly pro-Union Loyal League and federal Judge William F. Turner. In a letter to Secretary of the Interior James Harlan, the Judge criticized McCormick for favoring Copperheads and rebel sympathizers over loyal Union men in his appointments of two members to the Yavapai County Board of Supervisors and the territorial treasurer.[6] Turner also opposed the retention of Mr. Woolsey, a pro-Southern man from Alabama, as head of the militia. The Judge also disdained the way in which McCormick, as editor and controller of the *Arizona Miner,* had brazenly puffed up the "Secretary" and "Acting Governor." "He first delivers the Governor's Message to the Legislature," Turner wrote, "and then in the next number of the *Miner* publishes, as editorial, two columns of eulogy of the Message written by himself. In this way, he hopes to win the entire territorial machine and have everything his own way."

Another objection to McCormick was that he "put the bottle to his neighbor's mouth," to win support, though he himself was not a drinker. Instead of governing by precept and example to check vice, he was accused of catering to a depraved class of saloon patrons for selfish ends. For all these reasons, Turner withdrew his earlier endorse-

---

[6]*U. S. Statutes at Large,* Vol. XVI, 41st Cong., 2nd Sess., 1870, Chap. 29, Sec. 4, p. 77. This act gave territorial governors the power to fill certain vacancies.

ment of McCormick, and the Loyal League struck the Governor's name from its rolls.[7] If the Washington administration was influenced by these arguments, there was no indication, for it took no action and McCormick continued in office.

In his address to the joint session of the Third Legislative Assembly, the Governor reported that the 1866 census showed an increase in the population to 5,526. He suggested that the growth of the territory necessitated the building of county courthouses and jails if order and justice were to be served. McCormick expressed confidence in the great mineral potential of the territory but feared that development was possible only if the Apache menace were ended, either by crowding the Indians out by a large influx of population to the mines or by removing them with a bigger military force than the Pacific Department Commander, Major-General Irvin McDowell, had been able to send to Arizona. The Governor remarked with some ire that the faithless mail contractors were almost as inimical as the hostile savage in holding up progress and prosperity; the first one, he said, "so deliberately disregarded the contracts and the convenience of the people, that the service was a mere burlesque and provocation." On another topic, finance, Governor McCormick showed concern over the territorial indebtedness of $21,051.40. He urged a limitation of expenditures to extreme necessities.[8] The legislature had little difficulty complying with this direction since there were practically no schools or roads to maintain and Uncle Sam was footing the bill for salaries.[9]

Among the legislative acts passed in 1866 was one which authorized each board of supervisors to levy a special road tax for constructing county highways. The Yavapai County Supervisors were also permitted to levy a tax of fifty cents for each hundred dollars of assessed property to erect a jail and other needed public buildings in Prescott. Congress was memorialized by the legislature to establish additional mail routes and to repeal the law whereby Pah Ute County was created, prior to its annexation to Nevada.

Again Congress was not very receptive to the demands of a remote territory, but did enact several laws of benefit to Arizona. Money was appropriated for the purchase of agricultural implements and other

---

[7]Letter of Judge William F. Turner to Secretary of the Interior James Harlan, from Prescott, Arizona, January 26, 1866. Record Group 59, Territorial Papers: Arizona, Vol. I.

[8]"Message of the Acting Governor, Richard C. McCormick," *Journals of the Third Legislative Assembly,* 1866, p. 204.

[9]*U. S. Statutes at Large,* Vol. XIV, 39th Cong., 1st Sess., 1866, Chap. 28, pp. 22 and 24; and Chap. 208, p. 204.

articles that would assist the Indians to settle down in civilized pursuits. Congress also gave some consideration to the need for transportation in 1866 when the Atlantic and Pacific Railroad was incorporated and granted lands as aid in the construction of a transcontinental railroad that was to cross northern Arizona along the 35th-parallel route.[10]

Among the incorporators of this company were two future governors of the Arizona Territory, John C. Frémont and A. P. K. Safford. King S. Woolsey and Coles Bashford were also in the group. The law prescribed the route to be followed and provided a hundred-foot right-of-way as well as twenty alternate sections of public land on each side of the track for every mile of railroad built through a territory. The company was permitted to receive title for lands after each twenty-five miles of completed construction. The 1866 statute stipulated that the main line of the railroad was to be completed by July 4, 1878. To avoid taxes, however, the Atlantic and Pacific did not take out the patents to which it was entitled until after it was consolidated with the Atchison, Topeka, and Santa Fe in 1879. The railroad was not finished across Arizona until 1883. By that time the company had claimed some ten million acres in the territory. Coles Bashford, the delegate to Congress when the Atlantic and Pacific was incorporated, had died, and Governor McCormick had long since departed from Arizona. Technically, of course, the A and P was not entitled to a land grant because the July 4, 1878, deadline for completion of the railroad had not been met as specified in the 1866 charter. But when the legal question was submitted to the U. S. Attorney General, he ruled that Congress had not expressly provided for forfeiture and that only a special act of Congress could cause the land donation to be withheld. Since no special act had been passed, the railroad was not denied the land.

Meanwhile, the Fourth Legislative Assembly convened at Prescott on September 4, 1867. McCormick again stressed the need for more soldiers to subjugate the hostile Indians of the territory. He suggested that the ratio of one man per hundred square miles was insufficient but that the military defense could be improved if the small, temporary posts, by which at least one-half of the troops were rendered unavailable, were replaced by a few large, strategically located forts "from which troops can be hurled in force against any part of the Indian country and kept there until the end sought is fully attained." He said that

> while the war in the East continued it was not to be expected that much attention would be given to the frontier but now there would seem to

[10]*Ibid.* Chap. 278, pp. 292-99.

be no excuse for neglect to overcome the one great barrier to our prosperity, unless, as it is sometimes asserted, the Government does not deem the country worthy of occupation and development. Those who are familiar with its rare mineral resources, its rich fertile valleys, its unrivalled pastoral lands, its equable and salutary climate, its genial skies and all its capabilities and possibilities, taken as a whole (notwithstanding its large extent of desert and mountain) consider the assertion absurd.

McCormick favored placing the Indians on reservations over the policy of extermination advocated by many Arizona pioneers. He urged the establishment of an extensive reservation in the eastern portion of the territory and the assignment of sufficient troops to make escape an utter impossibility.[11] The members of the legislature shared the Governor's concern. Memorials were sent to Congress asking for permission to raise a regiment of volunteer troops and for an appropriation to construct military roads. It was to be several years, however, before the federal government was persuaded to subdue the hostile natives and place them upon reservations.

Among the laws passed by the Fourth Legislative Assembly in 1867 was one which made it a crime to use deadly weapons in any fight or quarrel. The same law forbade the indiscriminate discharge of any pistol or gun in the public streets or highways. This legislature also passed the first bill creating school districts in Arizona; each board of supervisors was empowered to set up a district wherever there were at least one hundred people within a four-square-mile area; a tax not to exceed one-half of one percent of the assessed valuation of taxable property could be levied for support of schools. The funds collected could be used to purchase, build, or rent rooms and to hire competent teachers.

The first district organized under this law was in Tucson. Arizona's Public School District Number 1 was organized by the Pima County Board of Supervisors on November 18, 1867. The Supervisors named John B. "Pie" Allen, William S. Oury, and Francisco S. León to the first public-school board to function in Arizona. An old adobe building was rented, and Augustus Brichta, a well educated California Forty-niner from New York, was employed as Tucson's first tax-supported public schoolteacher. The board tried to raise funds to match the $500 voted by the First Legislative Assembly in 1864, but the drive fell

---

[11]"Message of Governor Richard C. McCormick," *Journals of the Fourth Legislative Assembly,* 1867, pp. 3-46; see also, U. S. House, *Letter of the Secretary of the Treasury* [Hugh McCulloch] *Transmitting Report Upon the Mineral Resources of the States and Territories West of the Rocky Mountains,* 39th Cong., 2d Sess., 1867. House Exec. Doc. 29, pp. 135-38.

short, raising only $350, and therefore the district could not qualify for the legislative grant. As a result, the Tucson school was able to operate for only about six months in 1868. Brichta enrolled approximately sixty Mexican boys as pupils and certainly deserves credit for having made the first real attack on illiteracy in the territory. For four years, following his endeavors, there was no tax-supported school in Tucson.

A group of Spanish mothers, however, who were worried about the association of their daughters with American children who had "unaccountable bad manners," sponsored a private school in 1869. And the next year they welcomed the Sisters of St. Joseph who opened the "Sisters Convent and Academy for Females" at St. Augustine Church under the auspices of the Reverend J. B. Salpointe, Catholic Bishop of Arizona. An advertisement in the *Arizona Citizen,* on September 9, 1871, indicates that the school offered a broad curriculum and carefully regulated the lives of the students. The course of instruction included orthography, reading, writing, grammar, ancient and modern geography, use of globes, composition, sacred and modern history, astronomy, mythology, rhetoric, botany, intellectual and natural philosophy, chemistry, arithmetic, algebra, bookkeeping, French, music on piano forte, drawing and painting, plain or ornamental needle work, tapestry, hair and lace work, and making of artificial fruit and flowers.[12] Quite a comprehensive selection of studies! Each young lady, besides the uniform dress, was to be "provided with four dresses, a white swiss veil, a blue sun-bonnet, six changes of underclothing, towel, wash basin and pitcher, four table napkins, fork and goblet, work-box furnishes, letter paper, postage stamps and pens." Board and tuition was $125 for a five-month session. This amount was more than many parents in pioneer Arizona could pay. The free public school system still awaited its crusader, who turned out to be McCormick's successor in the governor's seat, A. P. K. Safford.

Another act of the Fourth Assembly was to "permanently" establish the capital in Tucson, effective November 1, 1867.[13] The residents of Prescott naturally resented this change. Their ill feeling was vented in an editorial in the *Arizona Miner* that not only charged that this legislature was fraudulent, but went so far ' as to print that several members were bribed and that Governor McCormick was pledged Tucson support if he should run for delegate to Congress.[14] There may or may not have been foul play involved. Whatever the case, the fact

---

[12]*Arizona Citizen,* September 9, 1871.
[13]*Acts, Resolutions and Memorials,* Fourth Legislative Assembly, pp. 25-26.
[14]*Arizona Miner,* January 18, 1868.

Old Capitol in Tucson. No longer standing, this building was located on Ochoa Street in what is now the civic-center area of downtown Tucson.

The original petition for Tucson School District 1 to the Pima County Board of Supervisors, November 3, 1867.

remains that McCormick did carry Pima County by a large_ enough majority to win election as delegate in 1868. Running as a Republican, he received 932 votes in Pima County. The Democrat John A. Rush was favored on only 71 ballots in that county though he carried the three less-populated counties by heavy margins. The perennial candidate, Samuel Adams, again ran a poor last.

The Fifth Legislative Assembly convened at the new capital in November, 1868. Indifferent to charges of "fraud" and "bribery," Tucsonans were as elated as the Prescott residents were disappointed. They felt that the end justified the means, especially since they had been cheated out of the capital in the first place. There is an old story that the legislature met in the Congress Hall Saloon. In truth they did not, though undoubtedly some of the members occasionally dropped in to lubricate their vocal chords and to wipe their large mustaches. Actually the capitol was in the adobe building belonging to Hiram S. Stevens, located on Main Street opposite Tully, Ochoa, and Company's store. It is said that the lawmakers filed their papers in crevices which they carved with pen knives between the adobe bricks. Certainly, the meeting rooms were not elegant, but neither was Tucson at that time. There were no sidewalks, no lawns, no paving, and few trees; buildings were placed flush with roads.

Governor McCormick evidently observed some progress, however. In his executive message to the territorial legislature he said, "There is a gratifying improvement in social life throughout the territory. In the chief towns the houses are of a better character than a year or two since and the ranchmen who have prospered have generally improved their structures. There is a growing disposition to live rather than stay here, to build homes and make them attractive, to cultivate household affections and loves, and society is assuming that organization which is necessary to pleasing and profitable existence."[15]

But in contrast to these sentiments, the Governor again spoke at length on the need for federal assistance to quell the hostile Apache. This time his pleas hit especially close to home since A. M. Erwin, who had been elected to the fifth legislature, was killed by Apache Indians before the session convened. As in previous messages, McCormick insisted that the Apache could be combatted by a regiment of picked Arizonans that Congress would have to authorize. He emphasized the necessity for ending the Indian depredations and getting railroad and telegraph lines through the territory so that the mines and agricultural

---

[15]"Message of Governor Richard C. McCormick," *Journals of the Fifth Legislative Assembly,* pp. 32-43.

lands could be developed. He mentioned the Vulture Mine at Wicken-burg as well as the new and prosperous farming settlements of Phoenix and Florence as examples of Arizona's great potential.[16]

After McCormick's address, his last official opening speech as Governor, the legislature went into action. The usual petition to Congress seeking military protection was passed. Memorials asking for land courts to decide the validity of Spanish and Mexican land grants and for $100,000 to build a territorial capitol were also sent. Another interesting measure enacted by the fifth legislature provided for a tax of from five to twenty-five dollars on all dance halls to help defray Arizona's governmental costs.

It was hard to maintain a quorum in the lower house because many of the lawmakers who were elected did not attend. Only one of six Yavapai members appeared at the new seat of government in Tucson. Yuma and Mohave were each one short in representation. Two late arrivals enlivened the session with stories about their experiences in getting to Tucson. These men were Octavius Gass of Callville, who represented Mohave in the Council, and Andrew S. Gibbons of St. Thomas, who was not officially a member of the House since his county of Pah Ute had been lost to Nevada. Departing from St. Thomas on November 1, Gass and Gibbons floated down the Colorado River in a fourteen-foot boat. They passed through the dangerous rapids of the Black Canyon and slept in the boat at night to avoid possible Indian attack. After arriving at Yuma they had trouble finding transportation to Tucson, mainly because a stagecoach had been recently attacked by Indians and the passengers massacred. When the legislature adjourned, Gibbons bravely traveled the five hundred miles to his home by horse-back, but the less-courageous Gass returned to Callville by way of California and Utah.

There was no legislative session in 1869, because McCormick moved to Washington to begin his first term as delegate to Congress, and his successor, A. P. K. Safford, did not arrive in time to call the lawmakers together. During this interim, Congress provided for biennial instead of annual sessions of the territorial legislatures.[17]

As a delegate to Congress, McCormick was active in securing several reforms which benefited Arizona as well as other western territories. In 1873, for example, he was successful in guiding a bill through Congress that transferred the administration of the territories

[16]*New York Times,* December 3 and 5, 1868.

[17]*U. S. Statutes at Large,* Vol. XV, 40th Cong., 3d Sess., 1869, Chap. 121, p. 300; and *ibid.,* Vol. XVI, 41st Cong., 2d Sess., 1870, Chap. 29, pp. 76-77.

from the Department of State to the Department of the Interior. In this undertaking he had the blessing and support of Secretary of State Hamilton Fish, a member of President Grant's cabinet. The Secretary wrote to McCormick in March, thanking him for his efforts, saying that the bill "will give relief to this Department and put the Territorial business where it properly belongs."[18]

Another cause to which McCormick successfully devoted his efforts concerned the salaries for territorial officials. In a speech before the House in January, 1873, he called upon his experience in Arizona as secretary and governor to deplore the insufficient compensation given to officers in the territories.[19] "I see no reason," he said, "why the Governor of a Territory should be obliged to involve himself head over heels in debt, why the Secretary of the Territory should go out of office in debt, or why a member of a territorial legislature should be obliged to incur debt for the simple reason that the Congress of the United States has hitherto not provided anything like an adequate compensation to them . . . . "[20] McCormick explained that the salaries of legislators were too small to meet the daily expenses of board and lodging in the capitals of the territories. He said that he had often made loans to members who couldn't return to their homes without borrowing money. Furthermore, many good men refused to serve in the legislature for fear of pecuniary embarrassment.

Convinced by arguments such as these presented by McCormick, Congress, in 1873, increased the compensation for territorial legislators to six dollars per day.[21] The annual salaries of governors and secretaries were raised to $3,500 and $2,500 respectively.[22] Though Congress did not always appropriate the amounts specified in later years, the enactment of the law and the transfer of the territorial administration to the Department of the Interior are a credit to the legislative ability of Delegate McCormick.

While in Washington, McCormick worked effectively for closer

---

[18]Letters of Secretary Hamilton Fish to Honorable Richard C. McCormick, February 17, 1873 and March 1, 1873, Hamilton Fish Papers, Vol. VII, Library of Congress.

[19]Letter of Delegate R. C. McCormick to Governor A. P. K. Safford (in Nevada), from Washington, D. C., April 22, 1869. [Photostatic copy in the Arizona Department of Library and Archives.]

[20]*Congressional Globe*, 42d Cong., 3d Sess., 1872–73, Part 1, January 8, 1873. pp. 412-13.

[21]*U. S. Statutes at Large*, Vol. XVII, 42d Cong., 2d Sess., 1872, Chap. 48, p. 416.

[22]*Revised Statutes of the United States, 1873–74*, 43d Cong., 1st Sess., 1874, p. 327.

ties with the national administration. During his first term he secured from the Treasury Department a much needed sub-treasury, or federal depository, at Tucson, and money order offices at Tucson, Prescott, and Arizona City from the Post Office Department.[23] He persuaded the Forty-first Congress to establish the Gila Land District and the Forty-second to extend the military telegraph from San Diego into Arizona.[24] Carried away by an ambition to be a United States senator, however, he was much premature in proposing statehood for the still-undeveloped territory; but in most of his actions, he succeeded in bringing the wild Arizona territory into a closer relationship with the rest of the country.

---

[23]*Weekly Arizonan,* November 27, December 11, 1869. (The "i" was dropped from *Arizonian* with the April 24, 1869 edition.)

[24]*U. S. Statutes at Large,* Vol. XVII, 42d Cong., 3d Sess., 1873, Chap. 227, p. 528.

Chapter 4

The Federal Ring:
Political Parties and Elections

Though small in stature, the red-haired and energetic McCormick was long on brains, charming personality, and political "savvy." Without doubt, he was the "idea" man in the territorial government from the beginning. His speeches and official work reveal much of the image that he patterned for Arizona. Along with Governor Goodwin and other federal appointees, he charted the course for the new territory in the first decade of its existence. In the first place, he believed, like the historian William Hickling Prescott, that it was the manifest destiny of Anglo-Saxon culture to triumph in this region over Spanish and Indian civilizations. Secondly, he believed that mining would be the basis for a settled life in a frontier region that hitherto had been the haunt only of warlike Indian tribes and roving fur-trappers, with here and there a ranch or an isolated military post. Hoping that Arizona could emulate the successful mining economy of California, McCormick advocated a *laissez-faire* policy to attract capital. He felt that with no tax on the gross products of the mines and with the passage of legislation to protect property rights, people would be eager to embark upon laborious and precarious mining operations. And most assuredly, Arizona could make its contribution to the nation if the actual production of metallic currency should be "sufficient to preserve the vitality of our national finances during a period of unprecedented trials."[1]

McCormick and the other federal appointees used their public offices to promote the economic development of the territory. As agents of the national government they sought appropriations from Congress to subsidize railroad, highway, and Colorado River transportation, and to subdue the hostile Indians. While firmly establishing federal authority,

---

[1]Richard C. McCormick, "Independence and Progress," An Oration Delivered at Prescott, Arizona, July 4, 1864. In Richard C. McCormick Collection, Arizona Pioneers' Historical Society.

they sought the cooperation of local business leaders and voters of the territory. Applying the axiom "in union there is strength" to political relations, the "federal ring" discouraged partisan politics and attempted to mollify the Spanish-Americans and the Southern Democrats, some of whom were ex-Confederate rebels who had migrated to Arizona after the war. Playing down the name "Republican," McCormick, Goodwin, the Bashfords, and Safford labeled themselves by such ambiguous terms as "Union," or "Independent." Identifying the main functions of a frontier government as economic development, protection of life and property, and the maintenance of law and order, Arizona's pioneer politicians quickly discerned that a nonpartisan coalition of leading citizens was the best approach for achieving territorial unity.[2]

Mention has been made of Goodwin's appointment of ex-Confederates W. S. Oury, as mayor of Tucson, and King S. Woolsey, as commander of the territorial militia. The powerful Tucson merchants, who in turn were closely associated with the Spanish-American community, were also assiduously cultivated for membership in the "coalition ring." Perhaps the best examples were Pinckney Randolph Tully and his business partner, Estevan Ochoa, who, for more than twenty years, operated the strongest mercantile firm in the territory. Though chosen a member of the Democratic Central Committee that was organized in 1873, Tully accepted appointment as territorial treasurer, the same year, from Governor Safford.[3] During the 1870s the firm of Tully and Ochoa profited immensely from its political alliance with the "federal ring" — as did other freighting and general merchandise firms such as Lord and Williams and Hooper, Whiting and Company. The territorial newspapers are full of references to the business activities of these firms which had the "pull" to secure army and Indian contracts. As early as 1870, for example, the *Weekly Arizonan* (Tucson) reported that the four-year-old company of Charles H. Lord and W. W. Williams was averaging between ten and fifteen thousand dollars worth of business per week.[4]

McCormick himself soon realized that there was more personal power in the delegate's job than in the governor's chair. In 1866, he supported Coles Bashford, a trusted henchman, as an "Independent" for the position. With some exceptions, the local Democrats buried partisan feeling and voted for the "ring" candidate, even though they

---

[2]Howard R. Lamar, "Carpetbaggers Full of Dreams: A Functional View of the Arizona Pioneer Politician," *Arizona and the West*, Vol. 7, No. 3 (1965), p. 193.

[3]*Arizona Citizen*, February 22, July 12, 1873.

[4]*Weekly Arizonan*, January 22, 29, 1870.

*These two men were respected
Tucson business partners who
had a powerful influence in
Arizona politics in the 1870s.*

Pinckney R. Tully

Estevan Ochoa

knew that Bashford was a staunch Republican.[5] The significance of this action is revealed by the fact that the "Democracy" held county conventions and nominated candidates for local offices; its cooperation with the "ring" in the delegate's race was by design, not from indifference. When McCormick ran as the "ring" candidate in 1868, however, the honeymoon was over, though the Governor himself maintained a façade of aloofness to the political parties. The northern Yavapai County Democrats, at a mass meeting in Prescott, called a territorial convention to assemble at Wickenburg on April 11 for the specific purpose of nominating a true Democrat to run for delegate to Congress at the June election.[6]

In praising the selection of John A. Rush, a member of the House in the fourth territorial legislature, the *Arizona Miner* (then edited by the vitriolic John H. Marion and no longer in McCormick's hands) said that the Democratic nominee would not attempt "to carry water on both shoulders" like his opponents. Referring to McCormick, the newspaper asked the voters to "put a quietus upon the last member of the clique of money making sharpers who came here from the East to ride, rough-shod, over the people of this Territory." Hurling such epithets as "nondescript opponents," "aristocratic, scheming demagogues who have fattened at the public crib," "carpetbag intriguers," and "professional dodgers" at the McCormick "ring," the *Miner* stated that Arizona had been shamefully represented in Washington by "three milk and water gentlemen" (Poston, Goodwin, and Bashford) and urged the election of a man whose interests were identified with those of Arizona and who was not afraid to acknowledge his allegiance to the Democratic Party.[7]

The "ring" was accused of fraud in the election of 1868. McCormick lost every county except Pima and probably won it with illegal votes. The *Miner* reported that one hundred soldiers voted for him at Camp Crittenden, "twenty of whom went afterwards, to two different precincts, and cast their votes for him. The same is true of nearly all the troops in Pima County."[8] The same newspaper also charged that hundreds of non-citizens of Mexican origin at Tucson, Tubac, and other places voted for him as many as three times in one day.

In 1870, McCormick ran for re-election on the same simple platform which had "carried him to victory" two years earlier. He promised

---

[5]*Arizona Miner,* September 26, October 13, 1866.
[6]*Ibid.,* March 14, April 11, 1868.
[7]*Ibid.,* April 18, 1868.
[8]*Weekly Arizona Miner,* October 29, 1870.

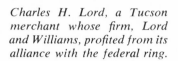

Charles H. Lord, a Tucson merchant whose firm, Lord and Williams, profited from its alliance with the federal ring.

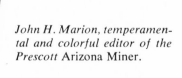

John H. Marion, temperamental and colorful editor of the Prescott Arizona Miner.

to "vigorously labor to procure from Congress and the Departments those measures of assistance to which the people are entitled and which are essential to the speedy and successful development of the rich resources of the Territory." He was endorsed by the nonpartisan Pima County People's Convention which was composed of delegates chosen from the precincts of Tucson, Tubac, Adamsville, Florence, Apache Pass, Camp Grant, the San Pedro ranches, and San Pedro Crossing. The delegates met in the courthouse in Tucson on October 14.[9] All of the candidates nominated at this convention won over their Democratic opponents in the November contest. In the race for sheriff of Pima County, for example, Charles H. Ott defeated Granville Oury, a dyed-in-the-wool Democrat whose later campaigns for other offices were to be more successful.[10]

A Democratic Convention had also met in Tucson, on September 17. The chairman, Oury, gave a lengthy address in which he set forth the "necessity of organizing the Democratic party for resistance, offensive and defensive, against Black Republican usurpation." A platform was adopted in which were listed the many wants of the people of the territory and the abuses to which they had been subjected "through the intrigues of corrupt officials." The convention then nominated a slate of candidates for county offices, and for delegate selected Peter R. Brady, a well-educated and respected resident of Tucson who had been active in business and politics since his arrival in Arizona in 1853.[11]

The Prescott *Weekly Arizona Miner* and the Tucson *Weekly Arizonan* jumped on the Democratic bandwagon. Prescott was still angry because McCormick had been instrumental in getting the capital moved to Tucson in 1867, but the Tucson paper made a sudden switch on the question of partisan politics. Going along, at first, with McCormick's Tucson organ, the *Arizona Citizen,* the editor of the *Arizonan,* Pierson W. Dooner, wrote, as late as the day of the convention: ". . . It is a mistake to suppose that the time has come at which party distinction is necessary. . . . We have no political voice outside the Territory, nor are we likely to have for years; while within our Territory no field for political strife exists. A common cause demands that we act in concert. . . ."[12]

By October, however, Dooner editorialized in a different vein. "It

---

[9]*Arizona Citizen,* October 15, 22, 1870.
[10]*Ibid.,* October 22, 1870.
[11]*Weekly Arizonan,* September 24, 1870.
[12]*Ibid.,* September 17, 1870.

Peter R. Brady, Democratic legislator and federal officeholder. He was one of the first Anglo settlers in Arizona, arriving in 1853.

R. C. Mac. to J. B. Allen, Jan. '69—"Pima county did me a favor, I did Pima county a favor; Pima county ows me nothing, I owe Pima county nothing. Good bye Mr. A.; I'll write you from Washington."

Nov. 18. '70—It has been satisfactorily ascertained that P. R. Brady is Deiegate elect; Mac. wants another office; he starts for Washington.

— Arizona Pioneers' Historical Society

"The Carpet-Bagger en Route." This woodcut, ridiculing Delegate McCormick, appeared in the Weekly Arizonan *on October 29, 1870, and was the first political cartoon in Arizona.*

John Wasson, editor of the Arizona Citizen *and a defender of the federal ring.*

is time," he said, "the people of Arizona choose for officers, men from among themselves. There is no just reason why we must be represented by starved-out politicians who can have nothing in common with us and would not remain a single hour in Arizona if divested of official patronage. It remains for the Democrats to explode the carpet-bag system of representation. . . ."[13]

John Marion of the *Miner* heaped on more coals; he devoted almost a full front page on October 29 to the alleged corruption of McCormick as secretary, governor, and delegate. John Wasson, editor of the *Citizen* and "ring" friend of McCormick's successor in the governor's chair, A. P. K. Safford, was just as bitter in defense of the independent People's ticket. This Tucson editor labelled Oury's charge that the officials had been sent to the Territory with instructions "to rob to the best of their ability" as basely false. He stated that the federal appointees in Arizona were "men of high character" who were not lacking success in the East.[14] And so the banter went back and forth between the rival editors, none of them pulling any punches.

McCormick's supporters were once again accused of election frauds. Watched more carefully in Pima County in 1870, the "ring" bought a few votes there at a "price varying from two to ten dollars," but picked up the bulk of its illegal votes in Yuma County. With the help of a wholesale merchandise firm, Hooper, Whiting and Co., at Arizona City, about four hundred ineligible Indians of both sexes were run through the polls. The indignant Dooner wrote facetiously about this fraud: "We believe in the right of women to vote . . . but it would appear more gallant on the part of Mssrs. Hooper, Whiting and Co., had they first extended this right to the white ladies of Arizona City and compelled the squaws to remain for next season."[15] The *Citizen* and other McCormick backers countered "that the pot was calling the kettle black" since the Democrats had picked up a lot of illegal votes for their candidate, Brady, in Phoenix, Adamsville, and elsewhere in the territory.[16]

But the *Arizonan* was relentlessly unforgiving. After stating that McCormick's "owners," who had bought the election for not less than ten thousand dollars, were "unscrupulous, hungry interlopers" who enjoyed "their omnivorous appetites for plunder" and after calling McCormick himself "a Republican of the blackest dye" who played

[13]*Ibid.,* October 1, 1870.
[14]*Arizona Citizen,* November 26, 1870.
[15]*Weekly Arizonan,* November 19, 1870.
[16]*Arizona Citizen,* November 26, 1870.

the "independent dodge" for selfish aims, the paper gave the Delegate the following discourteous send-off to Washington:

> Exit Mac — He has gone! The little carpetbagger has "vamoosed." Clothed in apostasy and degradation from having sacrificed the trust of honest men; mired down in filth and debris of bartered principle ... he flees from the scene ... Away! Away! ... Know ye contractors that fraud has sent from Arizona a merchantable article in the person of McCormick ... make good use of it whilst you may — for another of the same brood shall never yelp for Arizona.[17]

As we shall see further on, however, circumstances worked to McCormick's advantage during the next two years. The "ring" rebuilt a following in opposition to President Grant's Indian "Peace Policy." Both Delegate McCormick and Governor Safford supported the vigorous policies of General Crook over the peaceful methods of the President's emissaries, Indian Commissioner Vincent Colyer and General O. O. Howard. It was the mutual feeling of both the "ring" and the people of Arizona that the national government was unsympathetic to their desire to stop forever the Apache depredations. The territory was united to the extent that McCormick was re-elected without opposition in 1872.[18]

The truce was only temporary, for by the next year, as the result of General Crook's intensive campaigns against the hostile Indians, Arizona was nominally at peace. The pressures that had kept the "federal ring" in power since 1864 began to ease. McCormick wisely chose not to run again and four "Independents" clamored to fill the vacancy. None of the candidates sought party endorsement in 1874 because every man who had ever run for delegate to Congress on a partisan basis in Arizona had been defeated.[19]

Feeling that their party would have a majority if organized, however, the Democratic members of the seventh territorial legislature had assembled for this purpose in a caucus at the courthouse in Tucson on February 15, 1873. Resolving that a territorial convention would be held in Phoenix on the first Monday in May, 1874, the legislators asked each county to elect delegates and select one member to serve on the Territorial Central Committee for each one hundred voters. The resolutions passed by the caucus were signed by the chairman, W. F. Henning of Yuma and Mohave counties and by the secretary, J. T. Alsap. Other signers were King S. Woolsey of Yavapai and Maricopa;

---

[17]*Weekly Arizonan,* November 26, 1870.
[18]*Arizona Citizen,* November 16, 1872.
[19]*Ibid.,* October 31, 1874.

Fred Henry, William Cole, Thomas Stonehouse, and John H. Behan of Yavapai; John W. Sweeney, Mark Aldrich, Hiram S. Stevens, and Juan Elías of Pima; and Granville H. Oury of Maricopa.[20]

The work of these pioneer party organizers was all in vain, however, since the convention which met in Phoenix proved to be a farce. The *Miner* summarized the event thusly: "The abortive attempt of a few would be leaders to force themselves into power under the prestige of the mere name Democracy has gained a notoriety sublimely ridiculous."[21] The convention elected Peter R. Brady chairman and then proceeded to vote down a motion to adjourn a day so that delegates from Yavapai and Yuma counties might be present. Two candidates for delegate to Congress were nominated: John A. Rush of Maricopa by Granville H. Oury, and Hiram S. Stevens of Pima by John Bartlett of the same county. Because Oury had five "proxy" votes to add to his own and two others, Rush was nominated by an 8 to 7 count but refused to either accept or reject the nomination.[22]

In an address at Prescott the following week, Judge Rush explained that Stevens was running as an "Independent," even though he had signed the agreement in 1873 calling for the convention in Phoenix to nominate a Democratic candidate. Then, more than two months later, on July 24, Rush announced that he would not run.[23] The Democrats were thus left without a candidate to head local tickets which had been nominated by county conventions. Yet, though apparently thwarted, the party did elect a large number of people and built a nucleus for an organization that was ready to function when the influence of the federal ring finally dwindled away in the 1880s.

In the November elections for delegate, Stevens received 1,442 votes to 1,076 for C. C. Bean, 638 for John Smith, 13 for Charles Trumbull Hayden, and 7 for D. G. Beardsley.[24] If there had been party primaries in territorial days, "Independents" Stevens, Hayden, and Beardsley would have been pitted against each other for Democratic favor, while "Independents" Bean and Smith would have vied for the Republican nod. The territorial convention system, unsuccessfully tried by the Democrats in 1874, became the accepted means of nominating partisan candidates for delegates to Congress in 1880 and was used throughout the remainder of the territorial period by both Democrats

---

[20]*Ibid.*, March 1, 1873.
[21]*Weekly Arizona Miner*, July 24, 1874.
[22]*Arizona Citizen*, May 9, 1874; *Weekly Arizona Miner*, May 8, 1874.
[23]*Weekly Arizona Miner*, May 15, July 24, 1874.
[24]*Arizona Citizen*, December 19, 1874.

Hiram S. Stevens, Tucson merchant, territorial legislator, and delegate to Congress.

William H. Hardy, a Mohave County merchant, supervisor, and legislator.

and Republicans. The county conventions, with the delegates being sometimes chosen by primaries, continued to function to nominate local candidates very much as the Democrats had used it since the late 1860s.

There was one easily identifiable characteristic of the election of 1874 that made it similar to previous contests — attempted fraud, this time in Yavapai County. If 650 fraudulent votes for Mr. Bean had been accepted by the Yavapai Board of Supervisors, Stevens would have been swindled out of a certificate of election. The disputed votes were brought to the county seat at Prescott from the Little Colorado and Lower Lynx Creek precincts — 385 from the former and 317 from the latter. Witnesses testified that no election was held at Lower Lynx Creek and that only 106 votes, some illegal, were cast in the other precinct. Supervisors George D. Kendall, Thomas Ruff, and A. O. Noyes listened to lawyers argue the pros and cons and, when shown the glaring discrepancies in the returns, voted to reject them.[25]

The *Miner* called upon the next legislature for a strict voter-registration law. In 1875, Governor Safford also called the attention of the Assembly to the necessity of enacting a registry law. Otherwise, he said, elections would turn into "riotous assemblages, in which the several contending parties will meet trying to rival each other in the perpetration of frauds."[26] It was 1877, however, before a legislature strengthened the law concerning the registration of voters — requiring them to show either evidence of citizenship or intention of becoming a citizen and to have their names on the Great Register before election day.[27] Meanwhile, another election fraud was nearly perpetrated in 1876.

The Yavapai Supervisors were not so inclined to assist Stevens in the election of that year. Except for a technicality in the Arizona statutes, which required the secretary of the territory to accept the canvass of votes for the office of delegate to Congress that was submitted by the county recorder, Stevens would have been defeated by Republican William H. Hardy.[28] The latter was a pioneer Mohave County merchant and freighter from Hardyville, a town he himself had founded on the Colorado River; among other things, Hardy had served in both houses of the territorial legislature, contracted with the government to furnish supplies to military posts, established a ferry across the

[25]*Weekly Arizona Miner,* November 20, 1874.

[26]"Governor's Message," *Journals of the Eighth Legislative Assembly,* 1875, p. 32.

[27]*Acts, Resolutions and Memorials,* Ninth Legislative Assembly, pp. 64-66.

[28]*The Compiled Laws of the Territory of Arizona...1864 to 1871,* Sec. 36, p. 255.

Colorado, and promoted a stage line from Hardyville to Prescott.[29]

A conflict developed when Recorder William Wilkerson certified the ballots returned from all the precincts, whereas the Yavapai County Board of Supervisors, sitting as the Board of Canvassers, threw out the two precincts of Clifton and Little Colorado where the count was 168 for Stevens, 3 for Granville H. Oury, and none for Hardy. Since Stevens had only a plurality of 145 votes over Hardy (Stevens, 1,194, Hardy, 1,049, and Oury, 1,007), he couldn't have won without the disputed precincts. But under the law, the supervisors could legally canvass only the votes for county, township, and precinct officers — not for the federal office of delegate to Congress.[30] Nevertheless, by a two-to-one decision the board had attempted to throw out the precincts because the voters had not paid their poll taxes. Actually, the taxes were not due until December 31 and were not universally paid by people in the territory anyway. Besides, the same argument could have been used to knock out several Hardy precincts too, if the Board had been consistent.[31]

John Wasson, an intimate member of the "McCormick-Safford ring," was quick to charge the Yavapai Supervisors with attempting fraud in Mr. Hardy's behalf. Wasson and the "ring" nominally supported the "Independent" Stevens in 1874, 1876, and 1878, even though he was actually a Democrat and a local politician who represented Arizona's interests rather than those of the federally oriented clique.

In most respects Stevens had the aura of a native son. A Tucson merchant with limited education, he had been a resident of the territory for nearly twenty years. Born in Vermont, he enlisted in the First United States Dragoons while still in his teens and came to New Mexico to fight Apaches. During his four years in Washington, D.C., as delegate, he showed his "home rule" inclinations by securing the passage of a law enabling the elected territorial legislature to pass a measure over the federally appointed governor's veto by a two-thirds vote.[32] And in recognition of Arizona's growth in population to about 40,000 in 1878, he succeeded in getting congressional approval for an increase

[29]George H. Kelly, "Cap't. Wm. H. Hardy," in *Legislative History of Arizona, 1864–1912* (Phoenix: Manufacturing Stationers, 1926), pp. 340-41.

[30]*Acts, Resolutions and Memorials,* Seventh Legislative Assembly, 1873, Sec. 20, p. 51.

[31]*Arizona Citizen,* December 23, 1876.

[32]*Ibid.,* February 26, July 1, 1876; and *Congressional Record,* 44th Cong., 1st Sess., 1876, pp. 919, 3620, 3755, 4550, 4755. For other accomplishments of Stevens, see *Arizona Citizen,* August 26, 1876.

in the size of the territorial Council from nine to twelve members and the House from eighteen to twenty-four.[33]

Stevens was still wearing his political veil in 1878 when he ran for a third term and was defeated by John G. Campbell, a staunch Democrat who also chose to run as an "Independent."[34] Another member of the "Democracy," King S. Woolsey of Phoenix, entered the free-for-all race on the same basis. A. E. Davis, an Independent Republican, completed the field.[35] Both Campbell with 1,452 votes and Davis with 1,097 ran ahead of Stevens with 1,090. Woolsey brought up the rear with 822. The *Citizen* and the "ring" still played the nonpartisan tune and supported Stevens, perhaps as the candidate least likely to disturb them. Admitting that the incumbent was neither a great orator nor a great party leader, the paper contended that a non-voting delegate was a political nullity and should be expected to do little more than look after the business of his constituents.[36]

On the other hand, the *Miner* of Prescott reluctantly endorsed Campbell, a Yavapai County stockraiser and merchant. Observing that he was in fact bitterly Democratic in sentiment and in all his affiliations, the paper accepted his promise, as a "free and Independent" candidate, to serve all the people, and not merely one political party. In choosing Campbell for the delegate's office, the *Miner* had to overlook its disdain for one of his strong supporters, namely Granville Oury who had declared publicly that he "wanted to see the capital raised out of the d——d town of Prescott."[37] A factor in Campbell's favor was that he was a long-time resident. "His earthly possessions are in Arizona," said the *Miner,* "and on the principle that, 'where our treasures are, there will our hearts be also,' he is strictly and emphatically an Arizonan."[38] Technically, however, Campbell was still a citizen of Scotland, from which country he had migrated at the age of fourteen, and hence he served illegally as delegate to Congress. The oversight on this point is understandable since he presumed, though erroneously, that citizenship had been granted to his father, and therefore automatically to him too as a teenage son.

Campbell's single term in Congress was also clouded by election-

----

[33]*U. S. Statutes at Large,* Vol. XX, 45th Cong., 2d Sess., 1878, Chap. 329, p. 193.

[34]*Arizona Daily Miner,* April 22, October 4, 1878.

[35]*Ibid.,* May 8, 1878.

[36]*Arizona Citizen,* October 26, 1878.

[37]*Arizona Daily Miner,* October 14, 1878.

[38]*Ibid.,* April 22, 1878.

day irregularities, this time in the St. Johns area and in Yuma. Though elated over Campbell's victory, the *Miner* was disappointed in having to report how Barth and Co. "had driven in 300 cows, 3000 sheep, and with Campbell's cash, and some of their bad whiskey," purchased the votes of "all who were willing to sacrifice their manhood for such trash." On top of this was the scandal in Yuma. There the Campbell campaigners not only used whiskey, money, and fallacious reports damaging to the other candidate's character, but also enlisted the aid of a Catholic priest. The latter "was out electioneering and walking his subjects to the polls as he would drive so many sheep, and all in the interest of 'our' Campbell."[39]

During the election of 1878, several leading Democrats chided the Republicans for not cooperating in the formation of political parties in Arizona. A. E. Fay of the *Arizona Star,* for example, wrote that the success of the Democratic organization would have been assured "had the Republicans shown any disposition to organize and run candidates on party principles." He charged that many Republicans were in the thralls of the carpetbag federal officials and shared the spoils with them. The *Miner* answered Fay by saying that Democrats were simply excusing futile efforts to get the machinery of their own party organized. Continuing in a facetious vein, the *Miner* said that Republicans, who had never shown any disposition to organize in the territory, "ought to be ashamed of themselves for thus offending the poor, innocent Democracy and preventing their organizing by . . . doing as they pleased about it. . . ."[40]

In 1880, however, the party lines were finally drawn. In that year, Granville Oury, a lifelong Democrat and oft-frustrated party organizer, ran on the Democratic ticket and was elected to the first of two terms as delegate to Congress. Oury and his Republican opponent, Madison W. Stewart, were each nominated by a partisan territorial convention meeting in Phoenix. Looking forward to the nominating conventions in the summer of 1880 and the first election ever held in Arizona at which both candidates were placed in the field by the political parties prevailing in the states, the *Miner* expressed the feeling of many people when it wrote: "Let us have for once in the history of Arizona, a square, fair fight between two gentlemen whose political sentiments are at extreme variance. . . ."[41]

The Democrats were organized first. During the Tenth Legislative

[39]*Ibid.,* November 13, 1878.
[40]*Ibid.,* May 28, November 16, 1878.
[41]*Weekly Arizona Miner,* June 25, 1880.

*A Democratic political cartoon showing Granville
Oury ready to "bust" the federal ring.*

Assembly, meeting in Prescott in 1879, some of the Democratic members joined with a few others and appointed a Territorial Central Committee. County organizations were effected and finally, on June 28, 1880, the territorial convention convened, complete with parade and a spirited contest among prospective candidates for delegate to Congress. After thirteen roll calls failed to give anyone a two-thirds majority, the name of Hugo Richards was withdrawn and Oury was nominated unanimously.[42] The successful nominee was a well-known lawyer who had represented Arizona in the Confederate Congress in 1862 at Richmond, Virginia, and fought in the Southern army. After the Civil War was over, however, he took the oath of allegiance to the United States, and served in various county and territorial offices, including that of speaker of the House.[43] Commenting on the Democratic candidate, a

---

[42]*Phoenix Herald,* July 2, 1880.

[43]U. S. House, "Granville Henderson Oury," *Biographical Directory of the American Congress, 1774–1961,* 85th Cong., 2d Sess., House Doc. 442, p. 1414.

Republican orator, Clark Churchill, exclaimed, "The mountain has labored and brought forth a mouse." The speaker labeled Oury "an unreconstructed rebel, who believes that the war for the dissolution of the Union is still going on. . . ."[44]

The Democrats, however, believed that with an organized party they were in the majority and could elect Oury and his running mate for superintendent of public instruction, Ivy H. Cox. The campaign was launched at a torchlight rally of some two hundred people who gathered after adjournment to listen to the party's orators: Oury, Cox, A. C. Baker, Morris Goldwater, and Delegate John G. Campbell who, though he had not been nominated for re-election, promised to work for the "Democracy."[45]

Equally confident, the Republicans also organized. Their movement had grown from the grass roots like wildfire. It started with a "Republican Club" in Prescott which in turn called a county convention, composed of fifty-two delegates representing every precinct.[46] The Yavapai convention nominated a full slate of candidates with whom the Republicans hoped to fill the courthouse offices. When the success of this meeting attracted the attention of Republicans all over the territory, the Yavapai County Committee (Edmund W. Wells, Clark Churchill, W. N. Kelly, J. P. Hargrave, and Henry A. Bigelow) responded to the interest with alacrity by calling a territorial convention to meet in Phoenix on August 23, 1880.

Delegates came from all the seven counties and were in their seats when ex-Governor A. P. K. Safford, McCormick's successor from 1869 to 1877, banged his gavel to begin the proceedings. Safford explained his reason for switching to Republican partisanship, having formerly supported the "ring" policy of party aloofness; he said that he had favored Democrats in his appointments as governor, but now that the "Democracy" was ready to take the advantage, all past favors were forgotten.[47] William H. Hardy was elected permanent chairman of the convention and W. J. Osborne secretary. Then came the main business of the convention, the nomination of a candidate for Congress. This was disposed of quickly as Madison W. Stewart, a businessman from Pima County who had served as speaker of the House in the tenth legislature, defeated his only rival, DeForest Porter, a federal

---

[44]*Weekly Arizona Miner,* October 22, 1880.

[45]*Phoenix Herald,* July 2, 1880.

[46]*Weekly Arizona Miner,* June 11, 1880.

[47]Open letter from William H. Hardy, printed in *Weekly Arizona Miner,* June 30, 1882.

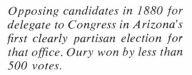

Opposing candidates in 1880 for delegate to Congress in Arizona's first clearly partisan election for that office. Oury won by less than 500 votes.

Granville Oury, Democrat

Photos — Arizona Pioneers'
          Historical Society

Madison W. Stewart, Republican

judge in the Second Judicial District from 1873 to 1882 and later mayor of Phoenix.

No nomination was made for the office of superintendent of public instruction that the legislature had created in 1879; the thinking of the delegates was that this office should be separated from any political or religious influences.[48] However, the temporary appointee, Moses H.

---

[48]Act No. 61, *Acts and Resolutions,* Tenth Legislative Assembly, 1879.

Sherman, was heartily endorsed by the convention and recommended to the voters. After adjournment, a grand ratification meeting was held on the public plaza where the Phoenix Brass Band entertained several hundred people in the light of huge bonfires and Acting Governor John J. Gosper introduced several speakers. The occasion would have been complete if Governor John C. Frémont, the first Republican candidate for President, had been present. The Phoenix ratification meeting was duplicated in other parts of the territory, the one in Prescott being climaxed with a hundred-gun salute.[49]

The Democratic press wasted no time in trying to rename the territory's newest party.[50] They referred to the Republican organization as the "Ring Party," the "Monopoly Party," the "Grab Party," the "Dishonest Party," and the "McCormick Party" — some of the sobriquets having more of a national significance than a territorial one. The Democratic campaigners made a point of the fact that Stewart was a relative newcomer to the territory; they also questioned his eligibility to be delegate because he had acquired considerable wealth selling goods to Uncle Sam. Stewart himself partially disposed of this issue by withdrawing from all government contracts.[51]

In offering Stewart to the electorate, the Republicans initiated a campaign argument that they were to use often during the territorial period — namely, that a delegate of that party would be more effective in dealing with a Republican Congress and President than any Democrat could be.[52] But after the shouting was over and the ballots cast, it was apparent that neither of the newly organized groups had developed much loyalty — that is if "straight ticket voting" is a criterion of party success. The *Citizen* reported that most voters were "scratching," many to the extent that they in effect changed their tickets from Republican to Democratic or vice versa.[53] The final tally gave Oury a majority, 4,095 to 3,606, over his Republican opponent.[54] The period of control by the first "federal ring" seemed to be drawing to a close.

In Congress, Oury served on committees important to Arizona, particularly those concerned with mining and Indian affairs; but like most non-voting delegates from the territories, he was unable to accomplish much for Arizona — a point that the Republican press mentioned

---

[49]*Daily Arizona Citizen,* August 24, 1880, and *Weekly Arizona Miner,* October 22, 1880.

[50]*Weekly Arizona Miner,* October 15, 1880.

[51]*Arizona Citizen,* October 2, 1880.

[52]*Ibid.,* October 30, 1880.

[53]*Ibid.,* November 6, 1880.

[54]*Ibid.,* December 4, 1880.

again and again during the next election campaign in 1882. The *Citizen* called him "the great incompetent" and the *Miner* concluded that the only thing that he had done in two years was draw ten thousand dollars in salary.[55] The latter paper compared him unfavorably with ex-Delegate McCormick, whose greatest obstacle had been the fact that he represented a thinly-populated territory of 20,000 which could not command much respect. In contrast, the population in Oury's time was four times as great and the territory was producing large quantities of precious bullion. So, once again, the Republicans suggested that a delegate of their party could command the confidence of the dominant Republican majority in Congress and better attend to the material wants of the territory: mail facilities, geological surveys, public buildings, highways, and others.

The Democrats, however, played up the fact that Oury was a native son. L. C. Hughes, a Tucson Democrat who later became territorial governor, told a rally in his town that Oury "ought to be re-elected in preference to Porter because he came to this country on a mule twenty-five years ago." On the other hand, the Republican candidate had come as a carpetbagger with a federal commission in his pocket. The electors must have agreed, for Oury carried all of the ten counties except Yuma and Apache, garnering a total of 6,121 votes to 5,141 for the Republican candidate, DeForest Porter.[56]

Oury did not run again in 1884, and Curtis C. Bean, a Republican who could boast of an eighteen-year residence in the territory, defeated Colonel C. P. Head, a leading merchant of Prescott. Bean was a well-known pioneer mining man from Yavapai whose public record as a member in the Council of the Tenth Assembly was undistinguished. During the campaign, Bean's opponents reminded the voters of how he had unsuccessfully tried to secure the passage of a bill, which was placed in his hands by the friends of Governor Frémont, to create the office of territorial mineralogist — a plum intended for the Governor with a remuneration of as much as $3,000 per year, in addition to his federal salary.[57] The Republicans countered by describing Head as "an old fogy" and a "second edition of Grant Oury, minus a heart" who "has no use for the poor man, the miner, the prospector or the ranchman, save when he is in need of their votes."[58] Bean was elected,

---

[55]*Arizona Weekly Citizen*, October 22, 1882; *Weekly Arizona Miner*, September 8, 1882.
[56]*Arizona Weekly Citizen*, December 10, 1882.
[57]*Ibid.*, November 1, 1884.
[58]*Ibid.*, October 18, 1884.

Curtis C. Bean, legislator from Yavapai County and Republican delegate to Congress.

— Sharlot Hall Museum

6,747 votes to 5,595, and carried along his running mate for superintendent of public instruction, Robert L. Long.[59]

Bean's career, as a one-term delegate to Congress, was hardly more illustrious than that of his Democratic predecessor. He did succeed, however, in getting a right-of-way through the Pima and Maricopa Indian reservations for a railroad to connect Phoenix with the Southern Pacific at Maricopa. He failed, though, in his effort to prevent the passage of the Harrison Act of 1886 that limited territorial indebtedness and thus curbed any possibility for the legislature to grant subsidies to local railroads. Nevertheless, though the actual accomplishments of Oury and Bean were insignificant, it should be pointed out that their election, as well as that of Stevens before them, symbolized the rise of provincial "native" politicians who were destined to replace federal appointees as the political leaders of the Arizona territory.

It should also be mentioned that the end of "ring" rule had caused economic reverberations that resulted in the demise of several business firms which had fattened on government patronage. Hooper, Whiting, and Company sold out to local men; Levi Bashford, brother of Coles who had died in 1878, moved to San Francisco; Lord and Williams was forced into bankruptcy and Safford's bank (Safford, Hudson, and Co.)

---

[59]*Ibid.*, December 6, 1884.

also failed. Even the formerly prosperous Tully and Ochoa Company closed.[60] The arrival of the Southern Pacific in Tucson in 1880 caught the latter concern with a large stock of high-priced goods and a big volume of uncollected debts.

Ironically, the coming of the railroad combined with the Tombstone silver strike and a cessation of Indian hostilities to bring an influx of new people and leaders into the territory — just as the oldtimers were ready to take over. Some of the new arrivals were opportunists and federal appointees, but others came to stay and vie for political leadership. The old group, headed by Governor John C. Frémont and called "graspers," attempted to establish another coalition, nonpartisan government; the Frémont machine was too busy trying to make "barrels of money," however, to win the support of the electorate.[61]

A newcomer who came to stay and who did well in Arizona politics was a Kentucky-born lawyer named Marcus Aurelius Smith who settled in Tombstone in 1881. Physically a small man, like McCormick, he was to succeed where the latter failed in that he became one of Arizona's first U. S. senators when statehood was achieved in 1912. A died-in-the-wool Democrat, a forceful speaker, and a wonderful campaigner who could appear to be all things to all people — his enemies called him "Marcus Octopus Smith" — he was elected delegate to Congress eight times between 1886 and 1910. Only two other men, Republican

---

[60]Accounts of the business failure of Lord and Williams can be found in the *Phoenix Herald,* October 28 and November 11, 1881. See the *Arizona Daily Star,* May 11, 1884, for a story on the fall of Safford, Hudson, and Company. The bankruptcy of William Zeckendorf was reported in the *Arizona Daily Star,* February 24, 1883, and in the *Arizona Gazette,* March 1, 1883. The collapse of the Tully and Ochoa Company is discussed in Lockwood's *Life in Old Tucson,* p. 249. The following excerpt from the *Arizona Champion* (Flagstaff), August 8, 1885, on Charles H. Lord is especially intriguing: "A few years since, the firm of Lord and Williams, of Tucson, was all powerful, and to a certain degree dictated to civil and military authorities as to the management of Territorial affairs. Finally the house, through extravagance and bad management of the would-be dictators, went to the ground. Dr. C. H. Lord was arrested on charge of perjury, etc., and while under bonds to appear before a judicial tribunal and answer to said charges, escaped into Mexico, and was finally reported dead. It was then that U. S. District Attorney Zabriskie consented to allow the matter to be dismissed from the courts and forgotten. Not so, however, with certain insurance companies, with whom he held policies to the amount of $60,000. They instituted inquiry and found out that the cunning Charles was not among the ghosts, but a living reality. To escape punishment and secure a fortune, the Doctor reported himself dead and buried among the orange and cocoa fringed forests of Mexico. Old friends of the (dead) live Lord will be pleased to know that his spirit is still among those of earth."

[61]*Daily Arizona Citizen,* June 10, 1879; see also, *Weekly Arizona Miner,* June 30, 1882, for a letter written by W. H. Hardy, criticizing the Republican federal officials in Arizona for appointing Democrats as court clerks, etc.

The Election of 1886

The territorial newspapers usually took sides in political campaigns. In these endorsements, the Tucson Weekly Citizen *on October 16 and the* Arizona Daily Star *on October 29 listed the territorial and county elective offices and names of candidates they were supporting. Newspapers in other towns had their slates too. (Right) The official Democratic ballot for Precinct No. 1, Pima County, for the general election. Straight-ticket voting was encouraged with this type of ballot.*

Governor Murphy for one term and Democrat ex-Confederate soldier John F. Wilson for two terms, were elected to that office during that entire period.

Generally speaking, Smith was as symbolic of the last half of the territorial period as McCormick was of the first part. McCormick's image was that of eloquent spokesman for the nonpartisan, federally focalized "ring" that wished to weave Arizona tightly into the national pattern. Smith, on the other hand, was identified with the local movement for home rule and for release from subservience to the federal government. Whereas the "ring" strove to promote social and economic development to the point that Arizona might qualify for statehood, the "local-righters" subsequently contended that the territory had achieved this condition and, accordingly, merited equal standing in the Union of States. The story of Delegate Smith and Arizona's fight for statehood is taken up in later chapters. Meanwhile, our narrative returns to McCormick's successor in the governor's chair, A. P. K. Safford.

Safford's selection as governor came after McCormick had consulted with the Nevada congressional delegation (Senators William Stewart and James W. Nye and Congressman Thomas Fitch) and Senator Aaron A. Sargent of California. The decision to recommend Safford to President Grant for the position came during McCormick's four-month junket in 1867 to discuss Indian affairs with territorial delegates at Salt Lake City and with Generals Halleck and McDowell at San Francisco.[62] McCormick and his Nevada friends were interested in promoting a railroad through Arizona, and trusted Safford, then the surveyor general of Nevada, to assist them in this endeavor.[63]

So that Safford might have the proper advice on territorial matters, McCormick sent him a list of his "ring" friends, subtly called "intelligent pioneers and sound counsellors," with whom the new governor should confer. Among the prominent people mentioned were C. H. Lord, Peter Brady, Stephen Ochoa, J. M. Barney, and Colonel C. P. Stone of Pima County; H. A. Bigelow, Levi Bashford, John Howard, and James Grant of Yavapai County; Thomas J. Bidwell and C. H. Brinley of Yuma County; and C. W. C. Rowell and Alonzo E. Davis of Mohave County.[64] Men such as these made it possible for McCormick to exercise extensive political influence during three territorial adminis-

---

[62]Letter of Governor McCormick to Secretary of State Seward, from Prescott, A. T., June 25, 1867. Record Group 59, Territorial Papers: Arizona.

[63]Letter of Delegate McCormick to Governor Safford, from Washington, D.C., August 4, 1869. Arizona Secretary of State, Territorial Records, Department of Library and Archives, Phoenix, Arizona.

[64]Letter of McCormick to Safford, April 22, 1869, *ibid.*

trations: Goodwin's, his own, and Safford's. It was during Safford's term, however, that the coalition "ring" that was formed in 1865 reached an apex of power through its control over federal patronage during the Indian wars.

— Arizona Pioneers' Historical Society

Official ballot for a Pima County precinct in the election of 1892, and Pima County returns by precinct for the election. Note the third-party candidates on the ballot for the Council and House of the Legislative Assembly. Greaterville was a mining town in the Santa Rita Mountains southeast of Tucson.

Chapter 5

Arizona Goes to School:

The Safford Administration

The third territorial governor, Anson Peacely-Killen Safford, had several distinctions. Besides being known as the "Father of the Arizona Public Schools," he was, at five feet, six inches in height, one of the smallest men to occupy the executive position. He also held the office longest, serving from April 7, 1869, to April 5, 1877. As a farm boy in Vermont and Illinois, he had had little opportunity for formal education. But by the time he arrived in Arizona, at the age of thirty-nine, he was a well-read and much-traveled official.

The experience that prepared him for his work in the pioneer territory began in 1850 when he joined the rush to the California gold fields. Interested in civic affairs, he became involved in public improvements projects and in politics. In 1855, he ran as a Democrat for the Assembly but was defeated by the American, or Know Nothing, Party. The following year, however, he was elected to the first of two terms in the California legislature at Sacramento. In the Ninth Assembly he was chairman of the Committee on Education and worked for a law to provide for the preservation of school lands from waste or injury.[1] Then, in 1862, he migrated to Nevada mining fields and was soon elected recorder of Humboldt County, where, on several occasions, he also acted as an Indian fighter. He also spent two years traveling in Europe in pursuit of culture and health. After returning to Nevada in 1867, he became the United States surveyor-general for that state. Two years later he was appointed to the governorship of Arizona by President Grant.

Conditions in the territory were chaotic at the time Safford became

---

[1]California, Legislature, Assembly, *Journal of the Ninth Session of the Assembly of California*, p. 254; *History of Placer County, California with Illustrations and Biographical Sketches of Its Prominent Men and Pioneers* (Oakland, Calif.: Thompson and West, 1882), p. 111; and *California Blue Book, 1907* (Sacramento, Calif.: State Printing Office, n.d.), p. 615.

Anson P. K. Safford, governor of Arizona Territory, 1869 to 1877.

— Arizona Pioneers' Historical Society

governor. John Wasson, then Surveyor-General of Arizona, described the situation thusly:

> He [Safford] found the territory almost in a state of anarchy. Many officers refused to obey the laws. The payment of taxes was resisted by some. Outlaws were coming from Sonora and robbing and murdering settlers along the border and as far north as the Gila River. The Apache Indians were atrocious in their thefts and murders and the military authorities were nearly useless. The commanding officer and many subordinates were not in sympathy with the people. Such eminent generals as Sherman and Sheridan regarded the territory about worthless and only fit for Indians. There was no public school system in operation and but one public school (at Prescott) in the whole territory.... There was not a railroad on the east nearer than Kansas.[2]

This uninviting situation called for a strong administrator and the "Little Governor," as Safford was affectionately called, proved equal to the task. Upon assuming his office he began familiarizing himself with the condition of affairs in the territory. He then journeyed to Washington, D.C., at his own expense and successfully appealed to Congress for help and for authority to discharge his duties until another legislature could convene.

The Governor's long and informative message to the Sixth Legislative Assembly, which finally convened at Tucson on January 11,

---

[2]Original manuscript in personal files of E. E. Williams, in the Arizona Pioneers' Historical Society; see also, John Wasson, *In Memory of A. P. K. Safford,* a brochure printed at Pomona, Calif., 1891.

1871, indicated that he had been quite actively attending to his job during the interim. He told the legislature that the question of paramount importance still confronting the territory was the hostility of the Apache Indians. After tracing the bloody history of Indian warfare and mentioning the inadequacy of the federal troops, up to that time, to subdue the Apache into submission, he said,

> I am of the opinion that volunteers raised among our own people, inured to the climate, acquainted with the habits of the Indians and the country, and fighting for their homes and firesides, would be found efficient, and in the end more economical than the regular troops. In the month of August last, the Indians made a simultaneous movement along the southern overland road. Two stage drivers were killed, one stage captured, and all on board were murdered; a train was taken and all with it killed, and a stage station twenty-two miles east of Tucson, was taken, and but one of the inmates escaped alive. Several others were killed about that time. The condition of affairs became so alarming that the citizens of Tucson contributed a sum sufficient to place a small company in the field; they were mostly Mexicans by birth and not mounted. I took command of the company, and acted a part of the time in conjunction with Captain E. Miles and his command of the regular army; and also, for a time with Lieutenant Cushing. We were in the field twenty-seven days . . . . I believe that a few companies of this class of our citizens would be found invaluable in subduing the hostile Indians.[3]

Even though Safford's militia returned with nothing to show for six hundred miles of "chasing," he had great faith in the local volunteers. However, it was the regular Army with a new commander, Colonel (later General) George Crook, and with new methods that eventually subdued the hostiles. But even in this Safford played a part since he and Delegate McCormick had worked together in securing the removal of the inactive General George Stoneman in June, 1871.[4]

The seriousness of the Apache depredations in 1869 and 1870 was emphasized by a special committee of the Arizona legislature made up of J. T. Alsap from the Council and T. J. Bidwell and F. H. Goodwin of the House. In a memorial to Congress requesting assistance to fight the implacable savages, the committee included a compilation of over eighty affidavits attesting to the depredations, signed by Army officers and reliable citizens who resided mainly in Pima County, with the view of fairly and forcibly making known the condition of affairs in the

---

[3]*Journals of the Sixth Legislative Assembly,* 1871, pp. 39-56; see also, letter of Secretary Coles Bashford to Comptroller R. W. Taylor, from Tucson, Arizona, August 28, 1870, Record Group 217, Territorial Letters Received, Vol. 10; see also, *Arizona Citizen,* October 8, 1869, for Safford's proclamation asking for cooperation of citizens to ride down Apache troublemakers.

[4]*Arizona Enterprise* (Florence), February 23, 1889.

territory. At the risk of losing immigration and capital from the states, the legislators reported

> that our citizens have been murdered on the highways and in their fields; that hundreds of thousands of dollars worth of property have been taken off and destroyed, and that murders and robberies are almost of daily occurrence. We find that some of the most fertile portions of our territory are being abandoned by the settlers, on account of the repeated and destructive raids of the Apache Indians. We find that the U. S. mails have been frequently captured by the Indians, and the mail carriers killed; stations upon mail routes have been attacked by the Indians and those in charge murdered and the stations destroyed. To sum up the evidence, it is our opinion that during the year 1870 the Apache Indians have been and are *now* in more active hostility than at any time since the territory has been under the American Flag.[5]

Though most of the affidavits contained accounts of Apache treachery, a few of them, quoted below, amply justify the concern of Governor Safford and the people of Arizona:

> Charles A. Shibell, sworn, and says he resides at Tucson, is assistant Assessor of Internal Revenue; that the following depredations of the Apache Indians have come under his observation the past year: In August, 1870, while coming from Camp Goodwin to Tucson, on the Rio Grande mail road, he found the mail coach destroyed and the following persons murdered and mutilated: John Collins, William Burns, and two U. S. soldiers. They were scalped, one partially burned, and another with his eyes gouged out; and he believes this Territory is now in a defenseless condition.[6]

> N. B. Apple, sworn: Is a freighter, and resides in Tucson; that in the years 1869 and 1870 had several animals stolen by the Apache Indians; that on the 18th of December, 1870, his train, while in company with the train of Tully & Ochoa, was attacked by not less than sixty Apache Indians, nine miles east of the Cienega Station; the Indians killed one man, and captured thirty-seven head of work cattle, and also one mule and three saddle horses. The value of the property taken was about $2000. In September, 1869, my wagonmaster and teamsters buried seven men at the Nogales, near the boundary line, that had been killed by Apache Indians . . . . Considers the roads extremely dangerous. Officers of the U. S. Army invariably have large escorts and travel safely.[7]

> William Morgan, sworn: He is a farmer and resides at Sonoita Valley, Pima County, Arizona, and is a member of the present Legis-

---

[5]*Memorial and Affadavits Showing Outrages Perpetrated by the Apache Indians in the Territory of Arizona During the Years 1869 and 1870* (San Francisco: Francis & Valentine, 1871; published by authority of the Legislature of the Territory of Arizona), p. 5.

[6]*Ibid.,* p. 9.

[7]*Ibid.,* p. 17.

lature. The following depredations have been committed in his neighborhood by the Apache Indians, to-wit: In May, 1869, E. G. and G. Pennington (father and son) were killed while plowing in their field, and all of the horses, mules, and other movable property belonging to the farm was taken. In November, 1869, Benjamin Aikin and a Mexican (name unknown) were murdered while harvesting corn, and all their property taken. The same year, Joaquin Tapia and Jos. Catterson were murdered while traveling on the road. Joseph Goldtree, who was traveling with them, escaped with his clothing riddled with a bullet and arrow holes. In the same year Thomas Vonday was murdered while standing in the door of his house and the house was robbed . . . . [8]

Governor Safford himself testified that he did not consider any portion of the territory safe from depredations, stating that the Apache Indians depended principally for their support on theft and robbery and would not accept any terms of peace until they were thoroughly subjugated by military power. The Governor stressed the cruelty of the Apaches and illustrated this point by describing a scene he had observed — the charred remains of a white man who had been burned alive, except for his scalp, which was tied to a pole.[9]

The marauding Indians were not the only group harassing settlers. About two weeks after the Sixth Assembly opened, Safford sent the lawmakers a request for authority to place an armed force of twenty men in the field to pursue Mexican outlaws and to escort freight teams and travelers.[10] "Dangerous and insecure as is nearly every highway in the Territory on account of the Apache Indians," he wrote, "I consider none more so than the Gila road." He said that the road from Gila Bend to Fort Yuma, a distance of 150 miles, was infested with Mexican robbers. To substantiate his plea for help, Safford quoted from letters he had received from such well-known pioneers as Colonel King S. Woolsey and Colonel James M. Barney. The latter, who then lived at Arizona City, summarized the situation thusly: "The Mexican outlaws are overrunning the country and if the present condition of affairs continues, they will soon drive off the Station Keepers, stock, and men, and the road itself will soon become impassable. They have already driven off between Gila City and Stanwix Station about one hundred head of mules."[11]

---

[8]*Ibid.,* p. 7.

[9]*Ibid.,* pp. 29-30; see also, letter of Governor Safford to General W. T. Sherman, from Washington, D. C., March 10, 1870. [Photostat copy in the Arizona Department of Library and Archives.]

[10]Letter of Governor A. P. K. Safford to the House of Representatives of the Territory of Arizona, January 27, 1871, Safford Papers, Arizona Pioneers' Historical Society.

[11]*Ibid.*

Next to the Indian and outlaw trouble, Safford considered the need for free, public schools to be the most important problem in the territory. He thought that, with almost two thousand children between the ages of six and twenty-one, the fact that there was not even one public school in the territory was mortifying and humiliating. He commended the efforts of S. C. Rogers in maintaining a private school at Prescott and the Sisters of St. Joseph for their girls' school in Tucson. But, he made it very plain that the legislature should adopt a system of free schools for the whole people, and that, as soon as it was put in operation it should by law compel the attendance of every child of sound mind and proper age.

Almost all the legislators were opposed to the Governor's plan for a compulsory tax to support one or more schools in each county for a term of six months each year. They argued that the people were too poor and distressed from Indian depredations to go along with such a plan and that previous efforts to establish schools had failed. Safford answered these objections by saying that without education the coming generation would be no more capable of self-government than the Apache. And he contended that the statutes then on the books were too indefinite and non-compulsory to bring results. Applying all his gifts of personal persuasion, the Governor got the legislature to pass a watered-down bill on February 17.

Based upon a California statute, the act of 1871 was the first to provide for a general or territorial tax for the support of schools, and it has served as the basic law for subsequent educational enactments.[12] To begin with, it levied a general territorial tax of ten cents on each hundred dollars of property and directed that this be paid into the territorial treasury "as a special fund for school purposes." The law provided also that the tax was to be levied and collected "at the same time and in the same manner as other territorial revenues," thus placing school taxes on the same level as other taxes. In other words, the schools were recognized as one of the necessary requirements of modern government, to be provided for just as were law enforcement branches or the executive offices. The law of 1871 ordered that the county board of supervisors should levy a county tax not to exceed fifty cents per hundred, to be collected as other taxes, and it provided further for the enforcement of this action if the county authorities failed to act.[13]

---

[12]U. S. Bureau of Education, *History of Public School Education in Arizona,* by Stephen B. Weeks. Bulletin No. 17. (Washington, D. C.: G.P.O., 1918), pp. 20-21.

[13]"An act to establish public schools in the Territory of Arizona," *The Compiled Laws of the Territory of Arizona Including the Howell Code and the Session Laws from 1864 to 1871,* compiled by Coles Bashford (Albany, N. Y.: Weed, Parsons & Co., 1871), pp. 223-30.

In each school district a board of three public-school trustees was to be elected, in whose hands, when organized, was placed the direct management of the schools. The trustees were to take the school census every year, were to provide and furnish schoolhouses, and when territorial and county money was not sufficient to keep schools open "for at least three months in each year" they might levy a district tax sufficient to make up the shortage. By a two-thirds vote also the district might levy a further tax to extend the term beyond three months and to erect schoolhouses. New districts might be established on petition of ten families. A uniform series of textbooks was adopted and the required subjects to be taught listed as spelling, reading, grammar, arithmetic, geography, and physiology.

The school law of 1871 was simple but clear. As the ex-officio superintendent of public instruction, the governor was given definite responsibility in promoting the best interests of the schools. He apportioned the mandatory territorial tax to the counties and recommended how much additional money should be raised by them. He appointed probate judges who served as ex-officio county superintendents of schools and also appointed county boards of examiners who assisted the judges in examining and licensing teachers. Though disappointed that the law did not go farther in providing funds, "the Little Governor" set out on an educational crusade immediately after the legislature adjourned. Notwithstanding the inadequate roads, the scattered population, and the hostile Apaches, he made trips, often alone, to nearly every settlement in Arizona in the course of the next six years and encouraged the people to organize public schools.

The first school under the law of 1871 was opened at Tucson in March, 1872, several months after the Pima County Supervisors had selected William F. Scott, James E. Baker, and Francis H. Goodwin as trustees. This group was better financed than the earlier Tucson school board. Property owners in the school district had paid $739.40 in school taxes and Pima County's share of the territorial school funds under the new law was $695.23 (for the 503 children in the county). Since there was only one public school in the county, the total operating budget was $1,434.63. A well-educated Swiss immigrant named John Spring was chosen as the first teacher. He was a Civil War veteran who had come to Arizona with the Army in 1866. His school was a one-room adobe building on the corner of McCormick and Meyer streets for which the trustees paid sixteen dollars a month. The crude furniture and equipment included some splintery desks and benches, two brooms and a sprinkling pot for the dirt floor, and some ash flogging sticks brought by parents who urged the teacher to use them liberally. One can imagine that, when the enrollment in the one-room school reached its peak of 138, Spring faced a real challenge. This was espe-cially so since most of the students were of Mexican origin who had to first learn English and who ranged in age from six to twenty-one.[14] There was a shortage of textbooks but Spring made good use of a couple dozen Ollendorf's *Grammars* which the Governor had brought in from the East.

Safford took a special interest in one of the pupils, the twelve-year-old Ignacio Bonillas. He missed the boy on one of his frequent visits to the school and offered to furnish him with books and paper if he returned to school.[15] Ignacio fed the Governor's mules, blacked his boots, and swept his office to pay for these items. After the new Congress Street School was built, Ignacio became an assistant teacher in Spanish and mathematics and helped the Governor in his corres-pondence with officials in Mexico. The boy later attended Massachussets Institute of Technology. Then the blacksmith's son became the first ambassador to Washington, D.C., from Mexico, and was a member of President Carranza's cabinet. This was a boy who could not have gone to school except with Safford's help and encouragement. Is it any wonder that John Spring wrote that Safford should be revered by future generations as the "Father of our Public Schools"?

The success of Spring's school brought about the first public school for girls who did not attend St. Joseph's Academy. In 1873, Mrs. Josephine Brawley Hughes, wife of L. C. Hughes, who was the editor of the *Arizona Star* and later governor, opened a school in the old Pioneer Brewery building in Levin Park in Tucson. Though not in good health, Mrs. Hughes kept the institution going until replacements arrived in the persons of Miss Maria Wakefield and Miss Harriet Bolton. These pioneer teachers were enticed from California in 1873 by the persuasive Safford and his good friend, John Wasson — Surveyor Gen-eral of Arizona and editor of the *Citizen* — who later married Miss Bolton. On October 26, the women left Stockton for San Francisco where they boarded a steamer for San Diego. From there, after five days and nights of continuous stage riding, the longest stop being twenty minutes to change horses and to partake of the wretched food provided at the stations, they arrived in Tucson. Wasting no time, they were soon at work and by November 22 were teaching forty-two boys and twenty-one girls in separate rooms of a building rented by the trustees from Sam Hughes, older brother of the newspaperman.[16]

In 1875, the new "way-out-of-town" Congress Street School was

---

[14]*Weekly Arizona Enterprise* (Tucson), November 27, 1892.
[15]*Arizona Citizen,* March 15, 1873.
[16]*Ibid.,* November 22, 1873.

built on what is now the northwest corner of Sixth Avenue and Congress where Dave Bloom's and the S. H. Kress Company were located in the 1960s. Women in the community were especially proud of this new building since they had raised most of the funds through food sales and a benefit dance. On one occasion a cake was sold and resold until it netted $200. The men also cooperated. The lumber used in the front porch, for example, was donated by Army officers stationed at Fort Grant and hauled free of charge more than one hundred miles by teams belonging to Tully and Ochoa. For a brief time the Congress Street School was the best in Arizona.

Prescott was the town that built a better one by 1876. Only three years earlier, Safford had induced Moses H. Sherman to come to Prescott from his native Vermont to teach. The men in Prescott had been interested in education from the first and cooperated in helping Sherman establish the first graded school in Arizona. The overcrowding problem, so common today, was soon evident and the citizens of Prescott voted bonds and constructed a two-story brick building in which several teachers taught with Sherman as principal. It was the best-equipped school in the territory and the pride of the town. From its hallowed walls Sherman went on to become the first full-time territorial superintendent of public instruction in 1879, by appointment of Governor John C. Frémont, and later a prominent businessman in Los Angeles.

Safford's enthusiasm for education was catching fire elsewhere in the state though most of the school buildings were of an impromptu nature. An abandoned saloon, for example, was the school room in Ehrenberg where Mary Elizabeth Post taught for five months in 1872. She later wrote that "sometimes an old prospector who had been used to visiting the saloon would wander in, and when he saw the new use to which his old stomping ground had been put he was more embarrassed than the young teacher and her pupils."[17] A New Yorker by birth, Miss Post had come to Arizona from San Diego at the urging of John Capron, at that time the government contractor for the stage between San Diego and Mesilla, New Mexico. She traveled by stagecoach to Yuma and went upstream to Ehrenberg on a steamer operated by Captain Isaac Polhamus. She found herself the only American woman in town, but with the help of a Spanish Californian she began learning the Spanish language of her pupils as they learned English. Following her tenure in Ehrenberg, Miss Post began almost forty years of teaching in Yuma. There her first schoolhouse was an old adobe courthouse of

[17]Frank C. Lockwood, *Pioneer Days in Arizona* (New York: Macmillan Co., 1932), p. 250; C. Louise Boehringer, "Mary Elizabeth Post — High Priestess of Americanization," *Arizona Historical Review*, Vol. 2, No. 2 (1929), pp. 92-100.

Two early schoolhouses in Arizona Territory. The Congress Street School (above) in Tucson was built in 1875 far from the then center of town on the northwest corner of Sixth Avenue and Congress Street. Requiring almost continuous repairs, and occupying land that was becoming valuable business property, the building and the site it occupied were sold in 1900. The first building actually built as a school in Phoenix (below) was constructed in 1873 on what is now Central Avenue between Monroe and Van Buren streets. By 1883 a larger building was needed and this structure was demolished.

Moses H. Sherman, the first superintendent of public instruction for the Territory of Arizona.

— Arizona Pioneers' Historical Society

three rooms, one of them a jail. Unlike most women teachers who came to Arizona, Miss Post never married but remained "La Maestra" to her appreciative pupils.

A courthouse was also the site of the first class held in Phoenix in the fall of 1871. Mr. J. R. Darroche, the first teacher, was appointed county recorder in 1872, a year before the school building was erected on Center (now Central Avenue) between Monroe and Van Buren streets. Miss Ellen Shaver from Wisconsin was the first teacher to preside over the educational endeavors of Phoenix school children in the new building.[18] She had thirty-five students, twenty-four girls and eleven boys. The Phoenix correspondent of the *Arizona Weekly Miner* described the school:

> The new school house is an adobe, 20x30 in the clear and 16 feet high, with a good shingle roof. There are three windows on each side, one large double door in one end and a fire-place in the other. The floor is of dirt, but the trustees intend to put in a plank floor as soon as they can procure the lumber. The building, so far, has cost about $1,400 and it is computed that it will take $200 more to finish it. Last week Judge Alsap, the county superintendent, purchased a small supply of books for the use of the children, and intends to send into California for a new set in a short time.[19]

---

[18]*Arizona Miner,* November 21, 1873.
[19]*Ibid.,* November 29, 1873.

— Sharlot Hall Museum

Members of the Ninth Legislative Assembly of the Territory of Arizona, 1877.
Top to bottom, left to right (members of the council in roman) — Row 1:
E. G. Peck, J. W. Dorrington, J. A. Parker; Row 2: *M. G. Samaniego, Hugo*
Richards, William S. Head, C. B. Foster; Row 3: *D. A. Bennett,* Levi Ruggles,
John A. Rush, George D. Kendall, *John H. Marion;* Row 4: *James P. Bull,*
Lewis A. Stevens, King S. Woolsey *(President of the Council),* M. H. Calder-
wood *(Speaker of the House),* Andrew L. Moeller, *S. C. Miller;* Row 5: *George*
H. Stevens, F. H. Goodwin, F. G. Hughes, José M. Redondo, *Estevan Ochoa;*
Row 6: *W. S. Ohnesorgen, W. W. Hutchinson, G. Hathaway, George Scott.*

In 1875, Miss Shaver married John Y. T. Smith of Camp McDowell and became the mother of three "little Smiths." She was followed in the adobe school by Mrs. Alabama Fitzpatrick and Miss Carrie G. Hancock, a sister of the man who surveyed the original townsite of Phoenix, Captain William Hancock.

Throughout his administration (1869–1877), Governor Safford labored for good, tax-supported schools. In his last message, to the Ninth Legislative Assembly in January, 1877, he pointed out some of the advances that had been made in education. He said that the rising generation had kept steady pace with the increase in population and wealth. He was pleased that at least 1,450 children out of the 2,955 reported on the census taken in May, 1876, had learned to read and write.[20] This was a marked and gratifying decline in illiteracy from previous years.

The ninth session of the territorial legislature, not only the last under Safford's tutelage but also the last to convene at Tucson, turned out to be a prolific body. It enacted some seventy-nine laws, beginning with an act to move the capital back to Prescott, in addition to three joint resolutions, and three memorials. Among the laws passed were ten divorce measures and a wide variety of legislation, ranging from an act providing for a fifty-dollar fine for anyone who permitted his hogs to run loose in any town in the territory, to an act authorizing Maricopa County to issue $15,000 in bonds for the purpose of building wagon roads from Phoenix — one to Globe City, another to Yuma via Agua Caliente, and two to Prescott, one route via Wickenburg and the second via the Black Canyon. A memorial to Congress asked that the people of Grant County, New Mexico, be given their wish for annexation of their county to Arizona. Another act authorized the Governor to pay a $300 reward to W. W. Standifer and J. W. Evans for having apprehended and arrested M. V. Alexander and Thomas Berry. The latter two men were highwaymen who robbed a stage and the United States mail in Skull Valley (Yavapai) on January 4, 1877.[21]

Governor Safford had expressed concern over outlawry in his message to the ninth legislature. In recommending a severe policy to check crime in the territory he said that highwaymen "are a scourge to civilization, a disgrace to humanity, and should be swept from the face of the earth as remorselessly as the most ferocious wild beast. I would recommend that highway robbery be made a capital offense, punishable

---

[20]"Message of Governor A. P. K. Safford," *Journals of the Ninth Legislative Assembly,* 1877, pp. 30-46.

[21]*Acts, Resolutions and Memorials,* Ninth Legislative Assembly, 1877.

The Territorial Prison at Yuma as it looked about 1890. Some of the cells were cut out of natural rock — notice the ventilators on top. The wire fence on the right separated the women's area from the men's.

with death."[22] The Governor seemed pleased to report that the new penitentiary on a barren bluff overlooking the Colorado near Yuma was as secure a place for the confinement of prisoners as could be found in most of the states. The eighth legislature, in 1875, had favored Yuma over several other cities in deciding to locate the territorial prison there. That body had authorized the sale of $25,000 in bonds to defray the cost of construction, though only $21,265.62 was made available since the bonds were purchased by the highest bidder, a man from San Francisco, at 85 and 1/16 cents on the dollar. Safford reported that two stone cells and an adobe building containing two prison rooms which could hold thirty prisoners had been erected, though only eight men were incarcerated the first year. Convicts assisted in building their own quarters as well as a water reservoir, housing for the superintendent and guards, and a wall that was five feet, six inches at the base. Safford asked for an additional appropriation and estimated the future operation cost at $475 per month, not an exorbitant amount even in those days.

The man who is sometimes called the "father of the territorial prison" was José M. Redondo, a prominent pioneer of irrigation and cattle raising in Yuma County. Redondo was first elected to the Council in 1864, but was informed after reaching the capital at Prescott that

---

[22]"Message of Governor A. P. K. Safford," *Journals of the Ninth Legislative Assembly,* 1877, p. 41.

it was necessary for members to be citizens of the United States. Disappointed because of this oversight, he returned home to complete the process leading to citizenship which he had already begun. As soon as he was a naturalized American, he ran successfully for the lower branch of the Seventh Legislative Assembly which met in 1873. Among other things, he distinguished himself as the only man in the House to vote against the bill granting a divorce to Governor Safford from his wife Jennie. Then, in 1874, he ran for the Council, defeating his friend and a reluctant candidate, Michael Goldwater, by a vote of 187 to 112. David Neahr ran third in the same race with 65 votes.[23]

In the legislature that convened in Tucson the following January, Redondo and Representative R. B. Kelly, also of Yuma County, secured the passage of the prison bill. Except for them, the territorial penitentiary would have been located elsewhere. As a matter of fact, the fifth legislature, on December 7, 1868, had approved a law to establish the institution in the "immediate vicinity of the town of Phoenix in the county of Yavapai."[24] But no funds were set aside for construction at that time, since it was expected that the federal government would defray the cost. Then, in 1875, Phoenix lost an opportunity to become a penal colony when its spokesman, Representative Granville H. Oury, was outmaneuvered. The latter attempted to correct the financial defect in the 1868 law by introducing a measure to authorize the bond issue mentioned above. At that point, the Yuma strategists had the bill amended to read "Yuma" instead of Phoenix. The law, as amended and passed, also provided, much to the disgust of Governor Safford, that the legislature would appoint the board of prison commissioners.[25]

By a joint vote of both houses, Redondo was appointed, along with William H. Hardy of Mohave County and Neahr of Yuma, to serve on the first board and supervise the construction of the prison. Hardy, as noted above, was a well-known businessman and politician whose career in governmental activities spanned most of the territorial period. Neahr, then of Yuma, later surveyed one of the first additions to the city of Phoenix, an area west of the downtown section between

[23]*Arizona Sentinel,* November 7, 1874; Barry Goldwater, "Three Generations of Pants and Politics," a speech before the members and guests at the annual meeting of the Arizona Pioneers' Historical Society, Tucson, November 3, 1962 [typewritten copy in the Goldwater File, APHS]; and *Journals of the First Legislative Assembly,* pp. 99-100.

[24]*Acts, Resolutions and Memorials,* Fifth Legislative Assembly, p. 19.

[25]*Acts, Resolutions and Memorials,* Eighth Legislative Assembly, pp. 116-20; and Mulford Winsor, "José Maria Redondo," manuscript in the Arizona Department of Library and Archives, pp. 31-32.

Members of the Council of the Eighth Legislative Assembly. Top to bottom, left to right, Row 1: *Lewis A. Stevens (Yavapai), King S. Woolsey, president (Maricopa), J. P. Hargrave (Yavapai);* Row 2: *Alonzo E. Davis (Mohave), J. M. Redondo (Yuma), John G. Campbell, later delegate to Congress (Yavapai);* Row 3: *Sidney R. DeLong (Pima), William Zeckendorf (Pima), Peter R. Brady (Pima).*

Seventh and Fifteenth avenues, and is particularly notable for the names he gave his ten children: Freedom, Freeson, Freeman, Freeborn, Freeling, Fannie, Freecome, Fida Mary, Freeland, and Freechild.

The prison was completed and partially occupied by the time Governor Safford reported to the Ninth Legislative Assembly in 1877. It was not as full as it might have been considering that the Territory of Arizona had more than its share of lawbreakers. This criminal element, however, did not deter the rapid development of the country. The territory was prosperous when Safford left office in 1877. That year may be counted as something of a turning point in Arizona's history. The Indians had in the main been pacified, although outbreaks occurred after this date; the Southern Pacific Railroad was coming in from the west; many rich mines were being discovered, and prospectors were swarming into the territory. Since there was relative safety from the Indians, stockmen were bringing in herds of cattle and sheep to graze on fresh pastures, and the export and import trade was growing rapidly. Northern Arizona received the bulk of this new immigration. The change in the balance of power from south to north was signalized by the removal of the capital from Tucson back to Prescott in 1877 and by the scarcity of Mexican-American representation after that date.

Changes in education were also forthcoming. For one thing, the larger schools, like that at Prescott which had hitherto paid all its expenses as it went, now discounted the future by selling bonds to meet the cost of building schoolhouses. The progress in education in Arizona during the period after 1877 was to be more closely connected with the material development of the territory than with the personnel in office, as had been the case during Safford's administration. In the 1880s, more rich mines were discovered and the ore was carried over better roads to the two railroads that traversed the territory from east to west. With the mineral and other resources opened to development, the population more than doubled, and more people meant more school children, more school revenue, and of necessity better schools and a higher state of civilization.

While governor, Safford yearned to share personally in the prosperity of the territory. So after eight years in office, he declined a third term and again turned to mining ventures to seek a fortune. Along with his good friend, John S. Vosburg, a Tucson gunsmith, he became interested in the Tombstone mines that had been discovered by Ed and Al Schieffelin and Dick Gird. Safford was able to enlist eastern capital for development of the rich discoveries and for a time served as president of the Tombstone Gold and Silver Milling and Mining Company.[26]

---

[26]*The Banker's Magazine,* Vol. XIII, 3d Series, No. 11 (May, 1879), p. 908.

Later he disposed of his holdings in the mines for about $140,000 and left Arizona in the early 1880s for Philadelphia and New York City where he interested capitalists in a real estate development in Florida.[27] Along with these eastern friends, he bought a four-million-acre tract of land and founded the city of Tarpon Springs. Safford returned to Arizona in late 1881 and married Miss Soledad Bonillas, sister of Ignacio Bonillas, at Tucson. This was his third marriage in the Old Pueblo. In 1873 the legislature had divorced him from Jennie L. Tracy whom he had married in the "Governor's Mansion." His second wife was the former Miss Margarita Grijalva of Magdalena, Sonora, Mexico, whom he married in December, 1877. She died in New York City in January, 1880, after giving birth to a daughter, Margarita, who later graduated from Smith College and operated a bookshop in Boston.

The *Tombstone Epitaph,* on January 12, 1882, succinctly described Safford's last visit to that city as follows:

> Ex-Governor A. P. K. Safford arrived by yesterday's coach from Benson, and is a guest at Brown's hotel. It is reported that Gov. Safford has closed out all his Arizona interests, and will hereafter devote himself exclusively to the development of the gigantic reclamation and colonization schemes that he is interested in in Florida. As governor of this territory he gave some of the best years of his life, and in his new field of enterprise he will carry with him the good wishes of the entire people of Arizona.[28]

Safford died at Tarpon Springs on December 15, 1891, following a lingering illness. A thousand-pound granite boulder from his native Vermont marks his grave.

Two years before his death, Safford was seriously considered by President Benjamin Harrison for reappointment to the governorship. Though apparently reluctant to become a candidate, he consented "at the earnest solicitation of the people of Arizona who represent the bone and sinew rather than the politicians of the Territory."[29] His candidacy was the impetus for a barrage of letters, both in support and in opposition, into the Appointments Division of the Interior Department. The opponents, headed by M. B. Duffield, were not great in number but were exceptionally derogatory and cast a shadow upon the ex-governor's chances for appointment. In contrast, the hundreds of petitioners in his

---

[27]Letter from A. P. K. Safford to Sam Hughes of Tucson, from Tarpon Springs, Florida, December 31, 1888. Record Group 48, Appointment Papers.

[28]*Tombstone Epitaph,* January 12, 1882.

[29]*Arizona Enterprise* (Florence), February 23, 1889; see also, letter of A. P. K. Safford to Sam Hughes from Tarpon Springs, Florida, December 31, 1888, Record Group 48, Appointment Papers.

*Two of the three wives of Gov-
ernor A. P. K. Safford — Mar-
garita (Grijalva) Safford (above),
his second wife, and Soledad
(Bonillas) Safford (below), his
third wife.*

Henry C. Hooker, prominent Arizona cattleman and founder in 1872 of the famed Sierra Bonita Ranch in the Sulphur Spring Valley.

— Arizona Pioneers' Historical Society

behalf represented a broad cross section of Arizona — leading business-men, ranchers, legislators, miners, and citizens of Mexican origin.

John Wasson, ex-surveyor of Arizona, wrote a eulogic letter to the President recommending the selection of his long-time friend. After reviewing Safford's administration and his outstanding achievements, Wasson candidly suggested that the politically sagacious ex-governor "will do more to bring Arizona into the Union as a Republican State than any other man can do."[30] The mayor of Tucson, the Honorable W. E. Stevens, struck a similar note when he wrote that Arizona Republicans could unite behind Safford to "give confidence and respect to the party and Territory."[31] The mayor of another city, Ignacio Bonillas of Magdalena, Sonora, Mexico, also enthusiastically endorsed his old benefactor. Writing that Governor Safford had financed his

---

[30]Letter of John Wasson to President Benjamin Harrison, from Chino, San Bernardino Co., Calif., February 22, 1889, *ibid.*

[31]Letter to Hon. W. E. Stevens to Senator William Stewart, from Tucson, Arizona, December 28, 1888, *ibid.*

education at the Boston School of Technology, Bonillas credited Safford with establishing a system of education in Arizona. He also made mention of Safford's popularity in Sonora, saying that the Mexican people gratefully remembered him for his success in ameliorating the onerous condition caused by the constant Apache depredations and disorderly element on the border. "We do not forget," Bonillas said, "that it was through his efforts that the Chiricahua Indians were removed to San Carlos from the Chiricahua reservation, whence they constantly invaded our defenseless settlements carrying to them death, destruction and panic."[32]

Whereas Bonillas praised Safford for his cooperation with Mexican authorities, many persons in Arizona admired him even more for his tendency to overlook protocol when action was needed. They commended him for his prompt and effective action on several occasions to alleviate border troubles in spite of possible international repercussions. Henry C. Hooker — a pioneer Arizona cattleman — Sam Hughes, and several others signed a letter of support for the ex-governor's candidacy.[33] They recalled how on one occasion he paid $500 for the kidnaping of a notorious Mexican who had murdered a man in the Picacho area and who was afterwards sentenced to imprisonment for life. When the Sonoran government protested to Washington via Mexico City, Safford was asked to explain why he had violated our treaty with Mexico. He replied that the Sonora government had refused to surrender some of the most notorious criminals and that unless these desperadoes could be punished, honest men and women could not live along the border. Not only did he defend his action that violated the treaty, but he put his job on the line in pledging himself to continue the same policy to protect the decent people on both sides of the international line. Safford's supporters also liked the way in which he unswervingly advocated a strong military plan to remove the Indian danger. His disagreement with the relatively mild policies of Generals Stoneman and Kautz, and with the "peace policy" of Vincent Colyer, the secretary of the Board of Indian Commissioners, had been publicized, both pro and con.[34]

The war of words that Safford and Editor Wasson had waged with

---

[32]Letter of Ignacio Bonillas to Senator William Stewart, from Tucson, Arizona, February 15, 1889, *ibid*.

[33]Letter of Samuel Hughes, F. H. Goodwin, H. C. Hooker, and C. H. Vail to the Editor of the *Enterprise*, from Tucson, February 21, 1889, printed in *Arizona Enterprise* (Florence), February 23, 1889.

[34]U. S. Board of Indian Commissioners, *Peace with the Apaches of New Mexico and Arizona, Report of Vincent Colyer, 1871* (Washington, D. C.: G.P.O., 1872).

General August V. Kautz, Commanding General of Arizona, was bitter and not necessarily to the advantage of the Governor's candidacy in some circles. Wasson's *Citizen* had gone so far as to advocate on April 15, 1876, that there should be indiscriminant "slaying of every Apache man, woman, and child until every fastness should send to high heaven the grateful incense of festering and rotting Chiricahuas."[35] But Kautz did not relish the thought of an all-out Indian war and was also opposed to the civilian idea of concentrating Indians of different ethnic backgrounds on one reservation.

For these reasons, Governor Safford used his influence to have John Clum, the young Indian agent at San Carlos, selected for the job of removing the wild and nomadic Chiricahuas to the latter place. Only after receiving explicit orders did Kautz reluctantly dispatch his 6th Cavalry and Indian Scouts to assist in moving the Indians from the reserve near Fort Bowie that General O. O. Howard had promised to them by treaty in 1872 "so long as the grass shall grow."[36] Displeased with Kautz's tactics, Safford sarcastically stated that without a new commander it would take the entire Army twenty years to pacify the Apaches.

The Governor's public allegations of inefficiency on the part of the military, especially the charges in his message to the Ninth Legislative Assembly, prompted the General to take up the pen in his own defense. Writing to the *New York Times* (April 2, 1877), for example, he said that many of the reports of Indian depredations were unfounded and that the remainder were exaggerated; that the troops had done their duty faithfully; that the Governor's charge that the military had done nothing was not true; that no twenty men, or half that number of citizens, had been killed in the previous six months. Kautz charged that Safford was seeking his removal in behalf of the "Indian Ring" of Tucson.[37] The latter group were contractors who feared that Kautz would reveal how they had been lining their pockets by fleecing the Indians on the reservations — feeding them poorly, thus causing many to run away to make a living by wreaking depredations on the inhabitants of the exposed frontier. The General also intimated that the "Ring" wanted the headquarters moved to Tucson — having lost the capital and

---

[35]*Arizona Citizen*, April 15, 1876.

[36]Andrew Wallace, "General August V. Kautz in Arizona," *Arizoniana*, Vol. 4, No. 2 (1964), pp. 54-65; see also, "Report of Brigadier General O. O. Howard, U. S. A., of his first visit as commissioner to the Apaches of Arizona and New Mexico, with papers accompanying," U. S. House, *Report of the Secretary of Interior*, 42d Cong., 3d Sess., 1872, House Exec. Doc. No. 1, pp. 533-43.

[37]*New York Times*, April 2, 1877.

political control of the territory, the contractors wished to enjoy the military patronage.

In spite of his attempts to justify his policies, however, Kautz was held responsible by the Commanding General of the Army, William T. Sherman, for the murders in southeastern Arizona. In March, 1878, Kautz was replaced by the more popular, though probably less able, General Orlando Bolivar Willcox. But by this time the stars of Kautz's enemies had also fallen; Indian Agent Clum had resigned and Safford had left the governorship. The record of the Kautz-Safford feud had been indelibly written, probably to the glory of neither antagonist.

Chapter 6

Receding Red Man:

The Apache Problem in the 1870s

By the end of the 1870s, the story of the cruel Apache depredations and the bloodthirsty efforts of the whites to either exterminate the Indians or concentrate them on reservations was well known. But at the beginning of that decade, the problem was little appreciated outside the isolated Southwest. With no railroad or telegraph facilities in the territory and only limited political influence in Washington, the Sixth Legislative Assembly felt compelled to dramatize the savage state of war that existed in Arizona. At the risk of discouraging immigration and the investment of Eastern capital to develop the rich natural resources of this region, the pioneer legislators memorialized Congress with a desperate plea for more military protection. Summing up the personal affidavits of Army officers and a large number of reliable citizens, including Governor Safford, the investigating committee of the Assembly wrote that "during the year 1870 the Apache Indians have been and are now in more active hostility than at any time since the Territory has been under the American flag."[1]

Is it any wonder that Safford was disgusted with President Grant's "peace policy"? Mercy for the red man was a popular Eastern cause, but the people of Arizona, particularly in Tucson, were screaming for vengeance. Brevet (temporary) General George Stoneman, an experienced cavalry officer in the Civil War, and later governor of California, had inclinations, like Safford, to take aggressive military action to subdue the hostile Apache. But when he assumed command of the newly created Department of Arizona, which had been a sub-district of the Department of the Pacific before April 15, 1870, he was bound by instructions from Washington to follow a policy of appeasement. He was directed to set up so-called "feeding stations" where Indians who

---

[1]*Memorial and Affidavits Showing Outrages Perpetrated By The Apache Indians in the Territory of Arizona, During the Years 1869 and 1870, p. 5.*

General George Stoneman, commander of the military department of Arizona, 1870-71. With John Marion, he toured the Territory in July, 1870, inspecting conditions. His report, published the following spring, which recommended the abandonment of seven of the fifteen military posts in Arizona and minimized the Indian problem, caused such a storm of protests from the citizenry that he was removed from command and replaced by General George Crook. Stoneman later was elected governor of California.

— Arizona Pioneers' Historical Society

surrendered were issued rations until permanent reservations could be established. After visiting Camp Verde, in the heart of the Apache country, in late July, Stoneman organized a party of twenty-five men at Fort Whipple to inspect the other military posts in Arizona.[2] His report on this trip aroused the wrath of the impatient pioneers when it was finally published in the *Arizona Citizen* on April 15, 1871.

Instead of spilling Apache blood, the general called for the abandonment of seven posts in the territory, including Forts Whipple, Lowell, McDowell, and Crittenden. He explained that each of these posts was expensive to operate and could be dispensed with advantageously by the government without detriment — except to those people in the immediate vicinity who were disposing of their hay and grain to the government at exorbitant prices. The only posts he proposed to keep were three in the hostile Indian country — Forts Verde, Thomas, and Grant; three located on the great mail routes and roads through the territory — Fort Bowie, Camp Hualpai, and Camp Date Creek; and two infantry posts that controlled the Colorado River Indians — Forts Mohave and Yuma.

Stoneman criticized merchants who were fleecing the government

---

[2]J. H. Marion, *Notes of Travel Through the Territory of Arizona,* Donald M. Powell, ed. (Tucson: University of Arizona Press, 1965), p. 13; Stoneman's report, dated October 31, 1870, appeared in the *Arizona Citizen* on April 15, 1871, and in the *Arizona Weekly Miner* on May 6, 1871.

by selling the Army such shoddy goods as blistered, discolored, and warped glass; stationery bearing the "condemnation" mark; water buckets, invoiced as "gutta percha," that were made of paper; and blankets, labeled as "woolen," that were actually manufactured from buffalo hair gathered on the Great Plains. There was no excuse for the mercantile firms that engaged in this type of business practice. However, as we shall see, the reservation system recommended by Stoneman resulted in corruption on a much larger scale on the part of "carpetbag" Indian agents who connived with a "ring" of federal officials and contractors.

In all fairness to the Arizona Army commander, however, it should be stated that many of the economy measures he recommended were justified; and, in the end, the system he promoted led to a solution of the Apache problem. Certainly, it was better for the Indian to be settled on a reservation raising corn than to be on the warpath raising scalps. But pioneers who lived in fear of Indian murders and depredations felt that Stoneman was too soft on the Apaches. They denounced his recommendations because he proposed a diminution of pressure on the wily hostiles. John H. Marion, the editor of the *Arizona Miner* who had accompanied Stoneman on his inspection tour, expressed the feeling of most people when he called the report "astounding and sickening."[3] Several other newspapermen bemoaned the fact that most of the two thousand troops in the Arizona command were being used to build roads and improve military posts and even suggested "a sort of complicity in the Arizona outrages."[4]

Whereas Stoneman was reluctant, almost apologetic, in mentioning the subject of the "irrepressible Indian" to authorities in Washington, Governor Safford talked to Secretary of War Belknap and General Sherman and reported that these officials were not weary of hearing about Indian atrocities in Arizona.[5] Unfortunately, their assistance came too late. The vengeful citizens of Tucson, despairing of any punitive action on the part of the Army, took matters into their own hands. Out of their rage and frustration came one of the most shameful episodes in the annals of Arizona — the Camp Grant Massacre on April 30, 1871.

The events leading up to this terrible blotch on white civilization are worth noting. First, Stoneman was directed by the President through General William T. Sherman, in command of the Army of the United States from 1868 to 1883, to modify his tactics to correspond with the

---

[3] *Arizona Miner,* May 6, 1871.
[4] *Arizona Citizen,* April 22, 1871.
[5] *Ibid.,* April 29, 1871.

Eskiminzin, chief of the Aravaipa Apaches. It was this group which was attacked during the Camp Grant Massacre.

— Arizona Pioneers' Historical Society

federal Indian policy of "moral suasion and kindness, looking to their Christianization."[6] Accordingly, the Arizona officer requested supplies of meat and corn to entice the red man to stay on reservations. The word spread and soon Indians flocked to their military benefactors, especially in the southern part of the territory.

In February, 1871, Lieutenant Royal E. Whitman, a New England Civil War officer who had no clear concept of frontier hatred for the Apaches, was approached at Camp Grant by five old Apache squaws looking for a boy who had been taken captive by the soldiers. The lieutenant received the women courteously and later agreed to a peace talk with their chief, Eskiminzin. Informed by this Indian leader that the Aravaipa Apaches did not wish to settle down on the White Mountain Reservation that Stoneman had established, Whitman permitted them to surrender and to live in their old home in the Aravaipa Canyon near the San Pedro River. Every second day — later every third day — Whitman counted the number of Indians and issued them rations. He also arranged for them to be employed in farming, in gathering hay for the post, and in work for neighboring ranchers.[7]

At the capital and population center, Tucson, news of the

---

[6]*Ibid.,* April 1, 1871.

[7]James R. Hastings, "The Tragedy at Camp Grant in 1871," *Arizona and the West,* Vol. 1, No. 2 (1959), p. 150.

impromptu reservation was at first hailed as a constructive step in solving the Indian question.[8] The attitude changed when, on March 10, 1871, Indians attacked a baggage train going from Camp Grant to a temporary Army station in the Pinal Mountains; one soldier and a Mexican civilian were killed and sixteen mules were driven away. Ten days later, at a ranch near Tubac, L. B. Wooster was murdered and a young woman, Trinidad Aggera, was kidnapped. Citizens were appalled by the latter incident; and newspaper reports of Indians roaming freely up and down the Santa Cruz Valley aroused them even more. The indignation was expressed by the editor of the *Arizona Citizen* who asked, "Will the Department Commander longer permit the murderers to be fed by supplies purchased with the people's money?"[9]

Enraged citizens of Tucson organized a "Committee on Public Safety" under the leadership of a former mayor, William S. Oury. The older brother of Granville Oury, who was also a colorful and powerful figure in territorial politics, William Oury had an interesting background. A native Virginian, he joined Moses Austin in Texas at the age of sixteen and missed being at the Alamo when it fell because Colonel Travis sent him for reinforcements. He fought with Sam Houston at San Jacinto, however, and then had several narrow escapes as a Texas Ranger buddy of the famous "Big Foot" Wallace. In 1849, he made the trek to the California gold fields and, seven years later, decided to settle in Tucson after stopping in that town en route to his home in Texas.[10]

A strongly partisan Southern Democrat and a natural leader, Oury was soon involved in politics. As noted above, he was appointed mayor of Tucson by Governor Goodwin and also was elected sheriff. While holding the latter office he was accused of selling 105 muskets and 18,000 rounds of ammunition, belonging to the Territory of Arizona, in Sonora for $2,000 in gold; the weapons had been placed in his hands for distribution among the inhabitants in the county for their protection against hostile Indians. It was not until 1869 that Territorial Treasurer J. B. Allen succeeded in collecting even a portion of the money received by Oury for the purchase of arms, and even then it required an act of the legislature to compel him to disgorge.[11]

Politically, Oury hated the Republican Safford and fought the

---

[8]*Arizona Citizen,* March 11, 1871.

[9]*Ibid.,* March 25, 1871.

[10]Colonel C. C. Smith [grandson of Oury], "Some Unpublished History of the Southwest," *Arizona Historical Review,* Vol. 4, No. 1 (1931), pp. 7-20.

[11]Lockwood, *Life in Old Tucson,* p. 101.

Governor's school program at every turn. The two politicians shared one common belief, however — that the hostile Indians were the main deterrent to the economic development of the territory. Safford wanted a part in mining bonanzas like those he had seen at Virginia City, Nevada; Oury owned a ranch south of Tucson where Apaches frequently stole stock until he and his cowboys opened fire on a small band that had killed a steer in one of his corrals. Though Safford did not openly propose or condone the Camp Grant Massacre as the best means of removing the Indian menace, the evidence indicates that he approved.[12]

A few days before the terrible mass murder, the aroused citizens of Tucson sent a delegation headed by Oury to General Stoneman asking for more protection; but the latter simply reiterated his instructions from Washington.[13] So, left to their own devices, Oury and his friends proceeded to organize a punitive expedition. Meanwhile, the *Citizen* published a running account of depredations and, on April 15, 1871, the editor forthrightly blamed Whitman's Aravaipa charges for two raids. He said that there could be no "reasonable doubt but Camp Grant-fed Indians made the raid on San Xavier last Monday and because they were followed, punished and deprived of their plunder, they went to Grant, rested on Wednesday, and in stronger force on Thursday attacked the San Pedro settlements."[14] A week later, the *Citizen* charged the government with fattening the Indians, and accused Green, the commandant at Camp Apache, of supplying them with guns and ammunition. Green added fuel to the quarrel with a tactless letter to the editor in which he degraded Arizona as "a rocky, mountainous desert, not fit even for the beasts of the field to live in."[15]

Words gave way to action as Oury and Juan Elías gathered together 148 men — 48 Mexicans, 6 Americans, and 94 Papagos — on April 28, 1871. With a wagonload of grub, guns, and ammunition, furnished by Sam Hughes, the expedition traveled on foot and by night.[16] Reaching their destination at daybreak on Sunday, April 30, the group divided and surrounded the Aravaipa camp. The Papagos attacked the unsuspecting victims in their wickiups with clubs, and the Apaches who

---

[12]Safford's Adjutant General, Sam Hughes, supported the plan and distributed arms and ammunition to Oury's men in the living room of the Hughes residence in Tucson. See Mrs. Samuel Hughes, "Reminiscences . . . ," *Arizona Historical Review,* Vol. 6, No. 2 (1935), p. 72.

[13]*Arizona Citizen,* April 1, 1871.

[14]*Ibid.,* April 15, 1871.

[15]*Ibid.,* April 22, 1871.

[16]Hughes, *Arizona Historical Review,* Vol. 6, No. 2 (1935), pp. 71-73.

Samuel Hughes, adjutant general of Arizona during the Safford administration. A native of Wales, Hughes arrived in Tucson in 1858, where he became a prominent merchant and active civic leader. He served several terms on the board of Tucson School District No. 1 during the 1880s, and at various other times was territorial treasurer, Pima County treasurer, and alderman for the City of Tucson.

— Special Collections, University of Arizona Library

escaped to the nearby bluffs were shot down by the Americans and Mexicans. The assault was so swift and fierce that approximately one hundred dead could be counted within a few minutes.[17] All but eight were women and children since most of the men were away hunting in the hills. The wounded who were unable to get away had their brains beaten out and nearly all the bodies were mutilated; one young infant, for example, was shot twice and one of his legs was nearly hacked off. A number of women were killed while asleep on bundles of hay they had collected to bring in that morning; at least two of the best-looking ones were raped.

After the massacre, Dr. Conant B. Briesly, the post surgeon, was dispatched with twelve men by Lieutenant Whitman to render medical aid and to bring in any wounded that might be found. On arrival at the charred scene, however, the doctor found that the assailants had done their work too thoroughly.[18] Less than thirty of the Apache children, captives of the Papagos, were spared. The "memorable and glorious morning of April 30, 1871," as Oury described it, was over and the men started for home.[19] After a reception, organized by Sam Hughes at the

[17] C. C. Smith, *Arizona Historical Review,* Vol. 4, No. 1 (1931), p. 19.

[18] "Testimony of Dr. Conant B. Briesly, United States Army," September 16, 1871, U. S. Board of Indian Commissioners, *Peace with the Apaches,* pp. 33-34.

[19] C. C. Smith, *Arizona Historical Review,* Vol. 4, No. 1 (1931), p. 20.

Nine Mile Water Hole, the Americans and Mexicans came on into Tucson and the Indians went back over their trail to San Xavier.

Easterners were shocked by the brutal massacre on the Aravaipa. President Grant described the attack as "purely murder" and ordered an investigation. He informed Governor Safford that martial law would be proclaimed in Arizona if the perpetrators of the crime were not brought to trial before the civil authorities.[20] Accordingly, at the December term of court, 104 members of the expedition were indicted and tried before Judge John Titus at Tucson. The hurried proceedings proved to be a farce; after five days of testimony the jury reported a verdict of "not guilty" in the record time of nineteen minutes.[21]

It was almost impossible at that time to convict a person for killing an Apache. In fact, the judge's extraordinary charge to the jury virtually instructed them to exonerate the defendants. In essence he said that justice on the wild frontier was not the same as in the quiet, populous, and strongly policed communities of the East. The jury was directed to consider the attack a justifiable and defensive act, he explained, if the evidence showed that the Indians had been persistently assailing, despoiling, and murdering Papago, Mexican, and American residents of Arizona. If the Government of the United States did not give these residents protection from Apache spoliation and assaults, then the sufferers had "a right to protect themselves and employ a force large enough for that purpose." Judge Titus was convinced that the Oury expedition was legal. The leading newspapers in the territory, while deploring the killing of women and children, also attempted to rationalize and commend the ferocious carnage at Camp Grant.[22]

The massacre made it almost impossible for any federal Indian policy to meet with universal approval. The peaceful persuasion approach was given a setback; but at the same time, the Army was obliged to refrain from pursuing aggressive warfare against the hostiles because of the heated state of Eastern opinion. Yet, nearly all factions — unrepentant Westerners, sympathizers with the cause of the mistreated Indian, residents of Tucson, and territorial officials — spoke out in unison for the dismissal of General "Economy" Stoneman, the symbol of Army ineffectiveness against the Apaches. The Arizona Department commander was the most unpopular man in the territory, with the pos-

---

[20]Reported in the *Arizona Citizen,* June 24, 1871.

[21]*Daily Alta California,* February 3, 1872. A complete transcript of the trial appeared in this newspaper. Some of it is also cited in Thomas E. Farish, *History of Arizona* (Phoenix: Filmer Brothers, 1915), Vol. 8, pp. 161-63.

[22]See, for example, the *Arizona Citizen,* May 6, 1871, and the *Arizona Miner,* June 10, 1871.

sible exception of Lieutenant Whitman, who had written a widely-publicized letter in defense of Camp Grant Indians accused of depredations against white settlers.[23] In a trip to the national capital, Governor Safford, with the help of Delegate McCormick, Senator Stewart of Nevada, and others, secured a replacement for Stoneman — General George Crook.[24]

In his *Autobiography,* Crook later wrote that he had previously refused the command of the Department of Arizona; he informed his superior in San Francisco, General George H. Thomas, that he was tired of Indian work and that the notoriously bad climate of Arizona would be injurious to his health. He said the same thing to Thomas's successor in charge of the Department of the Pacific, General Schofield. Then Governor Safford visited Crook in the city by the Golden Gate en route to Washington; when given the same story, the Governor assured Crook that he would not urge the matter in the capital. On the contrary, however, Safford got the California delegation to see President Grant, and the latter assigned Crook to Arizona over the objections of both Secretary of War Belknap and General Sherman, who felt that a higher-ranking officer should get the appointment.[25] Crook was only a lieutenant-colonel at the time but was known as an aggressive Indian fighter — the type of leader desired by Governor Safford.

Yet, no sooner had Crook arrived in Arizona to begin his duties than he received word from Washington of the impending arrival of Vincent Colyer, the first of two "peace commissioners" sent to Arizona by President Grant. Colyer, a Quaker and President Grant's principal adviser on Indian matters, was sent to the territory because of his sympathy for the Indian. Given complete powers, even above the military, he prejudged the "massacre affair" and telegraphed ahead to have the area around Camp Grant created as a temporary Indian reservation. The *Citizen,* on August 12, 1871, articulated the opposition of many Tucson residents to Colyer's coming visit to Arizona; reporting the news that the commissioner's house in Washington had been struck by lightning, the newspaper said facetiously, "Unfortunately Vincent was not hit."[26]

Diplomatically, Colyer was not the ideal person for the government

---

[23]Letter of Lieutenant Royal E. Whitman to Col. T. G. C. Lee, May 17, 1871, in U. S. House, "Report of the Commissioner of Indian Affairs, 1871," *Report of the Secretary of the Interior,* 42d Cong., 2d Sess., 1871-72, House Exec. Doc. No. 1, Part 5, pp. 485-87.

[24]A. M. Gustafson (ed.), *John Spring's Arizona* (Tucson: University of Arizona Press, 1966), pp. 243-45; see also, *Arizona Citizen,* July 8, 1871.

[25]Martin F. Schmitt (ed.), *General George Crook: His Autobiography* (Norman: University of Oklahoma Press, 1946), p. 160.

[26]*Arizona Citizen,* August 12, 1871.

to send to Arizona in 1871. His belief that the Apaches were innocent victims of oppression and that the whites were wholly to blame for past hostilities may be partially vindicated by history, but was an unwelcome view in Arizona at the time. Furthermore, his anti-slavery feelings — well known because of a famous painting he did of John Brown and because of his work in raising six million dollars through Y.M.C.A.S for the sick and wounded of the Union Army — did not endear him to the people in a territory where a strong Southern sentiment still existed.

In the light of some of the rabid editorials that assailed him, it is just as well that Colyer toured Arizona with a military escort. The *Miner,* for example, strongly criticized the mild Quaker, stating that the people "ought, in justice to our murdered dead, to dump the old devil into the shaft of some mine, and pile rocks upon him until he is dead. A rascal who comes here to thwart the efforts of military and citizens to conquer a peace from our savage foe, deserves to be stoned to death, like the treacherous black-hearted dog that he is." Colyer refused· to take such criticism by the press seriously; he even resented the proclamation of Governor Safford wherein the latter attempted to quiet the public furor by asking the people to extend a fair and tolerant welcome to the new representative of the federal government.[27]

In his report on the Indian situation in Arizona, Colyer wrote that the newspapers of Tucson and Prescott had erred in giving the impression that his policy of kindness to the Indian was unpopular. He said that the "hardy frontiersman, the miner and the poor laboring man" prayed for peace. It was his belief that the newspapers only reflected the opinions of those who prospered from the Indian wars — "the traders, army contractors, barroom and gambling saloon proprietors of the two towns."[28]

While there may be some basis in fact for some of Colyer's statements and certainly no question of his sincerity, it is also true that he came to Arizona with preconceived views and scorned any testimony to the contrary. Journeying through the territory with his Army guard of only fifteen men, he met with several bands of destitute Apaches who assured him of their peaceful intentions and desire to be placed under government tutelage. As reservations for these Indians, Colyer selected Camp Apache for the Coyoteros, Camp Grant for the Aravaipas and the Pinals, Camp McDowell for the Tontos, Camp Verde and Date Creek for the Mohave Apaches, and Beale's Springs for the Hualapais.

Considering his mission accomplished, Colyer went on to California

---

[27]U. S. Board of Indian Commissioners, *Peace with the Apaches,* pp. 50-51.
[28]*Ibid.,* p. 19.

General George Crook, commander of the military department of Arizona on two separate occasions, 1871-75, and 1882-86.

in October, followed by the curses of Arizonans, but satisfied in his own mind that the Apache problem was settled. His sojourn in the territory was perhaps for the betterment of the Indian situation in that it emphasized the need for taking the Apaches off the warpath and confining them on reservations; the harm came in the long suspension of Crook's operations against the hostiles.

The General had stepped aside while Colyer had responsibility for bringing peace to the territory. He realized that the farce of peace and war could not be played successfully on the same stage at the same time — especially since the Indians only considered themselves at peace with the military post that gave them food, clothes, and protection. The *New York Tribune,* departing from the typical Eastern pro-peace policy, sarcastically summarized the military point of view, which most people in Arizona supported, saying that "it stands to reason that Mr. Colyer and his peace agents have no business looking after Apaches while Crook and his fighters are hunting them. Either give up the Indians to General Crook or give up Colyer to the Indians."[29]

After the departure of Colyer from the territory, General Crook resumed preparations for an "all out war against the savages." During the lull he had organized and trained five companies of the Third Cavalry, which were ready for action, under the command of the ablest and most ambitious younger officers in Arizona. The troops ranged in

[29]Quoted in the *Arizona Citizen,* September 30, 1871.

size from twenty-four to about seventy; an auxiliary scouting party consisted of fifty Mexicans and Indians.[30] The force had been toughened by a summer march of some seven hundred miles through much of the enemy country. Traveling by way of Fort Bowie, north to Camp (later Fort) Apache, thence over the Mogollon Rim to Camp Verde, and finally to Fort Whipple (his departmental headquarters) and Prescott, Crook had an opportunity to study the terrain, develop an efficient pack train service, and to create an *esprit de corps*.

At Camp Apache he enlisted a group of Apache scouts to help ferret out incorrigibles. Apaches were divided into different clans that were sometimes at war with each other; and one band often proved to be quite willing to aid the soldiers in fighting other Apaches. Also, Crook was able to sell his scouts on the idea of functioning like police officers to round up renegades to force them to become good citizens. As department commander, Crook was given directions by General Sherman to pursue rigorously the renegades who did not settle peacefully on reservations. Accordingly, he placed an Army officer over each of the reservations created by Colyer, and ordered all Indians to be in the internment areas by February 15, 1872, if they were to avoid serious punishment. Many of the hostiles complied in hope of being fed, clothed, and sheltered. But in the midst of this round-up, President Grant reverted to pacifism and sent Brigadier General Oliver Otis Howard to continue the peace policy begun by Colyer.

Unlike his predecessor, however, Howard wanted evidence from both sides on the Indian question. Whereas Colyer listened avidly only to stories of incidents that would strengthen his position — such as the Camp Grant affair, Woolsey's Massacre at Bloody Tanks in 1864, the unjust imprisonment of Cochise by Lieutenant George Bascom in 1861, and the killing of Mangas Coloradas by the Walker party in 1863 — the new commissioner also considered accounts of Apache outrages on the whites. In several communications to General Crook after his arrival, he explained the President's desire to settle all troubles peaceably; but he also instructed Crook to deal vigorously with all incorrigible hostiles who refused to submit to civilization on the reservations.[31]

A Civil War hero who had lost his right arm in the Battle of Fair Oaks, Howard headed the Freedmen's Bureau in the South during

---

[30]*Arizona Citizen,* June 24, July 8, 1871.

[31]Letters of Brig. Gen. O. O. Howard to Gen. George Crook, from Prescott, A. T., May 9, 1872 and May 11, 1872, U. S. Bureau of Indian Affairs, *Annual Report of the Commissioner of Indian Affairs to the Secretary of the Interior for the Year 1872,* pp. 168, 171; see also, U. S. House, *Report of the Secretary of the Interior,* 42d Cong., 3d Sess., 1872-73, House Exec. Doc. No. 1, Vol. 1, p. 214.

Reconstruction and became widely known in humanitarian circles as the "Christian General." Arriving in Yuma in March, 1872, he was guided to central Arizona by C. H. Cook, a successful missionary to the Pimas. At Fort McDowell he conferred with Crook and then went on to Camp Grant. There he found a thousand Indians, under the care of Major E. W. Crittenden, ready to flee because their children who were taken at the time of the Camp Grant Massacre had not been returned; the Indians also asked for a new reservation in a more healthy and desirable locality with Lieutenant Whitman in charge. Unable to meet their demands at that time, Howard promised them a conference of Indians, white citizens, and military officials at the post on May 21.[32]

True to his word, Howard went on to the territorial capital at Tucson for a visit with Governor Safford and to arrange for the return of the captive children. Then on the appointed day, Howard opened a council at Camp Grant to consider the Indian demands. Present were General Crook; the Superintendent of Indian Affairs, Dr. Herman C. Bendell; Governor Safford with a large delegation of citizens, both Mexican and American; and representatives of the Pimas, Maricopas, Papagos, and Apaches.[33] Nine days were spent in considering the grievances. Disagreement arose on the fate of the captives. Safford sided with the Mexicans of Tucson who wanted to keep the six children which they had adopted. Howard decided, however, to leave the children at the agency, at least until the President could make a final decision — which was to return the children to their tribal relatives.[34]

Howard also complied with the Indian request for a new reservation. A peace treaty provided for the abolition of the Camp Grant reservations and the establishment of the San Carlos Agency as a division, south of the Gila River, of the White Mountain Reservation. On the other hand, the request for Whitman's restoration was denied on the grounds that too much partisan feeling existed against him and that the new agent, E. C. Jacobs, was gaining the confidence of the Indians.[35]

---

[32]Letter of Brig. Gen. O. O. Howard to Secretary of the Interior Columbus Delano, from Pima Villages, May 3, 1872, p. 168, and April 23, 1872, p. 173; and report of Ed. C. Jacobs, U. S. Special Indian Agent, to Howard, from Camp Grant Reservation, May 20, 1872, pp. 173-74, all in *Annual Report of the Commissioner of Indian Affairs to the Secretary of the Interior . . . 1872.*

[33]*Arizona Citizen,* May 25, 1872.

[34]*Ibid.,* September 7, 1872; and O. O. Howard, *My Life and Experiences Among Our Hostile Indians* (Hartford, Conn.: N. D. Worthington & Co., 1907), p. 162.

[35]Ralph H. Ogle, *Federal Control of the Western Apaches, 1848–1886* (Albuquerque: University of New Mexico Press, 1940), p. 106 [hereafter *Federal Control*]; and "Report of Brigadier General O. O. Howard, U.S.A., of his first visit as commissioner to the Apaches of Arizona and New Mexico . . . ," June, 1872, in *Annual Report of the Commissioner of Indian Affairs to the Secretary of the Interior . . . 1872,* pp. 148-78.

While at Camp Grant, General Howard persuaded seven Indians with high tribal standing in bands of the Pima, Papago, and Apache to accompany him to Washington, D. C., to see the "Great White Father." His purpose was to show the chiefs the futility of resisting the government and to impress them with the Eastern civilization in hopes that they would return to Arizona as ardent missionaries for the white man's way of life.[36] After three weeks of talks in the nation's capital during the summer of 1872, the delegation returned home, each chieftain the possessor of a new, blue suit of clothes, a bronze medal, and a Bible. Administrative officials who met with the Arizona group were sympathetic to a continuation of Howard's policy of getting the Indians on reservations, but felt that a treaty with Cochise, chief of the hostile Chiricahuas, was needed to assure the peace.

Back in Arizona with the Indian leaders, Howard continued his visits to the reservations and succeeded in arranging a meeting with Cochise — the most dramatic event of his experience in the territory. It was Captain Thomas J. Jeffords, known as "Red Beard" to the Apaches, who led him to the Chiricahua chief. Known best today, perhaps, as the hero in Elliott Arnold's famous novel, *Blood Brother,* Jeffords came to Arizona in 1862 after an early career as a steamboat captain on the Mississippi. He gained the admiration of Cochise when, as superintendent of the Overland Mail Company division between Tucson and Fort Bowie, he came alone into the Dragoon Mountains stronghold to seek protection for his stagecoaches. The friendship which began on that visit was sealed by an Apache blood rite and endured until Cochise's death in 1874.

Jeffords is probably the only white man who could have convinced his "blood brother" to meet with General Howard. Accompanied only by his aide-de-camp, Captain J. A. Sladen, Howard was led by Jeffords and two Apache guides across the Chiricahua Mountains and the San Simon desert into the Dragoon Mountains for a parley with the aging war leader. During the course of the next eleven days in October, 1872, Cochise recited grievances, which dated back to the Bascom affair in Apache Pass in 1861, and agreed to a treaty. In return for a reservation in the Sulphur Spring Valley for his Chiricahua Apaches, with Jeffords as the agent, Cochise promised permanent peace. "Hereafter," he was quoted as saying in his native tongue, "the white man and the Indian are to drink of the same water and eat of the same bread."[37]

---

[36]"Report of a council held by the chiefs and head-men of the Pima and Maricopa Indians at the U. S. Indian agency, Gila River Reservation, A. T., on 11th of May, 1872," *Annual Report . . . Commissioner of Indian Affairs . . . 1872,* pp. 167-68.

[37]*Ibid.,* pp. 175-76, 222.

Unperturbed by criticism in the territorial capital where people were convinced that Cochise deserved punishment, Howard proceeded to visit other reservations and made further plans to carry out Grant's "peace policy." He was disappointed to learn of conditions at Fort Grant: a high rate of sickness prevailed, guards had fired upon Indians causing some to leave the reservation, and certain employees had been drinking heavily in the presence of Indians. To rectify the situation, Howard replaced the unpopular agent, E. C. Jacobs, with George H. Stevens, a friend of both the Indians and white settlers. In addition, he ordered that all Indians be transferred from the pestilence-ridden Camp Grant area to San Carlos by January 1, 1873.

In order to reduce the large proportion of land set aside for the Indians, Howard also set the same date for the abolition of Colyer's temporary reservations, or "feeding posts," at McDowell, Date Creek, and Beale's Springs. At the same time, the San Carlos division of the White Mountain Reservation was reduced to an area within fifteen miles of the south bank of the Gila. So, when Howard departed for Washington to submit his comprehensive report, dated November 7, 1872, only two reservations remained, besides the Chiricahua reserve, upon which to concentrate all the different Apache tribes: the White Mountain with its San Carlos subdivision, and Camp Verde.[38]

Unfortunately, the Indian question was still unsolved. In his message to the Seventh Territorial Legislature on January 17, 1873, Governor Safford said: "The hostility of the Indians strikes at the life of our people, retards immigration, prevents development of our resources, and impoverishes the masses." He explained that the destruction of life and property had not decreased in the previous year and that, in the small valley of Sonoita, seventeen out of a population of thirty had been murdered by Apaches. The Governor reviewed the federal government's efforts to induce the Apaches to live on reservations. "General Howard," he said,

> offered the olive branch of peace to every hostile Indian in the Territory, and the government is feeding, and clothing all who accepted it; and now General Crook is following, and with the sword, compelling those who have not accepted terms of peace to do so. The great obstacle to the subjugation of the Apaches, has been the lack of any definite and fixed policy; but now one appears to have been settled upon . . . . [39]

---

[38]Letter of Howard to Dr. Herman C. Bendell, Superintendent of Indian Affairs for Arizona, from Sacaton, A. T., October 16, 1872, *ibid.,* p. 168.

[39]"Message of Governor A. P. K. Safford," *Journals of the Seventh Legislative Assembly,* pp. 35-36.

Safford's confidence in General Crook's ability to bring about a lasting peace seemed to be justified. In the previous months he had struck the enemy some hard blows, apparently trying to make up for lost time.

Convincing the turbulent Apaches that murder and plunder made for an unprofitable livelihood, thoroughly occupied General Crook. While the "peace policy" was still in effect, he especially sought to punish the Indians responsible for the Wickenburg Massacre, an incident that had helped to convince people in the East that there might be bad Apaches in Arizona as well as bad whites. The incident occurred on November 4, 1871, when a stagecoach bound for California, with seven men and a woman aboard, was attacked on the Ehrenberg road, nine miles west of Wickenburg. Six of the men, including a well-known scientist and *New York Tribune* correspondent named Fred W. Loring, were killed. The two wounded survivors, William Kruger and a Miss Mollie Sheppard, probably were able to escape because the attackers began an orgy on the "firewater" they found in the lucrative loot.

In spite of the testimony given by the survivors, however, Vincent Colyer, who had departed for California the month before, tried to fix the responsibility for the outrage upon "Mexican bandits"; his story was circumstantially corroborated by the fact that the horses, harnesses, clothing, and ammunition — things that greatly aroused Indian acquisitiveness — were not bothered by the plunderers.[40] Nevertheless, the traditionally pernicious Apache-Yumas and Apache-Mohaves along Date Creek, north of the mining camp of Congress, were blamed. And Crook's pursuit of suspects among the Date Creek reservation Indians led him into a treacherous "peace talk" at which he nearly lost his life. Adroit though the Indians were in plotting, they could not, however, cope with the "Old Grey Fox," as the general was called. At a signal — the lighting of a cigarette — the Apaches, sitting in a semicircle, were to remove concealed guns to kill Crook and any whites nearby. The plan would have succeeded except for a tip from the Hualapais. Instead of Indian fireworks, the smoke signal brought some casually stationed, veteran mule packers into action. So hot was the ensuing fight, the Indians fled for the surrounding hills.[41]

Crook continued to bring pressure on the Apache renegades but waited until the middle of November, 1872, to commit all his troops in an intensive campaign. He wanted to encircle the Apache bands, who

[40]Joseph Miller, *The Arizona Story* (New York: Hastings House, 1952), pp. 41-44.

[41]John G. Bourke, *On the Border with Crook* (Chicago: Rio Grande Press, reprint, 1962), pp. 167-68.

had been finding safe refuge in the Tonto Basin in central Arizona, at a time of year when they could not escape to mountain fastnesses. With detachments of soldiers converging upon the area from seven different Army posts, Crook was able to pursue the escapees relentlessly — raiding their rancherías, destroying their reserves of corn, mescal, and jerked meat, and forcing them to starve or surrender.

The first major encounter in the campaign was the "Battle of the Caves" near the end of December, 1872. On this occasion, an advance party of troops located a band of Apaches, just before daylight, singing and dancing around fires on a cliff ledge on the southern slope of the Mazatzals near the Salt River. The soldiers fired, killing six, but the rest of the Apaches fled into the shallow cave which was protected by a parapet of boulders. Asked to surrender, the warriors defiantly refused and fought back with their firearms, arrows, and lances. After awhile, the troopers discovered that rifle bullets shot against the slanting roof of the cave would splinter and ricochet among the Indians. Cries from within the cave soon made it apparent, however, that the pellets were killing women and children as well as men. But the second demand for surrender was answered with the strains of a weird chant and shouts of derisive hatred. So the battle continued.

Sometime after daylight a detachment of cavalry reached the crest of the cliff above the cave and began dropping huge rocks which shattered into thousands of pieces and wrought fearful havoc. The resistance ended, the soldiers charged the stronghold at noon, only to behold a sickening sight! About thirty Indians, some of whom had shielded themselves behind piles of dead bodies, survived the carnage. And about half of these were dying. Only eighteen women and children lived long enough to leave the Salt River canyon as captives. In all, some seventy-five met death.[42]

The spectacular affair at Skull Cave, as it is now called, was followed by a successful January campaign in the Superstition Mountains and a March engagement on Turret Peak. The latter occurred following the movement of a large band of Apaches from the Wickenburg area where they had been harrying settlers. The troops were pursuing them relentlessly, partly because of the murder of three people near Wickenburg. One of these, an eighteen-year-old British immigrant named George Taylor, had been atrociously tortured before being used for bow-and-arrow target practice; he had been rolled in cactus, his ears and eyelids cut away, and his body stuck full of splinters that were set on fire. After committing this cruel deed, the savages escaped with stolen horses

---

[42]*Ibid.*, pp. 190-201.

and cattle and finally took refuge on the top of Turret Peak, a circular, columnar-shaped mountain west of the Verde River in Yavapai County, where they fancied that no enemy would dare follow.

The soldiers, however, who were under the command of Major George Randall, crawled up the mountain at night on their stomachs. The angle of the incline was about 45 degrees. That, together with the loose rocks, made the ascent very difficult, for great care had to be taken so as not to make any noise. As the sun rose, the men charged the Apaches, some of whom were so panic-stricken that they jumped down a steep precipice and were dashed to death.[43]

The Turret Peak action and the battle at Skull Cave were the two affairs that broke the resistance of the Tonto Apaches. In both instances, the raiders were caught by surprise just after attacks upon white settlements; they suffered great losses in strongholds which had been considered impregnable.

By the beginning of April, 1873, most of the Apaches began assembling near Camp Verde, begging for amnesty.[44] In return for protection and food, the Indians agreed to remain upon reservations and accept the rule of the civilian agents, who had replaced the military supervisors in December, 1872, when the Department of the Interior assumed the duty of management of the Apache reservations. For the first time in three centuries, the trails of Arizona were free from Apache killers. The peace lasted through the tenure of General Crook, that is, until March, 1875, when he was transferred to the Department of the Platte to fight the Sioux.

Governor Safford expressed the appreciation of Arizona residents in his biennial message to the ninth legislature on January 6, 1875. "General Crook," he said, "in the subjugation of the Apaches, has sustained his former well earned military reputation, and deserves the lasting gratitude of our people."[45] Crook was given a farewell demonstration at Hatz's Hall in Prescott; around his picture, on the wall behind the platform, was a festoon of flags and these words in evergreen: "Brave, Generous, and True."[46] Among the people honoring the departing general was his successor and West Point classmate, General August V. Kautz. The latter became involved in serious controversies with Governor Safford, as mentioned earlier; in 1878 he was replaced by General O. B. Willcox.

The impression should not be left that General Crook was con-

---

[43]Schmitt, pp. 177-78.
[44]*Arizona Miner,* April 12, 1873; and Ogle, *Federal Control,* p. 116.
[45]*Arizona Miner,* January 8, 1875.
[46]*Ibid.,* March 26, April 9, 1875.

cerned only with the conquest of the red man. A philanthropist too, he believed that the Indians should be treated as human beings and as individuals rather than as nameless members of a tribe. The General was the target of the contractors' rancor because he promised to buy directly from the Apaches any crops of hay or corn that they could raise on the reservation; under the Crook system, the Indians would be self-supporting and receive the full reward for honest toil, rather than be wards of the government and victims of the avaricious white traders. Crook also tried to establish the customs of white civilization. Along this line, cleanliness was encouraged in the villages of the reservations and the mutilation of squaws was forbidden; a prominent Hualapai leader was sentenced to imprisonment because he insisted on cutting off the nose of one of his wives — the penalty among some tribes for adultery by the woman.

But not all of Crook's attention was given to the improvement of the Indians. He broke up military camps which had been hotbeds of fever and pestilence and constructed first-class wagon roads to connect all the Arizona posts. He brought in the first long telegraph line, which ran from San Diego to Fort Yuma and thence to Maricopa Wells — one branch extending to Prescott and Fort Whipple, the other going via Tucson to a crossing on the Gila near San Carlos.[47] During his campaigns, Crook directed his scouting parties to map the trails; as a result, many parts of the territory heretofore unknown were now mapped. Other plans, including a scheme to beautify the military posts with vines and trees, were never carried out because of Crook's transfer to another field.

Unfortunately, General Crook's successful campaigns to establish peace in Arizona had been followed by a period of chaos on the San Carlos Reservation. For nearly two years, authority alternated between the incompetent civilian agents sent out by the Department of the Interior and military agents who were forced to accept responsibility for running the reserve. Not until John P. Clum, who was appointed agent on the recommendation of the Dutch Reformed Church, arrived in August, 1874, was a strictly civilian "peace policy" established. Clum believed that the government's war of extermination had failed and was determined that the Apaches would get a square deal from that time on.[48]

To rid the reservation of the necessity for military interference, the new agent, then only twenty-three years old, organized a native court and a small body of Indian police to replace supervision by soldiers.

[47]*Arizona Citizen*, April 12, September 13, December 6, 1873.
[48]*Ibid.*, July 18, 1874.

Agent John P. Clum with Indians on the San Carlos Reservation in 1875. After resigning as agent in 1877, Clum went to Tucson and then to Tombstone, where he served as mayor and established the town's newspaper, the Tombstone Epitaph.

Rounding out his plan for self-government, Clum invited each band of Apaches to elect a representative to meet with him as a council. At first there were only approximately eight hundred Indians on the reservation to be governed; but, in 1875, the Bureau of Indian Affairs inaugurated a new policy of "transfer" whereby the San Carlos population soon swelled to 4,200 Apaches of mixed tribes — Coyoteros from Camp Apache and the Tontos and Yavapais from Camp Verde. The Camp Grant Indians had already been transferred, leaving only the Chiricahuas on their own land.

General Crook, who was still in Arizona when the Camp Verde reservation was abandoned, opposed the new policy as unsound.[49] At Verde, the Indians had cleared and irrigated land upon which they were beginning to produce their own food supply. There was hope that they might soon be self-sustaining; but it was not to be. The influence of the "Tucson Ring" of corrupt federal officials and contractors prevailed and the 1,400 disillusioned Apaches at Verde were moved.

The selfish reasoning of the "Tucson Ring" was that contractors couldn't make enormous amounts of money selling supplies to the agencies if the Indians supported themselves. The "Ring" had little concern for the local merchants in the Verde area who sold grain and flour to the agency, even though Delegate McCormick, in behalf of the suppliers, joined Crook for awhile in opposing the abandonment of the Verde reservation. John Bourke, author of *On the Border with Crook,* also sympathized with the Crook point of view and wrote accordingly: "It was an outrageous proceeding," he said, "one for which I should still blush had I not long since gotten over blushing for anything that the United States Government did in Indian matters."[50]

During most of the 1870s, the government had followed a policy of placing the maximum number of Indians on a minimum amount of land. This policy of "concentration" proved to be undesirable at San Carlos because the mingling of diverse groups, both nomadic and sedentary types, within the same confines, led to disorder and unrest — especially after the turbulent Chiricahuas were ordered to San Carlos in March, 1876, from their coveted rangelands and possibly rich mineral lands. The order for removal was not surprising, considering the fact that the Chiricahuas had gone on the plunder trail again.

Jeffords, who was still the Indian agent, was compelled by a shortage of government rations to permit the Indians to hunt for their

---

[49]U. S. Bureau of Indian Affairs, *Annual Report of the Commissioner of Indian Affairs for 1875,* p. 215.

[50]Bourke, p. 217.

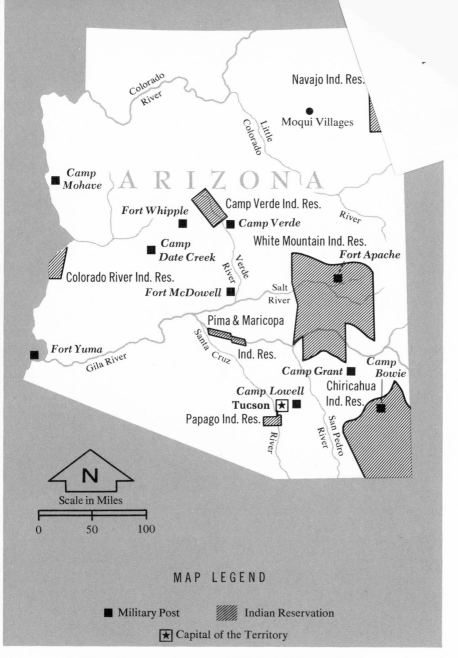

Colorado River

Navajo Ind. Res.

Little Colorado

● Moqui Villages

A R I Z O N A

■ Camp Mohave

Fort Whipple

Camp Verde Ind. Res.

■ Camp Verde

River

White Mountain Ind. Res.

Camp Date Creek

Fort Apache

■

Colorado River Ind. Res.

Verde River

Fort McDowell ■

Salt River

Pima & Maricopa

Santa Cruz

Ind. Res.

Fort Yuma

Gila River

■

Camp Grant ■

Camp Bowie

Camp Lowell

Chiricahua Ind. Res.

Tucson ★ ■

Papago Ind. Res.

San Pedro River

River

N

Scale in Miles

0   50   100

MAP LEGEND

■ Military Post   Indian Reservation

★ Capital of the Territory

Indian Reservations and Main Military Posts
in Arizona, 1874

The Commissioner of Indian Affairs reported the population on the reservations in 1874 as follows: Navajo (also in New Mexico), 9,068; White Mountain, 2,814; Chiricahua, 930; Papago, 6,000; Pima and Maricopa, 4,300; Camp Verde, 1,544; and Colorado River, 1,450. Tucson was the territorial capital from 1867 to 1877.

own provender in the Dragoon Mountains. Unfortunately, one band made a raid into Sonora and returned with precious metals, part of which was invested with an unprincipled trader at Sulphur Spring for whiskey. A leader of these renegades was Pionsenay, who became inebriated and killed his two sisters. A few days later, he did penance by killing the trader and led the restless bucks on a series of devastating forays in the San Pedro Valley. When Jeffords and cavalry from Fort Bowie were unable to capture the marauders, Governor Safford intervened; he requested that the federal authorities dismiss Jeffords, close the reservation, and remove the Chiricahuas (most of whom were innocent of any misdeeds) to San Carlos. In a telegram to John Wasson, editor of the *Arizona Citizen* who was lobbying in Washington, D. C., he said that no one but Clum had "the nerve, ability, and confidence" to perform the mission.[51]

Evidently alarmed over the possibility of a bloody uprising, Congress quickly provided funds. The fearless young agent, Clum, promptly volunteered his Indian police, marched them to Tucson where they entertained the terrified townsmen with a realistic war dance, and departed for parleys with the Chiricahuas on the reservation. As Clum approached, the Indians held a council to decide the question of war or peace. The peaceable advice of Tahzay and his brother Nachee (sons of Cochise who were true to their father's vow to keep the peace) prevailed. The old war chiefs, including Skinyea, were killed. Presenting no resistance to Clum, 325 Chiricahuas started on the six-day journey to San Carlos on June 12; they were resigned to their fate, though unhappy for being moved in punishment, so they thought, for the misconduct of a small portion of their number.

When the people of Cochise departed for their new reservation, a closely related band of Chiricahuas led by Geronimo, Juh, and Nolgee, fled into the Sierra Madre Mountains of Mexico. Some of the braves joined the Southern Apaches who usually lived either in Mexico or the southern part of New Mexico. By the end of 1876, the plundering of these errant warriors was notorious. Using the Hot Springs Reservation in New Mexico as a rendezvous for rest and government rations, the renegades stole horses and cattle on both sides 'of the border. On March 20, 1877, Clum received orders from Commissioner of Indian Affairs John Q. Smith to arrest the renegades and bring them to San Carlos.[52]

---

[51]Ogle, *Federal Control,* p. 166.

[52]Woodworth Clum, *Apache Agent: The Story of John P. Clum* (Boston: Houghton Mifflin, 1936), pp. 204-205; and John P. Clum, *The Truth About Apaches* (Los Angeles: n.p., 1931), pp. 38-39.

After notifying General Kautz, whom he intensely disliked, Clum journeyed to the Hot Springs agency with about forty Apache police. En route he was joined by Captain Clay Beauford whose Apache scouts increased the total force to about one hundred men. On April 21, Beauford arrested fourteen Apaches who were considered dangerous. Among the captives were Geronimo, Gordo, and two Indians who had stolen seven horses on the San Pedro two weeks earlier. Then, Victorio, the successor to Mangas Coloradas as leader of the Warm Springs Apaches, surrendered and agreed to go to San Carlos.

Between his 343 followers and Geronimo's 110, Clum had over 450 Apaches to march to his Arizona reserve. Discourteously refusing the assistance offered by General Kautz, via telegram, Clum returned to San Carlos with his Apaches to continue his feud with the Army. On June 9, he sent the following message to Commissioner Smith: "If your department will increase my salary sufficiently and equip two more companies of Indian police for me, I will volunteer to take care of all Apaches — and the troops can be removed."[53]

Fearing the loss of a protective military force, the Arizona press reacted unfavorably to Clum's proposal. The *Arizona Miner* said that "the brass and impudence of this young bombast is perfectly ridiculous."[54] A leading Tucson merchant, formerly a good friend of the San Carlos agent, probably inadvertently expressed the viewpoint of the "Federal Ring" when he asked, "What are you trying to do, ruin my business? If you take the military contracts away from us, there would be nothing left worth staying for. Most of our profit comes from feeding soldiers and army mules."[55]

Peremptorily turned down by the Indian Office on his radical proposal, the stubborn Clum resigned and rode away from San Carlos and the bewildered Apaches on July 1. Not one to relinquish the public stage, however, he proceeded to widen the breach between civilian and military authorities; he furnished his friend, Editor John Wasson of the *Arizona Citizen* in Tucson, with personal correspondence from his files and an open letter of his own in which he condemned Generals Kautz, McDowell, Sherman, and others who had charged him with inefficiency in the administration of the San Carlos reservation.[56] This kind of unreasonable action served only to distract from Clum's successful and

[53]John P. Clum to Commissioner of Indian Affairs John Q. Smith, June 6, 1877, quoted in Woodworth Clum, *Apache Agent*, p. 253.

[54]*Arizona Miner,* June 15, 1877.

[55]Woodworth Clum, *Apache Agent*, p. 254.

[56]*Arizona Weekly Citizen,* August 18, 1877.

highly dramatic tenure as agent and to focus attention on the disruptive factors already prevalent at San Carlos.

Indian morale was low because of the constant bickering of the authorities, the lack of supplies furnished them, the jealousies existing among the diverse tribes, and intrusions of the whites on reservation lands. The Warm Springs Apaches were especially dissatisfied and 310 men, women, and children broke out on September 1, 1877. Then, in 1878, Geronimo, who had been released from the guardhouse by the new agent, H. L. Hart, slipped away with some Chiricahuas to pillage and murder for the next year and a half.

Not the least cause for the Indian hostilities was the graft by government officials and the greed of contractors and mine speculators who coveted Indian mineral lands. In the words of an expert observer, General Crook, who was restored to the command of the Department of Arizona when the Apaches were in a dangerous state of discontent and unrest in 1882, "Greed and avarice on the part of the whites – in other words, the almighty dollar – is at the bottom of nine-tenths of all our Indian troubles."[57]

Crook's incriminating conclusions were well illustrated in the case of a goodly number of covetous miners who invaded reservations to develop mineral lands belonging to the Indians. These mine entrepreneurs were usually successful in securing a reduction of the reservations through political channels. Governor Safford, always a spokesman for the mining interests, felt that mine development was essential to the growth of Arizona. He joined forces with Delegate McCormick and Surveyor-General Wasson, who was also the editor of the *Citizen* in Tucson, to have certain areas returned to the public domain.[58]

As early as 1872, Charles Lesinsky and E. M. Pearce brought in over one hundred men and some $75,000 worth of equipment to begin taking copper ore from the eastern portion of the White Mountain Reservation in the vicinity of modern-day Clifton. A petition from Lesinsky, dated December 10, 1873, to have the mine separated from the reservation, started political manipulations between territorial and federal Indian officials. Indian Commissioner Smith, after receiving many requests in behalf of the petition, asked Agent James E. Roberts, on April 20, 1874, to reply by telegram regarding the desirability of the White Mountain reserve. Instead of replying immediately, Roberts

---

[57]Bourke, p. 464.

[58]*Arizona Citizen,* November 8, 1873; and letter of Safford to E. M. Pearce, July 14, 1874, in U. S. Dept. of the Interior, Letters Received by the Office of Indian Affairs, Arizona Superintendency [on microfilm No. 169, University of Arizona Library].

went to Tucson to confer first with Governor Safford and then with Attorney General Louis C. Hughes. The latter wrote to Lesinsky and attempted to extort a bribe for the "trouble, responsibility, expense" involved in "segregating" the land. And in a personal conference which was arranged a few days later, he told the mine operator that "all United States business is conducted on the basis of buy and sell."[59] Lesinsky informed Wasson of this "scheme upon the part of Roberts and Hughes to extort money," reportedly $5,000, and the Tucson editor immediately exposed the scandal to Commissioner Smith and in the July 25 issue of the *Arizona Citizen*.[60]

Though Wasson did not accuse Roberts of any malfeasance, he charged Hughes with extortion in connection with the performance of the duties of his office. The territorial Attorney General denied the charges but was, nevertheless, removed from office by Governor Safford. In the letter of dismissal, the Governor wrote that he was convinced Hughes was in collusion with some agent of the government "to blackmail said Lesinsky and Pearce, and if possible cause them to pay money for relief, which of right they were entitled to demand and obtain without expense, except as prescribed by law."[61] The Governor also revoked Hughes's commission as a notary public for Pima County.

Roberts, one of the Dutch Reformed agents sent out by Washington in accordance with Grant's "peace policy," was unscathed by the scandal. An investigation of the Indian Commission found him to be an "unconscious victim of a plot." However, his drunkenness and inability to control lawlessness on the reservation resulted in the seizure of the Camp Apache agency by Captain F. D. Ogilby. The perplexed Commissioner Smith solved the dilemma by transferring the Coyoteros, as we have seen, to Agent Clum at San Carlos.[62] It is regrettable that during this whole episode involving the reduction of the White Mountain Reservation — the intrusions by the mine developers, the corruption and maneuvering by the politicians, and the agent-military rivalry — there was little consideration given to the rights of the Indians!

Any defender of the red man's cause had plenty of opportunity to take up the gauntlet. The Anglo invasion of Apache territory was not limited to the Clifton area. By 1875, miners began encroaching upon the western boundary of the reservation. Camps and sawmills

---

[59]Ogle, *Federal Control*, pp. 130-31.

[60]Letter of Lesinsky to Wasson, July 13, 1874, U. S. Dept. of the Interior, in Letters Received by the Office of Indian Affairs, Arizona Superintendency; and *Arizona Citizen*, July 25, 1874.

[61]*Arizona Citizen*, August 1, 1874. The Governor also revoked Hughes's commission as notary public for Pima County.

[62]*Annual Report of the Commissioner of Indian Affairs for 1875*, p. 216.

subsidiary to them were operating well inside the reserve. Two modifications of the boundary had been made to accommodate the advancing mining frontier, but these changes probably served only to encourage further intrusion.[63]

Two miners, Charles McMillan and Theodore Harris, discovered a rich silver lode near the headwaters of the San Carlos River, a few miles north of the new community of Globe. The boom town of McMillanville, which was quickly developed on the site, had a five-stamp mill by 1879 and a population of fifteen hundred according to the census of 1880. By that time, McMillan and Harris had dug out $60,000 worth of precious silver on land to which they had no legal right and sold their interests to a Santa Rosa, California, company for $160,000. It was probably no real consolation to any Apache who might have learned that McMillan drank himself to death within a few months and that Harris quickly lost his fortune on the San Francisco Mining Exchange, after which he returned to Globe where he washed dishes in a restaurant for a living.

The mad rush of the covetous miners to McMillanville was followed by two other intrusions. A wave of Mormon immigration entered the southeastern part of the Apache reservation in the late 1870s. This group diverted enough water from the Gila River for development of the rich agricultural district around present-day Safford to cause partial crop failures for the aspiring Apache farmers downstream.[64] Then, in March, 1881, coal was discovered in the southern part of the reservation and desperate miners rushed in, coming within fourteen miles of the agency at San Carlos. This time, however, the agent, J. C. Tiffany, was successful in securing military aid to oust the invaders and in making a lease agreement whereby the Apaches were to enjoy royalties from all minerals taken from the reservation.[65]

When General Crook returned to Arizona in the summer of 1882, Indian affairs were in a deplorable condition. Two years earlier, Victorio, leader of the Warm Springs Apaches, had made his final exit from San Carlos, determined never to return. Until his death in Chihuahua at the hands of Mexican troops in October, 1880, the chief conducted a reign of terror in southeastern Arizona, New Mexico, and Chihuahua. Then Nana, though seventy-three years of age, gathered together the

---

[63]*Arizona Citizen,* September 18, 1875.

[64]Ogle, *Federal Control,* p. 203.

[65]Report of Indian Agent J. C. Tiffany to Commissioner of Indian Affairs Hiram Price, September 6, 1881, from San Carlos, in U. S. Bureau of Indian Affairs, *Annual Report of the Commissioner of Indian Affairs, 1881,* pp. 6-11.

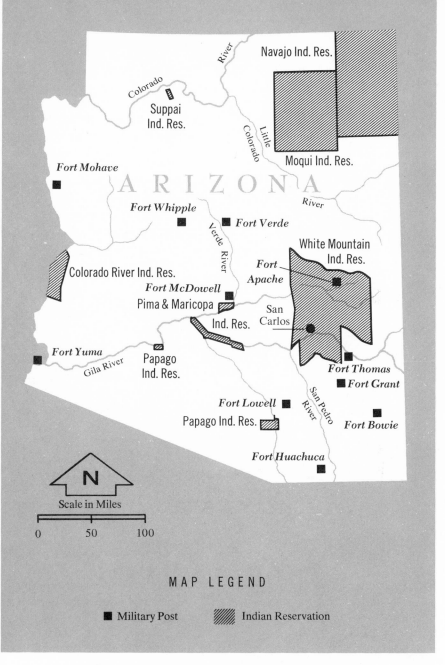

Colorado River

Suppai
Ind. Res.

Navajo Ind. Res.

Little Colorado

Moqui Ind. Res.

Fort Mohave

A R I Z O N A

River

Fort Whipple

Fort Verde

Verde River

White Mountain
Ind. Res.

Fort
Apache

Colorado River Ind. Res.

Fort McDowell

Pima & Maricopa

Ind. Res.

San
Carlos

Fort Yuma

Gila River

Papago
Ind. Res.

Fort Thomas

Fort Grant

Fort Lowell

San Pedro River

Papago Ind. Res.

Fort Bowie

Fort Huachuca

N

Scale in Miles

0   50   100

MAP LEGEND

■ Military Post   ▨ Indian Reservation

Indian Reservations and Main Military Posts
in Arizona, 1882

The Commissioner of Indian Affairs reported the Indian population in 1882
as follows: Navajo (also in New Mexico), 16,000; Moqui (Hopi), 1,813; White
Mountain, 4,133; Papago, 6,000; Pima, Maricopa, and Papago, 4,249; Suppai,
214; and Colorado River, 1,026.

remnants of Victorio's band and some stray Chiricahuas — a group large enough to keep the entire region on edge.[66]

In 1881, the discontented San Carlos Indians were deeply stirred by the incantations and prophecies of a White Mountain medicine man named Nock-ay-del-klinne (meaning "one bound to command") who predicted that he could resurrect several old warrior chiefs who had died. Failing to do this, he explained that all the whites would have to be driven from Apache land before his powers could perform the miracle. Meanwhile, continued ceremonials, including dances and the liberal drinking of tiswin, excited the Indians to a state of fanaticism. At this stage, troops under General Eugene A. Carr were sent to arrest Nock-ay-del-klinne, only to be surprised in an attack near the Indian village of Cibicu in what is now Navajo County on August 30. The medicine man was killed but his followers, reinforced by several of the U. S. Indian scouts who turned against their employers for the first time, hastened to attack Fort Apache. Though this venture was unsuccessful due to lack of leadership, another group of Cibicu warriors under Chief Nantiatish made a murderous and destructive raid into Pleasant Valley and the Cherry Creek region, burning ranch buildings and stripping the country of stock.

When news of the uprising reached Washington, General Sherman rushed reinforcements in from New Mexico and California. His desire for a "war of extermination" was forestalled only by the timely action of Commissioner of Indian Affairs Hiram Price.[67] The latter, contending that the Apaches were merely victims of circumstances, set aside a peace zone on the reservation to protect innocent Indians. The hostiles, however, were overawed by the massive troop movements and also took advantage of the safety area. General Willcox, then in charge of the Department of Arizona, and General Ranald S. MacKenzie, the New Mexico commander in charge of the field operations, were thus unable to strike the decisive blow demanded by Sherman.

A grand jury in Tucson, which investigated conditions on the reservation, concluded that the constantly recurring outbreaks of the Indians and their subsequent depredations were due to the criminal neglect or apathy of the Indian agent at San Carlos.[68] J. C. Tiffany, it appeared, had defrauded the government and his Indian wards in every possible way. His malfeasance was the more alarming since he was

[66]Schmitt, p. 243.

[67]U. S. Bureau of Indian Affairs, *Annual Report of the Commissioner of Indian Affairs, 1883,* pp. 7-10.

[68]*Arizona Star,* October 24, 1882.

— Special Collections, University of Arizona Library

Ration day at San Carlos 1883 (above). Similar scenes took place on other Indian reservations. It is interesting to note that the dress of the Apache women is remarkably similar to the style that many of them were still wearing in the 1960s. The village of San Carlos (below) on the reservation of the same name as it appeared in the 1880s.

appointed by the reform-minded Secretary of the Interior Schurz on May 4, 1880, with the approval of the Dutch Reformed Church. He performed meritoriously for six months in organizing a Sunday school and in formulating plans for a school building, irrigation ditches, full rations, the use of the labor of Indians with guardhouse sentences, and a general revitalization of the farming projects started by his predecessors. But Tiffany quickly learned how to use the power vested in an Indian agent to commit administrative irregularities to his financial advantage.

On several occasions he signed bills of lading for supplies never furnished and split the profits with crooked government contractors; one time he receipted for more than 15,251 pounds of sugar when only 2,168 pounds were delivered, and for 3,349 pounds of coffee when none was received. An official of the Treasury Department discovered in March, 1881, that the agent had established a ranch near the San Carlos-Globe road and was burning his brand on government cattle. R. S. Gardner, who investigated the agency affairs the following August, found that the charge was not only true but that the cattle were fed on government grain and cared for by salaried employees from the reservation; moreover, the ranch was the center for the distribution of public wagons and animals to private individuals. Gardner found graft at the agency, too, especially in the handling of agency supplies. In some instances heavy consignments of goods, including blankets which were intended for distribution to the Indians, were delivered directly to the post trader at Fort Thomas, one J. B. Collins, instead of to the San Carlos agency; yet, the agency storekeeper receipted in full to the obliging freighters.

The Tucson firm of Lord and Williams worked closely with Tiffany and on one occasion the agent threatened to expose Dr. C. H. Lord if the latter didn't send a clerk to San Carlos to make the books agree; the collusion was evidently not air-tight, however, for ex-Delegate to Congress Poston wrote to Commissioner of Indian Affairs Hiram Price, on September 25, 1881, that Lord and Williams, with Washington patronage and a connection with Governor McCormick, had been "the curse and disgrace of this Territory for seventeen years."[69]

Tiffany was also profiting from private coal-mine operations by furnishing Indian labor, wagons, tools, and supplies. In the meantime, the reservation Indians were neglected, half-fed, discontented, and turbulent. They received only a fractional part of what was appropriated

---

[69]Ogle, *Federal Control*, p. 212.

for them and, as a result of Tiffany's abominable administration, came to the fatalistic conclusion that no justice could be expected at the hands of the white man. Within a week after Tiffany was permitted to resign without punishment "for reasons of business necessity and health," Chief Nantiatish attempted to start a general uprising. Though rejected by most of the bands, he attacked San Carlos, killing J. L. Colvig and three of his Indian police. The insurgents, some sixty in number, staged an abortive attack on McMillanville and then fled the reservation. On July 17, a cavalry unit from Fort McDowell caught up with them in a deep canyon in what is now the southeastern corner of Coconino County and virtually ambushed them in the "Battle of the Big Dry Wash." After Nantiatish and more than twenty-five of his braves were slain, the survivors fled in panic back to the reservation.[70]

With the Chiricahuas in Mexico and the reservation Apaches sullen and demoralized almost to the point of desperation, General Crook was reassigned to the Department of Arizona and assumed command at Whipple Barracks on September 4, 1882. Shortly thereafter, he saddled his mule, named Apache, and started across the mountains to the White River Reservation to learn about the Indian grievances first-hand. After sitting with them in a series of powwows, Crook concluded that "the Apaches displayed remarkable forbearance in remaining at peace."[71] He later wrote his opinion of Tiffany and other "Ring" grafters by saying that "the greed and rapacity of the vultures who fatten on Indian wars have been a greater obstacle in the path of civilization than the ferocity of the wildest savages who have fought them."[72]

But he tried to convince the disaffected leaders that war was exactly what evil men desired in order to exterminate the Indians and seize the reservation lands. He explained the necessity of reestablishing his former system of "strict accountability," with each peaceful Apache wearing a tag and answering to frequent roll calls. In this way, every good Indian who wanted to settle down and raise corn would be known, and be safe; those who wanted to rebel and raise scalps would also be known, and be hunted. In order to make the Indians self-supporting and thereby less dependent upon the grafters, Crook found it expedient to relax his system and let the Indians scatter to the more fertile spots on the reservation. Though he placed them under the supervision of

---

[70]*Ibid.*, p. 215; and U. S. House, *Report of the Secretary of the Interior*, 47th Cong., 2d Sess., 1883, House Exec. Doc. No. 1, Vol. ii, p. 150.

[71]U. S. Department of War, *Annual Report, 1883,* p. 160.

[72]Ralph H. Ogle, "The Apache and the Government — 1870's," *NMHR*, Vol. 33, No. 2 (1958), pp. 81-82.

Lieutenant Charles B. Gatewood at Camp Apache and Captain Emmett Crawford at San Carlos, he expected the Indians to govern themselves insofar as possible, to maintain their own police, and to hold their own trials. He forbade the brewing of tiswin and promised that soldiers would be used on the reservation only if the Indians found it impossible to maintain order.

The results of this self-sustaining system were indicated in Crawford's report from San Carlos in 1883. In that year, the White Mountain Apaches raised 2,500,000 pounds of corn; 200,000 pounds of barley; 180,000 pounds of beans; 135,000 pounds of potatoes; and similar proportions of other crops. So propitious was Crook's return to Arizona that there were no depredations committed by Indians until March, 1883, when the Chiricahuas returned from their hideout in the Sierra Madres of Mexico. As we shall see in a later chapter, three and a half more years were to elapse before the Chiricahua renegades were subdued and exiled to Florida, in September, 1886, by Crook's successor of a few months, General Nelson A. Miles.

With the end of the Apache campaigns and the settlement of the red man on reservations, the Indian problem that had delayed the settlement of Arizona was finally remedied. Some critics of government policy referred to the reservations as "concentration camps" and pointed out the injustice of confining people to a restricted area who had been accustomed to complete freedom of movement. But there was really no alternative. With the white population penetrating every part of the Southwest, conflict was unavoidable between the Indians on the one hand and prospectors, ranchers, and settlers on the other. Few of the whites had any respect for the rights of the aborigines and usually regarded them as treacherous, bloodthirsty enemies — and not without reason. A people like the Apaches, who had survived for centuries on plunder, did not readily change. As General Crook said: "It should not be expected that an Indian who has lived as a barbarian all his life will become an angel the moment he comes on a reservation and promises to behave himself, or that he has that strict sense of honor which a person should have who has had the advantage of civilization all his life. . . ."[73]

Governor Safford expressed the feeling of most Arizona pioneers when he told the sixth territorial legislature in 1871 that "the Apache Indians have never manifested the least disposition to live on terms of peace, until after they have been thoroughly subjugated by military

---

[73]Bourke, p. 464.

power."[74] Yet, the Indian often had little choice. He was treated as a nonentity except when on the warpath, commanding respect for his rights only as long as he inspired terror for his rifle or scalping knife. Certainly, no one could condone the rascality of the grafting agents, contractors, and federal officials who fattened themselves on appropriations intended for those Indians that were willing to lead peaceful and orderly lives. The difference between savagery and the type of civilization brought by these rapacious "vultures" and "vampires," as Crook called them, was often hard to discern.

---

[74]*Arizona Citizen,* January 11, 1873; and "Message of Governor A. P. K. Safford," *Journals of the Sixth Legislative Assembly, 1871.*

Chapter 7

A Lawyer Takes Over:

The Hoyt Administration

When Governor Safford retired from office in April, 1877, he was replaced by Secretary of the Territory John Philo Hoyt. The new head man, then only thirty-five years of age, was a handsome, scholarly, and charming gentleman. Born and reared on an Ohio farm, he enlisted in the Union Army during the Civil War. After his discharge he studied law and then moved to Michigan where he gained political experience as a prosecuting attorney and as speaker of the house in the legislature. In 1876, he was appointed secretary of the Arizona Territory by President Grant and distinguished himself by compiling a code of laws for the legislature in 1877, a task for which he received $1,000 in remuneration. He followed the arrangement of the Howell Code while enlarging upon and amplifying the code compiled by Coles Bashford in 1871. The Hoyt Code was considered quite useful and serviceable by territorial lawyers and remained relatively unchanged for ten years.

Hoyt received his commission as governor in April but requested that he be permitted to continue as secretary of the territory until such time as his successor arrived to relieve him. In a letter to Secretary of the Interior Carl Schurz on April 23, 1877, he explained that several lawsuits relative to removal of the capital from Tucson to Prescott were in process.[1] Since the litigation was in the name of the territorial secretary, as the representative of the Arizona government, Hoyt did not consider it consistent with his duty to the public and the parties involved to leave the office vacant; he emphasized that Safford was still faithfully discharging the gubernatorial duties. Permission granted,

---

[1]Letter of Secretary John P. Hoyt to Secretary of the Interior Carl Schurz, from Tucson, April 23, 1877, Record Group 48, Appointment Papers.

Portrait of John P. Hoyt, governor of Arizona Territory, 1877 to 1878. This oil painting hangs in the Capitol.

— Arizona Department of Library and Archives

Hoyt did not take the oath as governor until May 30, after the new secretary, John J. Gosper, arrived.[2]

Shortly after he became governor, Hoyt requested an opinion from Schurz as to the propriety of public officials engaging in the private practice of law.[3] While secretary of the territory, both he and Governor Safford took civil cases that did not conflict with their official duties. Upon assuming the governorship, Hoyt continued working for clients by whom he had been retained while still secretary and he even presented arguments before the Supreme Court of the Territory. However, some of the persons, representing the opposite side in a case in which he was engaged, took exception and alleged that the authorities at Washington did not expect governors to try private cases in courts. Though he cited the precedent set by his predecessor, Hoyt wanted, nevertheless, to be above reproach and asked Schurz if there were any rule or understanding in the Interior Department forbidding him to appear as counsel in civil suits. Upon receiving instructions from the

[2]Letter of Governor John P. Hoyt to Secretary of the Interior Schurz, from Tucson, Arizona, May 30, 1877, *ibid.;* see also, letter of Comptroller R. W. Taylor to Secretary John J. Gosper, from Washington, D. C., June 15, 1877, Record Group 217, Territorial Letters Sent, Vol. 9.

[3]Letter of Governor Hoyt to Secretary of the Interior Schurz, from Prescott, Arizona, July 18, 1877, Record Group 48, Appointment Papers.

latter to desist from being involved in any case as an attorney, the Governor complied, though he did not approve of the decision.[4]

Hoyt had been highly recommended for the governorship by Safford, McCormick, Delegate Hiram S. Stevens, Surveyor-General John Wasson, Chief Justice C. G. W. French, and others. He had little opportunity, however, during his short tenure of slightly more than a year to demonstrate his executive potential. This was especially so since there was no meeting of the Legislative Assembly during his administration. Only occasional references to his mainly routine activities appeared in the territory's four newspapers, two of which (the *Salt River Herald* of Phoenix and the *Arizona Silver Belt* of Globe) began publication during his administration. The following excerpt from Tucson's *Arizona Citizen* gives us a picture of the man in office:

> Governor J. P. Hoyt, who has been looking after school matters in Southern Arizona, passed two days in Florence since our last issue and left yesterday morning for Phoenix and Prescott . . . . The Governor has been traveling about the Territory recently to acquaint himself with the people and with the condition and necessities of every section. . . . Governor Hoyt found schools generally in a healthy and prosperous condition and will use every endeavor to maintain them in their present satisfactory state. The Governor desired to make a more extended trip through Southern Arizona and to visit the military posts and the San Carlos Indian agency, but some important duties called him to Prescott, where among other delicate matters he was to examine and decide the case of J. A. Lewis who will be hanged on April 12, unless pardoned.[5]

Incidentally, the *Citizen* praised Governor Hoyt in the April 19 issue for commuting Lewis's sentence to life imprisonment and condemned those men in Prescott who disgraced themselves by hanging the prisoner in effigy.[6]

As governor, Hoyt deserved some commendation for attempting to repair the deteriorated relationship between the territorial government and the U. S. Army stationed in Arizona. He was congratulated for his attitude by Major General Irvin McDowell, the commander of the Division of the Pacific and the Department of California. In a letter dated July 20, 1877, the General acknowledged receipt of a communication from Hoyt and complimented him in this manner: "I . . . am much gratified to hear your wish to bring about a better state of feeling between the military and civil authorities in Arizona than has unfortunately existed there for a few years past; certainly such a

[4]Hoyt to Schurz, September 21, 1877, *ibid.*
[5]*Arizona Citizen,* March 29, 1878.
[6]*Ibid.,* April 19, 1878.

This Washington hand press was used to print Arizona's first newspaper, The Weekly Arizonian, *which appeared at Tubac on March 3, 1859. Later, according to William S. Oury, it was acquired by L. C. Hughes to print the* Arizona Star. *Now it is in the museum at Tubac State Park.*

— Special Collections, University of Arizona Library

result will be much to the credit of your administration and of great benefit to the country. . . ."[7]

The Indian and other problems of Arizona did not require Governor Hoyt's constant attention. During the winter of 1877–78 he took a leave of absence for several months to take care of both personal and public affairs in the East.[8] Besides tending to his important business interests in Michigan, he sought dental care, not wishing to entrust his aching teeth to any dentist in the territory. Hoyt also conferred with Delegate Hiram S. Stevens in Washington, D.C., in regard to legislation to which he considered the people of Arizona entitled. But much of his leave time was devoted to superintending the indexing and publication of *The Compiled Laws of the Territory of Arizona, 1864–1877,* upon which he had worked while secretary. Richmond, Backus, and Company, Printers, of Detroit, needed his assistance in order that the

---

[7]Letter of Major Irvin McDowell to Governor John P. Hoyt, from San Francisco, July 20, 1877, Record Group 48, Territorial Papers.

[8]Letter of Hoyt to Schurz, from Prescott, Arizona, October 25, 1877, Record Group 48, Appointment Papers.

compilation might be completed for the amount authorized and at the earliest possible date. In January, 1878, he asked for an extension of his leave. He was supported in his request by Delegate Stevens and ex-Governor Safford who explained the necessity for completing the law code as speedily as possible.[9]

While Hoyt was in office, some vitally important events were taking place: the Tombstone and Bisbee mining districts were opened, and the eastward-building Southern Pacific reached Yuma as the whistle of a railroad locomotive was heard for the first time in Arizona on September 30, 1877.[10] Even though the seat of government was moved back to Prescott in accordance with the law passed by the ninth legislature, Tucson, the largest city in the territory with a population then of less than 6,000, was looking forward to a boom when the track was extended eastward from Yuma. With the advent of the railroad, an influx of foreign population and capital was sure to follow. Already, by 1878, Tucson contained many enterprising citizens who were acquiring property and realizing large profits from business adventures and mining investments. The mercantile houses were prospering since Tucson was the market and trade center for the southern portion of the territory and northern Sonora.

But the great wealth of this region was yet to be gathered in. A correspondent for the *New York Times* who took the tedious, jarring, jolting, unforgettable, seventy-two-hour stage trip in a crowded so-called mudwagon from Yuma to Tucson in 1878, wrote that train service would reduce this journey to fifteen hours.[11] Businessmen and visitors were to be further accommodated by the construction of a new telegraph line. The wires then in use in the territory had been built for the use of the Army Signal Service and the military posts. Civilians could use them when they were not in use by the military, but the lines were so poorly constructed that breaks were frequent and repairs exceedingly slow. The people of the territory deserved more dependable telegraph service.

With improved transportation and communication on the way, the economic future of Arizona seemed bright. Unfortunately for Hoyt, however, he was not to be a part of the development because he was

---

[9]Letter of Hoyt to Schurz, with postscript by A. P. K. Safford and Delegate Hiram Stevens of Arizona, from Washington, D. C., January 17, 1878, *ibid.*

[10]Telegram of Major-General Irvin McDowell to Adjutant-General of the Army, from San Francisco, October 3, 1877, U. S. House, *Location of Southern Pacific and Texas Pacific Railroads,* 45th Cong., 2d Sess., 1877, House Exec. Doc. No. 33, p. 22.

[11]*New York Times,* December 28, 1878.

less famous than the man who wanted, needed, and got his job. On June 12, 1878, he was replaced by the well-known John C. Frémont, "the Pathfinder," explorer of the West, former senator from California, and the first man ever to run for President on the Republican ticket. An article in the *Arizona Citizen* on June 21, 1878, contained the following observations on the change:

> The nomination of General Frémont for the governorship of Arizona is understood to have been made independently of the wishes of the Arizona people and in opposition to the friends of the present Governor, John P. Hoyt, who is said to have given general satisfaction to the citizens of the Territory by his administration of its affairs. Governor Hoyt has been nominated for the top job in Idaho, but ... his displacement from his present position is regarded as another breach of civil service reform promises, the President [Hayes] having appointed Frémont purely from personal motives. It is well known that the latter has been unfortunate in his business affairs and lost all his property. He is said to be anxious to go to Arizona, attracted, it is believed, by the mineral prospects of the country.[12]

Hoyt declined the governorship of the Idaho Territory, because he didn't like the idea of replacing Governor Mason Breyman, who, he thought, had been unfairly removed. In addition, Hoyt reasoned that the failure of the Senate to act upon his nomination when it was submitted by President Hayes would tend to prejudice the people of Idaho against him to the extent that it might be difficult to properly discharge his official duties. In a letter to Secretary of the Interior Schurz, Governor Hoyt expressed a desire to be appointed to some other position, the emolument from which would be commensurate with that of the office of the governor.[13] Tendered only the Idaho executiveship, however, Hoyt decided to leave the federal service temporarily.[14] He remained in Arizona until after the arrival of his successor and in October, 1878, was honored jointly with Frémont at a gala ten-dollar-a-plate banquet and dance by the citizens of Prescott. Gracefully relinquishing his office, Hoyt moved to the Washington Territory in 1879. There he served successively, and successfully, on the territorial and later the state Supreme Court, as a banker and real estate promoter in Seattle, as president of the Constitutional Convention, and as first a regent and then a professor of law at the University of Washington. Arizona's loss was Washington's gain.

---

[12]*Arizona Citizen,* June 21, 1878.

[13]Letter of Hoyt to Schurz, from Prescott, Arizona, June 25, 1878, Record Group 48, Appointment Papers.

[14]Letter of Hoyt to Schurz, from Prescott, Arizona, August 23, 1878, *ibid.*

Chapter 8

Part-Time Governor and Carpetbagger *Par Excellence:*

The Frémont Administration

Arizona's fifth chief executive, John Charles Frémont, perhaps did less for the territory than any other governor, probably because he considered himself too important for the position. His long, illustrious career stretched back sixty-five years to his birth in Savannah, Georgia. His dashing father, Charles Frémon, was a Royalist-sympathizing refugee from the French Revolution who had been held prisoner by the British in the West Indies before his arrival in America. His mother was the runaway wife of John Pryor, an aging Revolutionary War veteran. After seven years his father died and young "Charley," as he was called, grew up in Charleston, South Carolina. A good student, he entered Charleston College in the junior year at age sixteen, but an infatuation for a West Indian girl caused him to neglect his studies. He was expelled three months before graduation for what the faculty called "habitual irregularity and incorrigible negligence." But soon his ambition reasserted itself. He graduated and then taught mathematics to midshipmen who were assigned to ships. After an extended voyage to Latin America on the sloop-of-war *Natchez,* he was employed by the Corps of Topographical Engineers.[1]

His first trip west for the government was made in 1838 with the distinguished foreign scientist, Joseph Nicollet, to examine the plateau country between the upper Mississippi and upper Missouri rivers. After returning to Washington, D.C., Frémont fell in love with Jessie Benton, the daughter of the powerful Senator Thomas Hart Benton of Missouri. He eventually married Jessie in 1841. The following year he was placed in full command of an expedition to find new routes to the Pacific and to estimate the value of the Oregon country, a pet project

---

[1]Allen Nevins, *Frémont: Pathfinder of the West* (New York: D. Appleton-Century Co., 1939). This book, though incomplete on the Arizona phase of Frémont's career, is considered to be the classic biography on the Pathfinder. The family name was Frémon; the "t" was added when John was still a boy.

— California State Library

— Arizona Department of Library and Archives

— Sharlot Hall Museum

John C. Frémont as he was photo-graphed in his younger years while ac-quiring fame as an Army officer and explorer of the West, and as he appeared in his late sixties while serv-ing as governor of Arizona Territory, 1878-82. The bust is of his wife, the redoubtable Jessie Benton Frémont.

of the Western-minded Senator Benton. Two more expeditions which took Frémont to California added further luster to his "Pathfinder of the West" glory but ended in court martial.

While he was in California the Mexican War broke out and he assisted Commodore Robert F. Stockton in the conquest of that region. Then, after Colonel Stephen W. Kearny arrived on the scene, Frémont supported Stockton in a dispute over authority and functioned as governor at Los Angeles while Kearny set up headquarters at Monterey. But when Kearny received reinforcements from New York, the Pathfinder was arrested and returned to Washington as a prisoner. Charged with "insubordination, prejudicial conduct, and mutiny," he was convicted and sentenced to be dismissed from the service. President Polk approved the verdict, except for mutiny, but restored Frémont in rank. In protest, Frémont resigned and sought consolation in two privately financed expeditions to survey a southern route for a railroad to the Pacific. The first ended in disaster during the severe winter of 1848–49 with the loss of one-third of the men and all the equipment. Later, after serving as California's first United States senator, 1850–51, Frémont succeeded in leading an expedition over the desired route, though little geographical knowledge was gained. Neither virtual failure on these later expeditions nor the court martial could, however, diminish Frémont's widespread popularity. His exploits had captured the imagination of the people in a period when the Far West was the center of public attention. So, in 1856, he had the distinction of being the first nominee of the new Republican Party for President, but lost the election.

Misfortune again plagued Frémont during the Civil War. He was relieved of his command in St. Louis after prematurely freeing the slaves in his military district — the type of action that President Lincoln thought might cause the border states to leave the Union. Transferred to West Virginia, he was defeated in a battle with the Confederates under Stonewall Jackson and soon resigned his commission as a major-general. Turning to railroad speculation after the war, Frémont became president of the Atlantic and Pacific that was later part of the Santa Fe system through Arizona. His financial schemes often brought him wealth he would quickly dissipate in other ventures. By 1878, his losses as one of the incorporators of the Texas Pacific Railroad Company forced him to turn from the financial world to statesmanship in order to alleviate his poverty. His friends persuaded President Hayes to appoint him governor of the Arizona Territory.

Hayes had been an ardent admirer of "the Pathfinder" for years. Back in 1849 he even changed the name of Sandusky, Ohio, to "Frémont"; and during the Civil War he served under his hero in the Valley

Campaign in West Virginia. Hayes also knew that the Republican Party had owed Frémont a political debt for a long time. It seems that in 1864 a convention of radicals, western Germans, and War Democrats was encouraging Frémont to run for President on a third-party ticket. If he had done so, his candidacy might have drawn enough votes from President Lincoln to elect General George B. McClellan, the Democratic candidate. Lincoln's worried friends delegated Senator Zachariah Chandler and the famous poet, John Greenleaf Whittier, to talk with Frémont. Convinced by Whittier's argument that "there is a time to do and a time to stand aside," Frémont declined to run.

Having thus stepped aside for the good of the party, he felt no compunction about asking for a political appointment as Arizona's territorial governor in his hour of need fourteen years later.[2] Frémont appreciated what was for him a meager salary of $2600 a year,[3] but probably welcomed even more the opportunity to revisit the West and perhaps to recoup his fortune in mine speculation. He made no secret of this. In a letter to Secretary Carl Schurz, he wrote, ". . . I suppose that nothing more is now required in the way of acceptance than to repeat my acknowledgements to the President and yourself for the honor conferred upon me, which many reasons outside of the appointment itself make important to me."[4]

Frémont journeyed to Arizona in an air of glory. There were banquets in his honor at Chicago and Omaha, a reception at San Francisco, and friendly demonstrations at railroad stops all along the way to the terminal at Yuma. At the San Francisco reception the tables were decorated with numerous designs illustrating well-known scenes in the general's life. Among the guests present were several members of the regiment that Frémont commanded in 1846–47. The *New York Tribune* (August 2, 1878) reported that Governor Frémont responded to hearty applause with a short speech. "The Governor is no speaker," wrote the reporter, "but he has a striking presence and a ruddy complexion. His three-score years sit lightly upon him, and were it not for his snow-white hair, he might readily pass for a man of forty. He began by narrating the causes that led to the acquisition of California. He showed how the rich territory was only saved from falling into the hands of England by loyalty, pluck, and enterprise of the pioneers from

---

[2]Bert M. Fireman, "Frémont's Arizona Adventure," *The American West,* Vol. 1, No. 1 (1964), pp. 8-19.

[3]*U. S. Statutes at Large,* Vol. XX, 45th Cong., 2d Sess., 1878, Chap. 329, p. 193; and *ibid,* Vol. XXI, 46th Cong., 2d Sess., 1880, Chap. 225, p. 225.

[4]Letter of Governor J. C. Frémont to Secretary of the Interior Carl Schurz, from New York City, July 9, 1878, Record Group 48, Appointment Papers.

— Sharlot Hall Museum

The return of the capital to Prescott by action of the Ninth Legislative Assembly contributed substantially to the growth of the community. This is how Prescott looked in 1878.

Eastern States." He thanked his friends for the esteem and assurance which their reception gave to him and said that he would depart for his new duties in Arizona with renewed hope and confidence.[5]

From the Yuma railway terminal he rode in an Army ambulance wagon. At Kelsay Station he was met by Governor Hoyt who briefed him on territorial affairs before scurrying back to Prescott to organize an official reception. Frémont made a grand entry, riding with Hoyt in the town's only "barouche" (a four-wheeled, low-bodied, pleasure vehicle with folding top) followed by three ambulances in which Mrs. Frémont, Mrs. Hoyt, Mr. and Mrs. Gosper and the Frémont party were seated.

The new first family, including their daughter Elizabeth and their son Francis Preston Frémont, who was suffering from tuberculosis, were cordially received by the people of Prescott. The Frémonts were domiciled temporarily in the well-furnished home vacated for them by Thomas Fitch, a local lawyer and legislator who had once served in Congress from Nevada and represented Brigham Young as a lobbyist in Washington, D.C. Before long, however, the family rented a hilltop house for which they paid ninety dollars a month. They employed a Chinese cook, Ah Chung, at forty dollars a month but were unable to keep family horses because of the high cost of hay. Mrs. Frémont

---

[5]*New York Daily Tribune,* August, 1878.

entered into the congenial social life with army wives and delighted school children with stories of her travels. Because her health was adversely affected by the high altitude, however, she returned to New York before a year elapsed. From that vantage point she was able to assist her husband in business affairs involving Arizona mining investments. On the other hand, the mountain air quickly restored Frank's health. Within a year after he came to Arizona he was able to obtain a commission as a lieutenant in the Army and was stationed in the Dakota Territory. The Governor himself enjoyed a return to outdoor life and thought nothing of spending a twelve-hour day in the saddle on trips inside the territory.

Frémont had been governor six months and in the territory about half that time when the Tenth Legislative Assembly convened in Prescott in January, 1879. In his first official message to the lawmakers he commented on the future possibilities of the territory.[6] Concluding that the development of potential resources depended upon the improvement of transportation, he recommended the expenditure of half a million dollars for the construction of good roads. He also advocated the establishment of a government assay office and a refinery at Prescott so that the expensive process of transporting raw bullion to distant San Francisco would not be necessary. He told the legislature that he had already suggested in a special report to the Secretary of the Interior that engineers be employed to determine when and how water might be obtained for irrigating farmlands in Arizona. With his characteristic liking for large projects, he mentioned the possibility of diverting Gulf of California water into the desert area which is known today as Imperial Valley.

Frémont's plan was to extend the Gulf by tapping its northern end and letting it run into and fill up the Colorado Desert. This was an old idea that had been long discussed. Centuries before, water had flowed freely into the area; but the sediment that was deposited at the mouth of the Colorado River down through the ages gradually piled up in sufficient quantity to dam off the northern part of the Gulf. The water in the unfed reservoir slowly evaporated, leaving a dry basin 130 miles by 30 miles in width, and this, together with surrounding slopes soon became a bladeless desolation while the river, turning southward, emptied into the Gulf many miles below. Between the arid waste and the present head of the Gulf are some thirty miles of soft earth, just above sea level, through which Governor Frémont proposed to cut his connecting canal.

6"Message of Governor J. C. Frémont," in *Journals of the Tenth Legislative Assembly,* 1879, pp. 40-48.

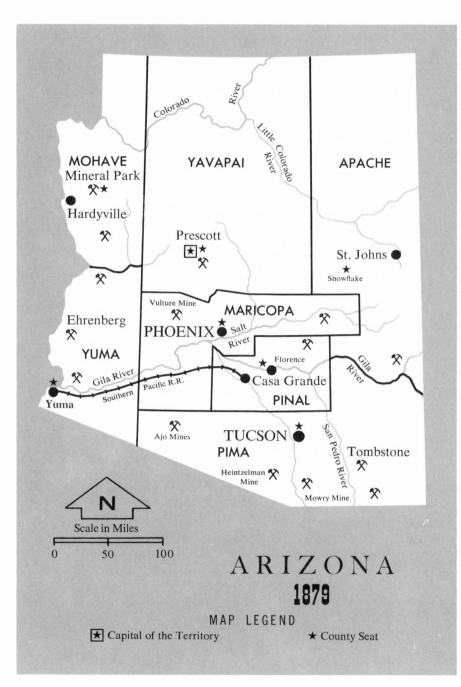

MOHAVE
Mineral Park
Hardyville

YAVAPAI

APACHE

Colorado River

Little Colorado River

St. Johns
Snowflake

Prescott

Vulture Mine

MARICOPA

Ehrenberg

PHOENIX
Salt River

YUMA

Florence

Gila River
Southern Pacific R.R.

Casa Grande

Yuma

Ajo Mines

TUCSON
PIMA

PINAL

Gila River

San Pedro River

Tombstone

Heintzelman
Mine

Mowry Mine

N

Scale in Miles

0   50   100

ARIZONA
1879

MAP LEGEND

★ Capital of the Territory   ★ County Seat

From 1877 to 1887 the capital was once again located at Prescott.

One benefit to be gained was a highway of commerce, but a broader purpose was to restore the natural harmonies and balances that had been disturbed by the drying up of the sea. The flooding of the valley would, supposedly, restore the climate, temperature, and atmospheric conditions to what they had been centuries before, and by increasing the rainfall would bring fertility and comfort to all the surrounding region.

In commenting upon Frémont's proposals, an editorial writer of the *New York Tribune* (April 12, 1879) contended that the plan was not as good as one suggested a few years earlier by the *Overland Monthly* whereby fresh water from the river would be diverted into the desert. Frémont's canal could then be added only if the river flow proved to be insufficient. While suggesting that the physical questions involved in Frémont's plan were interesting, the *Tribune* doubted that the international questions that needed to be negotiated with Mexico would be worked out immediately. "Governor Frémont will be many years older before the tides will ebb and flow in the desert sea," the paper concluded.[7]

Few of Governor Frémont's serious proposals were considered by the legislature, and the antagonistic editor of the *Arizona Citizen* wrote that Frémont was "as ignorant as the Ameer of Afghanistan of Arizona Affairs."[8] According to the Tucson *Citizen,* the Governor would have gotten more response from the legislature if, for example, he had asked that specific roads be built rather than seeking a large sum of money for roads in general. The Tucson newspaper also opposed the establishment of government mining facilities at Prescott, explaining that some town on the railroad would be a more practical location. And Frémont's scheme for watering the California desert was not considered to be of benefit to Arizona. Whether or not the criticisms were justified, the legislature was more inclined to devote its time to the passage of either private bills or measures of concern to only a part of the territory. Seventeen couples were divorced, for example, and eight persons were given a change in name. Most prominent of the latter was Colonel Clay Beauford, formerly a scout for the U. S. Army, who had been engaging in the cattle business under the name of Colonel W. C. Bridwell, the family name which he preferred.

The Assembly passed an act licensing gambling that provided for the payment of a $300 quarterly fee, half to go to the territory and half to the county. This latter bill was sought by the politically powerful

[7]*New York Daily Tribune,* April 12, 1879.
[8]*Arizona Citizen,* March 6, 1879.

gamblers and saloon-keepers and was sponsored by the president of the Council, Fred G. Hughes of Tucson, who divided his time between office-holding and gambling. Another law concerning gambling was passed in jest and was never mentioned on the books. It seems that Representative J. D. Rumburg of Maricopa County introduced a bill to outlaw horse racing in Arizona after he had lost a large sum of cash on the horses. The other legislators were aware of Rumburg's far-from-innocent reputation and treated the measure as a joke. Each snickering representative stood to defend the measure's merits but asked that his county be exempted. The last speaker, John T. Alsap, Rumburg's Maricopa colleague, facetiously requested that Maricopa County be exempted also — except for a certain piece of land on the Black Canyon road which, as it turned out, was owned by Rumburg.[9] The land is not many furlongs from the modern Turf Paradise where many a disappointed racing fan has probably wished that Arizona had a statute similar to the original version of Rumburg's bill.

The most conspicuously different piece of legislation, however, was the authorization of the Arizona Lottery, patterned after the one held in Louisiana. The scheme was promoted by Tom Fitch, the talented and persuasive member of the Assembly from Prescott. Fitch suggested that the lottery, as a painless means of raising money, would relieve the burdened property taxpayers. He had little difficulty in convincing Hughes, a professional gambler, to introduce the bill in the Council. The law created the Arizona Development Company to function under the supervision of the governor as the lottery commissioner, a job for which he was to receive a $100 fee. Michael Goldwater, of Prescott, was appointed treasurer. Ostensibly, the object of the lottery was to raise funds for the construction of state buildings and public schools.

The people seemed to accept the idea enthusiastically at first, even though the capital, Prescott, would be the only immediate beneficiary while other parts of the territory would have to wait three years to receive school construction aid. Several newspapers opposed the lottery, however, including the *Arizona Citizen* of Tucson, edited by John Clum, and the *Territorial Expositor* of Phoenix, published by James A. Reilly. The *Citizen* seemed to smell corruption when it asked why only $32,000 ($31,250 in 282 prizes according to the law) were to be distributed when 12,000 tickets in five-dollar denominations (a total receipt of $60,000) were to be sold.[10] Actually, however, there were three kinds of tickets — whole tickets for $5.00, halves for $2.50, and quarters for

[9]*Arizona Republic,* May 24, 1964.
[10]*Arizona Citizen,* March 7, 1879.

$1.25 — which totaled $31,250. When the tickets were sold, twelve thousand slips of leather were to be mixed in a huge glass wheel and 282 pieces drawn to be placed in a smaller glass wheel. Then the winners were to be picked, the top prize being $10,000. But the drawing never occurred, largely because public confidence was shaken by the vitriolic newspaper editorials. The lottery was postponed and ticket holders were advised that J. Goldwater and Brother of Prescott would redeem tickets at full cash value. The entire loss on the lottery scheme was borne by Mike Goldwater. In the words of his famous grandson, Barry, "There was only one loser in this episode — my grandfather. He ran advertisements in the territorial press offering refunds for every ticket sold. He paid for all the advertising, for the printing of the leather tickets, and ate his humble pie alone when he was bitterly censored in the press for associating with men like Frémont and Fitch. . . . Ledgers of our family business contain records of this money-losing fiasco."[11]

The *Expositor* was typical of the newspapers that heaped coals upon all the people connected with the lottery; it facetiously announced the demise of the scheme as follows: "What has been buried under a lot of public condemnation has been resurrected and its decaying carcass again made to stink in the nostrils of honest men. It seems that the postal authorities very properly prohibited the circulation of Arizona Development [lottery] literature through the United States mails."[12] Frémont had been informed by Secretary Schurz of the postmaster general's rulings. The Governor was advised that he couldn't hold the position of territorial commissioner since federal statute forbade any federal officeholder, except a postmaster, from accepting an appointment from a territorial government; and the transmission through the mails of circulars such as those which advertised the Arizona lottery was also considered unlawful.[13] Frémont received Schurz's forwarded letter in New York City and replied when he reached Washington, D.C. He explained that he had not been sufficiently informed on the lottery scheme and thus disclaimed any part of it.[14] The next legislature washed its hands of the whole matter by repealing the lottery act in 1881.

Frémont was more interested in his personal mining promotions.

[11]Goldwater, "Three Generations of Pants and Politics," in Goldwater Collection, Arizona Pioneers' Historical Society.

[12]*Territorial Expositor,* July 29, 1879.

[13]Letter of Secretary of the Interior Schurz to Governor Frémont, from Washington, D. C., April 23, 1879, Record Group 48, Letter Book.

[14]Letter of Governor Frémont to Secretary of the Interior Schurz, from Washington, D. C., May 27, 1879, Record Group 48, Territorial Papers.

After the Tenth Assembly adjourned he left for the East, officially on a special mission in behalf of the territory but also to raise capital for mine development.[15] The legislature had appropriated $2,000 to send the Governor and Charles Silent, a fellow speculator who was conveniently a member of the Arizona Supreme Court, to Washington, D.C. Their mission was to persuade President Rutherford B. Hayes and Secretary of the Interior Carl Schurz to withdraw an order extending the Gila River Indian Reservation into the fertile Salt River Valley. Farmers in the Phoenix-Tempe-Mesa area did not want the Indians to deprive them of water that would be needed to develop agriculture in that area and therefore were vitally dependent on the success of the Governor's mission. Frémont did not let them down but used his influence in the nation's capital to good advantage in getting the order rescinded.

He was also successful in his private project of interesting Eastern investors in Arizona mining property. His personal business kept him out of Arizona for nearly six months in 1879 and people were beginning to wonder if they had a governor only *in absentia*. Arizona's Delegate to Congress, John G. Campbell, voiced this antagonistic feeling when he said of Frémont, "So far we cannot tell what sort of Governor he will make as he has spent most of his time in the East." In March, 1880, Frémont began another extended Eastern junket which took him out of the territory for seven months. He did not return until near the end of October and consequently had only about two months to become acquainted with the territorial problems and prepare his message for the eleventh legislature which met at Prescott in January, 1881.

Except for a recommendation that divorce be left to the courts, this message was mainly devoted to suggestions of activities that might help promote Arizona's economic development.[16] The Governor proposed that a legislative committee be appointed to prepare a statement on the opportunities for settlement and economic development in the territory. He urged the Assembly to seek federal aid to develop water-storage projects that would enable vast wastelands to be occupied by settlers.[17] He said that the mines were Arizona's greatest interest and asked the legislature to encourage the investment of capital by levying no taxes upon the mining products.

---

[15]Letter requesting leave of absence, from Governor Frémont to Secretary of the Interior Schurz, from Prescott, Arizona, January 25, 1879, Record Group 48, Appointment Papers.

[16]"Message of Governor Frémont," in *Journals of the Eleventh Legislative Assembly,* pp. 34-37.

[17]*New York Times,* January 17, 1881.

Stress was also placed upon the advantage of increasing trade with Mexico. With the intention of keeping relations with that republic on a friendly basis, Governor Frémont sent a special message to the legislature on February 21, 1881. He described the chaotic conditions along the Mexican border where organized bands of outlaws were threatening the security of life and property on both sides of the line. He said, "I think it is urgent to put into the field a force of one hundred men, to be retained in service for three months, or for such time as in the discretion of the executive the safety of the citizens and the peace of the border may absolutely demand." This request for volunteers was denied by the legislature on the grounds that federal troops under General Willcox were sufficient to handle the situation.

However, the Eleventh Assembly did pass a multitude of other bills, 103 to be exact. The counties of Cochise, Gila, and Graham were created.[18] The towns of Phoenix, Tombstone, and Prescott were incorporated and several counties were authorized to issue bonds for construction of a courthouse, jail, or other needed buildings. Gambling by minors was prohibited. The governor was authorized to contract for the care of insane patients at the rate of six dollars per week. The legislature also appropriated $2,000 to gather information regarding the resources of Arizona and appointed Patrick Hamilton to compile this data; the result was a very valuable and readable book called *The Resources of Arizona,* published in 1884.[19] The repeal of the bullion tax probably created the greatest interest outside the territory. The *San Francisco Bulletin* criticized the Arizona legislature for passing this measure and Governor Frémont for signing it. The newspaper argued that it was unfair for nonresidents of Arizona to exploit the mines, under the protection of the laws, without contributing a dollar in taxes to the support of schools or government.

In another instance the local press ridiculed a memorial resolution introduced by J. F. Knapp, the speaker of the House from Yuma. This memorial, if it had passed, would have asked Congress to attach all of Arizona except Yavapai, Mohave, and Apache counties to Southern California. Though never seriously considered by the Assembly, the resolution, nevertheless, served to point out the ill-feeling that still existed between the northern and southern sections of the territory. Probably the question that stirred up the most controversy in the

---

[18]See the *Arizona Bulletin* (Solomonville), Special Illustrated Edition, January 12, 1900, for the history of the first county elections, etc. in Graham County.
[19]Patrick Hamilton, *The Resources of Arizona* (San Francisco: A. L. Bancroft, 1884).

eleventh session was the creation and naming of new counties. Captain Sharp of Maricopa was particularly ired by the name "Cochise" because he said that he had suffered too much from the "depredations and murderous attacks of that bloodthirsty savage" to immortalize him by giving his name to a county.[20]

A newspaper correspondent for the *Arizona Weekly Star,* who observed and reported on the Assembly, wrote an interesting personal account of the legislators at work.

> Since the passage of the two bug-bears of the session — the Cochise and Gila County bills — nothing bothers us; . . . trouble slips off our backs like water from a duck's wing. Decorum is a word known as or supposed to exist somewhere in the dictionary, which in conjunction with dignity, imply a characteristic unknown to the 11th Territorial Assembly. Not that we are riotous, for the Sergeant-at-Arms has not been called upon to make an arrest, nor has a call of the House been asked. We are punctual in attendance; but we do ignore the etiquette usually prevailing in Assemblys. We all smoke — that is the members do — and anyone not knowing that this was a Legislature, and visiting us, would certainly think that it was a reading room, and that of a second or third class hotel. Smoke from pipes — and some of them are powerful strong — cigars, and cigarettes fill the air from the hour of convening to that of adjourning. Members tilt back their chairs and complacently cock their feet up on the table in front of them, read the papers, write letters, hold audible caucuses, on the side, speak and vote away from their tables; and in fact do whatever their sweet fancy may dictate. And, mind you, the House is no exception. . . . The Council is just as bad, even worse, as one member has the habit of walking up and down the aisle between the tables, puffing a cigar like an over-loaded locomotive on a 100-foot grade, with his head dropped on his breast in profound meditation. It is shrewdly surmised that he is revis-ing in his mind whether he belongs to or represents Pima or what is to be Cochise County. But these are merely crudities of Territorial legislation, and in no way interfere with good honest work which the Assembly is doing. For, as a body, they will rank with that of average legislatures, and maybe are a cut above the average.[21]

The legislators hailed from diverse backgrounds, as the following examples illustrate. One who had led a most interesting life was Murat Masterson, President of the Council. He was born at sea in 1846, his father being from Virginia and his mother from France. Most of his boyhood was spent on ships traversing the sea lanes of the world. When the Civil War broke out he became a blockade runner and was captured off the coast of Florida near the St. John's River. After his release

---

[20]*Arizona Star,* February 10, 1881.
[21]*Ibid.*

he joined the Army and served during the remainder of the conflict. In the postwar period he studied law and was admitted to practice in Lexington, Kentucky. He then "hung up his shingle" in St. Joseph, Missouri, and, in 1875, moved to the Pacific coast where he resided in San Diego. The next year he came to the Arizona Territory and was soon elected to the position of Yavapai County district attorney and then to the Council.

B. O. Thomas, who represented Maricopa County, had devoted most of his life to the stage business. Born in Virginia and raised in Ohio, he filled an official position at the Ohio State Prison before becoming associated with stage companies in Ohio and Missouri. From 1862 to 1868 he was superintendent of Holliday and Company's overland stage. He then served in the same capacity for two years with Wells Fargo & Company, which purchased the Holliday business. Prior to his election to the legislature, Thomas had lived in Arizona only about five years. During part of this time he was connected with the California and Overland Stage Company and also filled one term as sheriff of Maricopa County.

Another man from afar was Solomon Barth of Apache County, who was born in Prussia in 1843. Coming first to California, Barth migrated to Arizona in 1862 where he sold merchandise at La Paz and then at Antelope Hill, Wickenburg, and Prescott. He moved to New Mexico but returned after nine years to become the first settler at what is now the town of St. Johns and to engage in freighting and stockraising. A highlight of his early pioneer experiences in the territory was his campaigning with Col. Woolsey against the Apaches, notably in the battles at Bloody Tanks and Tonto Basin. And so it went through the list of lawmakers. Nearly all were pioneers — like the people whom they represented.[22]

On March 17, 1881, Frémont sent a telegram to President Garfield complaining that the adjourned Eleventh Assembly was largely Democratic and that many of their acts were contrary to the best interests of the territory and in violation of the express prohibition of Congress. The Governor said that he had incurred the hostility of the Assembly by opposing this type of legislation. He understood that the lawmakers had wired Washington requesting his removal and asked the President to inform him at Tucson if this were so.[23] Governor Frémont left Prescott to live at 245 Main Street in Tucson where he felt that the

---

[22]*Ibid.*, February 3, 1881.

[23]Telegram from Governor Frémont to the President, from Prescott via Maricopa Wells, March 17, 1881, Record Group 48, Appointment Papers.

lower altitude would relieve his "mountain fever." But his residency there was short, for he soon departed again for the East.[24] Purportedly, his trip was for the purpose of buying arms for the territory to use in fighting the Apaches. More likely, however, he was simply neglecting the duties of his office to promote his mining interests. Specifically, he was seeking financial backing so that he could exercise his six-months' option to buy copper deposits at Jerome, but he failed to get the needed capital. Also, his efforts to sell land in the San Pedro Valley belonging to the José Elías family never materialized.

While in New York City in the summer of 1881, Frémont was interviewed by a reporter of the *New York Tribune* and had an opportunity to air publicly some of his views on the situation in Arizona.[25] He was asked to express his opinions on the recent Indian outbreaks in the Southwest and the border troubles. Though hesitating to reveal the full contents of a letter he had written to the Secretary of the Interior on these matters, the Governor attempted to summarize the information he thought the American people were entitled to have. Tracing the history of border troubles that had existed for several years, he suggested that peace and good order along the international line would require the employment of a small but active force. "In view of the increasing lawlessness on the frontier and of representations made to our Government by Mexico," he said, "I asked the Legislature at the last session for 100 men to enforce the law. But the bill introduced for this purpose passed only one House, and left me unprovided with any means to maintain order on our boundary."

Frémont explained that on paper the governor of a territory was impowered to call out the militia, but that no such force had been organized in Arizona and that no arms were available for it in the territory, even if the governor were to assume the responsibility for calling it out. Furthermore, he continued, the Army commander was interdicted by the *posse comitatus* act from using U. S. troops to quell lawlessness.

As to the Indian problem, Frémont said that the solution was not simple because the mountainous terrain of much of the Southwest was favorable to the Indian type of warfare. He said that small bands had been very successful in their depredations in the previous three years and that, if the fighting should be expanded, a disproportionately large force, considerable time, and loss of valuable life would be required

---

[24]File No. 538, 1881: Frémont, *ibid*. (This file contains requests for leaves of absence and leaves granted.)

[25]*New York Times,* August 25, 1881, p. 8.

to end it. He thought that, since the irreconcilable Indians were a common problem to both the United States and Mexico, the two republics should cooperate in maintaining peace and prosperity along the border. As a possibility along this line he offered another one of his novel plans. He said that he had suggested to the Secretary of the Interior the expediency of an arrangement with the Mexican government by which the peninsula of Lower California might be used as a reservation into which to gather all the Apache tribes. The peninsula is 700 miles long, the Gulf on one side and the Pacific Ocean on the other, with a breadth at the northern end of only 150 miles. Alternating posts on either side of the border maintained by the respective governments would effectually bar the Indians from all egress, and within these limits they could be controlled and taught to be self-supporting. To emphasize the possibility of his plan, Frémont recalled that early Spanish missionaries had found the Gulf shore well-populated and thriving.

Just as with his scheme to turn the California desert into a lake, however, nothing came of the Governor's proposal to solve the Indian problem. But the idea did stir up a controversy. The *New York Times,* in editorializing on the subject, stated that Arizonans shamefully and purposely exaggerated tales of bloodshed and slaughter. The paper reported that indignation meetings had been held in several Arizona cities to protest against the maintenance of Indian reservations in the territory, but concluded that the vociferous demands of the settlers for immediate removal of the Indians should be resisted.[26]

About the same time that the *Times* editorial was published, Acting Governor John J. Gosper, Secretary of the Arizona Territory, submitted his official report to the Secretary of the Interior.[27] In strongly recommending that Frémont be required to either return to his post or be asked to resign, Gosper was really asserting his own ambition to be governor in name as well as in fact. His lengthy report on conditions in Arizona and his suggestions upon subjects to which the attention of Congress should be called would indicate that Gosper had been performing all the duties of the office. In regard to the Indian policy in the territories, he thought that the citizens in Arizona favored transferring the whole question of managing the Indians to the War Department. He said that the Indian problem in this territory could never

---

[26]*Ibid.,* October 3, 1881.

[27]"Report of the Acting Governor of Arizona, October 6, 1881, to the Secretary of the Interior," in U. S. House, *Report of the Secretary of the Interior,* 47th Cong., 1st Sess., 1881, House Exec. Doc. No. 1, Part 5, pp. 915-37.

be brought to a satisfactory conclusion until the warlike spirit of the more savage tribes was broken. "I have been upon the San Carlos Reservation in times of fullest peace," he wrote,

> and have looked into the faces of chiefs, and through an interpreter have conversed with them, and have not failed to discover the restless and unsatisfied spirit, chafing like the lion in the cage, under the unnatural restraint to which they were compelled to yield. Their wild and untamed natures demand the fullest liberty to roam unmolested through the valleys, over the mountains, and along the streams of their birth-places and early associations. Unfair and unjust treatments, and ignorance of the Indian character to some extent, on the part of authorities placed over him, mingled with an uncontrollable desire for the liberty of a lifetime to roam unmolested, to hunt and chase undisturbed, is the motive that actuates him to steal away from their narrow confines, and to commit murder and theft in efforts to regain possession of their old and accustomed haunts.

Gosper charged that some designing Indian agents and government contractors aggravated the Indian problem with fraud and deception. He thought that a regular Army officer, his whole career at stake, would be more just to all parties than a civilian who expected to hold his agency or contract for a short time only.

Just as Gosper believed that the administration of Indian affairs could be improved in Arizona, so he was forthright in recommending changes to rectify certain shortcomings in all three branches of the territorial government. Starting with the legislature, he wrote that the quality of men who entered that body were on the whole mentally and morally inferior because of the low per-diem pay of $4 and mileage allowance of 15 cents.[28] He said that the cost of living in this territory was proportionately much higher than in the states and some of the other territories and that $4 per day would scarcely meet the absolutely necessary expenses of members during their temporary stay in the capital. Gosper believed that if Congress returned to the old pay of $6 per day a more industrious and intelligent class of citizens would be encouraged to leave their homes and businesses to serve the public in the legislature. As it was, he inferred, many candidates were running with the expectation of securing from some extra-legal source, honorable or otherwise, a reasonable compensation for their services. Both the Tenth and Eleventh Assemblies voted their members additional money from the territorial treasury, a positive prohibitory law of Con-

---

[28]*U. S. Statutes at Large,* Vol. XX, 45th Cong., 2d Sess., 1878, Chap. 329, p. 193; see also, letter of the Acting Comptroller to Secretary John J. Gosper, from Washington, D. C., July 16, 1879, Record Group 217. Territorial Letters Sent, Vol. 10.

gress notwithstanding. Governor Frémont approved the bill passed by the Tenth but vetoed the one submitted by the Eleventh Assembly. The latter body, however, showed its collective wrath by passing the illegal measure over the Governor's veto by a two-thirds vote, though the Auditor rightfully refused to issue the requested warrants on the treasury in this instance.

Gosper also recommended that Congress revise the federal statutes to allow the territory the privilege of electing its own governor.[29] With perhaps a back-handed slap at Frémont and a bid for his own candidacy, he wrote,

> A very strong prejudice exists in this Territory against so-called "carpet-bag" officials, and a spirit of distrust and uncertainty exists in the minds of our citizens in the case of new, untried, and stranger officials coming into their midst from abroad. Many of them come simply for the purpose of enjoying the honor and emolument of the term of office for which they are appointed, and very naturally do not feel that same deep concern for the public welfare they would if permanent residents and property-holders in the Territory.[30]

He thought that a law that allowed citizens to choose an executive from among their number would be widely hailed with proud satisfaction and that the best interests of the public would be enhanced.

Gosper also made a recommendation in regard to the judicial branch of the territorial government, and in this instance Congress eventually took action. After consultation with the leading lawyers and the judges themselves, he proposed that an additional, or fourth, U. S. judgeship be created. His reasoning was that three districts were too large and that an increased population justified another position. But the most important reason which he gave was that the three judges sat as the Supreme Court with appellate jurisdiction in cases arising from the three district courts; with a fourth district, three judges would be available for each appeals case and the man from whose lower court the case came would not have to sit in judgment a second time. It was obvious from this and other recommendations for congressional action suggested by Gosper that he knew what was going on in the Arizona Territory. Though it was never to be his destiny to hold the title of governor, his chances of receiving the appointment were brightened by Frémont's continual absenteeism.

---

[29]*U. S. Statutes at Large,* Vol. XII, 37th Cong., 3d Sess., 1863, Chap. 56, p. 665.

[30]"Report of the Acting Governor of Arizona, October 6, 1881, to the Secretary of the Interior," in U. S. House, *Report of the Secretary of the Interior,* 47th Cong., 1st Sess., 1881, House Exec. Doc. No. 1, Part 5, p. 918.

By the summer of 1881 the people of Arizona were becoming disgruntled and impatient over the prolonged absence of their "carpetbag" governor from his duties. Secretary Gosper had been contributing to the unrest for a long time. As early as August 8, 1879, for example, the *Arizona Citizen* printed a letter Gosper had received from the doctor in charge of the asylum at Stockton, California. The doctor simply reviewed the condition of Arizona's insane patients in that city but emphasized that he had been unable to communicate with Governor Frémont.[31] Then in the report to the Secretary of the Interior on October 6, 1881, mentioned above, Gosper strongly recommended that the regularly appointed governor of Arizona be required to return to his post or be asked to resign.[32] Obviously, the Secretary's motive in this request was partly selfish, since he had written a few weeks before, on March 17, 1881, to the new President, James A. Garfield, and solicited the governorship for himself. He wrote then that both Frémont and his predecessor, Governor Hoyt, had been absent so much of the time that the Secretary was forced to do their work without the honor of having the glory or salary.

In asking for promotion in the line of "civil service" to the governorship when a vacancy occurred, Gosper dropped the names of ex-President Grant and several other important people who could recommend him. He also cited his war record: "I was a volunteer in the Union service, and left a sacrifice upon the battlefield, my left leg, and am now using a wooden one as a substitute." His experience as an elected secretary of state in Nebraska was mentioned as further evidence of his qualification.[33] Accompanying telegrams were sent in his behalf by two members of the Territorial Republican Committee, William A. Hancock and John H. Smith of Phoenix, by Mayor John P. Clum of Tombstone, and by Judge DeForest Porter.

Later in the year, after Chester A. Arthur had succeeded to the Presidency, Secretary Gosper wrote a letter in which he set forth his reasons for expecting to be appointed governor. Again stressing his war mishap, he said that he had been secretary for nearly five years, during which time he was acting governor three-fourths of the time. He claimed to have twelve of the territory's sixteen newspapers behind him for

---

[31]*Arizona Citizen,* August 8, 1879.

[32]"Report of the Acting Governor of Arizona to the Secretary of the Interior, October 6, 1881," in U. S. House, *Report of the Secretary of the Interior,* 47th Cong., 1st Sess., 1881, House Exec. Doc. No. 1, Part 5, pp. 915-37.

[33]Letter of Secretary of the Territory John J. Gosper to President James A Garfield, from Prescott, Arizona, March 17, 1881, Record Group 48, Appointment Papers.

either secretary or governor and only one (the *Arizona Miner*) in opposition.[34] However, the reverse was closer to the truth according to Charles W. Beach, editor of the *Miner,* who wrote that only the *Phoenix Herald,* Gosper's own newspaper, was zealously tooting his horn. Beach bitterly hated Gosper and printed many editorials condemning him. In one issue he attacked him in these words:

> The *Tucson Citizen* thinks Gosper would do for Governor. Now has Gosper offered to trade the capital for the support of the *Citizen?* Would Gosper do such a thing? We believe he would. We don't want a man who would give one cent towards procuring the appointment wherein bribery might be construed. Mr. Gosper has not the least qualification for the place. He is unlettered and can't write ten words grammatically. Worse, he cannot spell, punctuate or present a document of a public nature in an enlightened and correct manner. He has the brass to present himself before an audience and repeat his old stereotyped harangue, and that's all there is in him. We want a man for Governor who has ability and honor, neither of which is possessed by the Secretary. While Fremont was still in the gubernatorial chair he circulated petitions asking for the position. This of itself should condemn the man. But his brazenness has no bounds. However, it is useless to discuss this matter so far as Gosper is concerned, for he will never see the parchment making him Governor of this Territory.[35]

The author of these words was one of the most interesting characters in Arizona history. Charles Beach came to the territory in 1864 from New Mexico, where he had commanded volunteers in the battles of Glorieta and Valverde during the Civil War and where he learned his trade as a printer from ex-Governor Ross. In 1876 he bought the *Miner* from T. J. Butler and operated that well-known journal for seven years. Following this, he engaged in the stock business in Yavapai County and also in contracting. He was the principal builder of the Prescott and Arizona Central Railroad and served as the road's superintendent when it was finished.[36] His life was full of incidents, not the least exciting of which was the terrible courthouse fray in Prescott on December 3, 1883. Beach's mother-in-law was suing the hot-tempered Patrick McAteer over water rights on Kirkland Creek which flowed through the adjoining ranches of both the plaintiff and the defendant. During the course of testimony before Chief Justice Charles C. G. W. French, Mrs. Kelsey's lawyer, Attorney General Clark Churchill, called the defense counselor, Charles B. Rush, a liar. Rush hurled an ink-

---

[34]Letter of Secretary Gosper to President Chester A. Arthur, from Prescott, Arizona, November 17, 1881, *ibid.*

[35]*Arizona Daily Miner,* November 10, 1881.

[36]*Phoenix Herald,* September 18, 1889.

*John J. Gosper (left), the secretary of the territory during Frémont's adminis-
tration, and acting governor much of the time, and a bitter enemy of Charles
W. Beach (right), editor of the* Arizona Miner *for seven years.*

stand at Churchill and then grabbed him by the throat as W. O.
"Buckey" O'Neill, the court reporter, and others came to the latter's aid.
At the same time, the wild McAteer drew a large double-edged knife
and commenced to cut in every direction. He first stabbed a seventy-
year-old man and then drove his blade into the left side of Beach's neck,
barely missing the jugular vein. O'Neill received a severe cut on the
hand while attempting to take the knife from the assailant and was
cornered against the wall, about to be knifed to death when Beach drew
a .38-caliber Colt and shot the mad McAteer in the back.[37] Probably
few other court trials in American history were so bloody. The old
man's arm had to be amputated, McAteer died a month later, and
several participants in the drama were left with scars, many with bumps
and bruises. Beach lived until 1889 when he was killed by George W.
Young, who blamed the former editor for alienating the affections of
his wife. When murdered, Beach was sitting in his room one evening
at Mrs. Taylor's lodging house, writing a letter to his young son who
was with his mother in Los Angeles. According to a report the next
day in the *Prescott Courier,* the assailant emptied the contents of a
shotgun through the window. The greatest portion of the shot struck
Beach in and around the left eye, knocking him over and killing him
instantly.[38]

---

[37]*Ibid.,* December 3, 1883.
[38]*Prescott Courier,* September 18, 1889.

Such was the life and demise of the man who was attacking the Secretary and Acting Governor in his newspaper columns in 1881. Actually the Gosper-Beach enmity had been simmering for some time, partly because Beach, though he was a Republican like Gosper, felt that his newspaper did not get its fair share of printing contracts awarded by the territorial Secretary. Then, during 1880, Beach filed charges against Secretary Gosper with the Interior Department, alleging that he had defrauded the government. As the secretary, Gosper purchased all the territorial supplies. After investigating, Beach disclosed that in one instance Gosper paid a bill amounting to $550 but submitted a voucher to the Interior Department for $1,100. Beach also said that Gosper charged the government for 250 copies of journals when he only paid for 125 copies, and charged for 500 copies of the printed laws when he only furnished half that number.[39] Beach's friend, A. M. Smith, asked for an investigation of all the affairs of the Secretary and wrote to Secretary of the Treasury John Sherman that Gosper "is a disgrace to his position morally, personally and officially and is held in utmost contempt by those who are compelled to associate with him."

Smith objected to the manner in which one Robinson, an agent of the Treasury Department, supposedly investigated Beach's charges.[40] After the agent arrived in Prescott, he was given the red-carpet treatment by Gosper. On his second day in town Robinson was airing himself behind a fast team of horses with the Secretary at the reins. During the two weeks the Washington official was in town collecting evidence to sustain or refute the charges, the local citizens observed a close intimacy between the "emissary" and the "investigated." As a result, those who had intended to assist in furnishing facts to substantiate the charges, including Beach and Smith, had no confidence in Robinson and declined to sign affidavits. Gosper publicly asserted, "in his usual bombastic way," that nothing would be done further in the matter.[41] According to Smith, Gosper seemed to be making certain that no one interviewed Robinson at the last minute by departing on the same stage with him.[42]

In his own defense, Gosper wrote to Secretary Sherman on November 19, 1880. He admitted that he had committed some errors in trying

---

[39]Letter of A. M. Smith to Secretary of the Treasury John Sherman, from Prescott, Arizona, October 12, 1880, Record Group 217, Territorial Letters Received, Vol. 15.

[40]Letter of Thomas Robinson to First Comptroller William Lawrence, from Prescott, Arizona, September 8, 1880, *ibid.*

[41]Letter of Smith to Sherman, *ibid.*

[42]*Ibid.*

to fulfill the duties of both the offices of secretary and governor, but he denied having defrauded the government of one dollar. He said that Beach's complaints were groundless and that Beach himself was mercenary, malicious, narrow-minded, and quarrelsome.[43] In a letter to President Arthur almost a year later, Gosper was more specific in his condemnation of the *Miner* editor, writing that Beach was untruthful, unreliable, and motivated by purely personal motives. He said that Beach was a gambler and an open consort with abandoned women, that he had been arrested and fined in police court for striking one of these women with a chair, and that he was the father of an illegitimate child by a Mexican woman.[44] This may well have been a case of the pot calling the kettle black because Beach's cohort, A. M. Smith, had accused the Secretary of a similar act of moral turpitude.

In another defensive letter, written on November 30, 1881, to Secretary of the Interior S. J. Kirkwood, Gosper apologized for giving the Phoenix *Herald,* a newspaper in which he had an interest, a share of territorial printing. He explained that no fraud was intended. The *Herald* and *Miner* were simply the only two Republican papers that applied for the work that was shared between them at no additional cost to the government. "At the time the newspaper of which I was part owner shared in the patronage in my hands as secretary," he wrote, "I was ignorant of the law prohibiting me from participating in any manner in any contracts which passed through my hands. I should have known the law but did not."[45] Gosper mentioned to Kirkwood the fact that his friends, ex-Governor Safford and Senator Saunders, had informed him that the Interior Department opposed continuing him in official life as a federal appointee because of the public printing incident. And in this letter he seemed to see the handwriting on the wall when he wrote, "If I am not appointed Governor of this Territory — or Secretary either — it will make but little difference to me. I have abundant means of support and can make more and take more comfort out of office."[46] Two years later, however, the government was threatening to sue the then ex-Secretary Gosper if he didn't submit the necessary vouchers to close out his accounts. At that time he asked for an extension and wrote to the first comptroller in the Treasury Department that "I have been completely overwhelmed with the cares and disappoints of a business failure,

---

[43]Letter of Secretary John J. Gosper to Secretary of the Treasury Sherman, from Prescott, Arizona, November 19, 1880, *ibid.*

[44]Letter of Secretary Gosper to President Arthur, from Prescott, Arizona, October 8, 1881, Record Group 48, Appointment Papers.

[45]Letter of Secretary Gosper to Secretary of the Interior S. J. Kirkwood, from Prescott, Arizona, November 30, 1881, *ibid.*

[46]*Ibid.*

and have neglected the matter of clossing [sic] the government accounts."[47]

Gosper continued to submit the proper vouchers but by 1885 had net yet accounted for all of $7,622.75 with which he was charged at the time he left office in 1882. In a letter to the first comptroller he again requested a postponement of his case in United States court, stating that he was willing and able to settle without suit in order to save costs. In all fairness to Gosper, it should be explained that most of the apparent shortage consisted of payroll money for the extra twenty days of the 1881 session. Since U. S. Treasury money had not arrived, the Secretary issued to the lawmakers certificates that were cashed at a bank in Prescott at a small discount. The money was finally forwarded from Washington and the certificates redeemed. For some reason, however, the certificates were not credited to Gosper's account.[48] The Secretary was perhaps more guilty of careless bookkeeping than of dishonesty. But while the clouds of doubt and bickering hovered over his career, others sought the governorship which Frémont had neglected.

A leading candidate for the territory's top job seemed to be Thomas J. Butler who briefly introduced himself by letter to President Arthur in March, 1881: "I respectfully ask the nomination for the Governorship of Arizona Territory," he wrote, "based upon fitness for the office, fifteen years citizenship in the territory, my position and consistent Republicanism, my unimpeached and unimpeachable record for ten years in the office of Territorial Treasurer . . . . "[49]

Beach, who supported his candidacy, described him in a series of editorials in the *Arizona Daily Miner* as a Republican gentleman of culture and refinement, a scholar, and a man of great executive abilities who was familiar with Arizona's laws, indebtedness, and problems. Taking an indirect slap at Gosper, the editor said that Butler "is no chronic office seeker, is competent to make a living in or out of office, and above all things is an *honest* man."[50] In a letter to President Arthur in support of Butler, the *Miner* editor said that the territory had been long and shamefully neglected. While recognizing Frémont's capability to be a useful chief executive, Beach commented that he had failed to be one because he was constantly absent from the territory, but that the

---

[47]Letter of late-Secretary Gosper to First Comptroller William Lawrence, from Prescott, Arizona, September 27, 1883; and letter of Solicitor of the Treasury to Lawrence, October 30, 1883, Record Group 217, Territorial Letters Received, Vol. 17.

[48]Letter of John J. Gosper to First Comptroller M. J. Durham, from Prescott, Arizona, November 14, 1885, *ibid.*, Vol. 18.

[49]Letter of T. J. Butler to President Arthur, from Ebbitt House, Washington, D.C., March 11, 1882, Record Group 48, Appointment Papers.

[50]*Arizona Daily Miner*, November 2, 4, 10, 22, 1881.

Thomas J. Butler, treasurer of the Territory of Arizona and unsuccessful applicant for the position of governor.

— Sharlot Hall Museum

Acting Governor was an unprincipled, dishonest public servant.[51] The President was also asked to consider R. C. Powers, formerly governor of Mississippi and a two-year resident of Arizona, for the office of secretary.

While Beach refrained from severely degrading the incumbent Governor Frémont in this letter, only four days before he had written a scathing denunciation in the *Miner*. He wrote that Frémont

> was instrumental in getting the iniquitous lottery bill passed and sanctioned the omnibus divorce bill, which separated seventeen couples from the bonds of matrimony without the knowledge of many of the contracting parties, and the very Honorable John J. Gosper, who now fauningly asks a re-appointment or promotion, was one of those persons who took advantage of a noble wife, living in a distant country [Lincoln, Nebraska] and severed in an unlawful way his marital relations. . . . Arizona is entitled, we contend, to consideration at the hands of President Arthur, and in placing over this people a Governor that man should be without stain or blemish of character. We present the name of Hon. T. J. Butler as the man most fitting for the position of Governor.[52]

Advocates of other candidates pulled no punches in criticizing Governor Frémont. William Herring of Tombstone, who supported

[51]Letter of Charles W. Beach to President Arthur, from Prescott, Arizona, November 8, 1881, Record Group 48, Appointment Papers.

[52]*Arizona Daily Miner,* November 4, 1881.

Judge W. H. Stilwell for the gubernatorial position, wrote a stultifying letter to Postmaster General Thomas L. James on August 22, 1881, in which he requested a change. Saying that he expressed the unanimous sentiment in the territory, Herring not only mentioned Frémont's absenteeism but labeled him as "positively incompetent" to quell the disorders along the border south of Tombstone that threatened to lead to international difficulties.[53]

J. W. Moorhead, another Tombstone resident who was backing Col. James G. Howard — formerly of Los Angeles — to replace the incumbent, wrote a satirical letter which was printed in the *Los Angeles Herald*. He said that Howard would be

> a striking contrast to the present weak and inefficient Governor, John Charles Frémont, who has devoted the last twenty years of his life to proving himself to be a first class visionary. Since General Frémont has been appointed Governor of Arizona his actions have resembled those of a hen on a hot griddle. When he was first appointed he was so long in getting out to the territory that every one supposed that he was one of the lost sheep of little Bo-peep; but like those patient but errant quadrupeds of the nursery rhyme, he turned up, after a great while. Since then he has been popping from Arizona to New York and Washington, and from those cities back to Arizona, in a bewildering manner. It has never been safe to assume that Governor Frémont was in Arizona, and the public business, if the office is not a veritable sinecure, must have suffered greatly.[54]

The writer went on to say that Col. Howard would stay in the territory and stimulate the investment of capital

> in the most inviting mineral region of the American continent. The very fact that John Charles Frémont was prominent as the advocate of an investment proposition would damn it in all the centers of capital in the East. The Eastern capitalist remembers John Charles's magnificent Mariposa & Memphis & El Paso projects, and he has not forgotten what miserable fiascos they were. . . . Frémont has been a detriment rather than a help to Arizona. He has given an empirical and speculative air, by his personal advocacy, to projects which would probably prove to be the best paying propositions on the American continent.[55]

Finally presented with the alternative of returning to duty or stepping aside for another, Frémont submitted his resignation to the President on October 11, 1881:

---

[53]Letter of William Herring to Postmaster General Thomas L. James, from Tombstone, Arizona, August 22, 1881, Record Group 48, Appointment Papers.

[54]Letter of J. W. Moorhead to Attorney General Wayne McVeigh, from Tombstone, Arizona, May 24, 1881, *ibid.*

[55]*Ibid.*

New York, 61 Broadway
October 11, 1881

To the President of the United States
Mr. President

I have the honor to tender my resignation of the office of Governor of the Territory of Arizona, and request to have it take effect on the 1st of November, or earlier if the convenience of the government should require it.

My intended resignation has been for some time delayed for the reason that the recent Indian hostilities in Arizona might have made it seem inopportune. But as I have now done in Washington all that the limited power of the Governor enabled me accomplish, and as the Governor of the Territory has neither force nor money at his command nor authority nor voice in the settlement of Indian difficulties, my experience in Indian affairs could not be put to any practical use. Under the circumstances private interests alone remained to be considered and these required me to resign my commission.

I have the honor to be
Very respectfully
Your obedient Servant

J. C. Frémont
Governor of Arizona Territory[56]

Gosper continued functioning as governor without the title until Frederick Tritle was selected on March 8, 1882, to replace Frémont officially. Nearly all the other principal officeholders were also either removed or invited to send in their resignations. The position of secretary of the territory was given to H. M. Van Arman and that of surveyor general held by Wasson was bestowed upon General J. W. Robbins. Internal Revenue Collector Thomas Cordis was replaced by S. W. Fisher, U. S. Marshal C. P. Dake gave way to Z. L. Tidball, and District-Attorney E. B. Pomeroy was succeeded by Colonel James A. Zabriskie. Judges DeForest Porter and W. H. Stilwell lost their judicial districts to Judges Daniel Pinney and Wilson W. Hoover. With the exception of Zabriskie all the appointees were from outside the territory. This almost universal removal of faithful officers without cause resulted in widespread dissatisfaction among Republicans. Detecting a possible winning issue in the fall election, Democrats began protesting against the Republican administration in Washington that sent in strangers to fill offices and thus deprived the people of Arizona a share in the management of their own affairs.[57] The strategy paid off as enough Republican voters defected to permit Granville H. Oury, the Democrat candidate, to be re-elected as delegate to Congress in 1882.

---

[56]Letter of Governor John C. Frémont to the President, from New York City, October 11, 1881, *ibid.*

[57]*New York Daily Tribune,* October 27, 1882, p. 5.

Governor Frémont was not in Arizona at the time his tenure in office was terminated; but all of his luggage was shipped to New York, except for some instruments which were accidentally sent to California. It seems that in 1879 Frémont had asked Secretary of the Interior Schurz to use his influence to requisition a sextant, an artificial horizon, and an aneroid barometer from the Navy Department. Ostensibly, Frémont wanted these items to fix certain geographic points more accurately and thus to increase materially the value of his annual reports to the Interior Department. He later explained, however, that the instruments were for his personal use and for purposes not at all within the sphere of his duties as governor; and, for that reason, he had not turned them over to Governor Tritle, who was requested to return them to Washington nearly two years after his predecessor had vacated the office.[58]

Probably the most important matter occupying Acting Governor Gosper's attention during the interim before Tritle's appointment was the disorder along the border caused by the so-called "cowboys," a name applied to armed bands of desperadoes, cattle thieves, and highway robbers. In a letter to Secretary of the Interior Kirkwood that was transmitted to President Arthur, Gosper attempted to analyze the causes of the lawlessness.[59] He wrote that the people of Tombstone and Cochise County, in their "mad career after money, have greatly neglected local self-government until the more lazy and lawless elements of society have undertaken to prey upon the more industrious and honorable classes for their subsistence and gains." He explained further that the civil officers of Cochise County and Tombstone contributed to the public disturbances by winking at crime for the sake of personal gain. It was generally believed that officers of the law were often in league with the "cowboy" element and were paid well to leave the outlaws unmolested. Gosper considered the two rival newspapers censurable too, because they took sides in the strife between the Sheriff of Cochise and the Earp brothers of Tombstone, largely for selfish reasons; county printing was given to one for its support and city patronage to the other for its hearty endorsement.

Still another cause of the general lawlessness was a class of people

---

[58]Letter of Governor Frémont to Secretary of the Interior Schurz, from Prescott, Arizona, September 26, 1879; Governor Frederick Tritle to Secretary of the Interior H. M. Teller, from Prescott, Arizona, January 31, 1884; Secretary of War Robert Lincoln to Secretary Teller, February 17, 1884, Record Group 48, Territorial Papers, Letters Received.

[59]Letter of Acting Governor John J. Gosper to Secretary of the Interior Samuel J. Kirkwood, from Prescott, Arizona, November 29, 1881, in U. S. House, *Lawlessness in Parts of Arizona,* 47th Cong., 1st Sess., 1882, House Exec. Doc. No. 58, pp. 1-5.

described as the "Good-Lord and Good-Devil kind, who carry water on both shoulders and under the guise of respectability." While pretending to observe the laws, this class secretly handled the stolen property (mostly beef cattle) of the cowboys and openly sold it to honest citizens afterward. Also, the owners of hotels, saloons, and restaurants who raked in the money spent by the "cowboys" often sympathized with this lawless element. Gosper, like Governor Frémont, thought that "if the military could be legally put in pursuit of these bands of outlaws they would soon be broken up and compelled to follow the pursuit of peace or be brought to punishment."

In a second letter to Secretary Kirkwood, the Acting Governor recommended that the *posse comitatus* act be amended to permit the use of the military as part of a posse to assist the civil authorities in the territories to maintain order. He thought it somewhat ridiculous that the ten cavalry companies stationed near Tombstone should be forbidden by federal statute from helping to rout the territory's lawbreakers.[60] President Arthur apparently concurred in Gosper's suggestions and asked Congress on April 26, 1882 (after Tritle had assumed the governorship) to amend section 15 of the act of June 18, 1878, chapter 263, to allow the use of military forces to enforce territorial laws.[61] Informed by the Senate Judiciary Committee that no further legislation was needed and that the President had ample power to put down the lawlessness in Arizona, Arthur issued a proclamation on May 3, 1882.[62] In this proclamation, the President asserted his right to employ the land and naval forces to enforce the faithful execution of the laws of the United States in any state or territory. He admonished all Arizona residents who were obstructing justice, or aiding those who were, to disperse by May 15. Though, as we shall see, the effectiveness of this action was questionable, at least Gosper had succeeded in calling national attention to Arizona's breakdown in law and order.[63]

General Frémont lived at Tarrytown-on-the-Hudson in New York during his final years. He hoped to wind up his affairs and spend the balance of his life in California. But at the age of seventy-seven he had an attack of ptomaine poisoning and died five days later on July 13, 1890. These last years of his life were a struggle to keep solvent. Whereas his former partner, Judge Charles Silent, grew wealthy from the

---

[60]Letter of Acting Governor Gosper to Secretary of the Interior Kirkwood, from Prescott, Arizona, December 19, 1881, *ibid.*, p. 2.

[61]*Lawlessness in Arizona*, 47th Cong., 1st Sess., 1882, House Exec. Doc. No. 188, pp. 1-3.

[62]*New York Times*, May 2, 3, 1882.

[63]*Arizona Daily Star*, May 3, 5, 1882.

Verde copper mines and other mineral enterprises, Dame Fortune seemed always to elude "the Pathfinder." He was buried, not in the uniform of his rank, but in ordinary civilian clothes and without military display. His wife declared him "grandly unselfish, it was a life to honor." The rather small part the Arizona venture filled in his life is perhaps best illustrated by his epitaph. Of the fifty lines chiseled on the monument marking his grave at Piermont Cemetery, Rockland, New York, one sums up his Arizona experience: "Governor of Arizona Territory 1878 to 1882."[64]

---

[64]George A. Zabriskie, *The Pathfinder* (Ormund Beach, Florida: The Doldrums, Publishers, 1947), p. 21.

Chapter 9

Cowboys, Indians, and the Thieving Thirteenth:
The Tritle Administration

Frederick A. Tritle, the sixth territorial governor, was the first to make Arizona his permanent home and to become thoroughly conversant with the interests of this frontier region. A transplanted Pennsylvanian, he practiced law in Iowa before moving to California in 1859 and on to Nevada the following year. As a Virginia City stockbroker, he was soon well known in business and mining circles and became involved in Nevada politics. He served in the upper house of the state legislature but was unsuccessful in his candidacy for the governorship of the Sagebrush State. His political fences were well mended, however, and in 1882 his old friend, Senator John P. Jones, secured his appointment as governor of the Territory of Arizona from President Chester A. Arthur.

Tritle had been in Arizona since 1880 and was already an ardent booster for the territory at the time of his selection. He welcomed his new office as a forum from which he could better tell the world about Arizona's mineral resources. Possessing both a boundless zeal for the future of his adopted land and practical acumen as a mining man, he worked to secure capital to develop the mines. His enthusiasm is well illustrated by an incident which occurred at a Boston banquet which he attended while on an eastern trip. The first toast of the evening was, "The Governor of the Oldest Commonwealth to the Youngest." Everyone knew that the speaker was referring to Massachusetts as the "oldest" and Governor Bullock of that state stood up to respond. But before the easterner could adjust his spectacles, Tritle rose and graciously thanked the startled Bostonians for the honor given Arizona in calling upon him, as the representative of the oldest commonwealth, to welcome the Governor of the young state of Massachusetts. And then he explained that Arizona had a civilization and a degree of government long before the first Indians roamed through the forests of New England.

The twin problems of law-breaking "cowboys" and hostile "Indians" must have given Tritle some doubt about the state of that civilization, however. Nearly everyone — editors, Army officers, the President, Congress, the people, and Governor Tritle — had some idea for remedying the chaotic situation in which Arizona found itself when Tritle assumed his duties. He favored the organization of a local ranger group, similar to the Texas Rangers, to curb violence in the territory. But neither Congress nor the Arizona legislature seemed willing to support his plan with appropriations. And since President Arthur's proclamation was really toothless and downright resented by people in Tombstone and elsewhere in the territory, the citizens were left to their own resources until the Army was directed to quell the Indians once and for all. Small groups of militia were formed in Tombstone, Tucson, Globe and other towns to combat either the Indians or the outlaws.

Shortly after Tritle took office, some hostile Apache Indians murdered several citizens in Pima County and fled to Chihuahua. After Sheriff R. H. Paul of that county asked for assistance, on May 1, 1882, to execute a warrant of arrest for the Indians, Governor Tritle designated a group of deputies, which were organized by the Pima County Board of Supervisors, as the First Regiment of the Militia of the Territory of Arizona under the command of Captain William J. Ross of Tucson. These "Tucson Volunteers," about fifty in number and with proper warrants issued by the authorities of Pima County, entered the Mexican state of Sonora en route to Chihuahua. But on June 5, 1882, Ross and his followers were arrested by General Bernardo Reyes of Sonora, and their arms taken from them. Reyes gave the captain a receipt for forty-eight rifles and five carbines, Springfield pattern, and ordered him to return unarmed to Arizona with his command. Embarrassed, if not humiliated, by the incident, Governor Tritle exercised his authority as commander-in-chief of the militia and negotiated through Secretary of State Frelinghuysen for the return of the arms to William C. Davis, Chairman of the Pima County Board of Supervisors.[1]

No one knew better than Tritle how helpless the territory was to enforce law and to keep the Indians at peace. About the time that the Tucson militia was being organized, he reported to Secretary of the Interior Teller on the Indian and "cowboy" situation in Arizona. Already he had asked Congress, through President Arthur, for an appropriation of $150,000 to be used for a force of rangers in the field to prevent cattle stealing, smuggling, and to overtake and punish roving bands of

---

[1]Letter of Governor F. A. Tritle to Secretary of State F. T. Frelinghuysen, from Prescott, Arizona, June 30, 1882. Disturbances Along the Mexican Border, Record Group 48, Territorial Papers, Arizona.

Frederick A. Tritle, governor of Arizona Territory from 1882 to 1885.

— Arizona Department of Library and Archives

Indians.[2] The Governor wrote that the territory did not have enough money for office rent and clerk hire, let alone to arm any militia, and that the U. S. Army, even if used as a posse, would move entirely too slowly to be of service. The rangers, he thought, would give the citizens security and make the settlement of the territory possible.

Tritle also advised the Interior Secretary that the government's Indian policy must be changed. He wrote that the San Carlos Reservation was a sort of "West Point" where the Apaches were being educated more in the science of war than in the science of peace. They were fed, clothed, and drilled. Then, at regular intervals, they left the reservation with guns and ammunition, murdering numbers of citizens before the military could overtake them.

To rectify this situation, Governor Tritle suggested that the Indians be disarmed, that a strong military force be placed around more plainly marked boundaries, that the policy of not issuing passes be continued, and that all Indians found outside the boundaries be killed as hostiles. "If these do not prevail," he said,

> removal from the territory must be insisted upon. The people are becoming so exasperated that I am convinced that unless some satisfactory disposition be made of the question, as well as of the Indian,

---

[2]Letter of Governor Tritle to President Chester A. Arthur, from Tombstone, Arizona, March 31, 1882, U. S. House, *Lawlessness in Arizona,* 47th Cong., 1st Sess., 1882, House Exec. Doc. No. 188, p. 2.

that a secret force will be organized to kill them upon the reservation. Such a course is now countenanced by prominent citizens and I should be powerless to prevent it. From such data as I have I am convinced that 120 to 150 persons have been killed in the last raid in Arizona, New Mexico, and Sonora. The prosperity of the Territory greatly injured, and the possibility of immediate return of the Indian from Mexico will prevent all work in exposed parts of the Territory. The prompt action of the Government in increasing our military force has awakened a sense of gratitude by the taking away, or if not that, disarming of the indian [sic] would be a much greater cause of rejoicing.[3]

Stories of Indian atrocities were being printed frequently in the newspapers of the territory. The "Clifton tragedy" of April, 1882, illustrates the danger involved in trying to develop a mine or ranch near the Apache reservation. The *Arizona Daily Star* (April 25, 1882) printed a report from Ft. Thomas on the incident:

The Indians attacked a party near Gold Gulch, about two miles and a half from the Longfellow mine on the 21st, killing S. D. Packard, Jno. P. Risque, Capt. Jno. Slosson & S. H. L. Trescott. They then attacked an ox train of O. K. Smyth, of Shakespeare, near Church's camp about a mile and a half from Clifton, and killed five teamsters and took away about one hundred mules. Last Saturday morning they attacked some ox teams near Wall's ranch and killed about twelve men.[4]

Tritle was on leave of absence from the territory during most of June and July, 1882, but after his return he again showed concern because of the Indian problem. He reported that at least five more citizens had been killed by bands from San Carlos. A feeling of insecurity existed among people living near the reservation and work had been abandoned on some mining properties near Clifton because no teams were available to transport the ore and supplies.[5]

The "cowboy" lawlessness, especially in Cochise County, worried Tritle as much as the Indian raids. In his letter to President Arthur, which he wrote from Tombstone while investigating the breakdown of law and order in that part of the territory, he suggested that the conditions called for strong remedies. He said the people were so intimidated and had lost so much confidence in government and local law officers that few would express an opinion adverse to the depredations of the criminal element. In addition to recommending the volunteer militia,

---

[3]Letter of Governor Tritle to Secretary of the Interior H. M. Teller, from Tucson, Arizona, May 4, 1882, and May 13, 1885, Record Group 48, Territorial Papers.

[4]*Arizona Daily Star,* April 25, 27, 1882.

[5]Letter of Governor Tritle to Secretary of the Interior Teller, from Prescott, Arizona, August 10, 1882, Record Group 48, Territorial Papers.

mentioned above, to aid the sheriff and marshals in preventing stage robberies, smuggling from Mexico, cattle stealing, and similar acts of lawlessness, Governor Tritle asked for other relief. He wanted specific authorization from Congress to summarily remove from office any county officer that he found to be corrupt, inefficient, and incompetent. Territorial statute prevented him from doing this.[6]

Editor L. C. Hughes of the *Arizona Daily Star* concurred in Governor Tritle's plan for putting a force of rangers into the field to suppress lawlessness. In a number of editorials on the situation in Cochise County he said that ruffianism had usurped peace and order and that the pistol and shotgun gave it law. "The officials of Cochise County with all the available strength which they can muster," he wrote on March 30, 1882,

> seem to avail nothing in putting down the blood thirsty class infesting that county. Ex-city [Earps] and United States officials have taken to the hills as so many Apaches. A lot of loose, marauding thieves are scouring the country killing good, industrious citizens for plunder. The officials are out in every direction, but nothing is accomplished. The killing of Peel, Schildy, and another party yesterday, near Contention, by unknown parties; the outlawry of the Earps, and the sanguinary conflict between Sheriff Breckenridge and posse with two thieves, and the lamentable result, is causing the people to understand the frightful condition of affairs. It is the re-enacting of the scenes of New Mexico and southwestern Texas of two years ago, and we can see no more speedy, certain and effective remedy than the organization of a body of rangers with the authority to settle the whole business, with the least possible expense to the Territory.[7]

Like the editors, the military leaders were also concerned about the condition in Arizona. General William Tecumseh Sherman, of Civil War fame, visited the southern and eastern tier of counties in Arizona.[8] He was surprised at the lawless and disorderly state of society. The civil officers did not have sufficient forces to make arrests, to hold prisoners for trial, or punish them when convicted. Like former Secretary Gosper, he thought that soldiers could be effectively used if the federal statute which forbade their use as a *posse comitatus* were repealed. If Congress did not promptly rescind that law, however, he favored Governor Tritle's volunteer militia plan. The General wrote to Attorney General B. H. Brewster and asked for "careful study and lively interest" in the possible legal alternatives that might be invoked to curb the nefarious activities

---

[6]Letter of Governor Tritle to President Arthur, from Tombstone, Arizona, April 26, 1882, U. S. House, *Lawlessness in Arizona,* 47th Cong., 1st Sess., 1882, House Exec. Doc. No. 188, p. 2.

[7]*Arizona Daily Star,* March 30, April 18, 1882.

[8]*Ibid.,* April 11, 1882.

of the robbers and thieves who made use of the international boundary to escape pursuit.[9]

A few weeks after receiving the recommendations of Governor Tritle and General Sherman, President Arthur asked Congress to repeal the statute which forbade the use of the Army as a *posse comitatus*. After being informed by a Senate committee that he already had authority to quell the Arizona insurrections, Arthur issued his controversial proclamation of May 3, 1882. Bluntly threatening to use the military forces if the lawbreakers in Arizona did not disperse, the President said in part,

> Whereas it has been made to appear satisfactory to me by information received from the Governor of the Territory of Arizona, and from the General of the Army of the United States, and other reliable sources, that in consequence of the unlawful combinations of evil disposed persons, who are banded together to oppose and obstruct the execution of the laws of the United States within that territory and that the laws of the United States have been therein forcibly opposed and execution thereof forcibly resisted; and whereas, the laws of the United States require, whenever it may be necessary in the judgment of the President to use the military forces for the purpose of enforcing a faithful execution of the laws of the United States, he shall forthwith by proclamation, command such insurgents to disperse and retire peaceably to their respective abodes within a limited time. . . . [10]

The new editor of the *Tombstone Epitaph,* Samuel Purdy, was vitriolic in opposition to the President's proclamation but was obviously off base when he wrote that Arizona was one of the most powerful sections of the country and all it wanted was to be left alone. So hastily did Purdy rush to Cochise County's defense, he forgot that the *Epitaph* had reported four holdups and robberies, five shootings, and eight killings in its columns within the previous three months. He described the proclamation as

> nothing more or less than a vicious advertisement operating against the value of our resources and the interests of our people. The latter should join in an indignant protest addressed to the President and Governor, denying the premises alleged in the proclamation, and stating that all we ask is to be let alone. Why Governor Tritle, who, it is alleged, is speculating in Arizona mines, should so act as to deter the investment of capital in the territory, is difficult to determine. Very likely he did not stop to consider the probable effects of his action.[11]

---

[9]Telegram of General W. T. Sherman to Attorney General B. H. Brewster, from Tucson, Arizona, April 11, 1882, U. S. House, *Lawlessness in Arizona,* 47th Cong., 1st Sess., 1882, House Exec. Doc. No. 188, p. 3.

[10]*Ibid.,* pp. 1-3.

[11]*Tombstone Epitaph,* May 2, 1882.

Other editors also objected to the proclamation but generally for different reasons — because they believed in local autonomy in quelling the lawlessness or because the proclamation in itself was useless. Whatever the truth, however, the "cowboy" problem gradually subsided, and the Army did not have to intervene. The demise of some of the "cowboy" leaders in the famous battle of the O K Corral in Tombstone and the departure of the Earps from the territory in March, 1882, had probably expedited a return to law and order, even before the proclamation was issued.[12]

While Tritle was out of the territory during the summer, a stand of one hundred arms arrived at Prescott. It was customary for a state or territory to pay the freight on such issues furnished by the federal government. However, Acting Governor H. M. Van Arman, the territorial secretary, had no funds for this purpose.[13] After telegraphing the War Department and getting no help, he was able to locate the necessary money. In notifying the Treasury Department of this, he briefly touched upon the problem of finances in the Territory of Arizona: "Thanks for telegram," he said, "I have found a way out of the difficulty and will get the guns. The territory is quite poor in purse although rich in mineral wealth. All the citizens have a holy horror of being assessed, or paying taxes. . . . "[14]

Financial and accounting problems plagued Van Arman during his entire tenure as secretary. When he assumed his duties, on April 17, 1882, he had no funds even to pay postage.[15] He secured a draft for $550, the balance of the 1881-82 appropriations for that office, which he had discounted locally as ex-Secretary Gosper told him was the custom. Van Arman said that he had to commence his official duties as if he were the very first secretary of the territory. Gosper's records and vouchers for expenditures were either missing or not in proper shape. There was nothing to guide him except some general instructions from the Treasury Department. He found his office located in a schoolhouse on a hilltop remote from the business portion of the town. The school directors wanted him to vacate the premises, which he did on the first of June. There was no insurance at all when Van Arman took over but

---

[12]Douglas D. Martin, *Tombstone's Epitaph* (Albuquerque: University of New Mexico Press, 1951), p. 173.

[13]Letter of Acting Secretary of War William E. Chandler to Acting First Comptroller of the Treasury J. Tarbell, Washington, D. C., July 22, 1882, Record Group 217, Territorial Letters Received, Vol. 16.

[14]Letter of Secretary H. M. Van Arman to First Comptroller William Lawrence, from Prescott, Arizona, July 25, 1882, *ibid.*

[15]Letter of Secretary Van Arman to First Comptroller Lawrence, from Prescott, Arizona, May 29, 1882, *ibid.*

As Prescott continued to grow, many of the original flimsy structures were replaced by substantial buildings. This picture was taken in the early 1880s.

he took out a $2000 policy on the supplies and furniture, which he purchased for the legislature. The insurance cost $18, but he thought it a good bargain since the Assembly met in a frame building; he considered the Prescott fire extinguishing service entirely worthless, even though Prescott was a wooden town and needed the best possible protection. There was no safe, either, in which to store the archival records and the articles of incorporation which companies filed with the Secretary's office. Van Arman located a good double-door safe for $450 but again had some difficulty finding the funds to purchase it.

The allocation of printing was another financial problem that frustrated Van Arman as it did most of the territory's secretaries. The strongly partisan Van Arman insisted upon controlling the bill-printing patronage for the benefit of his Republican Party. He wrote to the first comptroller, also a Republican appointee, that he would not give a dollar's worth of bill printing to any but Republican papers unless instructed to do so. "I do not wish to aid in sustaining party papers, which lampoon not only the Republican party generally, but all Federal officials indiscriminately and personally," he wrote. "In this stand I hope that I shall have your support and do not compel me to aid Democrat newspapers. The House is Democratic and the Council is Republican. The House seems afraid that the Democratic Editor won't get enough printing and try to coerce me. I will not be thus coerced. I see no need of a Democratic party except to irritate good men. Every member of that party in this territory has a rebel record or else is a foreigner. Of either class I am not an enthusiastic admirer, and was too long in the Union army to be afraid of them."[16] This was strong language! Except for a federal law requiring the Secretary to award contracts to the lowest bidder for the printing of session laws and journals, the Democratic newspapers in the territory would not have been given much consideration. As it turned out, however, the contract for printing the session laws of the Twelfth Assembly went to a firm in San Francisco and the printing of the journals was awarded to the State Journal Publishing Company of Lincoln, Nebraska, without regard to politics. Van Arman's only exasperation was due to the Nebraska firm's failure to follow his instructions, not to the party affiliation of the printers. He had asked that all but twenty-five copies of the journal be bound in an economical paper cover at ten cents per binding. Instead the company bound all 250 copies in half-sheep at forty cents each. "How such a blunder could have been made is beyond my comprehension," he said,

> unless it be that I wanted the composition to be set as solid as possible and as a specimen, sent to the printer a copy of the Vermont Senate Journal which I found in the Library here in which the type were set solidly and compactly, but this book was half bound and possibly they inferred that they must copy exactly from the model as the Chinese in making a pair of pants for the captain of a China steamer, did, with his old pair for a pattern, and to keep the new ones exact, put a big patch on the seat to look like a corresponding patch on the old ones.[17]

The journals contained the first message of Governor Tritle to the legislature. In this opening address to the Twelfth Legislative Assembly in January, 1883, Governor Tritle showed that he had carefully studied the problems of struggling Arizona.[18] Sincerely concerned with the future of the territory, he stressed the importance of its natural resources. Having been personally involved in mining, particularly at the Comstock Lode in Nevada and then at Jerome in Arizona, his first interest was naturally in the mining industry. However, he urged the development of other resources too. He was the first governor to recognize the value of timber in the territory's economy and asked the legislature to regulate the exploitation of the forest reserves. Like previous governors, he suggested that a Congressional appropriation be sought for the construction of artesian wells. He advised also that a survey be made of mineral

---

[16]Letter of Secretary Van Arman to First Comptroller Lawrence, from Prescott, Arizona, January 18, 1883, *ibid.*

[17]Letter of Secretary Van Arman to First Comptroller Lawrence, from Prescott, Arizona, May 23, 1883, *ibid.*

[18]"Messages of Governor Frederick Tritle," in *Journals of the Twelfth Legislative Assembly,* 1883, pp. 26-47.

springs to determine if any of the waters might be of benefit to certain ailments.

Looking to the future happiness and enjoyment of the people, the Governor recommended that ample provision be made for stocking streams and lakes with fish most suited to each locality. And finally, he encouraged the legislators to enthusiastically advertise the territory's assets to all classes of people who might like to make Arizona their home. In this latter connection, he emphasized the advantages already resulting from the new railroads — the reduced cost of transportation, the settlement of lands, and easy access into and out of the territory for people as well as commerce. The Atlantic and Pacific was soon to cross northern Arizona, and the Southern Pacific, of course, was completed across the southern part. To encourage trade over the rails that linked the S.P. with Sonora, Tritle urged that Congress be memorialized to negotiate a reciprocity treaty with Mexico whereby merchandise could be exchanged without payment of tariff duties.

Another matter to which Governor Tritle called the attention of the legislature was the unrestrained lawlessness existing in Cochise and neighboring counties.[19] Prior to his administration, scores of outlaws had been either driven to the Tombstone area from the states or been attracted by reports of amazing mineral discoveries upon which they could prey. As evidence of public sentiment in regard to the prevailing crime wave, he quoted several leading newspapers. One of them, the *Tombstone Epitaph* (April 4, 1882), gave this summary: "The recent feuds in Cochise County make it incumbent upon, not only officials, but all good citizens as well, to take such positive measures as will speedily rid this section of that murderous, thieving element which has made us a reproach before the world, and so seriously retarded the industry and progress of our country."[20]

Tritle reported that, after consultation with many citizens, he had requested federal funds to place a force of mounted police or rangers in the field to pursue and arrest criminals. He said that Congress had failed to act, however, and the public-spirited people of Tombstone took matters into their own hands, contributing over $5,000 to maintain a small armed force under Deputy U. S. Marshal John H. Jackson.

Because of this activity and a Presidential proclamation requesting the outlaws to desist, Tritle believed that law and order had been largely restored in Arizona. He urged the legislature to reimburse the Tombstone citizens and to pass a resolution expressing gratitude to President

[19]*Ibid.*, pp. 123-26.
[20]*Tombstone Epitaph,* April 4, 1882.

Arthur. By the time he addressed the next legislature, in 1885, he was to be more preoccupied with Mormon polygamy than with highwaymen, stage robbers, or cattle thieves.

The Twelfth Legislative Assembly took Tritle's advice and commended the President for his assistance in suppressing banditry, but followed few of the other recommendations. Many of the hundred-plus laws, resolutions, and memorials that were passed concerned the various counties and towns. The counties of Maricopa and Graham, for example, were each authorized to build a courthouse and a jail. The former was permitted to purchase ten acres of land for a county hospital and the seat of Graham was moved from Safford to Solomonville, where it remained until switched back by a vote of the people in 1915. Other acts incorporated Prescott and provided punishment for persons carrying deadly weapons in any of the towns or villages of Apache or Graham counties.

To encourage agriculture, the legislature authorized the Governor to pay $500 to any person who, in the year 1883, raised the greatest yield of cotton on any five acres, provided that the yield was in excess of 200 pounds per acre.[21] In his message two years later, Tritle reported that the money had been awarded to Felix G. Hardwick of Tempe, who produced 3,390 pounds on five acres of land. He also announced that a reward of $3,000 was granted to C. L. Whitney of Pinal County for sinking an artesian well.[22]

Arizona's progress up to 1884 was publicized to easterners by an exhibit at the World's Industrial and Cotton Centennial Exposition in New Orleans in that year.[23] The importance of the mining industry was emphasized by a display of 50,000 specimens of minerals including a piece of copper ore, from the vicinity of Bisbee, weighing 7,300 pounds and containing 33 percent copper. A *New York Tribune* correspondent at the exposition reported that Arizona's copper yield had increased between 1880 and 1884 to twenty-five million pounds. The same writer noted that Arizona's climate made year-round work in the mines and fields possible. He called the attention of his newspaper's readers to a canal being constructed in the Salt River Valley that would irrigate 100,000 acres. Improved land selling for $15 to $25 per acre was said

---

[21]*Laws, Resolutions and Memorials,* Twelfth Legislative Assembly, p. 149.

[22]"Message of Governor Frederick Tritle," in *Journals of the Thirteenth Legislative Assembly,* 1885, pp. 131 and 175.

[23]*Journals of the Thirteenth Legislative Assembly,* pp. 145-47; see also, *Weekly Arizona Miner,* February 13, 1885.

to be worth as much as productive lands in southern California that brought $100 an acre.[24]

Not only did the reporters at the exposition focus attention on the rapid economic progress being made in a territory that was comparatively unknown to most eastern people, but they also printed stories on the needs of Arizona. The lack of enough railroads, and the high rates of transportation, were temporary problems that could be partly overcome by the proposed construction of two north-south railroads. Territorial representatives in New Orleans took advantage of an opportunity to complain that Congress was failing to meet its responsibilities to the territory. Though the delay in clarifying whether certain lands could be settled and exploited was caused by legal problems involved in grants of vast tracts to the Atlantic and Pacific and the Texas and Pacific railroads, and by Mexican land-grant claims — some of which were fraudulent — the would-be settlers were naturally impatient. The federal government was also blamed for not stopping the cattle stealing on the border.

In brief, a lot of wrong impressions about Arizona were corrected by the New Orleans exhibit. It lasted two years and was still open to visitors when the thirteenth legislature convened in Prescott in January, 1885. There was no lack of topics for conversation as the lawmakers got acquainted and prepared for an exciting session. Nearly everyone in the territory was discussing the Mormon question that had been dramatized by polygamy trials a few months before. During the previous summer, in 1884, about two thousand Mormons arrived in the territory to settle. Altogether, there were probably five thousand who had quietly started towns and villages in the territory.

Opponents of the church believed that the Mormon leaders were craftily attempting to control politics in all the western territories and states. The L.D.S. Church had been sending out colonies of its members from Utah for several years. In Idaho a majority of the legislature was Mormon, and in Wyoming the church had enough political strength to affect the choice of a delegate to Congress. Not wishing the same policy to succeed in Arizona, many people began persecuting the new migrants. Within a few days after their arrival five of the Mormons were arrested, tried, convicted of polygamy, and sentenced at Prescott. Three of the

---

[24]*New York Daily Tribune,* December 29, 1884; see also, *Arizona at the World's Industrial and Cotton Centennial Exposition, New Orleans, 1884–85* (Chicago: Poole Brothers Printers, 1885), a souvenir of the Atlantic and Pacific Railroad. 67 pp.

defendants, one of them a bishop, were heavily fined and sentenced to the penitentiary for three and a half years. The remaining two, who were elders, pleaded guilty, and escaped with a fine of $500 and imprisonment for six months. One of the men who suffered the heavier punishment left two wives and twelve children in great poverty, but, according to his story, would have pleaded guilty if the church leaders at Salt Lake City had not forbidden him to do so under threat of excommunication. Defending the Arizona treatment of the Mormons, the *New York Times* editorialized:

> This is a good beginning. . . . In no other way can the growth of polygamy in Arizona be checked. It may not be possible to exclude from the Territory those who believe that polygamy is sanctioned and required by Divine revelation, but a vigorous enforcement of the new law now, before the Mormon immigrants have become a powerful factor in political contests, will probably prevent them from practicing polygamy in the Territory. The successful treatment of the matter in Arizona should lead the authorities of Idaho, Wyoming, Nevada, and Colorado to bring their polygamists before the courts without delay.[25]

Another topic of discussion in the opening days of the thirteenth session was the long trip taken by legislators from the southern counties by way of California. They had been warned that the flooding Gila and Salt rivers could not be crossed safely and therefore took the round-about train route in order to reach Prescott in time for the opening session. After hearing a report from a joint committee on mileage, the thirteenth legislature tried to "bulldoze" the reluctant Secretary, H. M. Van Arman, into paying about $4,000 more in travel allowances than he thought they were entitled to. The biggest requests were from five members from Pima County who claimed $330 each, or fifteen cents per mile for 2,200 miles of travel to and from Prescott.[26] From Maricopa they had taken a Southern Pacific train west and then returned on the Atlantic and Pacific (Santa Fe) via Needles to Ash Fork and thence by stage to the capital.

The testimony given by one of the Pima representatives, E. W. Risley, who journeyed from fifty miles beyond Tucson via Los Angeles, is illustrative of the dilemma that faced the Secretary who had to secure U. S. Treasury funds to pay the bills.[27] Risley swore that he had

---

[25]"Colonies of Polygamists," an editorial in the *New York Times,* December 7, 1884.

[26]Report of Joint Committee on Mileage, attached to letter of Secretary H. M. Van Arman to First Comptroller William Lawrence, from Prescott, Arizona, January 26, 1885, Record Group 217, Territorial Letters Received, Vol. 18.

[27]Affidavit of E. W. Risley, January 22, 1885, attached to letter of Secretary H. M. Van Arman to First Comptroller William Lawrence, from Prescott, Arizona, January 26, 1885, *ibid.*

intended taking the stage north of Maricopa via Phoenix to Prescott. But he was informed in Tucson by U. S. Marshal Zan L. Tidball and Associate Justice W. F. Fitzgerald, both of whom were preparing to leave for Prescott to attend the Supreme Court, that the road via Maricopa was totally impassable. Tidball had heard via telegram that the Salt River was four miles wide and ten feet deep, and that the ferries were out of repair and unable to cross. Judge Fitzgerald had decided to take the roundabout way via railroad even though he had to pay the fare out of his own pocket since he was not allowed mileage. Having heard this news, Risley and his colleagues also decided against taking a chance on getting through on the stage. The affidavit of J. S. Armstrong, a member from Maricopa County, seemed to substantiate the wisdom of their decision. He testified that in crossing a portion of the river he was submerged and would have drowned except for the swimming ability of his horse.

After writing to the first comptroller of the Treasury in Washington for instructions, Van Arman settled with most of the legislators on the basis of his estimates of accurate distances, allowing for all necessary detours on account of swollen streams and impassable roads.[28] But the Secretary was particularly irked by the claim of F. K. Ainsworth, President of the Council who represented the Northern District of five counties as a float councilman. Ainsworth lived in Prescott but insisted that he had a right to mileage from any county he selected and filed a claim for 1,700 miles, or $255.[29] One can sympathize with Van Arman because Congress only granted him $25,690 to pay all legislative salaries and expenses.[30]

The dispute over mileage claims was not the only problem that confronted the Thirteenth Assembly. Both branches were evenly divided politically. Though the legislature convened on January 12, a permanent organization was not achieved until January 19 in the House and two days later in the Council. After writing for instructions, Secretary Van Arman once again assumed his role as "watchdog of the treasury" and paid the members their four dollars per diem only from the dates when they were sworn in — a total of $208 for those in the Council.[31] By the closing days of the session, however, the lawmakers had more than

---

[28]Telegram of Secretary Van Arman to First Comptroller Lawrence, from Whipple Barracks, February 12, 1885; and letter of Van Arman to Lawrence, from Prescott, Arizona, March 4, 1885, *ibid.*

[29]Letter of Van Arman to Lawrence, from Prescott, Arizona, January 26, 1885, *ibid.*

[30]*U. S. Statutes at Large,* Vol. XXIII, 48th Cong., 1st Sess., 1884, Chap. 331, p. 177.

[31]Letter of Van Arman to Lawrence, March 4, 1885, Record Group 217.

evened the score. Van Arman wrote that he outfitted a new hall for the legislature and spent more money for stationery and other items to supply the extravagant body than he had anticipated.

After the Assembly completed its organization, Governor Tritle delivered his address to its members. The Governor emphasized his interest in agriculture and recommended that Congress be asked to provide for a geological survey of the territory to locate probable sources of water supply. In his words: "The determination of suitable localities and the possibility of storing water in reservoirs in different parts of this territory, whereby large tracts of land, now non-productive, may be reclaimed, would, in my judgment, be of the utmost value to our industrial interest."[32] The Governor indicated that evidence of some progress was shown in the exhibits at the first territorial fair, held in November, 1884.

Among other noteworthy topics to which Tritle called the attention of the Thirteenth Legislative Assembly was his proposal that Congress be asked to purchase from Mexico land to provide an outlet to the Pacific Ocean for Arizona; this suggestion was to be mentioned often in future years though nothing ever became of it. In asking for a more stable and permanent militia, Tritle told the legislature that, to stimulate interest, he was personally offering $50 to the best company in a competitive drill to take place at Prescott on February 22, 1885.[33] The Governor also requested the lawmakers to enact legislation to protect the territory's stock from the Texas cattle fever which was then prevalent in the Lone Star State. His recommendation that a site be selected and a university established appealed to the solons, because here was an opportunity for some alert politician to grab off a political plum for his constituents. Formerly, many towns had depended on a nearby fort and military spending for economic health. But now that the Apaches were almost subjugated, businessmen dreamed of a branch railroad or a money-spending territorial institution to keep the profits rolling in. By 1885 the commercial war for new sources of revenue was on and the legislative chambers in Prescott were the battleground. At the time, the two big prizes were considered to be the capital and the insane asylum. A university and a teachers' college were rated as spoils of secondary importance. A favorite quip was, "Who ever heard of a professor buying a drink?"

Though variously known as the "Bloody Thirteenth" or the "Thieving

---

[32]"Message of Governor Frederick Tritle," in *Journals of the Thirteenth Legislative Assembly*, 1885, p. 135.
[33]*Ibid.*, pp. 155-57.

Thirteenth" because of its extravagant expenditures, this legislature inaugurated and parceled out several institutions that are still a credit to Arizona. When the shouting was over and the smoke-filled rooms were aired out, the capital was still at Prescott and the prison at Yuma. Phoenix captured the coveted insane asylum with an appropriation of $100,000, though critics argued that it would have been cheaper to continue sending patients to Stockton, California, where a charge of six dollars per week each was made for their care. Tempe was given the teachers' college and an appropriation of $5,000. Tucson had to be content with the university and a $25,000 grant, or one-fourth of the amount provided for the asylum. Other spoils were also voted to placate different sections of the territory. Yuma was promised a new levee along the Colorado, and Florence received a $12,000 bridge over the Gila. The latter project turned out to be a complete waste of money since the then-water-filled river went on one of its famous rampages and cut a new channel, leaving the bridge "high and dry" in the desert.[34]

Though receiving one of the smallest appropriations, the people of Tempe seemed pleased with the Arizona Territorial Normal School. As a matter of fact, the town's leading businessman, the educationally minded Charles Trumbull Hayden, regarded a teachers' college as more important than a university in frontier Arizona. Like ex-Governor Safford, he felt that there was an urgent need to train teachers for the public schools. Politically alert, Hayden selected one of his employees, a young Southern newspaperman named John S. Armstrong who had originally come to Arizona from Virginia and Washington, D.C., to teach the Pima Indians, to run for the legislature.[35] Cleverly pledging to seek both an asylum and a university for Maricopa County, Armstrong was the top vote-getter and the only Democrat elected from what was then a predominantly Republican county.

In Prescott he skillfully used his influence as Chairman of the House Committee on Education to win a 16-to-7 vote in the House and a 10-to-2 triumph in the Council for the establishment of the normal school at Tempe. Earlier in the session, he had taken the dusty, two-day stage trip from the capital to Tempe to inform Hayden that there was a chance to get the insane asylum. But the elder Hayden, according to his son, the long-time U. S. Senator Carl Hayden, sent Armstrong hurrying back to the capital with emphatic instructions to bring home the normal school. He supposedly told the young legis-

---

[34]*Laws of the Territory of Arizona,* Thirteenth Legislative Assembly, pp. 270-72.

[35]*Arizona Gazette,* September 3, 1884.

Professor H. B. Farmer (seated, center) and students of the first class at Tempe Normal — now Arizona State University. The school opened on February 8, 1886, with thirty-three students.

lator that "Stockton, California, was known to most people only as the place where insane people are confined." Phoenix might want to risk that reputation, but not Tempe.

Armstrong's Prescott mission was accomplished, but Tempe had only sixty days under the law to secure a school site of twenty acres. Fortunately, George and Martha Wilson sold their twenty-acre cattle pasture for a meager $500, a personal sacrifice since they were people of modest means who depended on the land to maintain their butcher shop. Wilson continued to graze the land for awhile, however, and then was employed as caretaker for the buildings and grounds, a position he held twenty-five years until his death in 1916. Today the George W. Wilson Hall on the Arizona State University campus stands as a memorial to the man whose sacrifice enabled a modern educational institution to begin.[36]

Tucson was slower to appreciate its share of the spoils, the university. The people of the Southern District, which was then one of the political units for electing Council members, had elected an able lawyer, C. C. Stephens, to the upper house, in high hopes of getting the capital back from Prescott. But the entire Pima delegation was delayed in reaching Prescott. According to Stephens, "We were obliged

[36]Ernest J. Hopkins and Alfred Thomas, Jr., *The Arizona State University Story* (Phoenix: Southwest Publishing Co., 1960), pp. 33-82.

to work our way around on the railroad to Ashfork, then stage it through the horrible rigors of an Arizona winter, making 56 miles in 48 hours, being stuck for one-third of that time in Hell Canyon without anything to eat or drink." During the interim, the backers of Prescott had been wining and dining the other legislators, and by trading and jockeying practically had the capital secured. Sensing this, Stephens, Selim Franklin, and others in the Pima delegation then joined the opposition in pledging themselves in support of retaining the capital at Prescott. Stephens even helped to give the asylum to Maricopa County by his vote in the Council.

Actually, the Pima legislators had met with Tucson business leader J. S. Mansfeld even before leaving Tucson. In assessing possibilities for an institution, they decided that a university might be the only plum available for Tucson though the capital, asylum, or prison would be more desirable from the standpoint of appropriations to bolster the local economy. But the citizens of the Old Pueblo were furious. At a mass meeting they clamorously decided to seek the capital and sent the redoubtable Fred Maish to Prescott with a "sack," or slush fund, of $4,000 to influence the legislature. The mission "paid off" in that the lower house passed a bill to move the capital back to Tucson. Stephens, however, refused to renege on his pledge to fellow Council members and so the capital remained in Prescott until moved to Phoenix in 1887.

Some of Stephens' friends knew he was "sitting on a hot seat" and thus helped him to secure the university. The indignant *Arizona Daily Citizen,* however, bitterly attacked him in editorials. In one of these the editor wrote, "If C. C. Stephens thinks he can kick Pima County from one end of the Territory to the other, utterly ignore her and the wants of the people as if he were an avowed enemy, instead of a servant pledged to faithfully represent her interests in the Legislature and then after all his contemptible acts seek to smooth things over by the sop of a Territorial University, that nobody asked for and which at best can be realized in a far distant future, he will find that it will not go down."[37] When Stephens returned to Tucson and attempted to explain his actions, an enraged audience drove him off the rostrum with a shower of ripe eggs, rotting vegetables, and supposedly, a dead cat.

Unlike the *Citizen* and many Tucson residents, however, the *Arizona Daily Star* welcomed the idea of a school of higher learning in the Old Pueblo. "It will not only add to the importance of our city, but bring hither several hundred students from abroad who would live

---

[37]Quoted in Douglas D. Martin, *The Lamp in the Desert: The Story of the University of Arizona* (Tucson: University of Arizona Press, 1960), p. 23.

C. C. Stephens, member of the Thirteenth Legislative Council who helped gain the University of Arizona for Tucson — much to the disgust of Pima County residents who wanted either the capital or the insane asylum.

— Special Collections, University of Arizona Library

here at least ten months of the year. To have such an institution would be of equal importance to having the capital located here."[38]

The real burden of acquiring the university rested upon Selim Franklin because the bill faced strong opposition in the House and seemed doomed to defeat. In a straightforward speech near the end of the session, he blasted the legislature for its corruption and extravagance, going so far as to say that they deserved to be called the "thieving thirteenth" or the "bloody thirteenth." He pleaded with the House to wash away its sins by establishing an institution of learning. The enthusiasm of the speaker and the tumultuous applause of a favorably stacked gallery carried the bill through the House without a dissenting vote. Tucson was not impressed and, except for J. S. Mansfeld, the university might have been lost. Three appointed regents refused to serve and had to be replaced by the new Governor, C. Meyer Zulick, before a quorum was reached. J. S. Mansfeld, a naturalized citizen from Prussia and a vigorous friend of schools; Probate Judge John S. Wood, at that time the ex-officio county school superintendent; M. G. Samaniego, a mail contractor and cattleman; Charles M. Strauss, a former Tucson mayor; and R. L. Long attended the first meeting of the regents. They chose Dr. John C. Handy, a well-educated Tucson physician and surgeon for the Southern Pacific, to head the new university as chancellor.

The law creating the school, however, provided that the county,

---

[38]*Arizona Daily Star,* March 11, 1882.

Old Main Building on the University of Arizona campus about 1890.

town, or private citizens must provide a forty-acre campus site or the appropriation would lapse. Finding no interest in providing this land, Mansfeld, on May 3, 1886, picked out a desert site on a low mesa east of Tucson and then persuaded the owners to offer forty acres of the mesquite-covered land to the regents. The three donors were B. C. Parker, E. B. Gifford, and W. S. "Billy" Reid.[39] Interestingly enough, the first two were gamblers while Reid owned the finest saloon in Tucson. When the deed was filed on November 27, 1886, the University of Arizona was established in fact, though there were yet no students, no teachers, and no buildings.

The creation of the university and other institutions was part of the more constructive work performed by the Thirteenth Legislative Assembly. There were many other acts to commend it also. For example, two branch railroad lines were sanctioned to connect important towns to main lines. A subsidy of $292,000 in Yavapai County bonds was authorized to connect Prescott with the Atlantic and Pacific; another of $200,000 in Maricopa County bonds was provided to give Phoenix access to the Southern Pacific at Maricopa. A third railroad, which was not built, was also given approval by the Assembly, but only after a period of squabbling, especially among the Maricopa County legislators. The men from that county were divided on the question of whether Phoenix should be connected with the Southern Pacific to the south

---

[39]Martin, *Lamp in the Desert,* p. 25.

or with the more distant Atlantic and Pacific (now the Santa Fe) to the north.

Representative DeForest Porter favored and successfully maneuvered for the Maricopa and Phoenix road while J. S. Armstrong wavered between the two plans. On the other hand, Councilman Robert B. Todd consistently worked for a subsidized railroad that would ultimately connect the county-seat towns of Phoenix and Prescott; he introduced a bill that would have provided a $3,000 per-mile grant for a road to the northern boundary of Maricopa County somewhere in the vicinity of Wickenburg. Porter foiled Todd's efforts, however, by gaining possession of the original bill and absenting himself while the battle raged; he even reported himself ill when the doorkeeper was sent to escort him to the hall on the last day of the session. So, Todd had to be satisfied with a less satisfactory substitute law.[40]

By this measure, the Maricopa County Board of Supervisors could not issue bonds for the railroad north of Phoenix without the consent of the people at a special election to be held within ninety days. But this plebiscite was never held. The Southern Pacific, fearing competition from the Atlantic and Pacific if a north-south road should crisscross Arizona, promised a cut in passenger fares and freight rates. Accordingly, in May, 1885, Senator Leland Stanford, the President of the Southern Pacific, announced a reduction in local passenger fares from ten to five cents per mile for round trips of more than ten miles. Then, in July, freight rates from San Francisco to Maricopa were cut by 20 percent.[41] This action seemed to counter the argument heard at the time that access to competitive lines was necessary to bring about lower rates. At least no vote was called for by the supervisors and another ten years elapsed before Phoenix was connected to Prescott by rail.

The two railroads authorized by the thirteenth legislature were constructed, however. The Maricopa and Phoenix was built by N. K. Masten, the financial agent of the Southern Pacific who put together his own organization known as the Maricopa and Phoenix Railroad Company. The story of the road's beginning is almost like a modern television plot. The deadline for starting construction was the last day of October, 1886. As the deadline neared nothing had been done, and the principal officials of the company were out of the territory. Fortunately, the resourceful chief engineer, Herbert R. Patrick, took a team of horses, a garden plow, and a scraper to Maricopa to break ground and save the

---

[40]*Journals of the Thirteenth Legislative Assembly,* 1885, p. 961; and *Laws of the Territory of Arizona,* Thirteenth Legislative Assembly, Act. No. 96, pp. 259-65.
[41]*Weekly Arizona Miner,* May 15, July 3, 1885.

DeForest Porter, Phoenix lawyer, judge, mayor, and legislator.

— Arizona Pioneers' Historical Society

subsidy. When C. S. Masten, the superintendent of construction and brother of N. K., arrived late from San Francisco because of a washout along the Southern Pacific tracks, he must have been delighted. As he stepped off the train, he saw three hundred feet of six-inch grade along the new right-of-way.

With the arrival of more equipment, construction continued, but not without difficulty. Freight wagons were lost in the quicksands and rising waters of the Gila River. The Pima and Maricopa Indians at first refused to grant permission for a railroad line to go through their reservation lands. Stakes driven by the surveyors were pulled up almost as fast as they were put in, sometimes overnight. But after several weeks, Delegate Curtis Bean succeeded in getting a right-of-way bill passed by Congress. When bags of silver, the only medium of exchange acceptable to the natives, arrived from Washington, a meeting was arranged at the railroad camp. The scantily clad Indians assembled under the cottonwood trees to accept payment for land comprising the right-of-way. With this clearance, the line was completed to Tempe and reached Phoenix on July 4, 1887.[42] The last spike was driven by Captain William A. Hancock, the pioneer who had surveyed the original site of that city.

---

[42]*Arizona Republican,* May 28, 1909, and August 31, 1926; *Congressional Record,* 49th Cong., 1st Sess., 1884, pp. 4107, 6408, and 7428; *Congressional Record,* 49th Cong., 2d Sess., 1885, pp. 283 and 778; also, James T. Simms, "Reminiscent Notes on the Building of the First Railroad to Phoenix," *The Sheriff,* XII, No. 3 (September, 1953), p. 61.

For the first time, Phoenix, which then had a population of about three thousand, was free from total dependence upon animal-drawn stage-coaches and freight wagons for transportation.

Governor Tritle himself took the lead in organizing the second road — the Prescott and Arizona Central. He wanted cheaper transportation for the United Verde Copper Company in which he had an interest. Because of the low price of copper and the high cost of hauling ore in wagons — pulled by fourteen-mule teams — from the almost-inaccessible Jerome region to the Atlantic and Pacific Railroad, the company's profits were not what the stockholders had been led to expect. The only apparent way to reduce production expenses was to bring the railroad closer to the mine, but the problem was to raise sufficient money to construct a branch line to Prescott from some point on the main line. In order to attract Eastern capital and to obtain beneficial legislation, Tritle first organized a group of local promoters — including such well-known politicians and businessmen as N. O. Murphy, Clark Churchill, C. P. Head, Levi Bashford, John G. Campbell, Edmund Wells, E. P. Clark, Hugo Richards, Nathan Ellis, Alfred Eoff, J. N. Rodenburg, and F. K. Ainsworth.[43] After incorporating under the laws of the territory, the company surveyed and mapped a route. Then, Ainsworth, who was President of the Council, introduced and secured the enactment of the subsidy bill providing for the construction of a railroad in Yavapai County.[44] The board of supervisors of that county was required to sell bonds and pay $4,000 for each mile of standard-gauge track completed, payments beginning when ten miles of the seventy-three-mile road had been graded and the rails laid.

Two Eastern financial groups, which had been contacted by the original local corporation, vied for the opportunity to invest in the new project. By the summer of 1887, however, the rival New York and Minneapolis syndicates had united to back railroad-builder Thomas S. Bullock. Tritle, Thomas J. Butler, and W. N. Kelly, all of Prescott, emerged as leaders in a new board of directors. The new group then proceeded to acquire right-of-way and issue $750,000 in first-mortgage bonds. With money derived from both the sale of these securities and from the $292,000 in Yavapai County bonds, Bullock finished the branch railroad before the legal deadline. By January 1, 1887, he had linked together discarded lightweight rails — purchased from the Atlantic

    [43]Wallace W. Elliott & Co., *History of Arizona Territory Showing Its Resources and Advantages* (San Francisco: Wallace W. Elliott & Co., 1884), pp. 321-22. [Reprinted by Northland Press, Flagstaff, Arizona, 1964]
    [44]*Laws of the Territory of Arizona,* Thirteenth Legislative Assembly, Act No. 81, pp. 193-99.

The "Governor Frederick H. Tritle," one of two locomotives used in the festivities celebrating the completion of the Prescott and Arizona Central Railroad on January 1, 1887.

and Pacific — all the way from Prescott Junction (now called Seligman) on the main line to the capital city.[45]

On that day, a large crowd gathered in Prescott to participate in commemorative activities. A procession of fire companies, civic societies, a band and soldiers from Fort Whipple, and local citizens in carriages or on horseback paraded to the depot. Then two antique locomotives — the "Governor Frederick H. Tritle," belonging to the Prescott and Arizona Central, and the "Pueblo," an Atlantic and Pacific engine — pulled up with whistles blowing while a hundred-gun salute was being fired at the fort. Governor C. Meyer Zulick, Tritle's successor, drove a gilded spike into the last wooden tie, painted red and white for the occasion, and greeted the enthusiastic celebrants. Chief Justice Sumner Howard of the Arizona Supreme Court also spoke, as did Bullock and Thomas J. Butler, the grand marshal for the day. Butler, a local businessman and a director of the Arizona Central who had served as territorial treasurer in the Tritle administration, drew loud applause when he praised his former chief as the man whose influence and labors had contributed most to the consummation of the enterprise. After the honors had been done the company provided a fitting climax for the event with an excursion to Seven Mile House.[46]

---

[45]Lucile Anderson, "Railroad Transportation Through Prescott," unpublished master's thesis, University of Arizona, 1934, pp. 16-38.

[46]*Arizona Weekly Journal-Miner,* January 5, 1887.

The return of the "Tritle" to Prescott with about two hundred sightseers was the end of a perfect day but the beginning of a short life for the Arizona Central. For a few years, "Old Reliable," as the road was facetiously called, opened up the country around Prescott for development. But it was forced out of business by a rival company which built a road south from Ash Fork, on the main line of the Atlantic and Pacific, to Prescott and thence on to Phoenix. Known as the Santa Fe, Prescott, and Phoenix, the latter road was promoted by the Murphy brothers, Frank and Nathan Oakes, partly to supply transportation for the Congress Gold Mine, located about fifty miles southwest of Prescott. Frank Murphy had been retained as superintendent of this mine by Joseph "Diamond Joe" Reynolds, a wealthy steamboat and railroad man from St. Louis who had invested in it. Reynolds died of pneumonia he contracted while on a trip to the Congress mine in 1891, leaving a substantial interest in the property to Murphy. The latter, with the added inducement of a twenty-year tax-exemption law for new railroads passed by the sixteenth legislature in the same year, eventually succeeded, despite the panic of 1893, in getting eastern capital with which to carry out the plans started by Reynolds for a north-south railroad.[47] Passing through Congress and Wickenburg, the new first-class line reached Phoenix on February 28, 1895.

By that time, the Prescott and Arizona Central was no longer in operation. Only worthless railroad mortgage bonds and unpaid Yavapai County bonds were left as reminders. Bullock never exercised his privilege of extending the road from Prescott to the Maricopa County line. One reason was that he could not convince the legislature to change the Hassayampa-Wickenburg route specified in the 1885 subsidy act. He preferred the Black Canyon route that he thought would serve more mining regions and be less expensive to construct.[48] Disappointed, he left for Mexico to build a more profitable railroad.

Unfortunately, the thirteenth legislature, which had authorized needed railroads and institutions for Arizona, also had an unsavory reputation. Several fights in the legislative halls and in neighborhood watering places gave the body the name "bloody thirteenth." An incident that M. M. Rice, a reporter for the Tucson *Star* and Prescott *Courier,* described in his reminiscences, serves to illustrate the pugnacious nature of the session. It seems that Captain Welford Chapman Bridwell, a Council member from Graham County, was relaxing at one

---

[47]U. S. Dept. of the Interior, *Report of the Governor of Arizona* [Nathan O. Murphy] *to the Secretary of Interior, 1901,* p. 11; and Lucile Anderson, pp. 71-101.
[48]Anderson, pp. 36-37.

Welford C. Bridwell, who was known as Clay Beauford when he was chief of the San Carlos Apache police. He had his name changed to Bridwell by the Tenth Legislative Assembly. Later, he represented Graham County in the Council.

— Arizona Pioneers' Historical Society

of the Prescott public resorts between meetings. Though he was not one to carry the proverbial chip on his shoulder, he, nevertheless, was ever ready to resent an insult and thrash an aggressor; he did so on one occasion, causing quite a commotion in the process. When one Professor Arnold, a Frenchman and a lobbyist for the Arizona Copper Company of Clifton, cast aspersions at him for having had his name changed from Clay Beauford by the Tenth Assembly, Bridwell reacted quickly. The surprised Frenchman found himself sprawled on the floor with smashed eyeglasses and a bloody nose. Humiliated but still antagonistic, the Frenchman challenged Bridwell to a duel; the latter accepted and, being the challenged party, chose a weapon which he knew well — the Colt. When it came to gunplay, the Frenchman reneged, but offered to fight with his own familiar poignard in French style. Since no weapons of this kind were available and because mutual friends intervened, apologies of a sort were exchanged. With wrath assuaged, the matter ended over full goblets of Mumm's Extra Dry.[49]

The name of "thieving thirteenth" was not so easily dismissed, however. A United States grand jury sitting in Tucson condemned the legislature and reported some startling facts to Judge W. H. Barnes of the First Arizona Judicial District sitting in Tucson. The jury discovered that the legal limitation of $4,000 for the operating expenses of any one

---

[49]M. M. Rice, "Reminiscences," written in March, 1927; typescript in the files of the APHS.

legislature had been exceeded by $46,744.50. It charged that the outrageous appropriations were the result of a venal conspiracy and cited the example of a shorthand reporter who was paid $500 for three days work by a special act of the legislature.

Another United States grand jury meeting at Prescott in December, 1885, added its criticism of the "thieving thirteenth" after hearing the testimony of twenty-one witnesses. This latter jury found that the printing bill of $19,967 was exhorbitant and at rates in excess of those paid by private business.[50] An expenditure of $3,076.80 for territorial newspapers delivered to members was considered a waste also. A mileage bill to and from the farthest corner of the territory for a councilman-at-large who lived just across the street from the capital was hardly acceptable either. Furthermore, the employment of fifty-one clerks, four pages, and eight janitors above the number prescribed by the federal statute of 1861 was labeled a wanton and illegal squandering of public funds. On this matter of clerks, the jury wrote, "There was appropriated and paid for these excess clerks the sum of $23,700. From the testimony of a number of these clerks, corroborated by the further testimony of members, we find that very little actual work was done, and for the reason that the work did not exist. In many instances the clerks testified that they expended little or no time in committee rooms, or in the discharge of committee duty. Several never reported except to sign the payroll for payment due them for their fictitious services." A number of employees and contractors stated to the jury that they had "loaned" money to various legislators with no idea of being repaid. There was talk of criminal prosecution of several legislators but no charges were ever brought against them.

Governor Tritle was not directly implicated in any corruption, but his honor and integrity were often questioned near the end of his tenure. J. L. Biggers, the district attorney at Prescott, wrote on August 13, 1885, that the formerly popular Tritle had become, in about a year's time, one of the most unpopular governors of the territory. According to Biggers, the Governor had surrounded himself with some unprincipled characters and was almost continually under the influence of bad whiskey. And, of course, he could not evade the fact that he had been associated with the corruption of the thirteenth session. "The whole people are anxiously awaiting a change," said the District Attorney.[51]

In a petition signed by a number of Arizona citizens, Tritle was accused of violating sections 1887 and 1888 of the *U. S. Statutes* by

[50]Letter of Governor C. Meyer Zulick to Secretary of the Interior L. Q. C. Lamar, from Prescott, Arizona, December 2, 1885, Record Group 48, Territorial Papers.

[51]"Brief Charges Against F. A. Tritle," Record Group 48, Appointment Papers.

encouraging and approving exhorbitant appropriations for such things as clerk hire and territorial printing. He was castigated in the same petition for lobbying in the Assembly for the passage of subsidy bills to benefit corporations in which he had an interest. More specifically, the Tucson and Port Lobos Railroad, in which he owned a third of the stock, was granted lands from which the company derived $50,000 without spending a dollar on the road. And then W. S. Davis of Willcox signed an affidavit charging the Governor with making partisan political speeches and using the influence of his office to advance the interests of the Republican Party in the 1884 elections. All of these charges and complaints were filed with the Secretary of the Interior. Actually, however, Tritle was not removed because of any of these charges, but was replaced for political reasons, as was customary whenever a new administration took over in Washington.

Tritle submitted his resignation to Secretary of the Interior Lamar on October 7, 1885, so that President Cleveland could appoint a Democrat without any embarrassment. He wrote from Tucson, rather than the capital, since he was in the process of visiting localities that were liable to Indian attack. In his letter to Lamar, the Governor proudly reported that he had placed a small mounted militia in the field to cooperate with General Crook's forces for the purpose of informing citizens of any danger that might arise. Ranchers and prospectors who resided in remote areas away from larger settlements were of special concern. Tritle regretfully informed the Secretary, however, that no appropriation had been made by Congress to defray the expenses of the militia; he had been compelled to personally guarantee the payment of all expenses that might be incurred for equipping and provisioning the force. He volunteered to continue on as Governor until this important work was finished and suggested, in the event his successor were selected at once, that the service of the militia be extended until the need for the men no longer existed.[52]

In October, 1885, President Grover Cleveland appointed Conrad Meyer Zulick, Arizona's first Democratic governor, to succeed Tritle. As usual there were a number of disappointed aspirants for the position. The most prominent Arizona resident who applied was John G. Campbell, a big property owner and taxpayer in northern Arizona who had been in the territory for twenty-two years. As a devoted Democrat, a former member of the Yavapai Board of Supervisors and of the territorial House of Representatives (1868–1874), and a former treasurer of the territory and a delegate to Congress, Campbell had the experience

---

[52]Letter from Governor Tritle to Secretary of the Interior Lamar, from Tucson, Arizona, October 7, 1885, *ibid.*

and qualifications.[53] He was endorsed by members of the legislature and by many leading citizens.[54] Another application (now in the Appointment Papers of the Department of Interior in the National Archives) was in the form of a petition signed by thirty-nine voters of Vandalia, Illinois, endorsing a Mr. R. G. Moss. However, the following interesting note was written in the margin: "Mr. Moss is an old gentleman, who has conceived an insane desire to be appointed Governor of Arizona. We are afraid that his mind is seriously affected. Please acknowledge receipt of the petition and say to him that there are so many applications ahead of his that he should not be disappointed if he is not appointed. He could not fill the office. Yours, C. M. Ashcraft."[55]

Another unusual application was that of a New Yorker named E. H. Colman. He began his letter to President Cleveland in this way: "You may recall the writer as the first man who had the honor of shaking your hand at your reception at 2 P. M. today, and who mentioned briefly that he was a manufacturer of goods that come in direct competition with European goods but that his faith in the administration and the Democratic Party was sound and had given him no uneasiness. You replied, 'We will take care of you, Sir.' "[56] After listing some popular business and church leaders in New York who would endorse him and describing how he had personally settled a number of families in New Mexico, Colman asked to be considered for the position of Governor of Arizona. His letter seemed to be as much a pitch for the protective tariff as a request for an appointment.

Tritle remained in the territory after leaving office, and was for awhile actively engaged in railroad promotion and mining operations. He devoted much of his time to the United Verde mine at Jerome, an investment in which he had become involved while governor. The United Verde ultimately made millions for Senator William A. Clark of Montana who bought the property and developed it after 1889. But for Tritle and his associates it was not a paying proposition. He returned to politics, serving first as recorder of Yavapai County from 1894 to 1897 and then as supervisor of the census in 1900. He died in Phoenix in 1906.

---

[53]U. S. House, *Biographical Directory of the American Congress, 1774–1961*, 85th Cong., 2d Sess., House Doc. 442, p. 655.

[54]Letter of John G. Campbell to Secretary of the Interior Lamar, from Prescott, Arizona, April 6, 1885, Record Group 48, Appointment Papers.

[55]Petition for Mr. R. G. Moss, April 18, 1885, *ibid.*

[56]Letter of E. H. Colman to President Grover Cleveland, from Willard's Hotel in Washington, D.C., July 27, 1885, *ibid.*

Chapter 10

The First Democrat:

The Zulick Administration

Conrad Meyer Zulick, the seventh Governor of the Territory of Arizona and the first of three Democrats to serve in that capacity, was born in Pennsylvania in 1839. He served with distinction during the Civil War and rose to the rank of colonel, the youngest person of that rank then in the military service.[1] After the war he resumed his practice of law in Newark, New Jersey, and actively engaged in the political affairs of that state. He was appointed by President Andrew Johnson as collector of internal revenue for Essex, N. J., and in 1879 was elected surrogate judge of Essex County. The latter victory was a tribute to his personal popularity since he was the only successful Democratic candidate in a Republican county. Zulick repeatedly declined his party's nomination to Congress and for governor of New Jersey but sought instead the Arizona position to which he was appointed.[2]

Zulick won the gubernatorial appointment over such outstanding Democratic candidates as John G. Campbell, Charles Trumbull Hayden, and Granville H. Oury. The last was recommended by a large number of senators, congressmen, and Arizona residents, but he also had considerable opposition from George L. Lynde, a large Tucson taxpayer, and from certain citizens of Willcox.[3] Zulick also had numerous blue-ribbon endorsements.[4] Senator John R. McPherson of New Jersey, for example, wrote in his behalf:

> This is to certify that I have known . . . Col. C. Meyer Zulick . . . for the past 20 years during his residence in New Jersey. He is a good

---

[1] Letter of C. Meyer Zulick to Secretary of the Interior L. Q. C. Lamar, from Prescott, Arizona, May 14, 1886, Record Group 48, Appointment Papers.

[2] *Arizona Citizen,* October 24, 1885.

[3] Appointment Papers of Granville H. Oury, Charles T. Hayden, and John G. Campbell, Record Group 48, Appointment Papers.

[4] Letter of Zulick to Secretary Lamar, from Tombstone, Arizona Territory, April 5, 1885, *ibid.*

lawyer — an active and influential party man. A gentleman of high character and good social position. He is now a resident of Arizona and intends to make that his future home. If appointed he will deal justly by all and so conduct the affairs of the Territory as to reflect credit upon himself and the appointing power.[5]

William A. Farish, in a letter to Senator McPherson urging support for Zulick's appointment, wrote that the Democratic Party was torn by internal dissensions and was as disorganized as an unwieldy mob. He said that Col. Zulick was the only public man who possessed the requisite qualifications to turn this mob into a victorious army. In recommending the injection of new blood, Farish wrote that "the old cancer and sores must be removed. The barnacles must be brushed off or Arizona will forever remain a republican territory. The democratic majority in the Territory is conceded to be over five thousand (5000) votes, yet in the last election our nominee for delegate to Congress, a most excellent gentleman, a business man of wealth, suffered a most humiliating defeat."[6] He was referring to the defeat of C. P. Head, a prominent merchant of Prescott, by Curtis C. Bean, a Republican and a mining man who also lived in Yavapai County. Another strong Zulick supporter was J. H. Behan, a Tombstone lawman, who also wrote to Senator McPherson. "Having for 22 years seen the Territory governed by second class Republican adventurers," he said, "I am anxious, very anxious, to see what a first class Democrat can do for us in reforming abuses and promoting modes and measures for the public benefit. . . . "[7]

Zulick was proud to be known as a Democrat partisan who had worked for the election of Grover Cleveland. His legal residence had been in Arizona for less than a year at the time of his appointment in October, 1885, but he had been in and out of the Southwest for four years looking after business interests.[8] No governor ever entered upon his duties under more peculiar circumstances. At the time of his selection, Zulick was a prisoner below the border at Nacozari, Sonora. He had gone there to straighten out the financial difficulties of clients who had lost money in mine development. But instead, he became a hostage of the mine employees. Under the Mexican law, a manager could be

---

[5]Letter of Senator John R. McPherson to Department of the Interior, n. d., *ibid.*

[6]Letter of William A. Farish to Senator McPherson, from Deming, New Mexico (Tombstone, Arizona, return address). April 29, 1885, *ibid.;* Bean carried eight of the counties in 1884; defeating Head by a vote of 6,747 to 5,595, *Arizona Weekly Citizen,* December 6, 1884.

[7]Letter of J. H. Behan to Senator McPherson, from Tombstone, Arizona, September 14, 1885, Record Group 48, Appointment Papers.

[8]Letter of Zulick to Senator McPherson, June 8, 1885, *ibid.*

Conrad Meyer Zulick, governor of Arizona Territory from 1885 to 1889.

— Arizona Department of Library and Archives

jailed until the wages of the workers were paid. So Zulick was placed under house arrest in his own residence.

His escape from this embarrassing situation was organized by W. K. Meade of Tombstone, who had just learned of his own selection by President Cleveland to be United States marshal for Arizona. Meade's first move, after he received notice of Zulick's appointment to the governorship, was to contact M. T. "Doc" Donovan, a former scout and dispatch bearer with General Crook during the Apache wars who was then ranching in the Sulphur Spring Valley. Presented with the problem, Donovan agreed to take a mountain wagon and a team of mules down to Sonora to bring Zulick back. Being familiar with the country, the ex-scout was able to pull into the mining camp at night. At 2 A.M. he walked by the guard who was sleeping soundly on the porch and awakened the surprised Zulick. The latter put his trust in Donovan, whom he did not know, and climbed quietly into the wagon. Moving slowly in order not to give away the escape, the men crossed the border a few miles from what is now the town of Douglas. Then "Doc" broke the news to his passenger and congratulated him on his appointment. The New Jersey Dutchman was moved to tears and thanked Donovan for his kindness. After stopping to cook breakfast on United States soil, they continued on to Tombstone. When they pulled up at the Occidental Hotel a crowd gathered around the wagon and carried Zulick into the lobby. That night Thomas Gregory and his wife gave a dinner at their restaurant for the Governor that was attended by all the notables of that famous town. Within a short time, Donovan was rewarded for his deed with a commission as deputy marshal under Meade.[9]

Traveling by buckboard via Tombstone and Tucson en route to the capital, the Governor was lavishly praised by the territorial press. At Tucson he was honored with a banquet and dance at San Xavier. Perhaps the controversy that developed later over the failure of his Democrat Party hosts to pay the fiddlers was an omen for the future. Certainly, the following eulogy printed in the *Arizona Weekly Citizen* on October 24, 1885, was in contrast to the criticisms that he was soon to receive: "Governor Zulick has made a good impression on the people of this city and irrespective of party affiliations feel confident that the interests of Arizona are perfectly secure in his executive control. He will enter upon his official duties with the best wishes and moral support of every resident of the Territory."[10] Long before the end of his turbulent three-and-a-half year administration, however, he was being described as a "failure" and a political "trickster of the smallest calibre."

Whereas the appointment of Governor Zulick was well received at first by Arizona Democrats, there was some opposition to the new Secretary, James A. Bayard. The *Arizona Weekly Citizen,* for example, was outraged by the placing of a man with little training in such an important position solely because he was the son of U. S. Secretary of State Thomas F. Bayard. The younger man was a primary teacher in Delaware at the time of his selection for the Arizona position. In earlier years he had "followed the profession of a dude; then he started out to be a tough, succeeding so well as to be able to kick the glass out of hacks when he was on a spree, and winding up now and then in the police station on charges of disorderly conduct. His next effort was to try to get in jail as a fighter. He had nearly succeeded when he was bundled off to Delaware as a school teacher."[11]

A lack of previous political experience was not Secretary Bayard's only handicap. After taking office he discovered that his predecessor had failed to leave a file of territorial accounts. The disbursement of federal funds presented a second problem. The law required that each territorial secretary place all public money with the most convenient U. S. depository — in Arizona's case, San Francisco. The money had to be transported to Ash Fork by rail and on to Prescott by stage. Since Wells Fargo & Co. refused to be liable for money entrusted to their care, the loss, if any, would fall directly upon the Secretary. Another

[9]Reminiscences of Albert S. Reynolds in the Reynolds File, APHS.
[10]*Arizona Citizen,* October 24, 1885.
[11]*Arizona Star,* October 24, 1885.

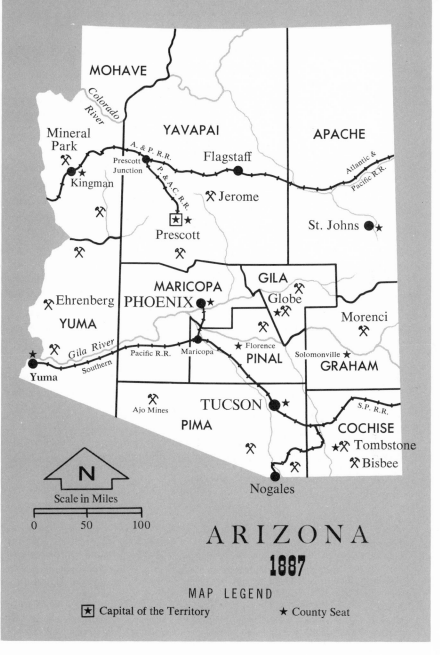

MOHAVE

YAVAPAI

APACHE

Colorado River

Mineral Park

A. & P. R.R.

Prescott Junction

Flagstaff

Atlantic & Pacific R.R.

Kingman

P. & A.C.R.R.

Jerome

St. Johns

Prescott

Ehrenberg

MARICOPA

PHOENIX

GILA

Globe

Morenci

YUMA

Gila River

Pacific R.R.

Maricopa

Florence

Solomonville

Southern

PINAL

GRAHAM

Yuma

Ajo Mines

TUCSON

S.P. R.R.

PIMA

COCHISE

Tombstone

Bisbee

Nogales

N

Scale in Miles

0   50   100

A R I Z O N A
1887

MAP LEGEND

★ Capital of the Territory   ★ County Seat

The Prescott and Arizona Central and the Maricopa and Phoenix railroads both began operation in 1887. At that time the capital was at Prescott; but two years later it was moved to Phoenix, and the legislators from other parts of the territory took the train, via Los Angeles, to the new seat of government. Note that the original county seats of Apache, Graham, Mohave, and Yuma counties had been changed by 1887.

possibility, drawing drafts against the San Francisco deposit and cashing them in Prescott banks, was also undesirable since the local charge for converting San Francisco drafts was one-half of one percent; the Treasury Department would not allow for this expenditure and Bayard was unwilling to pay the fee out of his own pocket. Frustrated by these alternatives, the Secretary asked permission to deposit U. S. drafts with the Bank of Arizona, which had agreed to cash them at face value.[12] Other executive matters were not so easily solved, however.

One of the first problems faced by Governor Zulick was the smuggling carried on between Arizona and the state of Sonora in Mexico. In a letter to Secretary of the Interior L. C. Q. Lamar, the Governor said that smugglers could easily cross the long border along the Mexican line without hindrance from the U. S. customs officials. Citing examples, he wrote: "There are within Arizona 20,000 inhabitants of Mexican origin, the national drink of whom is Mescal, a liquor distilled from the cactus plant, thousands of gallons of which is annually consumed by them, all of it being manufactured within the borders of our sister Republic, hardly a gallon pays duty; hundreds of thousands of cigars and quantities of tobacco, to say nothing of cattle, horses, mules, etc. which are also smuggled in."[13]

Zulick had studied the report of the last U. S. grand jury for the Second Judicial District, under the date of October 28, 1885, and quoted the following extract from it:

> Although we have been unable to gather sufficient facts to find more than one indictment for smuggling, yet that smuggling is extensively carried on all along the frontier admits of no doubt. In fact, so common has it become that it is no longer regarded by many reputable citizens as a crime, but is oftentimes engaged in as a legitimate business. That no real effort has been made by the general government to abate the evil, which operates severely against merchants and importers, who endeavor to conduct their business according to law, is shown by the fact that the government has but one mounted inspector to guard the line from El Paso, Texas, to San Diego, California, a distance of about 1200 miles. The government should furnish a special agent of the Treasury with a sufficient force of assistants to enable him to suppress this illegal traffic and promptly enforce the revenue laws, or on the other hand, allow beef cattle, cigars, mescal and tobacco to be imported from Mexico free from duty.[14]

---

[12]Letters of Secretary James A. Bayard to First Comptroller M. J. Durham, from Prescott, Arizona, November 4 and December 16, 1885, and September 9, 1886, Record Group 217, Territorial Letters Received, Vol. 18.

[13]Letter of Governor C. Meyer Zulick to Secretary of the Interior Lamar, from Prescott, Arizona, November 25, 1885, Record Group 48, Territorial Papers.

[14]*Ibid.*

Zulick proposed that four mounted inspectors be assigned by the Department of the Treasury to duty along the borders of Cochise and Pima counties; that they be selected on the basis of their familiarity with the country, and their knowledge of the trails and bypaths leading into Mexico; that they speak the Spanish language and be frontiersmen who might camp where night overtook them. The Governor thus set forth the problem and his solution to it, though little was actually done by the federal government to ameliorate the situation. The U. S. Senate, however, seemed aware of a border problem, in a resolution passed unanimously on May 5, 1886. Since no treaty provision existed between the two republics in regard to the reclamation of livestock that crossed the unobstructed boundary line, the solons feared that citizens of the two countries might become embroiled in arguments over ownership. The resolution stressed the desirability of reaching some agreement with Mexico so as to maintain peace and good will.[15]

Already the two countries were attempting to solve another mutual problem, the atrocities being committed by Chiricahua Apaches who had escaped from the San Carlos Reservation on May 17, 1885. An immediate reason for this latest Indian outbreak was a fear of being punished for having made and consumed a sort of "home brew" called tiswin, though boredom with confinement to an agrarian life on the reservation was probably a more underlying cause for the beginning of fifteen months of bloody savagery. Forty-two braves, led by Natchez, Nana, Chihuahua, and Mangas (son of Mangas Coloradas), accompanied by over ninety women and children, departed hurriedly for Sonora. En route they left a trail of death and burning ranches through southwestern New Mexico, successfully eluding troops from Camp Apache dispatched to capture them.

General George Crook, apparently by this time convinced that his policy of gentle treatment and fairness had failed, received orders from the War Department to kill the Apaches on sight. Soldiers were strung out along the border to prevent the return of the hostiles, and two expeditionary forces under Captains Wirt Davis and Emmett Crawford, the latter in command of friendly Indian scouts, launched campaigns into Mexico from Fort Bowie. After four months of tenacious pursuing of the renegades, the exhausted forces returned to their base with little progress to report. Some of the hostiles began recrossing the border and Geronimo even slipped through to San Carlos, where he hoped to get recruits, but left with the addition of only two squaws.[16]

---

[15]*U. S. Congressional Record*, 49th Cong., 1st Sess., May 5, 1886.
[16]Ogle, *Federal Control*, pp. 230-41.

Geronimo (on the right with the long rifle), his son, and two other Apache braves. This picture was taken by the famous territorial photographer, C. S. Fly.

Governor Zulick, greatly perturbed by the situation, pleaded for help in a letter to Secretary Lamar on December 5, 1885. He wrote: "Acting in compliance with the expressed wish of the people of the Territory, who by letters, petitions, and telegrams are daily beseeching me to take action in their behalf, I feel compelled . . . to appeal through you to the President to relieve Arizonans from the presence of those murderous tribes of savages, whose bloody raids have made the record of this frontier a continued chapter of murder, rapine and plunder seldom written in the history of any country."[17] In reviewing the history of the Chiricahua and Warm Springs Apaches, the Governor explained that General O. O. Howard had succeeded in getting about 1,200 Indians, including 250 warriors, on the reservation in 1873. The Indians remained peaceful until 1875, when a portion of the tribe under Geronimo escaped and resumed depredations in the states of Sonora and Chihuahua as well as in Arizona and New Mexico until 1877, when they were captured, disarmed, and placed upon the reservation again. In subsequent years the Indians alternated at federally subsidized farming and the warpath.

Calling the savages "more daring, devilish, and defiant" in 1885 than ever before, Zulick described several incidents to illustrate his

---

[17]Letter of Governor Zulick to Secretary of the Interior Lamar, from Prescott, Arizona, December 5, 1885, Record Group 48, Territorial Papers.

concern for citizens of southeastern Arizona. Less than two weeks before he wrote to Lamar, a band of hostiles visited San Carlos and killed a white man and a boy almost within sight of Camp Apache. "The boy, who was the eldest son of a widowed mother, was found with his head beaten with rocks. The mother upon hearing of her son's ruthless murder became a raving maniac. All through Graham and Cochise Counties men, women, and children have been brutally murdered. Two days ago the Sheriff of Graham Co. and two companions were killed, and today I received a telegram from the town of Duncan that women with their babes in their arms were yesterday driven into town from their homes not half mile away. . . ."[18]

Governor Zulick praised the people for restraining from retaliatory acts of violence and for patiently waiting for the military to save them from death and ruin. At times these citizens were incensed enough to attack the Indians on the reservation who were aiding and abetting their friends and relatives on the warpath.

> There are now upon the San Carlos Reservation, which is a body of land 150 miles long by 100 miles wide, of Tonto, Mohave, San Carlos and Yuma Apaches 2939, of White Mountain Apaches 1600, these are all peaceable and nearly self-supporting. The Chiricahua and Warm Spring Indians alone have defied every attempt to civilize them. Their treatment upon the Reservation has been an advertisement to other tribes that the greater and more numerous the outrages they commit upon unoffending citizens the more immunities are granted them, when wearied with bloodshed they return with perfidious faith to San Carlos. When last year [1884] for the third time they had surrendered, they were placed upon that portion of the Reservation which had been claimed and occupied by the White Mountain Indians for a hundred years, were given improved farming utensils, seed and everything necessary to till the soil, while the White Mountains, who have remained peaceful and are nearly self-supporting, were left to plow with tin cans, old hatchets and anything else they could utilize for the purpose. The humane policy of the Government in supplying the Chiricahuas with the richest lands within the Territory, clothing and feeding them, has been repaid by treachery and bloodshed. . . [19]

Since the Chiricahua and Warm Springs Indians had broken every treaty stipulation and were a menace to civilization, Governor Zulick recommended that those still on the reservation be sent to a land unknown to them where they could be safely guarded and compelled to work. He further recommended a speedy trial and punishment for the wife of Mangas; as the medicine woman of the tribe, she had influenced the latest outbreak of violence and was a captive in the

---

[18]*Ibid.*
[19]*Ibid.*

hands of the army at Fort Bowie. Without attempting to interfere with the military, he also proposed an increase of the force then operating against the hostiles "sufficient to guard every water hole, mountain pass and exposed settlement in the country" with detachments of ten or twelve in a place; and that a sufficient force, composed mainly of Indian scouts enlisted from other tribes, should be employed to trail the renegades and hunt them to the death. Bemoaning the fact that not a single hostile Chiricahua had been punished, Zulick suggested that "a little hanging would be beneficial in the long run, for it would teach all Indians in this Territory that under no pretext whatever can they commit murder without being punished."[20]

Zulick was opposed to mob violence against the Indians, however, and was worried about inflammatory publications of some of the territorial press. On December 23, 1885, he issued a proclamation in which he discouraged incitement to unlawful deeds, such as an attack on the San Carlos reservation by the people of the territory. He said that

> no-wrong was ever corrected by sacrificing right. The peaceful Indians occupy the San Carlos reservation by authority of the law. The Federal Government will give protection to them and any unlawful attack upon them would aggravate our present troubles and subject us to the just condemnation of the civilized world. The hostile Chiricahua Apache renegades, murderers and thieves, I am officially informed, will be pursued until their capture or utter destruction is effected....[21]

Citizens in many Arizona towns, however, met to denounce governmental failure in handling the Indian situation. Most of the resolutions forwarded to Washington demanded a more vigorous pursuit of the Indian murderers and their surrender to civil authorities. There were references to corrupt federal officials and Indian "rings." The towns uniformly condemned the Indian reservations on which hostile Indians were maintained in idleness, were fed, clothed, armed, and given the opportunity to commit inhuman outrages as tribal amusement. Globe residents were particularly bitter in condemning the military's failure to quell the Indian disturbances; they blamed General Crook and his temporizing policy for the loss of many lives and recommended his transfer from Arizona.

Crook resigned his command on April 2, 1886, following a second campaign into Mexico. On January 11, a company of his Indian scouts under the command of Captain Emmet Crawford was fired upon by Mexican irregulars who were also pursuing the Apache renegades. Craw-

---

[20]*Ibid.*
[21]Letter of Zulick to Lamar, from Prescott, Arizona, December 24, 1885, *ibid.*

ford was shot through the head and was replaced by Lieutenant Marion P. Maus, who brought his Americans back to Arizona after arranging a conference for General Crook with Geronimo. The meeting was held on March 25, in the Cañon de los Embudos, south of the border near San Bernardino. Crook refused the chief's offer to go back to the reservation without any punishment. He agreed, however, to the surrender of the hostiles on the basis of two-years' imprisonment in the East and then a return to the reservation.[22]

Following the conference Crook departed for Fort Bowie, leaving Maus to escort the prisoners. Unfortunately, Indians purchased some mescal from a trader named Tribolet near the border. Geronimo and Nachite, who were among those who got wildly drunk, led a group of some twenty warriors and about as many women and children back to the Sierra Madres. Maus pursued the escapees but to no avail. In the meantime, the rest of the Indians were escorted to Fort Bowie, arriving on April 2. A few days later, all the Chiricahua prisoners at the post, seventy-seven in number, were sent to Fort Marion, Florida, for an indefinite time, in conformity with the wishes of President Cleveland and General Philip Sheridan, Crook's superior.[23]

Geronimo's escape fastened upon him the well-earned reputation of being an unreliable and honorless man. This incident also terminated the Arizona career of the officer who had done so much to bring peace to the mountains and desert of this territory. General Crook resigned his command in a telegram to General Sheridan. The latter had long been skeptical of Crook's faith in Indian scouts and was convinced by Geronimo's successful escape that the scouts were unwilling to fight and kill their people. Sheridan also insisted upon unconditional surrender of the Apaches, whereas Crook had promised them a short imprisonment in the East. Crook believed just as strongly that the strategy upon which he had conducted his operations would prove most successful in the end. Rather than change his methods he asked to be relieved.[24]

So it was not Crook, but General Nelson Miles who was commanding the Department of Arizona when the last chapter of the Apache wars was written. Miles found that Crook's methods had been essentially

[22]U. S. Senate, *Letter from the Secretary of War . . . Regarding the Apache Indians,* 51st Cong., 1st Sess., 1890, Sen. Exec. Doc. No. 88, Vol. IX, pp. 2-3 and 11-17.

[23]*Ibid.*

[24]Letter of Brigadier General George Crook to Lieutenant General Philip H. Sheridan, from Fort Bowie, Arizona, April 1, 1886, in Britton Davis, *The Truth About Geronimo* (New Haven, Conn.: Yale University Press, 1929), p. 217.

General Nelson A. Miles, commander of the military Department of Arizona when the Apache wars were finally brought to an end in 1886.

Signaling with the heliograph at Fort Bowie. This fort was station number one in General Miles's signaling system. Station number three was located north of Bowie on what is now appropriately called Heliograph Peak in the Graham Mountains.

correct but introduced a few innovations. He divided the country most frequented by the Apaches into districts of observation, each garrisoned with sufficient troops (from his total command of over 5,000 soldiers and 500 Indian scouts) to keep the section clear of hostiles.

The high mountain ranges and hot sun, which had been considered great obstacles in the subjugation of Apaches, were used to advantage. Miles established a system of twenty-seven heliograph stations to neutralize the advantage the savages had enjoyed through their system of smoke signals. Proof that the Army men really did their work in observing the movements of the Indians can be seen from the number of messages sent between May 1 to September 30, 1886 — 2,264, of which 802 emanated from Fort Bowie. On one occasion the men transmitted a message eight hundred miles over inaccessible mountain peaks in less than four hours. Finally, an expeditionary force of nearly one hundred carefully picked desert men and Indian scouts was organized under Captain H. W. Lawton to hunt down the renegades. For nearly three months this small column held grimly to the bloody trail of the Apaches. Then late in August, Lieutenant Charles B. Gatewood, with an escort from Lawton's force, met Geronimo under a flag of truce and secured his promise to meet with Miles near the border for a final surrender.

On September 4, General Miles met the renegades in Skeleton Canyon a few miles north of the line and accepted their surrender. The Indians were taken to Fort Bowie and then marched to Bowie Station, fourteen miles away, for entrainment to Florida as the Fourth Cavalry Band appropriately played "Auld Lang Syne." One reason for the surrender of Geronimo's band was that some of the warriors wanted to be with their families in Florida. A few weeks earlier the Chiricahuas at Fort Apache had been assembled on the pretext of a roll call to receive rations. They were placed under guard by the troops and escorted to Holbrook, Arizona, where the 382 individuals were placed on the train and sent to Fort Marion. The removal of the Chiricahuas brought a close to the last of a savage and formidable opposition that had impeded the progress of civilization in the Southwest for more than three centuries.

Governor Zulick was very .pleased with the deportation of the hostile Indians and wrote in his report to the Secretary of the Interior, on September 25, 1886, that the capture of the outlaws had already had a beneficial effect upon Arizona's industries.[25] About a month earlier

---

[25]U. S. Dept. of the Interior, *Report of the Governor of the Territory of Arizona to the Secretary of the Interior, 1886*, p. 3.

he had gone to Washington for consultation with Secretary Lamar in regard to the Indian situation. The Secretary did not need much persuading, however, in regard to the removal plan. His own son, special agent L. C. Q. Lamar, Jr., had investigated the San Carlos reservation with General Miles and found the presence of the Chiricahuas a definite threat to the peace of the Southwest.

Miles, and also Governor Edmund G. Ross of New Mexico, strongly advocated transferring the hostile Indians out of the Southwest. Expressing his gratitude for this kind of support, Zulick attempted to justify a policy of removal to the Eastern press. He told a *New York Times* reporter, for example, that the expulsion of the Chiricahuas was an "absolute and pressing necessity." His objection to forgiving Geronimo and letting him return once again to the reservation was supported by references to past experience. "It is estimated," he said, "that in the raids made by these Indians since their first surrender in 1878 there have been 2,500 persons murdered in Mexico, Arizona, and the adjoining Territories, besides the destruction of a vast amount of property." When the *Times* interviewer asked the Governor where the Indians should be sent, he replied, "This question the Government must answer. In that question I am not deeply interested. We have borne the burden of their presence for many years, and we are now only anxious that the burden be transferred."[26]

Governor Zulick did not become complacent after the deportation of Geronimo and the Chiricahuas. On November 6, 1886, he wrote a letter to President Cleveland protesting against the transfer of the 8th Infantry out of Arizona to the Department of the Platte. Zulick explained that there were still 47,000 Indians in the Department of Arizona, a border along the Mexican state of Sonora 330 miles long, and a population scattered over 113,000 square miles of the territory. Arizona people felt that a strong military garrison was needed for the protection of their life and property.[27]

The Governor sent another letter of protest the following April after Mr. Herbert Welsh and Captain John G. Bourke, who had been on General Crook's staff, visited Fort Marion, Florida, and recommended that the Indians there be transferred back to the West. He wrote to Secretary Lamar that a new and brighter day had dawned in Arizona with the expulsion of the Chiricahuas. "The long sigh of relief which our people gave over the exile of this band of assassins had scarcely died away," he said, "ere their return to the high dry plains

---

[26]*New York Times,* August 22, 1886.

[27] Letter of Governor Zulick to President Grover Cleveland, from Prescott, Arizona, November 6, 1886, Cleveland Papers, Library of Congress.

Geronimo at Fort Sill in 1905.

— Special Collections,
University of Arizona Library

country of the West is being agitated. I am not inclined nor is it my right to question the philanthropic motive actuating Mr. Welsh in his interests in these Indians, and his desire for 'opportunity and facilities for their improvement and civilization,' but I do respectfully protest against the starting of a new breeding pen for assassins in Arizona. . . . Mercy to them is cruelty to us." Zulick emphasized that hundreds of brutal deaths and thousands of dollars of destroyed property testified to Arizona's past efforts to humanize the savages. If there had to be additional sacrifices he suggested that the altars "be erected and the victims be immolated somewhere other than on the 'high, dry plain country of the West.' "[28]

The administration in Washington must have been in sympathy with Zulick's view since the Chiricahuas were not returned to the West until 1894, and even then they were brought only as far as Fort Sill in the western part of the Indian Territory of Oklahoma. Geronimo was eventually converted to Christianity at Fort Sill. Uniting with the Methodist Church, he made a public confession of his many bloody deeds committed on the warpath. He urged his people to give up dancing and other worldly amusements and to repent for their sins. Needless to say,

---

[28]Letter of Governor Zulick to Secretary Lamar, from Prescott, Arizona, April 8, 1887, Record Group 48, Territorial Papers.

Geronimo's conversion to peaceful ways caused quite a sensation among Indians of Oklahoma and the Indian Territory.[29]

The Indian problem is not the only one that plagued Zulick during his first year in office. His first difficulty arose over patronage. The Republican officeholders refused to vacate for new appointees, basing their claim to tenure on two-year appointments made by the Council. The directors of the insane asylum were particularly aggravating to Zulick. Accused of selling bonds voted by the Thirteenth Assembly at too low a price, the members refused to acknowledge the Governor's authority or to produce their books. A court decree finally ousted the board but only after considerable ill will had been generated by both sides.

Governor Zulick made a careful study of the activities of the thirteenth legislature and advised the Department of the Interior that money had been appropriated contrary to law. His purpose was to seek a legal interpretation of the federal statutes involved that he could use in preventing a recurrence of past evils.[30] He felt that the people's treasury had been plundered and asked Justice J. C. Shields of the Third Judicial District to call a United States grand jury to determine whether the last Assembly had confined itself to rightful legislation or had acted corruptly. As mentioned earlier, the jury substantiated Zulick's own analysis of the situation. The Governor, in his letter to Washington, emphasized that the legislature had voted themselves special compensation, $40 for each House member and $90 for each Councilman, even though the federal law specifically forbade legislators to receive any pay except the per diem and mileage appropriated by Congress.[31] He also mentioned the illegal expenditures for clerk hire, postage, furniture, and rent for committee rooms; he seemed particularly concerned about the $23,967 disbursement for printing when the federal statute allotted only $4,000.

Zulick also wrote to Senator Benjamin Harrison, Chairman of the Senate Committee on Territories, in response to the latter's request for information on the territorial debt. In the tabulated statement of bonded and floating indebtedness that he submitted appear the following items: insane asylum bonds, $100,000; Gila River bridge, $15,000; Apache

---

[29]*New York Times,* July 22, 1903.

[30]Letter of Governor Zulick to Secretary Lamar, from Prescott, Arizona, December 2, 1885, Record Group 48, Territorial Papers.

[31]*U. S. Statutes at Large,* Vol. XVII, 42d Cong., 3d Sess., 1873, Chap. 48, p. 416.

wagon road, $12,000; territorial university, $25,000. Outstanding warrants amounted to $120,948, upon which interest was being paid at the rate of 10 percent. The aggregate debt of the counties of the territory was $1,101,625. In concluding his report, Governor Zulick wrote:

> The enormous increase of the debt by bonds and appropriations may be properly characterized as useless and extravagant legislation, a wanton misappropriation of public funds to purposes from which the people receive no corresponding benefits. The insane of the Territory are cared for at the asylum at Stockton, Cal., for $6 per week each patient, which is much less than we could keep them ourselves had we the asylum built. We require neither university nor normal school. The wagon road and bridge bonds are properly county and not Territorial charges. The appropriations for the last Territorial Assembly in excess of Congressional appropriations for that purpose are in my judgment in clear violation of the Federal statutes. In conclusion, permit me to say we have a debt when all the appropriations of the last Assembly are provided for, of nearly $700,000, upon which the Territory must pay an annual interest of over $50,000, a result of recklessness and extravagance in legislative government.[32]

The fact is that Congress had done little to restrict financial operations of the territories, at least not in the fashion that states imposed limitations upon themselves. The one exception was the standardization of salaries in 1873, whereby "compensation other than that provided by the laws of the United States" to territorial governors, secretaries, and legislators was prohibited.[33] And even this law was circumvented after Congress cut down legislative expense allowances in 1879.[34] But on July 30, 1886, a statute, partially prompted by the extravagance of the Thirteenth Legislative Assembly of Arizona, was enacted to limit territorial indebtedness. Known as the "Harrison Act," the law did not restrict taxation but forbade the contraction of any debt in behalf of a territory except to pay the interest on the territorial debt, to suppress insurrections, or to provide for the public defense. In addition to indebtedness created for these purposes, the legislature could authorize a loan for the erection of penal, charitable, or educational institutions for such territory, providing that the total debt did not exceed one percent of the assessed valuation of the taxable property in the territory. Furthermore, no municipality, county, or other political subdivision of

---

[32]*New York Times,* January 5, 1886.

[33]*U. S. Statutes at Large,* Vol. XVII, 42d Cong., 3d Sess., 1873, Chap. 48, p. 416.

[34]Letter of Secretary James A. Bayard to Secretary Lamar, from Prescott, Arizona, November 6, 1886, Record Group 48, Miscellaneous File No. 252.

a territory could encumber itself with bond obligations in excess of 4 percent of the assessed valuation.[35]

The "Harrison Act" also prohibited territorial legislatures from enacting special laws such as granting divorces, changing the names of persons or places, locating or changing county seats, providing for the punishment of crimes or misdemeanors, regulating the rate of interest on money, summoning and impaneling grand or petit juries, incorporating municipalities, regulating the practice in justice courts, regulating the jurisdiction and duties of justices of the peace and so forth.

The first legislature to come under the restrictions of this act, and also the first to convene during the Zulick administration, was the Fourteenth Assembly. In his message to this body in January 1887, Governor Zulick commented upon the territory's prosperity and said that for the first time in its history, Arizona was relieved of the curse of hostile Indians and free to develop its many resources. He praised General Nelson Miles and Captains Crawford, Gatewood, Lawton, and Lebo for their capture of Geronimo and the shipment of his hostile band by rail to Florida. Zulick also mentioned the growth of the cattle industry and recommended a quarantine law to protect against diseased cattle from outside the territory.

Further reviewing events of his first year in office, the Governor reported that twelve new school districts had been formed to make a total of 130 and that land had been secured for the University of Arizona at Tucson. He pointed out that the prison operating costs had been reduced and recommended that the legislature economize wherever possible.[36] This latter advice apparently was well taken since the law-makers to whom he spoke became known as the "Measly Fourteenth." Whereas the thirteenth legislature appropriated $294,323.00, the fourteenth spent only $44,216.73.[37] Altogether, 102 bills were passed, two of which were vetoed: one creating a lottery corporation, and another giving a salary of $1,200 per annum to each of the federal judges in addition to his regular salary.[38]

An attempt was made to create another county, to be known as "Frisco" with a county seat at Flagstaff, out of Yavapai. The law-

---

[35]*U. S. Statutes at Large,* Vol. XXIV, 49th Cong., 1st Sess., 1886, pp. 170-71.

[36]Letter of Governor Zulick to Secretary Lamar, from Prescott, Arizona, March 19, 1886, Record Group 48, Territorial Papers: Arizona.

[37]"Message of Governor C. Meyer Zulick," *Journals of the Fourteenth Legislative Assembly,* 1887, pp. 229-30.

[38]Letters of Governor Zulick to Secretary Lamar, from Prescott, Arizona, March 1, 1887, and April 2, 1887, Record Group 48, Territorial Papers.

makers voted down the bill but a later legislature picked up the idea and carved Coconino County out of the area suggested. Perhaps the Fourteenth Assembly's outstanding accomplishment was its creation of a livestock sanitary commission and the passage of livestock laws to stop rustling and to control stock disease. By the provisions of the "Stock and Sanitary Law," every cattle owner was required to register his brands and marks with a county recorder and the board was given the duty of protecting the health of the domestic animals of the territory from all contagious or infectious diseases of a malignant character. For this purpose it could prescribe a quarantine which the governor proclaimed and enforced.[39] Armed with this authority, Zulick, on August 18, 1887, issued a proclamation against the importation of Mexican cattle. Because of the fact that infected European livestock had been dumped on the Mexican ranges, all cattle from Mexico were to be placed on a ninety-day quarantine at the border before a certificate of health could be granted permitting entrance into the United States.[40]

The Mexican government protested this proclamation to the U. S. Secretary of State. The minister of that country, Matias Romero, even suggested the possibility of a like reprisal on the commerce of the United States with Mexico. An international incident was perhaps forestalled when the Arizona Livestock Sanitary Board was advised that its quarantine was null and void because it conflicted with the constitutional power of Congress to regulate interstate and foreign commerce.[41] Though the federal government soon assumed jurisdiction, the principle of protection against imported livestock disease was established by the Arizona legislature. Never able to avoid controversy, however, Zulick was criticized by some Arizona cattlemen who grazed stock in Mexico. Colin Cameron, for example, was quoted by the *Tombstone Epitaph* (November 15, 1888) as saying that the Livestock Sanitary Board was unjustly discriminatory and was being used by the Chicago "beef pool" in an attempt to keep prices up.[42]

The livestock laws and other good work of the fourteenth legislature were generally overlooked by the newspapers that were condemn-

---

[39]*Revised Statutes of Arizona,* 1887, Pars. 2797-2819, pp. 504-508.

[40]*Tombstone Epitaph,* September 3, 1887. The Governor's proclamation is printed in full in this issue. See also, *Tombstone Prospector,* October 7, 1887.

[41]Letter of Mr. Matias Romero, Minister of Mexico, to Secretary of State Thomas F. Bayard, as translated at the Mexican legation, Washington, D. C., November 16, 1887; see also, letter of Governor Zulick to Secretary Lamar, from Prescott, Arizona, November 16, 1887, Record Group 48, Territorial Papers.

[42]*Tombstone Epitaph,* November 15, 1888.

ing the Zulick administration in bitter language. In this vein, the *Arizona Silver Belt* of Globe, on April 2, 1887, printed a letter written by a Democrat that stated in part that "it has become evident that Governor Zulick, in his capacity as executive of the Territory, is a failure, and that charges of political duplicity brought against him by an almost unanimous press are generally true."[43] He was accused of inconsistencies in first advocating the abolition of county courts while endeavoring to establish an equally, if not more, costly circuit-court system to create "fat" positions for his political henchmen. Then, in contrast to his veto of a lottery bill, on high moral grounds, he sanctioned all sorts of games of chance by signing a law permitting the licensing of gambling.[44] The letter writer contended that "the appointment, by the President, of Zulick as Governor was, to say the least, unfortunate."[45]

The *Arizona Daily Star* charged Governor Zulick with making a political deal with the Mormon Church, agreeing to prevent the enactment of territorial laws inimical to the Mormons or polygamy in return for the Church's support.[46] The charge had some basis in fact. In his message to the Fourteenth Assembly in January, 1887, the Governor recommended the repeal of the "test oath law" which had been passed two years before with the idea of disenfranchising members of the Mormon Church. "A man may be an advocate of bigamy or polygamy, or belong to the church that so believes," he said, "but until he puts forth his belief in practice he has offended no law. Legislation should control actions, not opinions." Zulick's arguments seemed sound to the Assembly and the law was repealed. However, a federal statute, the Edmunds Act, was sufficient to stop the practice of polygamy if enforced as it had been against five polygamists during the administration of Governor Tritle.[47] It was not polygamy that worried the *Star;* rather, a possible union of Church and State as a result of the Zulick-Mormon combine was the cause of concern.

According to a *Star* editorial, the Mormons held the balance of power between the political parties in Arizona. The newspaper predicted that at the next election there would be but one issue, whether the Church or State would control policy in Arizona; this situation would result in the political parties being Mormon or anti-Mormon. A

---

[43]*Arizona Silver Belt* (Globe), April 2, 1887.

[44]Letter of Governor Zulick to Secretary Lamar, from Prescott, Arizona, March 19, 1886, Record Group 48, Territorial Papers.

[45]*Arizona Silver Belt,* April 2, 1887.

[46]*New York Times,* October 31, 1887.

[47]*Ibid.*

circular letter, dated June 21, 1887, and distributed in Arizona by Bishop H. B. Clawson of Salt Lake City, indicated that the L. D. S. Church was fulfilling its part of a bargain with the Arizona Governor. The Bishop urged the Mormon Elders to support a Phoenix newspaper controlled by Zulick and five of his subordinates and edited by the Governor's private secretary. Clawson wrote as follows:

> Dear Brother: You will receive regularly for one year a free copy of the Phoenix *Gazette.* That journal is well-disposed to our people, and we have every reason to believe it will use an influence in favor of their being protected in the enjoyment of their rights. This being the case, besides its being ably conducted, we deem it worthy the support of our people throughout the section where you are located. If you will kindly use an influence in extending the subscription list of the *Gazette* it will be appreciated and probably conducive to the general good. . . .[48]

The evidence indicated that the Mormon colonizing efforts had been successful and that the Church held the political balance of power in Arizona. No charge of law violation was made, however. The *Star's* exposé of the Zulick-Mormon deal attracted considerable attention, mainly because the Tucson journal was a strong supporter of the Cleveland administration that had appointed Zulick.

The *Star,* whose editor, Louis C. Hughes, was later appointed governor, continued its attacks upon the private and public life of Zulick. In an editorial on February 11, 1888, under the title of "Why," the paper bitterly denounced him with a long list of alleged malfeasance and shortcomings. "Governor Zulick has more than a thousand times tried to explain why the people and the *Star* have declared against his administration of the affairs of the territory," the editorial began,

> but with all of his explanations he has utterly failed to convince the good citizens of Arizona that his successor should not be appointed. The last heard from Governor Zulick he was in Washington trying to explain why he had become so unpopular with the people. Our correspondent says: "that from the governor's talk it would appear his unpopularity was all due to Hughes and the *Star*." Now this is a mistake. It is all on account of Zulick himself. His conduct in private and public life and his misconduct in office.

Stating that if Zulick wanted the trust of the people he would have to explain a large number of things, the editorial asked why he issued the famous, unpopular proclamation of December 23, 1885, warning the people not to take the law into their own hands to punish the Apaches; and why he signed the bill appropriating money to publish

---

[48]*Arizona Daily Star,* October 30, 1887; and *New York Times,* October 31, 1887.

a codification of Arizona statutes when the appropriation was far in excess of the limit fixed by Congress.[49] Continuing its enumeration, the editorial also asked:

> Why he entered into a bargain with Richards, Marion, King and others to appoint them to offices with the understanding they were to resign within a few days after the legislature adjourned, that he might appoint members of the legislature in their stead who could not be confirmed by the legislative council?
>
> Why after his attempt thus to violate the law indirectly and the will of the people through their representatives (the confirming power), and the same was exposed, he carried out the compact with such brazen audacity by accepting the resignation of his stool pigeons and appointing the legislative parties to the combine?
>
> Why he appointed as auditor a member of the assembly in violation of the law, the emoluments of the office having been increased by the legislature of which the appointee was a member?
>
> Why he formed a lobby for the defeat of railroad legislation in the reduction of fares and freights, and boasted of his success in obstructing legislation on this subject, of all other questions the most important to the people?
>
> Why his legislative friends urged the passage of the lottery bill and voted for it, and then vetoed the same? . . .
>
> Why he recommended in his message the increase of the district judges' salaries, and when the legislature passed a bill in accordance with his message, he vetoed the same?
>
> Why he recommended the repeal of the county courts, and after their repeal, used all the influence of his office to foist upon the people a much more expensive and extravagant system of territorial courts? . . .
>
> Why sterling democrats in both branches of the legislature denounced him as dishonest, unreliable and unworthy of trust by either the party or the people, if not on account of his questionable combines during the time the legislature was in session? . . .
>
> . . . .
>
> Why he issued the quarantine proclamation against the importation of cattle from Europe and Mexico under the guise of law, when the intent of the proclamation was against Sonora only where there were no signs of any infectious diseases known among cattle in that state, and when he well knew the representations made to him was [*sic*] in

---

[49]The next Secretary, Nathan O. Murphy, reported that the excess expenditure amounted to $8,000. See letter of Secretary Murphy to the First Comptroller, from Phoenix, Arizona, May 24, 1889, Record Group 217, Territorial Letters Received, Vol. 20; see also, *U. S. Statutes at Large,* Vol. XXV, 50th Cong., 1st Sess., 1888, Chap. 615, p. 276, wherein $3,750 was appropriated for printing.

the interest of a few Arizona shippers who wanted to shut out Sonora cattle from the market?[50]

Why was it he contracted for the sale of the territorial funding bonds at par when he well knew they ought to and would bring from 5 to 10 per cent premium? . . .

After also questioning why the governor received $20,000 when the Vulture mine was sold even though he had no interest in the mine, and wondering whether he had used his official position to promote the sale or had threatened to hinder it "if his position was not recognized," the editorial included: "Why is it that every Federal official in the territory disapproves of his official course and the press with but three exceptions condemn his administration, and the people irrespective of party desire the President to appoint his successor?"[51]

Though much of the criticism of Governor Zulick was exaggerated, his days were numbered after Republican Benjamin Harrison defeated Cleveland in 1888. At that time, however, the new President did not take office until the March following his election. Thus, Zulick was still in office when the Fifteenth Legislative Assembly convened at Prescott on January 21, 1889. Even before the session assembled, a rumor circulated in the territory that a majority of both houses favored removing the capital to Phoenix. There, a commodious city hall had been erected that would comfortably accommodate the legislature and the territorial officials. On January 26, Zulick signed Legislative Act No. 1 that declared that "on and after the 4th day of February, in the year of our Lord Eighteen Hundred and Eighty-Nine, the permanent seat of Government and Capital of this Territory shall be, and the same is, hereby located and established at the City of Phoenix, in the County of Maricopa."[52]

Secretary James A. Bayard was aggravated because of the short notice which he received of the capital's removal. All his preparations, including renting of the hall from the Prescott City Council, purchasing legislative supplies, preparing the legislative hall, and receiving bills for public printing, had been made with the understanding that the session would be held at Prescott. All the government property under

---

[50]C. M. Bruce, Chairman of the Livestock Sanitary Board, explained the need for Governor Zulick's quarantine proclamation. He said that there was widespread pleuro-pneumonia in Europe which could be brought easily to Mexico because that country had no sanitary regulations. In regard to the charge that the quarantine was for another purpose, Bruce wrote, "I repel such insinuations with scorn and indignation. . . . " Letter of C. M. Bruce to Governor Zulick, from Prescott, Arizona, December 13, 1887, Record Group 48, Territorial Papers.

[51]*Arizona Daily Star,* February 11, 1888.

[52]*Acts, Resolutions and Memorials,* Fifteenth Legislative Assembly, 1889, p. 19.

his charge was there and he was frustrated at the thought of having to move it to Phoenix by February 4. Under the territorial statutes he was obliged to attend all sessions of the legislature and, therefore, had to box and ship out all the records, supplies, and furniture by February 1. His problem was complicated by the fact that the road between Prescott and Phoenix was impassable for freighting, and the government property had to be sent on the railroad by way of California. In a letter to the first comptroller in the Treasury Department, Bayard wrote, "I would respectfully submit that this act is most unwise and unjust in that public business is thereby delayed, Federal officers put to unnecessary trouble and expense, and a very bad precedent established, and would suggest that the matter be brought at once to the attention of Congress, the only body having power to amend this law."[53]

The removal act was not rescinded, however; the solons packed their gripsacks and, on January 29, began a joyous junket to the new capital. Scorning the quicker Black Canyon Stage, they traveled in royal style in two Pullman cars via Los Angeles.[54] It was not unusual at that time for the legislators to accept free passes from the Santa Fe and Southern Pacific since railroads regularly extended this favor in hope that no legislation adversely affecting them would be enacted. Of course, certain citizens of Phoenix, including happy Mayor DeForest Porter, willingly picked up the tab for entertainment en route. The new shining silk hats the travelers wore on the trip were undoubtedly part of the "good will" gesture, too.

The people of Prescott were understandably disgruntled with the Phoenix politicians as well as with the Governor. Editor John Marion of the *Arizona Miner,* who as a Democrat had staunchly supported Zulick, now bitterly assailed him. Actually, the Governor had not recommended removal in his opening message to the Fifteenth Assembly, though it was well known that he favored moving the capital. Anyway, Prescott's economy was flourishing and the territorial patronage was not nearly so important to the town in 1889 as it had been in 1867 when the capital was removed to Tucson.

However, Secretary Bayard did award the printing contract of the fifteenth legislature to Marion. Another Prescott printer, J. C. Martin of the Republican *Courier,* charged Bayard with crookedness since his bid for the work was about 40 percent lower than that of Marion.

---

[53]Letter of Secretary Bayard to the First Comptroller, Department of the Treasury, from Prescott, Arizona, January 25, 1889, and telegram from Prescott, January 26, 1889, Record Group 217, Territorial Letters Received, Vol. 20.

[54]*Arizona Silver Belt,* February 2, 1889; and *Phoenix Herald,* January 26, 1889.

Thinking that he would be given the contract on the basis of his lower bid, Martin proceeded to Phoenix when the legislature moved, secured a good and sufficient bond, and reported to Bayard. He informed the latter that a number of bills had been ordered printed and that he was ready to perform the work. In spite of all this preparation, however, the contract was given to Marion, whose newspaper was the organ of Bayard and the Democratic Party.[55] Bad blood had already been spilled between the Secretary and Martin; the latter had previously filed an affidavit with the first comptroller in Washington, D.C., charging Bayard with fraud in connection with a printing contract for the last Assembly in 1887. The Secretary had refuted this charge in explaining that Marion had been awarded that job too because he was on that occasion actually the lowest bidder. In writing to the first comptroller, he said, "I consider Mr. Martin neither honest or reliable, and were the matter in my hands should absolutely decline to receive a bid from him for any work to be done. . . ."[56]

Politically, Bayard was simply following the customary practice of awarding patronage to a friendly newspaper that would likely advance the interests of his party. And except for the moving of the capital away from Prescott, the *Miner* editor undoubtedly would have given the Zulick administration his wholehearted support.

The city hall in Phoenix, where the legislature reconvened on February 7, was located in the block bounded by Washington, Jefferson, First, and Second streets. Known as the Plaza, this block was originally set aside in perpetuity by the founders of Phoenix as a place for rest and contemplation. Their laudable desire was thwarted in 1887, however, when the first floor of the old city hall was constructed. Then, just prior to removal of the capital to Phoenix, the contractor, John J. Gardiner, began work on a second floor containing two ample rooms for the legislature. Borrowing $5,000 from the Valley Bank, Gardiner worked night and day for six weeks and had the quarters ready before the "refreshed" lawmakers arrived.

One of the more notable acts passed by the legislature, once the lawmakers got down to business, startled a few people by establishing the death penalty for the crime of train robbery. Modeled after the New Mexico law, this act was praised by no less a newspaper than the *New York Herald* (quoted in *Arizona Weekly Journal-Miner,* March

---

[55]Letter of J. C. Martin to the First Comptroller, Department of the Treasury, from Prescott, Arizona, March 11, 1889, Record Group 217, Territorial Letters Received, Vol. 20.

[56]Letters of Secretary Bayard to the First Comptroller, Department of the Treasury, from Prescott, Arizona, January 9, 19, 1889, *ibid.*

The old City Hall in Phoenix. The Legislative Assembly met here after moving from Prescott in 1889.

The Arizona Capitol under construction in 1900.

20, 1889). Along with a list of train robberies committed during the previous year, the paper commented that these lawless desperadoes were no better than murderers since every passenger was at their mercy and in danger of his life. Another law enacted by the Fifteenth Assembly prohibited the carrying of deadly weapons in towns. In still other acts, the legislature promised tax exemption for six years to any railroad that might be built to the Grand Canyon, and offered a subsidy of $3,000 for the development of any artesian well that would benefit agriculture. Qualifications, including ability to read and write English, were established for territorial officeholders. And a memorial was sent to President-elect Harrison recommending that all appointments to political and judicial positions in Arizona should be made from *bona fide* residents of the territory; the practice of sending indifferent strangers on sojourns to the West was condemned.[57]

The legislature also selected three commissioners — S. M. Franklin, C. W. Johnstone, and T. D. Hammond — to obtain a site for a capitol building. The land where the capitol still stands was chosen by the commission and donated to the territory. The original structure was built of stone quarried in Arizona — gray granite for the ground floor, and tufa, a porous, volcanic stone, for the upper stories. The capitol was not completed until 1901 and was first occupied by the Twenty-First Assembly.

Another bill passed by the fifteenth legislature directed that action begin on a matter that was to require even more time for fulfillment — the achievement of statehood. This law, known as Public Act Number 59, provided for a convention to draft a constitution for Arizona.[58] It was passed too late in Zulick's term of office to be implemented, however. The next governor, Lewis Wolfley, deemed the act an "unwise measure" and refused to issue the necessary proclamation calling for the election of delegates to a constitutional convention.[59] The supporters of statehood were enraged by Wolfley's action, but pointed in vain to the argument his predecessor had given to the fifteenth legislature. Pleading for the end of territorial status for Arizona, Zulick had said, "The time has now arrived when Arizona should be relieved from this state of tutelage and be endowed with the duties and responsibilities of statehood. The rapid increase in wealth and population, the energy

---

[57]*Acts, Resolutions and Memorials,* Fifteenth Legislative Assembly, Memorial No. 12 to President Benjamin Harrison, pp. 113-14.

[58]*Ibid.,* pp. 84-88.

[59]*U. S. Congressional Record,* 51st Cong., 1st Sess., 1890, XXI, pp. 2946 and 2950.

and patriotism of her people, are sure guarantees that she would wear the robes of state sovereignty with dignity and honor."[60]

Zulick, of course, was not alone in advocating statehood. Major J. W. Powell, the Director of the U. S. Geological Survey who earlier had written a graphic account of his 1859 expedition down the Colorado River, testified before the House Committee on Territories that irrigation was practical in arid regions such as Arizona. Before the same committee, Delegate Marcus A. Smith described in detail the development of agriculture, railroads, education, and mining in Arizona. He cited the census report of 1882, which, even discounting the fact that the Yavapai County figures had been exaggerated to secure greater representation in the legislature for this part of the territory, showed that the permanent population of Arizona was increasing rapidly. The 82,976 total in 1882 was a 100 percent increase in two years and Smith estimated that close to 100,000 residents were in the territory in 1889. In his presentation to the committee, Smith quoted liberally from Governor Zulick's reports to the Interior Department. The members were evidently convinced since they reported to the House on February 13, 1889:

> The statistics in reference to the Territory of Arizona have been set forth *in extenso* in the remarks submitted to the committee by the delegate from that Territory [Mr. Smith], which remarks are printed herewith, and to which careful consideration is respectfully requested. It will be found, when all the facts are known, that Arizona is now fitted for statehood, and in the future gives promise of rapid development and a large and stable population.[61]

The idea was incubated, though nearly a quarter of a century was to elapse before Arizona finally achieved statehood.

Near the end of the fifteenth legislative session, Arizona Republicans became worried that President Harrison, who was not inaugurated until March 4, 1889, would not remove Zulick in time for a Republican successor to make territorial appointments. Ex-Governor Tritle wrote an urgent letter to the Interior Department in which he explained the situation.[62] He wrote that the governor had the power to appoint the following territorial officers, with the advice and consent of the Council, to two-year terms: treasurer, auditor, superintendent of public instruction, attorney general, veterinary surgeon, commissioner of immi-

---

[60]"Message of Governor C. Meyer Zulick," *Journals of the Fifteenth Legislative Assembly*, 1889, pp. 24-25.

[61]U. S. House, *Admission of Arizona, Idaho, and Wyoming Into the Union*, 50th Cong., 2d Sess., 1889, House Report No. 4053, pp. 1-3, 41-53.

[62]Letter from F. A. Tritle, ex-Governor of Arizona, to the Department of the Interior, received March 1, 1889, Record Group 48, Appointment Papers.

gration, three directors of the insane asylum, three commissioners of the territorial prison, five livestock sanitary commissioners, five directors of the normal school, and thirteen regents of the university. "The Governor has no power of removal," said Tritle, "and when appointments have been made by the Governor, whether they shall have been confirmed or not, the incumbents will hold until the next Legislative Assembly convenes, and will also hold over thereafter until successors shall have been nominated by the Governor and confirmed by the Council."

Tritle wrote that the Fifteenth Assembly's session, limited to sixty days by federal statute, would expire on March 22. Unless a change were made in the offices of governor and secretary in time for the above offices to be filled with Republicans before that date, the Democratic appointees of Governor Zulick would hold over for two years. Then if a Democratic Council should be elected in 1890, its members would probably refuse to confirm the appointees of a new Republican governor. In this event, the Democrats then in office might conceivably remain in office to the end of the Republican national administration.

Another Arizona leader, Royal A. Johnson, president of the Republican Club, wrote a letter to President Harrison, in which he expressed a need for an immediate change in the office of governor. "I trust," he said, "that on account of the peculiar situation of affairs here, between C. Meyer Zulick and the Republican Council, he on the one hand threatening not to sign appropriations, and the Council on the other hand refusing to confirm the Democratic nominations, you may be pleased to appoint a Republican Governor at your earliest convenience, in order that he may qualify and get here by the 15th at the latest, as the Legislature will adjourn by limitation of term a few days later."[63] Harrison did not act promptly enough, however, and the legislature had to resort to its own devices to thwart the Democrats.

The Fifteenth Legislative Assembly is sometimes called the "Holdover Legislature" because the Republican members postponed adjournment at the end of the legal sixty-day session. Their objective was to give Harrison's Republican selection for governor, Lewis Wolfley, time to return from a trip to Washington. Wolfley arrived on April 8 and by April 11 the legislature had approved his appointments and adjourned. The new governor was left to work out his own destiny. The executive office in which he performed his administrative functions was only sketchily equipped, having as its only furniture one lounge,

---

[63]Letter from Royal A. Johnson to President Benjamin Harrison, Record Group 48, Territorial Papers.

a rattan chair, two old tables, a combination washstand, a typewriter, and such miscellaneous items as three tin spittoons, four record books (orders of the governor), one trunk, one copy of *Revised Statutes of Arizona,* and a large map of the United States.[64] Wishing to work in quarters more befitting his office, Wolfley began furnishing two 20 x 24-foot rooms at considerable expense to himself.[65]

The new Secretary, Nathan O. Murphy, informed the Treasury Department that the legislative furniture had to be hauled by wagon from Prescott when the capital was moved to Phoenix. The property was three weeks in transit over bad roads and arrived totally unfit for use. The articles were not worth the freight charges, being no more than flimsy pine desks, homemade and stained for appearance's sake. The people of Phoenix saved the day for the Fifteenth Assembly by loaning the necessary furniture.[66]

Zulick remained in the territory for several years after relinquishing his office and was elected as a councilman from Maricopa County in the Sixteenth Assembly. He eventually returned to New Jersey where he died in 1926. A state Senate resolution was introduced in 1915 to invite him to visit the state of Arizona, but it was defeated because of an old political grudge. Zulick was denounced at that time by State Senator Morris Goldwater of Yavapai County because of circumstances revolving around Prescott's loss of the capital. It was charged that the removal was accomplished through the bribery of members of the Assembly. The ex-Governor was undoubtedly disappointed in not receiving the invitation, especially since he had been in the vanguard in advocating statehood for Arizona.

In 1895 a large number of telegrams and letters were sent to President Cleveland, then in his second term, and to Secretary of Interior Hoke Smith, urging the reappointment of Zulick as governor. One of the letters was from the former territorial Secretary, James A. Bayard, who summarized Zulick's attainments:

> I occupied the position of Secretary of the Territory during his term of office and was thrown into constant and intimate relation with him,

---

[64]Affidavit of Governor Lewis Wolfley to the Treasury Department, from Prescott, Arizona, May 11, 1889, Record Group 217, Territorial Letters Received, Vol. 20.

[65]Governor Wolfley to Secretary of the Interior John Noble, from Phoenix, Arizona, March 24, 1890, Record Group 48, Territorial Papers.

[66]Letter of Secretary Nathan O. Murphy to the First Comptroller, Department of the Treasury, from Phoenix, Arizona, July 14, 1889, Record Group 217, Territorial Letters Received, Vol. 20; and letter of January 25, 1890, *ibid.,* Vol. 21.

and am in a position to know of what great and lasting benefit this administration has been in the Territory. By him the reckless extravagance which had marked the previous Republican administrations was done away with and the credit of the Territory which he found in an apparently hopeless condition, was restored in the position which her resources and population entitle her. By his wise and judicious recommendations in regard to Indian affairs, which were endorsed and carried out by the National Administration, the Territory was freed from the Chiricahua Apaches, fear of whose bloodthirsty depredations had for years prevented immigration to the Territory and practically destroyed the value of property of all kinds in the Southeastern portion. Under his administration population and assessed values of property largely increased, the rate of taxation decreased and Territorial warrants which he found selling at 80 cents on the dollar, he left in active demand at par. Beyond any other man in the territory he has the confidence of the business and professional classes and his appointment as Governor would be regarded as the guarantee of an honest and businesslike administration of the affairs of the Territory, and would in my judgment greatly strengthen the party in the Southwest. His record as an honest money man and a consistent opponent of free silver coinage would of itself be of great advantage to the party at this juncture. His ability and attainments are well known and as a lawyer and man of affairs his reputation is thoroughly established throughout the Southwest. . . .[67]

Though Governor Zulick was not reappointed, he probably would have been proud to accept as authentic Bayard's appraisal of his tenure in the Arizona governorship. However, most contemporary political leaders, in both parties, were less eulogistic in evaluating the Zulick administration. The regular elections, which were held in 1886 and 1888 to choose a delegate to Congress and county officers, gave his critics ample opportunities to attack his record.

The Republicans were most severe but not alone in their criticism. In their territorial conventions, composed of delegates from all the counties, they condemned the Governor because he was a carpetbagger and because of his partisanship.[68] They opened the 1888 convention in Tucson with a rousing song by the Phoenix Glee Club called "Good Bye, Grover, Good Bye," and then proceeded to castigate the Democratic administration in Washington for not fulfilling its pledge of "home

---

[67]Letter from former Secretary Bayard to Secretary of the Interior Hoke Smith, from Newport News, Virginia, July 10, 1895, Record Group 48, Appointment Papers.

[68]*Arizona Weekly Citizen,* September 25, 1886; and "Platform" of the Republican Party in Arizona, 1888, printed in the *Arizona Daily Star,* September 20, 1888.

rule" made in 1884 and for remaining silent on the question in its 1888 platform. Strongly advocating that federal offices in Arizona should be filled by residents of the territory, the Republican delegates denounced Zulick at great length. They accused him of promiscuously pardoning criminals (such as the Chinese murderer Wing Ti), of appointing an unnecessary and expensive code commission, and of encouraging corruption and extravagance by "trafficking" in political patronage — even to the point of giving jobs illegally to members of the legislature in return for support.

But, in the words of the Democratic editor of the *Arizona Daily Star*, L. C. Hughes, Zulick was "between the devil and the deep blue sea," for he was also conspicuously repudiated by his own party.[69] The 1888 Democratic territorial convention, though stacked with a large number of pro-Zulick delegates led by Councilman George H. Stevens of Graham County, refused to give him a vote of confidence and even voted, 84 to 30, not to endorse the administration of President Cleveland.[70] Like the Republicans, the Arizona Democrats wanted "home rule." They chose to follow Marcus A. Smith, the former district attorney of Cochise County, who had identified himself with local interests. Though Smith himself had been a resident of the territory only since 1880, he upset the incumbent Republican Delegate-to-Congress Curtis C. Bean in 1886. And in the next election, despite Republican gains that gave that party control of the territorial Council and a nearly even split in the House, the popular and invincible Smith overwhelmed another Republican, General Thomas F. Wilson, by the huge margin — for that time — of over 3,800 votes.[71] So Smith, not Zulick, was the champion of the Arizona Democracy and was kept in office continuously (except for three terms when he chose not to run in 1894, 1898, and 1902) until he was finally defeated by Republican Ralph Cameron of Coconino County in 1908.

Smith's Republican victims during his long ascendency in Arizona politics included, in addition to Bean and General Wilson, George W. Cheyney (1890), W. G. Stewart (1892), A. J. Doran (1896), Nathan O. Murphy (1900), Benjamin Fowler (1904), and W. F. Cooper (1906). Several prominent third-party candidates, most notably William O. "Buckey" O'Neill, the Populist aspirant in 1896, were also defeated. During his eight terms as delegate to Congress, Mark Smith could not

---

[69]*Arizona Daily Star*, September 20, 1888.

[70]*Arizona Weekly Citizen*, September 8, 1888.

[71]*Arizona Daily Star*, November 29, 1888.

cast one vote, but he was able to introduce a total of 277 bills, 35 of which were enacted into laws.[72] Though he was not privileged to be in office when statehood was finally obtained, his labors in Congress through the years contributed, as we shall see, to the ultimate enactment of that legislation. In his desire to add a star to the American flag for his adopted territory, he shared something in common with most Arizonans — and with C. Meyer Zulick too!

[72]Official Record of Mark A. Smith, Delegate from Arizona, 1887–1909 (scrapbooks of clippings and and typewritten excerpts from the *Congressional Record*), Vol. 1, p. 3. [Arizona Department of Library and Archives, Phoenix]

Chapter 11

Political Confusion:
The Wolfley Administration

By 1889 a large number of Arizona people were advocating home rule. The *Arizona Daily Citizen* spoke out on this point in reminding President-elect Benjamin Harrison of a pertinent section in the Republican National Platform of 1888. According to this plank, "all officers, pending preparations for statehood should be selected from bona fide residents and citizens of the Territory wherein they have to serve." The *Citizen* asked Harrison to make his appointments from Arizona voters and to reject carpetbag adventurers who sought Arizona only as a political or official field.[1] "If there is any one important event that may be expected to occur before March 15th, in which the people are interested," the paper editorialized, "it is the appointment of the new Governor. It is confessedly an important epoch in our history, as we believe the appointee will be a genuine resident of our Territory, and that his appointment will mark the inauguration of a happy era of home rule for Arizona." After stressing the need for the appointment of an intelligent, upright, native son to demonstrate the wisdom of home rule, the *Citizen* endorsed Lewis Wolfley, who applied for the governorship.[2]

His application met with considerable opposition from other candidates and vested interests. Among the men vying for the job was former Governor A. P. K. Safford.[3] He was turned down after the revelation of a letter he had written to the president of the Southern Pacific railroad; Safford had used only $5,000 of $25,000 given to him

---

[1]*Arizona Daily Citizen,* February 23, 1889.

[2]*Ibid.*

[3]Petition of 350 citizens of Cochise County, Arizona, to the Department of the Interior, received March 8, 1889; petition of Arizona citizens to President Benjamin Harrison, n. d.; letter of Professor John A. Spring to Senator W. M. Stewart of Nevada, from Tucson, Arizona, February 16, 1889, Record Group 48, Appointment Papers.

to "fix" the Arizona legislature and returned the balance with a statement that he had overestimated the lawmakers. A second applicant, Curtis Coe Bean, represented the territory in the forty-ninth Congress, 1885–87, where he secured a right-of-way through the Pima and Maricopa Indian reservations for the Phoenix and Maricopa Railroad. Defeated for reelection, he returned to Arizona, where he had been a resident since 1868, and resumed mining operations. Bean likely would have received the appointment as governor, but he decided to withdraw from consideration because of his financial problems and the strong dislike of his wife for the frontier.[4]

The third and successful contender, Wolfley, was in Washington, D.C., when he applied for the position in a letter to President Harrison on March 6, 1889, two days after the latter was inaugurated. ". . . I have been a resident of this Territory for the past six years," he wrote,

> and have become familiar with many of its wants and necessities and I became a candidate for this position at the earnest request of its inhabitants, in proof of which, I enclose herewith the endorsements of many of its prominent republicans and republican organizations, editorials from the oldest and most influential paper in the Territory (*Citizen* of Tucson), as well as an editorial from the leading democratic paper of the Territory (*Gazette* of Phoenix) showing the necessity and reasons for a change of administration. I entered the service in 1861 (3rd Kentucky Cavalry) and was mustered out in 1865, having served through the entire war. I respectfully refer to the accompanying endorsements of General Miles, to whom I am well known and who has a personal knowledge of the wants and needs of Arizona, to General Schofield, ensuring cordial action between the civil and military in the most serious questions of this Territory — Indian troubles — to General and Senator Sherman who have known me from childhood, to Hon. J. J. Belden of New York, William Penn Nixon of Chicago, and other endorsements. I am also well known to Secretaries Blaine and Noble.[5]

Wolfley's candidacy was bitterly fought by certain vested interests since he had antagonized several claimants to land grants which he had surveyed for the United States. One prominent cattleman, Brewster Cameron of the San Rafael Cattle Company, attempted to use his eastern connections — his uncle, Senator Don Cameron of Pennsylvania

---

[4]U. S. House, *Biographical Directory of the American Congress, 1774–1961*, p. 531.

[5]Letter of Lewis Wolfley to President Harrison, from Washington, D. C., March 6, 1889, Record Group 48, Appointment Papers; see also, letter of Brigadier General Nelson A. Miles, from San Francisco, March 4, 1889, *ibid.*; and letter of General W. T. Sherman (no address), from New York, February 22, 1889, *ibid.*

Lewis Wolfley, governor of the Territory of Arizona from 1889 to 1890.

— to prevent the confirmation of Wolfley's nomination.[6] He sent a number of affidavits to the Senate showing that Wolfley was guilty of perjury and of blackmailing settlers of lands he had surveyed. In reality, Cameron probably had reason to believe that Wolfley would not support his company's extensive land-boundary claims.

An attempt was also made to discredit Wolfley in connection with his government service in New Orleans during the period of reconstruction. It was charged that he had been removed in 1869, for unfitness, from the position of assessor in the First Internal Revenue District of Louisiana. Another of the charges was that he had been paid a stipulated amount per month by a distiller who wished to be left alone; this latter information was contained in a letter Senator Charles B. Farwell received from the distiller.[7] In spite of this opposition to his appointment as Governor, however, Wolfley's nomination was confirmed by the Senate on March 28, 1889, and on April 8 he took the oath of office.[8]

Several months after he assumed office, he wrote to President Harrison to explain the New Orleans incident and prove that he had not been fired. He said that he was young and hot-headed at the time and that he had been personally and bitterly attacked by his superior,

---

[6]Letter of William Penn Nixon to Secretary of the Interior John Noble, from Tucson, Arizona, March 13, 1889, *ibid.*

[7]*New York Times,* March 22, 1889.

[8]Letter of Secretary of the Interior Noble to the First Auditor, from Washington, D. C., April 24, 1889, Record Group 217, Territorial Letters Received, Vol. 20.

Commissioner E. A. Rollins, who had opposed his employment in the beginning. His removal was recommended by Secretary of the Treasury McCulloch after Wolfley officially called Rollins a "liar" and a "thief." Upon investigation of the incident, however, McCulloch withdrew the recommendation and Wolfley remained in office even after Commissioner Rollins had departed.[9]

The malicious charges filed against Wolfley were so ugly that Senator Orville H. Platt, chairman of the committee considering the applications, was actually discourteous to him. The Senator even handed a private card to President Harrison, saying, "W. J. Murphy thinks you have made a bad appointment for Arizona. I wish you would see him and hear what he has to say." The charges, which included perjured testimony by J. W. Elder, held up the appointment for three weeks. After listening to Wolfley's defense, however, even the obdurate Platt changed his mind and commended him to both the President and Secretary of the Interior John M. Noble as "an honest man." In the end, Wolfley was confirmed unanimously by the Senate.[10]

Governor Wolfley was the eighth man appointed to the top political job in the Arizona Territory. He was the only bachelor to hold the position and was the first appointee to be a resident at the time of his selection.[11] Born in Philadelphia in 1839, he was educated as a civil engineer and worked for railroads in Iowa and Ohio before joining the Union forces in Kentucky during the Civil War. Distinguishing himself in that conflict, he was encouraged by General Sherman to remain in the Regular Army with his wartime rank of major — quite an honor since most officers had to take lower ranks after the war was over. Wolfley chose civilian life, however, and became a federal revenue officer in New Orleans. Then in 1872 he moved to Colorado to engage in mining. He was also employed by the District of Columbia for awhile before coming to Arizona to make his home in 1882. Settling in Yavapai County, he made his livelihood in mining and surveying.

Since Wolfley was in the national capital at the time of his appointment, the Republican-controlled "holdover" Fifteenth Legislative

---

[9]Letter of Governor Lewis Wolfley to President Harrison, from Phoenix, Arizona, September 12, 1889, Harrison Papers, Vol. 86, Library of Congress.

[10]Letter of Governor Wolfley to President Harrison, from Phoenix, Arizona, May 28, 1889, Harrison Papers, Vol. 78.

[11]Earl Pomeroy, "Carpetbaggers in the Territories, 1861–1890," *The Historian,* Vol. 2, No. 1 (1939), pp. 53-64. McCormick claimed Arizona residence but had come to Arizona as a federal appointee to the office of secretary in 1863; his reference letters recommending him for the governorship came mainly from New York. Zulick also is sometimes classified as an Arizona resident at the time of his appointment, but he was still in New Jersey serving as a surrogate six months prior to the date on which his commission as governor was granted.

Assembly postponed adjournment until after he arrived and assumed the gubernatorial duties. The Council then rejected Zulick's appointments and approved the full slate of territorial officers nominated by Wolfley.[12] The new officers were: Secretary Nathan O. Murphy, Attorney General Clark Churchill, Adjutant-General William O. O'Neill, Auditor Thomas Hughes, Treasurer J. Y. T. Smith, Commissioner of Immigration John A. Black, Superintendent George W. Cheyney, and other less-important appointees. For some time, however, Arizona had two sets of officials. Wherever a building or institution was necessary to exercise the duties of office, the Democratic incumbents refused to yield, just as their Republican predecessors had refused four years earlier. They continued to exercise the duties and maintain possession, claiming, despite precedent to the contrary, that the legislature was confined to sixty consecutive days; they said that the Governor could appoint "during recess of the Council" only on the resignation or death of an incumbent and that they were therefore the "de facto," if not the "de jure" officers.

In defense of the Republican appointments made by the Fifteenth Assembly, the new Attorney General, Churchill, pointed out that the actions of previous legislatures that went beyond the "sixty consecutive days" limit had not been disputed. To challenge the holdovers, however, legal action was taken on different grounds. Since the term of the treasurer was indefinite and not fixed by law, a suit was filed to remove the Democratic incumbent from that position. Though the presiding judge, DeForest Porter of the Second Judicial District, was biased toward the Democrat, he had no alternative but to decide that Republican John Y. T. Smith was the legal treasurer. Nevertheless, Smith's predecessor stubbornly refused to yield the records of the office until threatened with confinement for contempt of court. Furthermore, Judge Porter was able to use the *Smith* vs. *Foster* case to the advantage of the Zulick appointees. In an *obiter dictum* concerning the Fifteenth Assembly, he declared that "any laws passed by the Legislature after the expiration of 60 days [consecutive] are null, unless Congress act upon them and make them valid."[13] Accordingly, the other Democratic officials refused to yield and the Republican aspirants preferred to wait for the appointment of sympathetic judges before taking further legal recourse.

Another reason for hesitancy in resorting to the courts for satis-

---

[12]*Journals of the Fifteenth Legislative Assembly,* 1889, pp. 219-21; see also, letter of Governor Wolfley to Secretary of the Interior Noble, from Phoenix, Arizona, April 18, 1889, Harrison Papers, Vol. 75.

[13]*Arizona Daily Citizen,* May 21, 1889.

faction was that U. S. Attorney General W. H. H. Miller had also previously sustained the theory that the legislature was confined to the sixty consecutive days. This opinion was given on March 16, 1889, just prior to Wolfley's becoming governor. "If the Attorney General is right in his opinion," Governor Wolfley wrote to Congressman I. S. Struble, Chairman of the Committee on Territories, "then Arizona is almost without law, including nearly all the bonded indebtedness, revenue, civil, and criminal laws. If Judge Porter is correct, that non-action of Congress, has legalized the old laws but that 'Congress action is necessary to legalize the acts of the 15th Legislature after the consecutive days' even then there still remains a very serious necessity for Congressional action."[14] The Governor asked for a speedy correction of the situation by Congress.

Meanwhile, territorial affairs suffered severely. If the Democratic contention that all legislative acts passed after March 21 were not legal, then the appropriation bill was void and many people would suffer. The boards of supervisors in the counties did not know how to proceed in levying taxes. There were two territorial boards of equalization in session, each claiming a legal right to act, one Democratic and the other Republican. It was the board's duty to assess railroad property for tax purposes and to certify the amounts to the county boards. But if each Board of Equalization made assessments, which should the counties accept? And what was to keep the railroad companies from refusing to pay taxes until the situation was clarified? The railroad taxes amounted to one-fifth of the total revenue of the territory and were depended upon by both the local and territorial governments.

Secretary Murphy reported to Secretary of the Interior Noble that

> every institution of the Territory is becoming demoralized, democratic officials being in charge and possession upon at least an uncertain tenure, there is a lack of discipline, and the conduct of affairs to say the least is very careless, besides under the circumstances funds are not available for the maintenance of these institutions. Grave irregularities are charged but it is impracticable to investigate, the democratic incumbents being in possession of all books and records. Politically the predicament is none the less serious. Governor Wolfley is handicapped by having all the territorial offices with one exception in the hands of the opposition, while the mugwumps and sore-head republicans are covertly aiding and comforting the obstructionists. . . .[15]

14U. S. House, Committee on Territories, "Condition of the Laws of Arizona and Reasons for Congressional Legislation." Letter from Lewis Wolfley, Governor of Arizona Territory, to Hon. I. S. Struble, Chairman, Committee on Territories. No date. [Printed copy in New York City Public Library.]

15Letter of Secretary Nathan O. Murphy to Secretary of the Interior John Noble, from Phoenix, Arizona, June 7, 1889, Record Group 48, Territorial Papers.

262

George H. "Little Steve" Stevens, secretary of the Territorial Prison Board and long-time territorial legislator.

— Sharlot Hall Museum

Murphy asked the support of the national administration and recommended three possible remedies: (1) the replacement of Democratic partisan judges with good Republicans; (2) an extra session of the legislature, though the federal statutes were ambiguous on the question of whether or not a special session of the territorial legislature could be called legally; or (3) reenactment by Congress of the territorial laws passed after March 21. The last solution seemed the least desirable because Congress would not convene in regular session until December; even then, immediate action by Congress would be unlikely and the delay would be too demoralizing as the affairs of the territory became more muddled.

Governor Wolfley telegraphed President Harrison May 20, 1889, asking permission to call a special session of the legislature.

> The First Legislature of this Territory sat six days over the consecutive time and most of the important legislation occurred in those six days. The Eleventh Legislature sat nine days over the consecutive days. Much of the important legislation was in these nine days. In view of the recent decision of the court we are not only left without any appropriations for the year 1889 and 1890 but my great and serious doubts are raised as to almost our entire laws. . . . In view of these serious complications I have the honor to urge upon you the above telegram believing that the emergency requires the most speedy relief possible. It may almost be said, that we are without Territorial laws or officers.[16]

---

[16]Telegram of Governor Wolfley to President Harrison, from Phoenix, Arizona, May 20, 1889, *ibid.*; see also, *Arizona Daily Citizen,* September 25, 1889.

The telegram aptly described the situation but brought no help from the President. Eventually the courts upheld the Wolfley appointments. But it was the withholding of salaries by the Republican-controlled treasury that brought about a gradual withdrawal of the stubborn Democrats from their offices. Some of them were eventually remunerated by later Democratic legislatures, though one, Secretary George H. "Little Steve" Stevens of the Territorial Prison Board, had already provided for himself by absconding with prison funds and escaping to British Columbia.

Elated over the chance to advance the interests of the territory with the full force of his Republican administration, Wolfley wrote to the President on July 5, 1890:

> After over a year's hard struggle with the Democratic "holdovers" we have today succeeded in ousting the last one. It has been a long hard fight, that, except by the greatest moderation might at any time have occasioned blood shed. It has given rise to a great amount of personal abuse from the Democrats, and in many ways has been used by dissatisfied, or unfriendly Republicans to misrepresent, and injure me. Through it all Attorney General Churchill (to whom too much praise cannot be given) and myself have proceeded only by legal means, and patiently waited the slow process of the law made slower by all the legal exceptions and delays that were possible. . . . From a party stand point I am satisfied that it has been both legally, and politically a losing fight for the Democrats. . . .[17]

The situation had been frustrating and discouraging, but not like the startling statements of one John Wier to President Harrison would indicate. This purported "owner of some of the biggest mines in Arizona" was quoted by the New York press in September, 1889, as saying that "a war has resulted" over the two sets of officials; "that Democratic ruffians were determined to make the life of Governor Wolfley as miserable as possible; that it was almost as much as a man's life was worth to be an active Republican in Arizona; the majority of the Democrats were of the desperado pattern, ready to shoot on the slightest vocation." The *Prescott Courier* responded to these remarks by saying that no one in Arizona knew anything of John Wier's "biggest mines" but did know that he was the "biggest liar" in the territory.[18] Governor Wolfley explained to the President that Wier was a perfect stranger to him and that his description of Democrats as desperadoes was unfounded in fact. "There is no section of the U. S.," he wrote, "where any and every one

---

[17]Letter of Governor Wolfley to President Harrison, from Phoenix, Arizona, July 5, 1890, Harrison Papers, Vol. 109.
[18]*Prescott Courier,* September 24, 1889.

is more free to state his political views and to exercise all his political rights than in Arizona."[19]

Nevertheless, political partisanship was a major concern to Wolfley throughout his brief tenure as governor. Even before he left Washington to assume his duties in Arizona, he discussed patronage with Secretary Noble and with Secretary of State Blaine. Both of these men advised him that he was expected "to bring Arizona into Republican line." Soon after his arrival in Phoenix he wrote to Assistant Postmaster General J. S. Clarkson asking the latter's cooperation in making appointments in Arizona that would help the Republicans. "The great trouble in our Territory," he said, "has been that the Federal appointments have each one been appointed by independent influences and instead of being a strength to the party have as a rule been a weakness owing to jealousness between them. . . . "[20]

Wolfley also wrote to Attorney General W. H. H. Miller in hope that the national administrators might cooperate in working out a uniform system for the distribution of patronage in Arizona that would assure a concert of action and harmony in the party.[21] In another letter to President Harrison, the Governor said that party lines had never been drawn in Arizona as in the states. The Republican Party officers in the territory had never been considered important because they had no voice in the selection of appointees. He wrote that "the practice of appointing strangers to the national positions, from various sources of influence, has to say the least of it, not added any strength to their respective parties." The appointment of the local people — each with his following of friends — under some cohesive plan would be an improvement, he thought.[22]

What Wolfley really wanted was to be consulted when federal offices in Arizona were to be filled. To his disappointment, however, his enemies in the party were often given an ear in Washington. The case of George Christ, who was appointed collector of customs at Nogales, was an example. Christ, along with Brewster Cameron, had opposed Wolfley's nomination, falsely charging that he had an interest in the Peralta Grant, and joined with the Democratic delegate to Congress,

---

[19]Letter of Governor Wolfley to President Harrison, from Phoenix, Arizona, September 26, 1889, Harrison Papers, Vol. 87.

[20]Letter of Governor Wolfley to Assistant Postmaster General J. S. Clarkson, from Phoenix, Arizona, April 16, 1889, *ibid.*, Vol. 74.

[21]Letter of Governor Wolfley to Attorney General W. H. H. Miller, from Phoenix, Arizona, April 16, 1889, *ibid.*

[22]Letter of Governor Wolfley to President Harrison, from Phoenix, Arizona, May 14, 1889, *ibid.*, Vol. 76.

Marcus A. Smith, to fight the Governor's bills which came before the House Committee on Territories. Wolfley sent a letter to the President in which he said that the appointment of Mr. Christ, his personal and political enemy, would "do more to unsettle our affairs than anything the Democrats could possibly do." He told the President that the Treasury Department had the record of an incident wherein Christ, as a mounted inspector on the Mexican border, had seized a band of cattle belonging to one Thomas Smythe; he quoted Senator Henry M. Teller as having repeatedly stated that the charges against Christ were serious enough to prevent his being appointed to any office.

Wolfley also called the President's attention to affidavits that had been filed with the Interior Department against Christ for having cheated his deceased business partner, a Mr. Nelson. Before his death, the latter had placed property in Christ's name for the benefit of the Nelson child. But Christ claimed it for himself and the poor child was on the charity of the Catholic Sisters in Tucson. In addition, the Governor dropped the names of several Chicago Board of Trade men who could substantiate the facts relative to some of Christ's fraudulent transactions in connection with a mining company of which he and others were members.[23]

So perturbed was Wolfley by the appointment of his enemy that he dashed off a number of letters in protest to Washington officials and Senators. The following comments to Assistant Postmaster J. S. Clarkson were typical: "Is it right or just that the National leaders of our party should so embarrass me?" he asked. "Place yourself in my position, and consider the situation; you have a large Department at your command; why not find some place in it for Mr. Christ if you think him entitled to consideration."[24] Already, however, Christ had been turned down for the Tucson postmastership after three hundred citizens of that city signed a petition remonstrating against it.[25] In light of Christ's unpopularity, as shown in the Tucson petition and a similar protest submitted by the voters of Nogales against his receiving the appointment there, it is surprising that President Harrison favored him with a job. His connections with Cameron and his past membership on the Republican National Executive Committee no doubt helped him.

Another appointment to which Wolfley objected — but which he at first had endorsed — was that of Richard E. Sloan, a young Florence

---

[23]Letter of Governor Wolfley to President Harrison, from Phoenix, Arizona, April 29, 1890, *ibid.,* Vol. 104.

[24]Letter of Governor Wolfley to Assistant Postmaster General Clarkson, from Phoenix, Arizona, April 30, 1890, *ibid.*

[25]Interview with D. A. Sanford, a prominent cattleman from Tucson, Arizona, at the Astor House in New York City, *New York Times,* September 24, 1890.

attorney destined to be the last territorial governor, to the position of judge of the First Judicial District.[26] Sloan replaced William H. Barnes, a Democrat, while the Wham payroll case was getting under way in Tucson. Five Gila Valley farmers and stockmen were indicted by a grand jury for robbing Major J. W. Wham of a box containing $26,000 in gold and silver, on May 11, 1889, while he was en route from Fort Grant to Fort Thomas. Judge Barnes reduced the bail of some of the arraigned men from $15,000 to $10,000.[27] This action enraged a large number of people, including the grand jury, which sent a telegram to the Department of Justice recommending Barnes's removal.

Wolfley's objections to Sloan's appointment were based upon legal technicalities, though his personal enmity toward Brewster Cameron, who was made clerk of the court under Sloan, was probably an important factor.[28] According to the federal statutes, "no member of the legislative assembly of any territory shall hold or be appointed to any office which has been created or the salary or emolument of which have been increased, while he was a member during the term for which he was elected, and for one year after the expiration of such term . . . . "[29] The Fifteenth Legislative Assembly, in which Sloan was a member of the Council, appropriated $7,200, to pay the district judges one hundred dollars per month each for holding court and presiding in the trial of territorial cases.[30] This was an increase of fifty dollars per month.

Wolfley was not alone in questioning Sloan's legal right to serve as judge. Marcus A. Smith, the delegate to Congress and also an attorney for the defendants in the Wham trial, wrote a letter to the House Committee on the Territories, on February 6, 1890, in which he asked, "Can the Judiciary Committee afford to ignore the plain letter of the U. S. law (Revised Statutes 1854) that renders R. E. Sloan ineligible for Associate Judge in Arizona? Sloan was a member of the Territorial Council and his term does not expire until January 1st, 1891."[31]

Several of Governor Wolfley's enemies took the Sloan-appointment controversy as an opportunity to attack him. James A. Zabriskie, who

---

[26]Letter of Governor Wolfley to President Harrison, from Phoenix, Arizona, October 7, 1889, Record Group 60, Appointment Papers.

[27]*New York Times,* October 19, 1889.

[28]Letter of Governor Wolfley to President Harrison, from Washington, D. C., December 24, 1889, Harrison Papers, Vol. 94.

[29]Letter of Delegate Marcus A. Smith to U. S. House of Representatives Committee on Territories, Washington, D. C., February 6, 1890, Record Group 60, Appointment Papers.

[30]*Acts, Resolutions and Memorials,* Fifteenth Legislative Assembly, 1889, p. 93.

[31]Letter of Delegate Smith, February 6, 1890, Record Group 60, Appointment Papers.

was Brewster Cameron's lawyer and United States district attorney during the Tritle administration, wrote a letter to Attorney General W. H. H. Miller in which he said that Wolfley "was always repudiated by the people here, and holds his position against their protest." Charging him with "almost destroying the Republican Party in Arizona by his ignorance, stupidity, and vindictiveness," Zabriskie said that the Governor did not have a supporter among the press. "The only paper that has sustained him [the *Citizen*] has been compelled from a sense of self-respect to withdraw its support," he continued. "If Governor Wolfley is permitted to serve out his term of office, and to continue his senseless war upon decent Republicans, there will not be sufficient strength in the Territory to organize a corporal's guard. . . . "[32]

The *Arizona Enterprise,* in Sloan's hometown of Florence, printed a scathing editorial condemning Wolfley on December 7, 1889. Referring to the breach in the cordiality that previously existed between the *Citizen* and Governor Wolfley, the *Enterprise* said that it did not blame the Tucson newspaper "for cutting loose from the rudderless craft that is drifting about the political sea without chart or compass," because no self-respecting journal could afford to daily apologize for the blunders of the erratic Wolfley. The Florence editor criticized the Governor for defying the laws of the territory, spurning the counsel of his party leaders, and attempting to set up a personal government. Since Wolfley had alienated even his staunchest friends who stretched forth a helping hand, the *Enterprise* concluded that "the sooner the President drops him into obscurity the more all good citizens and especially the Republican Party will applaud the act."[33]

Secretary Nathan O. Murphy, who was supposedly on the Wolfley team, told the Governor that he was unwise and unreasonable in one incident. He wrote from Washington, D. C., where he had gone on business:

> My dear Governor: I was very much surprised and pained this morning to learn of the statements made in regard to me to the Secretary of Interior by yourself and General Johnson. You have been certainly unjust to me, as I do not deserve your criticism. You know very well that my visit to Washington had nothing to do with the candidacy of Christ and that my knowledge of his affairs has come to me incidentally here and not of my seeking nor choice. I say frankly, as I have said before, that I believe the war on him is, to say the least, very unwise, but no matter what my position is in regard to him, I must certainly

---

[32]Letter of J. A. Zabriskie to Attorney General Miller, from Tucson, Arizona, December 9, 1889, *ibid.*
[33]*Arizona Enterprise,* December 7, 1889.

reserve the right of judgment for myself in the premises. I decline to be dictated to in these matters as I have frequently told you. Now Governor, I do not see how you can reconcile your action with my consistent friendship for you, of which the Secretary of Interior can tell you if he will. I do hope this recrimination business will end some-time and we can all work together for the good of the party and the Territory. . . .[34]

Even with his own Republican administration finally entrenched in office, Wolfley did not succeed as governor. His extreme partisanship soon split his own party into factions and gained the ill-will of nearly all the leading territorial newspapers. In a futile attempt to create a more favorable political atmosphere he and his followers established the *Arizona Republican*. The official status he gave this newspaper, how-ever, furnished just another reason for his removal from office before the end of his term.

Several of his activities in connection with the paper were of an unethical nature. He was accused, for example, of ordering the manager of the territorial prison in Yuma to require every new employee at that institution to turn over 10 percent of his wages for the support of the *Republican* in Phoenix. According to an article in the *Tucson Daily Citizen* (July 14, 1890), much indignation was expressed by the employees who were compelled to support a paper in which they had no interest or sympathy. Several of the guards were objecting bitterly and two of them consulted a lawyer as to the right of the administration to enforce such an order. In commenting upon this situation the *Citizen* said: "In justice to the governor, we must say that most of the executive blunders thus far have been the result of inexperience and want of mental caliber. If, however, the accusation made by the Yuma corres-pondent should appear to be well grounded, the governor's friends can-not possibly offer in extenuation the time worn excuse that 'the governor did the best he could, he was badly advised in the matter.' "[35]

Actually, Wolfley's administration had few accomplishments to its credit. Probably the outstanding achievement was the funding of terri-torial bonds, an action that saved Arizona taxpayers $59,006.40 in annual interest.[36] These bonds had become a complicated and heavy burden, drawing interest at 8 to 10 percent. Under Wolfley's guidance

---

[34]Letter of Secretary Murphy to Governor Wolfley, from Washington, D. C., May 12, 1890, Record Group 48, Territorial Papers.

[35]*Arizona Daily Citizen,* July 14, 1890.

[36]Funding the territorial indebtedness was permitted by federal statute. *U. S. Statutes at Large,* Vol. XXVI, 51st Cong., 1st Sess., 1889, Chap. 614, pp. 175-79; see also, *Acts, Resolutions and Memorials,* Eighteenth Legislative Assembly, 1895, p. 38.

all territorial indebtedness was funded at lower rates. The legislature in 1895 recognized Wolfley's work in this connection by passing a bill to reimburse him $5,000 for his personal expenses.[37]

A matter that gave the Wolfley administration some concern, but which turned out to be based more on fear than reality, was the return of the Apaches to the West. The Chiricahuas had been temporarily moved to Mount Vernon Barracks in Alabama from Florida while the federal government decided where to place them permanently. General Nelson Miles and the Indian Rights Association recommended that they be settled in a mountain region in the western part of North Carolina, perhaps on surplus lands that the Cherokee Indians were willing to sell. But Governor Fowle of that state protested to Secretary of War Proctor. Many North Carolinians were willing to tolerate the industrious, Christian Cherokees but not the wild, roving, savage Apaches. Fowle, in a letter to Proctor, suggested that Vermont would provide as good a place for security as would his state.[38] The Easterners rested somewhat more easily, however, after General Crook, who had been listening to the Indian tales of suffering and want, proposed that the Apaches be removed to Fort Sill in the Indian Territory. When informed that people in the West were all worked up over the contemplated transfer of Geronimo and his followers because they feared that the Indians would escape to their mountain fortresses and again terrorize the country, Crook said to a *New York Times* reporter:

> I certainly would not formulate a plan to move the Apaches if there was any probability of their turning like snakes upon the Government. The Apaches are broken in spirit and humbled to the dust. Geronimo the great warrior, is now a "heap good Injun." He is teaching a Sunday school class, and, as I understand, has lost all hatred of the white people. These Indians would be only too glad to accept this removal as an opportunity to further their civilization and better their condition.[39]

General Crook's proposal seemed to dispose of North Carolina as a solution and formed the basis for a recommendation to Congress by President Harrison that the Apaches be moved to the Indian Territory.[40] A Senate joint resolution, which provided for the transferral of 390 of the prisoners, 311 of whom were women and children, was passed and sent to the House where hearings were held by the House Committee on Indian Affairs. Much of the testimony was in contradiction to the recommendations made by General Crook, and also by General Howard.

---

[37]*Acts, Resolutions and Memorials,* Eighteenth Legislative Assembly, pp. 37-38.
[38]*New York Times,* September 28, October 27, 1889.
[39]*Ibid.,* January 28, 1890.
[40]*Ibid.,* February 2, 1890.

Lt. Col. H. W. Lawton, a subpoenaed witness, offered suggestions contrary to those of his superior officers. He said that sanitary conditions were very poor at Fort Sill and that the Indians could very easily reach their old haunts near the White Mountain Reservation if they should become dissatisfied with life in the Indian Territory.

Like many Arizona residents, the people of New Mexico were concerned. W. H. H. Llewellyn of Las Cruces, New Mexico, voiced the feelings of nearly all witnesses when he said that the people of New Mexico, while desiring the government to do the best it could for these Indians, protested against their removal to Fort Sill. He believed that Generals Crook and Howard were mistaken as to the possible danger involved and was sure that the return of Geronimo's band to the Southwest would retard that area's development and progress. Brewster Cameron, a witness from Arizona, took the same view. He said that, whereas General Crook had failed to capture the Apaches in his campaigns, General Miles had succeeded and sent them out of the territory. "Naturally," he testified, "the people of Arizona believed that the opinion of a man who captured the Indians, as to the danger of proximity to them, was better than that of a man who always failed in his campaigns against them."[41]

For once, Governor Wolfley and Cameron were on the same side. The Governor presented a large number of clippings from western newspapers showing that the sentiment of the people was that these Indians should not be returned to the West.[42] He said that the people of Arizona believed in and liked General Crook, but they thought that he made a mistake in recommending the transfer of the Indians.[43] Eventually, in 1894, the Chiricahuas were moved to Fort Sill and all fears and apprehension came to naught as the Indians settled down there to peaceful pursuits.

Unlike previous territorial governors, Wolfley did not have the problem of Indian depredations; nor did he have a meeting of the legislature during his short term. Unfortunately for him, much of his time was diverted by petty politics and to correspondence with federal officials. Though he no doubt contributed to his own downfall by writing too many letters to the Secretary of the Interior that were critical of Arizona politics, his reports contain some valuable information on conditions in Arizona in 1889–1890. In his report dated October 5, 1889, for example, he commented on the indefinite land-grant boundaries and urged Congress to take action so that the public lands out-

[41]*Ibid.*, February 11, 1890.
[42]*Ibid.*, February 16, 1890.
[43]*Arizona Gazette,* February 17, 1890.

side the grants could be legally settled. He also contended that the so-called Peralta Grant, a vast region extending across central Arizona into New Mexico, was a fraud and suggested that criminal action be brought against James Addison Reavis and his cohorts.

For years there had been troublesome uncertainty about ownership to certain lands in territories acquired from Mexico. Under the terms of the Treaty of Guadalupe Hidalgo (1848) and the Gadsden Purchase (1854), the United States was bound to recognize the validity of grants made by the Spanish and Mexican governments.[44] But the procedure for investigating and verifying titles was necessarily slow. After the surveyor general of the territory in which a land grant was located had investigated a claim, he reported to the Secretary of the Interior who in turn made recommendations to Congress for special legislation to either confirm or invalidate the grant. This process dragged on for decades, denying justice both to the claimants and to the United States government. In Arizona Territory, which was designated as a separate surveying district in 1870, successive surveyor generals, beginning with John Wasson, examined and reported on claims, only to have Congress take no action. Fortunately, nearly all of the grants in Arizona were confined to the southeastern part of the territory; they were also smaller and less numerous than the huge haciendas in New Mexico and California. Most of the Arizona grants had been long since abandoned as worthless by the original grantees and were claimed by speculators, usually from California, who traced down the heirs and purchased the rights for practically nothing.

Delegate Marcus Smith opposed the recognition of the Spanish and Mexican land grants and fought furiously against a bill in Congress to create a court of private land claims.[45] He believed that the court would put small claimants at a disadvantage and serve as a tool for the big land-grabbers. This argument was partly responsible for Smith's successful bid for reelection in 1888; it especially appealed, as we shall see, to settlers in the Salt and Gila River valleys whose property rights were threatened by a fraudulent claim filed with the surveyor general by James Addison Reavis five years earlier. The Fifty-first Congress, however, was not influenced by Smith's objections and established the court, giving its five judges original jurisdiction over cases involving land titles originating under the authority of the governments of Spain and Mexico.[46]

By 1904, all the claims were completely processed, though many

---

[44] *U. S. Statutes at Large and Treaties,* Vol. IX, p. 929; *U. S. Statutes at Large and Treaties,* Vol. X, p. 1035; and *Arizona Citizen,* March 25, 1876.

[45] *Congressional Record,* 51st Cong., 1st Sess., pp. 223 and 2826.

[46] *U. S. Statutes at Large,* Vol. XXVI, 51st Cong., 2d Sess., pp. 854-62.

had to be taken to the U. S. Supreme Court for final adjudication. Of more than eleven million acres claimed in Arizona, titles to only a little over 120,000 acres were confirmed. But most of the rejected acreage was in the spurious claim of Reavis, a master crook who first came to Arizona about 1880 as a subscription agent for the San Francisco *Examiner.*[47]

With a vivid imagination and a developed talent for forgery, Reavis nearly succeeded in pulling off one of the most gigantic swindles in all history.[48] After spending years in arduously altering, adding to, or replacing pertinent records in the official depositories of Spain and Mexico, the ex-Confederate soldier and Missouri streetcar conductor went to Tucson in March, 1883, to file a sheaf of documents with Surveyor General J. W. Robbins to prove his claim to the Peralta Grant. In essence, what Reavis had done was to invent a family lineage starting with one Don Nemecio Silva de Peralta de la Córdoba. According to the fictitious data accumulated by Reavis, Peralta was given the title of Baron de los Colorados by King Ferdinand VI of Spain in 1748, and also an extensive grant of land in the northern provinces to go with it. To establish a connection between himself and the Peralta family, Reavis explained how he acquired title to the Peralta Grant from George Willing, a mine developer from the East who had been in and out of Arizona several times since 1864. Willing, allegedly, had purchased the deed from a descendant of the original Baron de los Colorados, a poverty-stricken Mexican named Miguel Peralta. Actually, Miguel existed only as a character in forged deeds and transfers designed to place the Peralta grant in Reavis' possession. George Willing could not contradict the story since he died in Prescott the day after he recorded the deed in the Yavapai County courthouse in March, 1874. His death was reportedly due to "exposure and privation," though an investigation into his sudden and convenient demise might have revealed foul play.[49]

Besides Willing, there was another living character in the plot, this one a Cinderella-like creation of Reavis' fertile imagination. To strengthen his claim, he found a Mexican orphan girl, had her educated, and eventually made her his wife with the title of Baroness of Arizona. For a man who had forged official documents on two continents, it was no great challenge to change church birth records in California

---

[47]*Arizona Gazette,* May 9, 1881.
[48]See Donald M. Powell, *The Peralta Grant* (Norman: University of Oklahoma Press, 1960), for a full, documented account of the Reavis fraud.
[49]*Weekly Arizona Miner,* March 20, 1874.

to make his bride the last surviving descendant of the Peralta family. Before this alteration and other false documents were revealed, the Baron and his sophisticated, probably unsuspecting, lady were to make a deep imprint on Arizona history.

The "barony" they sought was no ordinary land claim. Stretching from the approximate location of Silver City, New Mexico, on the east, to a line just west of Phoenix, the Peralta Grant was about seventy-eight miles wide, its southern boundary passing approximately twenty-five miles north of Tucson. In addition to Phoenix, it included the towns of Tempe, Mesa, Globe, Clifton, Solomonville, Casa Grande, and Florence. The Southern Pacific Railroad crossed its southwest corner and the fabulously rich Silver King mine was located within its bounds. Though this huge claim had not been validated in any court, many frightened and gullible people began to pay Reavis varying amounts for quitclaim deeds to their homes, farms, mines, businesses, and even schools in the case of Florence.[50]

The fact that some brilliant, nationally famous lawyers, including Roscoe Conkling and Robert Ingersoll, scrutinized the fraudulent documents and found them to be good in law and unassailable in court only increased the hysteria. And when millionaires like Charles Crocker and Collis P. Huntington pronounced the claim valid and financed the Baron's wanderings over the world in search of historical evidence, what could the little fellow do? Even the editor of the *Arizona Gazette,* Homer H. McNeil, who was urging the people to fight for their rights, was one of the first to purchase a deed from Reavis and have it recorded.[51] The big contributors, of course, were the Southern Pacific, which paid $50,000, and the Silver King mine, which gave $25,000 toward defraying the cost of the Baron's expensive tastes.[52] With this kind of income, Reavis was able to live in courtly style. He maintained homes in St. Louis, Washington, Madrid, and Chihuahua City, and traveled widely at home and abroad in a manner befitting royalty.

Meanwhile, however, the investigation of the Peralta claim was being patiently conducted by the office of the surveyor general. When Republican J. W. Robbins died of tuberculosis shortly after beginning the work, he was succeeded by Royal A. Johnson, the chief clerk and a well-trained lawyer. The latter's sincere interest in the claim was

---

[50]*In the Court of Claims of the United States . . . J. A. Peralta Reavis and Doña Sofía Loreta Micaela de Maso-Reavis y Peralta de la Córdoba, His Wife, and Clinton P. Farrell, Trustee,* vs. *The United States of America, Petition of Claimants* [No. 16,719] (Washington, D. C.: Gibson Brothers, 1890).

[51]*Arizona Gazette,* July 26, 1883.

[52]*Petition of Claimants* No. 16,719, p. 19.

indicated by the advice which he gave to his father, a New York attorney, to refuse a retaining fee offered by Reavis. Johnson's job was given to Democrat John Hise during the first Cleveland administration, but Johnson was reappointed after the inauguration of President Harrison in 1889. And while Arizona leaders such as Thomas Weedin, the Democratic editor of the Florence *Enterprise,* and Clark Churchill, the Republican attorney general, were pointing out glaring discrepancies in the Peralta documents and publicly denouncing Reavis' pretensions at mass meetings, Johnson quietly completed his report.[53] The citizens and newspapermen who had been criticizing him for dallying, were suddenly his enthusiastic admirers when he finally released his carefully reasoned exposé of the fraudulent Peralta Grant in 1889. His analysis of the questioned documents disclosed several forgeries and historical inaccuracies which led him to the conclusion that the Reavis claim was spurious and should be disallowed.[54] To show their appreciation of Johnson's work in their behalf, the populace of Phoenix joined Governor Wolfley, in March, 1890, to give him a gala reception in the capital city.[55]

Their jubilation was five years premature, however. It was 1895 before United States Attorney Matthew Reynolds, assisted by his special counsel, a Mexican-born lawyer-investigator named Severo Mallet-Prevost, successfully presented the government's case before the Court of Private Land Claims in Santa Fe. On June 3 of that year, Chief Justice Joseph R. Reed read the decision declaring that Reavis' claim to a grant 236.4921 miles by 78.8307 miles in size was "wholly fictitious and fraudulent." He further decreed that the forged documents upon which it was based had been surreptitiously introduced into the records and archives of Madrid, Seville, and Guadalajara, and into the baptismal and burial records of the parish of San Bernardino and San Salvador in California.[56]

Reavis was then placed under arrest and, after a year of legal maneuvering, was convicted of conspiracy to defraud the government. He was fined $5,000 and sentenced to a short term in prison. As

[53]*Arizona Weekly Enterprise* (Florence), May 2, 1885; and *Arizona Gazette,* December 14, 1889.

[54]Royal A. Johnson, *Adverse Report of the Surveyor General of Arizona Upon the Alleged "Peralta Grant," a Complete Exposé of Its Fraudulent Character* (Phoenix: Arizona Gazette Book and Job Office, 1890).

[55]*Weekly Phoenix Herald,* March 27, 1890.

[56]U. S. Court of Private Land Claims, Santa Fe District, *James Addison Peralta-reavis and Doña Sofia Loreta Micaela de Peraltareavis, née Maso y Silva de Peralta de la Córdoba, husband and wife, Petitioners, vs. The United States, Respondent,* 1895, pp. 1057-61.

onvict No. 964 in the penitentiary at Santa Fe, Reavis must have
vondered if the prize which he had sought was really worth the effort.
f anything can be said in his favor, it might be that his grandiose
cheme at least gave Arizonans a better appreciation of the value of
heir lands. Though the pioneers were treated as trespassers on their
wn property, they never ceased in their labors to develop the water
nd mineral resources of central Arizona. As in any frontier community,
f course, they had many problems to cope with, the need for cheaper
nd faster transportation not being the least of them.

In his 1889 report to the Secretary of the Interior, mentioned
bove, Governor Wolfley stressed the need for north-and-south railroads
n Arizona that would bring the Southern Pacific and Atlantic and
Pacific into competition and result in moderate rates and the exchange
f goods within the territory. He thought it unnecessary that Phoenix-
rea residents should have to pay as much as $60 per-thousand-board-
eet of lumber from the Washington Territory while the same product
old for as little as $12 in northern Arizona. Similarly, why should
ay selling for $5 per bale in the Salt River Valley bring eight times
hat amount a hundred miles north? Wolfley also believed that more
nines would be developed if cheaper transportation were provided.
To solve the problem, he proposed that two railroads be built to connect
he Southern Pacific and the Atlantic and Pacific — one through Prescott
and Phoenix, and another through Globe to Tucson on the Southern
Pacific.

Wolfley's observations on the railroad situation were obviously
wise and farsighted, though not as much can be said for his opinions
on another matter — the participation of Mormons in Arizona politics.
He charged that the Church's leaders in Utah had adopted the plan of
sending "stakes," with about two thousand colonists in each, into surrounding territories to form a balance of power between the two
political parties. There were four stakes in Arizona: two in Apache
County and one each in Maricopa and Graham counties. Since the
Mormons voted as a block without regard to party, Wolfley considered
them "a most dangerous and unscrupulous factor in politics."[57] He
accused ex-Governor Zulick and the Democrats in the Fifteenth Assembly with having attempted to win their political adherence by repealing
a territorial law that disenfranchised all who taught or practiced polygamy. Though admitting that the Mormons were "industrious and ener-

---

[57]*New York Times,* October 22, 1889; see also, U. S. Dept. of the Interior,
Report of the Governor of the Territory of Arizona to the Secretary of the Interior,
1889, p. 4.

getic" people, Wolfley wrote that they were both morally and politically unwelcome; he urged Congress to reestablish the law that had been rescinded.

Whereas the Mormon impact on Arizona's culture — political economic, and social — has been immense and continuous, Wolfley did not last long as governor. He resigned because of a disagreement with the national administration on arid-land policy, on August 20, 1890 About a week later, the Washington correspondent of the *New York Times* reported, in a front page story, that the cause of Wolfley's resignation was an affliction that sometimes falls upon federal officeholders and that is familiarly known as "the big head." Though his selection as Arizona's chief executive was largely due to his friendship with Secretary Noble, Wolfley seemed to regard the governorship as a much higher office than Noble's cabinet position. Scarcely an order relative to the territories was issued by the Secretary that did not bring, by return mail, a long letter of protest or criticism from the Governor of Arizona. "Together with this propensity to carp at the doings of the Secretary," wrote the *Times* reporter, "the Governor developed a disposition to take charge of the Republican Party in Arizona. The local leaders of the party say that while he was a success as a meddler, he was a failure as a manager." Delegation after delegation went to Washington to plead for Wolfley's dismissal. But Secretary Noble was reluctant to recommend a change; that is, until one day when a letter came from the Governor protesting the Interior Department's latest circular regarding arid-land entries. Finally at the end of his patience, the Secretary telegraphed a request to the Governor for his resignation — which came post haste![58]

In his letter of resignation to the President, Wolfley continued to show vindictiveness toward his political enemies. "I am today in receipt of a telegram from the Honorable Secretary of the Interior," he wrote,

> informing me that you deem a change in this office necessary and requesting my resignation. Your wish shall be my law, but before retiring I desire an opportunity to answer any charges effecting my honor and integrity, not with intention of urging my retention, simply to protect what is dear to any honest man, my good name. I will reach Washington with this letter and will not embarrass you beyond this request, after which my resignation will be at your pleasure. Mr. President I have the satisfaction and consciousness of having done my duties at least fairly well. I doubt if any Governor ever entered office under the embarrassing circumstances that surrounded me, not alone from democratic source, on the contrary, almost entirely from republicans.

---

[58]*New York Times,* August 29, 1890.

Brewster Cameron and Wm. Christy who have done everything in their power to oppose and embarrass me and my administration and who I feel certain are now charging me with the party troubles made up themselves.[59]

Governor Wolfley was not without his defenders. The Commissioner of Immigration, John A. Black, wrote to Secretary Noble from Tucson on August 21, 1890, that prominent men all over Arizona were satisfied with Wolfley. Among these gentlemen were some who represented the large interests in southern Arizona. Black mentioned Lewis Williams, superintendent of the Copper Queen Mining Company — the third-largest copper mining company in the United States — and Superintendent E. B. Gage of the Grand Central Mining Company of Tombstone, in particular. Stating that there was scarcely a dissenting voice among the Republicans in the northern counties of the territory, the Commissioner described the Governor's tormenters as spiteful and jealous men with personal grudges who came mainly from Tucson and Phoenix. Like Wolfley himself, he pointed to Brewster Cameron as the main disturber of Republican ranks in the Tucson area, and William Christy in Phoenix.

The quarrel with Cameron, which needs some explanation, stemmed from Wolfley's employment as a surveyor and researcher on the San Rafael, a Mexican land grant in southern Arizona claimed by the Cameron family. Then on friendly terms with Brewster and his brother Colin, Wolfley was hired in 1885 to locate the original deeds for the grant. While searching in Mexico, according to Colin, he discovered something that would cloud the Cameron claim if revealed, and exacted $1,000 in blackmail for not disclosing his information.[60]

Four years later, during the Senate confirmation fight over Wolfley's application for the governorship, Brewster Cameron alluded to his dishonesty in a telegram to President Harrison that was also signed by James A. Zabriskie and George J. Roskruge. Failing to block the appointment, the Camerons agreed to a truce in the feud, but only after Secretary Noble promised them that Wolfley would not interfere in their interests. However, as we have seen, the personal squabble was never really removed from territorial politics during the Wolfley administration.

And just as the Cameron coterie was persistent in its antagonism toward Wolfley, so was the clique in Phoenix headed by William

---

[59]Letter of Governor Wolfley to President Harrison, from Phoenix, Arizona, August 20, 1890, Harrison Papers, Vol. 73.

[60]Jane Wayland Brewster, "The San Rafael Cattle Company, A Pennsylvania Enterprise in Arizona," *Arizona and the West,* Vol. 8, No. 2 (1966), pp. 141-42 and 150-51.

To the President. Phœnix, *August 20th* 1890.

I am today in receipt of a telegram from the Honorable Secretary of the Interior informing me that you deem a change in this office necessary; and requesting my resignation. Your wish shall be my law, but before retiring I desire an opportunity to answer any charges effecting my honor and integrity, not with the intention of urging my retention, simply to protect what is dear to any honest man, my good name. I will reach Washington with this letter and will not embarrass you beyond this request, after which my resignation will be at your pleasure. Mr. President I have the satisfaction and consciousness of having done my duties at least fairly well. I doubt if any governor ever entered office under the embarrassing circumstances that surrounded me. Not alone from democratic source, on the contrary, almost entirely from republicans, Brewster Cameron and Wm. Christy who have done everything in their power to oppose and embarrass me and my administration and who I feel certain are now charging me with the party troubles made by themselves.

Very respectfully
Lewis Wolfley

Facsimile of Governor Wolfley's letter of resignation. The original is in the official papers of President Benjamin Harrison, Library of Congress.

278

A Phoenix street scene in the 1890s with the courthouse in the background. A "natatorium" is a swimming pool, usually an indoor one.

Christy unrelenting. Commissioner Black wrote that Christy had unsuccessfully sought the governorship and still jealously coveted that office — reason enough for opposing the incumbent. Black tended to disparage the influence of both Christy and Cameron. Despite the air of animosity that prevailed in the party ranks, it was his opinion that most Republicans in the territory "very generally" supported Wolfley's policies. He advised Secretary Noble not to endanger the chances of the Republican ticket in the 1890 fall elections by changing governors. But his solicitations were in vain. The political confusion in Arizona became so intolerable that the administration in Washington decided to send in new blood.[61]

Wolfley's replacement, John N. Irwin, was confirmed by the Senate in October, 1890, with Secretary Nathan O. Murphy holding the reins of government pending arrival of the new governor. After leaving office, Wolfley organized the Gila Bend Reservoir and Irrigation Company to bring under cultivation land suited to growing oranges, lemons, and other semitropical fruits. Plans called for the eventual irrigation of about a million acres. But an untimely flood swept away a dam and caused Wolfley to lose control of the enterprise. Interestingly enough, he carried his claim for financial losses all the way to the United States Supreme Court. And when that august body ruled against

---

[61]Letter of Commissioner of Immigration John A. Black to Secretary of the Interior Noble, from Tucson, Arizona, August 21, 1890, in Harrison Papers, Vol. 73.

his interests, he petitioned Congress to impeach the justices. No action was taken upon his unusual request, however. Meanwhile, the ex-governor returned to surveying for awhile and in 1893 was awarded the contract to survey 414,000 acres of land along the Atlantic and Pacific Railroad, northwest of Flagstaff. Wolfley died in Los Angeles in 1910 from injuries received in a streetcar accident, and was buried in Prescott.

When Wolfley left office, Phoenix had been the capital of the territory for over a year. The following contemporary description written by John A. Black gives us a good picture of Arizona's political mecca in 1890.

> Nearly in the center of the Salt River Valley is situated the flourishing city of Phoenix, the county seat of Maricopa County, and the capital of the Territory. Its present population, including suburbs, is about 6,500, and is rapidly increasing. Surrounded by a wealth of flowers, fruits and foliage, it is one of the handsomest towns in the Southwest. Through the streets flow streams of pure water, while rows of handsome shade trees line both sides of many of its thoroughfares. So dense is this forest of verdure that the traveler approaching it from any direction will not see the houses until he is fairly within the town. The streets are wide and level, facing the cardinal points. The buildings, which were formerly adobe, are now nearly all of brick and wood; those erected during the last year being entirely of the latter materials.

> Washington Street, the principal thoroughfare of the city, is three miles in length, lined on either side for several blocks by handsome business houses. The City Hall is a handsome three-story brick building. It is situated in the center of a plaza three hundred feet square, and is surrounded by a blue grass lawn, ornamental shade trees and flowers. The Court House is likewise an imposing brick structure and occupies a block three hundred feet square, similar to that of the City Hall. There are three commodious and elegant public school buildings in the city.

> The attendance averages about 450 pupils. Several private schools are also well attended. At the Northwestern corner of the city the Methodist Church will soon commence the erection of a large college, nearly all financial preliminaries have been completed. Arrangements are being made to start, within a few months, an Indian school near the city, when several hundred aborigines are to be instructed in the peaceful arts.

> In Phoenix the Methodists have two places of worship; while the Catholics, Presbyterians, Baptists and Episcopalians have handsome structures devoted to religious purposes. The secret societies are well represented; there are lodges of Masons, Odd Fellows, Knights of Pythias, Ancient Order of United Workmen, Grand Army of the Republic, Chosen Friends and Good Templars. There are three daily newspapers, the *Herald, Gazette,* and *Republican,* each of which issues a weekly edition.

Phoenix is lighted by gas and electricity, and is supplied with street railroads and water works. It has a well organized and efficient fire department. There are two manufactories of artificial ice, three planing mills, one flouring mill and four banks. There are good hotels, and many good lodging houses. Business of every description is well represented in Phoenix; and it being the natural trade center of an extensive region, has a large and steadily growing traffic. During the past year a number of fine brick structures have been erected, and the work of improvement goes on without intermission. Phoenix is connected by rail with the Southern Pacific road, and additional railroad connections will soon be had with the Atlantic and Pacific road, thus giving the advantages of competition both East and West. A good toll-road is completed into the heart of the Bradshaw mountains, that will bring to Phoenix a large amount of mining business. Excellent highways lead off in every direction, radiating to Phoenix as do the spokes of a wheel to the hub.

Three miles east of the city is the Territorial Insane Asylum, a model institution of the class. To the west of the city are the capitol grounds, highly improved. No start has been made upon a building as yet, but an appropriation to the end is expected at the next session of the Legislature. In the lack of a capitol building, the upper floor of the City Hall is given over to the Legislature, and the main floor is, for the most part, occupied by the offices of the Governor and Secretary of the Territory.[62]

The pamphlets and letters that Commissioner of Immigration Black and others circulated in the East were designed to induce a mass migration of people to the territory.[63] The population of Arizona in 1890, however, did not reach the size that advocates of statehood had hoped for. The census showed that the number of people in the territory had declined since 1882 from an estimated 83,000 to about 57,000.[64] Governor Wolfley had ascribed the loss to the exodus of the mining population.[65]

There was much optimism in the territory, however. A Tucson correspondent of the *New York Times* expressed this dream for the future in a report stressing improved transportation. "In the early days," he wrote,

much of the travel was done by stage, but the railroad is rapidly driving

---

[62]John A. Black, *Arizona: The Land of Sunshine and Silver, Health and Prosperity, The Place of Ideal Homes* (Phoenix: Republican Book and Job Print, 1890), pp. 67-68.

[63]For example, see letter of John A. Black, Commissioner of Immigration, to Ernest Ingersoll, Esq., of New York, from Tucson, Arizona, November 8, 1889, in the New York City Public Library, Manuscript Division.

[64]*New York Times,* August 5, 1890.

[65]*Ibid.;* see also, U. S. Dept. of the Interior, *Report of the Governor of the Territory of Arizona* [Wolfley] *to the Secretary of the Interior,* 1889, pp. 3-4.

out the buckboard and the Concord coach. In the words of one of the venerable Jehus of those times, "Stage drivin' will soon be played out in Arizona and these infernal kyars will be runnin' to every town and minin' camp in the whole blessed country." Many were the pleasant hours passed on these old rattletraps, and many were the thrilling tales of the lonely ambush, the sudden attack, the groans of the dying, and the wild race for life over mountain, hill, and plain. The great route in the olden time and only means of communication was the Butterfield line . . . Now, two transcontinental railroads cross the territory, one in the north and the other in the south. The regions through which they pass are not very inviting, and the stranger gazing at the vast stretches of dry, treeless, plains and barren mountains is not apt to be favorably impressed with the country. But nearly every one of these mountain masses is rich in minerals, and north and south of these lines the country presents a very different appearance. Many prosperous towns have sprung up, cattle ranges have been established, and almost everywhere that capital has sought an investment it has been successful.[66]

The advertising program begun by Commissioner Black was obviously paying off in favorable publicity for Arizona. Fortunately, an elaborate pamphlet that he prepared on Arizona's resources went to press before the Sixteenth Assembly took office in January, 1891, and abolished his job for political reasons. He was a Republican appointee and, therefore, fair game for the large Democratic majority that gained control of the legislature in the election of 1890.

As usual, the contest for the delegate to Congress attracted the most attention during the 1890 campaign since it was the only race in which the whole territory could participate. The Republican candidate who tried unsuccessfully to unseat Mark Smith for this office was George W. Cheyney, the superintendent of public instruction in the Wolfley administration. As a member of the Council from Cochise County in the Fifteenth Assembly, Cheyney had voted for the removal of the capital to Phoenix and against the further subdividing of counties — thereby fulfilling two pledges his constituents had exacted from him. Though the capital removal was considered an unfriendly act toward Prescott, Cheyney's supporters explained that their candidate had a reputation for being loyal to the voters that he represented and would faithfully serve all Arizona if elected delegate. It was also argued by the same people that any influence which he might have with the Republican administration of President Harrison would be an improvement.

The Republican press emphasized this point, claiming that Delegate Smith had made no progress in four years toward securing legislation relative to Arizona's most vital interests — statehood, the silver ques-

---

66"The Wealth of Arizona," *New York Times,* December 22, 1890.

tion, a north-and-south road in the territory, reservoirs and public buildings, the legal settlement of Spanish and Mexican land-grant claims, the Mormon question, matters pertaining to public lands, and the survey of Atlantic and Pacific Railroad lands.[67] As an example of what a delegate might do in Washington to assist the territory, the *Arizona Citizen* pointed out that there were over ten million acres of lands belonging to the Atlantic and Pacific in Apache, Yavapai, and Mohave counties that would be placed upon the tax rolls if Congress could be persuaded to provide for a survey.[68]

Granted that the territory needed much more beneficial legislation from Congress than it was getting, it should be explained at this point that Smith was probably doing as much as could be expected from any non-voting delegate. Even though he succeeded in getting only four laws passed out of the eighty-seven bills and resolutions he introduced in the House, he was skillfully building a reservoir of good will, especially with Democratic leaders, that would pay dividends to Arizona at a later date.[69] Certainly, many full-fledged Representatives envied his influence and political acumen. The inability of Smith, or any other delegate for that matter, to accomplish more for the people whom he represented seemed to be due more to the territorial system than to the particular man in office or the party to which he belonged.

But Delegate Smith's critics went further than simply trying to label him inept as a public official. Several opposition newspapers censured him for "impropriety" because of his participation in the Wham payroll robbery case. And another journal accused him of duplicity on the Mormon question. In the first instance, the *Arizona Miner* said that it was highly unethical for Smith, an able attorney, to defend the men accused of attempting to rob the same government that was paying him a salary of $5,000 a year as delegate.[70] Emphasizing the same point, the *Arizona Republican* published a large picture on its front page, in which Smith was posing with the defendants, and asked derogatorily, "Which is Mark Smith and which are the Wham robbers?"

On the Mormon question, the *Citizen* called him a "political prestidigitator" who deceived the public with "slight of hand performances." In Tucson, Smith reportedly said that he "abhorred the teachings of Mormonism as much as any man could," conceding only that he

---

[67]*Arizona Weekly Citizen,* October 25, 1890.

[68]*Ibid.,* September 6, 1890.

[69]Official Record of Mark A. Smith, Delegate from Arizona, 1887–1909, Vol. 1, p. 3, Arizona Department of Library and Archives.

[70]*Arizona Weekly Journal-Miner,* October 1, 1890; and the *Arizona Republican,* October 31, 1890.

The Wham payroll robbery of 1889 as reenacted the day after the ambush. Owen Wister, author of The Virginian, *recounted this famous crime for* Harper's *and* Century *magazines. He saved this picture, taken by a local photographer.*

believed in fair play for them. Yet, in the Mormon stronghold of Graham County he was introduced by the president of the Stake as "the Mormon Savior and the expounder of the word before Congress." Obviously perturbed by the Delegate's successful vote-gathering techniques, the *Citizen* asked rhetorically, "How long will the public tolerate such double dealing? . . . The people are not such condemned lunatics as you think, Mark."[71]

But, just as the Wham jury brought in a verdict of acquittal to free Smith's clients, so the voters of Arizona gave Smith and the Democratic Party a smashing victory in 1890. With Mr. Smith going to Washington and his fellow Democrats taking control of the Sixteenth Assembly, the territory seemed assured of a reenactment of an oft-repeated political phenomenon: a Democratic delegate going east to grapple with a Republican administration, and a Republican governor coming west to deal with a Democratic legislature. Paradoxically, as we shall see, some success was experienced in each situation. Delegate Smith, in the face of certain opposition from the Senate Committee on Territories, was able to get a statehood bill passed by the newly-elected Democratic House in March, 1902. And Governor Irwin, with the help of Secretary Murphy (a strong resident Republican), cooperated with the "Sixteenth" to compile a creditable record.

---

[71]*Arizona Weekly Citizen,* November 8, 1890.

Chapter 12

The Last Carpetbagger:
The Irwin Administration

Arizona's ninth governor, John N. Irwin, was the last nonresident executive to be appointed for the territory. Born in Ohio on Christmas Day, 1843, he grew up in Keokuk, Iowa. Like several of the other governors, he served in the Civil War, first with the Ohio "Squirrel Hunters" and then with the Forty-fifth Iowa Infantry. After the war, Irwin studied law and practiced for awhile before going into business with his father in Keokuk. Expanding his investments, he became president of several companies, including the Mississippi River Power Company, and was soon involved in politics. He served five terms as mayor of Keokuk and two terms in the lower house of the Iowa General Assembly.[1]

In 1883, he was appointed governor of Idaho by the Republican President, Chester A. Arthur. During his tenure in the Idaho position, it was necessary for him to be absent from his duties for several months to settle the family estate, following the death of his father in Iowa. The government continued to pay his salary but Irwin returned the money to Washington, explaining that he had not earned it. Not knowing what else to do with the unexpected revenue, the Treasury Department placed it in the "conscience fund," along with the ill-gotten gains turned over by repenting thieves. The indignant governor vehemently protested against being thus associated with society's renegades, and eventually the money was credited instead to the public debt of the United States.

Irwin was appointed governor of the Territory of Arizona by President Harrison in October, 1890, but did not assume his duties until the following January. He later explained that the reason for his delay in departing from Iowa was the illness of his son who was in bed with scarlet fever; the house was quarantined and the Governor remained there until the physician gave him permission to leave with

---

[1]*Arizona Journal-Miner,* January 20, 1891.

his family.[2] Finally arriving by train with his wife and three children, he was greeted by Acting Governor Murphy and a company of the National Guard that stood at "present arms" as the Governor's party walked to waiting carriages. The Guard led a march to the Commercial Hotel, where quarters had been engaged for the family.[3] Later, Murphy conducted his new chief on a tour of Phoenix and oriented him on the affairs of state.

Murphy had taken charge of the executive department after Wolfley's dismissal and had already submitted the 1890 annual report to the Secretary of the Interior and delivered a message to the Sixteenth Legislative Assembly, which convened in the Phoenix city hall on January 19, 1891. In his address, the Acting Governor stressed the financial condition of the territory and urged the legislature to "either reduce expenses of government or increase the revenue, to prevent serious financial complications." He estimated the public indebtedness of Arizona (territorial, county, municipal, and school) at $3,427,000 and deplored the tax evasion so common in Arizona at that time. Stating that the actual property valuation of the territory was about $70,000,000 and that the listed value was only about $28,000,000, he said that no class of property should be allowed to escape bearing its equitable proportion of governmental expenses. Murphy bluntly recommended, for example, that a memorial be sent to Congress asking for a change in the law that exempted the Atlantic and Pacific Railroad from paying taxes on its unsurveyed lands. To reduce expenditures, he suggested that the cost of operating the territorial prison could be lowered $20,000 "by properly reducing the cost of maintenance, utilizing prison labor and reduction in the salaries of officers and guards."[4] He also said that expenses at the insane asylum could be cut $8,000 by cultivation of that institution's farm.

Murphy also recommended the adoption of the Australian secret ballot system for Arizona elections; the abolition of Spanish and Mexican fiestas, or religious holiday celebrations, because American participation in these events had made them "outrageous and a disgrace to the territory"; the construction of a bridge across the Salt River at Phoenix; the organization of a mounted police for protection against the few remaining Apache renegades; a reform school for incorrigible boys and

---

[2]Letter of Governor John N. Irwin to President Benjamin Harrison, from Keokuk, Iowa, November 2, 1891, Harrison Papers, Vol. 131.

[3]*Arizona Republican,* January 20, 30, 1891.

[4]"Message of Acting Governor N. O. Murphy," *Journals of the Sixteenth Legislative Assembly,* 1891, pp. 7-45; see also, *Arizona Daily Star,* January 23, 1891, and the *New York Times,* October 3, 1890.

John N. Irwin, governor of Arizona Territory from 1890 to 1892.

— Arizona Department of Library and Archives

girls; the prohibition of gambling on the first floor of any building; and the initiation of action to bring about statehood to Arizona.

The Acting Governor reported he had accidentally found the eleven "lost laws" that were passed by the previous legislature and filed by Zulick in a back drawer of the governor's desk without signature or veto. He explained that the Arizona Supreme Court had held the laws valid and that his intention was to have them printed, unless repealed, with the acts voted by the Sixteenth Assembly.[5]

The latter Assembly not only agreed to print the "lost laws" but also passed 106 new bills. The *Arizona Daily Star* (March 22, 1891) praised the legislators by writing that "the Sixteenth legislature as a whole was about the ablest body of representatives that has ever consulted the law making power of the territory and we believe there has been more good and less vicious legislation than at any previous legislature of Arizona."[6] Many of Murphy's recommendations were embodied into law.[7] A balloting and registration measure, for example, was approved to purify elections in the territory. The gambling statute was revised to provide a tax of $30 per month, to be collected in advance, "on each gaming table or apparatus of any kind whatever

---

[5]*Acts, Resolutions and Memorials,* Sixteenth Legislative Assembly, 1891, pp. 193-208.

[6]*Arizona Daily Star,* March 22, 1891.

[7]*Acts, Resolutions and Memorials,* Sixteenth Legislative Assembly.

such as monte, faro, pass faro, rondeau, roulette, twenty-two, keno, dice, red-and-black, lansquinette, tan, stud-horse, poker, or any other banking or percentage game"; gaming tables were prohibited at any fiesta, in any park or fair ground, and at any race track.

Volunteer fire service was promoted in the various towns of the territory by a law exempting volunteer firemen from jury duty. Cattle rustling was discouraged by a legal requirement that calves must be branded before sold and all cattle inspected before being shipped. Though a maximum passenger fare of six cents per mile was established by the legislature, new railroads were given a tax exemption for twenty years as an inducement to construct needed lines. Governor Irwin was strongly opposed to the tax incentive but was influenced to sign the bill by several representatives, including Captain J. H. Tevis, a Cochise County pioneer whose memoirs were later published in a book called *Arizona in the '50's*. Tevis was an eccentric character. Though he favored tax benefits to railroads, he wanted to economize by doing away with the territorial prison at Yuma. His plan for punishment was to hang the worst criminals and sentence those convicted of misdemeanors to the whipping post, leaving no need for a prison. He was not as successful with this idea as he was with the railroad bill, however.

The Sixteenth Legislative Assembly also passed a military code that provided that all able-bodied male inhabitants of the territory who were between the ages of 18-45 years and citizens of the United States, were liable for militia duty if needed. Another law authorized the formation and maintenance of a force of Arizona Rangers; it was 1901, however, before this group was finally organized under the command of Captain Burton C. Mossman. The legislature carved away at Yavapai County again, creating Coconino County out of the northern part and granting some more of the Tonto Basin to Gila County. On the other hand, a renewed attempt by Council President Fred Hughes and other legislators to create the County of Miles out of Cochise and Graham counties was again unsuccessful.

Not the least important of the acts passed by the Assembly was one providing for a convention to prepare a constitution that would be submitted to the people for ratification and then sent to Congress along with a request for statehood.[8] In accordance with this law, Governor Irwin issued a proclamation for the election of twenty-two delegates to be chosen by counties. Partisan nominations were made and, after an aggressive campaign, seventeen Democrats and five Republicans

---

[8]*Arizona Republican*, March 25, May 22, 1891; *Acts, Resolutions and Memorials*, Sixteenth Legislative Assembly, pp. 97-100.

were chosen. Among them were some of the ablest political leaders in the state — including Delegate-to-Congress Marcus A. Smith (Democrat), Judge Will H. Barnes, Superintendent of Public Instruction George W. Cheyney (Republican), and ex-Governor Tritle (Republican).[9] All of the delegates, except Tritle, assembled in Phoenix in September, 1891. Though the convention was Democratic in its makeup, it had the cooperation of Murphy and other popular Republicans. The principal bone of contention between the parties was on the question of the "Idaho Test Oath" as applied to Mormons exercising the right of suffrage. The latter group, some twelve thousand in number out of an optimistically estimated population of nearly seventy thousand people, held the political balance of power in Arizona. Since most of the Mormons voted the Democratic ticket at that time, the Republican delegates argued for the inclusion of the "oath" in the constitution, hoping, thereby, to disenfranchise any Mormon who refused to renounce polygamy.[10] The convention failed to include the oath, however, in the document that was submitted to the voters in December and adopted by a count of 5,440 to 2,280.[11]

The constitution as finally approved was tinged with Populism. It was never seriously considered by the conservative easterners who objected to provisions for the establishment of silver as legal tender in the payment of state debts, state aid to railroads and corporations, and state control over rivers and canals.[12] But the Arizona electorate was satisfied and ready to join the Union under the 1891 constitution. Whether the territory would be accepted or not depended on the Congress and how a new state, predominantly Democratic, would fit into the picture of national politics in 1892. The Republican-controlled Fiftieth and Fifty-first Congresses, which admitted six Republican western states in 1889 and 1890, had given way to a divided Congress. The Democrats had a majority of 235 seats to 88 for the opposi-

---

[9]*Arizona Republican,* September 8, 1891; U. S. Dept. of the Interior, *Report of the Acting Governor* [Murphy] *of Arizona to the Secretary of the Interior,* 1891, p. 40. A good unpublished work on the Constitutional Convention of 1891 is Walter W. Walker, "Arizona's Struggle for Statehood with Emphasis on the Proposed Constitution of 1891" (unpublished master's thesis, American University, Washington, D. C., 1964). A copy is in the Arizona Department of Library and Archives.

[10]*Arizona Daily Citizen,* October 14, 1891; U. S. Dept. of the Interior, *Report of the Acting Governor of Arizona to the Secretary of the Interior,* 1891, p. 40.

[11]*Arizona Daily Star,* December 2, 1891.

[12]*Journals for the Constitutional Convention of the State of Arizona, 1891,* Phoenix, Arizona. [Arizona Dept. of Library and Archives] See particularly Article II, Section 16; Article IV, Section 39; and Article XVIII, Section 1. (Also in U. S. House, *Admission of Arizona into the Union,* House Report No. 168, 53rd Cong., 1st Sess., pp. 11-30.)

tion in the House, but were still outnumbered by the Republicans in the Senate in the Fifty-second Congress (1891–93). The partisan nature of this body became apparent after Delegate Marcus A. Smith introduced an Arizona statehood bill in the House on March 14, 1892.[13] Amidst Democratic applause, his bill was passed by a lopsided vote of 173 yeas to 13 nays. But when it was referred to the Senate Committee on Territories, the bill was quietly put to death.[14]

The times were not propitious for adding a Democratic star to the flag in 1892. Nor, paradoxically, was the situation improved in 1893 when both houses of Congress and the Presidency were in Democratic hands for the first time since the Civil War. Why the second Cleveland administration did not grab the opportunity to add two senators and three electoral votes to the Democratic majority can be understood only in relationship to Arizona's stand on the free-silver issue. The territorial convention of 1891 had inserted in the constitution a section (Section 16) declaring gold and silver on an equal footing as legal tender for all debts and obligations contracted within Arizona.[15] This part of the 1891 document was in defiance of Article I, Section 10 of the federal Constitution that prohibits any state from passing laws impairing the obligation of contracts.

One of the authors of section 16 was Delegate Smith, whose personal stand on the silver question was made a matter of record in a speech in the House of Representatives on March 24, 1892, when he said, "I favor the reopening of our mints to the free coinage of silver and gold at a fixed ratio."[16] With Arizona and its chief spokesman definitely labeled as "free silverite," there was scant chance that the gold supporters of the Cleveland administration would admit Arizona into the Union. Free silver, more than any other issue during the 1890s, was the stumbling block over which Arizona statehood was destined to fall. Smith's second enabling bill passed the House again on December 15, 1893, but died in the Senate without ever coming to a vote.[17]

Arizona Republicans were just as adamant for free silver. On election day, 1892, the Republican paper in Tucson, the *Arizona Daily Citizen,* carried a cartoon of the American eagle holding in its beak a banner on which was inscribed the words, "Statehood" and "Free

---

[13]*Congressional Record,* 52nd Cong., 2d Sess., XXIII, pp. 2071-2121 and 5088-89.

[14]*Ibid.,* p. 5089.

[15]*Arizona Republican,* September 28, 1891.

[16]*Congressional Record,* 52d Cong., 2d Sess., XXIII, Appendix, p. 38.

[17]*Congressional Record,* 53d Cong., 1st Sess., XXV, pp. 1669, 3123; and *ibid.,* XXVI, pp. 248, 258-67, 319, 8141.

This cartoon, in the November 8, 1892, issue of the Arizona Daily Citizen, *illustrated the determination of many Arizonans to have both statehood and the free and unlimited coinage of silver.*

Silver Coinage."[18] For weeks in the same paper, under the emblem of the Republican Party, appeared the party's declaration for free silver, statehood, and protection of American industry. Without doubt, the interest in free silver in the territory was more vital than the desire for statehood.[19] The only thing that Arizona gained from its early efforts for statehood was the knowledge that a more tactful approach to Congress would have to be made if statehood were to be achieved. It was not enough that the non-Indian and non-military population had reached 57,600 by the census of 1890, that railroad construction had broken down the barrier of isolation and opened the territory to settlement, that the problem of hostile Indians had been solved, or that law and order had been advanced along the international border.

Meanwhile, Governor Irwin was making a good impression on the people and newspapers of Arizona. The Graham County *Bulletin,* a Democratic paper, praised his wisdom in giving three places on the Chicago World's Fair Commission to newspapermen who "have labored to build up the territory and advance its interests." After his first visit to Tucson, the *Citizen* described his appearance there as a "right royal reception." A throng of about three thousand "puebloites" gathered on the courthouse lawn, which was appropriately decorated and lighted with a hundred Chinese illuminators, to obtain a glimpse of their gov-

---

[18]*Arizona Daily Citizen,* November 8, 1892.
[19]*Ibid.,* February 2, 1893.

ernor. Irwin was escorted to the reception by the philharmonic band and two companies of militia. After an introduction by Judge R. D. Ferguson, the Governor gave a speech that showed him to be "thoroughly conversant with the varied resources of this territory." The *Citizen* expressed its pleasure with the speaker: "Governor Irwin is a fluent and earnest orator, and speaks from conviction, and left the impression upon his audience that Arizona's executive chair is filled by a man thoroughly identified with their interests. . . . His reception last evening was as enthusiastic as it was deserving, and showed that he was not only popular but commanded the esteem of all classes."[20]

The *Arizona Daily Star* echoed these sentiments in reporting that Irwin, in the four months since he assumed his duties, had suppressed factional party bickering and placed the governor's chair on a high plane, above partisan politics. The *Arizona Republican* in Phoenix was just as free in its plaudits. In describing the Governor's address on Memorial Day, the paper said that it was a "masterly one and splendidly delivered. The chief executive has no superior as an orator in the territory." The *Florence Enterprise,* in an editorial on March 28, 1891, expressed the same feeling and complimented Governor Irwin for putting the welfare of all the people above party bias. "It is a strange and unusual circumstance that a Republican governor could completely harmonize the apparently wide partisan gulf existing in his official relations with an overwhelming Democratic legislature, especially in Arizona, and yet the people have just witnessed such a phenomenon."[21]

Not the least asset of the Irwin administration, of course, was the very capable Secretary Murphy, who served with distinction as acting governor on several occasions. Even before Irwin's arrival in the territory, Acting Governor Murphy had put in another bid for statehood in his *Annual Report to the Secretary of Interior.* He said that the population of the territory would reach 70,000 before the end of that present fiscal year. The mining industry had been very active during 1891 and Murphy reported that the mineral exports for the year would exceed those of any previous year. The copper, gold, and silver outputs were especially high, and new valuable deposits of superior onyx had been discovered.[22]

On June 15, 1891, Governor Irwin left for the East, leaving Secretary Murphy once again in charge. He went at the urgent request

---

[20]Newspaper clippings in Record Group 48, Appointment Papers.
[21]*Florence Enterprise,* March 28, 1891.
[22]*New York Times,* October 7, 1891; and U. S. Dept. of the Interior, *Report of the Governor of the Territory of Arizona to the Secretary of the Interior,* 1891.

of the Loan Commission, and many citizens, to secure a territorial loan. At the time, Arizona was badly in debt and its warrants were selling below par — when they could be sold at all. Irwin spent sixty days in New York negotiating in the financial interests of the territory and then went to his home in Keokuk, Iowa, to continue the transactions. There was some criticism of his long absence and he felt compelled to write letters of explanation to both the president and Secretary of the Interior Noble. He told the former that his intentions had been to remain in Iowa until the November election but would return to his job in Arizona to avoid misunderstanding.[23]

In a letter dated November 5, 1891, the President replied to Governor Irwin in these words:

> I have your letter of November 2d. I do not remember to have at any time said to Mr. Clarkson [Attorney General] that your leave could be extended until after the election. . . . I have no desire to press this matter further and I accept the explanation which you have offered. In appointing a resident of one of the States and not of the territory to be governor, I departed from the established rule and I felt that it was unfortunate in such case that they should be able to complain of absenteeism. Arizona has been in some respects misgoverned and is loaded with debt. I very much wish that your administration might put a check to extravagance, fund the debt and organize the territory upon a safe and prosperous basis. I still hope you may accomplish this result, in which work you will have my friendly cooperation. In referring to the delay attendant upon your first reaching the territory, Secretary Noble did not mean to complain of this, but only to say that this, added to a voluntary absence, gave increased force to the suggestion that you should return to the territory.[24]

While in New York, Irwin was honored by a complimentary dinner on July 28, 1891, and had an opportunity to extol the virtues of Arizona. Among other things, he said,

> It is not hard to make you believe our stories of its mines and its cattle, but when I come to tell you, especially those of you who have traversed the territory on the Atlantic and Pacific, or Southern Pacific Railroads, that every acre you saw from the car windows of so-called desert, where nothing grew but the cactus, the chuhua, or the mesquite, would produce, with water only, crops of grain and fruit that would reach a greater average per acre than the most fertile soil in the most fertile part of the United States; when I tell you that in the valley of the Santa Cruz and the Salt River crops of wheat and of barley have been

[23]Letter of Governor Irwin to President Harrison, from Keokuk, Iowa, November 2, 1891, Harrison Papers, Vol. 131.

[24]Letter of President Harrison to Governor Irwin, from Washington, D. C., November 5, 1891, *ibid.*

raised by the Indians for a time that runs back beyond the memory even of a tradition, and never one pound of fertilizer has been put upon this soil, you may be able, possibly, to comprehend its richness and fertility.[25]

The Governor extolled the prospects that the dense forests, minerals, and grazing lands furnished eastern capitalists. While expressing the utmost confidence in a great future for Arizona, he said that he could not tell how long it would be before that richly endowed section of the country became possessed of adequate facilities to develop its resources. Railroads and capital were both urgently needed and Irwin told his audience that the enterprising people of Arizona were looking to New York for both. "New Yorkers have got both the nerve and the capital to build railroads and open mines in an undeveloped country," he said. "We need greatly enlarged facilities of transportation in order to get our products to market. With an area of territory equal to New York State and New England combined we have only 1,100 miles of railroads. It is owing to this lack of transportation facilities that Arizona is today, perhaps, the least known of all the possessions of the United States."

He stressed the fact that Apaches were no longer a deterrent and that Arizona was civilized. "It is the simple truth," he said, "to say that life in Arizona — in its towns, its villages, and its farms — is safer today than life in New York. The life that can be led, and is led, by the American man and woman, by the American family in Arizona — in its mountains or in its valleys — is just as pure, just as sweet as is the life of any American family living in New York or New England."

Unfortunately for Irwin, he wasn't governor long enough to develop the territorial resources mentioned in his speech. His first mistake was to make most of his appointments from the opposition party, the Democrats, in hope of making everybody happy. As a result, neither party supported him. Most of his appointees were good men but a few were accused of corruption. His prison warden, for one, stole the furniture from the superintendent's house when he departed from the job. Governor Irwin was also severely criticized by several newspapers for releasing a number of prisoners about a year after he took office; his action probably would have been less objectionable if the pardons had been spread out over a period of time.[26]

---

[25]Walter S. Logan, *Arizona and Some of Her Friends: The Toasts and Responses at a Complimentary Dinner Given By Walter S. Logan at the Marine and Field Club, Bath Beach, New York, Tuesday, July 28th, 1891 to Governor John N. Irwin, Governor of Arizona. . . . ,* (n.p.; n.d.) pp. 10-16.

[26]*Arizona Journal-Miner,* May 17, 1892.

Tucson in 1892 as it appeared looking northeast from the Southern Pacific tracks toward the University of Arizona. The building on the far right at the back is Old Main on the campus.

The whole political situation was brought to the attention of the federal government and President Harrison decided to make his third Arizona gubernatorial appointment. He accepted the resignation Governor Irwin submitted on April 18, 1892. Irwin ended his letter: "I wish to thank you for your courteous treatment during my incumbency of this office and to express to you my best wishes for the continued success of your splendid Administration."[27]

The mantle of authority in Arizona was passed to Secretary Murphy who had applied for the governorship on April 4, after learning that Irwin intended to resign. In support of his application, Murphy said that he had been acting governor two-thirds of the time during the previous three years when Wolfley and Irwin were absent from their duties. He claimed to have the wholehearted support of the Republican Party and the affections of the people, having just received the unanimous endorsement of every county in the territory for delegate to the national convention. "I submit," he wrote, "that it will be impossible for a stranger to come here, who is not familiar with the duties of the office, or the needs and conditions of the territory, and render proper service, or give satisfaction to the people of the National Administration."[28] Murphy's solicitations were successful and he finally moved

[27]Letter of Governor Irwin to President Harrison, from Washington, D. C., April 18, 1892, Record Group 48, Appointment Papers.

[28]Letter of Acting Governor N. O. Murphy to Secretary of the Interior John Noble, from Phoenix, Arizona, April 4, 1892, *ibid.*

out of the secretary's office to become the chief executive in name as well as in fact.

Irwin was the last carpetbag governor to be chosen from outside the limits of the territory. He left Arizona, but not politics. In 1899, he was appointed minister to Portugal by another Republican President, William McKinley. Irwin died at Hot Springs, Arkansas, in 1905, and was buried at Keokuk, Iowa.

During his short residence in Arizona he became an advocate of statehood. In 1893, he wrote an article for the *North American Review* in which he not only pleaded the territory's cause for a star on the flag, but also showed a keen insight into the problems incumbent upon territorial status:

> The Territory of Arizona is knocking at the door of Congress and asks admission into the Union of States. The condition of a Territory is dependence upon the National Government. That of a State is independence in all things excepting when a constitutional limitation is imposed. A Territory is in vassalage. A State is in equality. A Territory is a child under tutelage. A State is a full grown man with no master. A State governs itself, elects its own officers and enacts its own laws. A Territory is governed by officials appointed by the President of the United States, and in the past these officers have usually been selected from the older States and have had little or no knowledge of the people or of the country they are sent to rule. A territorial legislature can, it is true, enact laws, but these laws are subject to the approval or disapproval of Congress, which knows little and cares less about the needs of a region hundreds of miles away. A Territory has no vote in Congress and no voice in the election of a President. A citizen of a territory is a citizen of the United States, but because he has crossed an imaginary line he has lost the privileges held by other citizens who remain in the States. A Territory is taxed, but has no representation. Its existence is an anomaly and as soon as it can fulfill the conditions it should be received into the Union and given all the rights and privileges of Statehood. . . . Arizona should be made a State because it meets all the requirements of Statehood. The Territory has the population to make a State, and the resources to maintain a State. . . .[29]

---

[29]John N. Irwin [ex-Governor], "Arizona," *The North American Review,* Vol. 156, No. 436 (1893), pp. 354-58.

Chapter 13

Home Rule at Last:
The First Murphy Administration

Nathan Oakes Murphy, the tenth and fourteenth Governor of the Territory of Arizona, was the only man who was twice accorded the honor of serving in the office. Born on a farm in Lincoln County, Maine, in 1849, and largely self-educated, he taught school in Wisconsin for awhile. Then following "the course of empire" westward in 1883, he reached Prescott to engage in mining and real estate activities with his older brother, Frank, who had settled there five years earlier.[1] Frank Murphy soon became one of the biggest businessmen in northern Arizona, being connected with the famous Congress Mine, the Bashford-Burmister Mercantile Company of Prescott, and the Santa Fe, Prescott, and Phoenix Railway. Both the Murphys were closely identified with the progress of Arizona and so Nathan's appointment to the governorship, in name as well as in fact, was acclaimed by the territorial newspapers. The *Arizona Sentinel* of Yuma (April 23, 1892), for example, said that "the people of Arizona have reason to rejoice that a man has been selected at least for the position whose every interest is identified with theirs, and one who will not act merely as a politician but always with the best interests of the whole Territory at heart."[2]

The short span of Murphy's first tenure in office was due to a change in national administrations. Cleveland defeated Harrison in 1892 and naturally chose to reward his Democratic supporters after the election. Murphy did have an opportunity to address the Seventeenth Legislative Assembly as governor, however. In a very able and progressive message, he again emphasized the financial condition of the territory. Pulling no punches, he said it was ridiculous that assessment rolls showed no material change from year to year, while in reality taxable property was steadily increasing, notwithstanding heavy losses in the

---

[1]*Arizona Republican,* Special Edition, August 1, 1892.
[2]*Arizona Sentinel* (Yuma), April 23, 1892.

cattle industry in the previous year because of drought. With the population expanding rapidly, more revenue was needed to bear the heavier expense of maintaining governmental, educational, and penal institutions. Not only did he believe that every property owner should pay his fair share, but he also recommended that the profits of mines should be taxed. On the other hand, he favored exempting new railroads from taxation because the building of a railroad in a thinly-settled frontier country was at best a hazardous undertaking and a financial risk.[3]

Also on the subject of taxation, the Governor made several suggestions that would advance the social tone of the territory and help pave the way for statehood. He proposed a "high license law" to regulate the sale of intoxicating liquors. His idea was to discourage drinking and to improve the character of saloons without appreciably decreasing the revenue. In a similar vein, Murphy advocated the repeal of the law licensing gambling and favored local option whereby each community could regulate such matters to create the moral climate desired. He deplored the fact that the schools were to such a great extent financed by the heavily taxed gambling fraternity, and contended that this situation retarded desirable immigration and blemished the good name of the territory.

Overlooking little of interest to the territory, Governor Murphy recommended the enfranchisement of women. He wanted a reformatory for youthful offenders of both sexes though one newspaper objected on grounds that the need was not sufficient at the time to justify the expenditure. He suggested that the vagrancy problem could be abated by a law allowing all conductors and brakemen to arrest tramps and turn them over to the nearest authority. He suggested a law to prohibit Indians from carrying arms when off the reservation.[4]

The Governor also recommended the removal of the territorial prison from Yuma to a more central location. He again explained that upkeep costs for the prison at Yuma were too great, and that in a different locality some useful employment might be found for convict labor that would not compete directly with free labor. Other governors were to repeat Murphy's arguments against convict idleness several times before the prison was moved.

The federal government did grant a request of Murphy's in 1893, however, to alleviate the situation at Yuma. Land was donated at the junction of the Colorado and Gila rivers to be used as a prison farm.

---

[3]*Arizona Journal-Miner,* February 17, 20, 21, March 4, 1893.
[4]"Message of Governor N. O. Murphy," *Journals of the Seventeenth Legislative Assembly,* 1893, pp. 14-36.

Nathan O. Murphy, governor of Arizona Territory from 1892-93 and from 1898-1902.

— Arizona Department of Library and Archives

Unfortunately, most of the soil was soon washed away by floods. No summer crops could be grown on the remainder because of spring floods, and winter crops could be irrigated only by carrying water in buckets. The farm's uselessness was finally confirmed in the report of Superintendent Herbert Brown in 1902. A more profitable enterprise was the manufacture of adobe bricks for use by the prison and for sale outside; but it was a problem securing a supply of adobe dirt from the nearby private landowners. The light manufacturing of clothing and shoes for the prisoners and for sale to the territorial insane asylum in Phoenix was another successful project. Ultimately, the failure of the Yuma prison to furnish steady work for the convicts was an important factor in the decision of the Twenty-Fourth Assembly in 1907 to move the institution. It was not until 1910, however, just two years before statehood was achieved, that the last inmates were transferred to the new penitentiary at Florence.

Having heard Governor Murphy's free and frank expression of his opinions on many subjects, the Seventeenth Territorial Assembly settled down to business. In all, the legislature enacted ninety-one laws, ranging from an act requiring irrigation canal owners to remove cockleburrs and sunflowers from the banks of their canals to another law temporarily exempting new railroads from taxation. Like many of the laws, the creation of a board to regulate the practice of dentistry seemed to indicate a willingness on the part of the legislature to prepare Arizona for the higher duties of statehood. Provision was made for a reform school at Flagstaff and for a territorial library in Phoenix. A museum to preserve the archeological resources of the territory was established on the campus of the University of Arizona at Tucson.[5]

Still another law authorized the Governor to offer a $5,000 reward for the capture, dead or alive, of the notorious Apache Kid, whose real name was Has-kay-bay-nay-ntayl, which means "brave and tall and will come to a mysterious end." The story of the bloody trail of the Kid and his charmed life in eluding the U. S. Cavalry, sheriffs' posses, and Apache scouts needs no embellishment. He was perhaps the most feared desperado in Arizona during the late 1880s and early 1890s. His outlaw career started when an attempt was made to arrest him for leaving the San Carlos reservation without permission to avenge the murder of his father, a chieftain named Toga-de-chuz. By that time he had established a good reputation as an Indian scout under the command of Al Sieber. It seems that the Kid's family had been placed on the White Mountain reservation by one of General Crook's army detachments when he was still a youngster. Naturally attracted to a warlike life, the boy attached himself as a kind of mascot to Clay Beauford, a former sergeant who was then chief of the San Carlos Police.

When the Kid was in his late teens, he was asked to enlist as one of Sieber's Indian scouts and was soon promoted to sergeant because of his expert trailing and his ability to handle other Indians. In 1882, he served with Sieber in the Battle of Big Dry Wash against the Coyotero White Mountain Apaches on the Tonto Rim, above Payson. And during the campaign against Geronimo he accompanied the gallant Captain Emmett Crawford into Mexico. After the capture of Geronimo in 1886, the Kid was stationed at San Carlos and was kept busy rounding up Apache renegades.

His sudden outbreak of savagery and donning of warpaint was perhaps due to several misunderstandings rather than to criminal intention. For one thing, he was faced with a conflict between his duties as a scout and his tribal obligation as the oldest son to exact blood vengeance for his father's murder. On one occasion he chose the latter and left the reservation to kill the prime suspect, an Indian named Old Rip. On another occasion the Kid was sent with his scouts to quell an Indian celebration which had become too wild. Instead, he joined with the Apaches in a drunken orgy. The treatment the Kid received following this episode was at least partially responsible for turning the once-proud Apache scout into the worst Apache outlaw.

---

[5]*Acts, Resolutions and Memorials,* Seventeenth Legislative Assembly, 1893.

The Apache Kid (center) photographed while serving as a scout in the campaign against Geronimo, 1885.

Al Sieber, famous German-born Army scout who served under Generals Stoneman, Crook, and Miles. He donned the buckskin attire for this picture, taken at Camp Verde in 1877, but did not wear such clothing otherwise.

The scouts were brought before Sieber and Captain F. E. Pierce, the commanding officer and Indian agent, to be publicly censured. Pandemonium broke loose after the scouts, who were still under the influence of liquor, were ordered to surrender their arms and be locked up in the guardhouse. When a shot was fired, the unarmed Sieber reached into his tent for a gun but was hit in the leg by a bullet that shattered his ankle bone so badly he was on his back for months and lame for life. Amid the confusion of this incident Sieber killed one scout. The humiliated Kid and his associates were tried and convicted of desertion in June, 1888. They were each sentenced to serve ten years in the Ohio state prison by Judge W. W. Porter but were all released within a few months following a United States Supreme Court test case decision holding that the Second Federal Judicial District Court at Globe had acted outside its jurisdiction in convicting "Captain Jack," one of the imprisoned scouts.

The local civil authorities in Gila County, however, were not satisfied with the government's disposition of the case and brought the Apache Kid and his companions to trial at Globe in October, 1889, before Judge Joseph H. Kibbey, Porter's successor and a future territorial governor. This time the men were sentenced to serve seven years each in the prison at Yuma for assault upon Al Sieber with intent to commit murder.

On November 1, Sheriff Glenn Reynolds of Gila County left Globe riding horseback beside a stagecoach bearing the Kid as well as several other Indian prisoners and a Mexican horse thief named Jesús Avott. The sheriff's plan was to transport the men by stage to Casa Grande where they would be transferred to a Southern Pacific train for the trip to Yuma. He was assisted by a guard named W. A. "Hunkydory" Holmes and Eugene Middleton, the driver and owner of the new, heavy-duty Concord coach — a sturdy, roomy vehicle with a paint job of forest green and bright yellow wheels. The first night's stop at Riverside, an adobe station across the Gila River nearly opposite the present site of Kelvin, was reached safely. But on the second day a tragedy occurred when the Indians, except for the Kid and one other Apache who were shackled, were let out of the coach to lighten the load going up a steep hill. Quick to seize advantage of the situation, the handcuffed Indians jumped upon Sheriff Reynolds with blood-curdling yells and killed him with the rifle they wrested from Holmes. The latter was not wounded, according to a coroner's jury, but apparently died on the scene from a heart attack. When Middleton looked back to see what had happened, he received a severe bullet wound in the head, the shock from which caused him to fall off the coach. He feigned death and later reported that the Kid probably saved his life by commanding the other Indians not to waste cartridges on him. Somehow Middleton managed to reach Riverside. The Mexican also escaped and finally reached Florence where many of the details of the bloody assault were revealed.

Before long one of the greatest manhunts in the history of the

Southwest was under way. With soldiers from several Arizona posts and sheriffs' posses searching for them, the escapees sought refuge in the Sierra Madre Mountains of Mexico. Governor Wolfley offered a $500 reward in 1889 for any of the Indians involved in the deaths of Reynolds and Holmes. Then, in 1893, $5,000 was offered for the Apache Kid after a bill introduced by Representative George W. P. Hunt of Gila County was passed by the Seventeenth Legislative Assembly.[6] The Kid, however, was successful in his suddenly invoked war against the white man, and was the only major Indian desperado in Arizona history that the Army failed to conquer. He returned frequently to the reservation on forays from his mountain fastnesses in Mexico, sometimes even appropriating a squaw, but cunningly evaded all pursuers.[7]

Unlike Geronimo or Cochise, each of whom was generally accompanied by a band of braves, the Kid preferred to plunder either alone or with a few companions. One of his methods was to observe his victim through a long telescope that he possessed, and wait in ambush. Although he was guilty of many robberies and murders, the Apache Kid was accused of many unsolved crimes that he never committed. But since he remained at liberty, his later years and death will probably always be shrouded in mystery.[8]

Just as the story of the Apache Kid was not confined to Governor Murphy's first administration, neither was the struggle for statehood. A few months before he left office, Murphy sent a letter to President Harrison in which he tried to convince the latter that the admission of Arizona to the Union would be a political boon to the Republican Party.

"As you probably know," he wrote in reference to Delegate Mark Smith's first statehood resolution which was pending in Congress in 1891 and 1892,

> the bill for admission of Arizona as a State passed the House last session and is now pending before the Senate Committee on Territories. There seems to be considerable objection in the Committee to reporting the bill favorably. I can say positively that if the bill is not reported and passed at the present Congress, it will certainly prove a serious administrative as well as party mistake. I think that I am competent to judge of this question, and I am not enthusiastic or over sanguine. Our Territory is very rapidly advancing in population and wealth, our growth in the last six months has been more than during the two years previous.

[6]*Journals of the Seventeenth Legislative Assembly,* p. 3.

[7]*New York Times,* May 10, 1896.

[8]A good work dealing with the Apache Kid is Jess G. Hayes, *Apache Vengeance* (Albuquerque: University of New Mexico Press, 1954).

It has been asserted that Arizona will retrograde like Nevada. We do not resemble closely the bankrupt state of Nevada in any particular, in latitude, altitude, climatic conditions, nature of soil, nor in natural productions. We are advancing in every material industry. Our assessable property is increasing, our debt has been funded into long lived, low interest bearing bonds. No good argument can be sustained whereby the Territory should not be admitted as a State. I am especially anxious for admission during your administration as President. It will help our party very much in the territory and it will improve our condition in every way. We have nothing whatever to lose politically or commercially. The incoming administration will admit if yours does not, and will take credit for a just and proper act and make our struggle for political success here all the harder. I most earnestly urge you to advise our friends in the Senate to act favorably upon these suggestions. . . .[9]

As we have seen, the Senate chose to postpone admission for Arizona, but Murphy continued his efforts with the Cleveland administration. On November 27, 1893, about six months after Murphy vacated the chief executive's office, a second statehood convention was held in Phoenix with Charles W. Wright of Tucson as chairman. After adopting a resolution to memorialize Congress for statehood, the convention appointed a delegation headed by ex-Governor Murphy to lobby the Arizona cause in Washington. En route to the capital Murphy stopped in New York City and displayed a large collection of photographic exhibits at the Holland House. The pictures, which were later examined by the Congress, showed the irrigating canals, fig and orange groves, the fields of grass, and some of the principal buildings of the territory.

In an interview by a reporter of the *New York Times,* Murphy said that "the Territory is fully ripe for Statehood, and had it not been for the uncertainty which existed in the last Congress as to which political party could control it, I believe it would have been admitted at that session." Asked if Arizona would be Democratic or Republican, he said, "It is doubtful Territory. If it became a State it would still be doubtful. For several years a Democratic Delegate to Congress has been chosen. I cannot tell whether it would elect Republican or Democratic Senators if it were admitted. The sentiment there is not so strongly for free coinage as in many parts of the West. Its mines produce more gold than silver. The output of gold last year was about $5,000,000."[10]

In another interview by the *Times* in Washington, D.C., Murphy's statements were amplified by the other members of his committee:

---

[9]Letter of Governor Murphy to President Benjamin Harrison, from Phoenix, Arizona, January 10, 1893, Harrison Papers, Vol. 155.

[10]*New York Times,* July 4, 1893.

James A. Fleming, President of the National Bank of Phoenix; J. L. B. Alexander of Phoenix; and Judge Rankin of Tombstone. After talking with these gentlemen, the reporter wrote that it was refreshing to find one section of the country to which hard times had not yet penetrated. There were few signs of the 1893 panic in Arizona, though promoters of schemes requiring the aid of Eastern bankers were somewhat handicapped by their inability to raise money. Speaking on the chances for statehood in the coming session of Congress, Murphy said,

> The fact of Arizona's stability in the present financial crisis, the wealth of her gold mines, the fact that she has always met her interest obligations promptly, and that within the year her debt has been refunded into 5 per cent bonds, which were sold at par, after exhaustive examinations by expert financiers, to my mind proves conclusively her capacity for self-government. It is believed that the population of the Territory has increased 20 per cent since the census of 1890. Congress should be just and recognize the rights of this deserving section of the country.[11]

It should be noted at this point that the question of statehood was a bipartisan issue with the Arizona residents who firmly believed in home rule. Republican Murphy, who served twice as governor (May, 1892 to April, 1893, and October, 1898 to July, 1902) and once as delegate (1895–1897), spoke the same language of states' rights as did "Mark" Smith. The rise of these two men to political prominence, and their cooperation in the statehood movement for over twenty years, symbolized Arizona's "coming of age." The image they attempted to create for Arizona was stated in the following preamble to the Constitution of 1893: "The spirit that has heretofore been known in Western countries as the 'frontier character' has, if it ever had an existence in Arizona, vanished before the intelligent toil, the patient industry, and the high culture of American bred citizens who have sought the territory for a home."[12] Propaganda for readers in the East, yes! But Murphy and Smith believed what they were saying and they frequently reminded their respective party leaders of commitments favoring statehood. Each man, of course, wanted his party to get the credit for adding Arizona to the Union.

The two major political organizations had for a number of years favored the admission of Arizona, and other territories, in their convention platforms.[13] A Republican plank in 1888 pledged the party to do

---

[11]*Ibid.,* August 18, 1893; see also, *Arizona Weekly Gazette,* August 18, 1892.

[12]See *Proceedings of the Arizona Convention for Statehood,* Phoenix, 1893, in the Arizona State Archives.

[13]Kirk H. Porter, *National Party Platforms* (New York: The Macmillan Co., 1924), pp. 149, 165, 186, 197, 216, 232.

all in its power "to facilitate the admission of the Territories of New Mexico, Wyoming, Idaho, and Arizona to the enjoyment of self-government as states, such of them as are now justified, as soon as possible, and the others as soon as they become so." Whereas Wyoming and Idaho received the coveted status in 1890, the two Southwestern states were destined to wait until 1912. In the meantime, the politicians — except for the Senate majority that had the votes for admission — continued to give at least lip-service in favor of admitting New Mexico and Arizona. In 1892, the Democratic convention approved the actions the House had taken in the Fifty-second Congress in passing "Mark" Smith's first statehood resolution and another bill to admit New Mexico; the Republican platform, in that year, more vaguely "favored the admission of the remaining Territories at the earliest practicable date."

By 1896, the Democrats came out for the immediate admission of Arizona, New Mexico, and Oklahoma. Four years later, the same party denounced the failure of the Republicans and the McKinley administration to grant statehood to these three territories. At the local level in Arizona, however, the shoe was on the other foot during the election of 1900 when Murphy and Smith opposed each other in a political contest for the first and only time during their careers. Smith had represented Arizona continuously in Congress since 1886 (except for one term served by Murphy who defeated two candidates from Prescott — Democrat John C. Herndon and Populist William O. "Buckey" O'Neill — in 1894, and for another term by Democrat John F. Wilson who won over the Republican, Rough Rider Colonel Alexander O. Brodie, in 1898). The ardent feeling of many Republicans for their standard bearer in the delegate race of 1900 was expressed by the *Arizona Daily Citizen:*

> Irritated by the reiteration of the question "What has Mark Smith done in his ten years in Congress?" the democratic press has raked up the fragment of a deed, in that Mark once passed a statehood bill through one house, only to have it die in the other. Great record, isn't it? Mark did it, even if he was aided at the time by a strong lobby from Phoenix, Tucson, and Prescott. One of the Arizona workers for statehood then in Washington was N. O. Murphy, there at his own expense. . . . When Mark was delegate, Arizona always had to send special delegations to Washington when anything was wanted. . . .[14]

After an aggressive campaign, during which both parties increased voter registration by paying out large sums for poll taxes, Smith was victorious. The *Citizen* took a "sour grapes" attitude in analyzing the election results. Assuming that "statehood was the republican shibboleth

---

[14]*Arizona Daily Citizen,* November 3, 1900.

of the campaign" because Smith had been tried on the question for ten years, the newspaper concluded, probably incorrectly, that the majority of Arizonans were satisfied with the territorial form of government.[15] Certainly, Smith proceeded to use what limited influence a voteless delegate could muster in behalf of statehood. Always one to see the question in larger perspective, he pooled his resources with Delegates Bernard S. Rodey of New Mexico and Dennis T. Flynn of Oklahoma to push the Omnibus Bill safely through the House in May, 1902.[16] The struggle over this measure, and the amendments that opponents in the Senate attempted to attach to it, is a story in itself and is related in a later chapter.

In a way, Murphy did his best work for statehood simply by doing a good job in the governor's chair. As the *Phoenix Herald* wrote about him on April 17, 1893, a few days after he was succeeded by Louis C. Hughes, "Governor Murphy has taken advanced ground on every question concerning the Territory and the tendency of his administration has been such as to prepare the Territory for those higher duties that we all hope will fall upon us soon to discharge."[17]

Murphy served too short a term as governor to accomplish all of his objectives. The main reason was because he could only mark time during the last five months, pending the inauguration of Cleveland and the appointment of a Democrat to the governorship. The President, however, did not complete the changeover as soon as Arizona Democrats would have liked. Delegate Marcus A. Smith, for example, wrote to Cleveland on March 22, 1893, and solicited his immediate attention to the selection of Murphy's successor. "It is absolutely necessary for the Democratic party in Arizona, that a Governor be appointed without delay," he urged.

> The Legislature is now in session and will adjourn on the 13th of April. The newly installed Governor must have several days in which to make a judicious selection of the important officers under his appointment. The Federal Statutes . . . provide . . . that the Governor of the Territory, by and with the consent of the Council, shall name the Territorial officers. When the Legislature adjourns there will be no Council to act in harmony with him. Mr. Harrison, five days after his inauguration, seeing the importance of this, appointed a Governor of Arizona, and removed your appointee by telegram (1889). The only necessity for this was one growing out of the political exigency. The Legislature held

---

[15]*Ibid.*, November 9, 1900.

[16]Howard R. Lamar, "The Reluctant Admission: The Struggle to Admit Arizona and New Mexico to the Union," in R. G. Ferris (ed.), *The American West: An Appraisal* (Santa Fe: Museum of New Mexico Press, 1963), pp. 166-67.

[17]*Phoenix Herald*, April 17, 1893.

Smith:—"I have always thought we couldn't make this race on this sort of track. I don't like it, but I'll do the best I can to help you through."

Herndon:—"I didn't expect this sort of track. I am sorry I entered."

Zulick:—"Come on, come on, this is in just my element. Everybody knows that I———!"

Political cartoon from The Arizona Republican, *November 5, 1894. In the same issue, Nathan Murphy, Republican candidate for delegate to Congress, answered charges that he was anti-Mormon with the following telegram from President Benjamin Harrison: "I recollect well your visiting me in Washington to urge the proclamation of amnesty for the Mormons."*

over the time prescribed by law, twenty-one days, (it being a Republican Legislature), in order to confirm the appointments, and avoid the question as to the power of the Governor to make an appointment without the consent of the Council. The Court, as now organized, was sent there by Mr. Harrison for the purpose, as we believe in Arizona, of sustaining this action. It is a notorious fact that that Court on every political question, had decided in favor of the Republicans. Now if you permit the Legislature to adjourn without appointing a Governor, the Court of Arizona is sure to hold that the Governor has no power to appoint a successor to the Republicans in office, there being no Council to confirm the appointments.[18]

Smith said that the future of the Democratic Party in Arizona depended upon having patronage to dispense. He told Cleveland that it was also in the interest of the national administration to have friends serving in the territorial offices. But whose friends? Smith and the stand-pat Arizona delegates supported D. B. Hill for the Democratic nomination in 1892, and the President was in no mood to reward his former opponents. He looked to the faction of the party that had been loyal to him and chose the diminutive editor of the *Arizona Star* (Tucson) as the new governor. The appointment highlighted a split in the ranks of the Democrats which cost them the office of delegate to Congress in 1894. The more liberal elements voted for William O. "Buckey" O'Neill, the champion of the newly organized Populist Party, rather than the nominee of the Democratic Convention, John C. Herndon. As a result, the Republican standard-bearer, ex-Governor Murphy, won the election with a plurality of 42 percent of the 13,465 votes cast in the territory. He went to Washington to represent Arizona while the Democrats engaged in an intra-party squabble — Hughes on the one side, with Smith, who chose not to run for reelection in 1894, and ex-Governor Zulick, the darling of the "wets," leading the opposition.

---

[18]Letter of Marcus A. Smith, Delegate of Arizona, to President Grover Cleveland, from Washington, D.C., March 22, 1893, Record Group 48, Appointment Papers.

Chapter 14

A Cleveland Democrat:
The Hughes Administration

Arizona's eleventh territorial governor, Louis C. Hughes, was in his late twenties when he first came to Arizona in 1871 to practice law. He was born in Philadelphia where his Welsh immigrant family settled after reaching America. One of ten children, he spent most of his early years in a Presbyterian orphanage after his parents died. At age ten he was indentured to a Calvinistic farmer and worked hard, his schooling being limited to a few months each year. Ardently opposed to slavery, he tried twice to enlist and was rejected for military duty in the Civil War because of his size before he was finally accepted by the 101st Pennsylvania Volunteers. After two years he was honorably discharged for general disability but served as a sergeant for several months in the protection of Washington, D. C.

Between tours of duty he enlisted in a government machine shop and acquired a trade. Known as the "little boy in blue" to the other workers, he was soon accepted as a journeyman and joined the Machinists and Blacksmiths Union #2 in Pittsburgh. It was here that he developed an altruistic spirit and became a leader in the labor reform movement in postwar years.

Favoring a reduction in work hours as a means of creating employment for the jobless veterans and free Negroes, he forwarded a petition to the U. S. Senate in 1866 with 7,000 signatures asking for an eight-hour day in government work. A bill providing for the shortened day was sponsored by Senator Henry Wilson of Massachusetts and passed by Congress as the first eight-hour-day law in the United States. Hughes also helped workers by organizing the first cooperative store in Pennsylvania. However, this activity, and the law studies he began, overtaxed his health and he moved to the milder climate of Tucson. With him came his wife of three years, Josephine Brawley Hughes, who opened the first school for girls in Arizona in 1872 and became known as the "Mother of Arizona."

Quickly launching himself into Arizona politics, Hughes served in succession as probate judge and ex-officio county superintendent, district attorney, attorney general for the territory, United States court commissioner, as a member and secretary of the Chicago World's Fair Commission (1892–93) and as a delegate to Democratic national conventions from 1884 to 1892. Beginning in 1877 and for thirty years thereafter he was also the editor and publisher of the Democratic *Arizona Star* (Tucson) and in 1892 was elected the first president of the Arizona Press Association. As an editor, Hughes advocated the removal of Apaches from Arizona to the swamplands of Florida, a policy the government later adopted.

He also agitated for the creation of a federal court of private land claims that, once it was established by the Cleveland administration, eventually invalidated claims to over twelve million acres of land held under Spanish or Mexican titles and returned this land to the public domain. Hughes persistently opposed licensed gambling and the liquor traffic, and took up the banner for woman suffrage as well as the movement for the initiative, referendum, and recall. The educational qualifications for voters that are now a part of the Arizona Constitution were also staunchly pushed at an early date in the columns of the *Star*. Hughes encouraged, too, the construction of homes and permanent settlement in the territory by his advocacy of building and loan associations, the first of which was organized in Tucson in 1887. And finally, he was "on the firing line" in every territorial political contest for thirty years.

Hughes's community activities stood him in good stead when he applied for the governorship. Dozens of letters were sent to Washington endorsing his candidacy. The Press Association of Arizona, regardless of politics, heartily supported him in recognition of his ability, integrity, and many years of service to the people of Arizona.[1] The national organization of the W.C.T.U. endorsed him in a letter signed by its president. General Nelson A. Miles, then with the Department of Missouri, and the G.A.R. sent letters in his behalf. Dr. H. H. Thompson of the Ohio Sabbath Association, Chairman Thomas D. Satterwhite and Secretary F. W. Oury of the Pima County Democratic Central Committee, Chancellor M. O. Freeman of the University of Arizona, Judge Richard E. Sloan, and a host of newspaper editors and Democratic Party officials helped to fill his application file with laudatory letters.

---

[1] Letter of the Press Association of Arizona, J. O. Dunbar, President, and N. A. Morford, Secretary, to Grover Cleveland, from Phoenix, Arizona, February 24, 1893, Record Group 48, Appointment Papers.

Louis C. Hughes, governor of
Arizona from 1893 to 1896.

Josephine Brawley (Mrs. Louis
C.) Hughes, photographed in her
later years. Reformer, suffragette,
newspaperwoman, and Arizona's
first woman public schoolteacher,
she is the only woman to be honored with a plaque hanging in the
halls of the Arizona State Capitol.

Morris Goldwater, who had already signed a petition for E. E. Burgess, said that he would welcome Hughes's appointment.[2]

John M. Fair, who was financially interested in Irrigation Enterprises, was another ardent supporter of the *Star's* editor. In a letter to President Cleveland, he explained that Mr. Hughes's almost solid support by the press of the territory would enable him to carry out needed reforms and assure the ascendancy of the Democratic Party in Arizona. Fair wrote that an energetic and vigilant press could counteract the Republican monied interests of the territory that controlled 80 percent of the mining, irrigation, cattle, banking, and land grants. He said that in Arizona,

> Democracy has divided itself, like politics in any frontier country, into two kinds; one party representing one band looking for spoils, while the other section has a higher motive and proclaims "a public office to be a public trust." To this latter class Mr. Hughes belongs. He has bent all his energies, and taken some risks in elevating Democracy above a mere scramble for office and the degrading influences and methods which usually attend such. . . . As a sample of his powerful work a reference to his connection with the Chicago convention will suffice. The Arizona Delegation was almost unanimous in favor of D. B. Hill, and went there in his interest. Mr. Hughes only could get there as Delegate at large — but he got there, and managed to swing the Arizona Delegation in the right direction at a very critical time, and it had great weight, and every delegate at the Convention knows.[3]

Hughes's chief rivals for the appointment seemed to be Foster Dennis, E. E. Burgess, and Thomas E. Farish. The latter was recommended to the Interior Department by Judge W. W. Porter. He was endorsed by a large number of people in California where he had served in the legislature, and by Benjamin J. Franklin, an attorney in Phoenix who was to succeed Hughes as governor. During the sparring for the appointment, Farish was accused of being a drunkard, a charge which several prominent Phoenix businessmen attempted to refute in a notarized statement.[4] Farish had been Governor Zulick's private secretary and was conversant with the affairs of the territory but was also a favorite of the so-called spoils section of the Democratic Party.

---

[2] Letters of Mrs. S. D. La Fetra, President of the W. C. T. U., to President Cleveland, from Washington, D. C., April 1, 1893; Morris Goldwater to L. C. Hughes, from Prescott, Arizona, February 18, 1893; T. J. Wolfley, editor of the *Arizona Republican,* to Cleveland from Phoenix, Arizona, March 3, 1893; Judge Richard E. Sloan to Cleveland, from Tucson, Arizona, March 5, 1893, etc., *ibid.*

[3] Letter of John M. Fair to President Cleveland, n. d., *ibid.*

[4] Letter of T. E. Farish to President Cleveland, from Phoenix, Arizona, March 4, 1893; letter of W. W. Porter to the Secretary of the Interior, from Washington, D. C., March 18, 1893; telegram of B. J. Franklin to President Cleveland, from Phoenix via Maricopa, March 23, 1893, *ibid.*

Not without enemies, Hughes had to fight hard for the appointment to the governorship, which he finally received in April, 1893. Several newspapers in the territory expressed gratification that President Cleveland chose to select Hughes. The Prescott *Journal-Miner,* for example, wrote that ex-Governor C. Meyer Zulick and Delegate-to-Congress Marcus Smith had fought against Hughes because "he is possessor of the manhood, intelligence, firmness of character and independence that would prevent them from using him as their tool, to advance their own ends to the detriment of the interests of the territory." In the same vein, the Florence *Tribune* wrote that "the appointment of Mr. Hughes is a triumph over the Democratic machine which has so long controlled matters in that party."[5]

Hughes was probably appointed, despite opposition from the Arizona Democratic Central Committee, because he had backed Cleveland at the national convention in 1892 and because of a photograph. It seems that one day the chairman of the committee, a gambler named Fred G. Hughes (no relation to L. C.) was in the Congress Hall Saloon in Tucson dealing a game of faro to a mixed racial group that included a Chinaman, a Negro, and two Anglo freighters. Frank Henry, a friend of L. C. Hughes, had a photographer take a flash picture of the scene and sent it to President Cleveland with this notation: "Here is Mr. Hughes' opponent's principal supporter at his daily work." Though not exactly ethical, this stroke of political sagacity helped gain Hughes the office.

The fight against Hughes continued, however, during the entire three years that he was in office. Before a month had passed, a bundle of charges was filed with Secretary of the Interior Hoke Smith. Delegation after delegation of Democrats began visiting Washington to urge the removal of Governor Hughes. The latter went to the capital several times to answer the accusations, and succeeded in convincing the Cleveland administration that he stood for law and order while his opponents represented the worst elements in the territory.

Most of the early charges were related to events several years old and the President declined to pay any attention to them. An example of an unsuccessful attempt of disgruntled politicians to traduce the character of the Governor came in 1894. He was charged with embezzlement in having received and retained the salary of the official interpreter, an office usually held by the governor's private secretary. After investigation, a grand jury exonerated Hughes from the charges. In reporting

---

[5]Quoted in *Arizona Citizen,* April 15, 1893.

the incident, the *Arizona Silver Belt* of Globe (January 12, 1895), wrote that the instigators of the charge should be "held in contempt by fair-minded people, while the attack on Governor Hughes only serves to increase the respect and approval which his administration merits."[6]

Governor Hughes wrote to President Cleveland that "it is the highest ambition of the present Territorial Government to give a clean and honest administration of high standing and thus far, outside of two federal appointments, this effort is receiving cordial and hearty support from all Territorial Federal appointees." Hughes said that Collector of Customs Samuel F. Webb had allied himself with some of the worst elements in the territory. Webb's deputy collector at Yuma, Mike Nugent, had been indicted while sheriff of Yuma County for failure to collect licenses from certain gambling houses, though he was not convicted because of a legal technicality. Webb's chief clerk of the Customs Service, Ed Mays, had served two years in the California State Prison at San Quentin for rape. One of the mounted inspectors, a Mr. Chalmers, was known as a chronic drinker and a disgrace to the Service. Governor Hughes also objected to Webb's unofficial activities. The latter and his brother, who was a mounted inspector, had controlling interest in the *Arizona Gazette,* which was maligning both the national and territorial administrations without cause.[7]

Another Cleveland appointee to which the Governor objected was Charles M. Shannon, Collector of Customs for the District of New Mexico. Shannon had been a member of the Council from Graham County in the Seventeenth Legislative Assembly. After the adjournment of that body, he allied himself with a few disaffected anti-Cleveland Democrats; he pledged himself to obstruct the Arizona territorial administration because Governor Hughes refused to appoint a number of legislators who were applicants for territorial offices. After his appointment as collector he disregarded the wishes of the Democratic Party. Living up to his pledge, he selected a man with an unsavory record as his chief deputy in Tucson, one B. M. Crawford. The latter had been indicted in the First Judicial District of the U. S. Court in 1889 for corruptly endeavoring to secure witnesses to give false testimony in the trial of the defendants in the case of the Wham robbery, in which seven soldiers were wounded and $26,000 taken from a federal paymaster.

The choice of Hughes and the leading Democrats for the deputy

---

[6]*Arizona Silver Belt,* January 12, 1895.

[7]Letter of Governor L. C. Hughes to President Cleveland, from Washington, D. C., October 21, 1893 (one of two letters), Cleveland Papers, Library of Congress.

job was B. C. Brichta, a young Tucson resident with a fine reputation. The Governor also objected to Shannon's appointees in New Mexico and told Cleveland that Shannon, who was supported only by the *Graham County Bulletin,* was a "menace to good government and the harmony of the Democratic Party in both Arizona and New Mexico."[8]

Though a lot of his energy was expended in political squabbling, Governor Hughes went about the business of his office and drew his $2,600 yearly salary.[9] In his annual report to the Secretary of the Interior in 1893, he explained that certain segments of the territory's economy were suffering because of the depression; but new developments in other channels had counterbalanced the losses. The Governor said that the shrinking in the value of silver had resulted in the closing of almost all the silver mines; the output during the year was less than $300,000, as against $6,278,895 in 1891. Owing to the absence of the usual rainfall — the drought extended over a period of two years — there was a loss in range-stock ranching of from 60 to 80 percent. However, the decline in the price of silver had stimulated prospecting and mining for gold with such good results that the territory was becoming one of the leading gold-producing regions in the Union. The loss in the cattle industry had been more or less compensated for by advances in agriculture and horticulture. The increased interest manifested in the reclamation of arid lands had been very pronounced.

An increase in the population to 65,000 was also considered a good indication that Arizona's prosperity had not vanished with the nation's panic. Hughes made a strong plea for the admission of the territory into the Union since it had every essential qualification for statehood. As to the politics of Arizona, the Governor said that the two parties were about equal in strength; and the territory could be trusted to give voice for gold as against silver since gold production was exceeding the silver output tenfold.[10]

During the summer of 1894, Governor Hughes went to the East in the cause of statehood. The *New York Times* interviewed him in the big city and printed the following interesting description:

> It would be a very long while, indeed, between drinks if the Governor of Arizona were to meet any other and bibulous Governor in the Astor House, where the former is at present staying. For Governor

---

[8]Letter of Governor Hughes to President Cleveland, from Washington, D. C., October 21, 1893, *ibid.*

[9]*U. S. Statutes at Large,* Vol. XXVIII, 53d Cong., 2d Sess., 1894, p. 185.

[10]U. S. Dept. of the Interior, *Report of the Governor of the Territory of Arizona to the Secretary of the Interior,* 1893; see also, *New York Times,* September 16, 1893.

Hughes of that Territory neither drinks nor smokes, and he has ideas on all subjects which he does not hesitate to express or put into practice. "That," said one of his constituents yesterday, a Mr. Fair, who is gifted with characteristic Far Western energy, but also in politeness that would do Boston credit, "is the very best Governor Arizona ever had. He isn't enormous physically, and his voice is soft and kindly, but he has rescued the Territory from semi-barbarism and overthrown the gamblers and the rumsellers who at one time held it by the throat, just as courageously as if he were six feet in height and could shout like a foghorn." Governor Hughes is truly not a large man, but is an exceedingly pleasant-mannered one, who wears glasses, a soft, full beard, and a white necktie. Indeed, he has the air of a clergyman, which impression is much heightened by his broad, white forehead, his clear-cut fashion of speech, his great earnestness and candor and agreeable quality of voice. . . .

"I have been East about a month," said the Governor yesterday, "and have spent three weeks of it at a watering place on the Jersey coast. I arrived here, however, from Washington, where I have been laboring in the interest of measures looking to the admission of Arizona to Statehood. There is, as you know, a bill at present in the hands of the Senate, favorably reported by a committee admitting us to that dignity."[11]

The bill Hughes mentioned was the one for which ex-Governor Murphy and his committee had been lobbying.

The *Times,* however, did not share the enthusiasm of the Arizona leaders for statehood. In an editorial, entitled "No Hurrah for Arizona," the paper quoted from the governor's annual report of 1894. Though Hughes favored admission of Arizona into the Union, he gave some very good reasons why the bill pending in the Senate should not pass. It was not the customary enabling act that would point toward statehood under Congressional authority in a step-by-step manner; it was a proposition to admit the new state outright with the imperfect constitution that had been hastily constructed and adopted by Arizona voters three years earlier in 1891. "A Constitution devised by a score of men on 30 days' time," went the editorial,

> might be a product of consummate wisdom, but in this case it was not. We have seen it charged that the convention of 1891 represented the railroad corporations and the gamblers and liquor sellers of the Territory. However, that may be, the Governor, while declaring that Statehood is paramount to all other issues with our people took very little interest in the subject when it was submitted to a vote, and had no serious idea that it was to be accepted by Congress. He is evidently cautious in his statements on account of the present popularity of the Statehood movement, but he says that it is "claimed" that certain provisions are "vague and indefinite and subject to conflicting construc-

---

[11]*New York Times,* August 7, 1894.

tions," and that others are "objectionable" for reasons which he gives. He recommends on his own responsibility that "Arizona's admission to Statehood be in line with usual precedents, to the end that every citizen now in Arizona may have a voice in the framing and ratifying of the Constitution of the State Government they so much desire to enjoy."[12]

The *Times* admitted that Hughes had given a good, lengthy case for statehood in his report, but opposed some of the arguments, including his estimate of the population at 70,000. This figure included 11,334 Mexicans and 1,362 Chinese and was less than half the ratio for a single member of Congress, and not, according to the *Times,* a promising constituency for two senators. The *Times* editorial stated that "this was, perhaps, the most rapid case of Constitution making on record."[13]

The Sixteenth Assembly, in March, 1891, had passed an act providing for a convention, to consist of 22 delegates.[14] These were chosen the following May, by a light vote. The convention met in September and finished the constitution within a month, and in December it was submitted to the people for a vote and ratified. The vote was 5,440 "yes" and 2,280 "no," the total being less than two-thirds of the votes cast at the previous general election.

Besides the objection to the hasty way in which the constitution was drawn up and ratified, there were criticisms against specific clauses. For example, a prominent Democrat, Peter R. Brady of the *Florence Enterprise,* and a leading Republican, Judge E. D. Tuttle of Safford, did not like the articles relating to water rights and irrigation; the proposed constitution provided that all owners of canals and ditches at the time of statehood could never be brought under the regulation of the state — a provision that would likely lead to endless litigation.

Another article to which senators objected, when the document was submitted to them, was the silver clause; the constitution made all debts, whether public or private, payable in either gold or silver. The senators felt that the territory was trespassing on the jurisdiction of Congress when it started regulating legal tender. The *Times* was probably summarizing the true feelings of many, including Governor Hughes and the Senate, when it wrote: "Arizona can surely wait long enough to have an enabling act passed under which a State Constitution may be framed with care and adopted with deliberation. The pending bill has been through the House and favorably reported by the Senate com-

---

[12]*Ibid.,* December 20, 1894; U. S. Dept. of the Interior, *Report of the Governor of the Territory of Arizona to the Secretary of the Interior,* 1894, pp. 60-61.

[13]*New York Times,* December 20, 1894.

[14]*Session Laws,* Sixteenth Legislative Assembly, 1891, pp. 75-78.

mittee, but it ought to go no further. Such haste in making States out of this kind of material verges on the ridiculous."[15]

Though Hughes took the oath of office on the last day of the Seventeenth Assembly in 1893, he did not have an opportunity to deliver his first executive message until January 21, 1895. Taxation, economy, education, and the moral standards of the territory were some of the topics about which the Governor spoke in this address. Like his predecessor, he deplored the high tax rate that resulted from low assessments, tax evasion, and exemptions. He recommended, though obviously in vain considering the historic lethargy of Arizona legislatures in tax matters, that all real and personal property be placed on the tax rolls at its appraised value and that all laws exempting property of any description from taxation be repealed.

Wishing to reduce the territorial debt without increasing taxes, he suggested that all unnecessary employees be eliminated. Prior to the Hughes administration, for example, all territorial institutions were governed by separate boards and commissions. He recommended, and the legislature enacted in this case, a law placing all territorial institutions, except the university and normal schools, under the direction of one board of directors of public institutions. Another saving was effected when prison maintenance costs were reduced by nearly a fourth. This was partly achieved by a parole law whereby a number of convicts were released on condition that they find honorable employment. According to the official records, only one person violated his parole.

Hughes devoted a considerable portion of his message to lauding the progress of schools in Arizona. Statistics compiled by Professor F. J. Netherton, Territorial Superintendent of Public Instruction, showed that there were 288 teachers and more than 11,000 students in the classrooms in 1894. The Governor complimented the people of the territory for their liberal support of public education and praised the Board of Regents for reorganizing the University of Arizona so as to reduce expenses by $6,500 while carrying on extra work. Finally, Governor Hughes made recommendations for the enactment of laws to regulate more strictly the sale of liquor, to prohibit gambling, to make the sale of lottery tickets a crime, and to provide for a Sunday rest law. He also urged that women be given the franchise and that provisions be made for the care of the deaf, dumb, and blind.[16]

Perhaps one of the most important laws enacted by the Eighteenth

---

[15]*New York Times,* December 20, 1894.

[16]"Message of Governor Louis C. Hughes," *Journals of the Eighteenth Legislative Assembly,* 1895, pp. 10-33.

Legislative Assembly was the one that set up the aforementioned board for the territorial institutions. Among several laws affecting schools was one allowing any school district with two thousand or more inhabitants to establish a high school. Another encouraged military instruction in the public schools for boys eleven or older who could be enrolled by their principals in the "American Guard" of the Territory of Arizona. Drill regulations for this organization were to conform to standards prescribed by the National Guard. Still another educational measure earmarked money for the education of the deaf, dumb, and blind.[17]

Other legislation dealt with the counties. Each county board of supervisors, for example, was instructed to give the care of indigents to the lowest bidder on lodging, food, medicine, and medical attention. On the last day of the session, the new county of Navajo was created from the west half of Apache County but only after a bitterly contested debate; Holbrook, heretofore a rival of St. Johns, was designated as the county seat. Two other new counties were proposed but not established: one to be called Papago with Nogales as the county seat, was finally created in 1899 as Santa Cruz County; the other often-suggested and defeated proposal would have carved a new county out of Graham and Cochise with Willcox as the seat.

Interestingly enough, the Eighteenth Assembly passed no appropriation bills because Speaker J. H. Carpenter of Yuma declared the House adjourned *sine die* at midnight of the sixtieth day with the measures unpassed. He chose to take this action to prevent consideration of a bill that would have taken the territorial prison from his constituents and moved it to Prescott.[18] Fortunately, the territorial auditors honored all accounts for the next two years and the probable illegality of expenditures was not seriously questioned.

Governor Hughes was connected with only one legislature but was ever an active crusader for reforms; that is, in between defenses against the incessant charges brought against him. The liquor traffic was a prime object of his scorn. In his 1895 *Report to the Secretary of the Interior* he wrote that "there are in the territory 635 saloons, seven wholesale liquor houses, and eighteen wholesale retail malt dealers, which paid a revenue of $16,294.62 to the United States for the year." The Governor went on to argue that strong drink was the chief cause for confinement of inmates in the territorial institutions. He reported that three-fourths of the 180 prisoners incarcerated at the prison in Yuma were there as a result of intemperance and that half the residents in the insane asylum

---

[17]*Acts, Resolutions and Memorials,* Eighteenth Legislative Assembly, 1895.
[18]"A Legislature Adjourns in Disorder," *New York Times,* March 23, 1895.

at Phoenix were victims of alcoholism. He further pointed out that the cost of operating these institutions constituted a large part of the territorial expenses.[19] Hughes's advocacy of prohibition won him friends in the East, including the famous Frances E. Willard who defended him after his dismissal from the governorship.

The removal of Governor Hughes from office was finally achieved by his political enemies on March 30, 1896. It followed, belatedly, an investigation made by two inspectors from the Department of the Interior the previous summer. Hughes said that the men "were from Georgia, and during almost their entire stay they were feasted and cared for by those inimical to me, especially the radical southern element, who do not in this country feel as kindly disposed to our Northern people, especially the old soldiers, as might be desired."[20] The inspectors spent three weeks building a case against the Governor. Before they left the territory the Governor attempted to refute the charges against him and offered to submit as much documentary evidence as necessary. The investigators hurried away, however, apparently content to submit a report based mainly upon the hearsay testimony given by the Governor's political enemies.

There had been charges that Hughes worked against the Democrat nominee for delegate to Congress in 1894 and that he had used undue influence with the territorial legislature to secure the passage of bills that he favored. Perhaps the chief reason for his dismissal, though, was his antagonistic policy to the Cleveland administration regarding the disposition of land that Congress had granted to Arizona for educational purposes. His problem was complicated in connection with the school-lands controversy because his name was supposedly forged on several telegrams sent to senators and representatives; the lawmakers were urged to defeat the President's veto on the Arizona school-land bill. The Governor denied having written anything against the veto.[21]

Not all of the Governor's opponents supported the efforts of those people who sought his removal. For example, William O. O'Neill, an unsuccessful candidate for Congress on the Populist ticket in 1894, wrote as follows to President Cleveland in defense of the Governor:

> As charges have been preferred against Hon. L. C. Hughes, Governor of Arizona, with a view to his removal, I deem it my duty to say in his behalf, that during his term of office Governor Hughes has given

---

[19]U. S. Dept. of the Interior, *Report of the Governor of the Territory of Arizona to the Secretary of the Interior,* 1895.

[20]Letter of Governor Hughes to Henry T. Thurber, Private Secretary to President Cleveland, from Phoenix, Arizona, June 15, 1895, Cleveland Papers.

[21]Telegram of Governor Hughes to Thurber, April 5, 1896, *ibid.*

that Territory a clean and economic administration of public affairs, which is admitted and meets with the approval of all except those who are his personal enemies. While I know, from personal experience as a candidate for Congress in that Territory during the last campaign, that Governor Hughes's views on the "silver question" are not in accord with the great mass of citizens in Arizona — a fact which has caused some in his own party to oppose him — and while I am politically opposed to him, I honestly believe that his removal at this time in the face of the reforms he has brought about, would be an act of official injustice.[22]

In reporting the story of Hughes's dismissal, the *New York Times* said,

The fight against Governor L. C. Hughes, the present occupant of the gubernatorial chair in Arizona, has been in progress for many months and delegations have repeatedly waited upon the Secretary of Interior asking his removal. Arizona appears to be a difficult Territory to govern judging by the number of Governors removed or asked to resign. Lewis Wolfley, as cousin of J. G. Blaine and John Sherman, who was appointed by President Harrison at the request of Secretary Noble was confronted one day by a letter from the Secretary of Interior saying that either Wolfley or Secretary Noble would have to resign, and the Secretary preferred that it should be Wolfley. The Governor promptly tendered his resignation. His successor, Governor Murphy, became almost equally unpopular. From statements made at the Interior Department there would seem to be warring interests involving land grants and irrigation claims which are bound to attack any person appointed to the Governorship of that Territory. Governor Hughes . . . undoubtedly had the active hostility of Marcus Aurelius Smith, the ex-Delegate from Arizona.[23]

Smith, though not an avowed candidate for the governorship, was boosted for the office by J. O. Dunbar, editor of the *Arizona Gazette* and T. E. Farish, secretary of the territory during the Zulick administration.[24] Another prospective gubernatorial possibility was E. F. Kelner, a wealthy Phoenix merchant and president of the Chamber of Commerce, who was not identified with any of the warring factions in the Democratic Party. He was warmly supported by many Democratic legislators in the Assembly.[25] But another noncontroversial candidate,

---

[22]Letter of William O. O'Neill to President Cleveland, from New York City, July 28, 1895, Record Group 48, Appointment Papers.

[23]"The Removal of Governor Hughes," *New York Times,* report from Washington, D. C., April 1, 1896.

[24]Letter of T. E. Farish (endorsed by J. O. Dunbar) to Secretary of the Interior Hoke Smith, from Phoenix, January 25, 1895, Record Group 48, Appointment Papers.

[25]"The Arizona Governorship," *New York Times,* report from Phoenix, March 11, 1895.

Benjamin Franklin, a Phoenix lawyer, received the President's nod.[26]
Meanwhile, Hughes's tenure as governor continued stormy to the end. The week before he vacated his position, he was assaulted on the streets of Phoenix by P. J. Clark, a newspaper correspondent. Clark struck Hughes in the face with his fist. The blow broke the Governor's spectacles, the glass from which cut the eyelid quite badly. Supposedly, Clark was deeply aggrieved at articles that had appeared in the *Arizona Star* that he believed the Governor had written. Also, he had been discharged from his Denver paper for sending in a scurrilous telegram about Governor Hughes; the paper printed the report but later apologized to Hughes.[27] Clark got off with a five-dollar fine for his assault on the Governor but was dropped from his membership in the Citizens League of Phoenix.[28]

The following article, which appeared in the *Arizona Silver Belt* on April 9, 1896, would indicate that Hughes was not even allowed to depart with dignity:

> The obsequious adulation which marks the reception of public officials in Phoenix was never more disgustingly shown than by the demonstration over the appointment of B. J. Franklin as governor. On receipt of the news from Washington, a thousand people congregated in the street in front of Mr. Franklin's office, cheering, throwing up their hats and acting the part of a lot of buffoons. "The people with bonfires, cannon and brass bands, went wild over the removal of Hughes and Franklin's appointment," so says the telegram sent to Mark Smith by B. A. Fickas, chairman of the Territorial Democratic central committee, and M. H. Williams, chairman of the Maricopa central committee. And what is the reason for the blare of trumpets and jubilation — because one gold bug is dethroned and another gold bug raised to the seat of authority.[29]

Though Hughes left office almost unhailed and unsung, he never stopped fighting. In a letter to President Cleveland he protested his dismissal without reason:

> I submit that your action could not have been more summary, or created in the public mind, grave doubts as to my integrity, as an official had I been guilty of the most heinous official crimes, and as a natural result a cruel wrong, has been inflicted upon myself and family. Taking into consideration my official record, and what I have accomplished in the interest of economy, the improvement of the public service and good government for Arizona, during my administration of

[26]"The New Governor of Arizona," *New York Times,* April 6, 1896.
[27]*New York Times,* April 1, 1896.
[28]*Arizona Silver Belt,* April 2, 9, 1896.
[29]*Ibid.,* April 9, 1896.

its public affairs. I am persuaded that I have been misrepresented to you or that you have been deceived or misinformed, as to the true conditions which existed in Arizona under my administration. . . .[30]

Those were emphatic last words to a President of the United States.

------

[30]Letter of Late Governor L. C. Hughes to President Cleveland, from Tucson, Arizona, May 14, 1896, in the Cleveland Papers.

Chapter 15

Another Gold Democrat:
The Franklin Administration

Benjamin Franklin, a descendant of a more famous man with the same name, was Arizona's twelfth territorial governor. Born in Maysville, Kentucky, in 1839, and trained as an attorney, Franklin began the practice of law in Leavenworth, Kansas, at the age of twenty. He was elected to the territorial senate in 1861, during the "bloody Kansas" days preceding the Civil War, but never served due to the outbreak of the war. When the South seceded, he joined the Confederate Army as a private and was promoted to captain under the command of General Braxton Bragg. After the war, he settled in Missouri where he managed a farm near Columbia, since he was not at first permitted the privilege of taking up the legal profession in that state. In 1868, however, he opened a law office in Kansas City with David J. Brewster, who afterward was an associate justice of the United States Supreme Court. Franklin himself served four years, 1871–75, as prosecuting attorney of Jackson County, Missouri, and in 1874 was elected to his first of two terms in Congress.[1] Prior to coming to Phoenix, in 1891, Franklin had also served for five years as the United States Consul at Hankow, China, and lived a short while in Los Angeles.[2]

Once settled in Phoenix, he quickly established a reputation as a faithful party worker. In 1894, he ran unsuccessfully for prosecuting attorney. In describing the campaign, his chief supporter for the governorship, Marcus A. Smith, said that Franklin was forced to run in 1894, but "fearlessly championed the whole policy of the President — denounced populists and populism and was like all the other Democrats defeated." In attempting to play down Franklin's loss at the polls, Smith said that "a wooden Indian marked "Republican" would in that

---

[1]U. S. House, *Biographical Directory of the American Congress, 1774–1961*, p. 912.

[2]*New York Times*, April 1, 1896.

election in this county [Maricopa] have beaten Andrew Jackson."[3] Many leading Democrats, and some Republicans, joined Smith in endorsing Franklin. Former judge W. H. Barnes, T. E. Farish, Maricopa County Supervisor W. L. George, Editor T. J. Wolfley of the *Arizona Republican,* and others wrote letters to Washington. The Democrats expressed concern over the future of the party, with Hughes at the helm, and asked for the appointment of a loyal party man who would dispense territorial patronage to good Democrats, not to partisan Republicans as Hughes had been doing.[4]

Cleveland must have been impressed because, when the time came for a change in April, 1896, he chose Franklin, after being assured that the latter, who was qualified in other respects, was a sound-money Democrat.[5] Cleveland favored the single gold standard and generally appointed men of like mind. Many Arizonans, however, including ex-Governor Zulick and the editor of the *Arizona Silver Belt* at Globe, sympathized with the Populists at that time and would have preferred a governor who favored the free coinage of silver.

As a result, considerable animosity developed between Governor Franklin and the Democratic majority in the Nineteenth Legislative Assembly that convened in January, 1897. The Governor was ill when the session opened but delivered a long message of approximately 20,000 words some ten days later. Counseling economy and cautioning against hasty legislation, he advised the lawmakers to follow the maxim of Jefferson that that government is best which governs least. Summing up the general conditions of the territory at the time he said,

> The financial depression that has prevailed throughout the country has of course affected Arizona, yet I feel safe in stating that a condition of more than ordinary prosperity exists within our borders. There has been a large increase in the output of our mines, the population during the last two years has increased nearly twenty thousand, and the cattle industry is in a more flourishing condition than it has been for a decade of years. Our agricultural development has been more than could have been expected considering the financial condition that has prevailed throughout the country.

---

[3]Letter of Marcus A. Smith to William Wilson, from Phoenix, Arizona, January 30, 1896, and letter of Marcus A. Smith to Secretary of the Treasury John G. Carlisle, from Phoenix, January 30, 1896, Record Group 48, Appointment Papers.

[4]Letter of W. L. George to Secretary of the Interior Hoke Smith, from Phoenix, Arizona, June 6, 1895, *ibid.*

[5]Letter of B. J. Franklin to Secretary of the Treasury Carlisle from Phoenix, Arizona, June 11, 1895, and letter of B. A. Fickas, Chairman of the Arizona Democratic Central Committee, to Carlisle, from Phoenix, Arizona, January 30, 1896, *ibid.*

Benjamin Franklin, governor of Arizona Territory from 1896 to 1897.

— Arizona Department of Library and Archives

Franklin estimated the population of Arizona at 101,000 and stated that thousands of immigrants would come if more capital could be obtained to bring water to the rich agricultural lands and to develop copper mines. Mining was still the most important industry with nearly a $14 million output in 1896, followed by stock raising with less than $3 million, and agriculture with about $2 million.[6]

In a way, Governor Franklin's address might be considered a plea for statehood. He believed that the territory was not only materially, but also socially and morally, ready to join the family of states. There were 16,936 children in school — more than 82 percent of the school-age population. The University at Tucson had 149 students in attendance in 1896–97 and was making rapid and substantial progress. There were fewer crimes and court cases per capita in Arizona than in the East, despite the fact that a total of only three policemen were employed in the cities of Phoenix, Tucson, and Prescott. Like the Governor, the legislature seemed to feel that statehood was coming. One of the most important bills passed by the Nineteenth Assembly provided for the construction of a capitol building. The measure that passed was introduced by Aaron Goldberg of Phoenix and provided for a bond

---

[6]"Message of Governor Benjamin J. Franklin," *Journals of the Nineteenth Legislative Assembly,* 1897, pp. 45-77.

— Arizona Department of Library and Archives

The Council of the Nineteenth Legislative Assembly in session in the Phoenix City Hall, 1897.

issue of $100,000.[7] Tom Lovell of Denton, Texas, received the contract and erected the structure which was first occupied in 1901 and is still used today. Additional bonds had to be sold to meet the total cost of $135,744.29.

The lawmakers were less liberal in appropriating funds to pay delinquent newspaper bills accumulated by the previous legislature, however. Even after ex-Governor Wolfley and several other prominent newspapermen personally appeared to seek recompense, the legislature voted that the newspapers were a nuisance rather than a benefit. The House jokingly passed a bill making it a felony, punishable by ten to twenty years in the Yuma penitentiary, to edit and publish a newspaper in the Territory of Arizona. The Council, of course, never gave the bill serious consideration and, later in the session, both houses voted to pay bills sent to the Nineteenth Assembly of $72 for dailies and $36 for weekly papers.

Strangely enough, another appropriation bill passed by the legislature resulted indirectly in the incarceration of the President of the Council, Fred G. Hughes, in the territorial prison. Hughes, who was

---

[7]*Session Laws of the Nineteenth Legislative Assembly,* 1897, pp. 38-42.

also an officer in the Arizona Pioneers' Historical Society, embezzled about two-thirds of $3,000 granted to this organization for the purpose of gathering relics and personal narratives of early pioneers.[8] Convicted in Pima County and imprisoned at Yuma, he was later pardoned and soon after was killed by a bolt of lightning.

One law passed by the Nineteenth Assembly aroused bitter criticism — the act which repealed the three sections of the penal code of Arizona that defined homicide and substituted a new definition.[9] The new law virtually acquitted all murderers, except where their trials were in progress or pending, whose crimes were committed prior to the enactment of this legislation. Among unprosecuted murderers, for which the law seemed to preclude a trial, were the dreaded Apache Kid and the accomplices of Black Jack. *The Arizona Weekly Journal-Miner* of Prescott severely reprimanded Councilman John W. Norton of Yavapai for introducing the bill, the Assembly for passing it, and Governor Franklin for signing it. The *Star* of Tucson labeled the law a "legislative and executive crime, for which the people must and will demand redress."[10] Law-abiding Arizonans were particularly perturbed since dozens of murders had been committed in the territory without severe punishment to the offenders. The new law made the prosecutor's job even more difficult.[11]

All in all, some 320 bills were introduced but only 88 were enacted into law. One of the more important measures codified and revised all the laws referring to livestock.[12] Cattlemen were pleased by several sections of the simplified law, especially by a new provision abolishing the county system of brand recording. The Livestock Sanitary Board was impowered to enforce registration in the *Territorial Brand Book* of all range-stock brands for which recognition was desired. The first cattleman to register under the law was Colin Cameron, of the San Rafael ranch in southeastern Pima County, who recorded his 6T brand.[13] Other honest cattlemen followed, recognizing that the law would help prevent brand duplications and serve as a deterrent to cattle rustling.

Another economic enterprise given encouragement by the Assembly

[8]*Ibid.*

[9]*Revised Statutes of Arizona,* 1887, Title III, Chap. 1, Sections 276, 277, 278, and 702; see also, *Session Laws,* Nineteenth Legislative Assembly, pp. 51-52.

[10]Editorial in Tucson *Star,* quoted in *Arizona Weekly Journal-Miner,* May 26, 1897.

[11]"Searching for Fugitive Prisoners," *New York Tribune,* May 12, 1897.

[12]*Session Laws of the Nineteenth Legislative Assembly,* 1897, pp. 9-34.

[13]Jay J. Wagoner, *History of the Cattle Industry in Southern Arizona, 1540–1940* (Tucson: University of Arizona Social Science Bulletin No. 20, 1952), p. 89.

was the railroad industry. One act exempted new roads from taxation for fifteen years and a second permitted the Santa Fe to absorb the Atlantic and Pacific Railroad, which was soon to be sold under foreclosure of mortgage. Much to the disgust of the legislature, Governor Franklin vetoed a number of other bills that would have granted tax privileges to certain private enterprises, which, unlike the railroads, were of a non-public nature. He refused to affix his signature, for example, to measures exempting beet factories, reduction works, and reservoir and canal projects from taxation for a number of years. Though Franklin appeared to be inconsistent, he was probably justified in signing the railroad exemption bill and vetoing the measures that would have given tax relief to private enterprises that are not entitled ordinarily to favored discrimination. The railroads were a necessity to the development of the territory's resources and of benefit to all the people — hence more entitled to government assistance.

Relations between the executive and legislative branches of government were already strained, but the Governor's vetoes resulted in an open rupture. The House passed a resolution, submitted by L. O. Cowan of Mohave County, declaring that "the best interests of the territory demanded an immediate change in the office of governor."[14] Even though the Council tabled the resolution and passed a substitute motion stating "that it has implicit confidence in the integrity and ability of our present governor, the Honorable B. J. Franklin," the Governor was extremely bitter and choleric. His unpopularity with the opposition in the legislature was not improved any when he charged certain members with bribery in connection with bills to increase salaries for county officials and to tax the net proceeds of mines. Franklin said that he was offered $500 by a Pima County lawmaker to support the salary measure which finally passed over his veto. In reference to the bullion tax, Franklin charged that a lobbyist of the Congress Gold Mining Company came down from Prescott with $6,000 to defeat the bill. Only $2,000 was needed and that was divided among nine members for their votes against the bill. The Governor was disappointed since he favored a levy on minerals that would have lifted some of the heavy tax burden from the shoulders of the stockmen and farmers. Thoroughly disgusted, he characterized the Nineteenth Assembly as the worst legislature that had ever met in Arizona.

Throughout the session, Governor Franklin labored under handicaps of legislative animosity and the fact that he was a gold Democrat

---

[14]*Arizona Silver Belt,* March 25, 1897.

in a free-silver state. But his hand was also weakened by the probability that McKinley, who had defeated Bryan for the Presidency, would appoint a Republican to the Arizona governorship.

Among the leading Republican aspirants for the gubernatorial appointment was Hiram M. Van Arman, who had served as secretary and as acting governor of the Arizona Territory from 1882 to 1886. He was recommended highly to the Senate by J. H. Carpenter, a member of the Council who had been speaker of the house in the Eighteenth Assembly. Among other things, Carpenter credited Van Arman with securing the election of Delegate Curtis C. Bean and swinging Arizona into the Republican column in 1884; and, according to the Councilman, Van Arman's campaign was partly responsible for the big Republican majority in Alameda County, California, that gave McKinley the electoral vote of that state.[15]

Another candidate with wide support was Isaac T. Stoddard whose appointment file in the National Archives is full of endorsement letters from such prominent people as Senator Henry Cabot Lodge and several New York congressmen. Stoddard, who was one of the most successful mine operators in Arizona, was boosted for the governorship as a nonpolitician. Among those who supported him along that line was George U. Young, editor of the *Williams News,* who wrote to President-elect McKinley, saying, "Government to be the best must be administered by the best and most capable men. To such a class Mr. Stoddard distinctively belongs. He has the ability in every way to fill the honorable position as Governor of the Arizona Territory." Besides having ability, according to the editor "the brightest jewel in his diadem of claim for that honorable position" was the fact that he had never been compelled "to base his existence upon public claims both fair and foul, but stands in the van as one of the most successful business men and managers in the southwest."[16]

Stoddard was never appointed governor, though he eventually became secretary of the territory during the administration of Governor Brodie. The successful candidate was Myron H. McCord, whose nomination was sent to the Senate on May 19, 1897.[17] Governor Franklin was taken to task by his critics for joining a group of affidavit makers who wished to defeat McCord so that their tenure of office might be

---

[15]Letter of J. H. Carpenter, Member of the Territorial Council, to Senator George C. Perkins, from Yuma, Arizona, December 15, 1896, Record Group 48, Appointment Papers.

[16]Letter of George U. Young, Editor and Proprietor of the *Williams News,* to Major William McKinley, from Williams, Arizona, February 17, 1897, *ibid.*

[17]*Arizona Weekly Journal-Miner,* May 26, 1897.

prolonged. After Attorney General Wilson had been sent to Washington to lobby against McCord, the *Arizona Weekly Journal-Miner* said that Franklin's meddling with the appointment of his successor was without parallel in Arizona history and that he "has demonstrated right along that he is a very small caliber politician and smooth bore at that."[18]

The paper recalled Franklin had promised, in the event of McKinley's election, that he would have his resignation in the new President's hands on inauguration day, March 4, 1897. But, according to the *Miner,*

> as the gubernatorial seat became warmer . . . under the portly form of his excellency, he realized more fully how good and how pleasant a thing it is to be governor. When McKinley's election was announced, the governor had forgotten all about his ante-election assertion and started his brain in motion to devise ways and means to hold office as long as he could. Realizing that his term in office was subject to the President, he planned to retain his appointees in office and as a result the tenure of office bill was involved and introduced in the legislature. There were enough democratic members in the legislature, however, possessed of sufficient principle and appreciation of decency in politics to defeat this measure. The next move was to join in the attempted defeat of Col. McCord and to this end the governor's attorney general was sent to Washington. Apparently realizing that the end is drawing near the governor, through the board of control, has taken up the completion of the Flagstaff reform school and has entered into a contract for that purpose, the object of which must be apparent to all, to hamper his successor. . . .[19]

On July 22, the Governor at last received his "Honorable Benjamin Franklin" telegram from Washington, D. C. He was informed that McCord had been confirmed by the Senate and had qualified before a justice of the Supreme Court of the United States as governor of Arizona. All records were to be turned over to Secretary Charles H. Akers, who had been directed by McCord to "act" as governor in his absence.[20] Interestingly enough, Akers claimed to be the governor, since McCord's oath was taken in Washington, D. C., outside the boundaries of Arizona. "I consider myself not the acting governor of Arizona," he wrote, "but governor in fact, through the removal of Governor Franklin, which under the law makes the secretary the governor." McCord, however, soon arrived and took office. Franklin continued to reside in Phoenix where he died on May 18, 1898.

---

[18]*Ibid.,* July 21, 28, 1897.

[19]*Ibid.*

[20]Telegram of Governor Franklin to Secretary of the Interior C. N. Bliss, from Phoenix, Arizona, July 22, 1897, Record Group 48, Appointment Papers.

Chapter 16

Spanish-American War Era:

The McCord Administration

The thirteenth territorial governor was Myron H. McCord, who was born in Ceres, McKean County, Pennsylvania, in 1840. When still in his teens, McCord went to Shawano County, Wisconsin. There he eventually prospered in the lumber business and became involved in a marital situation that was revealed years later in a sensational lawsuit in Phoenix after he died in 1908.

McCord's second wife, Sarah, was a school girl whom he met in Shawano and married after securing a divorce of questionable legality in Utah from Anna whom he had wed in 1861. Sarah preceded her husband in death in Phoenix and McCord then married Mary Emma Winslow, a family friend, and willed all of his Arizona property to her upon his death. The first wife, Anna, thereupon instituted proceedings against Mary Emma on the grounds that the divorce McCord had obtained nearly forty years earlier was invalid because she was not served with any papers before the decree was granted and because she had not waived her community property rights. Judge Edward Kent ruled against the plaintiff on the grounds that she had not proved her allegations and had been living for years as if she were divorced. The suit was a romantic chapter in local court history and threw some light on a facet of the governor's past life that was unknown to Arizonans.[1]

After his second marriage, McCord moved to Merrill, Wisconsin, in 1874, where he manufactured sashes, doors, blinds, and other wood products. A politically active Republican, he served in the Wisconsin State Senate in 1873 and 1874 and in the State Assembly in 1881.[2] After he was nominated for Congress by a Republican convention in

---

[1]Myron H. McCord File, Arizona Pioneers' Historical Society, Tucson, Arizona.
[2]U. S. House, *Biographical Directory of the American Congress, 1774–1961,* p. 1288.

1888, he made a speech that revealed some of his personality. "It is well known to all of you that I am not a public speaker," he said,

> that I am in no manner able to cope in debate with the intellectual giants and athletes who meet in the great arena. It is also well known to many that for more than thirty years I have wrought in the forests of Wisconsin, with little opportunity to delve among books of logic, of rhetoric or of elocution; hence I am no orator. But, Mr. Chairman, there is consolation in the fact that I am not selected to succeed a talking member, but a working member. There is consolation in contemplation of the fact that if the past is a criterion by which to judge the future, there will be no lack of talking talent in the next House of Representatives. . . .

McCord was elected, and though classified as a silent member of the Fifty-first Congress, he made personal contacts that stood him in good stead when he later asked to be appointed governor of Arizona.[3]

The person most important to his future career was William McKinley, the Congressman from Ohio who sat next to him. McCord gained the latter's friendship by championing his candidacy for the speakership against Czar Thomas B. Reed. Then, as a delegate to the Republican National Convention in St. Louis in 1896, McCord worked hard for the nomination of McKinley.[4] The new President remembered these favors and nominated McCord for governor, practically forcing a confirmation of the appointment when opposition developed in the Senate. By that time, 1897, McCord had been an Arizona resident more than four years. In that short time, he had established himself in both the economic and political life in Arizona; he was supported by dozens of groups for the governorship, not the least powerful of which was the Arizona Press Association.[5]

After moving to Arizona in 1893, he engaged in agriculture on a model farm near Phoenix, where he had about fifty acres in orange, apricot, and other fruit trees, as well as a patch of alfalfa. The hay from the latter was fed to range cattle that were fattened for the market. McCord also raised blooded cattle and, as an active member of the Arizona Livestock Association, often spoke in favor of bringing in good

---

[3]Speech of Myron H. McCord after his nomination to Congress in 1888. Copy in the Myron H. McCord File, Arizona Pioneers' Historical Society.

[4]Letter of McCord to William McKinley, from Phoenix, Arizona, November 9, 1896; letter of Charles H. Akers, Clerk of Yavapai Board of Supervisors to McKinley, from Prescott, Arizona, n.d., 1897; and letter of J. M. Ford, Chairman of Republican Territorial Committee to McKinley, from Phoenix, Arizona, January 1, 1897, Record Group 48, Appointment Papers.

[5]*Arizona Daily Gazette,* February 16, 1897; see also, *Arizona Journal-Miner,* February 1, 1897; *Tempe News,* February 17, 1897; *Yuma-Sun,* January 13, 1897; *Argus* (Holbrook), January 4, 1897; and *St. John's Herald,* January 25, 1897.

Myron H. McCord, governor of
Arizona Territory, 1897 to 1898.

— Arizona Department of Library and Archives

The three wives of Gover-
nor McCord — Anna M.,
his first wife (right), second
wife Sarah E. (left), and
Mary Emma (below).

— Arizona Pioneers' Historical Society

breeds (Herefords for the range and Shorthorns or Holsteins for the farm) to increase profits for the cattle industry. He had the solid endorsement of the Arizona Agricultural Association and the Livestock Board of Arizona when he sought the gubernatorial appointment.[6]

In 1895, McCord was appointed by Governor Hughes to be the citizen member and purchasing agent on the Board of Control. This board had two ex-officio members, the governor and the auditor, and was responsible for managing the territorial prison, insane asylum, and reform school. The board incurred much ill-will for a contract it signed with the State of Arizona Improvement Company, a corporation organized by Eugene S. Ives to dig a thirteen-mile irrigation canal above Yuma. By this contract, the company was to have the use of all available prison laborers for ten years at the low rate of seventy cents per day per man. The wages were payable, not in cash, but in "water rights," which simply meant that the territory could purchase water at the regular rates to irrigate any lands in the vicinity that it might possess when and if the canal were finished. The territory was to bear all the expense of maintaining, transporting, and guarding the prisoners. Furthermore, there was in the contract no stipulation that limited the work of the convicts to the canal project.

When Governor Franklin took office he refused to recognize the prison contract, describing it in terms too forcible to print. In litigation that followed, a decision of the Arizona Supreme Court that upheld the canal company's right to use the prison labor was reversed by the United States Supreme Court. Meanwhile, McCord became governor and attempted to make the contract seem more respectable by securing certain minor modifications in it with the company. The main stipulation was that the company should show its good intention of completing the canal by bringing in several thousand dollars worth of machinery. The Governor visited Yuma in December, 1897, after about a mile of the canal had been finished, and reported that the convicts were eager to work because four days of prison time was subtracted for each three days of work. The forty men, who worked on the canal during the day, were housed in a huge tent at night. Eventually there were a hundred convicts assigned to the project.[7]

Meanwhile, Buckey O'Neill of Prescott, a Populist leader, and Thomas E. Farish, the chief Democrat defender of Franklin's policies, assailed Governor McCord in the newspapers for reinstating the con-

---

[6]Letter of Charles W. Pugh, proprietor of the *Southwestern Stockman, Farmer, and Feeder,* to McKinley, from Phoenix, Arizona, February 20, 1897, Record Group 48, Appointment Papers.

[7]*Arizona Weekly Journal-Miner,* December 8, 1897.

tract. In an open letter, written on September 21, 1897, O'Neill went so far as to infer that the Governor would personally benefit by the contract and that he was deceiving the public. "The people of Arizona will never believe that you did it for nothing," he wrote. "They will not believe it because when you were a candidate for governor it was openly charged that if you were appointed you would be merely the tool to carry this contract into effect, a charge which you and your friends then emphatically denied. They will not believe it because of the dishonest manner in which you have sought to deceive them into believing that you were protecting their interest by modifying the contract, when in reality your acts have shown that you had no such intention."[8]

Whether McCord was the scoundrel that O'Neill portrayed him to be, or whether he sincerely hoped that completion of the canal would bring a bright future to the Yuma area, or both, made little difference in the end. Construction stopped soon after the company failed to receive a subsidy of about a thousand unsold city lots that it sought from the City of Yuma. The territory was left with $7,500 in "water rights" which could not be collected. Seven of eleven prisoners who had escaped were not recaptured and the territory lost $13,741 on the prison contract, with no way to recover the money.

The prison contract was not the only action of the Board of Control, during the years 1895 and 1896, that came under censure. A joint investigating committee of the Nineteenth Legislative Assembly reported that the board was guilty of a grave violation of duty on several counts. For one thing, a convict by the name of John P. Irving, who was originally imprisoned for obtaining money under false pretenses, was pardoned and given responsible duties at the prison. While negotiating with a Chicago firm for the purchase of electric plants for the asylum and the prison, Irving succeeded in getting a "rake off" from the company that cost the territory $1,175 in raised prices. McCord was at least guilty of authorizing the purchase without advertising to find the lowest bidder.

In another instance, McCord, acting in his capacity as the purchasing agent, obtained ten acres of land for the insane asylum from a real estate broker at a total cost of $630. Though this transaction was relatively small, the territory was the loser by $250 since the land was available for $380. The board was further accused of deliberately keeping its books in bad form to "cover up, not only mistakes that might occur, but palpable wrong as well."

Because of these charges, some of McCord's supporters began to

---

[8]Clippings in the McClintock File, Phoenix Public Library, Arizona.

drift away. Mayor Henry Buehman of Tucson, for example, wrote to President McKinley to ask that his recommendation of McCord for governor be withdrawn and to endorse heartily R. A. F. Penrose, who had strong support from his brother, the senator-elect from Pennsylvania, and other pro-silver Republicans.[9] Penrose had gone to Arizona to take a look at the country and had become a permanent resident in the southern part of the territory near the Mexican border.[10] His chances for the governorship looked temporarily bright after the committee leveled charges against McCord.

The evidence secured by the committee in several days of hearings was referred to a joint session of the House and Council that met in secret session. After hearing the committee's report, the Assembly adjourned *sine die* by a count of 24 "ayes" and 5 "noes" of those voting. This procedure seemed to imply that there was not sufficient evidence to censure McCord, even though his critics had the votes with twenty-one Democrats to three Republicans in the House and nine Democrats to three Republicans in the Council. According to President of the Council Fred G. Hughes and Speaker of the House D. G. Chalmers, no action, other than the above, was taken.[11]

All of the alleged breaches of official rectitude were brought to the attention of the U. S. Senate Committee on Territories when McCord was nominated for governor in 1897. The fight waged about him was bitter and relentless, especially on the part of Franklin's Democratic Attorney General, John F. Wilson, who went to Washington in an attempt to prevent the appointment. The *Arizona Weekly Journal-Miner,* siding with McCord, wrote that the "object in trying to defeat McCord is not in the interest of good government, but solely in the interest of Democratic officials" and that "Secretary [Charles M.] Bruce objects to retiring."[12]

Another contemporary newspaper, however, wrote that "the man who says he wants McCord for governor of Arizona in the interest of good government, needs watching. A hen roost is in danger when such a man is near it, and a watermelon patch is sure to be annihilated by his presence."[13] The opposition based its plea on the argument that no man with so many charges against him should be elevated to the office of governor.

---

[9]Telegram of Henry Buehman, Mayor of Tucson, to President McKinley, from Tucson, Arizona, March 17, 1897, Record Group 48, Appointment Papers.

[10]*New York Daily Tribune*, March 11, 1897.

[11]Letter of Fred G. Hughes and D. G. Chalmers to H. J. Cleveland, from Phoenix, Arizona, March 11, 1897, Record Group 48, Appointment Papers.

[12]*Arizona Weekly Journal-Miner,* June 2, 1897.

[13]*Ibid.*

Digging deep into McCord's past, the critics charged that his family had made an immense fortune in his former congressional district as a result of land legislation for which he was responsible. Senator John C. Spooner, who favored McCord's nomination, explained to the committee that it was true that McCord's brother had been prosecuted for fraud in connection with the so-called Omaha Indian lands in Wisconsin, but that not one aspersion had been cast upon Myron McCord in the eleven days of his brother's trial.[14] After McCord appeared before the committee and attempted to disprove the charges against him, an executive session of the Senate finally confirmed his appointment by a vote of 29 to 18 — a close one since a two-thirds majority was needed.[15]

He was obviously very ambitious to sit in the governor's chair, a job that paid only $2,600 a year. His expenses in securing the appointment were comparatively large; nearly two years after the Senate hearings, for example, he was sued by a Washington attorney who wished to recover $1,500 for legal services in securing the confirmation. Since he only served in the position about a year, the honorial aspect of the governorship overshadowed any monetary emoluments of the office.[16] Considering his hard fight for the job, McCord must have been encouraged by the following telegram sent by J. A. Kurtz of Phoenix:

> Appointment of McCord received with general rejoicing. Congratulatory telegrams coming in to his friends from all parts of Arizona. Hastily arranged but monster jollification in progress tonight. Phoenix never before gave such unanimous expression of approval of Presidential appointment . . . all trains and public conveyances to-night crowded by visitors. It's a glare of fireworks and bonfires. Business suspended. No trace left of hard fight made on new Governor. Late bitter opponents pleased with result and all republicans agree that appointment will unify republican factions of eight years standing.[17]

Returning to Arizona in late July, 1897, after filing a libel suit against a New York newspaper, McCord was given a rousing reception along the railroad route.[18] At Flagstaff almost the entire population turned out to greet him. At Williams he was welcomed by men of all political bearings, including a delegation from southern Arizona that came to accompany him to his home in Phoenix. Despite a torrential

---

[14]*Arizona Daily Citizen,* July 17, 1897; *New York Times,* July 17, 1897.

[15]McCord took two oaths, one before Justice Harlan of the U. S. Supreme Court in Washington, D. C., on July 21, 1897, and one before Chief Justice Truesdale of the Arizona Supreme Court on July 28, 1897. See note of Acting Secretary of the Interior Thomas Ryan to Auditor of the State and Other Departments, August 20, 1897, Record Group 48, Appointment Papers.

[16]Clipping from *Washington Evening Star,* about February 20, 1899, *ibid.*

[17]Telegram of J. A. Kurtz to McCord, from Phoenix, Arizona, May 19, 1897, *ibid.*

[18]*Arizona Weekly Journal-Miner,* August 4, 1897.

rain in Prescott, he was met by a large crowd which assembled at the depot. As the train pulled out the citizen's band struck up "Hail to the Chief." Obviously pleased, Governor McCord promised to visit the city often.

On Labor Day he returned to give one of many speeches for which he was in demand throughout the territory. In praising Frank M. Murphy and others for their efforts in completing the railroad that by that time connected the Salt River Valley to the Santa Fe, he said, "It took great skill and engineering because of the character of the country through which it must be built, and it took financial ability of the highest order to carry it to completion." He went on to say,

> Now, fellow citizens, this road and all the railroads in the territory are auxiliaries to the building of a state and they are appreciated and welcomed by all good citizens, but they are not sufficient. Permit me to repeat what I have said before. We want more railroads; we want more irrigation canals; we want more money to develop our latent resources and uncover our hidden wealth; we want our public affairs managed honestly, wisely, and economically, and we want many thousands of industrious, honest and worthy people to settle within our borders and help us build a state, and above all, we want the right to govern ourselves. All these things come with statehood.[19]

These farsighted words were printed in the *Arizona Weekly Journal-Miner* on September 8, 1897.

Governor McCord's tenure in office was destined to be short, however, and little progress was made toward his objectives. Perhaps the high point of his administration came with the outbreak of the Spanish-American War and his subsequent resignation to participate in what Secretary of State Hay called a "splendid little war." For the first time, Arizona was part of the United States when the country entered a war, and the state enthusiastically responded to the President's call to arms.

The governor received a request for only 210 volunteers, but about a thousand men had already been raised by the time Congress declared war on April 21, 1898. James H. McClintock, who was then engaged in newspaper work in Phoenix, recruited soldiers in southern Arizona and Mayor William O. "Buckey" O'Neill of Prescott sought enlistments in the northern part of the territory. The latter was one of the most illustrious pioneers in Arizona history.

Though a lawyer by training, O'Neill first worked as a typesetter for the Phoenix *Herald* after he came to Arizona in 1879. The following year he joined in the gold rush to Tombstone but soon became a

---

[19]*Ibid.*, September 8, 1897.

William O. "Buckey" O'Neill, Rough Rider, sheriff, newspaperman, miner, and Republican-turned-Populist. His equestrian statue adorns the courthouse grounds in Prescott.

— Sharlot Hall Museum

reporter for the *Epitaph* at the time when Wyatt Earp and brothers were "ramrodding" the town. Appalled by the wildness of the territory, Buckey looked for a home in California, in Hawaii, and at Santa Fe, New Mexico, before returning to Arizona to settle down. Serving as a circuit-court reporter for awhile, he saw a lot of the territory while traveling on horseback. Eager to return to newspaper work with his own publication, O'Neill opportunely recognized the need of cattlemen for a registry in which they could advertise their brands. This was before the legislature required that marks and brands be officially registered and advertised. So, in 1884, he established the *Hoof and Horn,* primarily a stockmen's paper, and offered a $100 reward for the capture of thieves stealing cattle with brands advertised therein.

As the paper's circulation grew, so did Buckey's popularity. He was elected probate judge and served as ex-officio county superintendent of schools. In this latter capacity he did some research which revealed that only three out of every ten children were attending school, and it was partly this information which prompted the legislature to pass Arizona's first compulsory school attendance law. In 1888, O'Neill was the successful Republican candidate for sheriff of Yavapai County. He gained fame as a fearless sheriff by tracking down and bringing to Prescott for trial, three of the four men who robbed an Atlantic and Pacific train at Canyon Diablo, between Flagstaff and Winslow, on March 21, 1889. Buckey trailed the outlaws into Utah with a small

NOTICE TO VOTERS To vote the straight ticket of any party, place an ✗ in the square underneath the name of the party or organization for ✗ which you wish to vote ☞ If you do not wish to vote the Straight Ticket put an ✗ in the square before the name of each candidate that you wish to vote for on the entire ticket. If you wish to vote for a person ✗ whose name is not printed on the ballot, write such in the blank space opposite the office he is a candidate for.

SAMPLE BALLOT.

Stub No.................... (To be torn off by Inspector.)

OFFICIAL BALLOT.
................................PRECINCT.   YAVAPAI COUNTY.
Election November 3, 1896.

NAME OF OFFICE VOTED FOR.	REPUBLICAN ☐	DEMOCRAT ☐	PEOPLE'S PARTY ☐	National Silver Party ☐
TERRITORIAL DELEGATE TO CONGRESS.	☐ A. J. Doran.	☐ M. A. Smith.	☐ Wm. O. O'Neill.	☐
COUNCILMAN.	☐ W. S. Head.	☐ John W. Norton.	☐ Robert DeLarge.	☐
REPRESENTATIVE.	☐ James Barton.	☐ Wm. J. Mulvenon	☐ Sam Foran.	☐ C. W. Anderson.
REPRESENTATIVE	☐ F. A. Tritle.	☐ D. J. Warren.	☐ W. J. Gilbert.	☐
REPRESENTATIVE	☐ Carl Holtzschue.	☐ G. W. Hull.	☐ W. H. Ferguson.	☐
SHERIFF.	☐ John S. Ross.	☐ Geo. C. Ruffner.	☐	☐
TREASURER.	☐ John Hartin.	☐ Dennis A. Burke.	☐	☐
RECORDER.	☐ Jos. I. Roberts.	☐ W. I. Johnson.	☐	☐
PROBATE JUDGE.	☐ A. E. Joscelyn.	☐ C. P. Hicks.	☐	☐
DISTRICT ATTORNEY.	☐ E. M. Sanford.	☐ H. D. Ross.	☐	☐
SUPERVISOR.	☐ Barney H. Smith	☐ G. H. Schuerman	☐ W. G. Shook.	☐
SUPERVISOR.	☐ W. G. Wingfield.	☐ T. M. Earnhart.	☐ James A. Strahan	☐

— Sharlot Hall Museum

Yavapai County sample ballot for 1896. Marcus Smith again won election for delegate to Congress, defeating both the regular party candidates. Other losers included former Governor Tritle who ran for representative in the Legislative Assembly.

posse and captured them after a gun battle. He was returning the four men on the train via New Mexico when one of the captives escaped by dangerously jumping off in a tunnel. The escapee was later arrested in Texas and subsequently imprisoned at Yuma with his partners in crime.

O'Neill was not so helpful to the railroads in his next political job, Yavapai County Tax Assessor, but did succeed in winning the hearts of the people. Whereas the Atlantic and Pacific had refused to pay its fair share of taxes, he assessed its land in the county at $1.25 per acre and sent the company a bill based upon the total valuation. The railroad protested and took its case all the way to the United States Supreme Court.

The "people's champion" refused to end his campaign against the railroads and, as a result, the party bosses refused him the Republican nomination for delegate to Congress. He bolted the party, however, and became the leader of the Populists, twice running for delegate — in 1894 and 1896 — and narrowly missing election the last time. Meanwhile, he also engaged in mining, making a fortune from an onyx deposit near Mayer and a copper mine in the Grand Canyon.

When war with Spain seemed imminent, Buckey's long-frustrated military aspirations came to the fore. Back in 1880 he had helped Major C. H. Vail organize a group of rangers in Phoenix to chase hostile Indians but was disappointed in that he saw no active service. In Prescott, he was captain of a militia company but apparently had no fondness for bloodshed since he fainted while helping to guard the scaffold where a murderer named Dilda was being hanged. Later he was the territorial adjutant general under Governor Wolfley.[20]

When Governor McCord received the April 3 call to arms, he put patriotism above prejudice and wired the War Department his nominations of O'Neill and McClintock as captains to command Troops "A" and "B" respectively. Alexander O. Brodie, a West Point graduate and formerly the head of the Arizona National Guard, was placed in charge of the entire battalion with the rank of major.[21] A third troop, lettered as "C," was organized after the recruits arrived in San Antonio to become part of the First United States Volunteer Cavalry, better known as the "Rough Riders." The new unit was captained by another

---

[20]*Report of the Adjutant General* [Brigadier General H. F. Robinson] *of the Territory of Arizona, 1898* (Phoenix: Dunbar and Ambler, 1899), p. 5.

[21]Telegram of Governor McCord to President McKinley, from Phoenix, Arizona, April 25, 1898, in the McKinley Papers, Vol. 116, p. 488, Library of Congress.

Major Alexander O. Brodie, commander of a battalion of Rough Riders and later governor of the Territory of Arizona.

McCord political enemy, J. L. B. Alexander, a prominent Phoenix attorney and Democrat.

The flag for the Arizona troops was made by the women of the Relief Corps of the Grand Army of the Republic, who worked all night to complete it. Lacking the proper cord, the ladies decorated the top with a cluster of tricolored ribbons.[22] This banner was the first to fly on Cuban soil and was carried by the conquering army into Santiago. Today it reposes in the governor's office in Phoenix — tattered, weather-beaten, and bullet-ridden.

Though led by a doctor and sponsored by a dude, few military outfits have gained as much fame as did the "Rough Riders." The regiment was nominally commanded by Colonel Leonard Wood, who had served in Arizona with the Regular Army during the Apache campaign and gained a great appreciation for the type of cowboys, ranchers, and miners that made up the "Rough Riders." The principal organizer of the unit was the glory-hungry Theodore Roosevelt, who resigned as Assistant Secretary of the Navy to serve as a lieutenant. Though totally lacking in military experience, Teddy used his political "pull" to secure his commission and to bypass physical requirements. He was actually so nearsighted that he took along a dozen pair of extra spectacles cached in handy spots.

---

[22]Jewell Nichols, "Arizona in the Spanish-American War," *Arizona Highways,* Vol. 15, No. 5 (1939), pp. 4-5.

After a short period of training near San Antonio, the First Cavalry moved to the embarkation point at Tampa, Florida. Amidst the confusion and congestion, the "Rough Riders" rushed onto a transport where they waited in the broiling sun almost a week. There were not enough troop ships and they didn't want to be robbed of a chance for action and glory. When the regiment left the harbor, the bands on other vessels sent them off to the tune of "There'll be a Hot Time in the Old Town Tonight." This was the Rough Riders' war song they had adopted while at San Antonio. The Spaniards were to hear the tune so often in Cuba they thought it was the Yankee national anthem.

Horses were left behind because of the lack of shipping facilities and the regiment became known as "Wood's Weary Walkers." The men carried the very accurate Krag-Jorgensen carbines, however, which were normally issued to mounted units, and were thus at least on an equal basis with the Mauser-armed Spanish. The Arizonans landed near Santiago on June 22, and fought through the thick of the Cuban campaign, including the famous charge led by Roosevelt up San Juan Hill in early July.

In that battle, Captain O'Neill was killed while carelessly standing, in full view of the enemy, behind the trenches where his men were concealed. Just before a sniper shot him, O'Neill supposedly told his sergeant, who had pleaded with him to lie down, "The Spanish bullet isn't molded that will hit me." Buckey's body was buried on the battlefield near San Juan Hill and later was moved to Arlington Cemetery. The twentieth legislature passed a resolution expressing sorrow over the untimely death of the courageous O'Neill and of other Arizona troopers who gave their lives in the Spanish-American War. A bronze equestrian O'Neill statue, which was erected in front of the Yavapai County Courthouse in Prescott in 1907, also commemorates the hero and his war buddies.

The Rough Riders were not the only troops raised in Arizona during the war. On July 9, 1898, Governor McCord resigned his office, effective August 1, to serve as colonel of a group known as the First Territorial Infantry, despite a petition signed by dozens of Arizona citizens and many letters requesting that he stay on as governor and decline the colonelcy.[23] Like Roosevelt, he had no military experience

---

[23]Letter of Governor McCord to President McKinley, from Phoenix, Arizona, July 9, 1898; and petition to Governor Myron McCord from ex-Governor L. C. Hughes, President M. M. Parker of the University of Arizona, *et al.*, enclosed with letter of Governor McCord to Secretary of the Interior C. N. Bliss, from Phoenix, Arizona, July 1, 1898, Record Group 48, Appointment Papers.

First Volunteer Cavalry officers at San Antonio. Major Brodie is third from the left in the front row and Theodore Roosevelt is third from the right.

The First Volunteer Cavalry, photographed at San Antonio.

but did have political "pull" with President McKinley.[24] Colonel McCord confined himself to administrative work, however, and a Regular Army officer, Lieutenant Colonel D. G. Mitchell, whipped the recruits into shape.

Arizona was allotted three companies (334 men and 12 officers), Oklahoma four, New Mexico four, and the Indian Territory one. The regiment trained at Fort Hamilton near Lexington, Kentucky, and was mustered out in February, 1899, at Camp Churchman, Georgia, without having seen any overseas service. The regiment lost more men from typhoid fever, however, than many units left on the battlefields of Cuba; and a verbal engagement was fought with citizens of Lexington who resented the presence of some of the soldiers.

Arizona also had soldiers in the Philippine campaign that followed the Spanish-American War. More than fifty men from Arizona served in the 34th U. S. Volunteer Infantry organized at Fort Collins, Colorado. Two former Rough Riders from Phoenix, J. E. Campbell and A. H. Stanton, led the Arizona company. R. C. Stanford, who was later elected governor of Arizona, was a sergeant in the Philippine campaign though he had been previously rejected for the "Rough Riders" because of his youth.

Stanford was one of the few veterans of the Spanish war who did well in politics. Another notable exception was Alexander O. Brodie who was appointed territorial governor in 1902. Isabella Greenway, the wife of Rough Rider Lieutenant John C. Greenway, served in Congress in the 1930s and her husband's statue is one of two allotted to Arizona in the national capitol's statuary hall.

Colonel McCord was never able to regain the governorship though he told the members of the First Territorial Infantry at a reunion in 1900 that he never regretted having resigned his office. Two other federal positions came his way. He was United States marshal, by appointment of President McKinley, from 1901 to 1905. At the time of his death in 1908 he had been a collector of customs at Nogales for two years.

---

[24]Letter of Governor McCord to President McKinley, from Phoenix, Arizona, May 7, 1898, printed in *The Arizona Bulletin,* May 13, 1898; see also, *New York Daily Tribune,* July 15, 1898.

Chapter 17

Murphy Encore:
The Second Murphy Administration

Nathan O. Murphy was in Washington, D.C., and called at the White House just after Governor McCord's letter of resignation was received. Actually it was not necessary that this document be accepted for it was accompanied by a request for a leave of absence. Many petitions and telegrams were sent by officeholders who worked under McCord asking that the resignation not be accepted. But President McKinley offered the governorship to Murphy on the spot, hoping thereby to avoid a barrage of Arizona job seekers like those who had besieged him before McCord was selected.

Murphy's appointment to a second term seemed to please most Arizonans. The Republicans were especially happy since they had almost given up hope of electing a county or legislative ticket in 1898 under McCord's leadership. The *Arizona Journal-Miner,* on July 20, 1898, stated that "the appointment of Governor Murphy can not fail to give universal satisfaction to residents of the territory. He served in this capacity under President Harrison. . . . During his entire term of office not a single fault was found with him, the democratic as well as the republican press of the territory commending him on his retiring from office for the able and impartial manner in which he had conducted the office."[1]

Murphy's second administration, however, was to reveal some glaring weaknesses in his character that brought upon him considerable wrath from the press. But in the beginning, he once again showed the intellectual qualities and leadership that made him, beyond a doubt, one of the ablest of the territorial governors.

The message that he delivered to the Twentieth Legislative Assem-

---

[1] *Arizona Journal-Miner,* July 20, 1898; see also, application letter of N. O. Murphy to President William McKinley, from Washington, D. C., June 13, 1898, Record Group 48, Appointment Papers.

Members and clerks of the Council, Twentieth Legislative Assembly, 1899. From left to right, first row — Chief Clerk E. J. Trippel, J. B. Finley (Pima), Aaron Goldberg (Maricopa), Morris Goldwater (President, Yavapai), *George A. Wolff (Navajo),* G. W. P. Hunt (Gila), *Charles C. Warner (Cochise);* second row—*J. M. Murphy (Mohave), D. K. Udall (Apache), J. H. Carpenter (Yuma), T. S. Bunch (Coconino), an unidentified clerk, Dr. A. C. Wright (Pinal), George O. Olney (Graham);* third and fourth rows—*clerks and other assistants.*

bly in January, 1899, was one of the most practical and comprehensive ever presented to an Arizona legislature. Avoiding generalities and platitudes, the Governor discussed the live issues affecting the territory. After complimenting the Spanish-American War veterans, he reviewed the financial condition of the territory and said that taxation and revenue constituted the greatest problem confronting the lawmakers. In no uncertain terms, he argued that the tax burden was not equitably distributed. He said that

> the small real estate owner, the farmer, the grazer, with a small band of cattle or sheep, cannot escape; they must pay, and frequently upon greater values than their property will sell for, but wealthy cattle or sheep owners, with large droves grazing upon untaxed public domain, do not always return to the assessor all of their property. The great corporations and the wealthy mine owners too often evade bearing their just proportion of the cost of maintaining the government which protects them. Simple justice, if nothing more, demands the equitable apportionment of taxes.

Murphy believed that the taxes on railroads should be increased as their profits grew and the market value of their securities rose. He further urged that mine operators be forced to pay for a fair amount of taxes, stating that it was wrong that Arizona's great riches in gold, copper, and silver should be dug from the ground to be distributed in huge dividends in the East and in Europe with scarcely any tax being paid in the territory. He suggested that either the profits of the mines be taxed or the property be assessed at a reasonable valuation. At the time he spoke, an estimated $100,000,000 in mines were listed on the tax rolls as worth only $2,000,000.[2]

The accomplishments of the legislature in the field of taxation did not measure up to the Governor's expectations. Numerous bills were introduced, for example, to regulate and tax the mines. Though many of these measures are now in effect in the state statutes, they were not enacted by the Twentieth Assembly. An attempt to reinstate the bullion tax on minerals taken from the mines failed. Another bill to create the office of mine inspector and to regulate hours of underground work was defeated also.

Murphy was more successful with two other recommendations. Opposing the use of the territorial building in Flagstaff for either a reform school or an asylum, he proposed that it be used for a normal school. The Assembly accepted his suggestion and speedily enacted a

---

2"Message of Governor N. O. Murphy," *Journals of the Twentieth Legislative Assembly*, 1899, pp. 440-63.

bill sponsored by the Speaker of the House, later U. S. senator, Henry F. Ashurst of Coconino County, to establish the Northern Arizona Normal School.[3] The first school term began on September 11, 1899, with twenty-three students. Professor A. N. Taylor of Jamestown, N. Y., was in charge with Miss Frances Bury assisting. Thus began the institution of higher learning known today as Northern Arizona University.

A second recommendation that appealed to the Assembly was Murphy's plea for a recodification of the statutes passed by previous legislatures. The lawmakers authorized the Governor to appoint a commission of three lawyers "to revise the laws and eliminate therefrom all crude, improper and contradictory matter and also to insert such new provisions as they may deem necessary and proper." In March, 1899, Governor Murphy appointed John C. Herndon of Prescott, Charles Wright of Tucson, and L. H. Chalmers of Phoenix to the commission. Judge R. E. Sloan was chosen in December, 1900, to fill a vacancy created by the death of Wright.[4] The commission's report was completed in time for submission to the next legislature in 1901 and was passed with minor modifications.

Altogether, sixty-nine new laws were passed by the Twentieth Assembly. One was a compulsory school-attendance law requiring parents or guardians to send their children between the ages of eight and fourteen years to a public school for at least twelve weeks each year; this measure was sponsored by Arizona's seven-term governor, the then-Councilman George W. P. Hunt of Gila County. Another law granted property-tax exemption for ten years to new railroads, and forbade freight-rate discrimination against local products. Water development companies were encouraged by tax exemption for an even longer period — fifteen years.

A bill creating the small county of Santa Cruz out of southern Pima County was introduced by Representative F. A. Stevens of the latter county and actively supported by a delegation from Nogales led by George Marsh, a prominent stockman and merchant.[5] The close vote on this latter bill is interesting today in that members of two families not known in later times for their political compatibility, namely Councilman D. K. Udall of Apache County and President of the Council Morris Goldwater, both voted "yea."

The legislature made several appropriations of a nostalgic nature.

[3]*Acts, Resolutions and Memorials,* Twentieth Legislative Assembly, 1899, pp. 30-35.

[4]*Revised Statutes of Arizona Territory,* 1901; see preface.

[5]*Acts, Resolutions and Memorials,* Twentieth Legislative Assembly, pp. 49-57.

Charles D. Poston

Money was set aside in one case to pay the burial expenses of a former territorial secretary and acting governor, John J. Gosper, who had died penniless in a Los Angeles Hospital. And a pension of $25 per month, increased to $35 two years later, was granted to the aged and destitute Charles D. Poston, the "Father of Arizona," then of Phoenix.

It seems appropriate to digress at this point to trace the career of this illustrious pioneer. After losing his seat as delegate to Congress to Governor Goodwin in 1864 and going down to defeat a second time in 1866, Poston became both a nationally and internationally recognized figure.[6] He attended the Paris Exposition in 1867 and then began practicing law in Washington, D.C., where he was known as a resourceful lobbyist as well as a professional journalist.

In 1868 he was appointed by Secretary of State Seward to deliver the Burlingame Treaty to the Emperor of China. He also had three other missions in the Orient: (1) to study farming methods in countries where irrigation had been practiced since ancient times; (2) to study population conditions with a view of making recommendations relative to immigration quotas; (3) and to discuss with Chinese officials the possibility of permitting American capital to exploit mineral resources in China. In no hurry, Poston was away from the United States for eight years. During the last five or six years of this foreign sojourn he worked as a correspondent for the *New York Tribune,* under the direction of his friend,

---

[6]U. S. House, *Biographical Directory of the American Congress, 1774–1961,* p. 1473.

Whitelaw Reid, who had become editor after Horace Greeley's death. The celebrated Philadelphia Exposition brought Poston back to his native country in 1876. The next year he returned to Arizona as the Federal Land Office registrar at Florence. He was paid only $500 a year, but had little business to attend to in the mud-dappled little pueblo of five hundred souls. For relief from the tedium he devoted his time to writing an allegorical book in verse called *Apache-Land,* which was published in 1878. The book contained some history though it was essentially an imaginative treatment of the author's experiences.

Besides his writing, Poston was preoccupied with raising money to construct a temple devoted to sun worship atop Primrose Hill, northwest of Florence. While traveling in India he had become a convert to Zoroastrianism and now wished to establish the sun- and light-worshipping cult of the Parsees, as they were called, in sunny Arizona. Poston sought help from the Shah of Persia in whose country the religion had originated back in ancient times. He received a polite return letter, through diplomatic channels, offering felicitations and best wishes from the Shah, but no money. And that about sums up the story of what his skeptical neighbors called "Poston's Folly." The fantastic project fell through, not for lack of sunshine, but for lack of funds. At his own expense he hired some Indian and Mexican workers with picks and shovels to carve a road out of the hillside. And a thirty-foot shaft was dug where he expected to be buried. To show his purpose, Poston unfurled a white flag with a blazing sun in the center on top of the butte. But no temple was ever erected.

His failure to make himself a high priest in the Order of the Sun as well as his inability to please Secretary of the Interior Carl Schurz in land-office business were reasons for another departure from the territory. This time he boarded the stage in Florence for San Francisco. Because of his thorough knowledge of the people and country of the Southwest, however, he was given a couple of federal border positions. He served successively as a United States consular agent at Nogales, Mexico, and as the government's military agent at El Paso, Texas. During the early 1880s Poston often sought the bright lights of Tucson and was among the celebrants when the Southern Pacific railroad arrived in 1880.

Two years later he was the chief participant in an event known as "Poston's bullet." The incident evolved from his having questioned the merit of a proclamation issued by President Arthur. This document threatened governmental intervention in Arizona if flagrant obstruction of law and order continued. Incensed by editorial criticism of his viewpoint in the *Arizona Daily Citizen* (Tucson), Poston stopped the editor,

J. A. Whitemore, in the barroom of Porter's Hotel. Drawing a six-shooter from the right pocket of his pantaloons, he fired a shot without any warning at Whitemore. Fortunately, the bullet missed its mark and imbedded itself in the wall: otherwise the "Father of Arizona" undoubtedly would have been charged with cold-blooded murder.

In the late 1880s Poston was connected with the Department of the Interior in Washington, D.C., but returned to Arizona, this time to Phoenix, in 1890, as a federal agricultural agent with a salary of only $50 per month. Following this job, he was appointed in 1895 by the Board of Regents of the University of Arizona to take charge of an experimental station on Grand Avenue in Phoenix. This position, which lasted about five months, was his last appointment to any office. Never one to be tied to the monotony of routine, Poston had returned to journalism and in 1894, when he was sixty-nine, contributed four historical articles to the *Overland Monthly* magazine on the founding of Arizona. (The articles were reprinted in book form in 1963 under the title, *Building A State in Apache Land.*)

He continued to write for other publications but his journalistic earnings grew pitifully small. He lost all his tangible property and, for lack of money, was unable to complete the requirements necessary to secure title to the homestead land that he claimed near the Papago Park "Hole-in-the-Rock." Forced to move from the Lemon Hotel, he spent his final years alone in a wretched adobe hut that fronted on an alley in the block in downtown Phoenix which is bounded by Adams, Monroe, First, and Second streets. Though twice married, Poston lived alone. He left his first wife in Kentucky where she lived for thirty-three years following a paralytic stroke. A daughter by this union was Poston's only source of subsistence for awhile. The second marriage, in 1885, to the youthful Miss Mattie Tucker of Phoenix, soon ended unhappily because of the great disparity in ages.

Whitelaw Reid, who wintered in Phoenix seeking relief from asthma and who later became U. S. Ambassador to Great Britain, visited Arizona's "first citizen" at the squalid hacienda. He found the quarters quite a contrast to the large stately home in which he himself lived at Sixth Street and Monroe, a block south of where Phoenix Union High School was later built. Moved by what he saw, Reid wrote down his observations, which were printed in the territorial newspapers and in the *San Francisco Call* (January 28, 1897). "When I pushed open the gate yesterday," he wrote, "a spry Mexican lad was searching for two rattlesnakes, that had escaped during the night. Colonel Poston explained apologetically that the Mexican had been forming the nucleus of an indigenous zoological collection." Reid went on to write that "at the far end of the yard is a long, low adobe house, all but one small room of which is tenanted by weaving spiders in wintertime and by tarantulas on the hot days. That single tiny room is at once the kitchen and boudoir of Arizona's first congressman — a learned, cultured gentleman, lawyer, traveler, author, explorer, soldier. His reception room is larger. It takes in the whole yard."[7] The concern of such a well-known newspaperman undoubtedly helped Poston to secure a pension.

The last entry that Poston penned in his diary read, "Legislature of Arizona at 20th session passed an act granting me a pension for life on account of public services. Approved 15th of March, 1899." He died in 1902 and was buried in Porter's Cemetery after contributions were solicited to save him from a pauper's grave. The Twenty-fourth Legislative Assembly in 1907 voted $100 to buy a suitably inscribed granite marker. Then, on April 26, 1925, his body was transferred to Poston's Butte, formerly Primrose Hill. Some 1,500 people, including Governor George W. P. Hunt, attended the last rites. A thirteen-and-a-half-foot-high pyramid, considerably smaller than the ones which Poston had seen and admired in Egypt, was erected by the state of Arizona in conjunction with the Maricopa Chapter of the D. A. R.

Returning to the actions of the Twentieth Assembly, we see that the legislature was not always as parsimonious as it was in the Poston pension bill. One appropriation measure, for example, set up a contingency fund that later became the object of much criticism because of the way it was misused by Governor Murphy and Auditor George W. Vickers. The law provided that as much as $6,250 could be expended by the governor "for the apprehension of criminals, or escaped patients from the Territorial Insane Asylum, and for other expenses incidental thereto, for the printing of election and other proclamations, and all necessary expenses." But Murphy ignored the purposes for which the fund was specifically intended and drew upon it without vouchers. An editorial in the *Citizen* accused him of disgracing his office, as the following passage indicates:

> It is clear that whenever the governor fell short in funds — or as the boys would say, got busted — that he called upon the faithful Dr. Vickers to give up a piece of the contingent fund. The people of the territory have cause to regret that the governor "went broke" so often in 1899. Luck must have been against him. Some nights he must have fingered the "blues" for next day he whacked the contingent fund for $300. Other nights he must have toyed with modest "reds" for his demands on the faithful auditor next day were for only $100 or $75.

---

[7]*San Francisco Call*, January 28, 1897.

Still again he must have monkeyed with the plebeian "whites" for it is of record that one some days he only touched the contingent fund for $25 or $35.[8]

The detected withdrawals were the inconsequential, "hen-roost-larceny" variety rather than bold, ambitious robbery. However, the President of the Council during this session, Eugene S. Ives of Yuma, accused Murphy of malfeasance in office and forwarded a report in 1902 to Delegate Marcus Smith for presentation to President Theodore Roosevelt. Ives charged that the Governor had illegally withdrawn $1,577.55 from the treasury for his personal use; that he had drawn out $1,129.50 to give his private secretary in addition to the latter's regular salary; and that, without authority of law, he caused thousands of dollars to be paid to the *Arizona Republican*. The newspaper was operated by Vickers and was either actually or virtually owned by the Governor or his brother, Frank M. Murphy. Naturally, the *Citizen* (January 26, 1902) and other newspapers eagerly printed accounts of Ives's accusations.[9]

The Attorney General could not be persuaded to bring charges against Murphy and the others. However, a law passed in 1901 permitted a citizen to bring action against public officials if the attorney general refused to do so. Accordingly, Thomas F. Wilson, a Tucson lawyer, filed a complaint against Murphy and Vickers for recovery of territorial funds. In a 1902 decision, Judge Edward Kent, a recent appointee from Maine to the position of chief justice of the Supreme Court of Arizona, dismissed the action against Murphy on the grounds that the liability for an illegal warrant on the treasury rested with the person drawing the warrant (Vickers) and not the person in whose favor the warrant was drawn (Murphy). Nevertheless, Murphy was guilty of arrant dishonesty; he had wantonly plundered the taxpayers' money. Unfortunately, the corruption disgraced his office at a time when Arizona was knocking at the door of the Union and also partly offset his own good work in behalf of statehood.

Some excuse for Murphy's laxity with territorial funds might be justified by the low salary and expense account appropriated for the governor's office by the Congress. Governor Murphy explained the problem in a letter to the Secretary of the Interior. "Section 1845 of the Revised Statutes of the United States fixes the annual salary of the Governor of a Territory at $3,500," he wrote,

> but Congress in a spirit of alleged economy appropriates year after year $2,600 and bars proceedings in the Court of Claims by specific terms

---

[8]*Arizona Daily Citizen*, n. d., clipping in the McClintock File, Phoenix Public Library.

[9]*Arizona Daily Citizen*, January 26, 1902.

of the appropriations act. This is a clear injustice, and it seems to me indirectly at least, a violation of law. $3,500 per annum is not enough when the labor and responsibility imposed are considered, but $216 per month as now allowed, is so manifestly inadequate that the injustice of Congress in this matter must appeal to any one at all familiar with the conditions. $2,600 per year hardly pays the necessary incidental expenses of the office, and no Territorial Governor can conduct the office properly without more or less pecuniary loss to himself. We are not allowed remuneration from the Territorial treasury, as the U. S. statutes expressly provide (Sec. 1855 Revised Statutes U. S.) that Territorial Governors "shall receive no compensation other than that allowed by the United States." No provision is made for a house to live in, and the $500 appropriated by Congress for contingent expenses is entirely insufficient. There is no provision made for the salary of a private secretary, except $50 per month by the Territory, and the balance of his salary has to be paid from insufficient contingent expense funds, and contributed by the Governor. The business of the Territory has grown into such proportions that there seems to be no reasonable excuse for not allowing Territorial Governors at least the salaries designated by statute.[10]

Murphy said that the subject had been brought to the attention of the appropriations committees several times, but that nothing had been done to correct the situation. The Governor's letter evidently had some influence on Congress because his salary was increased to $3,000 for the fiscal year 1900–1901.[11] However, his $500 allowance for contingent expenses remained the same for two more years; the amount was finally doubled, however, by the Fifty-seventh Congress in 1902.[12]

The twentieth legislature devoted much of its time to plans for the capitol building. The bond issue of $100,000 that was provided by the previous legislature was insufficient, so an additional $30,000 was appropriated. The contract was awarded to Mr. Tom Lovell of Denton, Texas, one of sixteen bidders, on February 13, 1899.[13] It stipulated that the Capitol Commission (E. B. Gage, president; Frank W. Parker, secretary; and Frank Talbot) would select the material to be used in the exterior walls. After visiting the stone quarries at Tucson and Rock Butte, and viewing the deposits of tufa near Kirkland, the commissioners decided to use granite for the sub-story walls and tufa for the superstructure. As the law required, the commission employed a competent builder to act as superintendent of construction. The man

---

[10]Letter of Governor N. O. Murphy to Secretary of the Interior E. A. Hitchcock, from Phoenix, Arizona, January 17, 1900, Record Group 48, Territorial Papers.

[11]*U. S. Statutes at Large,* Vol. XXXI, 56th Cong., 1st Sess., 1900, Chap. 192, p. 112.

[12]*U. S. Statutes at Large,* Vol. XXXII, 57th Cong., 1st Sess., 1902, Chap. 594, pp. 147-48.

[13]*Capitol Grounds and Building Commission Report,* 1899.

The Arizona Capitol as it looked in 1903.

employed, Jo Fifield, performed his services creditably. In other actions, the commission awarded Lovell an additional contract of $9,450.00 for plumbing, heating, wiring, and gas piping. A contract of $5,750 for elevator, electric motor, and enclosures was given to the Otis Elevator Comany. Combination gas and electric light fixtures were furnished by the Scoville Plumbing Company of Phoenix for $2,097. On August 4, 1900, Mr. Lovell turned the completed building over to the commission. Claims against the building continued to mount, however, reaching a total of $135,744.29. The deficit of $5,744.29 was dumped into the lap of the next legislature.[14]

A few weeks after the completion of the capitol, Arizona became involved in the political conventions and elections of 1900.[15] The Republicans nominated Governor Murphy as their candidate for delegate to Congress; he accepted with the understanding that he would retain the governor's job through the next legislative session (January to March, 1901) if elected to Congress.[16] The Democrats meanwhile engaged in what became one of the most ludicrous political fiascos ever enacted in Arizona.[17] From start to finish the convention, held in Phoenix in September, 1900, was a virtual riot.[18] It was marked by great bitterness between the factions supporting the incumbent Delegate, Colonel J. F. Wilson, and former occupant of the office, Marcus A. Smith. Two sets of officers were elected. The Wilson supporters chose Reese M. Ling of Yavapai County as chairman, and the Smith group elected C. M. Shannon of Graham County to the same position.[19] Two secretaries were also elected to help fill up the opera-house stage that was already crowded with people, including the sheriff and chief of police. According to one newspaper account, there were five or six persons on the floor at one time and the wildest excitement prevailed. Epithets were freely exchanged between the opposing factions, resulting in the drawing of pistols and knives. An array of police officers was called in to prevent carnage. From this melee resulted the nomination of both candidates.

Wilson was willing to withdraw but was persuaded by his wife to

---

[14]Capitol Commission, *Biennial Report,* 1900, pp. 1-9.

[15]*Arizona Daily Citizen,* September 24, 1900.

[16]Letter of Governor Murphy to Secretary of the Interior E. A. Hitchcock, from Phoenix, Arizona, September 26, 1900, Record Group 48, Appointment Papers.

[17]*Arizona Daily Journal-Miner,* September 12, 1900; and *Arizona Daily Citizen,* September 12, 1900.

[18]*Arizona Daily Journal-Miner,* September 13, 1900.

[19]*Ibid.*

Sample ballot from Yavapai County.

Circular advertising a Republican rally at Mayer in Yavapai County.

— Sharlot Hall Museum

— Sharlot Hall Museum

The election of 1900. This election was especially important because it pitted the territory's two outstanding politicians, Marcus A. Smith, and Nathan Oakes Murphy, against each other for the first and only time.

— Arizona Department of Library and Archives

— Arizona Pioneers' Historical Society

The Arizona Daily Citizen, *October 13, 1900, endorsed Murphy and the rest
of the Republican slate from top to bottom.* The Coconino Sun, *November 3,
also encouraged its readers to vote a straight Republican ticket. But the* Sun's
local rival, The Flagstaff Gem, *had the last laugh when its candidate, Mark
Smith, defeated Murphy, although the latter carried Coconino County.*

361

stay in the running rather than be a quitter. About a month later, however, he gave up. In reporting how "Mark Smith succeeded in taking the scalp of Colonel Wilson" in the delegate nomination controversy, the *Arizona Journal-Miner* said that a "deal" was made in the company of friends of the contestants. After the signing of the protocol and the attaching of the seal of approval, Colonel Wilson, with a delicate and half-hearted grasp, surrendered Democracy's whip to Mr. Smith and withdrew as a candidate for Congressional office.[20]

During the campaign that followed, Murphy toured the territory and attempted to answer some of the charges that had been leveled at him. At Jerome, for example, he tried to explain that he was not anti-labor just because he had vetoed a bill of the twentieth legislature that would have forbidden employers to issue blacklists of discharged workers. One newspaper, which printed an article on Murphy's visit to Jerome, said that the town had never witnessed such a demonstration. The magnificent opera house, with a capacity of nearly a thousand people, was overflowing to hear the Governor defend himself. If the frequent applause of the attentive crowd was an indication of approval for his remarks, Murphy apparently succeeded in disproving the charges that had been circulated about his being an enemy of the workingman.[21] But, as Murphy was soon to learn, a positive response to an admirable campaign speech was not tantamount to victory at the polls. There were more registered Democrats than Republicans in the territory and Smith won the election. Murphy carried only the northern counties. Maricopa, Pima, and the other southern counties gave Smith his majority.[22]

Murphy continued as governor and, in January, 1901, addressed the Twenty-first Assembly in the new capitol.[23] Though optimistic about the 100 percent increase in the territory's population to 122,212 during the 1890s and the prosperity of the mining industry, Murphy again asked for new laws and methods for assessing property. He said that the system of low valuations and high tax rates was wrong and misleading. And he was again very frank in saying that there was no justification in a system wherein mines worth $100,000,000 were assessed at only $2,000,000; mine owners who were reaping great profits in exploiting Arizona's underground wealth should be expected to contribute their fair share to the revenues of the state. Otherwise, however,

---

[20]*Ibid.,* October 12, 1900.

[21]*Ibid.,* October 25, 1900.

[22]*Ibid.,* November 9, 1900.

[23]"Message of Governor N. O. Murphy," *Journals of the Twenty-First Legislative Assembly,* 1901, pp. 296-320.

he governor has traveled throughout the territory in his
al car, handing great bunches of hot air to the people. The
s do not believe he is sincere with that cry of Murphy and
hood. Murphy in congress means more bonds, more taxa-
The people of Arizona will not vote to endorse the single
standard or the blacklisting of mines. Smith, Statehood
ilver will redeem Arizona.

This Democratic cartoon lampooning Governor Murphy's candidacy for delegate to Congress in 1900 appeared in The Daily Enterprise *on October 31, 1900.*

the Governor urged legislation favorable to the development of industries and the construction of railroads.

To conserve water for irrigation and thus enable farmers to bring more land under cultivation, he encouraged the Assembly to provide aid for the construction of storage reservoirs. In his report to the Secretary of the Interior, in 1901, the Governor made a similar proposal to upgrade the economic status of Arizona Indians. He recommended that water-storage projects be constructed, by the government, with canals leading to lands allotted to the Indians in suitable localities. By this plan, Murphy thought that most of the Indian reservation lands, with the possible exception of the Navajo, could be sold and settled by whites. The Indians would become self-supporting farmers and no longer would cluster around federal agencies, living in idleness on government rations as in the past.[24] In general, however, Murphy did not believe in federal reclamation.

He was severely criticized by many Arizonans when he went to Washington, D.C., in 1902, to lobby against President Roosevelt's recommendation for irrigation projects sponsored by the national government. The *Citizen* argued that Murphy "should have retired from the Governorship of Arizona before undertaking to promote the interests of the water stealers and land grabbers. He should have divested

[24]*New York Daily Tribune,* November 11, 1901; and U. S. Dept. of the Interior, *Report of Governor N. O. Murphy to the Secretary of Interior,* 1901.

himself of his official character before entering the lobby to advocate private monopoly at the expense of public interests."[25] Whatever his objectives, however, the Governor was not successful in obstructing federal legislation that soon enabled vast acreages in Arizona to be irrigated with water impounded behind Roosevelt and other dams. The Newlands Act was pushed through Congress in 1902 by the conservation-conscious President. This law provided that money derived from the sale of public lands in Arizona, and other sunbaked Western states, was to be used to build irrigation projects that would reclaim nonproductive, arid wasteland. Then money collected from the sale of water to farmers was to go into a revolving fund to finance more such enterprises.[26]

Another conservation program was initiated by the Department of the Interior to preserve forest lands — and hence the water supply — at the headwaters of the Verde and Salt rivers. While the Twenty-first Assembly was still in session, the Secretary signed an agreement with the individual owners of nearly one million acres of timber land, contiguous to similar lands already owned by the government, in the San Francisco Mountains region of northern Arizona. This agreement made possible the creation of the San Francisco Mountain Reserve of nearly two million acres of magnificent forests. The Interior Department's action was the outcome of a determined effort of residents in the Salt River Valley and south-central Arizona to oust sheep and cattle men from lands that supplied the irrigation waters for central Arizona. Previously, the federal government had owned only the alternate sections, and could not prevent the owners of stock and of timber from crossing these to gain access to their own lands. With the presence of thousands of sheep and cattle in the region, the underbrush was destroyed and the earth packed so hard that rainwater ran off in floods instead of soaking gradually into the soil. The struggle between the stockmen and lumbermen on the one hand, and the Salt River Valley people on the other, lasted four or five years.

Finally, the Santa Fe Railroad and others interested in the preservation of the forests negotiated and agreed to accept government lands elsewhere, contingent upon the withdrawal of the lands in question to form the forest reserve.[27] Watershed conservation was a necessary step in the development of irrigation, whether by the federal government or by local effort as Governor Murphy preferred.

[25]*Tucson Daily Citizen,* January 23, 1902.
[26]*U. S. Statutes at Large,* Vol. XXXII, 57th Cong., 1st Sess., 1902, Chap. 1093, pp. 388-90.
[27]"Forest Reserve in Arizona," *New York Daily Tribune,* January 28, 1901.

Just as the Governor failed to stop federally sponsored reclamation, so also he did not succeed in his plea to the legislature for the construction of a new and modern prison, at any location agreeable to the lawmakers, to replace the one at Yuma. That institution was deplorably inadequate to provide proper care for prisoners, but the legislature preferred to remodel it rather than erect proper buildings on a more desirable site. A bill providing a tax levy of 3.5 cents per $100 valuation for this purpose was passed over the Governor's veto.[28] This was not an unusual action for the Twenty-first Assembly, since it overrode the veto more than any other territorial legislature.

But the Twenty-first was not as obstinate on all matters recommended by the Governor. His request for a law permitting local option on the liquor traffic was granted, and the statute requiring the payment of the poll tax as a qualification for voting was repealed as suggested. Tax exemptions were given to sugarbeet factories for twelve years and to railroads for ten years, providing that ten miles of road were built annually. Other laws that met with Murphy's approval put the militia on a sound footing and organized a territorial police force. The National Guard was officially reestablished after operating for two years without financial support. The Adjutant-General, H. F. Robinson, was remunerated for personal expenses incurred during that time. The new militia code also provided him with a regular salary and authorized the payment of rent on company armories. Another law permitting the governor to form a company of mounted rangers, comprising a captain, sergeant, and twelve privates. The organization and work of this colorful force is discussed in the next chapter.

The formal housewarming of the new capitol on February 24, 1901, was a gala occasion. Special trains puffed into Phoenix with delegations of exuberant citizens. The dedication was performed in high style since $1,000 had been appropriated for that purpose. The capitol was baptized with flowers and a flood of oratory. Governor Murphy, Council President Eugene Ives, and Chief Justice Webster Street all spoke to the crowd from a lavishly decorated grandstand in the front of the building. Inside, the legislative chambers were garlanded in the green of northern pine and the semitropical shrubbery of the valley. One newspaper reporter described the festive atmosphere thusly: "Today all hands and the cook are engaged in dedicating the new capitol and this evening the structure will be 'dampened' in the most approved style. There will be a punch bowl in the Governor's office, another in

---

[28]*Revised Statutes of the Arizona Territory,* 1901.

the office of the Secretary, a third under Charlie Shannon's especial protection in the Council Chamber and still another with official backing in the Assembly Hall."

Perhaps the participants were making up for the omission of a cornerstone ceremony earlier. The capitol, still used by the state, is perhaps the only one in the fifty states without a cornerstone. A bronze tablet in a first-floor corridor gives essentially the same information that one would ordinarily find inscribed on such a stone.

A very important person visited the capitol a few months after its completion — President McKinley. Following a schedule laid out by Governor Murphy and the presidential secretary, George B. Cortelyou, he entered Arizona on a Southern Pacific train from the east during the night of May 7, 1901. His first stop, the following morning, was at the Congress Mine northwest of Phoenix. There the President's party was shown how gold was mined and milled into bullion and the First Lady was presented with a small gold bar as a souvenir. Later the same day, McKinley was whisked through a short appearance in Phoenix that included a visit to the capitol, a luncheon, a parade, and a trip out to the Phoenix Indian School. Ending his brief sojourn in the capital city at five o'clock, the President departed for California via Yuma, again traveling by night. Besides his wife, his entourage included representatives of the Associated Press, New York Sun Press Association, *Harper's Weekly, Leslie's Weekly, Collier's Weekly, Washington Evening Star, Washington Times,* Western Union, and Postal Telegraph Company. With this extensive coverage, the eyes of the states were focused, though for only a brief moment, upon Arizona.[29]

Other Easterners stayed longer, especially consumptives who were establishing colonies of canvas tents in every direction from Phoenix. The little settlement of Scottsdale, for example, consisted of some thirty-odd tents and a half dozen adobe houses in 1901. Situated on the direct road from Phoenix to Fort McDowell, protected by the stalwart proportions of Camelback Mountain, bordering on Paradise Valley, and possessed of an abundance of some of the best drinking water in Arizona, the site was recognized as one of the most admirable in the valley for the health seeker. With the artistic bungalow of Howard Underhill, of New York, and the tropically fruited ranch of U. S. Army Chaplain Winfield Scott (*not* the general of the same name) as centers, the temporary homes spread out over the desert for a good half mile.[30]

---

[29]Letters of George B. Cortelyou to Governor Murphy, from Washington, D. C., April 13, 1901; April 19, 1901; April 20, 1901; and April 24, 1901, McKinley Papers, Vol. 180.

[30]*New York Daily Tribune,* April 29, 1901.

Patients from all over the United States, including Justice Goebel, the brother of the assassinated governor of Kentucky, were being injected with experimental germicides, such as formaldehyde, in desperate hope of recovering from tuberculosis. A large percent of the people being treated by Phoenix physicians at the turn of the century were health-seekers of this type who lived in tents pitched on the surrounding desert.[31] It is not difficult to understand why so many people came to Arizona when one looks at the reports and other information Governor Murphy and Secretary Isaac Stoddard made available to Easterners.[32]

Governor Murphy occupied the chief executive's rooms in the new capitol a little over a year. In April, 1902, he submitted his resignation, purportedly to devote more time to his mining interests.[33] His tenure in office had been on shaky ground for several months, however. President Roosevelt had received innumerable letters from prominent people complaining of the Governor's conduct at a banquet; and more than once he expressed regret to friends that he had continued Murphy in office. With no small degree of satisfaction, Roosevelt appointed Alexander O. Brodie, his comrade of Rough Rider days, to take over the gubernatorial duties on July 1.

Brodie was undoubtedly a popular appointee. In all fairness to his predecessor, however, it should be mentioned that several leading residents and newspapers of Arizona had expressed hope that Murphy would be permitted to remain in office awhile. One of the political leaders of northern Arizona who favored his retention in office was Morris Goldwater, a Democrat. Writing to President Roosevelt on December 5, 1901, in behalf of the Board of Directors of the Prescott National Bank, Goldwater suggested that Murphy should be kept in office, at least until the expiration of his term. "His administration had been as good as any preceding one if not better," he said, "and he has in all things worked for the best interests of the Territory."[34]

In another part of Arizona, the *Tucson Citizen* was even more profuse in praising "Mr. Republican" at the time of his resignation in May. Contrasting him with others who had occupied the top office

---

[31]*Ibid.,* May 25, 1902.

[32]Interview with Secretary Isaac Stoddard, *New York Daily Tribune,* November 27, 1901; and U. S. Dept. of the Interior, *Report of the Governor of the Territory of Arizona to the Secretary of the Interior,* 1898 through 1901.

[33]Letter of Governor Murphy to Secretary of the Interior Hitchcock, from Phoenix, Arizona, April 21, 1902, Record Group 48, Appointment Papers; see also, *San Francisco Chronicle,* April 23, 1902.

[34]Letter of Morris Goldwater, Vice President of the Prescott National Bank, to President Theodore Roosevelt, from Prescott, Arizona, December 5, 1901, Record Group 48, Appointment Papers.

in the territory, the paper said that Arizona, on the whole, had been unfortunate in her chief executives and that not one who had held the office could be elected by the people. Claiming that most of the governors had been small-time politicians who sought the office for what there was in it, the *Citizen* said that N. O. Murphy, "with all his glaring defects and notorious shortcomings" had been intellectually the "ablest of Arizona's governors" and had a "knowledge of the territory that none of his predecessors possessed."[35] This was a magnanimous tribute from a newspaper that had often criticized Murphy in vitriolic language and which continued to taunt him.

Throughout the fall of 1902, the Tucson paper, confident of a Democratic victory in the coming election, challenged the Republicans to again nominate Murphy for delegate to Congress, a position to which he had been elected in 1894. "Who is so capable of defending the rape of the contingent fund during the last administration?" the *Citizen* asked.[36] And when Murphy came to Tucson from Prescott, in December, 1902, to campaign for the municipal ticket of his party, the paper blasted him with another charge. Stating that the ex-Governor, even though he was an able and far-seeing man, always kept "one eye, sometimes two, on the main chance," the *Citizen* charged him with having worked against the interests of Pima County when he was delegate to Congress. Referring to the Arizona Narrow-Gauge bonds, the paper said, "They are a steal pure and simple, and Oakes Murphy is responsible for saddling them on the county. Arrangements are now being made for the payment of interest on these fraudulent bonds." Continuing with its excoriation of Murphy, the *Citizen* alleged that "he wants to have his friends in office to assist in the collection of plunder. That is why ex-Governor Murphy is exerting himself for the election of the Republican ticket in Tucson."[37]

As we shall see, however, Murphy's main concern in working for the validation of the Pima County bonds mentioned by the *Citizen* was to establish the soundness of all bond issues in Arizona and, thereby, to encourage the investment of outside capital in the territory. But, assuredly, he was not personally disinterested; he and his brother Frank were trying to sell railroad securities and did succeed in building a line into Phoenix from the north in 1895. To say, however, that Murphy profited directly from the validation of the Pima County bonds was rather farfetched — even during the heat of a political campaign!

---

[35]*Tucson Daily Citizen,* May 7, 1902.
[36]*Ibid.,* September 10, 1902.
[37]*Ibid.,* December 6, 1902.

Perhaps the newspaper comments on the railroad bonds need some explanation. Back in the early 1880s many Tucson residents were anxious for another railroad to help guarantee the prosperity of the town as a trade center. The time was ripe for the people to be fleeced by a promotion scheme; and ready to "take" them was a big city slicker named W. A. Culver, a traveling salesman who could "charm the needles off a cactus." Culver told the interested citizens he was president of a new company called the Arizona Narrow Gauge Railroad Company that wanted to build a line from Tucson to Globe. In short order, on February 7, 1883, a petition signed by sixty-six enthusiastic individuals and firms of Tucson was presented to the Twelfth Legislative Assembly asking for a law to permit construction of the proposed road. Nine days later the legislature dutifully complied and passed an act directing the Pima County Board of Supervisors to exchange as much as $200,000 in 7 percent county bonds for first-mortgage bonds of the Arizona Narrow Gauge Railroad.[38] The law provided that Pima County would turn over county bonds worth $50,000 to Culver before a single spike was driven or a shovelful of earth was turned. Then, after each five miles of track were laid, another $50,000 worth of county bonds would be turned over to the company. In other words, the credit of Pima County was to be used to furnish the working capital for building the railroad.

Expressing the exuberance of the people, the *Arizona Daily Star,* on April 25, 1883, predicted that the opening of the narrow-gauge railroad to the north of Tucson would produce "the largest return on the investment of any enterprise ever inaugurated in Arizona." Explaining that the line was to be constructed through the richest mineral section of the territory, the *Star* said that it "will tap the coal fields which alone will create a large and profitable trade. The lumber fields beyond Globe will supply the market for Arizona for half a century.[39]

Unfortunately, this type of optimism for additional transportation into Tucson led to a catastrophic venture. During two periods of construction, in 1883 and 1886, grading never reached further north than the Pinal County line and rails were laid for a distance of only ten miles. Yet the company was able to secure a total of $150,000 in bonds from the Pima Board of Supervisors. Certainly, the bonds had been transferred without value received. Popular indignation over rumored corrupt practices brought a change of attitude to the board.

---

[38]*Acts, Resolutions and Memorials,* Twelfth Legislative Assembly, 1883, pp. 61-65.

[39]*Arizona Daily Star,* April 25, 1883.

In 1884, W. L. Vail was elected as a reform candidate and a motion was passed to suspend payment of interest on the bonds. Two years later, however, the company gave assurances that construction would be renewed. With the public again enthusiastic, and even hopeful that branch lines would soon be built to Florence and Phoenix, the board continued interest disbursements on the bonds. Building went on at a fast pace and, with the help of more northerly counties, the road might have been completed. But an amendment to a federal law passed in July, 1886, precluded that possibility.[40] This measure, introduced by Senator Benjamin Harrison, forbade any subdivision of a territory to use its credit or to borrow money for the benefit of any company. The Harrison amendment not only locked Pima County's door after the horse was stolen, but it also prevented Pinal County from shouldering its fair share of the railroad debt. Because of the amendment, the narrow-gauge road, designated as the Tucson, Globe, and Northern Railroad, was dead as a means of transportation. The ten miles of worthless track disintegrated rapidly. The rails were sold for taxes and used on a streetcar line in Hollywood, California. And, with the disappearance of the lone locomotive, eleven flat cars, and a water tank, went the last vestige of hope for completion of the railroad. However, litigation in the courts haunted Pima County taxpayers for years and holders of the bonds occasionally made demands on the county for at least the interest.

In 1894, the United States Supreme Court, in the case of *Lewis* vs. *Pima County,* upheld an 1892 decision of Judge Richard E. Sloan, presiding over the First Judicial District of Arizona, which declared the Pima County bonds void.[41] The basis for the decision was a Congressional act of 1867 prohibiting territories from granting private charters or special privileges. The implication in the Lewis case was that other similar obligations, such as the Yavapai railroad bonds, might be affected too. It was at this point that the Murphy brothers, N. O. and Frank, entered the picture. As president of the Santa Fe, Prescott, and Phoenix Railroad Company, Frank was indirectly interested in the Yavapai bonds that had been issued for a rival company, the Prescott and Arizona Central Railroad. He was planning an extension of his road through Phoenix to Nogales and feared that repudiation of the Yavapai railroad bonds would destroy public confidence and make it difficult for him to secure private aid. So in 1895, he asked for the privilege of speaking to the legislature and delivered an impas-

---

[40]*U. S. Statutes at Large,* Vol. XXIV, 49th Cong., 1st Sess., 1886, pp. 170-71.
[41]*Supreme Court Reporter,* Vol. XV, October 29, 1894.

sioned plea for sound finance and territorial integrity in meeting outstanding indebtedness.[42] The lawmakers of the Eighteenth Legislative
Assembly responded by memorializing Congress to pass remedial legislation. With Delegate N. O. Murphy zealously championing the cause,
Congress passed an act in 1896 that validated Pima County Narrow Gauge bonds, and other similar issues, by stating that "all bonds
and other evidences of indebtedness hitherto issued under the authority
of the legislature of said Territory, as hereinbefore authorized to be
funded, are hereby confirmed, approved and validated."[43]

Belatedly, in 1899, the territorial legislature asked for the repeal
of this 1896 act of Congress, explaining that the memorial of the
Eighteenth Assembly requesting the law was never intended to apply
to the Pima bonds that were considered fraudulent. But in two more
U. S. Supreme Court cases, *Utter* vs. *Franklin* in 1899[44] and *Murphy*
vs. *Utter* in 1902,[45] the validity of the Pima bonds was upheld; the
Territorial Loan Commission was ordered to refund the bonds. This
was finally done in 1903 and the bondholders then converted their
Narrow Gauge railroad securities, part of which had been purchased
at about fifteen cents on the dollar, for full-value territorial bonds
charged to Pima County.[46] The Pima Board of Supervisors refused to
levy a tax to meet the interest payments, but the U. S. Supreme Court
again decided against them in *Vail* vs. *Territory of Arizona* in 1907.[47]
Congress, however, in the Enabling Act of 1910, finally relieved Pima,
as well as Yavapai, Maricopa, and Coconino counties, from heavy
bonded indebtedness by providing that the proceeds from a grant of
1,000,000 acres of land given to the territory were to be used in
paying the principal and interest on their railroad bonds.[48]

Nathan Murphy, who had been criticized by Tucson newspapers
for assisting the bondholders against the public interest, had died two
years earlier. Newspaper accounts of his activities after leaving the
governorship indicate that he spent much time outside the state. In
1903, he was in the resort town of Atlantic City, New Jersey, for quite

---

[42]*Arizona Gazette,* March 21, 1895.

[43]*U. S. Statutes at Large,* Vol. XXIX, 54th Cong., 1st Sess., 1896, p. 262.

[44]*Supreme Court Reporter,* Vol. XIX, January 3, 1899, pp. 183-87.

[45]*Ibid.,* Vol. XXII, May 19, 1902, pp. 776-82.

[46]*New York Times,* March 14, 1903.

[47]*Supreme Court Reporter,* Vol. XXVIII, December 2, 1907, pp. 107-108.

[48]A good scholarly work on the history of the Arizona Narrow Gauge Rail-
road is Howard A. Hubbard, *A Chapter in Early Transportation History: the
Arizona Narrow Gauge Railroad Company* (Tucson: University of Arizona, Social
Science Bull. No. 6, 1934).

awhile. During his absence, his wife Sarah was granted a divorce by Judge Kent. The marital split between the Murphys was sensational news since both of them had been prominent in Phoenix social circles. In her petition, Mrs. Murphy alleged habitual drunkenness on the part of her husband.[49] An oft-married man, Murphy was not long in finding another bride. In April, 1904, he was wed to Miss Emma Sells of Washington, D.C., who had inherited the fortune of her brother, a wealthy coal merchant.[50] The bride was described by a reporter as being "middle-aged, prematurely gray, and extremely handsome."[51] After the ceremony, the newlyweds sailed for Italy and an extended honeymoon in Europe. By this time, Murphy lived more comfortably than he had back in 1884 when he married his first wife, Nellie Banghart, daughter of a Chino Valley pioneer. It would take considerable space to trace the intervening marital history of Nathan Oakes Murphy; his political career is interesting enough.

In 1905 he was back in Washington, D.C., to lobby against President Roosevelt's proposal of joint statehood for Arizona and New Mexico. He was quoted in the *Washington Post* as saying, "As long as that obnoxious proposition is before Congress I shall be in the vicinity, seeking to oppose it by every legitimate means."[52] Murphy was one of the territory's strongest advocates for separate statehood and had the support of the vast majority of the people on this issue.

---

[49]*Tempe News,* April 8, 1908; *Coconino Sun,* October 3, 1903.

[50]*Tempe News,* April 15, 1904; *Phoenix Enterprise,* April 13, 1904.

[51]*Phoenix Enterprise,* April 13, 1904.

[52]*Tucson Citizen* (formerly the *Arizona Daily Citizen*), December 5, 1905, contains quote from *Washington Post,* December 1, 1905.

Chapter 18

Law and Order:
The Arizona Rangers

Fourteen stouthearted men! Could a police force with so few officers rid the vast Arizona Territory of cattle thieves and outlaws? The optimistic Twenty-first Assembly had shown its faith, in March, 1901, when it authorized Governor Nathan Oakes Murphy to form a mounted company of lawmen to be known as the Arizona Rangers. While badmen jested and boasted that the Rangers would "turn up their toes before the next branding season," the Governor proceeded to organize the force — consisting of a captain, sergeant, and twelve privates.[1] Fully aware of the dangerous duties to be performed by these men, Murphy forsook partisan politics and appointed Burt Mossman, a cool-headed Arizona cattleman, as the first captain.

Mossman was well qualified for his position, having gained experience with outlaws while foreman of the huge Hashknife outfit at a time when it was fighting for its life against cattle rustlers.[2] Interviewed by a Tucson newspaper in late 1901, he explained the purpose of the Arizona Rangers. After correcting an eastern impression that the company was organized because the territory was a wild and lawless land overrun by desperadoes and Indians who terrorized peaceable settlers, he said, "The fact is that life and property in Arizona is safer than in many of the large eastern cities. The ranger company was organized to prevent cattle stealing and to rid unsettled sections of the Territory from the fugitives from justice who find a refuge there."[3]

By the turn of the century, rustling near the Mexican border was forcing many cattlemen out of business. Only the larger establishments, such as John Slaughter's San Bernardino Ranch in southeast Cochise

[1]*Revised Statutes of the Arizona Territory,* 1901, Pars., 3213-30, pp. 833-36.
[2]Frazier Hunt, *Cap Mossman, Last of the Great Cowmen* (New York: Hastings House, 1951).
[3]File of James H. McClintock, Phoenix Public Library.

County, William Greene's ranch in the southwest corner, and the Erie Cattle Company and Henry Boice's Chiricahua Cattle Company in between, had enough range riders to keep the large bands of rustlers away. The miscreants would sweep down from their mountain fastnesses and round up a small herd before a posse could be formed. There was a dire need for the formation of a permanent group that could protect law abiding residents from the depredations of these rustlers and to deter other ruffians from coming to Arizona. Outlawry begets outlawry and crooks attract crooks.

Already, for example, two daring train robberies had occurred in southern Arizona. At Cochise Station, in September, 1899, two cowboys named Billy Stiles and Matt Burts, at the instigation of two dishonorable officers of the law, Constable Burt Alvord of Willcox and William Downing of Pearce, held up a Southern Pacific train; they fled with between $2,000 and $3,000 in gold, silver, and jewelry. Then, in February, 1900, a Benson-bound train from Nogales was held up at Fairbank. These robberies undoubtedly frightened the railroads, which joined the cattlemen and miners in seeking a ranger force.

With the law-abiding citizenry behind him, the "dead game" Mossman commenced his duties with a determination to round up the sordid element or "bust." Asked how he intended to carry out the legislature's orders to rid the country of badmen, the Ranger Captain said,

> If they come along easy everything will be all right. If they don't, well, I just guess we can make pretty short work of them. I know most of them and the life those fellows are leading in the mesquite scrub and land holes to keep out of reach of the law is a dog's life. They ought to thank me for giving them a chance to come in and take their medicine. Some of them will object, of course. They'll probably try a little gun play as a bluff, but I shoot fairly well myself, and the boys who back me up are handy enough with their guns. Any rustler who wants to yank on the rope and kick up trouble will find he's up against it.[4]

The Rangers operated as a nonpolitical organization. To qualify, the members had to be good riders, ropers, and shooters.[5] Since they were supposed to be familiar with the type of men whom they were expected to apprehend, some of the Rangers who were hired had previous records that would not entitle them to distinguished recognition in genteel society. They were enlisted from different parts of the territory so that, wherever the force was called to serve in the line of duty, at least one member would know intimately the trails, waterholes, and

---

[4]George H. Smalley Papers, Arizona Pioneers' Historical Society. (Smalley was the private secretary to Governor Alexander O. Brodie, Murphy's successor.)

[5]Carl M. Rathbun, "Keeping the Peace Along the Mexican Border," *Harper's Weekly*, Vol. 50, No. 2604 (1906), p. 1632.

Burton C. Mossman, first captain of the Arizona Rangers.

— Arizona Pioneers' Historical Society

opography, as well as the character of the people. Ordinarily, however, hey carried on their investigations with their identity concealed. According to Joe Pearce, who replaced Ranger Carlos Tafoya after the latter was killed in a fight with the notorious Smith brothers on the Black River in Navajo County, the "Arizona Rangers had no uniforms, no dress parades, no flags, no saluting. We just had that five-pointed silver star badge which we wore most of the time under the vest or the jacket. When we went to arrest a badman, we placed the star in plain sight."[6]

The first headquarters of the Rangers was at Bisbee, because a great portion of the outlawry was centered around the international boundary. Here bandits crossed and recrossed from Mexico into the United States, seeking refuge from authorities on the side from which they fled. With an almost-unguarded line stretching hundreds of miles through desert country, opportunities for lawbreaking were unlimited. Smuggling of cattle, horses, merchandise, and Chinese coolies took place on a wholesale scale. Tombstone's wild and lurid days were past, but hordes of desperadoes drifted into Bisbee, Douglas, and other wide-open border camps to commit serious crimes. The Rangers cooperated with the *Rurales,* a Mexican patrol of several hundred soldiers headed by a naturalized Russian-Mexican colonel named Kosterlitski, to rid the border country of these undesirables. The *Rurales* were permitted to cross the border when in hot pursuit of renegades seeking sanctuary

[6]Mulford Winsor, "The Arizona Rangers," *Our Sheriff and Police Journal,* Vol. 31, No. 6 (1936), pp. 49-61.

Colonel Emilio Kosterlitski, commander of the Mexican Rurales.

Kosterlitski and his orderly in the Rurales' *camp at Cananea, Sonora.*

in the United States, just as the Rangers could cross into Mexico for similar purposes.

The Rangers were also charged with the responsibility of capturing fugitives from the New Mexico Territory and the States. Their first arrests were members of George Musgrove's band of outlaws, an affiliate of the infamous Black Jack gang, whose appalling record of train robberies, killings, and cattle thefts had created a reign of terror in western Texas and New Mexico. On this particular occasion, members of the gang headed by Witt Neil, alias "Shorty" Daniels, had robbed a post office at Tucumcari, in eastern New Mexico, and killed a boy bystander who had his hands up. Mossman was informed that the renegades were headed for the rough Blue River wilderness country, a favorite Arizona "cooling off" resort for outlaws. The Rangers who were assigned to the case took a special train to Clifton, unloaded horses, and joined a Graham County posse organized by Sheriff James V. Parks to search for the outlaws. Daniels was captured in bed with a Winchester by his side and enough ammunition for a small arsenal. The following day, George Cook and Joe Roberts were caught in the act of stealing twenty-five horses. After these arrests, the eastern Arizona mountains became a less popular robbers' roost.[7]

Under Mossman's leadership, the Arizona Rangers captured or drove out of the territory many notorious outlaws and made definite progress toward putting a stop to banditry. The organization placed 125 major criminals behind bars and killed one in line of duty during their first twelve months of service. But despite a lot of good work, the Rangers ran into unanticipated trouble. They were accused of being overbearing with sheriffs and local officers and brutal in making arrests. Admittedly, Mossman's men were tough and had a flair for gunplay. That's why they were selected. But a few instances of insobriety and brawling in Bisbee saloons did not endear them to the local populace — especially the professional gamblers who were, on one occasion, accused of crooked poker. Mossman defended his men and in the process earned the ire of the citizenry.

After one brawl, more than fifty persons signed a petition requesting that Governor Alexander Brodie, who succeeded Murphy in July, 1902, remove the Ranger Captain "for conduct unbecoming an officer." The paper never reached Brodie but would have made little difference anyway since Mossman had already submitted his resignation for political reasons. In September, he was replaced by Thomas H. Rynning,

---

[7]*Report* of Captain Burton Mossman of Arrests Made by Arizona Rangers from October 2, 1901 to June 30, 1902.

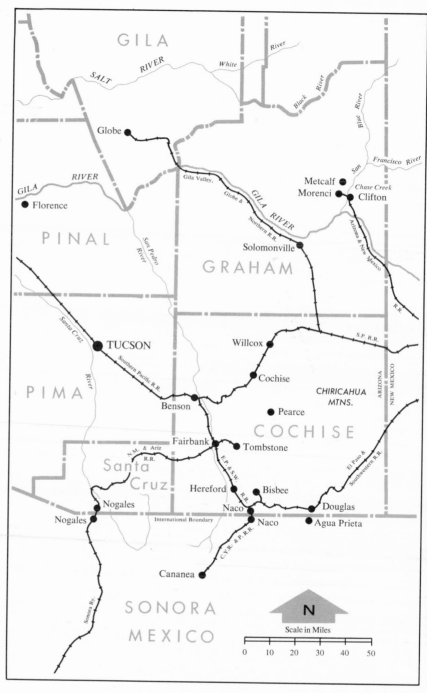

Southeastern Arizona in 1903.

a Rough Rider friend of both the new governor and Colonel Teddy Roosevelt, who had become President following McKinley's assassination.

But before Mossman left the service, he captured the Mexican murderer, Augustino Chacón, a bloodthirsty, ruthless killer unparalleled in Arizona's criminal annals. Estimates vary on how many murders he committed. But before Chacón died on the gallows at Solomonville, on November 21, 1902, he confessed to a Mexican official, who came to investigate the case, to having killed fifteen Americans and thirty-seven Mexicans in his lifetime. Certainly, his career was a bloody one! In 1896 he was convicted of murdering an officer named Pablo Salcido on Christmas Day, 1895, and was sentenced to hang. Ten days before the date of his execution in 1897, he dug out of the adobe jail in Solomonville and escaped into Mexico.[8]

To capture Chacón, Captain Mossman enlisted the aid of two former officers turned outlaw, Burt Alvord and Billy Stiles. The assistance of Alvord, who had led the life of a bandit in Mexico since his escape from a Tombstone jail in 1900, was especially valuable since he had on occasion been Chacón's partner in crime and knew the location of his hideout. Stiles, who was used as a go-between, had given himself up after the train robbery affair in Cochise County and had avoided trial by giving testimony damaging to his accomplices. Mossman, pretending to be an escapee from a Tucson jail, met his associates and Chacón at a prearranged location south of the border for the supposed purpose of crossing together into Arizona to steal horses from Colonel Bill Greene's ranch near Hereford.[9] After Alvord deserted the group on the pretense of looking for water, Chacón became suspicious and was reluctant to go further. Fearful of losing his long-sought prey, Mossman drew his six-shooter and arrested the murderer. He forced Chacón to ride handcuffed and with a rope around his neck across the border to Packard Station. The engineer whose train was flagged down must have been confused by the sight of one horseman (Stiles) leading the horse of another, who had a rawhide rope around his neck, the other end of the rope being, in turn, in the hands of a third horseman whose Winchester lay in the crook of his elbow. At Benson, Mossman turned his charge over to Graham County Sheriff Parks for the remainder of the trip to Solomonville and the scaffold.

Because his commission as a Ranger expired four days before he took Chacón, and because the arrest of a Mexican citizen on Mexican soil without process of Mexican law was a diplomatic offense, Mossman

[8]*Arizona Silver Belt,* November 27, 1902.
[9]*Ibid.,* September 4, 1902.

— Courtesy John D. Gilchriese

Captain Thomas Rynning and two of his Arizona Rangers meet Kosterlitski and some of his Rurales *on the border. This picture was probably taken in 1902.*

The hanging of Augustino Chacón at Solomonville.

— Arizona Department of Library and Archives

Thomas H. Rynning, successor to Mossman as captain of the Arizona Rangers.

— Arizona Pioneers' Historical Society

soon left for a New York City vacation. He remained in that city until the matter was resolved, and then settled down at Roswell, New Mexico, to direct extensive range-cattle operations.

Under his successor, Captain Thomas Rynning, the Ranger force was practically reorganized. The Rangers who were involved in the Bisbee fracas were dismissed and after nine months only three of Mossman's men remained. In accordance with a bill passed by the legislature in 1903, Governor Brodie authorized an increase in the size of the company to one captain, one lieutenant, four sergeants, and twenty privates.[10] Building a Rough Rider dynasty, Rynning promoted his sergeant, John Foster, to lieutenant, and advanced a Mossman holdover, J. E. Campbell, to a sergeant's position. Rynning also moved the Ranger headquarters from Bisbee to Douglas in compliance with the provision in the territorial statute that "the captain shall select as his base the most unprotected and exposed settlement of the frontier."[11] Douglas qualified as Ranger headquarters by this standard. Cattle thieves, murderers, and the worst *hombres* of two countries were attracted to the town by the nearness of the border as well as by the gambling halls, saloons, dance halls, and general debauchery. Most of the dives were

---

[10]*Acts, Resolutions, and Memorials, Twenty-second Legislative Assembly,* Act 64, secs. 1-10, pp. 104-106.
[11]*Revised Statutes of the Arizona Territory,* 1901, p. 835.

run by men who had plenty of notches on their guns and even some of the deputy sheriffs were blackleg gamblers and killers.[12]

One of the owners of the Cowboy Saloon, for example, was Lon Bass, a gunman and brother of the famous Texas outlaw, Sam Bass. Having no use for the law, Bass on one occasion threatened to kill a quick-drawing Ranger named W. W. Webb if the lawman came into his place of business. But the Ranger entered one night to investigate a shooting. When Bass thrust a gun into his face, Webb drew quick as a flash and shot the saloon owner through the heart. Another Ranger, Lonnie McDonald, who arrived on the scene with Rynning and Frank Wheeler, was wounded in the lung by a bullet fired from the gun of a crap-table dealer. Rynning cramped this assailant's style for awhile with a backhanded shot that broke his arm. Rynning then locked the saloon doors, drew a diagram of the action to use in Webb's defense, and used a stove shovel to help the nervous Hudspeth (co-owner of the establishment) scoop up the money that had been spilled from upturned tables. Webb was later declared innocent of any crime by a Tombstone court.

There was another point of view on the Webb incident, however. The *Arizona Silver Belt,* for example, considered the acquittal of Webb the most flagrant and deplorable miscarriage of justice that had occurred in Arizona. Quoting from the report of the crime and the coroner's inquest as published in both the *Bisbee Review* and the *Douglas International* on February 14, 1903, the *Silver Belt* said that five Rangers, including Webb, were going from one saloon to another drinking. "And anyone," the paper continued, "familiar with the delectable dives of the toughest town on the Mexican border, can readily picture this mob or gang of officers, conservators of the law armed with sixshooters, swaggering about, 'painting the town' and terrorizing the redlight district." Three of the men entered the Cowboy Saloon where Webb shot Bass. The testimony of the Rangers and of Samuel Henshaw, a bartender and musician who had entered the dive with them, was given more credibility in the Tombstone trial that followed than were the contradictory statements of seven witnesses. None of the saloon patrons or employees saw a weapon in Bass's hand and a Mr. Francis, the bartender on duty, testified that Webb fired a shot to scare him about seven minutes before he killed Bass. However, the burning of the saloon a few days after the incident removed any evidence that might have existed to corroborate the bartender's statement. In conclusion, the *Silver Belt* charged that the Ranger force had used its influence to clear

---

[12]Thomas H. Rynning, *Gun Notches, The Life Story of A Cowboy-Soldier* (New York: Frederick A. Stokes Co., 1931), pp. 202-203.

Webb and to remove the stigma from the name of the organization.[13]

Rynning's weekly reports to the governor are full of accounts of other exciting incidents. But the principal work of the Rangers was protection of the livestock industry. Working closely with the Livestock Sanitary Board and the Arizona Cattle Growers' Association, the Rangers attended roundups and served as livestock inspectors, especially along the border. The average distance traveled, on horseback, by each Ranger was about 390 miles per month. About a hundred rustlers were arrested during the years 1903–1904, while a great number of stolen cattle and horses were returned to their owners.[14]

The Rangers found that the cattle thieves who posed as honest ranchers were often the most difficult to apprehend. A cattleman named Taylor in Cochise County was a particularly good illustration of this point. According to Rynning, Taylor's neighbors had been unable to convict him of branding their calves, so Rynning and Johnny Brooks devised a means of detecting him. They roped thirteen unbranded calves belonging to neighbors near the Taylor spread in the Chiricahua Mountains, made slits in the gullet of each, and pushed in a Mexican half-dime. After driving the animals toward the suspected cow thief's headquarters, the Rangers left but returned several months later to check on their investment. Finding the calves with Taylor's brand, they had them transported to the county seat at Tombstone and arrested Taylor. Presented with the evidence, Taylor promised to leave the country if freed and to sell his ranch and cattle for $16,000, just about an eighth of the real value. The owners of the 7D and the Neil and Hershan outfits accepted this bargain so that the Taylor relatives could not continue stealing from their herds.[15] The Rangers could boast of many similar captures by the time Rynning reported to Governor Brodie in January, 1905, that cattle stealing was "practically wiped out in Arizona."

Wiping out cattle thieves was the particular business of the Arizona Rangers, but by no means the only duty. Arrests of all kinds totaled 1,052 during the fiscal year 1903-1904. In some instances, local sheriffs and judges refused to cooperate and the Rangers were forced to use extralegal methods to secure justice in the courts. Ranger Billy Olds, for example, straightened out a justice of the peace who was in league with cattle thieves in the thinly settled Tres Amigos border country west of Nogales. When the judge obviously favored some outlaws with

---

[13]*Arizona Silver Belt,* July 2, 1903.
[14]U. S. Dept. of the Interior, *Report of the Governor of Arizona to the Secretary of the Interior,* 1904, pp. 23, 75, and 79.
[15]Rynning, *Gun Notches.*

whom he was associated, Olds took command of the situation to prevent rustlers from running rampant in the area. He chained the crooked judge to a mesquite bush and proceeded to talk to the man about the error of his ways without interference. Leaving another Ranger to guard the judge, Olds went to get Rynning. When the Captain arrived, the enchained judge promised to administer justice impartially if released. And only upon that condition was he given another chance to grow up with the country.[16]

There were many other strange predicaments with which the Rangers had to cope. In one case they devised a unique plan to capture two renegade Papago murderers who were protected by their tribe. Disguised as cowboys on a roundup, Rangers Divilbess, Bailey, Beatty, and others drove a chuckwagon in close to the wanted Indians without exciting suspicion, and captured them alive. At another time, the Rangers helped avert a Mexican uprising that a revolutionary junta in Douglas was planning. A raid staged by Rangers and some federal officers netted twelve members of the organization, along with dynamite, percussion caps, arms, flags, and a mass of documents. This outstanding cooperation promoted good relations with the Republic of Mexico.

And still a third type of situation — in an unusual category — that tested the effectiveness of the Rangers was the mine strike. Probably the worst of several mine strikes that occurred during Rynning's four-and-a-half year period of duty came in 1903. On the first day of June of that year, the Mexican, Italian, and Slavonian miners of the Arizona, Detroit, and Shannon copper companies, operating at Clifton, Morenci, and Metcalf, walked out. The *Arizona Silver Belt* reported on June 4 that 1,500 miners struck and an additional 2,000 smeltermen, concentratormen, and other employees were affected by the action.[17]

The trouble developed from a compulsory eight-hour-day law for

---

[16]*Ibid.*, pp. 252-53.
[17]*Arizona Silver Belt,* June 4, 1903.

Bisbee, the center of much outlawry along both sides of the Mexican border, was the first headquarters for the Arizona Rangers. This picture was taken in 1908, a few years after headquarters had been moved elsewhere.

underground miners that had been enacted by the Twenty-second Legislative Assembly and that went into effect the day of the strike. The miners were paid $2.50 for a ten-hour day and demanded the same pay for the shorter day. James Douglas (father of Lewis Douglas, a former ambassador to the United Kingdom) of the Detroit Copper Company partially conceded, as did James Colquhoun of the Arizona Copper Company, to demands of the employees. They offered $2.25, or nine hours' pay under the old wage scale, for eight hours of work. The owners claimed that the ore being mined was of a low grade and wouldn't permit what amounted to a 25 percent an hour increase.[18]

Some newspapers in the state blamed the companies for the strike. *Our Mineral Wealth* (Mohave County), for example, said that the owners were using exaggerated figures relative to the cost of copper production; and "their pluck-me stores get back nearly all they pay out, yet they buck and snort around like they were in the last throes of poverty."[19] The *Arizona Democrat* (Phoenix), while professing opposition to strikes and lawlessness in any form, said that the mining companies were wholly responsible for the conditions that prevailed in the Clifton-Morenci area. The *Democrat* explained that the corporations had employed "illiterate, cheap labor foreigners" — mostly Mexicans — instead of American workers, and that the "chickens had come home to roost." In the same vein, the editor of the *Arizona Blade* (Florence) wrote that little sympathy could be extended to corporations operating in the United States and working foreign labor of the

---

[18]James Colquhoun, *The History of the Clifton-Morenci Mining District*, (London: John Murray, 1924).
[19]Reprinted in the *Arizona Blade and Florence Tribune*, June 20, 1903.

peon class. Stating that the low wages for which the Mexican and Italian immigrants were willing to work was the reason for their importation, the *Blade* said that "the employers brought them here and should be made to stand the brunt of any misdoing of their imported pets."[20]

The daily pay scale was the main item of contention, though W. H. Laustaunau, the real strike leader, also stressed other objectives while working the foreign laborers up to a dangerous pitch of excitement. He said that the miners' newly formed organization would not let the company employ workers who were not members of that society nor discharge a man without good reason. Furthermore, he argued, the company must not be permitted to assess hospital and insurance fees nor to increase prices at the company store unless there was a general increase in the market prices.[21] To some extent, unionism was an issue. The Mexicans and Italians had their own local organization but were not members of the Western Federation of Miners. As a matter of fact, representatives from this union's headquarters in Denver urged moderation when the strikers threatened to blow up the railroad bridges and to loot the company stores.[22]

The strike leaders — Laustaunau, Abram F. Salcido (president of the local group), and Frank Colombo (spokesman for the Italians) — had no desire to join the Western Federation. They feared that such action would deprive them of work since they would be forced to accept no less than the union scale; they were aware of the fact that the employers would not pay the scale to foreign laborers.[23] Whereas the operators in the Prescott area had agreed to pay an eight-hour-day scale to American miners, ranging from $2.50 for trammers to $3.50 for machinemen and pumpers, the Clifton-Morenci-area companies were offering, as mentioned above, only $2.25.[24] And this was considered high for foreign labor. At El Paso, just a few hours' train ride from Clifton, the Mexican common laborer received only a dollar for a ten-hour day; in Mexico the going wage ran from one dollar to a dollar and fifty cents, but that was in Mexican money which was then worth only forty to sixty cents in United States currency. From this viewpoint, some observers felt that the operators had the best bargaining position in the wage controversy.[25]

---

[20]*Arizona Blade and Florence Tribune,* June 20, 1903.
[21]*Copper Era* (Clifton), June 18, 1903.
[22]*Arizona Journal-Miner,* June 11, 1903.
[23]*Arizona Daily Star,* June 11, 1903.
[24]*Arizona Blade and Florence Tribune,* May 30, 1903.
[25]*Arizona Daily Star,* June 24, 1903.

Not everyone condemned the companies for using foreign labor, as did the *Arizona Republican* in Phoenix. This paper listed the names of the strike leaders (Laustaunau, Cruz, Colombo, Flores, Parrano, Montaza, Gonzales, Delao, Calderon, Costillo, Muerillo, and Montez) who were eventually arrested for inciting a riot, and then concluded its editorial with this withering comment: "All of them good American names!" In answer, the *Tucson Citizen* asked, "What's the matter with them? All of us can't be named Cochise, Sitting Bull, Billy the Kid, N. O. Murphy, Geronimo, Sims Ely, Rain-in-the-Face or Guv-ner Hughes." The *Citizen* went on to say that the "good American names" sounded "as if they were derived from the same genealogical tree as Christopher Columbus, Sebastian Cabot and Americus Vespucius."[26]

There was one thing that most Arizonans did agree upon, however, and that was that mob rule was inexcusable in a country where the people make the laws. An assault of rioters — whether strikers or anarchists — on the property of a corporation was not to be tolerated any more than an attack by robbers on a stagecoach.[27] But the miners were persistent. At Morenci, the storm center, the men were harangued into a potentially dangerous mob by inflammatory leaders. Meetings were held in an old lime-pit on top a hill above the town, and "Dago Red" flowed freely. Strikers in large numbers paraded the streets. Just as the situation seemed to be getting out of hand for the sheriff and some fifty civilians whom he deputized, Captain Rynning arrived with fifteen Rangers. Together, the two police forces kept peace until six companies of national guardsmen and several troops of regular cavalry took over. Acting Governor Isaac T. Stoddard, who was in charge of the territorial government while Brodie was absent on business in the East, had asked President Roosevelt for federal troops; his action was approved, apparently, by most of the people. The executive committee of the Western Federation of Miners, however, said that Stoddard was "guilty of treason to the principles of organized labor."[28] There might have been more sympathy for this latter point of view had the strikers not threatened to resort to violence.

Before the federals arrived, the Rangers had some excitement. On their second day in town, several hundred Metcalf strikers headed down Chase Creek Canyon to join the Morenci miners with pillage of the

---

[26]*Tucson Citizen,* June 16, 1903.

[27]*Arizona Journal-Miner,* June 15, 18, 1903.

[28]Letter of James Douglas, Detroit Copper Company, to Acting Governor Isaac Stoddard, June 9, 1903 (supplement, June 10, 1903) in Isaac T. Stoddard Miscellaneous Personal Papers, 1894–1913, University of Arizona Library, Special Collections.

The Detroit Copper Company at Morenci in 1901.

Detroit Copper Company's store as a possible object. Lieutenant John Foster detailed Rangers Bassett and Gray to intercept the Metcalf marchers and warn them against attempting to enter Morenci, while the other Rangers took positions outside the town. A slaughter was probably prevented only by a sudden cloudburst which brought a torrential wall of water rushing several feet deep down the canyon. The deluge sent the strikers scurrying for the hills and cooled their tempers for awhile. In destruction of property and in lives lost, the flood was a catastrophe, but against the marching mob it was a master, though unplanned, defense.[29]

Yet, on the next day, the strike situation was again foreboding. A large force of armed miners seized the Detroit Company's mill and disarmed the sheriff's deputies who were guarding it. But the course of events was reversed when Lieutenant Foster arrested the leading agitator, the above-mentioned Laustaunau (also spelled Laustenneau) who had been sent out of Chicago by an anarchist labor organization. This professional troublemaker, better known in later years as "Mocho" (crippled hand) to the Mexicans and "Three Fingered Jack" to the Americans, was locked up in jail. The following day he was joined by several other leaders and the strike was virtually over.

Altogether, eighteen men, including Laustaunau, were arrested and brought before Justice Chapman for arraignment. The strikers decided

---

[29]*Arizona Silver Belt,* June 11, 1903.

The Arizona Rangers — one man is missing — at the Morenci mine strike in 1903. Captain Rynning is at the far left. In 1962 the Winchester Company featured this picture, minus six of the men shown here, in a nationwide ad captioned, "19 Texas Rangers; only 18 Winchesters. Why?" (one man carried a Krag). When indignant Arizonans pointed out these were Arizona Rangers, the company apologized and gave a banquet in Phoenix to atone for its error.

to do without legal aid and designated "Three Fingered Jack" to be their spokesman and to cross-examine the territory's witnesses. The testimony of the twenty witnesses tended to show that "unparalleled scenes of bloodshed and crime" had narrowly been averted. Superintendent Alexander McLean gave the most damaging testimony. He swore that heavily armed men surprised him in his office and gave him one minute to close down the works. He also swore that the strike leader threatened to blow up the town with dynamite and to loot the ruins. The prisoners were held temporarily in the Solomonville jail and were taken later to Tucson, the Pima County jail being considered safer.[30]

"Three Fingered Jack" was convicted of inciting the miners to riot and was sentenced to serve a term in the Yuma prison where he became one of the most notoriously incorrigible inmates in the history of that institution.[31] From the beginning he agitated to upset the prisoners' routine by organizing work strikes and grievance committees to make impossible demands. He probably spent more time in the dungeon, called the "Snake Den," than any prisoner ever incarcerated in the so-called "Yuma Hell Hole." Once he did a stretch of eighty-eight straight days. After recovering from this ordeal he led an unsuccessful

[30]*Arizona Daily Star,* June 18, 1903.

[31]William and Milarde Brent, *The Hell Hole* (Yuma, Ariz.: Southwest Printers, 1962).

escape attempt during which Superintendent Griffith and his assistant, George Wilder, were beaten and nearly killed. The Yuma District Court added ten years to his sentence but about two years later Laustaunau died a lonely death in the "Snake Den." Meanwhile, Captain Rynning received an expensive gold watch from the mining companies for his part in curbing the copper strike. He, like "Three Fingered Jack," went to Yuma, but in a different capacity. In 1907, he was appointed superintendent of the territorial prison and relinquished his captaincy in the Rangers.

One of Rynning's last and very exciting experiences as a Ranger came in June, 1906, at the time of a strike in Cananea, Sonora, Mexico. The bad feeling that existed between the American bosses of William C. Green's Consolidated Copper Company and the Mexican workers exploded as the miners struck for higher wages. The very lives of the American colony, many of them women and children, were in danger.[32] Urgent messages requesting help were sent to Bisbee — some seventy miles away across the line in Arizona — to Douglas, and to El Paso. Also, U. S. Consular Agent Galbraith telegraphed U. S. Secretary of State Elihu Root on June 1: "Send assistance immediately to Cananea, Sonora, Mexico. American citizens are being murdered and property dynamited. We must have help. Send answer to Naco."[33] Though Superintendent J. T. Kirk already had hundreds of well-armed Americans in Cananea, the men of Bisbee quickly responded to the pleas for help. A second group of cowboys, miners, and other handy citizens gathered at Naco and tried to cross the line, only to be stopped by a small force of Mexicans. So it was up to the Bisbee force, under the leadership of Captain Rynning, to rescue the American nationals at Cananea.

Rynning's men, more than 250 in number, arrived at the border on an El Paso Southwestern Railroad train and probably would have stormed across the border, since they greatly outnumbered the defenders, if the Captain had not ordered a halt. Then, when Governor Yzabel of Sonora arrived from Hermosillo, Rynning explained the gravity of the situation in Cananea and offered his men as volunteers. The Governor was agreeable and, in order to avoid international complications, asked the Americans to cross the line as an unorganized mob. Once on Mexican soil, Yzabel swore them in as Mexican volunteers. Captain Rynning was appointed Colonel and seven members of his Ranger force were given officer commissions. This arrangement

[32]*Tucson Citizen,* June 4, 5, 1906; *New York Times,* June 4, 5, 1906; *Arizona Daily Journal-Miner,* June 2, 1906.
[33]*Tucson Citizen,* June 2, 4, 1906.

Harry Wheeler, the last captain of the Arizona Rangers, and later sheriff of Cochise County. In 1917, during a labor dispute in the Bisbee copper mines, he led the group responsible for the "Bisbee deportation" in which nearly 1,200 strikers and sympathizers were illegally deported from Bisbee.

— Arizona Pioneers' Historical Society

completed, the force proceeded to Cananea via the Cananea, Yaqui River, and Pacific Railroad.[34]

When the train steamed into the beleagured city there was wild rejoicing even though the real danger had passed. After charging and scattering the ranks of the Mexicans who were stationed in the hills surrounding the city, Rynning turned the policing duties over to Colonel Emilio Kosterlitski and his *Rurales,* who had arrived on the scene.[35] The riot was over as quickly as it had started. Rynning returned to Bisbee and his action, along with that of Governor Yzabel, was subsequently ratified and approved by both governments. The Captain's caution at the border probably had saved the incident from getting out of hand.

Rynning's successor as Captain of the Rangers was the colorful Harry Wheeler, the third and last commander of the group. Whereas Rynning was the careful, executive-type of officer who personally made few arrests, Wheeler was bold, daring, and eager to join in combat with lawbreakers.[36] In line of duty he was forced to shoot it out with several desperate men, though he boasted that he never shot first.

---

[34]*Bisbee Daily Review,* June 3, 1906; Rathbun, *Harper's Weekly,* Vol. 50, No. 2604, p. 1632; James H. McClintock, *Arizona: Prehistoric, Aboriginal, Pioneer, Modern* (Chicago: S. J. Clark Co., 1916), Vol. 2, pp. 584-85.

[35]*Arizona Daily Journal-Miner,* June 5, 1906.

[36]*Biennial Report of the Arizona Rangers.* 1905–1906. (Includes Rynning's report and a list of arrests.)

The first victim of his quick-gun action was a stranger named Bostwick who attempted to hold up the Palace Saloon on Congress Street in Tucson. Wheeler, then a sergeant, came upon the robber while the latter had a number of saloon patrons lined up against a wall. As Wheeler pushed open the swinging door, he and the robber exchanged fire but the Ranger's was the most effective. A shot grazed the bandit's head and another struck him in the chest. Bostwick's only shot whistled harmlessly by Wheeler as did two more shots from the gun of another robber stationed across the street as a lookout. The *Tucson Citizen* reported on February 28, 1907, that the second thug escaped, but Bostwick, who turned out to be an advance contract man for a wandering carnival company, lingered between life and death for a time before dying.[37]

On another occasion in the same month, Wheeler was twice wounded in a shooting scrape, but demonstrated remarkable coolness under fire and got his man. Wheeler was endeavoring to prevent an employee of the Helvetia Copper Company, a man named J. A. Tracy, from killing D. W. Silverton and his female companion, a woman with whom Tracy himself was infatuated, as the couple came to the railroad station in Benson to board a train for El Paso. The fighting occurred at six o'clock in the morning on the main street of the town after Wheeler commanded Tracy to drop his gun. The latter turned on the Ranger quick as lightning and in a matter of seconds inflicted two wounds, one in the thigh and another in the foot. Meanwhile, Wheeler had drawn and got four of his five shots into Tracy's body. After the battle the two men shook hands and wished each other a speedy recovery. Tracy, however, died on the train to Tucson. Wheeler was soon back in the saddle though he never completely recovered from his leg wound. But there was no letdown in Ranger activities.

The records show that the total number of arrests made by the Rangers during this period was greater than before, though there were not so many arrests for the more atrocious offenses. Douglas had been tamed already, so the new headquarters was moved to another border town, Naco, but Ranger law enforcement was not limited to that region. Many parts of the territory, for example, were concerned with the increasingly aggravating crime of horse stealing during Wheeler's tenure as captain. Cattle thievery, at least by organized bands of rustlers, was on the wane, partly because of previous Ranger harassment and partly because there was an exceptionally good market for horse flesh in Old Mexico and in the territories of Utah and New Mexico.

---

[37]*Tucson Citizen,* February 28, 1907.

The Rangers were constantly searching for stolen animals. On one occasion they spent twenty days in the saddle riding through the wildest parts of southeastern Arizona and western New Mexico, looking for the participants in an extensive horse-stealing operation. In the summer of 1908, Wheeler made a trip to Sonora where he found the country full of stolen horses. With the cooperation of Mexican authorities, he was able to recover a large number of the animals and return them to their owners in Arizona. In return for the Mexican assistance, Wheeler and his Rangers patrolled the border east of Douglas during the summer of 1908, thereby helping the *Rurales* to prevent hostile Yaqui Indian raiders from crossing the line.

No one was more disappointed than Wheeler when the last territorial legislature, meeting in 1909, abolished the company of Arizona Rangers.[38] In every legislature, following that of 1901, at least one bill had been introduced to wipe out the organization. But the need for an independent, mobile body of peace officers was so obvious that little headway was made by the opponents. Taxpayers in agricultural counties objected to the force on the grounds that they had little outlawry but had to share the expense for the benefit of other counties. Promoters of the territory argued that the Rangers advertised Arizona as a lawless country and thus deterred settlement. Certain local sheriffs and local police officers resented the prestige of the Rangers, as well as the fees they collected. In all fairness, however, it should be mentioned that many of these local law-enforcement officers were often inefficient and sometimes worked hand-in-glove with outlaw bands.

Other opponents of the Rangers contended that members of the force were frequently themselves in violation of statutory or moral law. The case of Sergeant Jeff Kidder, who was killed at Naco, Sonora, in April, 1908, was cited by critics. Though a courageous and capable Ranger, Kidder had come from Nogales, where he was on duty, to re-enlist. While waiting for Wheeler to return to headquarters at Naco, Arizona, he crossed the line into Mexico for a little recreation at a saloon and dance hall. There he engaged in a gun battle with two Mexican officers and was shot while wounding both of them. Attempting to reach the American side he was intercepted by Mexican line riders and police, beaten over the head with a Winchester, and brutally dragged to jail. Though moved to a private home at the request of an American officer, he died the next day. A Mexican investigation resulted in the dismissal of twenty policemen and line riders and the temporary closing

---

[38] *Acts, Resolutions and Memorials,* Twenty-fifth Legislative Assembly, 1909, Act 4, p. 3.

394

Thomas F. Weedin, Democratic legislator from Florence and, before that, publisher of the Arizona Enterprise *in that town.*

of Naco, Sonora, saloons. Yet, the stigma of Kidder's Mexican spree was not removed in the eyes of Ranger critics.

In spite of all the arguments against the Arizona Rangers, however, the bill of 1909 probably would have been defeated, like previous ones, except for the fatal element of partisan politics. Dissension between legislative and executive branches of the government during the administration of Republican Governor Joseph H. Kibbey led the lawmakers to strip the governor of all prerogatives possible, including the administration of the Rangers. The abolition bill was first endorsed by the Democratic caucus with the Maricopa County members forming the nucleus for the abandonment sentiment. The legislators from southern counties favored the territorial police force but failed to offer much resistance to the caucus position. It is likely that they didn't wish to jeopardize other desired legislation and that they agreed with several newspaper editorials which contended that the organization had to a considerable extent completed its intended objectives.

However, the legislative controversy over the bill was bitter and dramatic. Councilman Thomas F. Weedin of Pinal County introduced the bill to repeal the Ranger statute and led the fight for its passage.[39] His denunciation of Governor Kibbey's stinging veto of the measure

---

[39]"Message of Governor Joseph H. Kibbey to the Council of the Twenty-fifth Legislative Assembly," *Journal of the Twenty-Fifth Legislative Assembly,* 1909, pp. 94-111; reply of Councilman Thomas F. Weedin on pp. 111-22.

was both personal and vitriolic. The public in general expressed dissatisfaction with the legislature's action and Captain Wheeler was especially disappointed since his request for an opportunity to appear before a committee and answer questions about the Rangers was denied. So disappeared the Arizona Rangers in the arena of politics. The colorful force had effectively performed a great service in helping to establish law and order in the territory.

The Republicans went down crying "revenge," not only when the nonpartisan Ranger force was abolished but also when several offices held by members of their party were either eliminated or curtailed in power by the Democratic majority in the legislature. But the Democrats, alleging themselves to be friends of the taxpayers, answered by saying that the people wanted expenses cut wherever it was possible without injuring the public service. They said that the Republicans of Arizona had become so used to "bamboozling Democratic legislators into enacting laws raising their salaries and creating new offices for their party" that they resented Democratic economy. However, the fact that the territorial and federal officials had campaigned so bitterly against Delegate Smith in support of Ralph Cameron and the Republican ticket, in 1908, no doubt motivated the Democratic lawmakers to cut out as much Republican patronage as possible. The *Arizona Daily Star,* a Democratic paper in 1909, summarized the partisan battle by comparing it to the Washington struggle: "The Arizona Republicans probably realize how the Democratic congressmen feel when the Republicans under Cannon run the steam roller over their aspirations. Our legislators are getting quite proficient in handling the steam roller themselves."[40]

---

[40]*Arizona Daily Star,* February 3, 6, 7, 1909.

Chapter 19

Rough Rider in the Saddle:
The Brodie Administration

The fifteenth territorial governor, Alexander Oswald Brodie, first came to Arizona in 1870 as a second lieutenant in the First Cavalry. Fresh out of West Point, the twenty-one-year-old officer became one of General George Crook's most famous scouts during the days of Apache warfare in Arizona. On June 21, 1871, he won the personal commendation of the Secretary of War for his conduct during an engagement with a large band of hostile Apaches. Outnumbered, but occupying a good defensive position, Brodie's little force of troopers offered stubborn resistance and brought down many of the attackers with accurate firing. After eight hours of fighting, Brodie was able to extricate his command and return to Camp Apache.[1]

Sometime later, the vigorous and courageous Lieutenant Brodie undertook another dangerous mission. Offered a company of soldiers, he selected only one man upon whom he could rely and started out to bring sixty Apache braves back to the San Carlos Indian Reservation from which they had escaped. He located the Indians but was met by the enraged chief who threatened to shoot him. Showing no fear, Brodie quickly ended the parley by pulling his revolver and mortally wounding the chief. Convinced that the young officer meant business, the other Indians fell in line, as commanded, and marched sullenly back to the reservation.

In 1875, Brodie was promoted to first lieutenant and was transferred to Fort Colville, Washington. He resigned from the Army in 1877, a short time after the deaths of his wife, the former Kate Reynolds of Walla Walla, and an infant daughter. Afterwards, he operated a cattle business in Kansas for several years before turning to mining in Dakota and Arizona. From 1887 to 1890 he was the chief engineer and super-

---

[1]*Prescott Journal-Miner,* November 28, 1913. (From the *Army and Navy Journal*).

396

Alexander O. Brodie, governor of Arizona Territory, 1902 to 1905.

— Arizona Pioneers' Historical Society

intendent at the Walnut Grove Dam on the Hassayampa River, north of Wickenburg. This big structure was built to facilitate the mining of placers downstream, and impounded a body of water eleven miles in circumference. In February, 1890, when the dam was about completed, an immense flood caused it to collapse. The released floodwaters washed away a tent village near the base of the dam and swept destruction all the way to the Gila. Besides the property damage in the valley below that ran into the millions of dollars, dozens of lives were lost. Brodie's promised wife, the sole survivor of her family who were camped below the dam, narrowly escaped by climbing a cliff and, in a few months after the deluge, became Mrs. Brodie.

In 1891, Brodie was appointed by Governor Irwin as the first commander of the Arizona National Guard. He resigned after a year, when Murphy succeeded to the office of governor for the first time.[2] Shortly thereafter, he began gaining practical political experience in the capacity of county recorder of Yavapai. In the spring of 1898 a rich deposit of gold ore was discovered at Brodie's Crown Point mine. Yet when the first rumors of war came and a cowboy rode over from the railroad with news of the sinking of the *Maine,* Brodie pulled the pumps from the mine, saddled his horse, and rode to Prescott. He was appointed a major in the First Volunteer Cavalry (Rough Riders) and proceeded to organize a rugged group of men at Whipple Barracks.[3]

---

[2]Letter of Governor N. O. Murphy to Colonel A. O. Brodie, Col. of 1st Reg't., N.G.A., May 16, 1892, in the Brodie Papers, Arizona Pioneers' Historical Society.
[3]*Native American* (Phoenix), May 31, 1902.

ELECTION RETURNS.

November 8, 1898.

NAMES OF CANDIDATES.	Flagstaff	Williams	Challender	Bellemont.	Canyon Diablo.	Mormon Dairy.	Tubu City.	Fredonia.	Total Vote.	Majority.
For Delegate to Congress—										
A. O. Brodie, R...............	246	175	6	6	5	9	12	6		....
J. F. Wilson, D...............	187	123	3	7	8	3	2	15		....
For Council—										
E. T. Greenlaw, R............	200	157	6	5	2	7	2	3		....
T. S. Bunch, D....	225	138	3	8	10	7	12	18		....
For Assembly—										
H. T. Ashurst, D..............	303	227	....	9	....	....	....	21		....
For Sheriff—										
R. H. Cameron, R............	218	115	9	5	5	7	5	1		....
F. Fairchild, D...............	221	200	3	5	8	7	8	20		....
For District Attorney—										
Edward M. Doe, R............	225	131	6	7	3	8	12	2		....
James Loy, D.................	203	163	3	10	10	6	2	17		....
For Probate Judge—										
N. G. Layton, R..............	192	174	7	7	5	9	12	15		....
R. H. Jones, D................	231	127	2	7	7	5	2	6		....
For Recorder—										
Henry J. Sellers, R...........	141	156	6	5	1	5	2	....		....
T. E. Pulliam, D.............	289	145	3	9	11	9	12	21		....
For Treasurer—										
Harry Fulton, R..............	196	142	6	4	4	10	11	12		....
George Hoxworth, D..........	224	154	3	9	9	4	3	9		....
For Supervisors—										
John E. Davis, R.............	214	107	7	5	2	10	8	9		....
W. H. Anderson, R...........	196	90	7	6	1	11	12	8		....
J. C. Phelan, D..	205	193	2	7	9	3	4	12		....
J. B. Jones, D................	190	203	2	7	9	4	2	13		....
For Surveyor—										
J. T. McWilliams, R..........	180	115	6	....	2	....	....	6		....
W. H. Power, D	213	140	3	....	11	....	....	15		....
For Justices of the Peace—										
Samuel C. Black, R...........	110	....	....	....	....	....	....	....		....
J. A. Wilson, R...............	106	....	....	....	....	....	....	....		....
J. C. Milligan, D.............	137	....	....	....	....	....	....	....		....
D. R. Prime, D.	140	....	....	....	....	....	....	....		....
H. C. Hibben, Citizen........	229	....	....	....	....	....	....	....		....
For Constables—										
M. T. Black, R................	154	....	....	....	....	....	....	....		....
Guy C. Kilgore, R............	128	....	....	....	....	....	....	....		....
Jesse Gregg, D	199	....	....	....	....	....	....	....		....
Dan Hogan, D....	291	....	....	....	....	....	....	....		....

*Election returns for Coconino County in 1898, as given in
The Coconino Sun, November 12, 1898. Ashurst was incorrectly listed as "H. T." instead of "H. F."*

Rendering distinguished service in Cuba as commander of the first squadron, he was wounded in action at Las Guásimas and became a lieutenant-colonel of the regiment upon the promotion of Colonel Roosevelt, to whom he was second in command. Returning to Crown Point after the war, Brodie ran for delegate to Congress on the Republican ticket but was defeated by Colonel J. F. Wilson, a Democrat. However, his appointment in 1902, by his former commander in the Rough Riders, to be governor, was popularly received. One newspaper wrote that "Colonel Brodie is a man of fine character and his pleasant disposition attracts and holds friends wherever he goes. The people of Arizona have the highest regard for him, and his appointment as governor meets with the approval of all and is regarded as a reward which he well deserves."[4]

During the last half of 1902 Governor Brodie organized his administration, most of his appointees being new in government. Perhaps one of the most publicized of his actions prior to the opening of the legislature in January, 1903, was his pardoning of Pearl Hart, Arizona's most notorious female bandit. Though never a big-time woman outlaw like Oklahoma's Belle Starr, Pearl got more publicity in the newspapers and magazines when she was arrested and sentenced to the Yuma penitentiary than any other woman in the history of the territory.

An illiterate, mining-camp follower who could barely write her name, she was addicted to narcotics and was known as a real "tough cookie." With the help of a male companion, she held up a stagecoach in Kane Springs Canyon, between Globe and Riverside, in May, 1899. Pearl, whose real name was Taylor, took about four hundred dollars, besides watches and jewelry, from the passengers and rode off. A few days later, Sheriff Bill Truman of Pinal County caught up with the weary pair in the San Pedro Valley and recovered the loot. The man, who was tried under the false name of "Joe Boot," was sentenced in a Florence court to thirty years in prison at Yuma but was made a "trusty" and escaped after serving less than two years.

Meanwhile, Pearl was incarcerated in the Pima County jail at Tucson since there were no accommodations for women in the Florence jail. With the help of an accomplice, she cut her way through a light partition and fled. She got as far as Deming, New Mexico, before being recaptured and brought back to Florence for trial. The jury refused

---

[4]Newspaper clipping in the McClintock File, Phoenix Public Library. This file contains much of the personal correspondence between Brodie and his close friend, James H. McClintock, who is remembered as a Rough Rider, postmaster, historian, and newspaperman.

400

Arizona's famous woman bandit, Pearl Hart, photographed in the Yuma Territorial Prison. Note the rock background.

— Arizona Pioneers' Historical Society

to convict her of stage robbery, partly perhaps because she contended that she desperately needed money to visit her sick mother in the East. Judge Doan castigated the jury for failure to do its duty, however. Pearl was rearrested and another less sympathetic jury found her guilty on another charge, that of having robbed the stage driver of a revolver.[5]

She was sentenced to five years in the Yuma penitentiary. Though no great beauty, Pearl was the only female in the institution and thus became little short of an angel to the felons. Guards and trusties knocked themselves out to do special favors for her. Once she contrived to get a shortened sentence by doublecrossing an admirer named Adam Monroe, whom she induced to escape in a meat wagon. She informed another suitor, a guard, of the plot and Monroe was caught. Prison authorities knew that Pearl was a conniving woman, however, and were opposed to rewarding her at the time.[6] But in December, 1902, Governor Brodie paroled her on condition she leave the territory. The following article appeared in the *Yuma Sentinel* at the time: "Her ticket was bought straight through to Kansas City, where her mother and sister live, and the latter has written a drama in which Pearl will assume the leading role, arrangements having been made to play the Orpheum circuit, the initial performance to be given in Kansas City." In the

---

[5]Pearl Hart, "An Arizona Episode," *Cosmopolitan*, Vol. 27, No. 6 (1899), pp. 673-77.

[6]Brent and Brent, *The Hell Hole*, pp. 41-55.

drama, Pearl carried her Winchester and simulated her one-and-only stage holdup, which had been a washout, and then spoke to the audience about the horrors of the Yuma prison. The act was short-lived, however, and Pearl Hart disappeared from the public eye except for a brief stint with the Buffalo Bill show as a female rough-rider.

At the time that Governor Brodie pardoned the notorious female outlaw, he had about completed preparations for meeting the legislature in January, 1903. Like most political leaders today, he hired a ghostwriter. His "man Friday" was George H. Smalley, a newspaperman who was working for the Murphys on the *Arizona Republican*.[7] Smalley wrote speeches, messages to the legislature, the annual report to the Secretary of the Interior, and hundreds of letters, as well as magazine articles, one of which appeared in *Cosmopolitan* under the Governor's name.[8] He also was given special assignments during Brodie's administration. For example, he made the arrangements for President Roosevelt's visit to the Grand Canyon in May, 1903. After delivering a speech, Roosevelt requested the band to play the popular Rough Rider favorite, "Hot Time in the Old Town Tonight." When Smalley informed the President that the Mexican musicians knew only one American song, a funeral dirge, Roosevelt exclaimed, "The country is going to the dogs!"[9]

As a speech writer, the secretary was more successful. He had a hand in polishing Governor Brodie's first message to the Twenty-second Legislative Assembly, in January, 1903, which was widely acclaimed. The *Arizona Silver Belt* wrote that the message "is so completely divorced from politics as to disarm other than friendly criticism, and its recommendations reveal an intelligent and careful study of the conditions and needs of the territory, as well as a high sense of duty, at the present time none too common among influential public officials."[10]

From the beginning Brodie showed integrity and strong character by refusing to accept a special appropriation of the last legislature amounting to $750. This money was available to him for personal use, with no vouchers required, but he questioned the legality of the act

---

[7]Letter from A. O. Brodie to George H. Smalley, from Crown Point, Arizona, June 11, 1902, in the George H. Smalley File, Arizona Pioneers' Historical Society.

[8]Alexander O. Brodie, "Reclaiming the Arid West," *Cosmopolitan,* Vol. 37, No. 6 (1904), pp. 715-22; and Brodie, "The Rise of a Commonwealth on the Southwestern Frontier," *Bisbee Daily Review, World's Fair Edition,* n. d.; see also, George H. Smalley, *My Adventures in Arizona* (Tucson: Arizona Pioneers' Historical Society, 1966), p. 112.

[9]Smalley, "Reporter on Horseback," *Arizona Highways,* Vol. 24, No. 3 (1948), pp. 4-7; and Smalley, *My Adventures,* pp. 116-17

[10]*Arizona Silver Belt,* January 29, 1903.

*President Theodore Roosevelt with Governor Alexander O.
Brodie at the Grand Canyon in 1903.*

and declined to spend the money even though his salary was obviously inadequate to cover expenditures. Brodie was also quite frank and straightforward in his suggestions on taxation and for improving the financial status of the territory. He repeated the plea of previous governors for a tax on the output of mines that would not only bring in additional revenue but also be fair and proportionate in comparison to taxes paid by people engaged in other pursuits.

Governor Brodie made several suggestions in regard to the territorial institutions and offices. He asked legislative support for the Pioneers' Historical Society to secure and preserve historical data that would become increasingly more difficult to obtain as pioneers passed away. The new industrial school at Benson was reported complete except for final touches; the Governor recommended the use of short-term prisoners from the penitentiary to improve the grounds and to build a wall. The legislature's attention was called to two gifts of $5,000 each from James Douglas' Copper Queen Mining Company to the University of Arizona, one for the construction of a gymnasium hall and one for a hall of mechanical arts. The Governor made a special point in asking that his secretary be granted an increase in pay from $125 to $150 per month and be provided with more filing cases; in contrast to modern multi-million dollar state governmental operations, this request seems most interesting. Other proposals were that county supervisors and legislators be elected from districts and that the political parties hold primaries at the same time in the various voting precincts of the territory; these recommendations were enacted several years later but not by the Twenty-second Assembly.[11]

The legislature passed ninety-three acts plus ten memorials and joint resolutions.[12] Mention has already been made of the eight-hour-day law for underground miners and the measure increasing the number of Arizona Rangers. Railroad companies were forbidden to work their employees for more than sixteen consecutive hours and were permitted to hire police officers, more commonly known as "railroad bulls," to protect their premises. New railroads were again exempted from taxes for ten years. To encourage the generation of electric power, all dams and other appurtenances were exempt from taxation for nine years. The practice of operating company stores in mining districts and forcing the workers to accept coupons, script, punchouts, or store orders instead of lawful money was stopped.

---

[11]*Message of Governor Alexander O. Brodie to the Twenty-Second Legislative Assembly* (Tucson: Citizen Printing and Publishing Co., 1903), pp. 3-22.

[12]*Acts, Resolutions and Memorials,* Twenty-second Legislative Assembly, 1903.

The legislature also changed another practice which had benefited the territorial secretary's office. The Cowan bill took from the secretary the filing fees paid by new corporations, purportedly amounting to as much as $40,000–50,000 a year, and transferred the fees to the auditor's office for deposit in the territorial treasury.[13] Secretary Isaac Stoddard fought the Cowan bill and sought to hold the fees for his office.[14] A "stalwart" Republican, he was already incompatible with Brodie and Roosevelt — reform Republicans — and was eventually succeeded by W. F. Nichols in April, 1904.

Other legislation was passed to help make the Territory of Arizona a good a place to live as any state. Laws required that each physician and dentist should procure a license before practicing in Arizona, and established a territorial board of health as well as county boards of health. Several measures dealing with the schools were passed too. All of the school districts in the territory were required to fly the United States flag during school hours. A special tax was levied for operation costs and building construction at the Tempe Normal School. All school districts with as many as a thousand residents were authorized to hire drawing and music teachers.

Provision was made, also, for completion of the Arizona Industrial School at Benson. In December, 1903, the school opened under the superintendency of Frank O'Brien, who had been probate judge of Cochise County. Before a decade had elapsed, however, the institution was transferred to Fort Grant because the building at Benson had been poorly constructed and was considered dangerous for occupancy. Also, the site offered no facilities for farming or other industries. Another state institution, the overcrowded territorial asylum in Phoenix, was given much-needed assistance by a law providing for a loan of $100,000 to make improvements in facilities. The accommodations were inadequate for the more than 150 patients; many of the inmates were crowded into small rooms that were suitable for the habitation of only two people. Under these circumstances it was impossible for those in charge to classify and separate the patients suffering from different kinds and degrees of mental ailments. Accordingly, the legislature voted the fifty-year loan in order that more buildings could be erected and the grounds improved so that the unfortunates who were placed in the asylum might

---

[13]Manuscript of George H. Smalley in the Brodie Papers, Arizona Pioneers' Historical Society.

[14]Newspaper clipping dated October 31, 1911, in Miscellaneous Personal Papers, 1894-1913 of Isaac T. Stoddard, in the University of Arizona Library, Special Collections.

Members and employees of the Twenty-Second Legislative Assembly.

have some chance for recovery. Congress approved the legislation the following year.[15]

There were two bills in particular that brought protests from the public when they were introduced — one to grant woman suffrage and another that supported joint statehood with New Mexico. The voting measure supposedly passed the House as a joke. It cleared the Council on St. Patrick's Day but only after Governor Brodie had assured the members of that body that he would veto it, which he did. Brodie's veto was not based upon the merits of woman suffrage but on the argument that the subject was outside the power of the legislature and beyond the limitations of the Organic Act that permitted only males to vote.[16] Thus, the ladies had to wait for statehood before they could cast ballots.

Of all the bills introduced in the Twenty-second Legislative Assembly, few created as much excitement as the one endorsing joint statehood with New Mexico. This endorsement was passed by the Council and telegraphed to Washington, D.C., as a joint resolution. On the following day, however, it was unanimously repudiated by the territorial lower house. The House's telegram to Delegate Marcus A. Smith in the capital stated that "Arizona will always fight against any policy, even by implication, through which she may lose her name, identity, and history."

Prior to the Council's action, Smith, who was unalterably opposed to joint statehood, had sent a telegram (on February 26, 1903) to his friend Eugene S. Ives, the President of the Council, suggesting that the territorial legislature unanimously memorialize the next Congress against any jointure bill.[17] Ives, however, chose to attempt a flank movement rather than the frontal assault recommended by Smith. He firmly believed that the Fifty-eighth Congress convening in 1903 would pass a bill annexing Arizona to New Mexico against the consent of the people. Accordingly, he urged the legislature to advise Delegate Smith to accept a bill combining the two territories — providing that statehood would not be effective until the constitution of the new state had been first accepted by a vote of the people of each territory voting separately. In other words, under this proviso, Arizona herself could veto joint statehood.[18] But the Arizona House either did not understand or did not appreciate Mr. Ives's tactics. Like the governors of the territory,

---

[15]*U. S. Statutes at Large,* Vol. XXXIII, 58th Cong., 2d Sess., 1904, Chap. 817, pp. 146-49.

[16]*New York Times,* March 18, 20, 1903.

[17]Printed in the *Arizona Republican,* October 15, 1904, the *Tucson Citizen,* October 17, 1904, and the *Arizona Blade* (Florence), October 22, 1904.

[18]*Arizona Republican,* October 15, 1904.

Brodie and his successor, Joseph Kibbey, the lawmakers of the lower house chose to support Smith in his inveterate opposition to jointure with New Mexico.

Smith had spoken against joint statehood as early as May 9, 1902, when the House, sitting as a Committee of the Whole, was debating the Omnibus Bill that he and Delegates Rodey and Flynn had introduced. On that occasion, he argued against an amendment proposed by Congressman Jesse Overstreet of Indiana, one of the opponents of single statehood status for Arizona, New Mexico, and Oklahoma. To make the bill objectionable to even its advocates, Overstreet moved that the following section be included: "The inhabitants of all that part of the area of the United States now constituting the Territories of New Mexico and Arizona as at present described may become a State under the name of Montezuma, or such other name as may be finally determined by the convention to be elected under this act."[19]

Among other arguments against this motion, Smith said that the two territories were much too large for one state and had nothing in common except geographic proximity; he also pointed out the fact that each territory had its own capitol building, Arizona having just recently completed hers at great expense.[20] The Overstreet amendment was defeated 106 to 28 and the Omnibus Bill subsequently was passed in the House. In commenting upon the measure's success in that body, Bernard S. Rodey, the Republican Delegate from New Mexico, wrote: "Delegate Mark Smith of Arizona is entitled to credit for having procured the entire Democratic membership of the House to resolve in caucus to support the three bills as a party."[21]

But Smith's influence was not limited to the U. S. House of Representatives. In a letter to this writer, Senator Carl Hayden appraised Smith thusly: "During the years of his service, between 1887 and 1902, as the Delegate to Congress from Arizona, Mark gained the friendship of Senators who had sufficient influence in that body to prevent the enactment of legislation which provided for the admission of Arizona and New Mexico into the Union as one State."[22]

---

[19]*U. S. Congressional Record,* 57th Cong., 1st Sess., 1902, XXXV, Part 5, p. 5198.

[20]*The Statehood Bill,* Speech of Hon. Marcus A. Smith of Arizona in the House of Representatives, May 8 and May 9, 1902. Reprint, pp. 14-16.

[21]Letter of Bernard S. Rodey to M. A. Otero, Solomon Luna, and Frank A. Hubbell, May 10, 1902. Quoted in LaMoine Langston, "Arizona's Fight For Statehood in the Fifty-seventh Congress" (unpublished master's thesis, University of New Mexico, Albuquerque, 1939).

[22]Letter of Senator Carl Hayden to the writer, Washington, D. C., February 26, 1966.

And it was in the Senate where the real battle was fought. A coterie of Republican senators, headed by the powerful Albert J. Beveridge of Indiana, the chairman of the Committee on Territories, opposed statehood for Arizona and New Mexico. This group believed that the Southwest was some sort of "great American desert," inhabited by culturally incompatible, Spanish-speaking residents, and dominated by a few large absentee-controlled mining corporations and the big railroads — Southern Pacific and Santa Fe. At first opposed to statehood in any form, Beveridge and his cohorts on the Committee on Territories, by a strictly party vote of 6 to 4, in June, 1902, delayed a vote on the Omnibus Bill until the next session. The bill might have passed if brought to a vote since it had the solid support of all the Democrats in the Senate and about a dozen Republicans under the leadership of Matthew Quay of Pennsylvania.[23]

During the congressional recess, Beveridge took a subcommittee on a whirlwind investigating tour of the territories to verify his preconceived conclusions against statehood. In looking over the territory for adverse impressions, he spent only three days, including one in Phoenix searching for signs of urban depravity. Indeed, the committee moved with such speed that Delegate Smith acidly commented in a speech to the House in 1903: "I met the committee — I never could have overtaken it — at Phoenix and it remained one day . . . and 'investigated' a police judge and some census enumerators, and had an interpreter with them scouring the town to see whether some Mexicans could not be found who could not speak English and prove valuable witnesses for the purpose of the investigation."[24]

About a month after delivering this speech in the lame-duck session of the Fifty-seventh Congress, Smith left office for two years because of ill health; he was replaced by another Democrat, ex-Delegate J. F. Wilson, who had defeated the Republican candidate and former United States District Attorney, Robert E. Morrison, in the 1902 election. During this election, the national confusion over Arizona's possible admission into the Union was injected into the arena of territorial politics. The more biased newspapers of Arizona, both Democratic and Republican, tried to use the statehood question as an instrument for the election of their candidate as delegate to Congress. They seemed

---

[23]*Arizona Republican,* June 15, 1902; *Congressional Record,* 57th Cong., 1st Sess., 1902, XXXV, Part 7, pp. 7197-98 and 7357; *Tucson Citizen,* October 31, November 1, 5, 1902.

[24][Hon.] Marcus A. Smith, *Answer to Charges Against Arizona,* speeches given on January 28 and February 10, 1903 (Washington, D. C.: G.P.O., 1903, reprinted from *Congressional Record*), 13 pp.

John F. Wilson, Democratic delegate to Congress from 1899 to 1901 and 1903 to 1905.

— Special Collections, University of Arizona Library

to forget the fact that statehood was the end to be achieved — not just the means for the election of a political office-seeker. The Democratic journals were profuse in their praise for Marcus Smith in particular and the Democratic Party in general for promoting the statehood bill. These papers thought that the voters should show appreciation to the Democratic senators, who were called "attorneys for Arizona," in order to insure future support for the Omnibus Bill.[25]

On the other hand, the Republican newspapers contended that the Democrats in the Senate would support the bill anyway and that a Republican delegate was needed to draw the support of the Republicans in Congress for statehood.[26] Smith returned from a trip to Europe in time to campaign for Wilson and to assure the people that a delegate who could keep the support of the Democratic senators would be most useful in securing the passage of the statehood bill. In light of congressional activities after the election, however, it can be said that Morrison was more nearly correct when he said in a Phoenix address that "it would really make no difference which was elected as far as statehood was concerned."[27] The Democrats in the Senate would have favored the admission of the three territories even if Arizona had gone Repub-

[25]*Arizona Democrat,* October 8, 1902; *Phoenix Enterprise,* October 27, 1902; *Tucson Citizen,* November 1, 1902.
[26]*Arizona Daily Gazette,* June 26, September 27, 1902.
[27]*Ibid.,* October 16, 1902.

lican because, in the long run, Arizona and the other territories were more likely to send Democratic senators to Congress. Republicans who realized this would not have changed their opinions of the political aspects of the Omnibus Bill, unless Arizona had gone overwhelmingly Republican in 1902.

The Beveridge subcommittee investigation was of much greater importance to Arizona's statehood aspirations than was the 1902 election. A highly moral Progressive who had been greatly affected by muckraker literature, Beveridge used his "findings" to attack statehood as a scheme of business interests. In order to get the "facts" before the public, he explained to his friend, Albert Shaw, editor of the *Review of Reviews* and one of the best-known literary men in America, why some Democratic senators and Senator Quay were so eager to admit the territories. "The truth ought to be told," he wrote, "that a Democratic minority, standing as a unit now, knows that these territories will after the first Senators constantly send Democratic Senators to Congress and that is their only reason." Then he went on to flail Senators Quay and Bois Penrose of Pennsylvania and Senator W. A. Clark of Montana for pushing statehood to promote their personal mining and railroad schemes in Arizona and New Mexico.[28]

When a Pennsylvania political lieutenant of Quay's, William H. "Bull" Andrews, showed up in New Mexico and ran for delegate, in 1904, Beveridge was certain that his accusations were correct; Andrews was directing the building of a railroad, the bonds of which would advance in value in event of statehood. Senator Clark, of course, owned most of the stock in the United Verde Copper Company at Jerome and Senator Penrose's brother was interested in mines in southern Arizona.

Senator Beveridge reported a bill for the admission of Oklahoma shortly after the Fifty-seventh Congress convened again in December, 1902, but made no mention of Arizona and New Mexico. He seemed to like the so-called "American qualities" of the "Sooner" territory but harped upon the lack of schools, and the high degree of illiteracy in the other two territories.

One of Beveridge's friends, Senator Knute Nelson of Minnesota, spoke in the same vein in opposing Arizona statehood and was criticized facetiously by the *Arizona Republican* as follows: "We are informed that the verbatim notes of the Senate stenographer represented the honorable Knute Nelson, Senator from Minnesota and Norway, as

---

[28]Senator Albert J. Beveridge to Albert Shaw, November 3, 1903, quoted in Langston, pp. 33-35.

saying: 'Ay tank does fellairs en Arizona not beene enofe Amaracaines. To bay goot seetyzain, a fellair moost bay Amaracaine'."[29]

Senator Thomas R. Bard of California also joined the Beveridge tune, bluntly asserting that the people of Arizona and New Mexico were not intelligent enough to deserve statehood. Ex-Governor Murphy was so incensed by Bard's slander that he bitterly attacked the Senator in a public interview in San Francisco.[30] And the other half of Arizona's "one-two punch," Mark Smith, assailed him in Los Angeles. At a banquet in the latter city honoring Champ Clark of Missouri, in July, 1903, Smith humorously referred to the support given to Arizona by Senator Gallinger of far-away New Hampshire "while this man here [Bard] was saying: 'No, you cannot have statehood. You have some Mormons and some Indians down there.' " On the same occasion, Representative James McLachlan (a "Republican and accidental statesman," according to H. G. Otis, the anti-Arizona editor of the *Los Angeles Times*) piquantly said, "Mark Smith, God bless him! I'll never forget the eloquence with which he fought for statehood. The universal sentiment of this state was in favor of admitting Arizona to statehood."[31]

Following this incident, the Arizona press unleashed a barrage of editorials that helped to arouse the business community of southern California against Senator Bard and bring about his defeat in the state legislature in 1904. The following editorial in the *Tucson Citizen* was typical:

> In view of the admitted fact that Arizona pours not less than half a million dollars annually into the lap of Los Angeles, through the medium of summer visitors, and that Arizona's trade with California mounts to millions each year, Arizona feels that she has a right to complain to the people of California of the conduct of Senator Bard of that State when Arizona appealed for Statehood to the Congress. . . .[32]

Bard, along with Senators Nelson, Lodge, Aldrich, Platt, Hale, and others, supported Beveridge in his efforts to keep the Senate from acting upon the Omnibus Bill. They used filibuster techniques during 1903 and, on one occasion, Beveridge himself resorted to a very unorthodox device. For reasons of courtesy, no vote could be taken without the presence of the chairman of the Committee on Territories;

---

[29]*Arizona Republican,* January 20, 1903.

[30]Waldemar Westergaard, "Senator Thomas R. Bard and the Arizona-New Mexico Controversy," *Annual Publications,* Historical Society of Southern California, 1919, Vol. 11, pp. 11-13.

[31]*Ibid.,* p. 14; *Los Angeles Times,* July 26, 1903.

[32]*Tucson Citizen,* July 28, 1903.

so, at the crucial time, he secluded himself on the third floor of Gifford Pinchot's home for a week. The latter, who was President Roosevelt's Chief of the Forest Service, feared that statehood for Arizona and New Mexico would result in the wanton exploitation of lands and forest reserves, particularly in New Mexico.

The President himself shared Beveridge's feeling that the old Anglo-Saxon American was being threatened by other ethnic groups, including the Spanish in the Southwest, at the turn of the century; he, therefore, approved of the Senator's unusual parliamentary tactics to preclude action on the Omnibus Bill.[33] When the Phoenix city council learned that the President had committed himself to support the next ruse of the Beveridge coterie — the merger of Arizona and New Mexico into one state — it voted to change the name of Roosevelt Street to Cleveland Street.[34]

The goal of the anti-admission strategists in the jointure move was to make statehood so objectionable that those demanding it would of their own accord reject it.[35] By the spring of 1904, the statehood debate in Congress was being fought mainly along party lines, the Republicans for jointure and the Democrats against. On April 19, the House, on a strictly party division, passed a bill introduced by Congressman Edward L. Hamilton of Michigan to admit Oklahoma and the Indian Territory as one state and likewise the two territories of Arizona and New Mexico.[36] Delegates Bernard S. Rodey of New Mexico and Bird S. McGuire of Oklahoma approved of the measure, while J. F. Wilson of Arizona made a long, though futile, speech in opposition.[37]

The news of the Hamilton bill spread consternation in Arizona. Two groups were especially frantic: budding politicians whose opportunities would be limited with the state capitol located in Santa Fe; and the railroad and mining interests that had made plans to control a new state government of Arizona as outlined in the Omnibus Bill and that would be overwhelmed by a majority of the agricultural population of New Mexico, should the two territories be joined in one huge, Texas-like state.[38]

---

[33]Lamar, "The Reluctant Admission: The Struggle to Admit Arizona and New Mexico to the Union," in Ferris (ed.), *The American West: An Appraisal,* pp. 168-70.

[34]Westergaard, *Annual Publications,* Historical Society of Southern California, 1919, Vol. 11, p. 16.

[35]*Arizona Republican,* February 22, 27, 1903.

[36]*Congressional Record,* 58th Cong., 2d Sess., 1904, XXXVIII pp. 5-6, 4281, 5152.

[37]*Arizona Republican,* April 20, 1904.

[38]Howard A. Hubbard, "The Arizona Enabling Act and President Taft's Veto," *Pacific Historical Review,* Vol. 11 (1934), p. 315.

The Arizona press, of course, wasted no time in condemning the "asinine wisdom" of the House of Representatives. The *Tucson Citizen,* a Democratic publication at the time, said that the people of the territory would fight the merger scheme to the end and "depend on the Democrats of the Senate to prevent the consummation of the outrage."[39] The *Citizen* quoted two Arizonans, who had just returned from Washington, regarding the attitude of President Roosevelt on joint statehood. A Republican leader, Colonel William Herring, said that Roosevelt was not only favoring the proposition but was urging it upon the Republican members of both houses. Marcus Smith corroborated Herring's report, saying that "the merging of Arizona and New Mexico seems to be the President's pet scheme at this time." The *Citizen* urged the voters of Arizona to show their detestation of the conduct of the President and the Republican leaders by helping to defeat every Republican who ran for office in the fall elections.

The joint-statehood question was naturally an important issue in the electioneering for the post of delegate to Congress in 1904. The Democratic territorial convention scored an advantage in agreeing to run Marcus Smith, well-known for his Congressional battles to end the territorial status of Arizona. The convention also made a strong appeal for votes by endorsing William Randolph Hearst for the Presidency. Hearst, as a congressman from New York, had endeared himself to Arizonans by leading an investigating committee to the territory, following Beveridge's rushed tour in 1902, and by submitting a Democratic report favorable to single statehood to Congress. The Republican territorial convention nominated Benjamin A. Fowler for delegate to Congress; he was a leader in the movement to secure a dam in the Tonto Basin (Roosevelt Dam) and an irrigation project for the Salt River Valley. Governor Brodie and Judge Joseph Kibbey were chosen as delegates to the Republican national convention that nominated Theodore Roosevelt.

Because of the stand taken by the national Republican administration in favor of joint statehood and because of the failure of the Republican territorial convention to take a strong position on this issue, the Republican newspapers attempted to offset the Democratic advantage by questioning Smith's record on the issue. During the campaign Smith was accused of having joined with the former president of the territorial Council, Eugene S. Ives, in behalf of joint statehood in 1903. However, as we have seen, Ives came to the defense of his law partner and made public the telegram mentioned above whereby

---

[39]*Tucson Citizen,* April 20, 1904.

OFFICIAL BALLOT.

TUCSON PRECINCT NO. 1.

Election November 8, 1904.

PIMA COUNTY.

Name of Office Voted For.	REPUBLICAN.	DEMOCRATIC.	SOCIALIST PARTY.	PROHIBITION.	SOCIALIST LABOR.	INDEPENDENT
TERRITORIAL DELEGATE TO CONGRESS.	☐ Benjamin A. Fowler.	☐ Marcus A. Smith	☐ Francis A. Shaw	☐ O. Gibson.	☐ J. A. Leach.	☐
JOINT COUNCILMAN.	☐ E. M. Dickerman	☐ N. W. Bernard	☐ A. M. Feldman			
ASSEMBLYMAN	☐ L. G. Davis	☐ M. G. Samaniego				
ASSEMBLYMAN	☐ Hal. C. Kennedy	☐ S. W. Purcell				
ASSEMBLYMAN	☐ Thos F. Wilson	☐ Ed. C. Taylor	☐ A. G. Swanson			
SUPERVISOR.	☐ Phil. S. Hughes	☐ John N. Brown				
SUPERVISOR.	☐ C. F. Richardson	☐ Chas. E. Hardy				
SHERIFF.	☐ Nabor Pacheco	☐ F. E. Murphy	☐ A. C. Rosewell			
TREASURER.	☐ John W. Bogan	☐ Chas. F. Hoff				
RECORDER.		☐ Chas. A. Shibell		☐ A. M. Reeder		
DISTRICT ATTORNEY	☐ Benton Dick	☐ F. M. Hartman				
PROBATE JUDGE.	☐ W. J. Kirkpatrick	☐ Alonzo Haley				
COUNTY SCHOOL SUPERINTENDENT	☐ Thos. Hughes. Sr.	☐ C. O. Rouse				
SURVEYOR.	☐ Wm. B. Alexander	☐ C. Barthelemy				
JUSTICE OF THE PEACE.	☐ O. T. Richey	☐ Charles H. Tully				
JUSTICE OF THE PEACE	☐ W. H. Culver	☐ S. L. Rodgers				
CONSTABLE	☐ J. E. Dufton	☐ R. E. Kelly				
CONSTABLE.	☐ Frank Avila	☐ Manuel Orta				

— Arizona Pioneers' Historical Society

Official ballot for a Pima County precinct in the 1904 election.

Smith, then Delegate in Washington, had advised the legislature to memorialize Congress against joint statehood.[40]

The *Arizona Blade* (Florence), one of several newspapers that sided with the Democratic candidate in the controversy, printed the Ives telegram and the following arguments in Smith's defense:

> This nails another campaign lie that should not have fooled anyone in the first place. Mark Smith's position on single statehood for Arizona is so well known as to surprise one at the simplicity of the republican press in trying to misrepresent him on that question. He has thrice passed bills through Congress giving Arizona statehood, only to have them defeated in the senate by the republican majority and was one of the first men in Arizona to denounce, in vigorous terms, the joint statehood scheme. He has never missed an opportunity to speak against it in the press and on the platform.[41]

The Democrats tried to picture Smith as an "all Arizona man." It was claimed that, in contrast to Smith's many years of work in behalf of government reclamation of arid lands, beginning back in 1887, Fowler would be a "private serving man" for the landowners of the Salt River Valley. The latter's candidacy was not helped any when George Maxwell, a friend with whom he had done lobbying in Washington, made some statements in favor of joint statehood.[42] Smith, as usual, was elected, this time by a count of 10,394 to 9,522 for Fowler, and took his seat in Congress in March, 1905.

The *Arizona Republican,* which had supported Fowler, gave Smith a backhanded compliment after the election. Calling him one of the ablest campaigners in the United States, the paper said that Smith was especially effective with an Arizona audience. Because he had been campaigning in the territory for nearly twenty years, he knew perhaps a majority of the voters by name and how to appeal to the dominant feeling of the locality. "Smith's single text was the joint statehood bill," said the *Republican.* "He assured his party that his election was necessary to defeat the bill. . . . In addition to that, Smith had the solid support of the Mormon church in Maricopa and Graham counties."

Yet Smith carried only six of the thirteen counties, losing his own, Pima, by two hundred votes, as well as adjacent Santa Cruz in the southern part of the territory; he also lost Maricopa, then a Democratic fortress, by 250, in addition to the northern counties of Apache, Navajo, Coconino, and Yavapai. The *Republican* considered Fowler's race a creditable one considering that he was relatively unknown at the begin-

---

[40]*Arizona Republican,* October 15, 1904.
[41]*Arizona Blade,* October 22, 1904.
[42]*Ibid.*

The Coconino Sun

is 327. The complete returns will increase his plurality to 375. The democratic county ticket is elected, with two exceptions. Fisk, republican, is elected recorder by a large majority. Butler, republican, gets the long term as supervisor.

MOHAVE COUNTY.

A special from Kingman says: Although Kingman, the county seat, is normally democratic by three to one, it gave Smith but 10 plurality. Other precincts in the county have brought

kins 1433, Hull 1384, Anderson 1379, Bradley 1256, Biles 1216.

Sheriff—Lowry 1784, Roberts 1281.

Treasurer—Wright 1486, Cline 1182.

District Attorney—Ellinwood 1635, Clark 1309.

Recorder—Mosher 1707, Jordan 1081.

Probate Judge—Hicks 1607, Flora 1114.

School Superintendent—Jolly 1807, Perkins 977.

COCONINO COUNTY.

The Republicans Win the Majority of Their Ticket—A Full Vote Polled.—Two Precincts to be Heard From.

VOTE OF COCONINO COUNTY.
ELECTION NOVEMBER 8, 1904.

NAME OF CANDIDATES	Flagstaff.	Williams.	Maine.	Bellmont.	Grand Canyon.	Cañon Diablo.	Mormon Lake.	Grand View.	Sedona.	Fredonia.	Anita.	Tuba City.	Total.	Majority.
Del. to Congress—														
M. A. Smith, D..	257	180	13	4	17	5	12	..	7	..	..	..	486	
R. A. Fowler, R..	296	162	17	9	19	5	3	..	7	..	..	..	535	44
O. Gibson, P ..	...	...	..	..	..	..	..	..	..	..	..	..	....	
Francis A. Shaw, S..	...	...	..	..	..	..	..	..	..	..	..	..	....	
J. A. Leach, S. L..	...	...	..	..	..	..	..	..	..	..	..	..	....	
Council—														
J. F. Ruffin, D..	260	157	16	9	15	4	2	1	14	..	..	..	478	
John H. Page, R..	308	188	20	7	20	9	13	22	4	..	..	..	591	113
Assembly—														
Charles A. Neal, D..	379	244	17	7	21	9	4	7	..	..	..	..	597	167
John Clark, R..	260	92	14	7	11	2	11	17	7	..	..	..	430	..
Sheriff—														
A. T. Cornish, D. ..	212	135	14	5	18	5	1	5	4	..	..	..	419	..
Harry Henderson, R..	338	235	22	11	19	8	14	18	6	..	..	..	637	243
District Att'y—														
Henry F. Ashurst, D..	267	238	18	6	18	6	7	5	9	..	..	..	572	69
Edward M. Doe, R..	304	121	16	9	20	4	8	18	3	..	..	..	503	..
Probate Judge—														
R. H. Jones, D. .. .	223	146	9	4	7	4	1	3	8	..	..	..	405	..
A. E. Douglass, R..	349	193	26	12	25	10	14	18	4	..	..	..	651	246
Recorder—														
G. N. Baty, D..	204	122	6	4	9	2	1	2	3	..	..	..	353	..
Harry C. Hibben, R..	363	234	29	12	28	11	14	20	8	..	..	..	719	366
Treasurer—														
Thomas Devine, D..	347	200	18	9	20	8	6	3	9	..	..	..	622	190
Joseph R. Treat, R..	225	149	17	6	12	4	7	10	2	..	..	..	432	..
Supervisor—														
George Babbitt, D..	329	110	9	5	20	12	6	16	7	..	..	..	514	..
F. O. Polson, R. ..	240	184	26	11	13	1	8	17	4	..	..	..	504	..
Supervisor—														
Jacob Salzman, D..	202	222	5	2	15	4	4	2	5	..	..	..	461	..
Ralph H. Cameron, R..	314	145	29	13	28	7	11	19	7	..	..	..	568	..
Surveyor—														
W. H. Power, D..	206	134	13	4	..	6	3	4	8	..	..	..	468	..
E. E. Hall, R..	244	190	14	9	..	6	8	18	2	..	..	..	501	25
School Supt.—														
Harrison Conrad, D..	256	166	17	7	16	8	4	4	8	..	..	..	470	..
J. S. Amundson, R ..	308	172	18	9	18	4	11	19	2	..	..	..	561	91
Justice of Peace—														
L. L. Burns, D..	237	...	..	..	..	..	..	..	..	..	..	..	...	..
John O. Harrington, R	327	...	..	..	..	..	..	..	..	..	..	..	...	..
Constable—														
Thos. A. Gandos, D..	274	...	..	..	..	..	..	..	..	..	..	..	...	..
Wm. C. Bayless, R..	292	...	..	..	..	..	..	..	..	..	..	..	...	..

The election, while exciting, passed off without anything occurring to mar the day. The vote was an increased one over last year. There were something over 1100 votes cast in the county.

Flagstaff cast 606 votes as against 598 in 1902. Williams cast 387, as against 392 two years ago.

The republicans elected were John H. Page for the council. H. C. Hibben for recorder. Harry Henderson for sheriff. A. E. Douglass for probate judge. R. H. Cameron for supervisor. F. O. Polson for supervisor. E. E. Hall for surveyor. J. S. Anderson for superintendent of schools.

The successful democrats were C. A. Neal for assembly. H. F. Ashurst for district attorney. Thomas Devine for treasurer.

The precincts of Fredonia and Tuba have not been heard from in detail. A telegram from Fredonia states that 19 votes were cast and 17 were for the republican ticket, thus adding that number to each republican candidate and Tuba is expected to increase the vote for the republican ticket.

Election returns for Coconino County for the election of 1904, as given in The Coconino Sun, November 12, 1904. This list of candidates is especially interesting because of the number of famous names in Arizona history — Smith, Fowler, Ashurst, Babbitt, Cameron, and A. E. Douglass, for example.

ning of the campaign and the fact that the Democratic party had a majority of possibly two thousand in the territory.[43]

Governor Brodie did not, of course, have to run for his appointive office; he was, nevertheless, castigated by the Tucson Democratic newspaper for a personal pledge which he had made to the last Republican territorial convention. Brodie was charged with willfully deceiving the representatives of his party by stating that President Roosevelt did not favor the merging of Arizona and New Mexico.[44]

There was no doubt how the Governor himself stood on the question of jointure, however. When the territorial legislature convened in January, 1905, he spoke against the merger bill then pending in the United States Senate. He said that his two-year investigation of this subject showed conclusively that people of all classes and conditions opposed joint statehood. In response to Brodie's appeal, both houses of the Assembly unanimously passed and forwarded to Congress the following resolution protesting against the Senate proposal:

> We insist that such is without precedent in the American history. It threatens to fasten upon us a Government that would be neither of, by, nor for the people of Arizona. It would be a government without the consent of the governed. It humiliates our pride, violates our tradition and would subject us to the domination of another commonwealth of different traditions, customs, and aspirations. With the most kindly feelings toward the people of New Mexico, we must protest against this proposed union and would rather remain forever a territory than to accept statehood under such conditions.[45]

Though the question of joint statehood was the single most important matter confronting the Twenty-third Legislative Assembly, there were other concerns, too. By the time Governor Brodie addressed the legislature in January, 1905, much economic progress had been made in Arizona. He reported optimistically: "A review of the advancement of Arizona made in the past two years widens the source from which comes the pride we feel in our commonwealth. Industrial development has been most substantial; our mines have produced wealth beyond that of many states of the union; and in copper production I believe we occupy second place to Montana."

The Governor also lauded the federal government for having selected sites for the Theodore Roosevelt Dam on the Salt River and for the Laguna Dam on the Colorado.[46] With these projects, the agri-

---

[43]*Arizona Republican,* November 10, 1904.
[44]*Tucson Citizen,* April 20, 1904.
[45]*Journals of the Twenty-Third Legislative Assembly,* 1905, pp. 26-27.
[46]*New York Times,* April 3, October 15, 1903.

cultural future of Arizona looked good. Once again, however, Brodie was critical of the territory's tax system. He thought it unfair that mines producing $38,700,000 in ore should contribute only $178,000 in land and improvement taxes to the territorial treasury. Why shouldn't a mine operator also pay on his production, like the stockman on his cattle?[47]

Less than a month after addressing the legislature, Governor Brodie retired from office on February 14, 1905, to accept an appointment as the assistant chief of the Records and Pensions Bureau of the War Department in Washington, D.C.[48] In his place, President Roosevelt announced the promotion of Attorney General Joseph H. Kibbey to the governorship. Several days elapsed, however, before Congress got around to approving the appointment; during the interim, Secretary W. P. Nichols acted as governor. Unlike some of his predecessors, Brodie had managed to remain free of scandal and dissension. Even the Democratic legislature held him, a Republican, in esteem and presented him with a saber upon his retirement from office.

Brodie did not remain long in the nation's capital. Later in 1905, he was made a lieutenant-colonel and sent to the Philippines. There he served as military secretary and adjutant of the Department of Visayas and as a member of the Board on Church Claims. Returning to the States in 1907, he was assigned as adjutant-general of the Department of the Dakotas from 1907 to 1911 and in the same capacity in California until his retirement in 1913. His final years were spent in Haddonfield, New Jersey, where he died in 1918.[49]

The following story, which appeared in the *New York Globe,* indicates that Brodie never lost his love for Arizona after leaving the territory:

> Henry Miller in the first act of "The Great Divide" at Daly's theatre is now "toting" a big blue barrelled Colt's 45 revolver which has a history. The actor-manager came into possession of it in a peculiar way. A few days ago a bellboy at the Hotel Wolcott, where the actor-manager lives, brought in to Mr. Miller a card on which was written in a sprawly hand, "Col. Alexander O. Brodie, Arizona." The name was unfamiliar, but surmising correctly as it eventuated — that the caller was a citizen of the picturesque commonwealth in which the first and second scenes of "The Great Divide" are located, had come to express his opinion of the play, Mr. Miller decided to receive him. Presently a heavy tread echoed along

---

[47]*Journals of the Twenty-Third Legislative Assembly,* 1905.

[48]Telegram of Governor Alexander O. Brodie to President Theodore Roosevelt, from Phoenix, Arizona, February 1, 1905, Record Group 48, Appointment Papers.

[49]*Prescott Journal-Miner,* November 28, 1913; see also, Smalley manuscript in the Brodie Papers, Arizona Pioneers' Historical Society.

the corridor and there entered over six feet and 200 pounds of square shouldered, rugged humanity which threatened destruction. Mr. Miller then discovered that his visitor was none other than the redoubtable "Alec" Brodie, formerly lieutenant colonel of Roosevelt's Rough Riders, and later by appointment of his former commander, governor of Arizona. On his left hand was a livid scar, the reminder of a Spanish bullet received at Las Guasimas.

"I saw your show at Daly's last night," said Col. Brodie after the exchange of greetings, "and it reminded me so much of home I couldn't pass up the opportunity of coming around and telling you how much I enjoyed it. Why, when your curtain went up on your 'roof of the world' scene in the second act, I could almost feel myself back on the brink of the Grand Canyon. And as for the cabin in the first act, I've ranched it in many a one just like it. But there was one thing which was not right — your gun. Nobody out in Arizona carries a nickle-plated smoke wagon like yours. It would be too easy a mark. In the moonlight it would be a dead giveaway. Our revolvers are all blue barrelled, so as to be more easily concealed. Like this one."

And with a quick motion the Rough Rider produced from somewhere near the rear waist line a formidable looking weapon, dark blue in color, save as to the handle, which was black gutta percha and ominously notched.

"Now I want you to do me a favor," continued Col. Brodie. "And that is to wear this gun in the show. It'll play the part all right. See those notches? Well, they mean a dozen Greasers and Indians that this trinket has turned into good men. I never thought it would go on the stage, but I reckon my days of fighting Indians and Mexicans are over and that forty-five wouldn't be very happy if it had to lead an aimless life."

Mr. Miller accepted the offer gladly, and the shiny pistol which did service all last season at the Princess has been relegated to Daly's property room.[50]

---

[50]McClintock File, Phoenix Public Library.

Chapter 20

Water for the Valley:
The Kibbey Administration

Pleased with the Senate's unanimous confirmation of Joseph H. Kibbey as the sixteenth territorial governor of Arizona, the *Arizona Journal-Miner* editorialized on March 1, 1905:

> President Roosevelt has done many good things for Arizona, but nothing he has done has resulted in such general and manifest satisfaction as the appointment of Judge Joseph H. Kibbey to be governor of the territory. . . . His intimate knowledge of the needs and conditions of the territory affords him an immediate command of the situation and his recognized strength of character, tempered by an admirable tact, peculiarly fit him for the difficulties of his office. . . . To paraphrase an expression frequently heard lately in Prescott relative to Judge Kibbey's appointment, "Lucky Arizona."[1]

The newspaper's evaluation of Kibbey's eminent qualifications for the office were not unfounded.

A native of Indiana, Kibbey was born on March 4, 1853, at Centreville, and attended Earlham College, a Quaker institution at Richmond. Following brief experiences in teaching school in Arkansas and in merchandising in Illinois, he began reading law in the office of his father, a distinguished judge and friend of Abraham Lincoln. After practicing his chosen profession for more than a decade in Indiana, Kibbey moved to Arizona in 1888 as legal adviser of a large irrigation company at Florence. The next year he was appointed by President Benjamin Harrison — who knew Kibbey and his father — as an associate justice of the Supreme Court of Arizona. Serving as a trial judge in a district comprising Pinal, Graham, and Gila counties, he made an enviable record for his courageous and impartial decisions relative to mining and irrigation questions. Near the end of his tenure he was

---

[1] *Arizona Journal-Miner*, March 1, 1905.

brought to Phoenix to preside in the bitterly-contested case of *Wormser et al.* vs. *Salt River Valley Canal Company* (1892).[2]

This lawsuit arose out of a dispute between landowners and water-distributing companies over abuses by the latter in the delivery of water, particularly during periods of drought. The companies were accused of treating the public water supply as corporate property that they often allocated to their own members and denied to prior users. But the so-called "Kibbey Decision" in this case held, in brief, that the irrigator who first puts water to beneficial use has the prior right thereto as against later claimants; furthermore the "water belongs to the land" and is not the "floating" possession of the company to dispense as it chooses.

At first, the canal companies refused to accept their role as distributing agents only and circumvented the decree. As a result, the farmers of the Salt River Valley were unlawfully dominated and at the mercy of companies that controlled the public water supply as though it were their own. In 1901 and again in 1904, however, the Arizona Supreme Court upheld the "Kibbey Decision," and the doctrine of prior appropriation was then enforced.[3] Today, the principles that Judge Kibbey promulgated in his revolutionary decree are used by courts in much of the arid West to determine water rights.

Replaced on the bench by a Cleveland Democrat, Kibbey took up the practice of law in Phoenix. Among his clients were many so-called "old righters," who were seeking to recover water rights they thought had been taken from them by the Grand and Arizona Canal companies. Kibbey also became involved in politics, serving both as city attorney of Phoenix and as assistant district attorney of Maricopa County. In every campaign year he took to the stump in behalf of the party's candidates and, in 1902, was himself elected as a member of the upper house of the territorial legislature where he served as minority leader. In 1904, he was appointed to be attorney general of Arizona, having served as chairman of the Republican territorial committee during the same year.

But Kibbey's most outstanding contribution to Arizona history before becoming governor was in connection with the Salt River Valley

---

[2]*Wormser et al.* vs. *Salt River Valley Canal Company,* Case No. 708 (1892), Federal District Court for Arizona, 3d Judicial District, Phoenix. Decision, Joseph H. Kibbey, Judge. [Typewritten copy of decision is in the Arizona Department of Library and Archives.] See also, *Arizona Daily Gazette,* April 6-16, 1892, for the same decision, and *Arizona Weekly Gazette,* April 7, 1892, for a chart of allocations of water to the various canals for specific years.

[3]*Slosser* vs. *Salt River Valley Canal Company* (1901), 7 Arizona 376; *Thomas Brockman* vs. *The Grand Canal Company* (1904), 8 Arizona 451.

422

Joseph H. Kibbey, governor of Arizona Territory from 1905 to 1909.

Project, the nation's first multi-purpose reclamation project. Perhaps the fact that the Kibbey plan for the organization of the Salt River Valley Water Users Association has been the pattern for all similar groups that have been formed in connection with federal water-storage projects, is in itself a lasting monument to his work in irrigation law. Whereas many subsequent reclamation developments have been planned and engineered for previously unsettled public lands, the Salt River Project was organized to save an existing community.

Today when one gazes about at the green lawns, rich fields of cotton and alfalfa, swimming pools, and the burgeoning population, it is difficult to conceive that the "Valley of the Sun" was once confronted alternately with the uncontrolled disasters of flood and drought. By the 1890s, irrigation farming in the valley had reached the point where a water-storage plan was needed so that water from wet seasons could be saved for use in drier periods. The normal flow of the Salt River could not fill with a steady and sufficient supply all the canals that had been constructed. The fact that water was plentiful, if it could be controlled, was emphasized by the great flood of 1891. Torrential rains, in February of that year, brought the deluge; the Salt overflowed its banks, washed away the Tempe railroad bridge near Hayden's Butte, and damaged houses as far north as Jackson Street in downtown Phoenix.[4] As usual, the waters receded and rushed on to the Colorado River as quickly as they had risen.

---

[4]*Arizona Republican,* February 20, 1891.

Later in the decade, a long drought descended upon the valley. Water became such a precious commodity that armed, desperate men patrolled the canals to protect their rights. As the rivers dried up, at least a third of the 200,000 acres of farmlands was forced out of cultivation, livestock died, orchards became firewood, and families packed up and left, expecting settlements like Phoenix to die on the banks of the Salt River. Then the cycle of natural calamities was completed, and the misery compounded, when the rains finally came and turned the drought into a new disaster. A flash-flood destroyed the brush diversion dams along the river. But the water was gone as soon as it appeared, serving no purpose except to dramatize the need not only for water but for water control. Out of this background of destruction and despair came the realization that some means must be found to assure a permanent and dependable water supply if the valley were to prosper and continue to grow.

A huge storage dam in the mountains above the valley was the obvious answer. A good site had been located back in 1889 by a committee appointed by the Maricopa County Board of Supervisors. County Surveyor W. M. "Billy" Breakenridge (who had ridden with Sheriff John Behan during Tombstone's turbulent days), James H. McClintock, and John Norton (a farmer and superintendent of the Arizona Canal Company) had selected a good dam site on the Salt River below its confluence with Tonto Creek. But with plenty of water in the river at that time, the storage project was no more than a topic for discussion.

The idea was not forgotten, however. In 1896, the National Irrigation Congress, meeting in Phoenix, enthusiastically endorsed the project. Following this meeting, Arthur P. Davis, an engineer for the United States Geological Survey, surveyed the Tonto Basin site and described it as one possessing every requirement for a successful reclamation project.[5] Then in August, 1900, another committee (composed of Benjamin Fowler, a Glendale farmer and teacher; Vernon Clark, a young businessman; and John Norton) reported favorably on the project to a mass meeting of citizens in Phoenix.[6] The engineering problems of constructing a dam sixty miles from the nearest railroad and more than eighty miles from the land to be watered seemed formidable though not insurmountable.

Financing was a different story, however. There was not enough private capital available in Arizona to carry out a venture that would

[5]"Investigation in Arizona," by Arthur P. Davis, in U. S. House, *Second Annual Report of the Reclamation Service,* 1902–1903, 58th Cong., 2d Sess., 1904, House Doc. No. 44, p. 71.
[6]*Arizona Daily Gazette,* August 31, 1900.

The Salt River flood of 1891 washed out the Tempe Bridge, leaving Phoenix without train service for three months. The flood also caused extensive destruction in the capital city.

cost an estimated two-to-five million dollars. Yet, while various plans were being discussed and discarded as unworkable, conditions were getting worse. So, in the spring of 1901, when the flow of the Salt River was down to 800 miner's inches (a miner's inch is roughly 11 and 1/5 gallons per minute passing a given point), Fowler was sent to Washington, D.C., to plead the valley's cause and to request congressional authority for the Territory of Arizona to exceed its debt limit and to issue bonds for the construction of a dam.

At first discouraged, Fowler soon joined forces with two reclamation zealots from Nevada, a lobbyist named George Maxwell and Representative Francis Newlands. A climate for favorable legislation was generated by the succession of Teddy Roosevelt to the Presidency. Interested in the West, and an ardent protagonist of the preservation of the country's natural resources, Roosevelt asked for a federal irrigation law in his first message to Congress. And on June 17, 1902, he signed the Hansbrough-Newlands Reclamation Act.[7] As originally drafted, the bill would have provided federal loans for projects on public

---

[7] *U. S. Statutes at Large,* Vol. XXXII, 57th Cong., 1st Sess., 1902, Chap. 1093, pp. 388-90.

lands only, but Fowler and Maxwell convinced the lawmakers that the offer of assistance should also be extended to private lands already settled and cleared by homesteaders at their own expense. It seemed more important to save an existing community like the Salt River Valley than to create new ones. Before a loan could be obtained for any project, however, there had to be a party of the second part to contract for the money and to repay it in ten installments to the federal reserve fund, which was originally built up from the sale of public lands. Unfortunately, there was no precedent to follow.

There were many local problems to be considered before an organization could be formed. Some means had to be found to guarantee the prior water rights of farmers and the interests of eleven canal companies without abrogating the larger community needs. Men who had fought for water with guns and in the courts would not tolerate interference from the federal government and had to be convinced that a storage dam would be mutually advantageous for all. On August 2, 1902, Fowler, Maxwell, and Newlands spoke to a mass meeting at the courthouse plaza.[8] They emphasized that prior rights were valuable only where a water scarcity existed and that the new dam would supply plenty of water for both present users and the influx of people that was sure to come. Before the Phoenix meeting adjourned, Fowler was appointed to head a committee of citizens, who represented each of the eleven canal companies in the valley and the towns of Tempe, Mesa, Glendale, and Phoenix. The committee was formed to work out the means whereby the benefits of water storage might be secured. At this point, Judge Kibbey was employed as legal counsel to draft articles for the Salt River Valley Water Users' Association.

On February 4, 1903, the articles were published, and the association was legally incorporated five days later.[9] By mid-July, some four thousand landowners had signed the association's membership roster, pledging 200,000 acres — each acre representing a share of stock in the association — for the construction of the dam in Tonto Basin.[10] John P. Orme was elected the first president of the Water Users' and in October, Louis C. Hill, engineer for the U. S. Reclamation Service, arrived to take charge of the planning for what was to be the world's highest dam.[11]

---

[8]*Arizona Daily Gazette,* August 3, 5, 1902.

[9]See the Articles of Incorporation of the Salt River Valley Water Users' Association, 1903, in "Investigation in Arizona," *Second Annual Report of the Reclamation Service,* 1902–1903, 58th Cong., 2d Sess., House Doc. No. 44, pp. 76-87.

[10]*New York Times,* April 19, October 15, 1903.

[11]"Investigation in Arizona," *Second Annual Report of the Reclamation Service,* 1902–1903, p. 72.

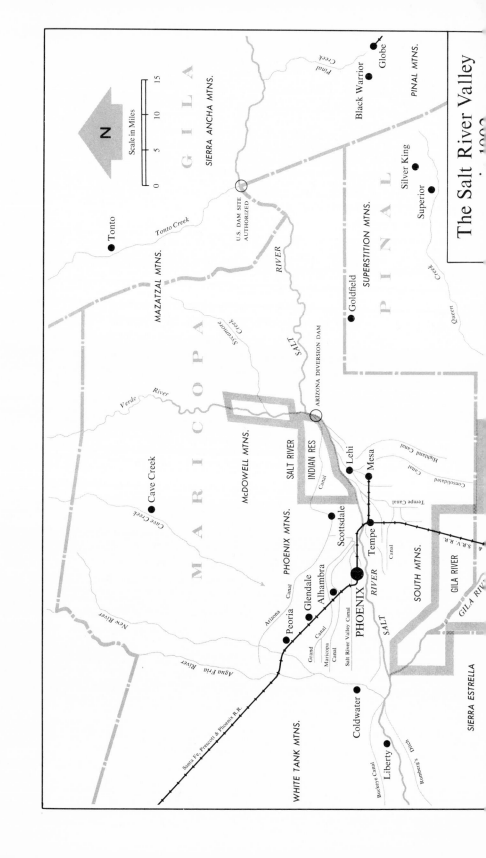

The Salt River Valley

There was much preliminary work to be done before construction could begin on the dam itself. Because of the remoteness of the dam site, 112 miles of access roads were built. The most important was the Roosevelt Road, now known as the Apache Trail, from Mesa.[12] Over this narrow, dangerous route, twenty-mule teams pulled huge, heavily laden freight wagons around sharp turns and over dizzying heights. A second road ran out of Globe, and another was built to a new sawmill, thirty miles away in the pine-covered Sierra Ancha Mountains. This sawmill furnished more than three million board feet of lumber for use at the dam. Another source of local materials was the large deposits of clay and limestone that were converted into cement at a mill built near the dam site. Fuel for the kiln had to be freighted from California, but electricity was furnished, for both the cement mill and the construction equipment, by an auxiliary dam erected twenty miles up the Salt River. Despite some difïculty with hot springs, which emitted a steam-like vapor that raised the temperature to as much as 130 degrees, a 500-foot tunnel was dug through solid rock to divert the river around the site.

On October 12, 1903, the Secretary of the Interior approved the awarding of contracts to the following: Wilcox and Rose, Riverside, California, for erecting a building for the manufacture of cement; Hendrie & Bolthoff, Denver, Colorado, for the electric motors required in the mill; Babcock Electric Manufacturing Company, for the generators for the temporary power plant; Stillwell-Bierce and Smith-Vaile Company, for the water wheels for same; Allis-Chalmers Company, for the machinery for the manufacture of cement; James R. Thorpe, for a telephone line from the Arizona dam to Livingstone.[13] While this preliminary work was underway, a contract was awarded to John M. O'Rourke & Co., of Galveston, Texas, on April 8, 1905, for the construction of what is known today as Theodore Roosevelt Dam.

One of the most unusual towns in Arizona history was built for the construction workers. Now under the waters of Roosevelt Lake, the site for the original town of Roosevelt was selected by the engineers who surveyed the region. It was divided into two parts, that nearest the

---

[12]Letter of Charles Walcott, Director of the U. S. Geological Survey, to the Secretary of the Interior, from Washington, D. C., January 19, 1904, Record Group 48, Territorial Papers; the road was authorized by an act of Congress on January 21, 1904, *U. S. Statutes at Large,* Vol. XXXIII, 58th Cong., 2d Sess., 1904, Chap. 6, p. 6.

[13]"Investigation in Arizona," *Second Annual Report of the Reclamation Service,* p. 72.

Stage stop in the original town of Roosevelt.

dam being reserved for the use of the government, while the rest was laid off in town lots. The rules laid down for settlers were simple but effective. Title to the lots remained with the government, and parties who moved in did so with the understanding that they would someday be flooded out. They also accepted the condition that the lots had to be immediately occupied with a residence or business. No saloons, gambling halls, or questionable businesses were permitted on the main street. Within a short time the town was settled, a school and a hall for religious and other meetings erected, a water supply and a sewage disposal system provided, a stage line and daily mail service from Globe secured, and telephone service with Globe (43 miles away) and Phoenix (75 miles away) established.

The usual businessmen — the baker, the druggist, and a liveryman — were soon operating.

When a barber drifted in, he took over a hot spring flowing from a nearby cavern and provided the inhabitants of Roosevelt with the luxury of a hot bath; the long line of citizens with towels and soap on Sunday morning attested to his shrewdness. The town hall was used for meetings of the Salvation Army, and as a church, a theater, a dance hall, and a restaurant. Morally, Roosevelt was ahead of most western towns. Drunkenness was practically unknown. Bloodshed at the lively dances was avoided by "fair play." Since men outnumbered the women three to one, each got a tag. Numbers 1 to 20 could be on the floor for the first dance, 21-40 for the next, and so forth. This "life as usual" approach of people who knew that their town would soon be unceremoniously torn down might have seemed profligate to Easterners, but not to the dam builders.[14]

As it turned out, a better location for the dam could not have been chosen. Between the steep walls and on a tough sandstone foundation, an arched gravity structure was built of native stone, some chunks as large as fifty cubic feet in size. A total of 343,000 cubic yards of stone and 338,000 barrels of cement was dumped into the world's largest masonry dam. However, due to floods that filled excavations and destroyed much equipment, the first stone was not laid until September 20, 1906, just a year after the planned beginning date. The dam was not completed until February 5, 1911, more floods having brought additional delays. It took nearly five years to complete the structure, which is 170 feet thick at the base, tapering to a 16-foot roadway at the top. Including spillways, it stretches more than a thousand feet across the mouth of the canyon and towers above 284 feet of flood water.

Other statistics reveal that seventeen men lost their lives in the construction of Roosevelt Dam. Several workmen drowned after falling into the river. Al Sieber, the famous scout, lost his life on February 19, 1907, purportedly when he was trying to save some of the Apache road builders under his supervision from a boulder that rolled down a hillside near the dam.[15] Five more men were killed during the construction of the Granite Reef diversion dam. The latter was built below the juncture of the Salt and Verde rivers to raise the level of the water and to divert it into two main canals. The Arizona Canal became the waterway for the north side of the valley; the South Canal served the needs of lands stretching from the Mesa-Tempe area westward to Laveen. The irrigation arterial system was constructed with the use of U. S. Geological Survey maps of valley lands in the vicinity of Phoenix and Mesa.[16] Altogether, the federal government advanced more than

---

[14]*New York Tribune,* May 1, 1905.

[15]Dan L. Thrapp, *Al Sieber: Chief of Scouts* (Norman: University of Oklahoma Press, 1964), pp. 400-401. There is some doubt about the cause of Sieber's death. Thrapp refers to some evidence indicating that the Apaches might have pushed the huge rock down on Sieber.

[16]"Investigation in Arizona," *Second Annual Report of the Reclamation Service,* pp. 72 *et seq.* Plates V and VI in this report are maps of the Salt River Valley.

$10,000,000 to construct the Roosevelt Dam, but the Salt River Project had repaid every dollar by 1955.[17]

While the dam was under construction, Joseph Kibbey served more than four years as governor of the Territory of Arizona. When he assumed his duties on March 7, 1905, the Twenty-third Legislative Assembly was already in session. Very quickly he took up the gauntlet left by Brodie and assumed leadership of the opposition to the joint-statehood-with-New Mexico movement, even though it had the endorsement of President Roosevelt.[18] His insistence upon a fair hearing for both sides was so well recognized, his difference with the President so consistent, and his attitude so dignified, that the battle with the national administration was eventually won without loss of confidence on either side. Kibbey officially stated his viewpoint on statehood three days after he assumed the governorship. In a written message to the legislature he suggested that Congress was not fully aware of the sentiment of the people in Arizona and recommended that the legislature authorize the holding of a special election to determine the true feelings of the voters on the statehood question.[19] Despite the Governor's letter, however, the legislature took no action in 1905.

The fight against joint statehood was not left solely to the politi-

Roosevelt Dam under construction in 1908.

— Arizona Pioneers' Historical Society

Theodore Roosevelt as Moses dedicating Roosevelt Dam on March 18, 1911. This cartoon appeared in the Arizona Republic *the following day.*

A MODERN INSTANCE

"And Moses lifted up his hand and with his rod smote the rock twice and the water came out abundantly and the congregation drank and their beasts also." Numbers 20:11

— Arizona Pioneers' Historical Society

cians. The railroad and mine owners used their influence against jointure, and, in so doing, voiced the sentiments of the large majority of Arizona citizens.[20] When another congressional delegation arrived in October, 1905, the Arizona investors rolled out the red carpet and received the group royally. A special train carried the visitors to places of interest in the territory. The train consisted of a buffet car, the private car of Superintendent McGovern of the Southern Pacific; the private car of Colonel Epes Randolph, superintendent of the Arizona branch lines of the Southern Pacific; the private car of F. M. Murphy, president of the Santa Fe, Prescott, and Phoenix lines; and three additional private cars occupied by the congressional party. During the first part of the trip, Walter Douglas, general manager of the Copper Queen

[17]See Stephen Shadegg, *Arizona: An Adventure in Irrigation* (Phoenix: Jahn-Tyler, 1949); Frank Crehan, "Historic Milestones in U. S. Reclamation," *Arizona Highways,* Vol. 37, No. 4 (1961), pp. 26-31; articles by Bert Fireman in the *Phoenix Gazette,* March 6, 1961, *et seq.;* "Reclamation's Golden Jubilee," *The Current News,* Salt River Project, Special Issue (April, 1952); and "Arizona Grows Where Water Flows," *Arizona Days and Ways* (*Arizona Republic* Sunday Supplement), March 12, 1961.

[18]"Roosevelt's Message Recommending Joint Statehood," in *Tucson Citizen,* December 5, 1905.

[19]*Journals of the Twenty-Third Legislative Assembly,* pp. 212-17.

[20]*Arizona Republican,* December 23, 1905.

interests in Arizona, and Superintendent S. J. Simmons, general manager of the El Paso and Southwestern Railroad, also had their private cars hooked onto the train.

The visitors were impressed by this welcome and especially by a novel reception given in their honor at Metcalf. There, a stope in one of the big mines was transformed into a banquet room and lighted by electricity; the legislators were served by well-trained Negro waiters in dress suits. In commenting on the tour, Congressman E. S. Minor of Wisconsin expressed the feeling of the entire delegation. After explaining that the men had come to Arizona unofficially to study conditions in the territory firsthand, he said, "I voted for a joint statehood bill once, but I will never do it again." To make certain, Marcus Smith, who was traveling with the visiting dignitaries and attempting to impress them with the territory's economic development, arranged for them to visit a natural wonder, the Grand Canyon, as a climax to their Arizona sojourn.[21] The combined efforts of Smith and the Arizona investors were evidently effective, for most of those who made the visit carried on an open fight against joint statehood after the opening of Congress in December.[22]

Nor were these touring congressmen the only ones who were convinced by firsthand observation that jointure was wrong. M. G. Cunniff wrote in a national magazine that "no other question anywhere in the United States is arousing half the red-hot enthusiasm that this is." Cunniff, who later moved to Arizona and served with distinction in the Constitutional Convention, toured New Mexico and Arizona in the fall of 1905. Preceding ten congressmen who came to find out what the people of these territories thought about joint statehood, Cunniff asked every person whom he met whether he favored joint statehood. In New Mexico the people were for "half a loaf" if they couldn't get single statehood. But in Arizona is was a different story. "Asking that question was like touching a match to a cannon cracker," he wrote.

> Men did not merely say, "We don't want joint statehood." They made speeches. They shot forth their reasons. They told stories. They made parables. Lawyers overwhelmed me with arguments, doctors analyzed the situation, storekeepers detained me to tell me all about it, conductors hung over rear seats of cars to discuss it; mining men, business men, teachers, editors, Democrats, Republicans, Prohibitionists, were all in the same mood. Sheriff Jim Lowry of Yavapai County, said to me in Prescott, "Sir, I'd like to see Arizona a state. But half a state with

---

[21]*Arizona Republican,* October 13, 1905.
[22]*Ibid.,* December 11, 1905.

New Mexico as the other half? Well, I'd rather see a territory till I die." This was the gist of what they all said. . . .[23]

Cunniff said the charge was true that the huge mine and railroad corporations in Arizona were opposing the merger of that territory with New Mexico because they feared heavier taxation from Santa Fe in the proposed state.[24] However, most of the people were not similarly motivated, according to Cunniff. "The explanation is simpler," he said. "Americans building a commonwealth take a jealous pride in its integrity. All Arizona asks is a square deal. The Foraker amendment to the statehood bill of last year provided that the question of admission be submitted to popular vote in both territories, each voting separately. This would be a fair method of settling the difficulty.[25]

These sentiments were expressed at length by a delegation of citizens, under the chairmanship of Dwight B. Heard, who went to Washington to protest against the union of Arizona and New Mexico into one state. One reason given by this group was "the opposition of at least 95 percent of the people of Arizona, as proved by the written protests of nearly every social, religious, political, and business organization within our Territory, and the petitions of protest signed by many thousands of our citizens." Differences in race, language, customs, laws, and ideals were cited as a further possible deterrents to successful amalgamation of the territories. Other reasons were the unwieldly size of the proposed state and the difficulty of adjusting the territorial debts since certain counties in New Mexico were practically bankrupt while Arizona bonds were selling above par.[26] After presenting extensive information on Arizona's economic and social progress, the Heard group summarized its request for separate statehood:

> In every line of industry, as we have shown, Arizona is making remarkable progress. Her population and wealth are rapidly and steadily increasing. Her agricultural valleys today are among the garden spots of the world and are rapidly filling up with the highest class of home-making citizens. As we have shown, the population of these valleys will be greatly increased when the vast irrigation works, now in actual con-

---

[23]M. G. Cunniff, "The Last of the Territories," *The World's Work,* Vol. 11, No. 3 (1906), pp. 7108-9.

[24]Robert Baker [ex-Congressman, New York], "Human Liberty or Human Greed?" *The Arena,* Vol. 35, No. 196 (1906), pp. 240-42; see also an article in the *New York Tribune,* December 25, 1905, about the feeling of Connecticut capitalists who had investments in Arizona, in regard to joint statehood; also, a story on low mine assessments in the Arizona territory, *New York Tribune,* January 19, 1906.

[25]Cunniff, *The World's Work,* Vol. 11, p. 7119.

[26]Dwight B. Heard, "Why Arizona Opposes Union With New Mexico," *The World To-Day,* Vol. 10, No. 4 (1906), pp. 409-18.

struction by the Government within Arizona's borders, are completed and the flood water stored for the purpose of creating thousands of new homes.

We have referred to Arizona's magnificent forests and the growing lumber industry under the wise control of the Government Bureau of Forestry. The showing in the livestock industry will compare favorably with that of any State in the Union.

We have shown the immense mineral resources of Arizona and the desirable class of home-making citizens in her mining towns and cities, as well as the rapid development of these mining sections along lines of permanent stability. The increase in Arizona's school population during the past decade of over 100 per cent is certainly most significant, and the substantial homes, modern brick schoolhouses, and splendid public and private buildings which are being constructed in all of Arizona's towns and cities, and her vast and rapidly developing resources, give the assurance of a future of which not only Arizona, but the nation will be proud. When she applies for statehood, as is her right as provided in the organic act, the Congress will find her coming bright and beautiful, fully equipped with population and wealth sufficient to completely satisfy the requirements of every fairminded American citizen, and worthy to have a star placed in the blue field of our national flag.[27]

Heard's committee was supported by petitions, resolutions, and protests from many different groups and organizations. Among these were the Arizona legislature, supervisors of several counties, the Tucson Chamber of Commerce, the mayors of Tucson and Phoenix, the Territorial Baptist Convention, Phoenix Presbyterian Church, Methodist Episcopal Church, Arizona Federation of Women's Clubs, Territorial Bar Association, Arizona Cattle Growers' Association, Miners' Association of Arizona, Phoenix and Maricopa Board of Trade, mass meetings of citizens in several Arizona cities, the Republican Central Committee, and the Democratic Central Committee. A good indication of the animosity of Arizona people toward joint statehood was indicated by a petition obtained at the territorial fair in Phoenix. The signatures of 3,200 people opposing joint statehood were obtained in the grandstand in thirty minutes' time.[28]

The Arizona cause was also supported by many leading politicians, including J. W. Babcock, one of the most influential members of the House and chairman of the Republican National Committee in the campaigns of 1894, 1898, 1902, and 1904. Babcock wrote an article

---

[27]"Memorial from Delegates from Arizona in Opposition to Joint Statehood of Arizona with New Mexico; Also a Statement in Detail Giving the Reasons Therefor" (February 12, 1906), U. S. Senate, *Protest Against Union of Arizona with New Mexico,* 59th Cong., 1st Sess., 1906, Senate Doc. No. 216, p. 17-18.

[28]*Ibid.,* p. 18.

or the *Independent* magazine in which he said that enactment of the joint-statehood bill would be "one of the greatest legislative outrages ever perpetrated in this country. . . . In my opinion," he wrote, "neither Arizona nor New Mexico is at this time ready for Statehood. . . . It will not be long before Arizona is fitted to come into the Union of States, but when she does reach that stage of preparedness every consideration of justice and fair play demands that she shall take her place in the sisterhood in her own right and unhampered by a union which could almost be called miscegenation, with comparatively an alien race. If let alone, Arizona's future is assured and will be glorious."[29]

Babcock told how the mayors of Arizona's cities, the county boards of supervisors, and delegates of various commercial groups met in Phoenix on May 27, 1905, to organize the Anti-Joint Statehood League. Still another group, a bipartisan meeting of the two political parties, had accentuated the almost universal feeling in the territory by adopting resolutions which declared in part, "We profoundly believe that the union of the two Territories as one State would be inimical to the best and highest interests" of both territories.[30] Babcock also mentioned the frequently heard argument that the Organic Act of February 24, 1863, promised Arizona separate statehood. This act provided: "That said Government shall be maintained and continued until such time as the people residing in said Territory shall, with the consent of Congress, form a State government, republican in form, as prescribed in the Constitution of the United States, and apply for and obtain admission into the Union as a State on an equal footing with the original States."[31]

Among those who argued that Congress was honor-bound to carry out the promise of the Organic Act was ex-Governor Nathan O. Murphy.[32] On December 4, 1905, the Tucson *Citizen* printed a copy of an interview given by Murphy to the *Washington Post* four days earlier. "Have you come to Washington, Governor, to make your regular fight against the consideration of Arizona and New Mexico into a single state?" he was asked. "You have guessed me correctly," Murphy answered.

> As long as that obnoxious proposition is before Congress I shall be in this vicinity, seeking to oppose it by every legitimate means. The people of Arizona are against it overwhelmingly and if a fair expression of the sentiment of New Mexico could be taken, a majority of its people would

[29]J. W. Babcock, U. S. Representative from Wisconsin, "Statehood Rights of Arizona and New Mexico," *The Independent,* Vol. 61, No. 2987 (1906), p. 505.

[30]*Ibid.*

[31]*U. S. Statutes at Large,* Vol. XII, 37th Cong., 3d Sess., 1863, Chap. 56, p. 665.

[32]Babcock, *The Independent,* Vol. 61, p. 507.

be found in the negative. Arizona is rich and prosperous and there
no other cloud on its horizon save the threat of being forced into a mo
distasteful partnership. If we cannot be admitted as a State on our ow
individual merit, all we ask is to be allowed to remain as we now are.[³]

On the other hand, two other ex-governors, Louis C. Hughes an
Myron H. McCord, were for joint statehood. They joined several othe
prominent Arizona residents in sending a memorial to Congress in whic
they protested against a vote on the question.[34] Several senators, how
ever, made effective use of Governor Kibbey's powerful brief of argu
ments in favor of requiring both territories to approve joint statehoo
before it could be granted. And when Roosevelt was finally persuade
to Kibbey's point of view too, the danger of joint statehood wa
diminished.

Arizona had some good friends in the Senate during the years c
intense anxiety when the Hamilton bill was being considered. Fore
most among them were Foraker of Ohio and Bard of California. A
we have seen above, Bard's opposition to the Omnibus Bill of 190
caused many Arizona merchants, newspapers, and politicians to inter
fere in California politics and prevent his reelection. A few Arizon
editors, however, had argued that "butting in" was "rather bad taste" -
especially since Bard was the only Republican senator in 1904 bol
enough to take a stand against joint statehood.[35]

He continued to oppose statehood in any form and argued effec
tively against merger when the joint-statehood bill came to the floor c
the Senate for discussion in the short session of the Fifty-eighth Con
gress. In a prepared speech on January 6, 1905, less than two month
before the end of his term, Bard vigorously protested against coercio
on the sound basis of reason and tradition. He said that neither territor
had indicated any desire for joint statehood and that Congress ha
never admitted any state accept upon evidence that its people wer
applying for admission. He reminded his attentive listeners that Arizon
and New Mexico combined would be equal in area to all the thirtee
states on the Atlantic seaboard from Maine to South Carolina and muc
too big for convenient and economical administration. His last an
strongest point was the argument mentioned above, that Arizona'
autonomy had been guaranteed forever when she was separated fror
New Mexico by the Organic Act of 1863.[36]

---

[33]*Tucson Citizen,* December 5, 1905.

[34]U. S. Senate, *Joint Statehood for New Mexico and Arizona,* 59th Cong., 1s
Sess., March 17, 1906, Sen. Doc. 254.

[35]*Arizona Daily Star,* July 3, 1904, and *Arizona Republican,* June 28, 1904.

[36]Hon. Thomas R. Bard, *The Autonomy of Arizona Guaranteed Foreve.*
speech in the U. S. Senate, January 6, 1905 (Washington, D. C.: G.P.O., 1905)

Marcus Smith, speaking to the House in the same vein on January 25, 1906, asked rhetorically, "Who is responsible for the bill anyway? Where did it come from? Arizona did not ask it, and her delegate here is certainly as well acquainted with her wishes and her interests as is the gentleman from Michigan [Mr. Hamilton]. . . . New Mexico did not ask it. Her Delegate here ["Bull" Andrews who was elected in 1904] was elected on a single statehood platform. . . . " Smith said further that no senator, including Beveridge of Indiana, had been commissioned to speak for either territory.[37]

In answer to Bard, however, Senator Beveridge delivered an oratorical masterpiece, entitled "Arizona the Great," in which he denied that Congress had ever assured separate statehood for Arizona. He argued emotionally that inhabitants, not sections, should determine representation. Visualizing a great Southwestern border state, he attempted to lure Arizonans by calling the new state "Arizona." Of course, the capital was to be in Santa Fe, an even-more-attractive bait for the citizens of New Mexico. In concluding his case, Beveridge showed his brilliant oratorical skill in these words:

> And what a glorious state this New Arizona would be . . . second in size and eminent in wealth among the states of the greatest of nations; Arizona standing midway between California and Texas, three giant commonwealths guarding the Republic's southwestern border; Arizona, scattering with one hand the fruits of the Tropics and with the other the products of the Temperate Zone; Arizona, youngest of the Union and the fairest; how proud of her the American people would be; how just a place she would hold in the nation's councils. Not querulous, irritable, and contentious because of the consciousness of her scant population, but large-minded, generous, and conciliatory, because of the knowledge of her greatness; not apologetic for her numbers, but serene in her popular equality with her associated states; not Arizona the little, but Arizona the great; not Arizona the provincial, but Arizona the national; not Arizona the creation of a politician's device, but Arizona the child of the nation's wisdom! How its people and the people of the Republic will glory in such an Arizona. For it is such an Arizona this bill will create.[38]

Despite this flamboyant and flowery appeal for joint statehood, Bard and Foraker induced the Senate to amend the joint-statehood bill so that the two territories might express separately their wish in regard to jointure. The House refused to concur in the amendment, however,

---

[37]Marcus A. Smith, *Speech of Hon. Marcus A. Smith of Arizona,* in the House of Representatives, January 25, 1906 (Washington, D. C.: G.P.O., 1905), p. 9. (Reprinted from *Congressional Record,* January 25, 1906.)

[38][Hon.] Albert J. Beveridge, *Arizona the Great.* Extracts from speech closing the Debate on the Statehood Bill in the Senate of the United States, February 6, 1905 (Washington, D. C.: G.P.O., 1905).

and so the whole matter remained in abeyance until January, 1906. Then the situation reversed itself; the House quickly passed the amended merger bill, but the Senate battle was renewed.

In June, after four and a half months of debates and committee hearings on the Hamilton joint-statehood bill, the Senate passed the "Foraker Amendment" and the original jointure bill, as thus revised. The senator who introduced the amendment, Joseph Benson Foraker, had become an Arizona ally in a roundabout way. Because of a bitter struggle with another Republican, Senator Marcus A. Hanna, for control of the Ohio legislature, Foraker had joined forces with Matthew Quay, the Pennsylvania senator who was using the statehood issue as a means of attacking the entrenched Republican machine in the Senate.[39] Quay, however, before his death on May 28, 1904, became an advocate of jointure as the quickest way to achieve statehood for New Mexico, the territory that he favored because of railroad interests there. Quay even promised to help Mark Smith become a senator in return for the latter's influence in getting Democratic senators to vote for the merger. But Smith, having no ambition to represent such a discordant state in Washington, refused the offer and confided in Foraker who assured him that the Hamilton bill "will never pass this Senate while my head is hot."[40]

Many months later, on February 9, 1906, Foraker introduced the above amendment, which was actually drafted by Smith, to allow the two territories to hold a referendum on the question, "Shall Arizona and New Mexico be united to form one State?" The amendment passed in the Senate by a vote of forty-two to twenty-nine after Foraker made an eloquent appeal to the Progressive's love of the referendum.[41]

If approved by the people, the law provided that the new enlarged territory would be named "Arizona" and the capital would be at Santa Fe, at least until 1915. The name "Arizona" undoubtedly pleased the *New York Times*. In an earlier editorial, on December 31, 1904, the paper had inferred that joint statehood was a foregone conclusion and had proceeded to speculate on a name for the baby state. Commenting on the suggestion of one correspondent that "Cibola" and "Arizona" be combined into "Cibara," the *Times* said that "Arizona" was too euphonious a name to live only in a penult; besides, "Cibola" was a reminder

---

[39]*Arizona Republican,* January 1, 1902.

[40]Letter of Mark A. Smith to George H. Kelly, from Washington, D.C., January 12, 1924, printed in Kelly, *Legislative History of Arizona,* pp. 295-99.

[41]*Congressional Record,* 59th Cong., 1st Sess., 1906, XL, pp. 2332, 3591-97; and *U. S. Statutes at Large,* Vol. XXXIV, 59th Cong., 1st Sess., June 16, 1906, Chap. 3335, pp. 278-85.

of Coronado's tragic mistake and "its exact location would be as difficult to find as were its seven cities by the gold-hungry Spaniards."[42]

In the election of November, 1906, there were 19,406 votes cast in Arizona, of which only 3,141 were for joint statehood and 16,265 were against it.[43] On the other hand, in the more thickly populated New Mexico, a majority of 26,195 out of 40,930 votes cast favored joining the Arizona and New Mexico territories into one state. Even considering the aggregate vote, however, the Arizona viewpoint won by a 1,664 majority. The heavier New Mexico vote wouldn't have been sufficient to swing the election even if Kibbey's plan of separate voting had not been adopted by Congress. But the result was close enough to justify the Governor's fears.

Just as the twenty-third legislature failed to act upon Governor Kibbey's suggestion for an Assembly-sponsored election on the statehood question, it also failed to enact many needed laws. The lawmakers seemed to be marking time until the matter of statehood was settled by Congress. Though economy-minded in most things, the legislature was somewhat extravagant in hiring attachés. The daily payroll, amounting to $350 at first, included such political appointees as the seventeen clerks in each house who were paid to sit in the gallery as an audience, and the three messengers who were assigned the job of blindfolding the Goddess of Liberty on the capitol building.

Among the more noteworthy laws was one establishing the Arizona Territorial Fair and appropriating money for the purchase of suitable ground for a one-mile race course and the erection of permanent exhibit buildings. Another measure set aside $500 for a properly inscribed sword to be presented to ex-Governor Alexander O. Brodie. Several laws indicated the advancing progress of frontier Arizona. One enactment, for example, prohibited the establishment or maintenance of saloons, gambling houses, and other places inimical to good morals within a radius of 4,000 feet of the center of the University campus.

42"Cibara Is Neat But Needless," *New York Times,* December 31, 1904.

43Letter of Governor Joseph H. Kibbey and Secretary William F. Nichols to Secretary of the Interior E. A. Hitchcock, from Phoenix, Arizona, November 26, 1906, Record Group 48, Territorial Papers; see also, "Biennial Message of Governor Joseph H. Kibbey to the Twenty-fourth Legislative Assembly," January 22, 1907, pp. 5-6, *ibid.;* letter of Secretary of the Interior Hitchcock to the U. S. House of Representatives from Washington, D. C., December 5, 1906, U. S. House, *Arizona's Vote on Joint Statehood,* 59th Cong., 2d Sess., 1906–1907, House Doc. 140; and letter of Governor H. J. Hagerman and Secretary J. W. Reynolds, to Secretary of the Interior, from Santa Fe, New Mexico, November 26, 1906, in *Certificate of the Governor and Secretary of the Territory of New Mexico as to the Election Upon Joint Statehood,* 59th Cong., 2d Sess., 1906–1907, House Doc. No. 194, pp. 1-3.

Another bill required that each dog owner, within a mile radius of the post office in each unincorporated city having a population of 1,500 or more, buy a license for his pet. It was made unlawful to furnish tobacco to anyone under sixteen years of age.

The rise in the caliber of the professions was indicated by a law requiring that all district attorneys must be learned in the law and licensed to practice.[44] For the most part, however, only bills and appropriations necessary to carry on the territorial government were given much attention. The Assembly ended its work on March 16, 1905.

Of course, political activities were not limited to the legislative chambers at the capitol. Even before the Twenty-third Assembly convened in January, the Tucson City Council had curbed gambling in that city by placing a high license tax on all public houses of chance. Douglas followed suit and, in November, 1906, the voters of Phoenix overwhelmingly gave the city fathers a mandate to end gambling. On the day following the election, Mayor L. W. Coggins expressed the popular sentiment in a statement to the press. "We will pass a gambling ordinance," he said, "that will prohibit every form of gambling, even to dice and slot machines. The intention is to sweep the city clear of the evil and put the gambling houses out of business."[45] The Phoenix gamblers had spent huge sums of money, paying as much as two to five dollars each for votes, in a desperate effort to stave off the inevitable. But the political influence of gamblers and their shark games had waned to the point that the prospects of an anti-gambling bill being passed at the next session of the legislature seemed excellent. And the suppression of gambling was indicative of the order, decency, and progress that had come to the territory.

After the Twenty-fourth Legislative Assembly convened in January, 1907, Governor Kibbey directed the attention of the legislature to the need for a higher standard of morality in the territory. He recommended the repeal of the law that permitted the licensing of public gambling. He also suggested that a law be enacted forbidding women and girls to frequent or to be employed in any capacity in or about saloons or in other places where intoxicating liquors were dispensed. The Governor said that

> the time has come, it must appear to us all, when more care should be taken in our deportment than has been the rule in our earlier and ruder days. Cities, towns and villages are growing up all over the Territory. Every year finds a larger number of children, whose education not alone

---

[44]*Acts, Resolutions and Memorials,* Twenty-third Legislative Assembly, 1907.
[45]*Tucson Citizen,* November 21, 1906.

in the schools, but in the formation of habits by association, example and observation, demands a more careful consideration than was accorded to it when our towns and villages were the abodes of men chiefly, or of but few women and children.[46]

The Governor's arguments were evidently convincing since both his recommendations were enacted into law. On the third day of the session, an anti-gambling bill was introduced to the then Republican-controlled Council by a Democrat and former president of that body, George W. P. Hunt. Eventually, the bill was passed by both houses and signed by the Governor. A second measure, which prohibited women from loitering in saloons, made the "painted singer" an extinct songbird.

The liquor traffic, as well as gambling, was also regulated by the Twenty-fourth Assembly to improve the moral climate in the territory. A uniform license of $300 a year was imposed upon every saloon. Prior to the passage of this law the liquor license varied from $12 quarterly for wayside inns selling hay and provisions to travelers, to $50 for saloons in the larger towns. The traveling saloon was virtually prohibited by a provision stating that no saloon could be maintained in a railroad town or camp unless it was established there five months before the arrival of the railroad. One county officer predicted quite a savings for the taxpayers as a result of this latter provision; he estimated that a traveling saloon carrying a $100 stock and paying a monthly license of $4.00 had cost the county as much as $5.00 a month in the prosecution of crime.[47]

The new laws to improve social conditions were not the result of any reform movement that swept the West. In the main, those responsible for the passage of the liquor-control and the anti-gambling laws were the persons who were active in seeking statehood. U. S. Representative Littlefield of Maine had given Arizonans the "big hint" by proposing a bill in Congress to make gambling in the territories a misdemeanor punishable by a $5,000 fine and one year's imprisonment. The champions of statehood hurriedly took up the gauntlet to muffle Mr. Littlefield's thunder. In the process, Delegate Mark Smith was reproved for challenging the Maine representative with more heat than tact. What Smith had said was this: "I will not wish it understood that I am here in sympathy with gambling, but I do protest against the gentleman from Maine, the farthest point in the U. S. from my home, coming here to meddle in our quarrels when, with prohibition in his own State, there

---

[46]"Biennial Message of Governor Joseph H. Kibbey to the Twenty-fourth Legislative Assembly," January 22, 1907, Record Group 48, Territorial Papers.

[47]"Social Reforms in Arizona," *Charities and The Commons*, Vol. 18 (June 22, 1907), p. 325.

are 150 saloons open in the town of Bangor, Maine. The gentleman should confine his philanthropies to his own State."[48] The possible prize of statehood was an attractive lure, especially since public opinion seemed to be behind reform and several Arizona cities had already enacted ordinances against gambling.

The greatest struggle in the 1907 session was on the question of mine taxation. No territorial governor was as forceful and determined on this subject as was Governor Kibbey. He hammered away at the idea that the mines should pay a fair share of taxes until public sentiment was aroused. In his annual report to the Secretary of the Interior in 1906, he reviewed efforts that had been made during the previous year to secure a more equal distribution of the burdens of taxation.[49] He reported that the Territorial Board of Equalization, at its yearly meeting in August, 1905, had attempted for the first time to equalize the assessed valuations of mines. After studying an abstract of the assessment role from each county, the board concluded that patented mines, together with their improvements, were assessed at not more than 3 to 5 percent of actual values. Except for railroads, other property had been assessed at from 40 to 75 percent.

To more nearly equalize the tax burden, the board raised the total assessments of the mines from $2,500,000 to $11,500,000, still well below the average of valuations placed upon cultivated and grazing lands, town lots, improvements, and livestock. However, several boards of supervisors refused to comply and Attorney General E. S. Clark applied to the Supreme Court of the Territory for a writ of mandamus to compel the local boards to put the equalization order in effect. The Supreme Court (Chief Justice Edward Kent and Associate Justices Richard Sloan and Frederick Nave) decided in favor of Clark's contentions in regard to the Board of Equalization's power to raise valuations, but refused a writ of mandamus on the grounds that the board had not raised assessed valuations on patented mines sufficiently to actually bring about true equalization of all property. Nevertheless, the county assessors met with the territorial auditor in February, 1906, and the mine assessments were increased an aggregate amount of $3,500,000.

During the previous month, the *New York Tribune* printed some revealing statistics on the assessed valuations of some of Arizona's largest mines. The United Verde Copper Mine valuation was assessed at $835,504, though its actual worth was about $150,000,000. The Con-

---

[48]Barton Wood Currie, "The Transformation of the Southwest Through the Legal Abolition of Gambling," *The Century Magazine,* Vol. 75 (Vol. 53, New Series), No. 89 (1908), p. 905.

[49]U. S. Dept. of the Interior, *Report of the Governor of Arizona to the Secretary of the Interior,* 1906, pp. 28-32.

gress Consolidated Mine was likewise inadequately assessed at $112,747 since it could not be bought for several millions. The Imperial Copper Company mines, which were reported as being worth $3,000,000, were assessed at only $75,000. Other well-known rich mines were also assessed much too low: Copper Queen Consolidated, $56,000; Calumet and Arizona, $67,000; Calumet and Pittsburg, $13,224; and Tombstone Consolidated, $79,000. The last named was bonded for $6,000,000. Obviously, increases in mine assessments were overdue.[50]

The largest increases were in Cochise County where the Board of Supervisors, carrying out the policy of the territorial Board of Equalization, ordered increases amounting to about 400 percent. Bisbee mining interests took their case to the United States Supreme Court where their attorney contended that the "elected" supervisors, who originally authorized lower assessments, more nearly represented the sentiment of the people than did the "appointive" Board of Equalization members who had been selected by Governor Kibbey. Justice White, upon hearing this argument, looked sardonically at the other justices whose countenances duplicated his expression. The mining attorney had lost his case for he failed to appreciate that the Supreme Court itself is an appointive body. The legal path was cleared for increased mine assessments.

Except for the dogged determination of Governor Kibbey, however, very little progress would have been made. In his message to the legislature in 1907, he said, "Farms, city and town lots, houses, shops and stores, banks, railroads, cattle, sheep, and horses, and all other smaller items of property are assessed at figures which at least approximate equality, and probably at least one-half their value. But the great mines, which produce more wealth and yield greater profits, many times over, than all other classes of property in the territory combined, pay but a small proportion of the taxes — in no event exceeding 8 or 10 per cent of their proper share." In a very straightforward manner the Governor went on to say, "It is easily conceivable, however, that a county assessor, or a county supervisor, who owes his election to assistance received from a mining company or to any other influential single interest may find it easy to believe that suggestions from that mining company or that other interest relative to its assessment should have too favorable consideration."[51]

A variety of bills was introduced in both houses to provide for

[50]*New York Daily Tribune,* January 19, 1906.

[51]"Special Message of Governor Joseph H. Kibbey on the Assessment and Taxation of Mines," March 1, 1907, *Journals of the Twenty-Fourth Legislative Assembly,* pp. 159-84.

more equitable valuation of the mines. One measure that finally passed became known as the "Doran bill" because it was sponsored by the President of the Council, A. J. Doran of Yavapai County. Though inadequate, this bill was signed by the Governor because it was a step in the right direction. It provided for two classes of mines, nonproductive and productive, the latter being one from which minerals worth $3,750 were extracted annually. The law required the county assessor to take 25 percent of the gross product, as determined by average market quotations in some reliable financial publication such as the *Engineering and Mining Journal* of New York City, as the assessed valuation of a mine. Nonproducing mines were to be assessed in the same manner as any other personal property.[52] Under this law the aggregate mine assessments rose to approximately $20,000,000. Kibbey's persistence had at least partially overcome the formidable lobby of such well-known mining men and attorneys as Frank Murphy of Prescott, S. W. French of Bisbee, C. W. Clark of Jerome, Ben Goodrich, and others.

The Kibbey administration was less successful in dealing with the railroads, however. Attempts of the Twenty-fourth Assembly to set up a railroad regulatory commission and to fix freight and passenger rates were defeated. The Board of Equalization was handicapped in trying to establish fair tax assessments for the railroads. In the case of the Santa Fe, Congress had fixed the rate of taxation by federal statute. Then the territorial legislatures had made exemptions from taxation to several lines in order to encourage construction.

The board was especially perplexed by the Santa Fe's status because that railroad was quite comparable in value to the Southern Pacific, and the latter was subject to territorial regulation. Both lines were in fine condition — ballasted roadbeds, the heaviest steel rails, and good concrete and steel bridges. Both were carrying a heavy traffic and their securities commanded high prices on the stock exchanges. Thus, there was no apparent reason why the valuations for the two lines should be appreciably different. Yet Congress had decreed that the Santa Fe should pay taxes at the rate of $175 per mile of track through the territory, which at the prevalent rates in the counties traversed, would amount to an approximate valuation of $5,500 per mile. On the other hand, the territorial board had been assessing the Southern Pacific at approximately $7,000 per mile. Obviously, it was unjust to assess the

---

[52]*Acts, Resolutions and Memorials,* Twenty-fourth Legislative Assembly, 1907, pp. 20-26; see also, U. S. Dept. of the Interior, *Report of the Governor of Arizona to the Secretary of the Interior,* 1907, p. 34.

S. P. at a higher rate than the Santa Fe. But actually the S. P. was also underassessed, considering the company's earnings; so the board raised its assessment to $11,000 per mile.[53] Equalization was postponed until another day.

Another action of the legislature in 1907 was to move the prison from Yuma to the vicinity of Florence.[54] A sum of $120,000 was appropriated to erect buildings on a site that was donated to the state. Most of the labor in constructing the high wall, detention and shop structures, and a concrete bridge across the nearby Gila River, was done by the convicts under the supervision of the Superintendent, T. H. Rynning. The Board of Control stimulated the men to work by subtracting two days from the term of imprisonment for each day on the job. Governor Kibbey supported this experiment with the prisoners and also introduced other prison reforms. He abolished stripes and solitary confinement and demanded that the prisoners be treated as human beings not beyond redemption, and neither as beasts nor as saints.

The need for these reforms and for the removal of the prison from Yuma were pointed out by a correspondent for the *Charities and The Commons* magazine shortly after the Assembly adjourned.

"After years of agitation against the situation and condition of the territorial prison at Yuma, Arizona," he wrote,

> the last session of the legislature passed a law providing for the construction of a new prison at Florence and for the removal within two years of the prisoners to that place. The present prison is located upon a low hill above the Colorado River at Yuma, which is reputed to be the hottest place in the U. S. It is composed of several acres of yard, surrounded by a high wall of adobe and mud bricks. The garden which was formerly maintained in the Colorado bottom has been entirely washed away by the river and there is little opportunity for providing the prisoners with work. The construction of the prison itself is not of the best, and it is totally inadequate to the purposes of an institution of its kind. A large proportion of the 375 prisoners confined are difficult or desperate characters and but for the known qualities of the superintendent, Captain Thomas H. Rynning, formerly in command of the Arizona Rangers, and the consideration shown to the men, serious trouble might break out at any time. In the absence of sufficient public work the prisoners are encouraged to work for themselves and a variety of articles are made of horse-hair, shells and onyx, and beaten silver. The beautiful hat-bands, hair bridles and quirts seen so commonly in Arizona are the work of the convicts at Yuma, and are often referred to as "state's prison bridles,"

---

[53]*Report of the Governor of Arizona to the Secretary of the Interior,* 1907, pp. 28-32.

[54]*Acts, Resolutions and Memorials,* Twenty-fourth Legislative Assembly, 1907, pp. 184-86.

etc. Over 60 percent of the prisoners are Mexicans, whose skill in handling horsehair is well known, and their presence accounts in measure for the quality of work produced, though many white men become equally skillful. At the noon hour or when there is no public work to perform, almost the entire population of the prison can be seen sitting in the shade of the high walls busily employed in plaiting horse-hair. The indeterminate sentence law, passed by the last legislature, though considered from other standpoints, was intended primarily for the improvement of prison discipline.[55]

Before the next and last territorial legislature met in January 1909, there was considerable politicking on the Arizona scene. Though the nomination of Taft at the Republican convention was assured, there was a factional fight in the territorial convention held in Tucson in April, 1908. A number of the Republicans opposed the Kibbey faction of the party and its proposals to send an instructed delegation to the national convention. Both factions supported Judge Richard Sloan but could not agree on other delegates. Governor Kibbey again met opposition in December, 1908, when he was nominated by President Roosevelt for another term as governor. His opposition, particularly enemies who had been antagonized by his successful work in raising mine taxes, were able to delay his confirmation by the Senate. Kibbey remained in office, however, until the newly elected Taft appointed Sloan as his successor in May, 1909.

Meanwhile, the Twenty-fifth Legislative Assembly convened and heard Kibbey express confidence that Arizona would be admitted to statehood within the immediate future. The Governor expressed satisfaction over the prosperity and financial soundness of the territory and estimated the population at 200,000. Though he decided to leave the subject of mine taxation as a problem for the new state government he did propose that the legislature create a railroad board to cooperate with the Interstate Commerce Commission in establishing freight and passenger rates.[56] Altogether, the Democrat-controlled Assembly passed 107 bills, including a measure introduced by Representative Frank DeSouza to set up the Territorial Railroad Commission that was succeeded later by the Arizona Corporation Commission.[57]

During most of this session, the legislature was highly partisan

---

[55]"Prison Reforms in Arizona," *Charities and The Commons,* Vol. 18 (June 22, 1907), pp. 333-34.

[56]"Biennial Message of Governor Joseph H. Kibbey to the Twenty-fourth Legislative Assembly," pp. 3-28, January 22, 1907, Record Group 48, Territorial Papers.

[57]*Acts, Resolutions and Memorials,* Twenty-fifth Legislative Assembly, 1909 pp. 16-23.

Members of the Council of the Twenty-fifth — and last — Legislative Assembly. Standing (left to right): F. S. Breen (Coconino), S. E. Day (Apache), William ⸬ *Morgan (Navajo), John R. Hampton (Graham), J. B. Finley (Pima and* ⸬ *anta Cruz), George W. P. Hunt* (President, *Gila), Bo. J. Whiteside (Sergeant* ⸬ *Arms);* seated: *Eugene Brady O'Neill (Maricopa), M. G. Burns (Yavapai),* ⸬ *ean St. Charles (Mohave), George W. Norton (Yuma), Ben Goodrich* ⸬ *Cochise), Thomas F. Weedin (Pinal).*

passing several bills over the Governor's veto. The Arizona Rangers organization was abolished in this manner though another bill permitted sheriffs in the various counties to appoint a limited number of "ranger deputies."[58] The office of territorial examiner was also abolished. Anti-administration legislators charged that the Rangers were influenced too much by the governor and that Examiner W. C. Foster had been overly active in the last political campaign. Another act, which was passed over the veto, provided for a literacy test – a test designed to keep Mexicans from registering to vote, for it was claimed that these people generally voted Republican.

Among the notable laws passed was one that carved the fourteenth and last county, Greenlee, from the eastern portion of Graham; the new county, because of rich mines in the Clifton and Morenci districts, assumed the total debt of Graham County as part of the price for its creation. The Pioneers' Home at Prescott was established for aged and infirm early settlers. Several new positions besides the Railroad Commission were provided, including the offices of the territorial historian and the territorial engineer. The latter was placed in charge of all roads, bridges, and road improvements to be constructed by the territory. This office was the beginning of the present Arizona State Highway Commission.

After the legislature adjourned, Kibbey marked time until his successor was chosen. Naturally, he would have felt honored to have been the last territorial governor. But he also wished to return to the private practice of law in Phoenix and did little in his own behalf to counteract the partisan and corporate pressures that his enemies were bringing to bear upon President Taft. On his last day in office, on May 6, 1909, he received a convincing indication of the high esteem in which he was held by territorial employees. He was presented a number of gifts by people who had served under him. Dr. J. A. Ketcherside, Superintendent of the Territorial Asylum, opened the ceremony by expressing his feelings of great respect for the governor and presented him with a beautiful cut-glass water service. Captain Rynning of the prison, on behalf of the employees of that institution, with a few well-chosen affectionate words, delivered a chest containing 254 pieces of silver to the governor. The chest was made of heavy cherry and was ornamented with handles of gold and the monogram "J.H.K." Then Attorney General Clark presented the departing executive with a gold watch from employees at the capitol. Obviously, Kibbey was popular with his subordinates. And, by most measurements, he should be classified as

---

[58]*Ibid.*

one of the best territorial governors. His administration was marked by the introduction of economy, by lower tax rates for the average tax-payer, and by efficient, honest administration. Arizona took a giant stride toward statehood during his term.

Chapter 21

Statehood at Last:
The Sloan Administration

Richard Elihu Sloan, the seventeenth and last territorial governor, came to Arizona in 1884 at the age of twenty-seven. Born in Preble County, Ohio, he was a graduate of Monmouth College in Illinois and the Cincinnati Law School. When in his early twenties, he went as far west as Colorado where he engaged in newspaper work and dabbled in mining, but returned to Ohio to study law. Lured a second time by the call of the West, he and L. H. Chalmers, another young attorney, went searching for a town where their legal talents would be more quickly recognized. Not finding the Pacific Coast cities to their liking, the "Buckeyes" came to Phoenix upon the recommendation of John M. Barrett, a newspaper acquaintance in San Francisco.

Sloan's first impression of Arizona was a dismal one. Coming in on the Southern Pacific, he got off the train at Maricopa. He later wrote as follows in his *Memories of an Arizona Judge:*

> Looking about me, I found what in a descriptive advertisement of this part of the Southwest had been called "the gateway to Phoenix and the Salt River Valley" to consist of a railroad station, a small frame building with a lean-to used as a Wells Fargo Express office, and across the road a stagecoach parked at the side of an adobe structure, which, as indicated by signs painted on its windowpanes, was used as a stage office, saloon, and an eating-house. So disappointing was the prospect that I was assailed with doubt as to my sanity in thus venturing into such a desolate place as Arizona appeared to be in search of a law practice, and it was with regret that I saw my train pull out from the station. If it had been possible then for me to have caught it, I think that I might have done so.[1]

Shortly after arriving in Phoenix by stage, Sloan and Chalmers opened a law office but had little practice except for Pierpont Miner,

---

[1]Richard E. Sloan, *Memories of an Arizona Judge* (Stanford: Stanford University Press, 1932), pp. 4-5.

Richard E. Sloan, governor of Arizona Territory from 1909 to 1912.

— Arizona Historical Foundation

their landlord who came regularly to collect the rent. The partnership was dissolved in 1885 when Chalmers joined the rival firm of Tweed and Hancock. The following year, Sloan moved to Florence and was soon appointed district attorney there. The ruggedness of the Arizona frontier at the time is well illustrated by Sloan's seventy-five mile journey to Florence by horseback. He had to wait a day to cross the flooding Salt River and then was soaked when his horse encountered a deep slough on the south side of the river and was compelled to swim. Traveling by way of Mesa, Sloan reached his destination exhausted since he was forced to walk the last twenty miles when his horse pulled up lame.

Rising fast in politics, Sloan was the keynote speaker in the territorial Republican convention in 1888 and in the same year was elected a member of the Council from Pinal County to the Fifteenth Legislative Assembly, where he voted to move the capital from Prescott to Phoenix. In 1899, he was appointed associate justice of the Arizona Supreme Court by President Harrison and was assigned to the First Judicial District with headquarters in Tucson.[2] The most important trial over which he presided was the Wham Payroll case. Eight Gila Valley farmers and stockmen, who were accused of robbing $26,000 in gold

[2]The Arizona Statewide Archival and Records Project, Division of Community Services, W. P. A., *The District Courts of the Territory of Arizona,* mimeographed, p. 37.

and silver from Major J. W. Wham en route from Fort Grant to Fort Thomas, were defended by Marcus A. Smith and Ben Goodrich. The defendants were freed by the jury, partly because of prejudice in the territory against prosecutions by the federal government.

After the expiration of his judicial term in 1894, Sloan moved to Prescott and reentered the practice of law. Three years later, however, he again was placed on the Supreme Court bench, this time by President McKinley.[3] He was reappointed in 1902 and in 1906 by President Roosevelt. In 1908 Sloan was chosen as one of Arizona's two delegates to the Republican National Convention and was instrumental in obtaining the adoption of a statehood plank for the territory. The judge's work at the convention enhanced his reputation to the point that the successful Republican presidential candidate, William Howard Taft, summoned him to Washington shortly after the inauguration to discuss the Arizona governorship.

Before his departure from Arizona, Sloan was encouraged by Governor Kibbey to take the position if it were offered to him.[4] The rest is history. In spite of the inadequate salary the job provided, Sloan accepted the appointment and returned to be greeted by enthusiastic admirers. From a reception at Flagstaff, where he debarked from the train and held a term of court, he went to Prescott. There he was received with a hilarious demonstration, the likes of which, according to the *Arizona Journal-Miner* (April 21, 1909), the city had not seen since it bade farewell to Buckey O'Neill and the Rough Riders. Introduced by Mayor Morris Goldwater, Sloan addressed an overflowing crowd in the opera house and emphasized the purpose of his tenure as chief executive in these words: "I bring back from Washington assurance of the highest and most trustworthy character that my term in office must of necessity be short; that statehood will not be delayed longer than may be necessary after Congress meets in December next. It is therefore important that every citizen should give some thought and attention to those things which must be done in preparation for this event. It is a time for unselfish and patriotic effort on the part of every citizen."[5]

Governor Sloan took his oath of office on May 1, 1909.[6] With no political debts to pay and with no legislature to influence, he concentrated on the question of statehood. In his annual report to the Secre-

---

[3]*Ibid.*
[4]Sloan, *Memories*, pp. 210-11.
[5]*Arizona Journal-Miner*, April 21, 1909.
[6]Sloan, *Memories*, p. 212.

Ralph Cameron, Republican delegate to Congress.

— Arizona Pioneers' Historical Society

tary of the Interior in 1909, he expressed hope that Congress would soon pass an enabling act.[7] His hope was realized on June 20, 1910, when President Taft signed such a measure. The final passage and enactment of the statehood bill in a Republican administration was no doubt expedited by Arizona's election in 1908 of a Republican, Ralph H. Cameron, to represent the territory as delegate in Congress. President Roosevelt, for example, was apparently influenced by this switch in partisanship to the extent that he advised Congress in his last message to that body on December 8, 1908, to admit Arizona and New Mexico as separate states. Taft also expressed sympathy for the desires of the people after his visit to Arizona in 1909, though he warned against the inclusion of any radical provisions in the new state's constitution.

The political weight of President Taft behind the statehood measure was probably the deciding factor in the bill's ultimate passage, since there was still formidable opposition to the enabling legislation. For example, one national magazine called the bill an "undesirable proposition" and said that there was not a man in public life in Washington, "whether President, Speaker, or heads of the committees on Territories," who favored such a measure purely on its merits. Deploring the possibility that four new senators might be sent from communi-

[7] U. S. Dept. of the Interior, *Report of the Governor of Arizona to the Secretary of the Interior,* 1909, pp. 5-6.

CAMERON LEADS REPUBLICANS TO VICTORY IN ARIZONA

A Mixed Ticket Is Again Elected in Coconino County

HON. R. H. CAMERON,
Arizona's Delegate to Congress.

WILLIAM H. CHOICE

Sherman the Era of Pros

[Telegram.]

BISBEE, A. T., Nov. 4, 1908.
Hon. F. S. Breen, Flagstaff, A. T.:

Cameron elected by 1,000. Please accept my sincere thanks for the good work Coconino did in this campaign in behalf of Ralph Cameron. Statehood for Arizona at short session should be our slogan until fulfillment.

HOVAL SMITH, Chairman.

THE ELECTION IN COCONINO.

The election in Coconino county passed off peacefully, although the different parties were very aggressive in supporting their respective tickets. Both parties were partially successful. Both Democrats and Republicans had hoped that there would be fewer split tickets voted this year than in former elections, but they were disappointed. The canvass of the votes did not indicate any party lines at all. Three of the Democratic candidates were elected by handsome majorities, while several of the Republican candidates are proud of the overwhelming vote they received.

The returns, however, show a gain for the Republicans, as they were successful in electing two more of their candidates than two years ago. The officers-elect for assembly, and district attorney will displace Democrats.

Another favorable result for the Republicans is that Hon. R. H. Cameron carried Coconino by a handsome majority, while two years ago the county gave Smith a majority of 145.

The officers-elect are all good men, who will serve the county's best interest. Some good men were defeated, but they took their defeat as an incidental matter, and went about their business with smiling faces, not wasting any time boring their friends with the story of how it happened.

COCONINO'S VOTE IN 1906.

We reproduce below the vote of Coconino county in 1906, which may be of interest to the readers in making comparisons.

Name of Candidate and office	Williams	Flagstaff	McMillan	Cliff Dwellers	Grand Canyon	Fredonia	Tuba	Sedona	Mormon Lake	Total
Del. to Congress—										
Cooper, r	236	130	27	43	2	8	3	1	1	417
Smith, d	246	207	34	6	4	15	5	3	4	592
Council—										
Lockett, r	290	166	25	19	13	19	14	4	4	496
Flynn, d	233	126	18	7	5	18	16	3	2	496
Assembly—										
Hilliard, r	197	190	21	30	1	5	2	7	7	1288
Williams, d	262	247	19	4	3	27	1	6	1	1504
Sheriff—										
Nellis, r	188	213	19	24	3	8	7	1	1	1518
Francis, d	314	133	5	7	5	21	8	5	8	1634
Dist. Att'y—										
Doe, d	232	112	27	40	3	9	5	2	3	1499
Ashurst, d	276	241	19	4	7	19	18	6	7	1674
Pro. Judge—										
Kint, r	281	150	28	15	6	8	35	10	1	6565
Newcomer, d	160	171	14	6	5	30	10	3	5	3442
Recorder—										
Hilken, r	237	99	27	41	2	9	34	4	1	1550
Boyce, d	250	250	19	5	3	21	17	4	4	4619
Treasurer—										
Trent, r	270	166	26	40	6	8	3	2	2	1536
Wilson, d	229	170	14	4	6	21	6	6	3	4504
Supervisor—										
Polson, r	150	136	29	27	2	9	27	4	1	1301
Harrington, r	238	94	28	40	2	8	3	5	2	1406
Gregg, d	248	212	31	3	22	17	4	6	4	4609
Kennedy, d	241	255	19	5	7	21	17	5	5	3625
Surveyor—										
Lamport, r	279	138	26	51	6	5	10	1	1	1280
Lockridge, d	173	171	14	5	2	31	7	3	3	4425
School supt.—										
Layton, r	170	54	21	41	5	33	4	1	1	1180
Carmody, d	314	255	29	21	2	8	10	3	3	3586

THE GREATEST PISTOL SHOT

For the third time for the presidency by an ceives 300 electoral votes has 64 more than the num ular vote was about 1,50 velt in 1904.

New York went Repu by 45,000.

Ohio, Indiana, Mary can; Colorado, Montana small majorities. Nebra majority.

Uncle Joe Cannon w withstanding the fierce fig branches of congress will The fight for the speakers ent indications are that Ca

He is now in the profess ranks.

Akard challenged Col. Bord ry, the well known French p shot, to a match for $500. The lenge was never accepted. W this is the first time Akard has played his wonderful shootin Arizona, it will not be his Directly after the fair he will a circuit of Arizona, giving e bitions, and Flagstaff is one of fortunate towns that will be inc ed in his itinerary. Mr. Aka manager, C. W. Clement, who the way is not a stranger in F staff, having had his family two summers, was here this v and made arrangements for Akard to give the Flagstaff peop

Cameron won the race for delegate to Congress, and *The Coconino Sun,* November 6, 1908, showed its pleasure with the election results.

Gentleman's Admission Card

The presentation of this card will admit you to Capitol Building and Grand Stand at City Hall, Reception of President W. H. Taft, October

No. 199 *13, '09, Phoenix, Arizona*

Admission card for a reception honoring President William Howard Taft.

ties that had not yet bred any national statesmen and whose condition of development did not justify that much representation, the *American Review of Reviews* said sarcastically,

> It is now proposed, at this very session of Congress, to pass the magic wand over the desert sands of Arizona and over the adobe huts of the humble Spanish-speaking people of New Mexico. . . . They will become full partners in that limited government at Washington which bought them for a song from Mexico and which ought to have dignity and firmness enough to keep them in their proper place of tutelage for perhaps forty years yet to come.[8]

The motives of both political parties were questioned. "Democrats have been so sure that they could control New Mexico and Arizona as States," said the *Review*, "that they have naturally wanted to bring them in by way of balancing the 'cowboy States' of the Northwest. . . . They are much less to be blamed than the Republicans." The two leaders of the latter party singled out for reproach were Teddy Roosevelt, who wanted to keep his promise to his Rough Rider friends, and President Taft, for waving the 1908 Chicago party platform in the face of Congress and demanding admission of the new states in time to give the credit to his administration well in advance of 1912.[9]

A statehood bill was first passed in the House in January, 1910, shortly after a ringing plea by Delegate Cameron, who said eloquently that "it is a matter of history that Arizona has been knocking at the doors of Congress for many, many years, and its just claims to recognition and inclusion in the Sisterhood of States have met with scant consideration, notwithstanding the numerous promises and pledges of the two dominant parties." He want on to argue that there were 37,000 qualified voters in Arizona who were being denied their inalienable right to join in the selection of a President and other national officers.

The wheels of legislative machinery grind slowly, however, and it was not until June 16 that the Senate passed the statehood measure. The vote was 64 to 0 with 27 solons abstaining.[10] The bill provided that the election of 1908 would be the last one held under territorial law, and that all officials then elected would hold over pending the admission of Arizona as a state. Delegates to a constitutional convention were to be chosen by county conventions, rather than by a

---

[8]"Two More Undeveloped States," *The American Review of Reviews,* Vol. 41, No. 3 (1910), pp. 268-70.

[9]*Ibid.,* p. 270.

[10]"An Act to enable the people of Arizona to form a constitution and state government . . . ," *U. S. Statutes at Large,* Vol. XXXVI, 61st Cong., 2nd Sess., 1910, Chap. 310, Arizona section, pp. 568-79.

direct primary, the election system which the Twenty-fifth Territorial Assembly had provided for Arizona in 1909. Despite criticism of this latter provision and of another stipulation requiring congressional approval of the new constitution, all Arizona was jubilant over the achievement of statehood.[11] Delegate Cameron, Governor Sloan and ex-Delegate Smith were honored in public celebrations.

Both political parties claimed credit for the final passage of the statehood bill. United States Attorney Joseph E. Morrison of Bisbee was typical of the Republicans who enthusiastically congratulated Cameron. "It seems entirely proper," he said, "that the people of Arizona should fully appreciate what the republicans, through their delegate to Congress, have done for them in securing statehood. We promised you statehood if you would elect Cameron; you elected Cameron and he has secured you statehood and in so doing, the republicans have fully kept their pledges, something that the democracy of Arizona did not do for twenty years."[12]

On the other side, the Democrats contended that credit for the passage of the statehood bill belonged to the senators of their party. For example, John P. Orme, the president of the Salt River Valley Water Users' Association who was in Washington when the bill passed, sang the praises of Senators Joseph W. Bailey of Texas and Francis G. Newlands of Nevada. He said that Bailey and his Democratic colleagues agreed not to oppose the administration's railroad bill in exchange for Republican votes on the statehood act. "Until Bailey got this promise there was no hope for statehood," Orme concluded.[13] Democratic newspapers reviewed the political history of both parties on the statehood issue. The *Bisbee Review* said that the Democratic national platform had declared in favor of statehood for Arizona for twenty years and that during all this time the Democratic members of Congress had been ready and willing to grant statehood, only to be met with determined opposition on the part of the Republicans. "On three different occasions," the *Review* said, "Hon. Mark Smith succeeded in passing a statehood bill through the house and the republican senate promptly killed the bill."[14]

Perhaps Smith himself, however, saw the statehood fight in a broader perspective. In his last speech in Congress, on February 15,

---

[11]*Arizona Daily Star,* June 23, 28, 1910. An editorial from the *Douglas International* criticizing the limitations of the statehood bill is reprinted in the latter issue of the *Star.*

[12]From the *Bisbee Review,* quoted in the *Arizona Daily Star,* June 24, 1910.

[13]*Arizona Democrat,* quoted in the *Tombstone Epitaph,* June 26, 1910.

[14]*Arizona Daily Star,* June 24, 1910.

1909, he reminded the Republicans that their platform of 1908 called for the "immediate admission of the Territories of New Mexico and Arizona as separate states in the Union." Then, despite the sweeping claims of partisan orators and newspapermen in Arizona, he said that the politics of the proposed states had nothing to do with the failure of the statehood bill to pass during his tenure as delegate. "The opposition here and elsewhere to the admission of these States is not that they are Democratic or Republican, but solely and alone because they are western."[15] Smith felt that the fight over statehood was geographic rather than political; the East was afraid that Arizona's senators and representatives, be they Democratic or Republican, would be fearless and plain-spoken.[16]

In his final plea for statehood as a delegate to Congress, Smith said, in part, "You have witnessed the struggle I have made to secure the blessings of liberty to my people. From early manhood my life has been dedicated to this holy cause, and I find myself now in poverty, with hair as white as the snows on her mountain tops, still pleading the cause of Arizona."[17] Nothing would have pleased Smith more than to have been Arizona's delegate in 1910 when Taft signed the statehood act. At the time of his death in 1924, the *Arizona Republican* editorialized on his part in the statehood struggle as follows:

> Mark Smith was always remembered as a state builder and one of the foremost characters of early Arizona. He was the idol of the democracy of the territory and the state, and was liked by the Republicans for his infinite geniality. That quality secured for him at the national capital a wide circle of friends in both the house and senate. No other territorial delegate, a representative without a vote, had ever possessed so much influence in Congress.[18]

Within a week after President Taft signed the Enabling Act on June 20, 1910, Governor Sloan called a special election for September 12 for the purpose of choosing fifty-two delegates to a constitutional convention.[19] In his proclamation he appealed to the voters to put aside partisanship and to choose the best man in each county without regard

---

[15]"Speech of Honorable Marcus A. Smith in the House of Representatives," February 15, 1909, *Congressional Record*, 60th Cong., 2d Sess., 1909, Appendix, pp. 18-19 (A Xeroxed copy of this speech was furnished the writer by Senator Carl Hayden.) See *Congressional Record*, 60th Cong., 2d Sess., 1909, Vol. XLIII, p. 2423, for the passage of the statehood bill in the House on February 15, 1909.

[16]*Arizona Daily Star*, June 23, 1910.

[17]"Speech of Honorable Marcus A. Smith . . . ," *Congressional Record*, 60th Cong., 2d Sess., February 15, 1909, Appendix, pp. 18-19.

[18]*Arizona Republican*, April 8, 1924.

[19]"A Proclamation of Election of Delegates to the Constitutional Convention, By the Governor of Arizona," June 28, 1910, Record Group 48, Territorial Papers.

to political parties or special interests. Many newspapers of the territory echoed the Governor's sentiments and urged the election of delegates whose deliberations would not be displeasing to the conservative-minded President and Congress; Taft, himself a brilliant constitutional lawyer, was especially opposed to any recall provision that would make judges subject to political control. Republicans in Arizona argued that the most important thing was statehood and that delegates should be chosen who would write a short, conservative constitution that would insure admittance to the Union at the earliest possible date.

In September, 1910, the same month as the election, Governor Sloan published an article in *Sunset* magazine entitled "The Forty-seventh Star" in which he described the economy of Arizona and pointed up the reasons why the territory deserved statehood.[20] In land area, it would be fifth among the states and first in the production of copper. There was enough water to irrigate a million acres of land and a population in excess of 200,000. Arizona was making rapid progress. Already there were two thousand miles of steam railways and a good public school system including a territorial university and two normal schools. There were about sixty newspapers and magazines in publication, and law enforcement was outstanding. With all these indications of a bright future, the Governor was naturally anxious that the constitutional convention not upset the apple cart by writing into the constitution radical ideas that might prevent Arizona from becoming a state. As it turned out, the progressives did not stop the attainment of statehood, but they delayed it, and the more conservative New Mexico won the flag's forty-seventh star that Sloan wanted.

The election for delegates followed a series of party conventions held in thirteen of the fourteen counties to decide on platforms and candidates. The direct primary system, which had been established by the territorial legislature in 1909, could not be used since the Enabling Act specified the use of the nomination plan provided in the 1901 code — the convention. Greenlee County had been created too late to be allotted delegates since the apportionment was based on the voting population as shown in the 1908 election for delegate to Congress. The issues in the campaign of 1910 were clear-cut. The electorate could choose a convention composed of men who favored a liberal constitution that might not be acceptable to Congress and the President, or one that would draw up a document pleasing to the national adminis-

---

[20]Richard E. Sloan, "The Forty-seventh Star," *Sunset,* Vol. 25, No. 3 (1910), pp. 267-72; see also, "Arizona's Outlook in the Family of States," *The American Review of Reviews,* Vol. 42, No. 4 (1910), pp. 484-85.

OFFICIAL BALLOT

TWIN BUTTES PRECINCT NO. 23   PIMA COUNTY

Election, September 12th, 1910

	REPUBLICAN	DEMOCRATIC	SOCIALIST PARTY	LABOR PARTY	INDEPENDENT
ate to the titutional nvention	S. L. Kingan *1124*	E. S. Ives *796*	J. P. Bailey *29*	A. A. Worsley *386*	
ate to the titutional nvention	W. F. Cooper *1119*	W. H. Sawtelle *794*	A. Philion *29*	B. C. Brichta *247*	
ate to the titutional nvention	C. C. Jacome *1107*	J. M. Ronstadt *797*	C. G. Fuller *57*		
ate to the titutional nvention	George Pusch *1091*	Thos. Kavanaugh *118*	Grant Allen *50*	George Angus *260*	
gate to the stitutional nvention	J. C. White *1089*	A. S. McKelligan *112*	J. J. Squire *11*	Tom Davenport *257*	

— Arizona Pioneers' Historical Society

An official ballot for a Pima County precinct in the election for delegates to the Constitutional Convention, 1910.

tration. The most controversial issue in the election was the question of direct democracy — the initiative, referendum, and recall.[21] These measures had been incorporated into the Oregon and Oklahoma constitutions, which were considered by many to be the most modern and progressive of that day. Speakers who had had experience with these experiments in direct legislation were imported into Arizona during the campaign to testify for one side or the other.

In at least one county the election expense seemed exorbitant to the territorial Secretary, George U. Young. He at first declined to pay bills submitted by three newspapers in Cochise County for the publication of election notices. These newspapers, and the amount of their bills, were: *The Bisbee Daily Review*, $1,404; *Douglas Daily Dispatch*, $1,527; and *Daily Prospector and Weekly Epitaph* (Tombstone), $1,350. A law passed by the Arizona Assembly in 1905 authorized

---

[21]E. E. Ellinwood, "Making a Modern Constitution," a Speech By E. E. Ellinwood delivered in the Opera House at Bisbee, Arizona, August 27, 1910. Copy in the Arizona State University Library.

the Board of Supervisors to publish notices of elections in newspapers representing each political party.[22] In this instance the Cochise Supervisors claimed that the Bisbee *Review* was Democratic, the Douglas *Dispatch* Republican and the Tombstone *Epitaph* Socialist. Secretary Young did not question the political affiliation of the first two but contended that the *Epitaph* had always been known as a Democrat publication; he charged that this paper was evidently claiming alignment with the Socialist Party in order to collect a printing bill that would otherwise be illegal. However, Secretary of the Interior R. A. Ballinger recommended payment of all the bills, even though the total amount seemed "quite large," since the law permitted publication of notices in newspapers affiliated with parties other than the Democrat and Republican. Secretary Young reluctantly accepted this advice and authorized payment.[23] By that time, the election was over, the delegates selected, and the constitution written.

The voters, influenced by the campaign oratory as well as by dissatisfaction with a territorial government only indirectly responsible to them, gave an overwhelming victory to the Democratic Party and its progressive platform. Forty-one of the fifty-two delegates elected were Democrats. Thirty-nine delegates, including Republican Bracey Curtis of Nogales, were pledged to support the initiative and referendum; thirty were honor-bound to vote for the recall. Thirty-three were directed by their Democratic county conventions to work for the adoption of a direct primary law for all officials.[24] Thus it was certain from the beginning that the constitutional convention would adopt several forms of direct democracy.[25]

After the election, the *Arizona Republican* stated that instead of statehood being a reasonable certainty it was now a remote possibility. It seemed doubtful to this newspaper that a convention with only eleven Republicans could write a constitution acceptable to a Republican Congress. The rival Democratic *Arizona Gazette,* however, was just as emphatic in describing the election as a "triumph of the people" over the corporate interests. For years it had been charged that the

---

[22]*Acts, Resolutions and Memorials,* Twenty-third Legislative Assembly, 1905, p. 140.

[23]Letter of Arizona Attorney General John B. Wright to Secretary George U. Young, from Tucson, Arizona, October 19, 1910; letter of Secretary Young to Secretary of the Interior R. A. Ballinger, from Phoenix, Arizona, November 28, 1910; and letter of Ballinger to Young, from Washington, D. C., January 16, 1911, Record Group 48, Territorial Papers.

[24]*Arizona Republican,* December 1, 1910; *Arizona Gazette,* October 10, 1910.

[25]"Two New State Constitutions," *The Outlook,* Vol. 96 (November 12, 1910), pp. 564-65.

Members of the Arizona Constitutional Convention, 1910. George W. P. Hunt, President of the Convention, is seated behind the two small boys. Vice President Morris Goldwater stands directly behind Hunt. The one woman in the group was not a delegate.

MEMBERSHIP OF THE
ARIZONA CONSTITUTIONAL CONVENTION, 1910

County	Political Party	Occupation	Residence
Apache			
Fred T. Colter	D	Cattleman	Eagar
Cochise			
John Bolan	D	Miner	Bisbee
S. B. Bradner	D	Switchman	Benson
P. F. Connelly	D	Railroad engineer	Douglas
D. L. Cunningham	D	Lawyer	Tombstone
E. E. Ellinwood	D	Lawyer	Bisbee
Thomas Feeney	D	Machinist	Bisbee
A. F. Parsons	D	Lawyer	Douglas
C. M. Roberts	D	Miner	Dos Cabezas
R. B. Sims	D	Plumber	Douglas
E. A. Tovrea	D	Butcher	Lowell
Coconino			
Edward M. Doe	R	Lawyer	Flagstaff
C. C. Hutchinson	R	Cattleman	Flagstaff
Gila			
George W. P. Hunt	D	Merchant	Globe
J. J. Keegan	D	Saloon keeper	Globe
Alfred Kinney	D	Capitalist	Globe
John Langdon	R	Machinist	Globe
Jacob Weinberger	D	Lawyer	Globe
Graham			
Lamar Cobb	D	Mining engineer	Clifton
A. R. Lynch	D	Lawyer	Safford
Mit Simms	D	Farmer	Solomonville
A. M. Tuthill	D	Doctor	Morenci
W. T. Webb	D	Farmer	Pima
Maricopa			
A. C. Baker	D	Lawyer	Phoenix
Lysander Cassidy	D	Lawyer	Phoenix
James E. Crutchfield	D	Minister	Phoenix
Alfred Franklin	D	Lawyer	Phoenix

MEMBERSHIP OF THE
ARIZONA CONSTITUTIONAL CONVENTION, 1910 (Cont'd)

County	Political Party	Occupation	Residence
Maricopa			
F. A. Jones	D	Traffic expert	Phoenix
B. B. Moeur	D	Doctor	Tempe
John P. Orme	D	Farmer	Osborn
Sidney P. Osborn	D	Clerk	Phoenix
Orrin Standage	D	Farmer	Mesa
Mohave			
Henry Lovin	D	Mining	Kingman
Navajo			
William Morgan	D	Cattleman	Lakeside
James Scott	R	Cattleman	Pinedale
Pima			
William F. Cooper	R	Lawyer	Tucson
Carlos C. Jácome	R	Merchant	Tucson
Samuel L. Kingan	R	Lawyer	Tucson
George Pusch	R	Cattleman	Tucson
James C. White	R	Railroading	Tucson
Pinal			
E. W. Coker	D	Lawyer	Florence
Thomas N. Wills	D	Cattleman	Mammoth
Santa Cruz			
Bracey Curtis	R	Banker	Nogales

(The only Republican elected on a platform favoring the initiative and the referendum.)

County	Political Party	Occupation	Residence
Yavapai			
M. G. Cunniff	D	Merchant	Crown King
Morris Goldwater	D	Banker	Prescott
Albert M. Jones	D	Sheepman	Seligman
A. A. Moore	D	Rancher	Walnut Grove
Edmund W. Wells	R	Lawyer	Prescott
H. R. Wood	D	Mining	Prescott
Yuma			
Fred L. Ingraham	D	Lawyer	Yuma
E. L. Short	D	Merchant	Bouse
Mulford Winsor	D	Newspaperman	Yuma

huge railroads and mines controlled the territorial legislature to the detriment of the homeowners, farmers, and laborers. But in this election, organized labor forced the Democratic Party to embrace the labor platform by calling the representatives of all unions together in Phoenix in July, 1910, and threatening to unite the unprivileged groups into a new Labor Party. In this case the politicians did not renege on their bargain.

The labor cause was popular in the convention, as Article XVIII, entitled "Labor," indicates. The measures included in this article established an eight-hour day for public employees, an employers' liability act and compulsory compensation for workers injured in hazardous occupations, and child-labor regulations; the exchange of labor "black lists" by employers was forbidden as was the hiring of aliens on public works. The recall of public officials was provided for in another section of the constitution, but was supported by Labor as a means of ousting judges who abused their power to issue writs of injunction in labor disputes. As a matter of fact, Labor had a vital interest in almost every part of the constitution. It was anxious, for example, to see corporations regulated and forced to pay their just share of taxes, and it wanted public school lands protected from private exploitation. The liberal and progressive nature of the whole constitution was due in no small part to the influence of Labor.[26] Few political bargains have been so successfully culminated as the one between Labor and the Democratic Party in 1910.

The day before the constitutional convention convened at the capitol on October 10, 1910, the *Arizona Republican* showed its alarm over what the progressive majority might do. Its fear that statehood might be sacrificed in exchange for the shadowy allurement of utopian schemes was illustrated in a cartoon adapted from one of Aesop's fables. A dog, labeled "constitutional convention," held a bone captioned "statehood," and peered from a bridge at his reflection in the water of "Populist-Socialistic Constitution." The cartoon was titled, "Will it drop the bone for the shadow?"[27]

The people, however, had elected an unusually capable group of men, many of whom were later successful in state politics. Three of the delegates were destined to become governor: George W. P. Hunt, Dr. B. B. Moeur, and Sidney Osborn. Mit Simms served as both secre-

---

[26]A. J. McKelway, "Social Principles of the New State Constitutions," *The Survey*, Vol. 25 (January 7, 1911), pp. 610-13; see also, the *Arizona Gazette*, December 2, 1910.

[27]*Arizona Republican*, October 9, 1910.

THE BIG QUESTION

WILL IT DROP THE BONE FOR THE SHADOW?

Cartoon in The Arizona Republican, *October 9, 1910. Many people feared that Arizona would lose its chance for statehood because of its populist constitution.*

tary of state and state treasurer; Mulford Winsor was the first land commissioner and director of library and archives; General A. M. Tuthill commanded the Arizona National Guard for years as adjutant general; John P. Orme was president of the Salt River Valley Water Users' Association; others served in the legislature and the courts. Among the business leaders, perhaps the names of Carlos Jácome, Morris Goldwater, and E. A. Tovrea stand out. The membership included both workingmen and the well-to-do, liberals and conservatives, pioneers and newcomers.[28]

When the delegates convened on October 10, they were called to order by the temporary president, Judge A. C. Baker. After some discussion over seating, Democrat Mulford Winsor facetiously stated: "It will be so arranged that the Republicans in this convention may be seated by themselves if they so desire in order that they may be free

---

[28]*Minutes of the Constitutional Convention of the Territory of Arizona* (Phoenix: Phoenix Printing Co., 1910), pp. 3-4; see also, *Arizona Gazette,* October 10, 1910.

from association with the unwashed Democratic majority."[29] However, it was decided that the delegates would select seats in the order that the names of their respective counties were drawn from a hat.[30] Some of the members had difficulty adjusting to the swivel armchairs. One leaned too far back and sprawled on the floor during the introduction of the first motion; E. W. Coker of Florence, who weighed 350 pounds, had difficulty in rising from his chair to make motions.[31]

Prior to the first day's session, each political party had chosen its candidate for president of the convention. Edmund W. Wells was selected by the Republicans and Hunt by the more numerous Democrats. The latter party had met in caucus at the Elks' Lodge and balloted four times before giving the nod to Hunt. His friend, Winsor, led in the first vote with fourteen, followed by Alfred Franklin, who was regarded as the spokesman for the Maricopa County delegation, with twelve; Hunt and Morris Goldwater each receiving seven. Most of Winsor's and Goldwater's supporters then swung behind Hunt.[32]

In editorializing on Hunt's subsequent election on the convention floor, Colonel Fred S. Breen of the Republican *Coconino Sun* wrote about his personal friend and political enemy on October 14, 1910:

> George Washington Peter Hunt [sic], of Globe, president of the last territorial council, was selected as presiding officer over the constitutional convention in the Democratic caucus, and owing to the fact that the Democrats have forty-four [sic] members and the Republicans eleven members, he was elected. Hunt is a good presiding officer, but belongs to the radical element of the party which it would seem are in the saddle. Unless there is a change in sentiment a constitution radical enough to suit the most radical will be made.

The conservatives were to express similar fears throughout Arizona during the sixty days of the convention.

The only other officers elected were Amos W. Cole as secretary and Morris Goldwater as vice-president. However, the last office was not provided for until December 8, the next to the last day of the convention; then it seemed desirable to provide a substitute in the event the president should be incapacitated and unable to set up an election so that the people might vote on the constitution.[33] All other employees were appointed, and interestingly enough, received more pay than did

---

[29]*Journal of the Arizona Constitutional Convention,* October 10–December 9, 1910, compiled by Con P. Colin, State Librarian of Arizona, November 1, 1925.

[30]*Minutes of the Constitutional Convention,* p. 8.

[31]*Arizona Republican,* October 12, 1910.

[32]*Minutes of the Constitutional Convention,* p. 8.

[33]*Ibid.,* p. 420.

George W. P. Hunt presiding over the Constitutional Convention in 1910.

Morris Goldwater, Vice President of the Constitutional Convention. A merchant who also had experience as a telegraph operator, Goldwater served at various times as a Democratic territorial legislator and as mayor of Prescott. He was the uncle of Senator Barry Goldwater.

the delegates. Congress had set the remuneration of the sergeant-at-arms, doorkeepers, clerks, pages, watchmen, and secretaries at five dollars per day. Morris Goldwater jokingly offered to resign his position as a delegate from Yavapai if he could be assured a position as an attaché at a dollar a day more than the delegates received. Miss Ethel Ming, a clerk, reminded him, however, that "the delegates get big chunks of honor."[34] Each member of the convention, for example, was presented with two souvenirs of the first day: a pearl-handled, four-bladed pocket knife, with the inscription "Arizona Constitutional Convention, October, 1910," and a pair of desk scissors with a similar inscription.

In 1963 the last surviving delegate of the Constitutional Convention, Jacob Weinberger, reminisced about some of the delegates when he visited Arizona from San Diego, where he was serving as a United States district judge. "A dyed-in-the-wool Democrat" was his recollection of Morris Goldwater. Sixty-one at the time of the convention, Goldwater was a six-term mayor of Prescott and a former president of the Arizona Council. A fine speaker and something of a wag, Goldwater proposed a resolution allowing speakers to have their utterances printed with directed interpolations by the secretary for shouts of "hear! hear!," "applause," "loud applause," and "laughter."

Weinberger remembered Hunt as a "behind-the-scenes manipulator who presided in the manner of a stoic, benign Buddha — if one can picture Buddha with a splendid handlebar mustache." Hunt led the five-man Gila County delegation that included J. J. Keegan, a saloon keeper; Alfred Kinney, a self-styled capitalist; John Langdon, a mechanic; and Weinberger, an attorney who at twenty-nine was the second youngest member of the convention, Sidney P. Osborn being the youngest at twenty-seven. Weinberger had an interesting background. Born in the part of Austria-Hungary which became Czechoslovakia, he migrated to the United States with his parents at the age of seven. The sixth of ten children, most of whom grew up in Denver, he went to Globe in 1905, when that town was a roistering mining community with forty-one saloons on Main Street. While he was an assistant county attorney, 1907–1909, a convict came gunning for him, only to be killed in one of these saloons by a sheriff's deputy.[35] Weinberger was elected a delegate from Gila County and served on committees dealing with the legislative and executive sections of the constitution. Altogether

---

[34]J. Morris Richards, *The Birth of Arizona* (Phoenix: Allied Print, 1940), p. 12.

[35]*Arizona Daily Star,* February 14, 1963.

HE ARIZONA REPUBLICAN

PAGES.   PHOENIX, ARIZONA, MONDAY MORNING, DECEMBER 5, 1910.   18 PAGES.

TITUTION OF ARIZONA IN ALMOST COMPLETED FORM

THE CONSTITUTIONAL CONVENTION IN ACTION

PEACE COMMISSION   DRUG CHARGES OF

Sketch of the Constitutional Convention of 1910 in session, from
The Arizona Republican, *December 5, 1910.*

there were twenty-one standing committees, the membership of which
was announced by President Hunt on October 13.[36]

Once organized, the convention operated much like a legislature.
Guided largely by the constitutions of other states, the members introduced what were called "propositions," which were assigned to the
appropriate standing committees for study. These measures, if approved,
were referred back to the convention, along with other measures initiated
by the committee, for debate in "committee of the whole." The latter
was simply the convention acting in a different guise with informal
rules to speed up action. After a proposition was reported favorably
to the convention from the "committee of the whole" and passed by a
formal vote, it was assigned to the Committee on Style, Revision and
Compilation. The latter committee was headed by the Harvard-educated
Michael Cunniff who had served as editor of *World's Work*. His ability
was attested to by the fact that he had been in Arizona only three
years before being elected to serve in the convention. With the assistance
of Mulford Winsor — a newspaperman from Yuma — Judge Wells of
Yavapai, Ellinwood of Cochise, and Baker and Franklin from Maricopa, Cunniff edited the wording of the constitution and deserves most
of the credit for its literary style.

Some of the propositions submitted by the delegates were approved
for inclusion in the constitution, others were not. The three most controversial provisions included in the document were the initiative,
referendum, and recall of elected officials; these measures were passed
without modification despite the valiant efforts of conservatives, ever-
mindful of President Taft's attitude, to exempt judges from the recall.
The determination of the progressive majority to go for "the shadow
rather than the bone," was accompanied by some apprehension as the
following unusual and original prayer of the convention chaplain, the
Reverend Seaborn Crutchfield, indicates: "Lord, we hope that President Taft will not turn down the constitution for a little thing like the
initiative and referendum; Lord don't let him be so narrow and partisan
as to refuse us self-government."[37] Crutchfield obviously had more faith
in the Lord than did Delegate William Morgan of Navajo County. The
latter was a free-thinker who stirred up a controversy by objecting
to any mention of the Deity in the constitution. Ridiculing all forms
of religion, he sensationally, though unsuccessfully, attempted to persuade the convention from exempting church property from taxation.

---

[36]*Minutes of the Constitutional Convention,* pp. 22-24.
[37]*Arizona Gazette,* November 28, 1910.

Michael Cunniff, chairman of the committee which edited the wording of the Constitution drafted by the Constitutional Convention.

— Arizona Pioneers' Historical Society

Among the delegates who opposed Morgan's proposals was J. E. Crutchfield, son of the chaplain and also a minister.

The younger Crutchfield himself failed to win the convention's approval for a measure he favored that would have made Arizona virtually dry. It was a simple proposition, to be added to the bill of rights, containing only the following words: "No law shall endanger the moral welfare of the citizens of the state." Instantly, the convention interpreted this single phrase as an attack upon the saloons, and Thomas Feeney of Bisbee was certain of it. With unusual haste the convention voted down the proposition by a substantial majority. Even though saloon doors were to continue swinging, Crutchfield must have felt some satisfaction in putting the convention on record, though indirectly, as affirming that saloons endanger public morals.[38]

A month before this abortive attempt to stop the sale of alcoholic beverages, a public hearing had been held on the issue of prohibition. A petition, signed by 3,200 women who asked for the inclusion of an article in the constitution forbidding the sale of intoxicating liquors, was read to the convention. The delegates were also made aware of a local-option election in Safford which gave the prohibitionists a victory margin of four to one.[39] Despite a lot of eloquent oratory favoring

[38]*Arizona Daily Star,* November 29, 1910.
[39]*Arizona Gazette,* October 20, 1910.

the submission of the prohibition question to all the voters of the territory, a proposition submitted by Alfred Franklin of Phoenix, providing that this be done, was defeated by a vote of 33 to 15.[40]

Another popular reform of the day, woman suffrage, made no more progress than did prohibition with the delegates at the constitutional convention. P. F. Connelly of Douglas introduced a proposition that provided for a special election and permitted women as well as men to vote on the question of woman suffrage. Connelly lost the support of many constituents because of his action. One telegram from "Democrats that supported you" told him not to come back to Douglas and concluded with these words: "You ought to be shot. We are sorry that the recall is not in operation." Another bitter telegram, from "Henry Sullivan and 200 others," called Connelly a "bum" and advised him to move to Apache County. A third uncomplimentary message, this one from "H. Jennings and the Bunch," suggested that he "go to England and tie up with Lady Worwock, Maxim Gorky and Emma Goldman." He was also promised a "model hobble skirt and a peach basket hat" upon his return to Douglas after the convention adjourned.[41]

But the suffragettes, despite this kind of opposition, kept the pressure on the delegates. One petition from Gila County had a list of signatures ten feet long. The territorial suffrage organization sent each delegate a postcard with the picture of a degenerate drunk opposite a young mother with these captions: "This man can vote" and "This woman cannot." When the proposition to submit the issue of woman suffrage as a popular referendum came to a vote, however, the delegates voted it down 30 to 19, much to the disappointment of the large number of ladies in the galleries.[42]

Another heated controversy in the convention arose from a report of the Committee on Education recommending the segregation of Negroes and whites. Many of the delegates who were southern-born, including Dr. B. B. Moeur, chairman of the committee and a future governor, favored segregation. But most of the members had the strong feeling for tolerance and racial equality that then prevailed in Arizona. The argument that segregation would be expensive also influenced them not to give it constitutional sanction.[43]

Perhaps the most important and fundamental work performed by the convention was that of establishing the three branches of govern-

[40]*Ibid.,* November 17, 1910.
[41]*Ibid.,* November 2, 1910.
[42]*Ibid.,* November 2, 17, 1910.
[43]*Ibid.,* November 22, 1910.

ment. The structure that was created gave the governor very meager power. No doubt the delegates remembered that the governors had for nearly fifty years been appointed by the federal government as political patronage and that the selections had not always been wise ones. Just as the people of the original thirteen colonies had distrusted the executive branch, for a similar reason, and put their faith in a more powerful legislature, so did the men at the constitutional convention in Phoenix.[44] Governor Sloan was disappointed since he advocated more centralization of powers and real control over the reins of government in the hands of the governor. He believed that there should be no elective boards or commissions, and very few elective offices. He thought the provision in the constitution requiring the governor to see that the laws are faithfully executed should be made to mean something. Only two executive offices — attorney general and state auditor — he believed, should be elective and independent of gubernatorial control. With the short ballot, the people could vote more intelligently and hold the governor responsible for his administration.

In order to prevent a political machine from perpetuating itself in office through the power of appointment, Sloan recommended that the governor be limited to one term of four years, or possibly six years at the most. Many political scientists today would agree that Sloan was astute, if not prophetic, in his observations on the governorship. However, it is doubtful if very many people, even Sloan himself, would advocate granting any chief executives as much authority as was bestowed upon him as the last territorial governor.[45]

Actually, Congress conferred upon him as much authority in the matter of taxation and the expenditure of revenue as has ever been exercised by any executive in this country. This grant of power was somewhat accidental in that the Enabling Act of June, 1910, contained a provision that no legislature should be elected in that year. This clause was inserted on the assumption that the territory would become a state in time to permit the election of a state legislature to levy taxes and to make the necessary appropriations. But admission to statehood was delayed, for reasons to be seen below, and Congress provided for this emergency by conferring upon the governor those fiscal responsibilities normally handled by a legislature. Concerning his experience at the time, Sloan later wrote "I learned by this experience, small though it was, that great economy may be brought about when one

---

[44]*Arizona Republican*, November 16, 1910.
[45]Sloan, *Memories*, pp. 214-15.

central power controls the expenditure of the state's money, and when a carefully prepared budget is not subject to assault by organized lobbies working on legislative committees which control legislation and appropriations."

The task of creating a legislature aroused more interest among the delegates than did the work on the executive branch. Several ideas were suggested for consideration. A comprehensive plan submitted by Lysander Cassidy, a Phoenix lawyer and delegate from Maricopa County, called for a one-chamber body of twenty-four members elected for two years. A candidate would have to be twenty-five years of age and an Arizona resident for at least five years. Remuneration would be six dollars a day for a sixty-day session. However, five dollars would be deducted each time a member failed to vote; he also had to take a pledge against log-rolling before receiving any pay. Cassidy's plan did not permit the legislature to repeal any measure approved by the people by a three-fourths vote. No act would take effect for ninety days unless it were an emergency.[46]

After much deliberation the constitutional convention established a bicameral legislature, consisting of the Senate with nineteen members and the House of Representatives with thirty-five. The five counties (Cochise, Maricopa, Pima, Gila, and Yavapai) that had the largest vote for the office of delegate to Congress in 1910 were each given two senators, while the other counties were to have one each. The number of representatives, which were apportioned to each county on the basis of the 1910 vote, varied from seven for Cochise to only one each for six counties. Population statistics indicate that the Democratic majority in the convention manipulated the legislative apportionment in favor of the Democrats. The five possible Republican counties (Pima, Santa Cruz, Coconino, Apache, and Navajo), with 58,411 people, were given thirteen legislators — seven representatives and six senators. In contrast, four safely Democratic counties (Mohave, Yuma, Yavapai, and Graham), with a combined population of only 38,056, were assigned fourteen legislators — nine representatives and five senators.[47]

But not all of the Democrats were satisfied. Delegate Sidney

---

[46]Papers of H. R. Wood, in Arizona Department of Library and Archives; see also, Calvin Brice, "The Constitutional Convention of Arizona" (unpublished master's thesis, Arizona State University, 1953), pp. 15-16.

[47]Letter of F. W. Hamm, Deputy Treasurer of Gila County, to Senator William A. Smith, Chairman of the Committee on Territories, from Globe, Arizona, April 27, 1911, in the Ralph H. Cameron Collection, University of Arizona Library, Special Collections; see also, *Constitution of Arizona,* Article IV, Division 2: Legislature, Sec. 1.

Osborn of Phoenix accused the convention of "throwing the hooks" into politically doubtful Maricopa; this county was given one less representative than Cochise though the population of each was approximately 34,500. The constitution provided, however, that the allotment of senators and representatives could be changed. And over the years several changes have been made. In 1953, for example, the size of the Senate and House was fixed at twenty-eight and eighty members respectively by a law referred to the people at a special election. A U. S. Supreme Court decision on June 15, 1964, however, declared unconstitutional any districting plan, in either house of a state legislature, that is not based upon population.[48]

The constitutional convention limited membership in the legislature to citizens who were at least twenty-five years of age and had been Arizona residents for three years. Compensation for a regular biennial sixty-day session was set at only seven dollars per day, though several delegates argued that a poor man could not afford to serve at that rate of pay.

After sixty days of wrangling over the structure of the government and other matters, the constitutional convention completed its assigned task on December 9, 1910.[49] The smooth-working Hunt faction had succeeded in constructing a progressive document and securing its approval at the convention by a vote of 40 to 12. All the Democrats signed the constitution except Ellinwood of Cochise and Tuthill of Graham. All the Republicans, except John Langdon of Gila County, refused to sign it. As a result of this alignment, three counties (Pima, Santa Cruz, and Coconino) had no signatures on the Constitution of 1910.[50] In the absence of Governor Sloan, who was in Washington, D.C., lobbying against the constitution as written, the historic document was signed and sealed by George U. Young, Secretary of the Territory of Arizona. Young also called the election by which the people could ratify or reject the constitution for February 9, 1911.

After his return to the territory, Sloan was quoted as saying that "Arizona stands just as much chance of annexation as a province of the Russian empire as it does of admission to statehood under the constitution." He said further, "There is no sentiment anywhere in the east or the south in favor of the initiative, referendum, and recall.

---

[48]*Davis* vs. *Mann* (1964), 84 Sup. Ct. 1453; see also, *Lucas* vs. *Forty-Fourth General Assembly of the State of Colorado* (1964), 84 Sup. Ct. 1472.

[49]*Minutes of the Constitutional Convention,* p. 435.

[50]*Ibid.,* pp. 434-45; see also, U. S. Senate, *Constitution Adopted by Arizona,* 61st Cong., 3d Sess., 1910-11, Sen. Doc. 798, pp. 1-41.

476

A cartoon reproduced in The Survey, *January 7, 1911, defending Arizona's progressive constitution.*

Culver in Los Angeles *Expr*

"THE PEOPLE'S WEAPONS."

At the conference of governors at Frankfort, I talked with the governors of Alabama, Georgia, and Virginia on this subject and found them strongly opposed to these innovations. Governor Harmon and Governor-elect [Woodrow] Wilson's utterances have been against them. Therefore it may be seen that the position of the administration would be strengthened by the rejection of the constitution on account of them."[51] Sloan's observations were affirmed by Delegate Ralph Cameron. In a statement to the press, the latter advised the Arizona electorate that ratification of the constitution as written would only delay statehood.[52]

Supporters of the constitution formed the Arizona Statehood League, with Hunt as president, to work for adoption by an impressive vote. The League sought outside assistance to plead its cause. A favorable letter from Ben Lindsey, the famous juvenile judge in Denver, was widely published in territorial newspapers; and William Jennings Bryan appeared in Phoenix, just two days before the election, to speak for the popular constitution that he thought would provide a "government of the people and by the people." The voters responded by giving the document their approval by a majority of 12,584 to 3,920. Many Arizonans were undecided and failed to vote, however, and the affirmative count represented only 49 percent of the total number of registered

[51]*Arizona Silver Belt,* December 22, 1910; *Arizona Gazette,* December 6, 1910.
[52]Ralph H. Cameron, open telegram to the press, February 11, 1911, Cameron Collection, University of Arizona Library, Special Collections.

THE SITUATION TO DATE

A cartoon from The Arizona Republican, *November 27, 1910. The chance for statehood appeared to be lost because of the progressive constitution drafted by the Constitutional Convention.*

voters.[53] The day after the election, a practical-thinking Governor Sloan told a jubilant Arizona that he still hoped for statehood under the 1910 Enabling Act, even though he was confident that the ratified constitution would not be approved by President Taft as long as it contained a provision for the recall of judges.

Despite a bombardment of petitions and letters that were sent to Washington asking for admission of Arizona to the Union, Sloan's analysis, unfortunately, was proved to be accurate. A joint resolution, providing for statehood, was passed by Congress only to be vetoed by President Taft on August 15, 1911. In his veto message to Congress, Taft said of the recall, "This provision is so pernicious in effect, so destructive of the independence of the judiciary, that it is likely to subject the rights of individuals to possible tyranny. It is so injurious to the cause of free government that I must disapprove the constitution containing it."[54]

Many journals of opinion in the country did not like Taft's veto. The *American Review of Reviews,* for example, said that "if the people of Arizona are indeed fit for Statehood, and if they should be allowed to send two Senators to Washington to help govern the entire country, they must surely be regarded as competent to settle for themselves the various details of their domestic government."[55] Describing the official reaction to the methods of popular government provided in the Arizona document, the same magazine said tauntingly, "The constitution of Arizona . . . was received with horror . . . Washington sneered at the initiative, sniffed at the referendum, and had spasms over the recall. It was bad enough for the people of Arizona to recall other elected officers whose official conduct they did not like; but to recall their judges would be subversive of justice. . . ."[56] The *Review* argued that the Arizona recall was an "orderly method by which the people could raise a question as to the conduct of men on the bench" and concluded that the alarm raised against it was unjustified.

Theodore Roosevelt took a similar dim view of Taft's veto. In an article in *The Outlook,* a publication he helped to edit, he said that Arizona deserved statehood in spite of the recall. Though he personally preferred the Massachusetts plan whereby a judge could be removed by the two branches of the state legislature, he felt that each

[53]Hamm to Smith, Cameron Collection, *ibid.*

[54]*Congressional Record,* 62d Cong., 1st Sess., 1912, XLVII, Pt. 4, pp. 3964-66.

[55]"Delaying Statehood," *The American Review of Reviews,* Vol. 44, No. 3 (1911), p. 266.

[56]*Ibid.,* p. 265.

AN EXECUTIVE ULTIMATUM

— Special Collections, University of Arizona Library

*President Taft was strongly opposed to the recall provision
in the Arizona constitution. This cartoon appeared in the*
Washington Evening Star, *April 11, 1911.*

state should be able to decide for itself how it wished the judicial system to be conducted. "Outside of this provision," Roosevelt wrote in reference to the Arizona recall, "no serious objection has been made to her Constitution, and personally, after considerable study of the document, I have come to the conclusion that it is an unusually good Constitution."

While recognizing that certain sections might meet with considerable dissent, the former President endorsed the constitution as being "above average" and "an admirable thing to have imitated in New York and elsewhere in the East." In summarizing his analysis of the situation, Roosevelt wrote:

> The whole question, therefore, narrows down to the point as to whether it is legitimate to reject Arizona's plea because she had done what Oregon has done, what California has announced she will do — that is, because Arizona desires, when she is a State, to have the same privilege which these two States possess and exercise. Moreover, it must be remembered that, if the people of Arizona desire to exercise the right of recall of the judges, their desire can be made effective immediately after their admission to statehood. . . .[57]

Taft was fully aware that a constitution without the objectionable recall could be amended after statehood to include it. But having done his duty, as he saw it, in stressing the necessity for an independent judiciary, he signed the Flood-Smith resolution on August 21.[58] This resolution provided for statehood on condition that the recall of judges clause be removed from the constitution by a vote of the people. One of the eight senators who voted against the resolution was Moses E. Clapp of Minnesota. While in Phoenix, on August 26, en route to California, he said, "The people of Arizona feel resentful because they were forced to take something they did not want . . . they will correct the wrong. The primary reason why I believe in the recall of the judiciary is because there is no place in an autonomy government for irresponsible power. And that is reason enough. The idea that there is to be an exclusive class that shall be granted certain privileges and immunities is bound to go."[59]

Several prominent Arizonans began charting the course that the

---

[57]Theodore Roosevelt, "Arizona and the Recall of the Judiciary," *The Outlook,* Vol. 98 (June 24, 1911), p. 378.

[58]"Joint Resolution to admit the Territories of New Mexico and Arizona as States into the Union upon an equal footing with the original States," House Resolution No. 8, August 21, 1911, in *U. S. Statutes at Large,* Vol. XXXVII, 62d Cong., 1st Sess., 1912, pp. 39-43; see also, *Arizona Gazette,* April 21, 1911.

[59]*Arizona Gazette,* August 29, 1911.

territory would follow to comply with the President's wishes. Eugene S. Ives, for example, stated it this way to the *Arizona Gazette:*

> We have the best constitution that was ever written, even with the recall out. It would be even better with the recall in. Simply to read it, so many good features are revealed, it would be an outrage to throw that constitution out simply because the President has taken his stand against the recall of the judges. We should take the judiciary recall feature out, and then pledge each of our representatives in the first legislature to support the proposed amendment reinstating the recall of the judiciary.[60]

Accordingly, at a general election held on December 12, 1911, the Arizona electorate amended the constitution by ratifying Article VIII, Section 1, to conform to the wishes of President Taft. The vote on the constitutional amendment was 14,963 for and 1,980 against.[61] Colonel Thomas F. Weedin, editor of the Florence *Blade-Tribune* and unsuccessful Democratic candidate for governor in the October 24 primary, expressed Arizona's scorn for Taft's attitude in an open poem which included these lines:

> We will tolerate your gall
> And surrender our recall
> Till safe within the statehood stall,
> Billy Taft, Billy Taft
>
> Then we'll fairly drive you daft
> With the ring of our horse-laugh
> Billy Taft, Billy Taft
>
> As we joyously re-install
> By the vote of one and all,
> That ever-glorious recall,
> Billy Taft, Billy Taft.

And that is the way it actually happened. On November 5, 1912, the voters reinserted the recall of judges in the constitution. In the election, Arizona exacted personal revenge against Taft by giving him fewer votes in his bid for reelection to the presidency than were given to his three opponents, Woodrow Wilson, Teddy Roosevelt, and Eugene V. Debs.

By the time of this election, Arizona had already been a state nearly nine months. It was on St. Valentine's Day, February 14, 1912, that President Taft signed the proclamation admitting Arizona to the

---

[60]*Ibid.,* August 26, 1911.

[61]Letter of W. S. Norvill, Secretary to the Governor, to the Secretary of the Interior, from Phoenix, Arizona, n. d., Record Group 48, Territorial Papers.

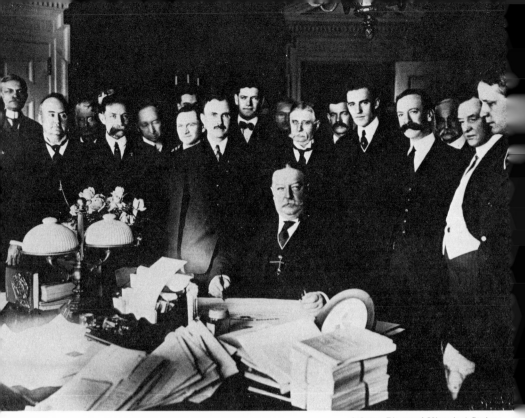

President William Howard Taft signing the Arizona statehood bill.

Union.[62] Sitting at his desk in front of grinding movie cameras, he affixed his signature at 10:02½ A.M. and handed the golden pen to Delegate Ralph Cameron. A few minutes later he sent the following telegram to Governor Sloan: "I have this morning signed the proclamation declaring Arizona to be a State of the Union. I congratulate the people of this our newest commonwealth, upon the realization of their long cherished ambition. Best wishes to the retiring and incoming officials."[63]

For over two months, a full slate of officers had been anxiously awaiting the chance to take over the reins of government. The successful candidate for governor was George W. P. Hunt who defeated Democrat Thomas F. Weedin in the October 25, 1911, primary, and Republican Judge Edmund W. Wells in the December 12, 1911, general election. The Hunt-Weedin contest was fought mainly by the newspapers and involved little personal animosity between the candidates.

---

[62]Taft's proclamation granting statehood to Arizona, February 14, 1912, in Record Group 48, Territorial Papers; see also, *U. S. Statutes at Large,* Vol. XXXVII, Part 2, 62d Cong., 2d Sess., 1912, pp. 1728-29.

[63]*Arizona Democrat,* February 14, 1912.

Hunt flailed the corporations, which he said had controlled territorial politics to the detriment of the people. He called for the election of men to the Corporation Commission who would not bow to the "big interests," or "coyotes" and "skunks" as he was calling them by the end of the campaign. Hunt's hometown newspaper, the Globe *Silver Belt,* supported Weedin and described him as a man who "writes and speaks good English, accomplishments that, while not wholly essential to honesty and clear thinking, are, nevertheless, graces that will befit a man who undoubtedly will become chief magistrate of the great state of Arizona." This observation was an indirect slap at the self-educated, unpolished Hunt. Undaunted by this type of criticism, Hunt appealed to the masses for support. He had indicated that he would follow this political philosophy before starting his campaign. He wrote to a friend, M. M. Rice, on August 25 that "I am going to try for the Governorship and I shall go all over Arizona and in my feeble way try and show and tell the people of Arizona that if I am elected Governor that all will have an eaqual [sic] show, the time has come in my mind that the common people of this Country should have a say in the affairs of the nation. . . ."[64]

In an interview with the press in Phoenix on September 25, he said, "I have been in Arizona thirty years. When I came here Globe was a little village. I had nothing but my two good hands and a determination to win out. I have now a store and a few other business interests at Globe that I have acquired by my own individual efforts. One of the Globe papers published the fact that I used to be a waiter. When I first came to Globe I did work in a restaurant. I am not ashamed of it. It was honest work. . . ." The *Arizona Republican,* which opposed Hunt, passed off his visit to Phoenix with this comment: "The Hon. 'GWP' Hunt is in town today, and so is the other circus [Ringling's]."[65]

After the primary was over, the press lost no time in aligning itself with the candidates of one party or the other. Among Hunt's chief supporters were Colonel Weedin's *Blade Tribune* and J. O. Dunbar's *Arizona Democrat* of Phoenix. An editorial in the latter on October 28, called for the election of the Hunt progressives.[66] "The *Republican,*" Dunbar wrote, "cannot mislead the people of Arizona into the belief that George Hunt is either ignorant or incompetent. It is true that

[64]Letter from George W. P. Hunt to M. M. "Mike" Rice, from Hotel Woodstock, New York City, August 25, 1911, in the M. M. Rice Papers, Arizona Pioneers' Historical Society.

[65]*Arizona Republican,* September 25, 1911. A good article on Hunt's life and career is Peter C. McFarlane, "The Galahad of Arizona: Governor Hunt," *Collier's,* April 15, 1916, pp. 21-27.

[66]*Arizona Democrat,* October 28, 1911.

484

George W. P. Hunt, first gover-
nor of the State of Arizona. This
picture was signed by Hunt on
August 7, 1914.

Mr. Hunt started life low down in the scale — in fact at the foot of the ladder — and today single-handed and alone no man in Arizona stands higher in the estimation of all classes of citizens than does George W. P. Hunt, the honored son of Gila county. . . ." On the same day, the *Arizona Republican* set the tone for the opposition press by declaring its support for Judge Wells and labeling Hunt a "socialist," and an "ambitious politician" who was "extremely illiterate."[67]

Running confidently, but scared, Hunt conducted a vigorous campaign. Covering the state with the other Democratic candidates, he advocated the judicial recall, economy in government, wise regulation of business and industry by the Corporation Commission, better educational facilities, and free textbooks for public school children. He recommended that the federal government construct reservoirs and irrigation systems in Arizona just as it assumed responsibility for rivers and harbors projects elsewhere in the country. The Hunt group stressed the need for better roads, not only for the wagons and carriages but also for the automobiles that were beginning to appear in the territory. Speeches on the road issue struck responsive ears, particularly since most of the travel between larger communities in the territory was done by rail in those days.

When the campaigning was over and the ballots counted, Hunt

---

[67]*Arizona Republican,* October 28, 1911.

Carl Hayden, a territorial sheriff of Maricopa County, member of the U. S. House of Representatives from 1912 to 1927 and United States Senator from 1927 to 1969. At the time of his retirement, he had served longer in Congress than any other man in American history.

— Arizona Pioneers' Historical Society

had been elected the first governor of the state of Arizona.[68] The four Phoenix precincts gave him only a one-vote margin, but returns from the whole territory were more decisive. He received 11,123 votes to 9,166 for Wells. Democrats also swept the other offices. Sidney P. Osborn was elected secretary of state over his Republican opponent, J. F. Cleaveland. A native-born Arizonan, Osborn, then only twenty-eight years of age, was the youngest man ever elected to that office in any state. Henry Fountain Ashurst and Marcus A. Smith were elected the state's first United States senators over the Republican candidates, Ralph Cameron and H. A. Smith.

In the race for Arizona's one seat in the U. S. House of Representatives, Sheriff Carl Hayden of Maricopa County led the ticket in defeating J. S. Williams, 11,556 to 8,485. This victory launched Hayden on a career in Congress that, at the time of his retirement in 1968, had not been equaled in length by any other man in American history.[69] In 1962, President John F. Kennedy, Vice-President Lyndon B. Johnson and other notables attended a testimonial dinner at the Hotel Westward Ho in Phoenix, marking Senator Hayden's fiftieth year in

[68]Letter of Norvill to Secretary of the Interior, Record Group 48, Territorial Papers; see also, *Arizona Gazette,* December 13, 1911.

[69]U. S. House, *Journal of the House of Representatives of the United States,* 62d Cong., 3d Sess., begun on December 2, 1912. Representative Hayden introduced about a dozen bills, mainly related to reclamation, Indian affairs, and private pensions for soldiers who had fought in Indian wars between 1864 and 1898.

Marcus Aurelius Smith

Henry Fountain Ashurst

Smith and Ashurst, both Democrats, were elected as the first United States Senators from the State of Arizona.

Congress. That same year he was reelected to another term in the Senate. Priding himself on being a "work horse, not a show horse," Hayden could look back with satisfaction to a prophecy made by the *Arizona Democrat,* on February 15, 1912. After reporting that he had turned over the Maricopa County sheriff's office to Jeff Adams, the *Democrat* said, "It is probable that Congressman Hayden will answer 'here' to the house roll call about a week from tomorrow. From that time until Congress adjourns he will be 'on the job' every minute for Arizona."[70]

After the election, Hunt thanked the people for confidence in the Democratic ticket and began a two-month wait for the President's official proclamation granting statehood. Taft had intended signing on February 13, but was persuaded by numerous officials to delay the signing until Valentine's Day because of the unlucky superstition connected with the number 13. When word of the signing reached Phoenix at 8:55 A.M., steam whistles at waterworks, gas plants, and laundries heralded the glad tidings. Residents of the state cast inhibition aside and left their homes to celebrate in the streets.[71]

One of the new senators, the usually loquacious Henry Fountain Ashurst, aptly expressed the feelings of most people when he was interviewed by a reporter of the *Arizona Democrat.* "I feel like a boy with a new toy," he said, "It is hard for me to express my feelings. The greater part of my life has been spent in Arizona. I have waited and hoped for statehood with the other people of this glorious commonwealth, and now that we have achieved our greatest ambition and stand upon an equal footing with the older states of the Union it is difficult for me to find words with which to express my sentiments."[72]

The frenzy had not subsided when Governor-elect Hunt appeared in the lobby of the Ford Hotel on West Washington Street at 11:15 A.M. to begin his previously announced walk to the capitol. Hunt's "stunt of pedestrianism" was supposed to set an example of thrift for everyone. Dressed in a brown suit with a carnation in the lapel, Hunt doffed his woolly hat to the smiling citizenry and waved aside an offer for a ride in one of the touring cars sitting nearby. Walking determinedly with his official family, Hunt was joined by scores of perspiring well-wishers in a march described as "spectacular in its simplicity."[73] In a few minutes the group reached the capitol and the new governor's walking

---

[70]*Arizona Democrat,* February 15, 1912.
[71]*Ibid.,* February 14, 1912.
[72]*Ibid.*
[73]*Arizona Republican,* February 15, 1912.

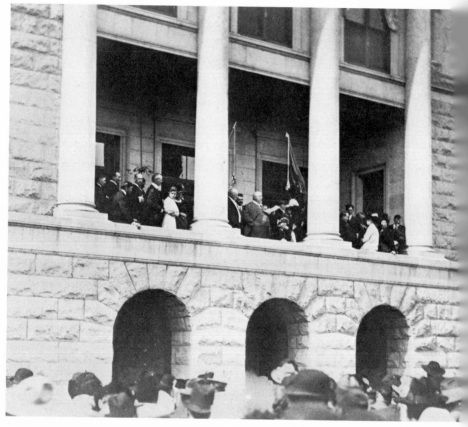

Hunt giving the address at his first inauguration as governor of Arizona.

Cartoon in the Arizona Gazette *on the fourth anniversary of the walk, entitled,* *"Governor Hunt On His Famous Economy Walk to the Capitol. He Uses An Auto Now and It Costs the Taxpayers $300.00 a Month."*

days were over; thereafter he was chauffeured in a $3,000 automobile that cost the taxpayers $300 a month.

Hunt was escorted by Governor Sloan to the speaker's platform in the front portico of the capitol where he took the oath of office just before high noon, February 14, 1912. In his first inaugural address, probably written by his friend Mulford Winsor, Governor Hunt sketched the tone of his administration. He said, "Arizona is progressive and Arizona is democratic. This fact has been clearly and simply demonstrated. I believe that I may without egotism suggest that my selection as the state's first chief executive is in a sense by reason of the views I have held and freely expressed, typical of that progressiveness, of that democracy. . . . "[74] At the conclusion of the inaugural ceremony, the governor held a public reception in his executive chambers. Standing on his right shaking hands with the public was William Jennings Bryan. The latter came up from Tucson where he had been visiting his son.

The featured program in the afternoon, following a colorful parade through the streets of Phoenix, was a two-hour address by Bryan to

---

[74]"Governor Hunt's Address," in the *Arizona Journal-Miner,* February 15, 1912; see also, *Arizona Democrat,* February 14, 1912.

"five thousand cheering people" at the city plaza. Speaking on the topic, "The Trend of Events Toward Popular Government," the "silver-tongued orator," who thrice had won the Democratic nomination for President, held his audience spellbound. Politics aside, the *Arizona Republican* described the address as "one of the greatest public speeches heard from a Phoenix platform in a month of pink moons."[75] But the crowning event of the day was the inaugural ball held on the new pavement in front of the Adams Hotel. A jubilant crowd danced under a canopy of electric lights to the music of a brass band from the Indian school.[76] Just before midnight the band played "Home Sweet Home" and brought to a close the greatest day in Arizona's history. The next morning Governor Hunt was at his desk at 6:30 to get the machinery of government organized and to receive callers. Most Arizonans felt that the "baby state" was in good hands.

The *Weekly Journal Miner* (February 21, 1912) summarized the inauguration story in these words:

> The ceremonies attendant upon the birth of the state and the induction into office of its first executive was entirely devoid of the pomp and display that usually accompany inaugurations. No uniforms glittering with gold lace were in evidence. The military was conspicuous by its absence, for the new governor is averse to ostentation. There was but meager display of even the silk hat and the frock coat, which only a few years ago invaded Arizona. It was a simple affair throughout — Phoenix has witnessed much more ceremonious functions.[77]

A few days later, the *New York Times* published the following article on Arizona's statehood that said many favorable things about Governor Hunt:

> Though the Constitution may contain some newfangled ideas, the execution of the laws of the new state of Arizona is in the hands of an old-line Democrat who believes in Jeffersonian simplicity. Many Democrats here are still sore from the two [sic] miles' walk Gov. W. P. Hunt gave them on inauguration day, when he insisted on going afoot from his hotel to the Capitol, where he took the oath of office. He has begun his administration in a way to show that simplicity will be his watchword. He promises to be a man of the people, and has given warning that corporation agents will be barred from the Capitol. Gov. Hunt got his Democracy in Missouri. He moved out of that State in the early eighties, however, and made his way to Arizona. He entered the town of Globe driving a burro on which were packed his few belongings. He had intended to go farther west, but settled down as a clerk

---

[75]*Arizona Republican*, February 15, 1912.
[76]*Ibid.*
[77]*Weekly Journal-Miner*, February 21, 1912.

in the Old Dominion Commercial Company's store, and remained to become the President and largest owner in the extensive business that was built up. . . .

Mrs. Hunt is very like her husband in her simple tastes. She was Miss Duett Ellison, daughter of a pioneer ranchman. She was in reality a cowgirl, and is a fine horsewoman and an expert with rifle and pistol. Her vacations are spent at the ranch of her father, 100 miles from Globe, and she is accustomed to go there on horseback, carrying her little daughter. She cares little for society, and will not be likely to take the leadership of the women of the capital in that respect, though she and her husband are sufficiently wealthy to make any display they might think needed.[78]

Meanwhile, ex-Governor Sloan quietly stepped down as Arizona's chief executive, somewhat startled, perhaps, by the horde of Democrats who moved into the capitol. The day after his retirement as territorial governor, President Taft named him judge of the United States for the District of Arizona.[79] The newly elected Democratic senators from Arizona objected, however, and Senate confirmation was held up, notwithstanding a favorable report by the Judiciary Committee, until the expiration of the Sixty-second Congress. The Sloan appointment, along with a large number of other Taft nominations, was never approved. But even without the appointment, Sloan had the distinction of having served on the federal bench longer than any other judge in the history of the Territory of Arizona. In 1913, he resumed the practice of law in Phoenix where he had begun his Arizona career nearly thirty years earlier.

---

[78]"Governor Hunt's Simplicity," *New York Times,* February 25, 1912.
[79]*Arizona Republican,* February 15, 1912.

Appendices

Appendix A

OFFICERS OF THE TERRITORY[1]

(Listed for the years when the legislature was in session)

	1st Legislative Assembly 1864 (Prescott)	2nd Legislative Assembly 1865 (Prescott)	3rd Legislative Assembly 1866 (Prescott)
Federal (Appointed by the President)[2]			
Governor	John N. Goodwin	Goodwin	Richard C. McCormick
Secretary	Richard C. McCormick	McCormick	James P. T. Carter
U. S. Marshal	Milton B. Duffield	Duffield	Edward Phelps
District Attorney	Almon Gage	Gage	Gage
Chief Justice	William F. Turner (Prescott)	Turner	Turner
Associate Justice	William F. Turner (Tucson)	Henry T. Backus	Backus
Associate Justice	Joseph P. Allyn (La Paz)	Allyn	Allyn
Territorial (Appointed by the Governor)[3]			
Adjutant General	(none)	(none)	William H. Garvin
Attorney General			Coles Bashford
Auditor			James Grant
Treasurer			John T. Alsap
Presiding Officers of the Elected Legislative Assembly			
President of the Council	Coles Bashford	Henry A. Bigelow	Mark Aldrich
Speaker of the House	W. Claude Jones	James S. Giles	Granville H. Oury
Delegate in Congress (Year of last election)			
	Charles D. Poston[4] (1864)	John N. Goodwin (1864)	Goodwin (1864)

[1]The officers were not all housed in the town where the capital was located. Each judge, for example, was assigned a different district. Source: **Journals** of the twenty-five legislatures.

[2]Other federal offices which existed during all or part of the territorial period were: Surveyor General, Collector of Internal Revenue, Assessor for Internal Revenue, Superintendent of Indian Affairs, Deputy Collector of Customs, Register of the U. S. Land Office (at Prescott, Florence for a short time, and Tucson), Receiver of the U. S. Land Office, and the Depositary at Tucson.

[3]Other offices appointed by the governor which existed during part of the territorial period were: Superintendent of Public Instruction (elective for a short time), Commissioner of Immigration, Superintendent of the Territorial Prison, Superintendent of the Territorial Insane Asylum, Captain of the Arizona Rangers, Territorial Veterinarian, Territorial Engineer, Territorial Geologist, Historian, Public Examiner, Superintendent of Public Health, as well as various boards and commissions.

[4]Charles D. Poston was elected to serve as delegate until March, 1865. John N. Goodwin was elected in September, 1864, to the first full term, 1865–67.

OFFICERS OF THE TERRITORY

(Listed for the years when the legislature was in session)

	4th Legislative Assembly 1867 (Prescott)	5th Legislative Assembly 1868 (Tucson)	6th Legislative Assembly 1871 (Tucson)

Federal (Appointed by the President)

Governor	McCormick	McCormick	A. P. K. Safford
Secretary	Carter	Carter	Coles Bashford
U. S. Marshal	Phelps	Phelps	Isaac Q. Dickason
District Attorney	(none)[5]		C. W. C. Rowell
Chief Justice	Turner	Turner	John Titus
Associate Justice	Backus	Backus	Isham Reavis
Associate Justice	Harley H. Cartter	Cartter	C. A. Tweed

Territorial (Appointed by the Governor)

Adjutant General	Garvin	Daniel H. Stickney	Samuel Hughes
Attorney General			James E. McCaffry
Auditor	Grant	Charles H. Lord	Lord
Treasurer	Alsap	John B. Allen	Allen

Presiding Officers of the Elective Legislative Assembly

President of the Council	Octavius D. Gass	John T. Alsap	Daniel H. Stickney[6] Harley H. Cartter
Speaker of the House	Oliver Lindsey	Thomas J. Bidwell	Marcus D. Dobbins

Delegate in Congress (Year of election)

	Coles Bashford (1866)	Bashford (1866)	Richard C. McCormick (1868)

[5]In his message to the fourth legislature in 1867, Governor McCormick explained that the two important federal offices of District Attorney and U. S. Marshal were often unoccupied because of the inadequate compensation allowed by Congress.

[6]Stickney died while the legislature was still in session.

OFFICERS OF THE TERRITORY

(Listed for the years when the legislature was in session)

	7th Legislative Assembly 1873 (Tucson)	8th Legislative Assembly 1875 (Tucson)	9th Legislative Assembly 1877 (Tucson)

Federal (Appointed by the President)

	7th Legislative Assembly 1873	8th Legislative Assembly 1875	9th Legislative Assembly 1877
Governor	Safford	Safford	Safford
Secretary	Bashford	Bashford	John P. Hoyt[7]
U. S. Marshal	Dickason	F. H. Goodwin	W. W. Stondefer
District Attorney	James E. McCaffry	McCaffry	E. B. Pomeroy
Chief Justice	Titus	E. F. Dunne	C. G. W. French
Associate Justice	Tweed	Tweed	Tweed
Associate Justice	DeForest Porter	Porter	Porter

Territorial (Appointed by the Governor)

Adjutant General	J. S. Vosburg	Vosburg	C. E. Curtis
Attorney General	McCaffry	(office abolished)	(none)
Auditor	A. C. Benedict	Benedict	J. S. Vosburg
Treasurer	Allen	Allen	P. R. Tully

Presiding Officers of the Elected Legislative Assembly

President of the Council	J. P. Hargrave	King S. Woolsey	Woolsey
Speaker of the House	Granville H. Oury	John T. Alsap	M. H. Calderwood

Delegate in Congress (Year of last election)

McCormick (1872)	Hiram S. Stevens (1874)	Stevens (1876)

[7]Hoyt succeeded Safford as governor in 1877, but no legislature convened while he was in office.

OFFICERS OF THE TERRITORY

(Listed for the years when the legislature was in session)

	10th Legislative Assembly 1879 (Prescott)	11th Legislative Assembly 1881 (Prescott)	12th Legislative Assembly 1883 (Prescott)

Federal (Appointed by the President)

Governor	John C. Frémont	Frémont	F. A. Tritle
Secretary	John J. Gosper	Gosper	H. M. Van Arman
U. S. Marshal	C. P. Dake	Dake	Zan L. Tidball
District Attorney	Pomeroy	Pomeroy	J. A. Zabriskie
Chief Justice	French	French	French
Associate Justice	Porter	Porter	D. H. Pinney
Associate Justice	Charles Silent	W. H. Stilwell	A. W. Sheldon

Territorial (Appointed by the Governor)

Adjutant General	William Bashford	Clark Churchill	Moses H. Sherman
Attorney General	(none)	(none)	Clark Churchill
Auditor	E. P. Clark	Clark	Clark
Treasurer	T. J. Butler	Butler	Butler

Presiding Officers of the Elected Legislative Assembly

President of the Council	Fred G. Hughes	Murat Masterson	Edwin H. Wiley
Speaker of the House	M. W. Stewart	J. F. Knapp	Winthrop A. Rowe

Delegate in Congress (Year of last election)

John G. Campbell (1878)	Granville H. Oury (1880)	Oury (1882)

OFFICERS OF THE TERRITORY

(Listed for the years when the legislature was in session)

	13th Legislative Assembly 1885 (Prescott)	14th Legislative Assembly 1887 (Prescott)	15th Legislative Assembly 1889 (Prescott-Phoenix)
Federal (Appointed by the President)			
Governor	Tritle	C. Meyer Zulick	Zulick—Lewis Wolfley
Secretary	Van Arman	James A. Bayard	Bayard—N. O. Murphy
U. S. Marshal	Tidball	W. K. Meade	Meade
District Attorney	Zabriskie	Owen T. Rouse	Rouse
Chief Justice	Sumner Howard	James Wright	Wright
Associate Justice	Pinney	W. W. Porter	Porter
Associate Justice	W. F. Fitzgerald	W. H. Barnes	Barnes
Territorial (Appointed by the Governor)			
Adjutant General	Sherman	J. F. Meador	William O. O'Neill
Attorney General	Churchill	Briggs Goodrich	Clark Churchill
Auditor	Clark	John J. Hawkins	Thomas Hughes
Treasurer	Butler	C. B. Foster	John Y. T. Smith

Presiding Officers of the Elected Legislative Assembly

President of the Council	F. K. Ainsworth	A. Cornwall	Charles R. Drake
Speaker of the House	H. G. Rollins	Samuel F. Webb	John Y. T. Smith

Delegate in Congress (Year of last election)

Curtis C. Bean (1884)	Marcus A. Smith (1886)	Smith (1888)

OFFICERS OF THE TERRITORY

(Listed for the years when the legislature was in session)

	16th Legislative Assembly 1891 (Phoenix)	17th Legislative Assembly 1893 (Phoenix)	18th Legislative Assembly 1895 (Phoenix)

Federal (Appointed by the President)

Governor	John N. Irwin	Murphy—L. C. Hughes	Hughes
Secretary	N. O. Murphy	N. A. Morford	Charles M. Bruce
U. S. Marshal	Robert H. Paul	Paul	W. K. Meade
District Attorney	H. R. Jeffords	Thomas F. Wilson	E. E. Ellinwood
Chief Justice	Henry C. Gooding	Gooding	Albert C. Baker
Associate Justice	Joseph H. Kibbey	Kibbey	Owen T. Rouse
Associate Justice	Richard E. Sloan	Sloan	J. J. Hawkins
Associate Justice[8]	Edmund W. Wells	Wells	J. D. Bethune

Territorial (Appointed by the Governor)

Adjutant General	E. S. Gill	Edward Schwartz	Schwartz
Attorney General	William Herring	Francis J. Heney	T. D. Satterwhite
Auditor	Hughes	H. C. Boone	C. P. Leitch
Treasurer	William Christy	J. A. Fleming	P. J. Cole

Presiding Officers of the Elected Legislative Assembly

President of the Council	Fred G. Hughes	T. G. Norris	A. J. Doran
Speaker of the House	C. S. Clark	Frank Baxter	J. H. Carpenter

Delegate in Congress (Year of last election)

Smith (1890)	Smith (1892)	N. O. Murphy (1894)

[8]A fourth justice was added to the Arizona Supreme Court in 1891.

OFFICERS OF THE TERRITORY

(Listed for the years when the legislature was in session)

	19th Legislative Assembly 1897 (Phoenix)	**20th Legislative Assembly 1899** (Phoenix)	**21st Legislative Assembly 1901** (Phoenix)

Federal (Appointed by the President)

Governor	B. J. Franklin[9]	N. O. Murphy	Murphy
Secretary	Bruce	Charles H. Akers	Akers
U. S. Marshal	Meade	William M. Griffith	Griffith
District Attorney	Ellinwood	Robert E. Morrison	Morrison
Chief Justice	Baker	Webster Street	Street
Associate Justice	Rouse	George R. Davis	Davis
Associate Justice	Hawkins	Fletcher M. Doan	Doan
Associate Justice	Bethune	Richard E. Sloan	Sloan

Territorial (Appointed by the Governor)

Adjutant General	Schwartz	H. F. Robinson	Robinson
Attorney General	John F. Wilson	C. F. Ainsworth	Ainsworth
Auditor	Leitch	George W. Vickers	Vickers
Treasurer	Thomas E. Farish	Thomas W. Pemberton	Pemberton

Presiding Officers of the Elected Legislative Assembly

President of the Council	Fred G. Hughes	Morris Goldwater	Eugene S. Ives
Speaker of the House	D. G. Chalmers	Henry F. Ashurst	P. P. Parker

Delegate in Congress (Year of last election)

Marcus A. Smith (1896)	John F. Wilson (1898)	Marcus A. Smith (1900)

[9]Franklin was succeeded by Myron H. McCord in 1897, but no legislature was in session during McCord's tenure.

OFFICERS OF THE TERRITORY

(Listed for the years when the legislature was in session)

	22nd Legislative Assembly 1903 (Phoenix)	23rd Legislative Assembly 1905 (Phoenix)	24th Legislative Assembly 1907 (Phoenix)

Federal (Appointed by the President)

Governor	Alexander O. Brodie	Brodie— Joseph H. Kibbey	Kibbey
Secretary	Isaac T. Stoddard	W. F. Nichols	Nichols
U. S. Marshall	Myron H. McCord	McCord	Ben F. Daniels
District Attorney	Frederick S. Nave	Nave	John L. B. Alexander
Chief Justice	Edward Kent	Kent	Kent
Associate Justice	Davis	Davis— Eugene A. Tucker	Frederick S. Nave
Associate Justice	Doan	Doan	Doan
Associate Justice	Sloan	Sloan	Sloan
Associate Justice		John H. Campbell[10]	Campbell

Territorial (Appointed by the Governor)

Adjutant General	Ben W. Leavell	Leavell	Leavell
Attorney General	Edmund W. Wells	Joseph Kibbey— E. S. Clark	Clark
Auditor	W. F. Nichols	Isaac M. Christy	John H. Page
Treasurer	Isaac M. Christy	E. E. Kirkland	Kirkland

Presiding Officers of the Elected Legislative Assembly

President of the Council	Ives	George W. P. Hunt	A. J. Doran
Speaker of the House	Theodore T. Powers	Wilfred T. Webb	Neill E. Bailey

Delegate in Congress (Year of last election)

John F. Wilson (1902)	Marcus A. Smith (1904)	Smith (1906)

[10]A fifth justice was added to the Arizona Supreme Court in 1905.

OFFICERS OF THE TERRITORY

(Listed for the years when the legislature was in session)

25th Legislative Assembly 1909
(Phoenix)

Federal (Appointed by the President)

Governor	Kibbey — Richard E. Sloan
Secretary	George U. Young
U. S. Marshal	
District Attorney	Alexander[11]
Chief Justice	Kent
Associate Justice	Nave—Ernest W. Lewis
Associate Justice	Doan
Associate Justice	Sloan—Edward M. Doe
Associate Justice	Campbell

Territorial (Appointed by the Governor)

Adjutant General	L. W. Coggins
Attorney General	John B. Wright
Auditor	W. C. Foster
Treasurer	Kirkland

Presiding Officers of the Elected Legislative Assembly

President of the Council	George W. P. Hunt
Speaker of the House	Sam F. Webb

Delegate in Congress (Year of last election)

Ralph H. Cameron (1908)

[11]Alexander was replaced by Joseph E. Morrison in 1910.

Appendix B

ROSTER OF JUDGES OF THE DISTRICT COURTS OF THE TERRITORY OF ARIZONA[1]

First Judicial District

William T. Howell (1864–65)
Henry T. Backus (1865–70)
*John Titus (1870–74)
*E. F. Dunne (1875–76)
*Charles G. W. French (1876–84)

*Sumner Howard (1884–85)
W. H. Barnes (1886–90)
Richard E. Sloan (1890–94)
J. D. Bethune (1894–97)
George R. Davis (1897–1905)

John H. Campbell (1905–12)

Second Judicial District

Joseph P. Allyn (1864–67)
Harley H. Cartter (1867–69)
Isham Reavis (1870–72)
DeForest Porter (1873–82)

Daniel H. Pinney (1882–85)
William W. Porter (1885–89)
Joseph H. Kibbey (1889–93)
Owen T. Rouse (1893–97)

Fletcher M. Doan (1897–1912)

Third Judicial District

*William F. Turner (1864–70)
Charles A. Tweed (1870–78)
Charles Silent (1878–81)
W. H. Stilwell (1881–83)
Wilson W. Hoover (1883)
A. W. Sheldon (1884)
W. F. Fitzgerald (1885)

*J. C. Shields (1886)
*James Wright (1887–90)
*Henry C. Gooding (1890–93)
*Albert C. Baker (1893–97)
*Hiram C. Truesdale (1897)
*Webster Street (1897–1902)
*Edward Kent (1902–12)

Fourth Judicial District

Edmund W. Wells (1891–93)
John J. Hawkins (1893–97)

Richard E. Sloan (1897–1909)
Edward M. Doe (1909–12)

Fifth Judicial District

Eugene A. Tucker (1905)

Frederick S. Nave (1905)

Ernest W. Lewis (1909–12)

*Chief Justice

[1]Works Progress Administration, **The District Courts of the Territory of Arizona.** Mimeographed publication, 1941, p. 37. There is a slight variation in dates given in this publication and in the **Arizona Reports** because the date of appointment, rather than the date for taking office, was usually listed in the latter.

504

Appendix C

MEMBERS OF THE
TWENTY-FIVE TERRITORIAL LEGISLATIVE ASSEMBLIES

FIRST LEGISLATIVE ASSEMBLY, 1864
(Prescott)

Council

	Name	Residence
First District	Mark Aldrich	Tucson
	Coles Bashford **(President)**	Tucson
	Patrick H. Dunne	Tucson
	Francisco S. León	Tucson
Second District	George W. Leihy	La Paz
	José M. Redondo	Arizona City
Third District	Henry A. Bigelow	Weaver
	Robert W. Groom	Groomdale
	King S. Woolsey	Agua Fria Ranch

House of Representatives

	Name	Residence
First District	Nathan B. Appel	Tubac
	John G. Capron	Tucson
	Jesús M. Elías	Tucson
	Gregory P. Harte	Tucson
	Norman S. Higgins	Cerro Colorado
	Gilbert W. Hopkins	Maricopa Mine
	Henry D. Jackson	Tucson
	W. Claude Jones **(Speaker)**	Tucson
	Daniel H. Stickney	Cababi
Second District	Thomas J. Bidwell	Castle Dome
	Luis G. Bouchet	La Paz
	George M. Holaday	La Paz
	Edward D. Tuttle	Mohave City
	William Walter	Mohave City
Third District	John M. Boggs	Prescott
	James Garvin	Prescott
	James S. Giles	Prescott
	Jackson McCrackin[1]	Lynx Creek

[1] In 1874 McCrackin discovered a rich silver mine in Mohave County where a peak is named after him. Somewhere along the line the i in his name became an e. See the **Arizona Sentinel** (Yuma), July 6, 1878.

505

SECOND LEGISLATIVE ASSEMBLY, 1865
(Prescott)

Council

	Name	Residence
Mohave County	William H. Hardy	Hardyville
Pima County[2]	Coles Bashford	Tucson
	Patrick H. Dunne	Tucson
	Francisco S. León	Tucson
Yavapai County	Henry A. Bigelow (President)	Wickenburg
	Robert W. Groom	Prescott
	King S. Woolsey	Agua Fria Ranch
Yuma County	Manuel Ravena	La Paz

House of Representatives

Mohave County	Octavius D. Gass	Callville
	Converse W. C. Rowell	Hardyville
Pima County[3]	Daniel H. Stickney	Cababi
Yavapai County	Daniel Ellis	Turkey Creek
	James S. Giles (Speaker)	Prescott
	Jackson McCrackin	Lynx Creek
	James O. Robertson	Big Bug
Yuma County	Peter Doll	La Paz
	Alexander McKey	La Paz
	William K. Heninger	La Paz

[2] In his election proclamation of August 4, 1865, Governor Goodwin directed Pima County to "elect one member of the Legislative Council, in place of Hon. Mark Aldrich, resigned, and nine members of the House of Representatives." George W. Pierce, who was elected to replace Aldrich, León, and Dunne, resigned before the second legislature convened at Prescott on December 6. Coles Bashford, President of the Council of the First Legislative Assembly, resigned on the first day after calling the Council of the Second Assembly to order. So Pima County was not represented in the Council during this session. See **Journals of the Second Legislative Assembly, 1865**, pp. 11, 15-16, 257-58.

[3] Eight elected representatives from Pima County did not attend: Simon Chambers, Juan Elías, Samuel Hughes (who received the highest number of votes), William J. Osborn, M. R. Platt, Manuel Smith, John W. Sweeney, and Henry McC. Ward. See Pima County Original Documents, Vol. 53: Election Returns, University of Arizona Special Collections. In regard to the Pima County delegation, the House passed the following resolution on the last day of the session: "Whereas no member elect from the county of Pima has attended this session of the Legislature, or shown to this house any reason for non-attendance, except the Hon. D. H. Stickney, who has been constantly in attendance during this session; and whereas without such attendance by said Hon. D. H. Stickney this House could not have organized nor have transacted any business whatsoever . . . we heartily endorse his course in the premises and that all true citizens and friends of this, our infant Territory, will applaud with us his unselfish devotion to the true interests and prosperity of the Territory." See **Journals**, p. 218, and **Arizona Miner**, Jan. 10, 1866.

THIRD LEGISLATIVE ASSEMBLY, 1866
(Prescott)

Council

	Name	Residence
Mohave County	William H. Hardy	Hardyville
Pah Ute County	Octavius D. Gass	Callville
Pima County	Mark Aldrich **(President)**	Tucson
	Henry Jenkins[4]	Tubac
	Mortimer R. Platt	Tucson
Yavapai County	Daniel S. Lount	Prescott
	John W. Simmons	Prescott
	Lewis A. Stevens	Prescott
Yuma County	Alexander McKey	La Paz

House of Representatives

Mohave County	Alonzo E. Davis	Hardyville
Pah Ute County	Royal J. Cutler[4]	Mill Point
Pima County	Oscar Buckalew	Calabasas
	Solomon W. Chambers[4]	Tubac
	James S. Douglas	Tucson
	Thomas D. Hutton[4]	Huavabi
	Michael McKenna	Tucson
	William J. Osborn	Tubac
	Granville H. Oury **(Speaker)**	Tucson
	Henry McC. Ward	Babocomari
Yavapai County	Underwood C. Barnett	Walnut Grove
	Daniel Ellis	Postle's Ranch
	William S. Little	Prescott
	John B. Slack	Turkey Creek
	Hannibal Sypert	Prescott
Yuma County	Marcus D. Dobbins	La Paz
	Robert F. Platt	Planet Mine
	William H. Thomas[4]	Arizona City

[4]Did not attend the session.

FOURTH LEGISLATIVE ASSEMBLY, 1867
(Prescott)

Council

	Name	Residence
Mohave County	William H. Hardy	Hardyville
Pah Ute County	Octavius D. Gass **(President)**	Callville
Pima County	Henry Jenkins	Tubac
	Mortimer R. Platt	Tucson
	Daniel H. Stickney	Tucson
Yavapai County	Daniel S. Lount	Agua Caliente
	John W. Simmons	Prescott
	Lewis A. Stevens	Prescott
Yuma County	Alexander McKey	La Paz

House of Representatives

Mohave County	Nathaniel S. Lewis	Hardyville
Pah Ute County	Royal J. Cutler	St. Joseph
Pima County	John B. Allen	Tucson
	Underwood C. Barnett	Tucson
	Solomon W. Chambers	Calabasas
	Philip Drachman	Tucson
	Francis M. Hodges	Tucson
	Charles W. Lewis	Tubac
	Marvin M. Richardson	Tubac
Yavapai County	Edward J. Cook	Prescott
	Allen Cullumber	Walnut Grove
	John T. Dare	Prescott
	James S. Giles	Prescott
	John H. Matthews	Kirkland Valley
	John A. Rush	Prescott
Yuma County	G. W. Hanford[5]	Eureka
	John Henion[5]	Williams Fork
	Oliver Lindsey **(Speaker)**	La Paz

[5]Did not attend the session.

FIFTH LEGISLATIVE ASSEMBLY, 1868
(Tucson)

Council

	Name	Residence
Mohave and Pah Ute Counties	Octavius D. Gass	Callville
Pima County	Henry Jenkins	Tucson
	Alexander McKey	Tubac
	Estevan Ochoa	Tucson
	Daniel H. Stickney	Casa Blanca
Yavapai County	John T. Alsap **(President)**	Prescott
	John G. Campbell[b]	Prescott
	F. M. Chapman[b]	Wickenburg
Yuma County	Joseph K. Hooper[b]	Arizona City

House of Representatives

Mohave County	U. C. Doolittle[b]	Hardyville
Pah Ute County	Andrew S. Gibbons	St. Thomas
Pima County	John Anderson	Apache Pass
	Sol. W. Chambers	Calabasas
	Robert M. Crandal	Tucson
	Jesús M. Elías	Tucson
	Francis H. Goodwin	Tucson
	John Owen	Tubac
	Hiram S. Stevens	Tucson
Yavapai County	Thomas W. Brooks[b]	Prescott
	Follett G. Cristie[b]	Prescott
	William S. Little[b]	Prescott
	E. Lumbley[b]	Wickenburg
	John Smith	Camp McDowell
	G. R. Wilson[b]	Phoenix
Yuma County	Thomas J. Bidwell **(Speaker)**	La Paz
	Oliver Lindsey	La Paz
	James P. Lugenbul[b]	Arizona City

[b]Did not attend the session.

SIXTH LEGISLATIVE ASSEMBLY, 1871
(Tucson)

Council

	Name	Residence
Mohave and Pah Ute Counties	Not represented	
Pima County	Francisco S. León	Tucson
	Estevan Ochoa	Tucson
	Hiram S. Stevens	Tucson
	Daniel H. Stickney[7] **(President)**	Santa Rita
Yavapai County	John T. Alsap	Phoenix
	Harley H. Cartter[8] **(President)**	Prescott
	Andrew J. Marmaduke	Prescott
Yuma County	John H. Phillips	Eureka

House of Representatives

Mohave and Pah Ute Counties	Not represented	
Pima County	J. W. Anderson	Florence
	Juan Elías	Tucson
	W. L. Fowler	Tucson
	F. H. Goodwin	Tucson
	William Morgan	Tucson
	Ramón Romano	Tubac
	Rees Smith[9]	Tubac
Yavapai County	J. H. Fitzgerald	Wickenburg
	Joseph Melvin	Verde
	James L. Mercer	Phoenix
	William J. O'Neill	Kirkland Valley
	John L. Taylor	Prescott
	G. A. Wilson	Phoenix
Yuma County	Thomas J. Bidwell	Ehrenberg
	C. H. Brinley	Arizona City
	Marcus D. Dobbins **(Speaker)**	Arizona City

[7]Died while legislature in session.

[8]Became president when Stickney died.

[9]Smith, a native of Ohio and one of the first American pioneers in California, was murdered near Tubac on June 15, 1871, by Mexicans who escaped to Sonora with stolen cattle. The contents of a sealed envelope, which he had left with the **Citizen,** revealed that he had expected to be killed by Indians in the sparsely-settled upper Santa Cruz Valley. The eleven-year-old son of Pete Kitchen was killed in the same area by Indians just a week before Smith's death. See **Arizona Citizen,** June 24, 1871.

SEVENTH LEGISLATIVE ASSEMBLY, 1873
(Tucson)

Council

	Name	Residence
Pima County	Mark Aldrich	Tucson
	Juan Elías	Tucson
	Levi Ruggles	Florence
	Hiram S. Stevens	Tucson
Yavapai County	J. P. Hargrave **(President)**	Prescott
	A. O. Noyes	Prescott
Yavapai and Maricopa Counties	King S. Woolsey	Agua Caliente
Yuma County	Thomas J. Bidwell	Ehrenberg
Yuma and Mohave Counties	W. F. Henning	Mineral Park

House of Representatives

Maricopa County	Granville H. Oury **(Speaker)**	Phoenix
Pima County	John B. Allen	Tucson
	William C. Davis	Tucson
	Lionel M. Jacobs	Tucson
	F. M. Larkin	Sanford (Adamsville)
	John Montgomery	San Pedro
	John T. Smith	Tubac
	John W. Sweeney	Florence
	J. S. Vosburg[10]	Tucson
Yavapai County	John H. Behan	Prescott
	William Cole	Bradshaw Mines
	Fred Henry	Peeples Valley
	Thomas Stonehouse	Williamson Valley
	Henry Wickenburg	Wickenburg
Yuma County	C. H. Brinley	Yuma
	J. M. Redondo	Yuma
	C. W. C. Rowell	Yuma
Yuma and Mohave Counties	George Gleason	Mineral Park

[10]Sometimes spelled Vosberg in the official records.

EIGHTH LEGISLATIVE ASSEMBLY, 1875
(Tucson)

Council

	Name	Residence
Maricopa County	King S. Woolsey **(President)**	Agua Caliente
Mohave County	A. E. Davis	Mineral Park
Pima County	P. R. Brady	Florence
	S. R. DeLong	Camp Bowie
	William Zeckendorf	Tucson
Yavapai County	John G. Campbell	Prescott
	J. P. Hargrave	Prescott
	L. A. Stevens	Prescott
Yuma County	J. M. Redondo	Yuma

House of Representatives

Maricopa County	John T. Alsap **(Speaker)**	Phoenix
	Granville H. Oury	Phoenix
Mohave County	S. W. Wood''	Mineral City
Pima County	S. H. Drachman	Tucson
	Jesús M. Elías	Tucson
	F. M. Griffin	Florence
	John Montgomery	Tres Alamos
	Alphonso Rickman	Tubac
	George H. Stevens	Eureka Springs
Yavapai County	Levi Bashford	Prescott
	Gideon Brooke	Prescott
	C. P. Head	Prescott
	A. L. Moeller	Prescott
	W. J. O'Neill	Kirkland Valley
	Hugo Richards	Prescott
Yuma County	H. Goldberg	Yuma
	R. B. Kelly	Yuma
	Samuel Purdy Jr.	Yuma

''Wood, a native of Illinois, was persuaded to come west by his cousin, Governor A. P. K. Safford, who appointed him probate judge of Mohave County in 1873. Wood and A. E. Davis made the arduous 650-mile trip from Mineral City to the capital at Tucson in a mule-drawn buckboard. See the Selwyn Willard Wood File, APHS.

NINTH LEGISLATIVE ASSEMBLY, 1877
(Tucson)

Council

	Name	Residence
Maricopa County	King S. Woolsey **(President)**	Agua Caliente
Pima County	F. H. Goodwin	Tucson
	F. G. Hughes	Tucson
Pinal County	Levi Ruggles	Florence
Yavapai County	George D. Kendall	Prescott
	Andrew L. Moeller	Prescott
	John A. Rush	Prescott
	Lewis A. Stevens	Prescott
Yuma County	J. M. Redondo	Yuma

House of Representatives

Maricopa County	M. H. Calderwood **(Speaker)**	Phoenix
	J. A. Parker	Phoenix
Mohave County	James P. Bull	Mineral Park
Pima County	D. A. Bennett	Tucson
	Estevan Ochoa	Tucson
	William Ohnesorgen	Don Pedro
	Mariano G. Samaniego	Tucson
	George H. Stevens	Eureka Springs
Pinal County	George Scott	Globe City
Yavapai County	C. B. Foster	Prescott
	G. Hathaway	Prescott
	William S. Head	Prescott
	W. W. Hutchinson	Prescott
	John H. Marion	Prescott
	S. C. Miller	Prescott
	Ed. G. Peck	Prescott
	Hugo Richards	Prescott
Yuma County	J. W. Dorrington	Yuma

TENTH LEGISLATIVE ASSEMBLY, 1879
(Prescott)

Council

	Name	Residence
Maricopa County	C. H. Gray[12]	Phoenix
Pima County	Fred G. Hughes **(President)**	Tucson
	J. M. Kirkpatrick	Tucson
Pinal County	P. Thomas	Globe City
Yavapai County	C. C. Bean	Prescott
	W. S. Head	Camp Verde
	W. A. Rowe	Gillett
	E. W. Wells	Prescott
Yuma County	F. D. Welcome	Yuma

House of Representatives

Maricopa County	John T. Alsap	Phoenix
	J. D. Rumburg	Phoenix
Mohave County	John H. Behan	Signal
Pima County	A. E. Fay	Tucson
	C. P. Leitch	Tucson
	James Speedy	Tucson
	Madison W. Stewart **(Speaker)**	Camp Grant
	Walter L. Vail	Tucson
Pinal County	W. K. Meade	Florence
Yavapai County	W. M. Buffum	Prescott
	John Davis	Camp Verde
	Thomas Fitch	Prescott
	Pat Hamilton	Prescott
	P. McAteer	Kirkland Valley
	E. R. Nicoles[13]	Williamson Valley
	J. A. Park	Prescott
	James Stinson	Snowflake
Yuma County	Samuel Purdy Jr.	Yuma

[12]Incorrectly listed as E. H. Gray in the **Journals of the Tenth Legislative Assembly.**
[13]Sometimes spelled Nichols in the **Arizona Miner.**

ELEVENTH LEGISLATIVE ASSEMBLY, 1881
(Prescott)

Council

	Name	Residence
Apache County	Solomon Barth	St. Johns
Maricopa County	A. C. Baker	Phoenix
	R. S. Thomas	Phoenix
Mohave County	A. Cornwall	Stockton
Pima County	B. A. Fickas	Tombstone
	B. H. Hereford	Tucson
	W. K. Meade	Tombstone
	H. G. Rollins	Tombstone
	George H. Stevens	Safford
Pinal County	J. W. Anderson	Florence
Yavapai County	Murat Masterson **(President)**	Prescott
Yuma County	J. W. Dorrington	Yuma

House of Representatives

Apache County	J. Barton	Clifton
	G. R. York	Clifton
Maricopa County	N. Sharp	Hayden's Ferry
	Peter J. Bolan	Phoenix
	John McCormack[14]	Globe
Mohave County	David Southwick	Stockton
Pima County	Thomas Dunbar	Tombstone
	E. B. Gifford	Tucson
	John Haynes	Tucson
	M. K. Lurty	Tombstone
	John McCafferty	Tombstone
	J. K. Rodgers	Smithville
	John Roman	Tucson
	M. G. Samaniego	Tucson
	E. H. Smith	Tombstone
	M. S. Snyder	Tucson
	H. M. Woods	Tombstone
Pinal County	A. J. Doran	Pinal
	Donald Robb	Globe
Yavapai County	George E. Brown	Prescott
	R. B. Steadman	Prescott
	L. Wollenberg	Prescott
Yuma County	J. F. Knapp **(Speaker)**	Yuma
	G. W. Norton	Yuma

[14]Sometimes spelled McCormick in the **Journals of the Eleventh Legislative Assembly.** McCormack was later a sub-commissioner at the World's Fair in New Orleans. He was shot and killed at Clifton in 1885. See **Arizona Gazette,** August 10, 1885 and **The Clifton Clarion,** August 12 and September 16, 1885.

TWELFTH LEGISLATIVE ASSEMBLY, 1883
(Prescott)

Council

	Name	Residence
Apache County	H. E. Lacy	Ft. Apache
Cochise County	Edwin H. Wiley **(President)**	Tombstone
Graham and Cochise Counties	Peter J. Bolan	Safford
Maricopa and Gila Counties	A. D. Lemon	Phoenix
Mohave and Yuma Counties	L. S. Welton	Mineral Park
Pima County	Fred Hughes	Tucson
	J. F. Knapp	Tucson
Pinal and Pima Counties	J. W. Davis	Florence
Yavapai County	F. K. Ainsworth	Prescott
	Morris Goldwater	Prescott
	Murat Masterson	Prescott
	Edmund W. Wells	Prescott

House of Representatives

Apache County	C. A. Franklin	St. Johns
Cochise County	J. F. Duncan	Tombstone
	W. H. Savage	Tombstone
	D. K. Wardwell	Huachuca
Gila County	William Graves	Globe
Graham County	Adolphe Solomon	Bowie
Maricopa County	J. P. Holcomb	Phoenix
	S. F. Webb	Mesa City
Mohave County	L. J. Lassell	Mineral Park
Pima County	R. C. Brown	Tucson
	J. H. Fawcett	Oro Blanco
	E. B. Gifford	Tucson
	D. Snyder	Harshaw
	Moye Wicks	Tucson
Pinal and Pima Counties	J. W. Anderson	Florence
Yavapai County	Alfred Allen	Prescott
	Robert Connell	Prescott
	John Ellis	Prescott
	E. H. Gobin	Prescott
	Nehemiah McCallum[15]	Prescott
	C. A. Randall	Prescott
	Winthrop A. Rowe **(Speaker)**	Prescott
	Charles Taylor	Prescott
Yuma County	J. W. Dorrington	Yuma

[15]See the **Great Register, Yavapai County, For 1882,** copy in State Library and Archives. The name appears as N. McCollum and R. McCallum in the **Journals** . . . and in the **Laws of the Territory,** 12th Legislative Assembly.

THIRTEENTH LEGISLATIVE ASSEMBLY, 1885
(Prescott)

Council

Name	Residence
Apache County	E. S. Stover	Apache
Cochise County	W. A. Harwood	Tombstone
Gila County	Alonzo Bailey	Globe
Graham County	W. C. Bridwell	Safford
Maricopa County	R. B. Todd	Phoenix
Mohave County	John Howell	Hackberry
Pima County	R. N. Leatherwood	Tucson
Pinal County	Thomas Weedin	Florence
Yavapai County	W. G. Stewart	Flagstaff
Yuma County	J. W. Dorrington	Yuma
Northern District[16]	F. K. Ainsworth **(President)**	Prescott
Southern District[16]	C. C. Stephens	Tucson

House of Representatives

Apache County	J. D. Houck	Springerville
	Luther Martin	St. Johns
Cochise County	W. F. Frame	Tombstone
	T. T. Hunter	Tombstone
	W. F. Nichols	Tombstone
	Hugh Percy	Tombstone
	D. K. Wardwell	Tombstone
Gila County	W. C. Watkins	Globe
Graham County	James Sias	Clifton
Maricopa County	J. S. Armstrong	Mesa City
	DeForest Porter	Phoenix
Mohave County	William Imus	Quijotoa
Pima County	E. W. Aram	Tucson
	G. W. Brown	Tucson
	S. M. Franklin	Tucson
	E. W. Risley	State Line
	H. G. Rollins **(Speaker)**	Nogales
Pinal County	Levi Ruggles	Florence
Yavapai County	D. J. Brannen	Flagstaff
	Julius A. Brown	Lower Agua Fria
	Robert Connell	Prescott
	L. P. Nash	Tonto Basin
	W. H. Robbins	Alexandria
Yuma County	Samuel Purdy Jr.	Yuma

[16]One member was elected at large from the five northern counties of Apache, Maricopa, Mohave, Yuma, and Yavapai. Another member was elected at large from the southern counties of Cochise, Gila, Graham, Pima, and Pinal. See **Laws of the Territory of Arizona,** 12th Legislative Assembly, 1883, pp. 218-20.

FOURTEENTH LEGISLATIVE ASSEMBLY, 1887
(Prescott)

Council

	Name	Residence
Apache County	J. H. Breed	Winslow
Cochise County	L. W. Blinn	Tombstone
Gila County	P. C. Robertson	Globe
Graham County	George H. Stevens	Solomonville
Maricopa County	L. H. Goodrich	Phoenix
Mohave County	E. L. Burdick	Mineral Park
Pima County	Charles R. Drake	Tucson
Pinal County	J. W. Anderson	Florence
Yavapai County	C. B. Foster	Prescott
Yuma County	Isaac Lyons	Yuma
Northern District	A. Cornwall **(President)**	Signal
Southern District	W. C. Watkins	Globe

House of Representatives

Apache County	J. Q. Adamson	Winslow
	James Scott	St. Johns
Cochise County	J. M. Bracewell	Tombstone
	M. Gray	Benson
	F. W. Heyne	Bisbee
	B. L. Peel	Tombstone
	Scott White	Dunn Springs
Gila County	Eugene J. Trippel	Globe
Graham County	D. H. Ming	Camp Thomas
Maricopa County	John Y. T. Smith	Phoenix
	Samuel F. Webb **(Speaker)**	Phoenix
Mohave County	P. F. Collins	Mineral Park
Pima County	A. A. Bean	Tucson
	R. N. Leatherwood	Tucson
	A. McKay	Tucson
	J. B. Scott	Olive Camp
	C. R. Wores	Tucson
Pinal County	A. J. Doran	Florence
Yavapai County	Henry T. Andrews	Lynx Creek
	W. H. Ashurst	Flagstaff
	O. C. Felton	Payson
	J. J. Fisher	Thompson Valley
	A. G. Oliver	Seligman
Yuma County	Charles Baker	Yuma

FIFTEENTH LEGISLATIVE ASSEMBLY, 1889
(Prescott-Phoenix)

Council

	Name	Residence
Apache County	E. J. Simpson	Holbrook
Cochise County	George W. Cheyney	Tombstone
Gila County	George T. Peter	Armer
Graham County	Burt Dunlap	Dunlap
Maricopa County	S. F. Webb	Phoenix
Mohave County	W. H. Hardy	Kingman
Pima County	Charles R. Drake **(President)**	Tucson
Pinal County	R. E. Sloan	Florence
Yavapai County	J. M. W. Moore	Prescott
Yuma County	John W. Dorrington	Yuma
Northern District	L. H. Orme	Phoenix
Southern District	George W. Hoadley	Bisbee

House of Representatives

Apache County	Charles Flinn	Winslow
	J. A. Johnson	Navajo
Cochise County	George H. Dailey	Tombstone
	Grant Hicks	Tombstone
	John O. Robbins	Tombstone
	J. O. Stanford	Tombstone
	Alexander Wright	Tombstone
Gila County	J. C. Jones	Globe
Graham County	George H. Stevens	Solomonville
Maricopa County	T. C. Jordan	Tempe
	John Y. T. Smith **(Speaker)**	Phoenix
Mohave County	Thomas Halleck	Signal
Pima County	J. J. Chatham	Nogales
	Louis Martin	Tucson
	J. S. O'Brien	Tucson
	H. B. Tenney	Tucson
	H. D. Underwood	Tucson
Pinal County	Louis DePuy	Florence
Yavapai County	C. D. Brown	Prescott
	J. L. Fisher	Prescott
	J. V. Rhoades	Flagstaff
	F. L. Rogers	Williams
	George P. Thornton	Williams
Yuma County	Samuel Purdy Jr.	Yuma

SIXTEENTH LEGISLATIVE ASSEMBLY, 1891
(Phoenix)

Council

	Name	Residence
Apache County	E. J. Simpson	Holbrook
Cochise County	J. V. Vickers	Tombstone
Gila County	George T. Peter[17]	Armer
Graham County	P. M. Thurmond	Solomonville
Maricopa County	C. Meyer Zulick	Phoenix
Mohave County	Foster S. Dennis	Kingman
Pima County	Fred G. Hughes (President)	Tucson
Pinal County	A. J. Doran	Florence
Yavapai County	J. C. Herndon	Prescott
Yuma County	A. Frank	Yuma
Northern District	Harris Baldwin	Prescott
Southern District	P. R. Brady	Florence

House of Representatives

Apache County	Frank Hart	Winslow
	J. T. Lesueur	St. Johns
Cochise County	S. M. Burr	Tombstone
	C. S. Clark (Speaker)	Tombstone
	Thomas Dunbar	Tres Alamos[18]
	F. W. Heyne	Powers (Rucker Canyon)
	J. H. Tevis	Bowie
Gila County	R. B. Moore	Globe
Graham County	D. Gough	Clifton
Maricopa County	L. H. Chalmers	Phoenix
	T. E. Farish	Vulture
Mohave County	M. C. Copeland	Kingman
Pima County	Thomas Driscoll	Tucson
	Gus A. Hoff	Tucson
	George Pusch	Tucson
	M. G. Samaniego	Tucson
	C. C. Suter	Tucson
Pinal County	J. B. Allen	Florence
Yavapai County	J. W. Dougherty	Prescott
	J. J. Fisher	Ferguson Valley
	W. A. Freeze	Prescott
	S. C. Mott	Prescott
	J. A. Vail	Flagstaff
Yuma County	C. H. Brinley	Yuma

[17]The name is seen several ways in the newspapers and official records: G. F. for G. T. and Peters for Peter. See the **Arizona Republican,** January 25, 1891, for short biographies of Peter and other members of the Sixteenth Legislative Assembly. The **Arizona Cattlelog,** February, 1964, also has a biography of Peter.

[18]Tres Alamos was located north of Benson. Dunbar was appointed postmaster there in 1875 and also ran a stage station for awhile.

SEVENTEENTH LEGISLATIVE ASSEMBLY, 1893
(Phoenix)

Council

	Name	Residence
Apache County	J. A. Hubbell	St. Johns
Cochise County	George W. Cheyney	Tombstone
Coconino County	F. R. Nellis	Williams
Gila County	E. J. Edwards	Globe
Graham County	Charles M. Shannon	Clifton
Maricopa County	W. T. Smith	Phoenix
Mohave County	Foster S. Dennis	Kingman
Pima County	W. M. Lovell	Tucson
Pinal County	A. J. Doran	Florence
Yavapai County	John J. Hawkins	Prescott
Yuma County	M. J. Nugent	Yuma
At Large[19]	T. G. Norris **(President)**	Flagstaff

House of Representatives

Apache County	R. C. Dryden	Winslow
	Luther Martin	Springerville
Cochise County	M. Gray	Rucker
	James Reilly	Tombstone
	Austin C. Wright	Bisbee
Coconino County	H. D. Ross	Flagstaff
Gila County	George W. P. Hunt	Globe
Graham County	A. D. Brewer	Morenci
	George Skinner	Safford
Maricopa County	Frank Baxter **(Speaker)**	Phoenix
	M. E. Hurley	Phoenix
	J. A. Marshall	Phoenix
	H. C. Rogers	Lehi
Mohave County	David Southwick	Music Mountain
Pima County	J. W. Bruce	Tucson
	R. N. Leatherwood	Tucson
	Charles Mehan	Nogales
	C. F. Schumaker	Tucson
Pinal County	W. T. Day	Vekol
	Thomas C. Graham	Kenilworth
Yavapai County	S. P. Behan	Prescott
	D. A. Burke	Prescott
	J. D. Cook	Prescott
Yuma County	D. M. Field	Yuma

[19]One member was elected from the entire territory. See **Acts, Resolutions and Memorials,** Sixteenth Legislative Assembly, 1891, pp. 111-12.

EIGHTEENTH LEGISLATIVE ASSEMBLY, 1895
(Phoenix)

Council

	Name	Residence
Apache County	F. T. Aspinwall	Winslow
Cochise County	B. A. Packard	Bisbee
Coconino County	E. J. Babbitt	Flagstaff
Gila County	E. J. Edwards	Globe
Graham County	Burt Dunlap	Dunlap
Maricopa County	Henry E. Kemp	Phoenix
Mohave County	William H. Lake	Kingman
Pima County	J. B. Scott	Tucson
Pinal County	Thomas Davis	Kenilworth
Yavapai County	John S. Jones	Chaparal
Yuma County	M. J. Nugent	Yuma
At Large	A. J. Doran **(President)**	Florence

House of Representatives

	Name	Residence
Apache County	Will C. Barnes	Holbrook
	George H. Crosby	Springerville
Cochise County	C. L. Cummings	Bisbee
	H. C. Herrick	Fairbank
	A. C. Wright	Benson
Coconino County	E. F. Greenlaw	Chalender
Gila County	George W. P. Hunt	Globe
Graham County	Joseph Fish	Safford
	George W. Skinner	Graham
Maricopa County	A. E. Hinton	Alhambra
	J. A. Marshall	Phoenix
	Niels Petersen	Tempe
	Perry Wildman	Tempe
Mohave County	O. D. M. Gaddis	Kingman
Pima County	N. W. Bernard	Arivaca
	H. K. Chenoweth	Nogales
	James Finley	Tucson
	M. G. Samaniego	Tucson
Pinal County	Thomas E. Baker	Schultz
	M. R. Moore	Arizola
Yavapai County	Thomas H. Brown	Congress
	G. W. Hull	Jerome
	J. C. Martin	Prescott
Yuma County	J. H. Carpenter **(Speaker)**	Yuma

NINETEENTH LEGISLATIVE ASSEMBLY, 1897
(Phoenix)

Council

	Name	Residence
Apache County	Solomon Barth	St. Johns
Cochise County	B. A. Packard	Bisbee
Coconino County	A. A. Dutton	Flagstaff
Gila County	George W. P. Hunt	Globe
Graham County	D. H. Ming	Ft. Thomas
Maricopa County	C. R. Hakes	Mesa
Mohave County	W. H. Lake	Kingman
Navajo County	F. T. Aspinwall	Winslow
Pima County	Fred G. Hughes (President)	Tucson
Pinal County	P. R. Brady	Florence
Yavapai County	J. W. Norton	Prescott
Yuma County	J. H. Carpenter	Yuma

House of Representatives

Apache County	J. B. Patterson	St. Johns
Cochise County	J. N. Jones	Bisbee
	J. J. Riggs	Willcox
	William Speed	Willcox
Coconino County	H. F. Ashurst	Williams
Gila County	Leroy Ikenberry	Globe
Graham County	J. K. Rogers	Pima
	George W. Skinner	Safford
Maricopa County	Aaron Goldberg	Phoenix
	J. C. Goodwin	Tempe
	P. P. Parker	Phoenix
	J. W. Woolf	Tempe
Mohave County	L. O. Cowan	Kingman
Navajo County	J. N. Smith	Snowflake
Pima County	A. C. Bernard	Tucson
	D. G. Chalmers (Speaker)	Tucson
	J. B. Finley	Tucson
	A. J. Preston	Tucson
Pinal County	C. P. Mason	Florence
	C. D. Reppy	Florence
Yavapai County	G. W. Hull	Jerome
	W. J. Mulvenon	Prescott
	D. J. Warren	Walker
Yuma County	Heil Hale	Yuma

TWENTIETH LEGISLATIVE ASSEMBLY, 1899
(Phoenix)

Council

	Name	Residence
Apache County	D. K. Udall	Springerville
Cochise County	Charles C. Warner	Bisbee
Coconino County	T. S. Bunch	Flagstaff
Gila County	George W. P. Hunt	Globe
Graham County	George A. Olney	Solomonville
Maricopa County	Aaron Goldberg	Phoenix
Mohave County	J. M. Murphy	Kingman
Navajo County	George A. Wolff	Winslow
Pima County	J. B. Finley	Tucson
Pinal County	A. C. Wright	Mammoth
Yavapai County	Morris Goldwater **(President)**	Prescott
Yuma County	J. H. Carpenter	Yuma

House of Representatives

Apache County	N. Gonzales	Springerville
Cochise County	Mike Gray	Pearce
	Henry Etz	Benson
	H. M. Woods	Bisbee
Coconino County	Henry F. Ashurst **(Speaker)**	Williams
Gila County	John C. Evans	Globe
Graham County	W. W. Pace	Safford
	E. M. Williams	Morenci
Maricopa County	J. W. Benham	Phoenix
	Sam Brown	Tempe
	Charles Peterson	Mesa
	Winfield Scott	Scottsdale
Mohave County	William Imus	Peach Springs
Navajo County	W. A. Parr	Winslow
Pima County	Alfred S. Donau	Anvil Ranch
	Otis Hale	Tucson
	George Pusch	Tucson
	F. A. Stevens	Tucson
Pinal County	James E. Arthur	Florence
Yavapai County	W. S. Adams	Jerome
	A. A. Moore	Walnut Grove
	J. J. Sanders	Richinbar
Yuma County	John Doan	Fortuna

TWENTY-FIRST LEGISLATIVE ASSEMBLY, 1901
(Prescott)

Council

	Name	Residence
Apache County	E. S. Perkins	St. Johns
Cochise County	C. C. Warner	Bisbee
Coconino County	M. J. Riordan	Flagstaff
Gila County	S. B. Claypool	Globe
Graham County	C. M. Shannon	Clifton
Maricopa County	J. M. Ford	Phoenix
Mohave County	M. G. Burns	Chloride
Navajo County	C. C. Campbell	Winslow
Pima and Santa Cruz Counties	J. B. Finley	Tucson
Pinal County	G. P. Blair	Mammoth
Yavapai County	H. T. Andrews	Prescott
Yuma County	Eugene S. Ives **(President)**	Yuma

House of Representatives

Apache County	Richard Gibbons	St. Johns
Cochise County	Mike Gray	Pearce
	Stephen (Steve) Roemer	Benson
	H. M. Woods	Bisbee
Coconino County	James Walsh	Williams
Gila County	C. L. Houston	Globe
Graham County	E. T. Ijams	Safford
	Andrew Kimball	Thatcher
Maricopa County	B. A. Fowler	Glendale
	J. P. Ivy	Phoenix
	P. P. Parker **(Speaker)**	Phoenix
	Charles Peterson	Mesa
Mohave County	Kean St. Charles	Kingman
Navajo County	William J. Morgan	Show Low
Pima County	Sam Y. Barkley	Tucson
	A. C. Bernard	Tucson
	Joseph B. Corbett	Tucson
Pinal County	Alexander Barker	Mammoth
	William Beard	Florence
Santa Cruz County	A. H. Noon	Nogales
Yavapai County	T. E. Campbell	Jerome
	O. L. Geer	Martinez
	F. R. Ward	Crown King
Yuma County	Jesse E. Crouch	Mohawk

TWENTY-SECOND LEGISLATIVE ASSEMBLY, 1903
(Phoenix)

Council

	Name	Residence
Apache County	Heber Jarvis	Eagar
Cochise County	B. A. Packard	Bisbee
Coconino County	Henry F. Ashurst	Williams
Gila County	A. H. Morehead	Globe
Graham County	H. B. Rice	Morenci
Maricopa County	J. H. Kibbey	Phoenix
Mohave County	John R. Whiteside	Chloride
Navajo County	J. X. Woods	Winslow
Pima and Santa Cruz Counties	Joseph B. Corbett	Tucson
Pinal County	E. W. Childs	Mammoth
Yavapai County	J. W. Burson	Constellation
Yuma County	Eugene S. Ives **(President)**	Yuma

House of Representatives

Apache County	N. Gonzales	Springerville
Cochise County	James A. Howell	San Bernardino
	J. M. O'Connell	Bisbee
	Stephen Roemer	Benson
Coconino County	John H. Page	Grand View
Gila County	Joseph B. Henry	Globe
Graham County	W. T. Webb	Pima
	Gus Williams	Clifton
Maricopa County	G. U. Collins	Phoenix
	J. D. Marlar	Phoenix
	Theodore T. Powers **(Speaker)**	Phoenix
	J. W. Woolf	Tempe
Mohave County	Kean St. Charles	Kingman
Navajo County	W. A. Parr	Navajo
Pima County	N. W. Bernard	Tucson
	L. O. Cowan	Tucson
	M. Lamont	Tucson
Pinal County	L. C. Herr	Florence
	P. A. Schilling	Ray
Santa Cruz County	B. J. Whiteside	Nogales
Yavapai County	Lucius R. Barrow	Prescott
	T. J. Morrison	Jerome
	W. A. Rowe	Walker
Yuma County	F. S. Ingalls	Yuma

TWENTY-THIRD LEGISLATIVE ASSEMBLY, 1905
(Phoenix)

Council

	Name	Residence
Apache County	Alfred Ruiz	St. Johns
Cochise County	Stephen Roemer	Benson
Coconino County	John H. Page	Grand View
Gila County	George W. P. Hunt **(President)**	Globe
Graham County	H. B. Rice	Morenci
Maricopa County	J. E. Bark	Phoenix
Mohave County	J. E. Perry	Kingman
Navajo County	Benjamin Downs	Winslow
Pima and Santa Cruz Counties	N. W. Bernard	Tucson
Pinal County	C. H. Cutting	Troy
Yavapai County	R. N. Looney	Prescott
Yuma County	M. J. Nugent	Yuma

House of Representatives

Apache County	J. B. Patterson	St. Johns
Cochise County	Charles Strong	Bisbee
	William Neville	Douglas
	N. E. Bailey	Naco
Coconino County	Charles A. Neal	Williams
Gila County	S. A. Haught	Rye
Graham County	Lamar Cobb	Clifton
	Wilfred T. Webb **(Speaker)**	Pima
Maricopa County	L. R. Krueger	Phoenix
	Watson Pickrell	Tempe
	M. A. Stanford	Phoenix
	John H. Pomeroy	Mesa
Mohave County	P. F. Collins	Fort Mohave
Navajo County	Q. R. Gardner	Woodruff
Pima County	Thos. F. Wilson	Tucson
	H. C. Kennedy	Tucson
	L. G. Davis	Tucson
Pinal County	J. G. Keating	Florence
	Alexander Barker	Mammoth
Santa Cruz County	T. L. Bristol	Nogales
Yavapai County	G. W. Hull	Jerome
	LeRoy Anderson	Prescott
	M. A. Perkins	Prescott
Yuma County	W. F. Timmons	Yuma

TWENTY-FOURTH LEGISLATIVE ASSEMBLY, 1907
(Phoenix)

Council

	Name	Residence
Apache County	John T. Hogue	St. Johns
Cochise County	Stephen Roemer	Benson
Coconino County	H. C. Lockett	Flagstaff
Gila County	George W. P. Hunt	Globe
Graham County	J. F. Cleaveland	Morenci
Maricopa County	Eugene Brady O'Neill	Phoenix
Mohave County	William G. Blakely	Kingman
Navajo County	Robert Scott	Show Low
Pima and Santa Cruz Counties	E. M. Dickerman	Tucson
Pinal County	Thomas F. Weedin	Florence
Yavapai County	A. J. Doran **(President)**	Prescott
Yuma County	Donald McIntyre	Yuma

House of Representatives

Apache County	S. E. Day	Fort Defiance
Cochise County	Owen E. Murphy	Bisbee
	Neill E. Bailey **(Speaker)**	Naco
	John H. Slaughter	San Bernardino
Coconino County	L. S. Williams	Williams
Gila County	John McCormick	Young
Graham County	W. W. Pace	Thatcher
	John R. Hampton	Clifton
Maricopa County	J. W. Crenshaw	Phoenix
	William Wallace	Riverside
	E. C. Bunch	Glendale
	W. D. Bell	Phoenix
Mohave County	Carl G. Krook	Sandy
Navajo County	William J. Morgan	Show Low
Pima County	Anthony V. Grossetta	Tucson
	Adolph Bail	Tucson
	David Morgan	Silverbell
Pinal County	J. I. Coleman	Kelvin
	Nott E. Guild	Kelvin
Santa Cruz County	B. J. Whiteside	Nogales
Yavapai County	G. W. Hull	Jerome
	D. A. Burke	Prescott
	Roy N. Davidson	Crown King
Yuma County	John B. Martin	Harquahala

TWENTY-FIFTH LEGISLATIVE ASSEMBLY, 1909
(Phoenix)

Council

	Name	Residence
Apache County	S. E. Day	St. Michaels
Cochise County	Ben Goodrich	Tombstone
Coconino County	Fred S. Breen	Flagstaff
Gila County	George W. P. Hunt **(President)**	Globe
Graham County	John R. Hampton	Clifton
Maricopa County	Eugene B. O'Neill	Phoenix
Mohave County	Kean St. Charles	Kingman
Navajo County	William J. Morgan	Lakeside
Pima and Santa Cruz Counties	James B. Finley	Tucson
Pinal County	Thomas F. Weedin	Florence
Yavapai County	Michael G. Burns	Humboldt
Yuma County	George W. Norton	Yuma

House of Representatives

Apache County	J. S. Gibbons	St. Johns
Cochise County	Fred A. Sutter	Bisbee
	Oscar W. Roberts	San Simon
	Neill E. Bailey	Naco
Coconino County	T. J. Coalter	Flagstaff
Gila County	John McCormick	Payson
Graham County	W. W. Pace	Thatcher
	Phil C. Merrill	Pima
Maricopa County	Sam F. Webb **(Speaker)**	Meridian
	J. C. Reed	Wickenburg
	Frank DeSouza	Phoenix
	J. W. Woolf	Tempe
Mohave County	S. W. Tobey	Chloride
Navajo County	Joseph Peterson	Lakeside
Pima County	John Doan	Silverbell
	Kirke T. Moore	Tucson
	William J. Hogwood	Tucson
Pinal County	C. L. Shaw	Casa Grande
	J. B. Bourne	Mammoth
Santa Cruz County	Frank J. Duffy	Nogales
Yavapai County	Perry Hall	McCabe
	G. A. Bray	Prescott
	George D. Morris	Prescott
Yuma County	R. A. Hightower	Yuma

Bibliography

MANUSCRIPTS, COLLECTIONS, AND ARCHIVAL MATERIALS

Arizona Department of Library and Archives, Phoenix

McCormick, R. C. [Delegate to Congress]. Letter to Governor
A. P. K. Safford, from Washington, D.C., April 22, 1869.
Photostatic copy of the original.

Arizona. Secretary of State. "Territorial Records." On microfilm.

Richmond, Jonathan [a member of Governor John N. Goodwin's party
from Michigan]. Letters, dating from October 13, 1863,
to May 31, 1865.

Safford, A. P. K. [Governor]. Letter to General W. T. Sherman, from
Washington, D.C., March 10, 1870. Photostatic copy of the original.

Smith, Marcus A. "Official Record of Mark A. Smith, Delegate from
Arizona, 1887–1909." Scrapbook of clippings and typewritten
excerpts from the *Congressional Record.* 4 vols. (Similar material,
giving Smith's record as U. S. Senator, is in vols. 5-30.)

Winsor, Mulford. "José M. Redondo." Typewritten ms. 44 pp.

Wormser, M., *et al.,* vs. Salt River Valley Canal Co., *et al.*
Case No. 708 (1892), Federal District Court for Arizona,
3d Judicial District. Decision, Joseph H. Kibbey, Judge.
Typewritten, signed copy of the decision.

Arizona Pioneers' Historical Society, Tucson

Ashurst, Henry Fountain. "Address . . . Commemorating the
75th Anniversary of the Founding of the University of Arizona,
March 12, 1885." 1960. Copy.

Brodie, Alexander O. Papers.

Cargill, Andrew Hays. Papers, including a personal narrative with
references to Governor Safford and other manuscript materials.

Goldwater, Barry M. File, containing some material on
Governor Frémont and a speech on the history of the
Goldwater family in Arizona.

Goodwin, John. Papers; and Carroll, F. L. Papers. These files contain
copies of letters from Governor Goodwin to General Carleton
and to other officials.

Hughes, Louis C. Papers, including letters and correspondence for the
period from September 20, 1909, to January 11, 1911.

McCord, Myron H. Volume of manuscript materials containing the
family tree, biographies of various members of the family,
photographs, and miscellaneous items on Governor McCord.

McCormick, Richard C. Collection of speeches, correspondence, and a
manuscript copy of newspaper items referring to Gov. McCormick.

Mansfield, J. S., Hughes, Samuel, and Goodwin, F. H. Pioneers' Society
Memorial Committee biography of the former A. P. K. Safford,
dated January 9, 1892.

MORROW [Senator], ROBERT E. and RICHARDS [Senator], J. MORRIS. Mimeographed copies of speeches entitled, "Remarks in the Arizona State Senate, March 7, 1960, Dedicating the New Senate Chambers," which pertain to the history of the territorial government.

REYNOLDS, ALBERT S. Collection of reminiscences, including the story of Governor Zulick's arrest in and escape from Sonora and pictures of President McKinley in Tucson.

RICE, M. M. Papers, including some correspondence with and about George W. P. Hunt and a manuscript on the "Bloody Thirteenth" legislature which Rice observed as a reporter.

SAFFORD, ANSON P. K. Papers, including letters written by Governor Safford while he was in office and in later years, as well as a manuscript written jointly with Samuel Hughes entitled, "The Story of Mariana Diaz."

SMALLEY, GEORGE H. Collection of some one hundred items. Smalley was Governor Brodie's private secretary. His daughter, Mrs. Yndia Moore, served as Secretary of the Arizona Pioneers' Historical Society for many years.

————. Letters from Alexander O. Brodie, including personal and official correspondence.

TRITLE, FREDERICK A. Collection of six scrapbooks of newspaper clippings covering Tritle's tenure as governor.

VOSBURG, JOHN S. Collection of items by a mining partner of Gov. Safford.

WILLIAMS, EUGENE E. Manuscript articles on the territorial governors.

Arizona, University of, Library, Special Collections

"Arizona (Territory). "Constitutional Convention, Verbatim Report." 4 vols. Presented to the University of Arizona Library by George W. P. Hunt, President of the Constitutional Convention. Typescript with penned corrections and annotations.

————. "Executive Records" (December, 1863–August, 1887). Manuscripts in "Records of the States of the U. S., a Microfilm Compilation Prepared By the Library of Congress." (R.S.U.S., Class E, Reel 1, Arizona). Original in Office of the Arizona Secretary of State. (This compilation contains day-by-day manuscript ledgers of proclamations, appointments, pardons, messages, and official letters of Governors Goodwin, McCormick, Safford, Hoyt, Frémont, Tritle, and Zulick, plus records of some other territorial officers.)

————. Governor. "Messages of Territorial Governors to Territorial Legislatures from 1864 to 1909." Partly typescript volume compiled by H. S. McCluskey, Secretary to George W. P. Hunt. The speeches of Governor Franklin (1897) and Governor Kibbey (1909) are printed.

_____. Legislative Assembly, House of Representatives. "Report of Committee appointed to examine the report of Isaac T. Stoddard, Secretary of the Territory, relative to fees accrued from the organization of public corporations, including testimony of witnesses," March 6, 1903.

CAMERON, RALPH. Collection of official letters and miscellaneous personal papers.

FRANKLIN, SELIM. "Early History of the University of Arizona," an address delivered on March 12, 1922. 9 pp.

HUGHES, LOUIS C. Letter-book of L. C. Hughes, Governor of the Territory of Arizona, covering the period April 21, 1893 to March 20, 1896. The letters are typescript and holograph carbons.

_____. Scrapbooks containing newspaper clippings relating to the political career of L. C. Hughes, 1892–1906. 3 vols.

POSTON, CHARLES D. "Diary of Charles D. Poston, covering the period 1850–1895." Manuscript in "Records of the States of the U. S., a Microfilm Compilation Prepared by the Library of Congress." (R.S.U.S., Class X.x., Reel 1a, Miscellaneous.)

SMITH, MARCUS A. Letter-book of Personal Correspondence, Tucson, Arizona, 1900–1905.

STODDARD, ISAAC T. "Miscellaneous Personal Papers, 1894–1913," containing family records and correspondence relating to his position as Secretary of the Territory of Arizona.

TUTTLE, EDWARD. "Journals and Letters of Edward Tuttle," photostatic reproduction of the original manuscripts deposited in the Huntington Library, San Marino, California. Among other interesting items, this collection includes the reminiscences of Tuttle as a member of the first legislature of the Territory of Arizona and personal letters, now of historical significance, to members of his family.

WEINBERGER, JACOB. "Material Pertaining to the Constitutional Convention of 1910," including two scrapbooks of official papers, propositions introduced, and newspaper clippings.

Bancroft Library, University of California, Berkeley

"Arizona Dictations," 132 items based upon interviews in Arizona, 1885–89, and filed by counties.

HOYT, JOHN P. "Leading Events Since the American Settlement of Arizona." Ms., 1878. This manuscript is a general commentary on the early years of the territory by a former governor, with interjections by a Mrs. Lewis who was present at the San Francisco interview. 35 pp.

California State Library, Sacramento, California

California Blue Book, 1907. State Printing Office, Sacramento, n. d.

CALIFORNIA. LEGISLATURE. ASSEMBLY. *Journal of the Ninth Session of the Assembly of the State of California,* 1858.

Henry E. Huntington Library, San Marino, California

ADAMS, SAMUEL. "The Exploration of the Colorado River — Original Manuscript Notes, July 12, 1869." Included is the letter of Frederick F. Low, Governor of California, to the citizens of Arizona, from Sacramento, California, December 10, 1864, in behalf of the candidacy of Samuel Adams for Delegate to Congress.

BROWN, ANGELINE M. Diary. A schoolteacher in the Tonto Basin on the Arizona frontier, 1880–81, the diarist was later employed as the Enrolling and Engrossing Clerk for the House in the Eleventh Legislative Assembly in 1881. Among other things, she wrote about how her husband, a member of the legislature, turned down a thousand-dollar bribe to vote for the repeal of the bullion tax on mine output.

BRINLEY, CHARLES HENRY. Letter to Abel Stearns, Esq., Los Angeles, from La Paz, Arizona Territory, May 2, 1863. Brinley wrote about the placer diggings at La Paz, transportation on the Colorado in 1863, the high prices, and the Apache problem.

MANSFELD, JACOB SAMUEL (a pioneer newsdealer in Arizona). "Literature in the Territory of Arizona in 1870." Ms.

Library of Congress, Washington, D. C.

Grover Cleveland Papers.

Benjamin Harrison Papers. Volumes of original letters, correspondence, and related items.

Andrew Johnson Papers.

William McKinley Papers. Official Letter Books.

Hamilton Fish [Secretary of State] Papers. Vol. VII, Letter Copy Book (November 25, 1872–March 18, 1873).

National Archives, Washington, D. C.

Record Group 48. General Records of the Department of the Interior. Appointment Papers: Arizona Territory, 1857–1907.

Record Group 48. General Records of the Department of the Interior. Letter Book Miscellaneous No. 13.

Record Group 48. General Records of the Department of the Interior. Territorial Papers: Arizona, 1868–1913.

Record Group 56. General Records of the Department of the Treasury. Correspondence with Committees of Congress, No. 6 (May 21, 1864–February 10, 1868).

Record Group 59. General Records of the Department of State. Territorial Papers: Arizona (April 4, 1864–February 3, 1872).

Record Group 59. General Records of the Department of State.
Territorial Papers: New Mexico
(January 2, 1861–December 23, 1864).

Record Group 60. General Records of the Department of Justice.
Appointment Papers: Arizona, 1863–1893. Boxes 23–28.

Record Group 217. Records of the U. S. General Accounting Office.
First Comptroller's Office, Division of Records, Warrants, etc.,
Register of Territorial Accounts
(February 23, 1864–August 23, 1881).

Record Group 217. Records of the General Accounting Office.
First Comptroller's Office, Division of Records, Warrants, etc.,
Territorial Letters Received, Vols. 8–21 (1864–91).

Record Group 217. Records of the General Accounting Office.
First Comptroller's Office, Division of Records, Warrants, etc.,
Territorial Letters Sent, Vols. 7–10 (October, 1861–June, 1880).

Record Group 217. Records of the General Accounting Office.
Treasury Auxiliary Ledger, Nos. 2 and 3.

Southwest Museum, Los Angeles, California

HAYDEN, CHARLES TRUMBULL. Letter to Mr. Joseph Fish, from
Tempe, Arizona, February 8, 1898. This letter is a brief
biography of the Hayden family up to 1898.

Miscellaneous

ELLINWOOD, E. E. "Making a Modern Constitution." A speech delivered
in the Opera House at Bisbee, Arizona, August 27, 1910.
Arizona State University Library, Tempe.

BLACK, JOHN A. [Commissioner of Immigration]. Letter to Ernest Ingersoll,
of New York, from Tucson, November 8, 1889.
New York City Public Library, Manuscripts Division.

HAYDEN, CARL [Senator]. Letter to the author, from Washington, D.C.,
February 26, 1966.

PUBLISHED DOCUMENTS — ARIZONA

ARIZONA (Terr.). *Acts, Resolutions, and Memorials* (also called
Session Laws):

Acts, Resolutions and Memorials, First Legislative Assembly, 1864,
at Prescott. (Includes copy of the Organic Act., vii-viii;
40 acts, 21 resolutions, 5 memorials.) 79 pp.

Acts, Resolutions and Memorials, Second Legislative Assembly, 1865,
at Prescott. (42 acts, 12 resolutions, 6 memorials). 72 pp.

Acts, Resolutions and Memorials, Third Legislative Assembly, 1866,
at Prescott. (34 acts, 9 resolutions, 5 memorials). 72 pp.

Acts, Resolutions and Memorials, Fourth Legislative Assembly, 1867, at Prescott. (31 acts, 6 resolutions, 8 memorials). 74 pp.

Acts, Resolutions and Memorials, Fifth Legislative Assembly, 1868, at Tucson. (30 acts, 5 joint resolutions, 7 memorials). 71 pp.

The Compiled Laws of the Territory of Arizona Including the Howell Code and the Session Laws from 1864 to 1871. [Sixth Legislative Assembly]. Compiled by Coles Bashford. Weed, Parsons & Co., Printers, Albany, N. Y., 1871.

Acts, Resolutions and Memorials, Seventh Legislative Assembly, 1873, at Tucson. (59 acts, 2 joint resolutions, 3 memorials). 177 pp.

Acts, Resolutions and Memorials, Eighth Legislative Assembly, 1875, at Tucson. (50 acts, 2 joint resolutions, 3 memorials. The appendix includes the Mining Laws of 1866, 1870, 1872, 1873, and 1874 and various treaties with Mexico: the Gadsden Treaty of 1854, etc.). 238 pp.

Acts, Resolutions and Memorials, Ninth Legislative Assembly, 1877, at Tucson. (79 acts, 3 joint resolutions, 3 memorials). 126 pp. plus index.

The Compiled Laws of the Territory of Arizona, 1864–1877. Arranged By Authority of an Act of the Legislative Assembly Approved February 9, 1877. John P. Hoyt, Compiler. Richmond, Backus & Co., Printers, Detroit, Michigan, 1877. 692 pp.

Acts and Resolutions, Tenth Legislative Assembly, 1879, at Prescott. (65 acts, 4 resolutions). 170 pp.

Acts and Resolutions, Eleventh Legislative Assembly, 1881, at Prescott. (103 acts, 7 joint resolutions). 193 pp. plus index.

Laws of the Territory of Arizona, Twelfth Legislative Assembly; also *Memorials and Resolutions,* January 8–March 8, 1883, at Prescott. (100 acts, 4 joint resolutions, 8 memorials). 303 pp. plus index.

Laws of the Territory of Arizona, Thirteenth Legislative Assembly; also, *Memorials and Resolutions,* January 12–March 12, 1885, at Prescott. (123 acts, 4 joint resolutions, 15 memorials). 376 pp. plus index.

Revised Statutes of Arizona, 1887. Prescott Courier Print, Arizona, 1887. (Laws codified by a commission made up of Cameron H. King, chairman; Ben Goodrich; and Ed. W. Wells. Acts passed by the Fourteenth Legislative Assembly, 1887, are included.) 905 pp. including indices.

Acts, Resolutions and Memorials, Fifteenth Legislative Assembly, 1889, at Prescott and Phoenix. Office of the Courier, Prescott, 1889. (63 acts, 2 joint resolutions, 15 memorials). 115 pp. plus index.

Acts, Resolutions and Memorials, Sixteenth Legislative Assembly, 1891, at Phoenix. (106 acts, 2 memorials, 10 concurrent and joint resolutions, and 11 acts of the Fifteenth Assembly known as the "Lost Laws," pp. 193-206). 208 pp.

Acts, Resolutions and Memorials, Seventeenth Legislative Assembly, 1893, at Phoenix. (91 acts, 7 memorials, 4 concurrent resolutions, 4 joint resolutions). 172 pp.

Acts, Resolutions and Memorials, Eighteenth Legislative Assembly, 1895, at Phoenix. (82 acts, 6 joint resolutions, 10 memorials). 149 pp. plus index.

Acts, Resolutions and Memorials, Nineteenth Legislative Assembly, 1897, at Phoenix. (78 acts). 140 pp. plus index.

Acts, Resolutions and Memorials, Twentieth Legislative Assembly, 1899, at Phoenix. (69 acts, 4 House Joint Resolutions, 5 memorials). 92 pp. plus index.

The Revised Statutes of the Arizona Territory, 1901, Containing Also the Laws Passed by the Twenty-first Legislative Assembly, the Constitution of the United States, the Organic Law of Arizona and the Amendments of Congress Relating Thereto. Press of E. W. Stephens, Columbia, Missouri, 1901. 1517 pp. including indices.

Acts, Resolutions and Memorials, Twenty-second Legislative Assembly, 1903, at Phoenix. (93 acts, 11 resolutions and memorials). 197 pp. plus index.

Acts, Resolutions and Memorials, Twenty-third Legislative Assembly, 1905, at Phoenix. (69 acts, 6 memorials, 6 joint resolutions). 167 pp. plus index.

Acts, Resolutions and Memorials, Twenty-fourth Legislative Assembly, 1907, at Phoenix. (102 acts, 8 memorials, 5 joint resolutions). 303 pp. plus index.

Acts, Resolutions and Memorials, Twenty-fifth Legislative Assembly, 1909, at Phoenix. (107 acts, 12 memorials, 4 resolutions).

————. *The Constitution and Schedule of the Provisional Government of the Territory of Arizona and the Proceedings of the Convention at Tucson.* Tucson: J. Howard Wells, Publisher, 1860. (Library of Congress microfilm, R.S.U.S., Arizona, D-2.) Although Arizona was not a separate territory in 1860, libraries list this under Arizona Territory to keep all pre-statehood material together.

————. *The 1864 Census of the Territory of Arizona.* Records Survey Division of Professional Projects, Works Projects Administration. Phoenix, 1938. Mimeographed.

————. ADJUTANT GENERAL. *Report of the Adjutant General* [Brigadier General H. F. Robinson] *of the Territory of Arizona, 1898.* Phoenix: Dunbar and Ambler, Printers. (Dated January 1, 1899, and addressed to Hon. N. O. Murphy, Commander in Chief.)

————. ARIZONA RANGERS. *Biennial Report,* 1905–1906.

————. CAPITOL COMMISSION. *Biennial Report,* 1900. Addressed to N. O. Murphy, January 1, 1901, by F. H. Parker.

————. CAPITOL GROUNDS AND BUILDING COMMISSION. *Report, 1899.* Addressed to Hon. N. O. Murphy, January 14, 1899, by F. H. Parker, Secretary.

_____. CONSTITUTIONAL CONVENTION (1891). *Journals for the Constitutional Convention . . . of Arizona, 1891.* Phoenix.

_____. CONSTITUTIONAL CONVENTION (1893). *Proceedings of the Arizona Convention for Statehood.* Phoenix, 1893.

_____. CONSTITUTIONAL CONVENTION (1910). *Journal of the Arizona Constitutional Convention, October 10–December 9, 1910.* Compiled by Con P. Cronin, State Librarian of Arizona, November 1, 1925.

_____. _____. *Minutes of the Constitutional Convention of the Territory of Arizona, 1910.* Phoenix: Phoenix Printing Co., 1910.

_____. _____. *Standing Rules, Constitutional Convention of the Territory of Arizona.* Phoenix: Arizona State Press, 1910.

_____. GOVERNOR. *Message of Governor Alexander O. Brodie to the Twenty-second Legislative Assembly.* Tucson: The Citizen Printing and Publishing Co., 1903.

_____. LEGISLATIVE ASSEMBLY. *Journals:*
Journals of the First Legislative Assembly, 1864, at Prescott. Office of the Arizona Miner, 1865. (Includes the Message of John Goodwin, pp. 33-45, and his official proclamation in appendix.) 250 pp.

Journals of the Second Legislative Assembly, 1865, at Prescott. Office of the Arizona Miner, 1866. (Includes the Message of Acting Governor, Richard C. McCormick, pp. 33-53.) 231 pp.

Journals of the Third Legislative Assembly, 1866, at Prescott. Office of the Arizona Miner, 1867. (Includes the Message of Governor Richard C. McCormick, pp. 31-48, and his proclamations, pp. 263-69.) 269 pp.

Journals of the Fourth Legislative Assembly, 1867. Office of the Arizona Miner, 1868. (Includes the Message of Governor Richard C. McCormick, pp. 3-46, and his proclamations, pp. 258-63, plus the Reports of the Territorial Auditor, pp. 251-53, and the Territorial Librarian, pp. 254-57.) 263 pp.

Journals of the Fifth Legislative Assembly, 1868, at Tucson. Tucson Publishing Co., 1869. (Includes the Message of Governor Richard C. McCormick, pp. 32-43, and his proclamations, pp. 267-72, plus Reports of the Territorial Auditor and the Territorial Librarian, pp. 249-66.) 272 pp.

Journals of the Sixth Legislative Assembly, 1871, at Tucson. Office of the Arizona Citizen, Tucson, 1871. (Includes the Message of Governor A. P. K. Safford, pp. 39-56.) 396 pp.

Journals of the Seventh Legislative Assembly, 1873, at Tucson. Office of the Arizona Citizen, 1873. (Includes the Message of Governor A. P. K. Safford, pp. 31-45.) 366 pp.

Journals of the Eighth Legislative Assembly, 1875, at Tucson. Office of the Arizona Citizen, 1875. (Includes the Message of Governor A. P. K. Safford, pp. 28-40.) 341 pp.

Journals of the Ninth Legislative Assembly, 1877, at Tucson.
Office of the Arizona Citizen, 1877. (Includes the Message of
Governor A. P. K. Safford, pp. 30-46.) 404 pp.

Journals of the Tenth Legislative Assembly, 1879, at Prescott.
Office of the Arizona Miner, Prescott, 1879. (Includes the
Message of Governor J. C. Frémont, pp. 40-48.) 442 pp.

Journals of the Eleventh Legislative Assembly, 1881, at Prescott.
(Includes the Message of Governor J. C. Frémont, pp. 34-37.)
1053 pp.

Journals of the Twelfth Legislative Assembly, 1883, at Prescott.
Journal Company, State Printers, Lincoln, Nebr., 1883.
(Includes the Message of Governor F. A. Tritle, pp. 26-47.) 684 pp.

Journals of the Thirteenth Legislative Assembly, 1885, at Prescott.
H. S. Crocker & Co., Printers and Stationers, San Francisco, 1885.
(Includes the Message of Governor F. A. Tritle, pp. 122-61.) 968 pp.

Journals of the Fourteenth Legislative Assembly, 1887, at Prescott.
Courier Book and Job Printing Establishment, Prescott, 1887.
(Includes the Message of Governor C. Meyer Zulick, pp. 222-48.)
652 pp.

Journals of the Fifteenth Legislative Assembly, 1889, at Prescott and
Phoenix. Courier Book and Job Printing Establishment, Prescott,
1889. (Includes the Message of Governor C. Meyer Zulick,
pp. 17-26.) 451 pp.

Journals of the Sixteenth Legislative Assembly, 1891, at Phoenix.
Herald Book and Job Office, Phoenix, 1891. (Includes the
Message of Acting Governor N. O. Murphy, pp. 7-45.) 586 pp.

Journals of the Seventeenth Legislative Assembly, 1893, at Phoenix.
Herald Book and Job Office, 1893. (Includes the Message of
Governor N. O. Murphy, pp. 14-36.) 490 pp.

Journals of the Eighteenth Legislative Assembly, 1895, at Phoenix.
Herald Book and Job Print, Phoenix, 1895. (Includes the Message of
Governor Louis C. Hughes, pp. 10-33.) 622 pp. plus index.

Journals of the Nineteenth Legislative Assembly, 1897, at Phoenix.
Herald Book and Job Print, Phoenix, 1897. (Includes the Message of
Governor Benjamin J. Franklin, pp. 45-77.) 608 pp. plus index.

Journals of the Twentieth Legislative Assembly, 1899. Press of
J. O. Dunbar, Phoenix, 1899. (Includes the Message of
Governor N. O. Murphy, pp. 440-63.) 903 pp. plus index.

Journals of the Twenty-first Legislative Assembly, 1901. Press of
the Arizona Republican, Phoenix, 1901. (Includes the Message of
Governor N. O. Murphy, pp. 296-320.) 570 pp. plus index.

Journals of the Twenty-second Legislative Assembly, 1903.
487 pp. plus index.

Journals of the Twenty-third Legislative Assembly, 1905, at Phoenix. Press of the H. H. McNeil Co., Phoenix, 1905. (Includes Governor Joseph Kibbey's special message and proposed bill authorizing an election on the question of joint statehood with New Mexico, pp. 212-15.) 650 pp. plus index.

Journals of the Twenty-fourth Legislative Assembly, 1907, at Phoenix. (Includes the Special Message on Taxation from Governor Joseph H. Kibbey, pp. 159-84.) Council *Journal,* 347 pp.; House *Journal,* 341 pp.; plus index.

Journals of the Twenty-fifth Legislative Assembly, 1909, at Phoenix. Press of Phoenix Printing Co., 1909. Council *Journal,* 458 pp; House *Journal,* 397 pp.; plus index.

_____. LEGISLATIVE ASSEMBLY. *Memorial and Affidavits Showing Outrages Perpetrated by the Apache Indians in the Territory of Arizona During the Years 1869 and 1870.* Published by authority of the Legislature of the Territory. San Francisco: Francis & Valentine, Printers, 1871. (Reprinted by Territorial Press, Tucson [1967?].)

_____. SUPERINTENDENT OF PUBLIC INSTRUCTION. *Report of the Superintendent of Public Instruction, Territory of Arizona, 1907–1908.* Phoenix.

_____. SUPREME COURT. *Reports of Cases Argued and Determined In the Supreme Court of the Territory.* Vol. 8 (1902–1904).

PUBLISHED DOCUMENTS — FEDERAL

BARD, THOMAS R. *The Autonomy of Arizona Guaranteed Forever.* Speech of Hon. Thomas R. Bard of California in the Senate of the United States, January 6, 1905. Washington: G.P.O., 1905. 27 pp.

BEVERIDGE, ALBERT J. *Arizona the Great.* Extracts from Speech of Hon. Albert J. Beveridge of Indiana closing the Debate on the Statehood Bill in the Senate of the United States, February 6, 1905. Washington: G.P.O., 1905. 31 pp.

SMITH, MARCUS A. *Answer to Charges Against Arizona.* Speeches of Hon. Marcus A. Smith of Arizona in the House of Representatives, January 28, 1903, and February 10, 1903. Washington: G.P.O., 1903. 13 pp. (Reprinted from *Congressional Record* for dates of speeches.)

_____. *Speech of Marcus A. Smith* in the House of Representatives, January 25, 1906. Washington: G.P.O., 1906. 16 pp. (Reprinted from *Congressional Record* for January 25, 1906.)

SUPREME COURT REPORTER (U. S.) Transcripts of cases heard by the U. S. Supreme Court.

U. S. ARMY. DEPARTMENT OF CALIFORNIA. *General Orders No. 35,* July 14, 1866, signed by Assistant Adjutant General R. C. Drum by command of Major General Irwin McDowell.

U. S. BOARD OF INDIAN COMMISSIONERS. *Peace With the Apaches of New Mexico and Arizona, Report of Vincent Colyer, 1871.* Washington: G.P.O., 1872.

U. S. BUREAU OF EDUCATION. *History of Public School Education in Arizona,* by Stephen B. Weeks. Bulletin No. 17, Washington: G.P.O., 1918.

U. S. BUREAU OF INDIAN AFFAIRS. *Annual Report of the Commissioner of Indian Affairs to the Secretary of the Interior,* 1867, and 1872 through 1883.

U. S. *Congressional Globe* and the *Congressional Record.* (Items relevant to the Arizona Territory and to delegates to Congress from this territory, 1863–1912).

U. S. COURT OF CLAIMS. *In the Court of Claims of the United States . . . J. A. Peralta Reavis and Doña Sofia Loreta Micaela de Maso-Reavis y Peralta de la Córdoba, His Wife, and Clinton P. Farrell, Trustee,* vs. *The United States of America, Petition of Claimants* [No. 16,719]. Washington, D.C.: Gibson Brothers, 1890.

U. S. COURT OF PRIVATE LAND CLAIMS, SANTA FE DISTRICT. *James Addison Peraltareavis and Doña Sofia Loreta Micaela de Peraltareavis, née Maso y Silva de Peralta de la Córdoba, Husband and Wife, Petitioners,* vs. *The United States, Respondent,* 1895.

U. S. DEPARTMENT OF THE INTERIOR. *Report of the Governor of the Territory of Arizona to the Secretary of the Interior,* annual, 1878–1910. (No report in 1880 and 1882). Frémont, 1878–79; Acting Governor Gosper, 1881; Tritle, 1883–85; Zulick, 1886–88; Wolfley, 1889; Murphy, 1890–92; Hughes, 1893–95; Franklin, 1896; McCord, 1897; Murphy, 1898–1901; Brodie, 1902–1904; Kibbey, 1905–1908; and Sloan, 1909–10.

U. S. DEPARTMENT OF WAR. *Annual Report,* 1883.

_____. *The War of Rebellion: A Compilation of the Official Records of the Union and Confederate Armies.* Four Series, 128 volumes. Washington: G.P.O., 1880–1901.

U. S. HOUSE. *Admission of Arizona, Idaho, and Wyoming Into the Union,* 50th Cong., 2d Sess., 1889, House Report No. 4053.

_____. *Admission of Arizona Into the Union,* 53d Cong., 1st Sess., 1893, House Report No. 168.

_____. *Arizona's Vote on Joint Statehood,* 59th Cong., 2d Sess., 1906–1907, House Doc. No. 140.

_____. *Biographical Directory of the American Congress, 1774–1961,* 85th Cong., 2d Sess., 1961, House Doc. No. 442.

_____. *Certificate of the Governor and Secretary of the Territory of New Mexico as to the Election Upon Joint Statehood,* 59th Cong., 2d Sess., 1906–1907, House Doc. No. 194.

————. Committee on Territories. *A bill to enable the people of Arizona to form a constitution and state government and to be admitted into the Union on an equal footing with the original States* [Introduced by Delegate Ralph Cameron, July 15, 1909], 61st Cong., 1st Sess., 1909, H. R. 11578. [Copy in the University of Arizona Library, Special Collections.]

————. ————. "Condition of the Laws of Arizona and Reasons for Congressional Legislation." Letter from Lewis Wolfley, Governor of Arizona Territory, to Hon. I. S. Struble, Chairman, Committee on Territories. No date. [Printed copy in New York City Public Library.]

————. ————. *Statehood for Arizona and New Mexico,* January 16-20, 1906.

————. *Journal of the House of Representatives of the United States,* 38th Cong., 2d Sess., 1864 through 62d Cong., 3d Sess., 1912–13.

————. *Lawlessness in Arizona,* 47th Cong., 1st Sess., 1882, House Exec. Doc. No. 188.

————. *Lawlessness in Parts of Arizona,* 47th Cong., 1st Sess., 1882, House Exec. Doc. No. 58.

————. *Letter of the Secretary of the Treasury* [McCulloch] *Transmitting Report Upon the Mineral Resources of the States and Territories West of the Rocky Mountains,* 39th Cong., 2d Sess., 1867, House Exec. Doc. 29.

————. *Location of Southern Pacific and Texas Pacific Railroads,* 45th Cong., 2d Sess., 1878, House Exec. Doc. No. 33.

————. *Report of the Secretary of the Interior,* 42d Cong., 2d Sess., 1872, House Exec. Doc. No. 1.

————. *Report of the Secretary of the Interior,* 42d Cong., 3d Sess., 1873, House Exec. Doc. No. 1.

————. *Report of the Secretary of the Interior,* 47th Cong., 1st Sess., 1882, House Exec. Doc. No. 1.

————. *Report of the Secretary of the Interior,* 47th Cong., 2d Sess., 1883, House Exec. Doc. No. 1.

————. *Second Annual Report of the Reclamation Service, 1902–1903,* 58th Cong., 2d Sess., 1903, House Doc. No. 44.

U. S. SENATE. *Constitution Adopted by Arizona,* 61st Cong., 3d Sess., 1910–1911, Sen. Doc. 798.

————. *Federal Census: Territory of New Mexico and Territory of Arizona,* 89th Cong., 1st Sess., 1965, Sen. Doc. No. 13.

————. *Joint Statehood for New Mexico and Arizona,* 59th Cong., 1st Sess., 1906, Sen. Doc. No. 254.

————. *Letter from the Secretary of War . . . Regarding the Apache Indians,* 51st Cong., 1st Sess., 1890, Sen. Exec. Doc. No. 88.

————. *Message of the President of the United States,* 38th Cong., 1st Sess., 1863–64, Sen. Doc. No. 49.

_____. *Message from the President of the United States Transmitting a Copy of the Constitution Adopted by . . . New Mexico . . . ,* 31st Cong., 1st Sess., 1850, Sen. Exec. Doc. No. 74.

_____. *Protest Against Union of Arizona with New Mexico.* 59th Cong., 1st Sess., 1906, Sen. Doc. No. 216.

U. S. STATUTES AT LARGE.

WATTS, JOHN S. *Territory of Arizona.* Speech of Hon. John S. Watts, of New Mexico, in the House of Representatives, May 8, 1862. Washington, D. C.: Scammel & Co., 1862. 7 pp.

BOOKS, ARTICLES AND OTHER SOURCES

ANDERSON, LUCILE. "Railroad Transportation Through Prescott." Unpublished master's thesis, University of Arizona, Tucson, 1934.

Arizona at the World's Industrial and Cotton Centennial Exposition, New Orleans, 1884–85 [A souvenir of the Atlantic and Pacific Railroad]. Chicago: Poole Brothers Printers, 1885. 65 pp.

"Arizona Grows Where Water Flows," *Arizona Days and Ways Magazine, The Arizona Republic,* March 12, 1961.

"Arizona's Outlook in the Family of States," *The American Review of Reviews,* Vol. 42, No. 4 (October, 1910), pp. 484-85.

ASHURST, HENRY F. *A Many-Colored Toga* (diary). Tucson: University of Arizona Press, 1962.

BABCOCK, J. W. [U. S. Representative]. "Statehood Rights of Arizona and New Mexico," *The Independent,* Vol. 41, No. 2987 (March 1, 1906), pp. 505-8.

BAKER, ROBERT [Ex-Congressman, N.Y.]. "Human Liberty or Human Greed?" *The Arena,* Vol. 35, No. 196 (March, 1906), pp. 409-18.

BANCROFT, HUBERT H. *History of Arizona and New Mexico, 1530–1888.* San Francisco: The History Company, 1889. [Reprinted in Albuquerque: Horn & Wallace, Publishers, 1962].

The Banker's Magazine, Vol. 13, 3rd Series, No. 11 (May, 1879), p. 908. (An item related to Governor Safford.)

BARNEY, JAMES M. "A Forgotten Incident in Arizona's Early Political History," *The Sheriff,* Vol. 8, No. 3 (March, 1949), pp. 10-11 and 23.

_____. "Phoenix: A History of Its Pioneer Days and People," *Arizona Historical Review,* Vol. 5, No. 4 (January, 1933), pp. 264-85.

BELL, HAZEL A. "Federal Relations of the Territory of Arizona 1963–1893." Unpublished master's thesis, University of California, Berkeley, 1929.

BLACK, JOHN A. *Arizona: The Land of Sunshine and Silver, Health and Prosperity, The Place for Ideal Homes.* Phoenix: Republican Book and Job Print, 1890.

BOEHRINGER, C. LOUISE. "Mary Elizabeth Post — High Priestess of Americanization," *Arizona Historical Review,* Vol. 2, No. 2 (July, 1929), pp. 92-100.

BOURKE, JOHN G. *On the Border with Crook.* New York:
Charles Scribner's Sons, 1891. [Reprinted in Chicago:
Rio Grande Press, 1962.]

BRANDES, RAY. *Frontier Military Posts of Arizona.* Globe, Ariz.:
Dale Stuart King, Publisher, 1960.

BRENT, WILLIAM, and BRENT, MILARDE. *The Hell Hole.* Yuma, Ariz.:
Southwest Printers, 1962.

BREWSTER, JANE WAYLAND. "The San Rafael Cattle Company,
A Pennsylvania Enterprise in Arizona," *Arizona and the West,*
Vol. 8, No. 2 (Summer, 1966), pp. 133-56.

BRICE, CALVIN. "The Constitutional Convention of Arizona."
Unpublished master's thesis, Arizona State University, 1953.

BRODIE, ALEXANDER O. "Reclaiming the Arid West," *Cosmopolitan,*
Vol. 37, No. 6 (October, 1904), pp. 715-22.

————. "The Rise of a Commonwealth on the Southwestern Frontier,"
Bisbee Daily Review, World's Fair Edition, n. d.

BROWNE, J. ROSS. *Adventures in the Apache Country.* New York:
Harper and Brothers, 1869. [Reprinted as *A Tour Through Arizona,
1864.* Tucson: Arizona Silhouettes, 1950.]

CLUM, JOHN P. *The Truth About Apaches.* Los Angeles, California:
n. p., 1931.

CLUM, WOODWORTH. *Apache Agent: The Story of John P. Clum.*
Boston: Houghton Mifflin Co., 1936.

COLQUHOUN, JAMES. *The History of the Clifton-Morenci Mining District.*
London: John Murray, 1924.

COLTON, RAY C. *The Civil War in the Western Territories.*
Norman: University of Oklahoma Press, 1959.

Confederate Victories in the Southwest: Prelude to Defeat
(from the *Official Records*). Albuquerque, New Mexico:
Horn & Wallace, Publishers, 1961.

CONNER, DANIEL ELLIS. *Joseph Reddeford Walker and the Arizona
Adventure.* Norman: University of Oklahoma Press, 1956.

CREHAN, FRANK. "Historic Milestone in U. S. Reclamation,"
Arizona Highways, Vol. 37, No. 4 (April, 1961), pp. 26-31.

CREMONY, JOHN C. *Life Among the Apaches.* San Francisco:
Roman and Company, Publishers, 1868.

CROSS, JACK L., SHAW, ELIZABETH H., and SCHEIFELE, KATHLEEN (editors).
Arizona: Its People and Resources. Tucson:
University of Arizona Press, 1960.

CUNNIFF, MICHAEL G. *The Last of the Territories.* New York:
Doubleday, Page & Co., 1906.

————. "The Last of the Territories," *The World's Work,* Vol. 11, No. 3
(January, 1906), pp. 7108-9.

CURRIE, BARTON WOOD. "The Transformation of the Southwest Through the
Legal Abolition of Gambling," *The Century Magazine,* Vol. 75
(Vol. 53, New Series), No. 89 (April, 1908), pp. 905-10.

DAVIS, BRITTON. *The Truth About Geronimo.* New Haven, Conn.:
Yale University Press, 1929.

"Delaying Statehood," *The American Review of Reviews,*
Vol. 44, No. 3 (September, 1911), pp. 264-66.

ELLIOTT, WALLACE W., & CO., publisher and compiler.
History of Arizona, Showing Its Resources and Advantages.
San Francisco: Wallace W. Elliott & Co., 1884.
[Reprinted in Flagstaff, Ariz.: Northland Press, 1964.]

FARISH, THOMAS E. *History of Arizona.* 8 vols.
Phoenix: Filmer Brothers, Electrotype Co., 1915.

FARLOW, ARCHA M. "Arizona's Admission to Statehood,"
Historical Society of Southern California, Annual Publications,
1913. pp. 132-53. [Los Angeles.]

FAVOUR, ALPHEUS H. *A Four Foot Shelf of Arizona Laws.*
Prescott, Ariz.: Prescott Historical Society, n. d.

FERRIS, R. G. (ed.). *The American West: An Appraisal.*
Santa Fe: Museum of New Mexico Press, 1963.

FIREMAN, BERT M. "Frémont's Arizona Adventure," *The American West,*
Vol. 1, No. 1 (Winter, 1964), pp. 8-19.

FISH, JOSEPH. "Labors for a Territorial Government,"
Arizona Historical Review, Vol. 1, No. 1 (1928), pp. 63-68.

FRÉMONT, ELIZABETH BENTON. *Recollections of Elizabeth Benton Frémont.*
New York: F. H. Hitchcock, 1912.

FRÉMONT, JESSIE BENTON. *Far-West Sketches.* Boston: D. Lothrop Co., 1890.

GOFF, JOHN S. "Charles D. Poston for Governor!" *The Journal of
Arizona History,* Vol. 8, No. 2 (Summer, 1967), pp. 45-53.

GRESSINGER, A. W. *Charles D. Poston: Sunland Seer.*
Globe, Ariz.: Dale Stuart King, Publisher, 1961.

GUSTAFSON, A. M. (ed.). *John Spring's Arizona.*
Tucson: University of Arizona Press, 1966.

HAMILTON, PATRICK. *The Resources of Arizona.* San Francisco:
A. L. Bancroft, 1884.

HART, PEARL. "An American Episode," *Cosmopolitan,* Vol. 27, No. 6
(October, 1899), pp. 673-77.

HASTINGS, JAMES R. "The Tragedy at Camp Grant in 1871,"
Arizona and the West, Vol. 1, No. 2 (Summer, 1959), pp. 146-60.

HANES, JESS G. *Apache Vengeance.* Albuquerque: University of
New Mexico Press, 1954.

HEARD, DWIGHT B. "Why Arizona Opposes Union with New Mexico,"
The World To-Day, Vol. 10, No. 4 (April, 1906), pp. 409-18.

HENSON, PAULINE. *Founding a Wilderness Capital: Prescott, A. T.*
Flagstaff, Ariz.: Northland Press, 1965.

HINTON, RICHARD J. *Handbook to Arizona: Its Resources, History, Towns,
Mines, Ruins, and Scenery.* San Francisco: Payot, Upham & Co., 1878.

History of Placer County, California with Illustrations and Biographical Sketches of Its Prominent Men and Pioneers. Oakland, Calif.: Thompson and West, 1882. (Contains information on the career of Governor A. P. K. Safford. Copy in the California State Library, Sacramento.)

HOLLISTER, OVANDO J. *Boldly They Rode: A History of the First Colorado Regiment of Volunteers.* Lakewood, Colo.: The Golden Press, 1949. [Reprint of book first published in 1863.]

HODGE, HIRAM C. *Arizona As It Is.* New York: Hurd and Houghton, 1877. [Reprinted under the title, *Arizona As It Was.* Chicago: Rio Grande Press, 1962.]

HOPKINS, ERNEST J. and THOMAS, ALFRED, JR. *The Arizona State University Story.* Phoenix: Southwest Publishing Co., Inc., 1960.

HOWARD, OLIVER O. *My Life and Experiences Among Our Hostile Indians.* Hartford, Conn.: N. D. Worthington & Co., 1907.

HUBBARD, HOWARD A. "The Arizona Enabling Act and President Taft's Veto," *Pacific Historical Review,* Vol. 3, 1934, pp. 307-22.

————. "Arizona's Struggle Against Joint Statehood," *Pacific Historical Review,* Vol. 11, 1942, pp. 415-23.

————. *A Chapter in Early Transportation History: the Arizona Narrow Gauge Railroad Company.* Tucson: University of Arizona Social Science Bulletin, Vol. 5, No. 3, 1934.

HUBBARD, PAUL G. "Life in the Arizona Territorial Prison, 1876–1910," *Arizona and the West,* Vol. 1, No. 4 (Winter, 1959), pp. 317-30.

HUFFORD, KENNETH. "P. W. Dooner: Pioneer Editor of Tucson," *Arizona and the West,* Vol. 10, No. 1 (Spring, 1968), pp. 25-52.

HUGHES, MRS. SAMUEL. "Reminiscences," *Arizona Historical Review,* Vol. 6, No. 2 (April, 1935), pp. 66-74.

HUNT, AURORA. *The Army of the Pacific: Its Operations . . . 1860–1866.* Glendale, Calif.: Arthur H. Clark Co., 1951.

HUNT, FRAZIER. *Cap Mossman, Last of the Great Cowmen.* New York: Hastings House, 1951.

HUNT, GEORGE W. P. "The Making of a State," *Sunset,* Vol. 31, No. 4 (October, 1913), pp. 681-83.

IRWIN, JOHN N. [Ex-Governor]. "Arizona," *The North American Review,* Vol. 156, No. 436 (March, 1893), pp. 354-58.

JOHNSON, ROYAL A. *Adverse Report of the Surveyor General of Arizona Upon the Alleged "Peralta Grant," a Complete Exposé of Its Fraudulent Character.* Phoenix: Arizona Gazette Book and Job Office, 1890. Includes "Argument of Clark Churchill Against the Claim."

JUDD, B. IRA. "The Apache Kid," *Arizona Highways,* Vol. 29, No. 9 (September, 1955), pp. 32-35.

KARTUS, SIDNEY. "Helen Duett Ellison Hunt," *Arizona Historical Review,* Vol. 4, No. 2 (July, 1931), pp. 39-43.

KEEN, EFFIE R. "Arizona's Governors," *Arizona Historical Review,* Vol. 3, No. 3 (October, 1930), pp. 7-17.

KEITHLEY, RALPH. "He Stayed With 'Em While He Lasted: the Saga of Buckey O'Neill," *Arizona Highways,* Vol. 14, No. 1 (January, 1943), pp. 4-5, 29-35; No. 2 (February, 1943), pp. 8-9 and 31-41.

KELEHER, WILLIAM A. *Turmoil in New Mexico.*
Santa Fe: The Rydal Press, 1952.

KELLY, GEORGE H. *Legislative History of Arizona, 1864–1912.*
Phoenix: Manufacturing Stationers, Inc., 1926.

KNOX, MERTICE B. "The Escape of the Apache Kid," *Arizona Historical Review,* Vol. 3, No. 4 (January, 1931), pp. 77-87.

LAMAR, HOWARD R. "Carpetbaggers Full of Dreams: A Functional View of the Arizona Pioneer Politician," *Arizona and the West,* Vol. 7, No. 3 (Autumn, 1965), pp. 187-206.

_____. *The Far Southwest, 1846–1912: A Territorial History.*
New Haven, Conn.: Yale University Press, 1966.

LANGSTON, LaMOINE. "Arizona's Fight for Statehood in the Fifty-Seventh Congress." Unpublished master's thesis, University of New Mexico, Albuquerque, 1939.

LEE, MARCIA HOOKER. "John A. Spring: Swiss Adventurer," *Arizoniana,* Vol. 3, No. 3 (Fall, 1962), pp. 50-52.

LOCKWOOD, FRANK C. *Life in Old Tucson, 1854–1864.* Los Angeles: The Ward Ritchie Press, 1943.

_____. *Pioneer Days in Arizona.* New York: Macmillan Co., 1932.

LOGAN, WALTER S. *Arizona and Some of Her Friends: The Toasts and Responses at a Complimentary Dinner at the Marine and Field Club, Bath Beach, New York, Tuesday, July 28th, 1891 to John N. Irwin, Governor of Arizona . . .*, n.p., n.d.

MANN, DEAN E. *The Politics of Water in Arizona.* Tucson: University of Arizona Press, 1963.

MARION, J. H. *Notes of Travel Through the Territory of Arizona.*
Edited by Donald M. Powell.
Tucson: University of Arizona Press, 1965.

MARTIN, DOUGLAS D. *The Lamp in the Desert.*
Tucson: University of Arizona Press, 1960.

_____. *Tombstone's Epitaph.*
Albuquerque: University of New Mexico Press, 1951.

McCLINTOCK, JAMES H. *Arizona: Prehistoric, Aboriginal, Pioneer, Modern.* 3 vols. Chicago: The S. J. Clarke Publishing Co., 1916.

McCORMICK, RICHARD C. *Arizona: Its Resources and Prospects.*
[Reprinted from a letter to the editor of the *New York Tribune,* June 26, 1865.] D. Van Nostrand, 1865. [Facsimile printed in Tucson: Territorial Press, 1968, Sidney Brinckerhoff, editor.]

McFARLAND AND POOLE (compilers). *A Historical and Biographical Record of the Territory of Arizona.* Chicago: McFarland and Poole, 1896.

McKELWAY, A. J. "Social Principles of the New State Constitutions," *The Survey,* Vol. 25, January 7, 1911, pp. 610-13.

MILES, GENERAL NELSON A. *Personal Recollections of General Nelson A. Miles.* Chicago: The Werner Co., 1896.

MILLER, JOSEPH. *Arizona Cavalcade: The Turbulent Times.* New York: Hastings House, 1962.

_____. *Arizona: The Last Frontier.* New York: Hastings House, 1956.

_____. *The Arizona Story.* New York: Hastings House, 1952.

MOWRY, SYLVESTER. *Memoir of the Proposed Territory of Arizona.* Washington, D.C.: Henry Polkinhorn, Printer, 1857. [Reprinted in Tucson: Territorial Press, 1964.]

MURPHY, NATHAN O. *Ex-Governor Murphy of Arizona Vigorously Protests Against Jointure with New Mexico — Prefers the Territorial Condition Indefinitely.* Published under the Auspices of the Arizona Anti-Joint-Statehood League. Prescott Journal-Miner Press, November 7, 1905.

NELSON, KITTY JO PARKER. "Prescott: Sketch of a Frontier Capital, 1863–1900," *Arizoniana,* Vol. 4, No. 4 (Winter, 1963), pp. 17-38.

NEVINS, ALLAN. *Frémont: Pathfinder of the West.* New York: D. Appleton-Century Co., 1939.

NICHOLS, JEWELL. "Arizona in the Spanish-American War," *Arizona Highways,* Vol. 15, No. 5 (May, 1939), pp. 4-5.

NOEL, THEOPHILUS. *Autobiography and Reminiscences of Theophilus Noel.* Chicago: Theophilus Noel Company Print, 1904.

OGLE, RALPH H. "The Apache and the Government — 1870's," *New Mexico Historical Review,* Vol. 33, No. 2 (April, 1958), pp. 81-102.

_____. *Federal Control of the Western Apaches, 1848–1886.* Albuquerque: University of New Mexico Press, 1940.

PATTEE, SAMUEL L. "Governor Hunt — A Personal Recollection," *Arizona Historical Review,* Vol. 6, No. 2 (April, 1935) pp. 44-48.

PEDERSON, GILBERT J. "The Founding First," *The Journal of Arizona History,* Vol. 7, No. 2 (Summer, 1966), pp. 45-58.

PEPLOW, EDWARD H. *History of Arizona.* 3 vol. New York: Lewis Historical Publishing Co., 1958.

POMEROY, EARL S. "Carpetbaggers in the Territories, 1861 to 1890," *The Historian* [Phi Alpha Theta], Vol. 2, No. 1 (Winter, 1939), pp. 53-64.

_____. *The Territories and the United States, 1860–1890.* Philadelphia: University of Pennsylvania Press, 1947.

PORTER, KIRK H. *National Party Platforms.* New York: The Macmillan Co., 1924.

Portrait and Biographical Record of Arizona. Chicago: Chapman Publishing Co., 1911.

POSTON, CHARLES D. *Building a State in Apache Land.* John M. Myers, ed. Tempe, Arizona: Aztec Press, 1963. (Originally published as four articles in *Overland Monthly* in 1894.)

POSTON, LAWRENCE III (ed.). "Poston vs. Goodwin, a Document on the Congressional Election of 1865," *Arizona and the West,* Vol. 3, No. 4 (Winter, 1961), pp. 351-54.

POWELL, DONALD M. *The Peralta Grant, James Addison Reavis and the Barony of Arizona.* Norman: University of Oklahoma Press, 1960.

"Prison Reforms in Arizona," *Charities and The Commons,* Vol. 18, June 22, 1907, pp. 333-34.

RATHBUN, CARL M. "Keeping the Peace Along the Mexican Border," *Harper's Weekly,* Vol. 50, No. 2604 (November 17, 1906), pp. 1632-34 and 1649.

REAVES, JOHN ARDEN. "Arizona Statehood — the Constitutional Convention," *Arizona: The New State Magazine,* Vol. 1, No. 4 (December, 1910), pp. 11-17. (This article includes pictures of the Constitutional Convention of 1910 at work, the territorial officers, the capitol building, and delegates.)

"Reclamation's Golden Jubilee," Salt River Project [Phoenix] *Current News,* April, 1952, special issue.

RICE, MIKE M. "The Thirteenth Arizona Legislature," *Arizona Historical Review,* Vol. 1, No. 3 (1928), pp. 80-96.

RICHARDS, J. MORRIS. *The Birth of Arizona.* Phoenix: Allied Print, 1940.

RICHARDSON, HAROLD C. "John C. Frémont: Territorial Governor," *Arizoniana,* Vol. 3, No. 2 (Summer, 1962), pp. 41-47.

ROCKFELLOW, JOHN A. *Log of an Arizona Trail Blazer.* Tucson: Acme Printing Co., 1933. [Reprinted by Arizona Silhouettes, Tucson, 1955.]

ROGERS, HARRIET. "The Establishment of Territorial Government in Arizona." Unpublished master's thesis, University of California, Berkeley, 1923.

ROOSEVELT, THEODORE. "Arizona and the Recall of the Judiciary," *The Outlook,* Vol. 98, June 24, 1911, pp. 378-79.

RYNNING, CAPTAIN THOMAS H. *Gun Notches: The Life Story of a Cowboy Soldier.* New York: Frederick A. Stokes Co., 1931.

SACKS, B. *Be It Enacted: The Creation of the Territory of Arizona.* Phoenix: Arizona Historical Foundation, 1964.

————. "The Creation of the Territory of Arizona," *Arizona and the West,* 2 Parts: Vol. 5, No. 1 (Spring, 1963), pp. 29-62; and Vol. 5, No. 2 (Summer, 1963), pp. 109-48.

————. "Sylvester Mowry," *The American West,* Vol. 1, No. 3 (Summer, 1964), pp. 14-24 and 79.

SAFFORD, A. P. K., AND HUGHES, SAMUEL. "The Story of Mariana Diaz," *Arizona Citizen,* June 21, 1873. (The original manuscript is in the files of the Arizona Pioneers' Historical Society.)

————. *The Territory of Arizona, A Brief History and Summary.* Tucson: The Citizen Office, 1874.

SANTEE, J. F. "The Battle of Glorietta Pass," *New Mexico Historical Review,* Vol. 6. No. 1 (January, 1931), pp. 66-75.

SCHMITT, MARTIN F. (ed.). *General George Crook: His Autobiography.* Norman: University of Oklahoma Press, 1946.

SHADEGG, STEPHEN C. *Arizona: An Adventure in Irrigation.* Phoenix: Jahn-Tyler, 1949.

SIMMS, JAMES T. "Reminiscent Notes on the Building of the Railroad
to Phoenix," *The Sheriff,* Vol. 12, No. 3 (September, 1953), p. 61.

SLOAN, RICHARD E. "The Forty-seventh Star," *Sunset,*
Vol. 25, No. 3 (September, 1910), pp. 267-72.

_____, AND ADAMS, WARD R. *History of Arizona.* 3 volumes.
Phoenix: Record Publishing Co., 1930.

_____. *Memories of an Arizona Judge.*
Stanford: Stanford University Press, 1932.

SMALLEY, GEORGE H. *My Adventures in Arizona.* Edited by
Yndia Smalley Moore [his daughter]. Tucson: Arizona Pioneers'
Historical Society, 1966.

_____. "Reporter on Horseback," *Arizona Highways,*
Vol. 24, No. 3 (March, 1948), pp. 4-7.

SMITH [COL.], C. C. "Some Unpublished History of the Southwest,"
Arizona Historical Review, Vol. 4, No. 1 (April, 1931), pp. 5-20.

"Social Reforms in Arizona," *Charities and The Commons,*
Vol. 18, June 22, 1907, pp. 324-25.

SPARKS, GEORGE F., BATEMAN, HERMAN E., AND BRANDES, RAY (editors).
"Three Years of the Diary of Henry Fountain Ashurst, 1910–1913,"
Arizona and the West, Vol. 3, No. 1 (Spring, 1961), pp. 7-38.

THRAPP, DAN L. *Al Sieber: Chief of Scouts.*
Norman: University of Oklahoma Press, 1964.

TUTTLE, EDWARD D. "Arizona Begins Law-Making,"
Arizona Historical Review, Vol. 1, No. 1 (1928), pp. 50-62.

"Two More Undeveloped States," *The American Review of Reviews,*
Vol. 41, No. 3 (March, 1910), pp. 268-70.

"Two New State Constitutions," *The Outlook,* Vol. 96, November 12, 1910,
pp. 564-65.

Union Army Operations in the Southwest: Final Victory (from the
Official Records). Albuquerque: Horn and Wallace, Publishers, 1961.

VAN PETTEN, DONALD R. *The Constitution and Government of Arizona.*
3rd ed. Phoenix: Tyler Printing Co., 1960.

WAGONER, JAY J. *History of the Cattle Industry in Southern Arizona,
1540–1940.* Tucson: University of Arizona Press, 1952.

WALKER, CHARLES S. "Causes of the Confederate Invasion of New Mexico,"
New Mexico Historical Review, Vol. 8, No. 2 (April, 1933),
pp. 76-97.

WALKER, WALTER W. "Arizona's Struggle for Statehood with Emphasis on
the Proposed Constitution of 1891." Unpublished master's thesis,
American University, Washington, D.C., 1964.

WALLACE, ANDREW. "General August V. Kautz in Arizona,"
Arizoniana, Vol. 4, No. 2 (Summer, 1964), pp. 54-65.

WASSON, JOHN. *In Memory of A. P. K. Safford.* Pomona, Calif., 1891.
[Brochure.]

WATFORD, W. H. "Confederate Western Ambitions," *The Southwestern
Historical Quarterly,* Vol. 44, No. 2 (October, 1940), pp. 161-87.

WESTERGAARD, WALDEMAR. "Senator Thomas R. Bard and the Arizona-
New Mexico Controversy," *Historical Society of Southern California,
Annual Publications,* 1919. Vol. 11, pp. 9-17. [Los Angeles.]

WILLIAMS, EUGENE E. "The Territorial Governors of Arizona,"
Arizona Historical Review, 5 parts: Vol. 6. No. 3 (July, 1935),
pp. 59-73; Vol. 6. No. 4 (October, 1935), pp. 50-60; Vol. 7, No. 1
(January, 1936), pp. 69-84; Vol. 7, No. 2 (April, 1936), pp. 84-87;
and Vol. 7, No. 3 (July, 1936), pp. 80-87.

WILLIAMSON, DAN R. "The Apache Kid: Red Renegade of the West,"
Arizona Highways, Vol. 15, No. 5 (May, 1939), pp. 14-15 and 30-31.

WINSOR, MULFORD. "The Arizona Rangers," *Our Sheriff and Police Journal,*
Vol. 31, No. 6 (June, 1936), pp. 49-61.

WOODY, CLARA T. "The Woolsey Expeditions of 1864,"
Arizona and the West, Vol. 4, No. 2 (Summer, 1962), pp. 157-76.

Works Progress Administration, The Arizona Statewide Archival and
Records Project, Division of Community Services Programs.
The District Courts of the Territory of Arizona.
Mimeographed, 1941. 38 pp.

WYLLYS, RUFUS K. *Arizona: the History of a Frontier State.*
Phoenix: Hobson & Herr, 1950.

ZABRISKIE, GEORGE A. *The Pathfinder.* Ormund Beach, Fla.:
"The Doldrums," publisher, 1947.

NEWSPAPERS

Territorial Arizona

Argus (Holbrook), January 4, 1897.

Arizona Blade (Florence), 1904.

Arizona Bulletin (Solomonville), Special Illustrated Edition, Jan. 12, 1900.

Arizona Citizen (Tucson), 1870–1912. (Known since 1929 as the
Tucson Daily Citizen, this paper has appeared also under the names
Arizona Daily Citizen and *Tucson Citizen.*)

Arizona Daily Star (Tucson), 1879–1912. (From 1877–79 the name was
Arizona Star.)

Arizona Democrat (Phoenix), 1901–1912. (The *Democrat* was purchased
in 1913 by the *Arizona Gazette.*)

Arizona Enterprise (Florence), 1885–1889.

Arizona Gazette (Phoenix), 1880–1912. (This newspaper evolved into the
Phoenix Evening Gazette, and later became the *Phoenix Gazette.*)

Arizona Graphic (Phoenix), September, 1899–February 10, 1900.
(Though short-lived, this publication was an excellent illustrated
periodical on the history and life in Arizona.)

Arizona Miner (Prescott), 1864–1912. (The exact names of the weekly
and/or daily *Miner* have been changed from time to time:
*Arizona Weekly Miner, Daily Arizona Miner, Arizona Journal-Miner,
Prescott Journal-Miner,* etc.)

Arizona Republican (Phoenix), 1890–1912. (This paper became the *Arizona Republic* in 1930.)

Arizona Sentinel (Yuma), 1872–1912. (The *Sentinel* merged with the *Yuma Examiner* in 1911 and has had variations in names.)

Arizona Silver Belt (Globe), 1878–1912. (This newspaper was moved to Miami, Arizona, in 1913.)

Arizona Star (Tucson), 1877–1879. (In 1879 the name was changed to *Arizona Daily Star.*)

Coconino Sun (Flagstaff), 1882–1912. (This publication was originally named the *Arizona Champion* and has also been known as the *Flagstaff Sun-Democrat.*)

Copper Era (Clifton), 1903.

Enterprise (Phoenix), 1898–1907. (The Democratic *Enterprise* merged with the *Arizona Democrat* in 1907.)

Expositor (Yuma and Phoenix), 1878–1881. (Beginning as the *Yuma Expositor,* this Democratic paper was moved to Phoenix in 1879 and became the *Territorial Expositor.*)

Florence Tribune, 1892–1912. (The independent *Tribune* was combined with the *Blade* in 1902 and became the Democratic *Arizona Blade-Tribune.*)

Native American (Phoenix), 1900–1912. (This periodical was published by the U. S. Indian Vocational School in Phoenix.)

Phoenix Herald, 1878–1899. (Published as the *Salt River Herald* until March 5, 1879, this paper was purchased by the *Arizona Republican* in 1899.)

Prescott Courier, September 18 and 24, 1889.

St. John's Herald, January 25, 1897.

Tempe News, February 17, 1897; April 15, 1904; and April 1, 1908.

Tombstone Epitaph, 1880–1912. (Because of consolidations with other newspapers, this famous journal went under the names *Tombstone Daily Epitaph and Republican* and the *Daily-Record-Epitaph* during the 1883–1887 period.)

Tucson Citizen. See *Arizona Citizen.*

Weekly Arizona Enterprise (Tucson), March 28, 1891, and November 27, 1892.

Weekly Arizonan (Tucson), March 9, 1861; November, 1869–December, 1870. Arizona's first newspaper, this publication was started on March 3, 1859, under the name *Weekly Arizonian,* as a voice for mining interests in the Gadsden strip. The paper was moved from Tubac to Tucson with the August 4, 1859 issue and an "i" was dropped from Arizonian with the April 24, 1869 edition.

Yuma-Sun, January 13, 1897.

Non-Arizona Newspapers

Daily Alta Californian (San Francisco), February 3, 1872.

Mesilla Times (New Mexico), May 11, 1861.

New York Daily-Tribune, 1875 through 1906. The *Tribune Index* is a valuable aid in locating items related to Arizona.

New York Times, 1851 through 1905. The *Times Index* is useful in finding articles pertaining to Arizona.

San Francisco Call, January 28, 1897.

Index

(Numbers in *italics* refer to pages in the appendices)